Androgynos

Günther Feuerstein

Androgynos

Das Mann-Weibliche in Kunst und Architektur
The Male-Female in Art and Architecture

Edition Axel Menges

Gefördert vom Österreichischen Bundes-
ministerium für Wissenschaft und Verkehr.

Supported by the Österreichisches Bundes-
ministerium für Wissenschaft und Verkehr.

© 1997 Edition Axel Menges, Stuttgart/London
ISBN 3-930698-74-9

Reproduktionen/Reproductions: Bild und Text
GmbH Baun, Fellbach
Druck und Bindearbeiten/Printing and binding:
Daehan Printing and Publishing Co., Ltd.,
Sungnam, Korea

Mitarbeiterinnen des Autors/Collaborators of the
author: Johanna Krenn, Elke Wikidal
Lektorat/Editorial supervision: Dorothea A. Duwe
Englische Übersetzung/English translation:
Michael Robinson
Gestaltung/Design: Axel Menges
Layout: Helga Danz

Die Liebe ist auf Erden das Mittel, zur Erlösung zu gelangen, aber diese Liebe muß ihrem Wesen nach androgyn sein, um den primordialen Androgyn wiederzufinden. Liebe ist nur dann wahr, wenn der Mann und die Frau innerlich weder Mann noch Frau sind. Busquet

Der Mythos vom Androgynen ist der einzige große anthropologische Mythos, auf dem die anthropologische Metaphysik aufgebaut werden kann. Nikolai Berdjajew

Love is the way to achieve redemption here on earth, but the nature of this love must be androgynous, in order to find the primordial androgyne once more. Love is true only when man and woman are inwardly neither man nor woman. Busquet

The myth of the androgyne is the only great anthropological myth upon which anthropological metaphysics can be built. Nikolay Berdyayev

1. Begriffe

1.1. Grundstrukturen

Die Frage nach der Grundstruktur alles Seienden erfährt in der Ideengeschichte der Menschheit, in Mythen, Religionen, Philosophien und Ideologien eine Fülle von Antworten.

In dieser Studie sollen zwei Kategorien von Konzepten im Hinblick auf die Kunst und die Architektur marginal behandelt werden. Es sind die **monistischen** und die **dualistischen** Grundmodelle.

Die scheinbare Polarität und die spannungsreiche Divergenz in dualistischen Systemen legen immer wieder den Versuch nahe, zu einer einzigen allumfassenden Struktur zu kommen, jedoch nicht im Sinne einer alternativen Entscheidung oder dogmatischen Festlegung, sondern im Sinne einer Synthese, einer Überlappung, einer Identität, einer »coincidentia«, die es uns vielleicht ermöglicht, den großen »Welträtseln«[1] näherzukommen. Sie vollends entschlüsseln zu wollen, ist eine Hoffnung, die unerfüllt geblieben ist und es vermutlich auch weiterhin bleiben wird. Zumindest in unserem Jahrhundert beginnt man jedoch zu begreifen, daß die »Annäherungen« an Problemlösungen bereits einen hohen Gewinn darstellen, wo doch die eigentlichen »Lösungen« unerreichbar scheinen.

Unbeantwortbar bleibt auch die Frage nach dem wertkategorischen Primat von monistischen und dualistischen Systemen. Es wäre aber auch gefährlich, diesen Primat für eine etwaige Synthese, für die »coincidentia« zu beanspruchen, zum einen, weil uns diese vergleichsweise selten begegnet, zum anderen, weil aus dem Spannungsfeld der beiden Modelle immer wieder eine fruchtbare Fülle von Ideen entspringt.

Ein Vergleich mit den religionsgeschichtlichen Thesen zeigt, daß eine Evolutionstheorie im mythisch-religiösen Bereich heute nicht mehr bestehen kann. Die Auffassung des 18. und 19. Jahrhunderts, wonach sich aus dem Animismus der Polytheismus und daraus der Monotheismus entwickelt haben, sind heute kaum mehr haltbar, ebenso wie die Auffassung, der Monotheismus stelle eine höhere Kulturstufe dar als der Polytheismus.

1.2. Urerfahrungen. Kategorien

1.2.1. Monistische Kategorien

Für das vorliegende Thema können, mehr als in anderen kulturhistorischen, philosophischen und religiösen Bereichen, gewisse Urerfahrungen des Menschen, insbesondere die Bedingungen seines Daseins, einen Ausgangspunkt bilden.

Die »Anschauung« der Natur, der Rhythmus des Lebens, die Fragen der Existenz sind in ihren detaillierten Ausprägungen einem historischen Wandel unterworfen, in den grundsätzlichen Kategorien jedoch seit dem Bestehen des Menschengeschlechts prägend für sein Bewußtsein, für Kultur und Religion.

Das Prinzip der Einheit und Einzigkeit alles Existierenden ist als eine These für die »Urerfahrung« kaum zu postulieren. Es mag zwar sein, daß der Mensch sich selbst schon sehr früh als unteilbares und einzigartiges Wesen erfahren hat, daß die Menschheit oder das Menschengeschlecht als ein kompaktes, monistisches System gesehen wurden. Vielleicht waren es auch die Natur oder der Kosmos, die als Einheit rezipiert wurden, doch finden wir gerade in diesen Bereichen auch die wichtigsten Ansätze zu dualistischen und pluralistischen Systemen.

Die Idee des Monismus hat im 19. und 20. Jahrhundert gleichwohl eine gewisse Aktualität behalten. **Ernst Haeckel** (1834–1919) definiert seinen Monismus aus der Sicht des Naturwissenschaftlers: »Die alte Weltanschauung des **Ideal-Dualismus** mit ihren mystischen und anthropistischen Dogmen versinkt in Trümmer; aber über diesem gewaltigen Trümmerfeld steigt hehr und herrlich die neue Sonne unseres **Real-Monismus** auf, welche uns den wundervollen Tempel der Natur voll erschließt. In dem reinen Kultus des Wahren, Guten und Schönen, welcher den Kern unserer monistischen Religion bildet, finden wir reichen Ersatz für die verlorenen anthropistischen Ideale von Gott, Freiheit, Unsterblichkeit.« (Haeckel, 1902)

Für ihn ist der »Monismus« ein »Band zwischen Religion und Wissenschaft«. (Haeckel, 1892)

Die Relation von Dualismus und Monismus sieht Haeckel unter dem Gesichtspunkt seines »natürlichen Systems«: »Alle verschiedenen Richtungen der Philosophie lassen sich, vom heu-

1. Concepts Employed

1.1. Basic Structures

The question of the basic structure of all existence meets with an abundance of answers in the history of human ideas: in myths, religions, philosophies and ideologies.

It is intended in the present study to give marginal treatment to two categories of concepts as they relate to art and architecture. These categories are the **monistic** and **dualistic** basic models.

The seeming polarity and tension-ridden divergency to be found in dualistic systems repeatedly suggest the idea of trying to arrive at a single, all-embracing structure, but not in the sense of an alternative decision or dogmatic determination, but rather that of a synthesis, an overlapping, an identity, a »coincidentia«, which may enable us to come closer to understanding the »Welträtsel«, the great mysteries of the world.[1] The hope of ever completely deciphering those mysteries remains unfulfilled and will probably continue to remain so. However, in the present century at any rate, people are beginning to understand that approaches to solutions of problems in themselves constitute a great gain, given that the actual »solutions« seem to be unattainable.

Another question which remains unanswerable is that of whether monistic and dualistic systems are pre-eminent ways of categorizing values. But it would also be dangerous to use this pre-eminence for the purpose of any synthesis, for a »coincidentia«, one reason being that we encounter such a synthesis only comparatively rarely, and the other being that a fertile abundance of ideas arises, again and again, from the field of tension produced by the two models.

A comparison with the theses occurring in the history of religion shows that it is no longer possible today for there to be any kind of theory of evolution in the mystical-religious field. The view held in the 18th and 19th centuries, namely that polytheism developed from animism, and monotheism from polytheism, is scarcely tenable today, and the same applies to the view that monotheism is a higher stage of culture than polytheism.

1.2. Primeval Experiences, Categories

1.2.1. Monistic Categories

Certain of man's primeval experiences, in particular the conditions of his existence, may form a more suitable starting point for the topic now being dealt with than they would for other areas of philosophy, religion and cultural history.

Man's »conception of nature«, the rhythm of life, and questions of existence, have been subject to change over the course of history where their detailed characteristics have been concerned, but their basic categories have shaped man's consciousness and his culture and religion ever since the human race has existed.

The principle of the unity and uniqueness of all that exists can scarcely be postulated as a thesis for the »primeval experience«. It is true that man may at a very early stage have experienced himself as an indivisible and unique being, and that humankind or the human race was seen as being a compact, monistic system. It may though also have been nature or the cosmos that was admitted as being a unity, but it is precisely in these areas that we also find the most important tendencies towards dualistic and pluralistic systems.

Nevertheless, the idea of monism retained a certain currency in the 19th and 20th centuries. **Ernst Haeckel** (1834–1910) defined his monism from a natural scientist's point of view: »**Idealistic dualism**, that old outlook on life, with its mystical and anthropinistic dogmas, is sinking in ruins; but the new sun of our **realistic monism**, which fully opens up to us the wonderful temple of nature, is rising sublimely and gloriously above this vast expanse of ruins. Within the pure cult of truth, goodness and beauty which forms the core of our monistic religion, we can find ample compensation for the lost anthropinistic ideals of God, freedom and immortality.« (Haeckel, 1902)

To him, monism is »a bond between religion and science«. (Haeckel, 1892) Haeckel looks at the relationship between dualism and monism from the point of view of his »natural system«: »When assessed from the modern standpoint of natural science, all the different tenden-

tigen Standpunkte der Naturwissenschaft beurteilt, in zwei entgegengesetzte Reihen bringen, einerseits die dualistische oder zwiespältige, andererseits die monistische oder einheitliche Weltanschauung. Gewöhnlich ist die erstere mit teleologischen und idealistischen Dogmen verknüpft, die letztere mit mechanistischen und realistischen Grundbegriffen. Der Dualismus (im weitesten Sinne!) zerlegt das Universum in zwei ganz verschiedene Substanzen, die materielle Welt und den immateriellen Gott, der ihr als Schöpfer, Erhalter und Regierer gegenübersteht. Der Monismus hingegen (ebenfalls im weitesten Sinne begriffen) erkennt im Universum nur eine einzige Substanz, die ›Gott und Natur‹ zugleich ist; Körper und Geist (oder Materie und Energie) sind für sie untrennbar verbunden. Der extramundane Gott des Dualismus führt notwendig zum Theismus; hingegen der intramundane Gott des Monismus zum Pantheismus.« (Haeckel, 1902)

Der Monismus ist zweifellos als eine historische philosophische Strömung anzusehen. Dies erhellt vor allem aus den divergenten Strömungen eines ontologischen Monismus, der als die einzig seiende Substanz entweder die Materie anerkennt und somit in den Materialismus mündet oder den Geist als wesenhafte Substanz postuliert und damit zum Spiritualismus führt. Der erkenntnistheoretische Monismus betont lediglich die Einheitlichkeit der Erscheinungswelt und führt zu keiner Aussage über das Wesen des Seienden.

1.2.2. Dualistische Kategorien

Der Ausgangspunkt aller dualistischen Modelle ist viel deutlicher aus den unmittelbaren **Lebenserfahrungen** zu erläutern, die auch dem Urmenschen geläufig waren. So werden möglicherweise die ersten Gegensatzpaare jene gewesen sein, die uns heute noch zutiefst bewegen: Tag – Nacht; Sonne – Mond; Licht – Finsternis; Himmel – Erde; Feuer – Wasser; Leben (Geburt) – Sterben (Tod); Ruhe – Bewegung; Frau – Mann.

Aus diesen realen Erfahrungen baut sich eine magisch-mythische Dimension auf, in der die Gegensatzpaare wieder ihren Ort haben: Seele – Leib; Geist/Gott/Götter – Mensch; gut – böse.[2]

In der religiösen Welt selbst können sich die Dualismen entfalten, etwa in der Form von metaphysischen Mächten, die einander komplementär oder antithetisch gegenüberstehen. Vielleicht zählt es aber auch zu den Urerfahrungen, daß diese Polaritäten keine scharfen Abgrenzungen ermöglichen: Im Guten ist auch Böses enthalten und umgekehrt, die Götter werden zu Menschen und umgekehrt, zwischen Tag und Nacht liegt die geheimnisvolle Dämmerung, Sonne und Mond ziehen in Partnerschaft oder Feindschaft über das Firmament und können gleichzeitig am Himmel stehen, nach dem Tode gibt es ein Weiterleben, und das Leben ist vom Tod geprägt.

Existieren diese Übergänge auch bei Mann und Frau, oder sind wir, auf Grund unserer biologischen Natur, auf eine scharfe Trennung angewiesen?

Wenn wir die menschliche Existenz nur aus den biologischen Fakten heraus zu deuten versuchen, bedarf die Tatsache der Geschlechterdifferenzierung keiner weiteren Erörterung. Wenn wir jedoch die gesamte Geisteswelt in die Betrachtung miteinbeziehen, so wird uns klar, daß die scheinbar eindeutige Differenzierung der Geschlechter die Frage nach den Übergängen, Grenzüberschreitungen, Synthesen, Koinzidenzen nicht überflüssig macht.

Gerade weil es, verglichen zu den Milliarden der bisherigen menschlichen Existenzen, nur wenige reale und biologische »Übergangsmodelle« zwischen Mann und Frau gibt, kommt der unübersehbaren Zahl an kulturhistorisch formulierten Modellen eine ganz besondere Bedeutung zu: Das »Androgyne« wird, weit über die bloßen Geschlechtsmerkmale hinaus, zu einem generellen Sehnsuchtsmodell menschlicher Bestrebungen.

»Die dialektische-teleologische Weltdeutung entspricht wesentlich den Motiven archaischer Erlösungsmythen: Der Wunsch nach Aufhebung von Entzweiung, z. B. auch in Dualismen wie Geist – Materie, Seele – Leib, Wahrheit – Schein, Absolutheit – Bedingtheit, Ich und außerhalb des Ich stehende Objektwelt ... entspricht der begrenzenden bipolaren Geschlechtsstruktur in der menschlichen Gefühlssphäre. Hier wie dort besteht der Wunsch nach Entgrenzung, Harmonie, Unendlichkeit und Vollendung in der Einheit.« (Raehs, 1990)

cies in philosophy can be placed into two opposing categories. The first is the dualistic or dis-united world-outlook on life, and the second is the monistic or integrated world-outlook. The former is usually linked to teleological and idealistic dogmas, and the latter to basic mechanistic and realistic concepts. Dualism (in its broadest sense) divides the universe into two entirely different substances: the material world and the immaterial God, who stands opposite that world as its creator, preserver and ruler. On the other hand, monism (again understood in its broadest sense) recognizes in the universe only one single substance, which is ›God and nature‹ at the same time; for this substance, body and spirit (or material and energy) are insepa-rably combined. The extramundane God of dualism necessarily results in theism; the intra-mundane God of monism, on the other hand, leads to pantheism.« (Haeckel, 1902)

Monism must undoubtedly be looked on as a historical philosophical movement. This mostly becomes clear from the divergent currents of an ontological monism which either ack-nowledges material as the only existing substance and thus passes into materialism, or else postulates the spirit as a really existing substance and thus leads to spiritualism. Epistemolog-ical monism merely emphasizes the integrity of the world of appearance, and does not result in a statement about the nature of what exists.

1.2.2. Dualistic Categories

The starting point of all dualistic models can be explained much more clearly from those direct **experiences of life** with which prehistoric man was also familiar. Thus the first contrasting pairs may have been those which still move us very deeply today: day – night; sun – moon; light – darkness; sky – earth; fire – water; life (birth) – dying (death); rest – movement; woman – man.

On the basis of these actual experiences, a magical and mythical dimension is built up in which contrasting pairs again have their place: soul – body; spirit/god/gods – man; good – evil.[2]

Dualisms can develop in the religious world itself, for example in the form of metaphysical powers which stand face to face with one another either complementarily or antithetically. But perhaps one of the primeval experiences is that these polarities do not enable any sharp de-marcations to be made: good contains some evil, and vice versa; gods become humans, and vice versa; there is a mysterious twilight between day and night; sun and moon move across the firmament in partnership or enmity, and may both be in the sky at the same time; after death there is an afterlife; and life is shaped by death.

Do these transitions also exist in men and women, or does our biological nature mean that we are dependent on the maintenance of a sharp division?

If we try to interpret human existence solely on the basis of the biological facts, the fact that there is differentiation of the sexes requires no further discussion. However, if we include the entire spiritual world in our observations, it becomes clear to us that, although there is a seemingly clear differentiation between the sexes, this does not mean that it is superfluous to ask about transitions, syntheses, coincidences, and crossings of borders.

Compared with the billions of human beings who have already existed, there have been only a few real, biological, transitional models half way between a man and a woman. The fact that there have been so few of them lends a particular significance to the immense number of models formulated in the history of civilization: far over and above the mere sexual character-istics, androgyny becomes a general model which human endeavour longs for.

»The dialectic-teleological interpretation of the world corresponds largely to the motives found in archaic myths of salvation: the wish for the elimination of disunion, for example in such dualisms as spirit – material, soul – body, reality – appearance, absoluteness – condition-ality, the ego and the world of objects outside the ego, ... corresponds to the limiting bipolar sexual structure in the sphere of human emotions. In both the former and the latter there is a wish for the overcoming of barriers, for harmony, infinity and perfection in unity.« (Raehs, 1990)

1.2.3. Pluralistic Categories

The primeval experience achieved through pluralism probably consists primarily in the aston-ishing variety of species: animals, plants, bodies of water, minerals, stars, and finally humans,

1.2.3. Pluralistische Kategorien

Die Urerfahrung über den Pluralismus liegt wohl in erster Linie in der erstaunlichen Vielfalt der Arten: Die Tiere, die Pflanzen, die Gewässer, die Mineralien, die Gestirne – und letztlich auch der Mensch manifestieren sich in einer fast unüberschaubaren Pluralität. Dementsprechend entwickeln sich oft hypertrophe pluralistische Mythologien, üppige Götterwelten, ein reich bevölkerter Heiligenhimmel. Nicht zuletzt aber ist das Sein, Denken und Handeln unseres Jahrhunderts mehr und mehr von pluralistischen Systemen geprägt.

1.3. Begriffe, Definitionen

Die Synthese von Mann und Frau in einem einzigen Lebewesen beschäftigt den Menschen offenkundig seit Jahrtausenden: Die Vereinigung der beiden Wesen, meist als Repräsentanten von »Prinzipien«, führt gleichsam zu Über-Wesen, Sonder-Wesen, die aber nicht nur in Mythen und Phantasien existieren sollen. Für diese Synthese haben sich vor allem zwei Begriffe herausgebildet: **Androgyne** und **Hermaphroditen**.

Androgyne sind doppelgeschlechtliche Wesen, »Mannfrauen« (oder »Gynander«, »Frauenmänner«), also Wesen, die männliche und weibliche Merkmale – oft in ungleicher Intensität – vereinigen. (Aurnhammer, 1986) »Androgynie« soll darüber hinaus die grundsätzliche und integrale Vereinigung unterschiedlicher oder entgegengesetzter Wesenheiten bezeichnen, im weiteren Sinne also nicht nur die Synthese des Männlichen und des Weiblichen.[3]

Andrea Raehs (1990) meint, daß man »im modernen Gebrauch des Begriffes ... bei einer Verschmelzung der spezifisch definierten Geschlechter sich eine neue, eine dritte Qualität erwartet, die über die Potenzen der beiden empirisch erfahrbaren hinausgeht«.

Raehs versucht, die Begriffe Androgyn und Hermaphrodit voneinander abzugrenzen. Sie sieht im Androgyn »einen verinnerlichten Hermaphroditen«, der ein »abstrakter Begriff« bleiben muß, während der Hermaphrodit eine »begreifbare Erscheinung« sei und am ehesten »durch die Darstellung als Zwitterwesen repräsentiert« und »auf körperliche Gegebenheiten« bezogen sei. Der Begriff »Androgyn« könne als eine idealisierte Form des Hermaphroditen angesehen werden, dürfe aber freilich nicht nur als eine »abstrakte Vorstellung«, die der »reinen Geisteswelt vorbehalten« sei, definiert werden. (Raehs, 1990)

Achim Aurnhammer (1986) bringt eine praktikable Definition: »Androgynie soll hier jede Relation zweier komplementärer Elemente heißen, die eins waren, eins sind oder eins sein möchten, sofern die Komplementarität geschlechtlich erkennbar ist.« Dieser letzte Satzteil wird im zweiten Teil der Studie, indem es konkret um eine androgyne Architektur geht, nur mehr begrenzt gültig sein. Im allgemeinen ist es so zu verstehen, daß keineswegs eine Liquidation des Sexuellen stattfindet, wenngleich die »Geschlechtslosigkeit« als ein Grenzfall der Androgynie zu erwähnen ist. »Androgynie bedeutet nicht die Aufhebung der Geschlechtlichkeit in einer neutralen Übergeschlechtlichkeit, sondern stellt eine Befreiung des Einzelnen aus kulturellen Fesseln dar.« (Ehmann, 1976)

Auch Ernst Silbermayr (1988) betont, »daß Androgynie ... nicht Geschlechtsneutralität bedeute, sondern die Freiheit, seine geschlechtliche Identität unabhängig von kulturell bedingten Stereotypen zu suchen bzw. zu finden«.

Der Begriff der Androgynie ist zu benachbarten Begriffen nicht genau abzugrenzen. Im allgemeinen aber wird er eher in der idealisierten Form, in einer geistigen Konzeption, im Religiös-Mythischen, im psychologischen und soziologischen Sprachgebrauch zu finden sein.

Gaston Bachelard charakterisierte in *La Poetique de la rêverie* (1960) das Wesen der Androgynie: »Qui parle d'androgénéité, frôle, avec un double antenne, les profondeurs de son propre inconscient.«[4]

Bisweilen wird »Androgynie« auch als Überbegriff verwendet, dem Hermaphroditismus und Bisexualität untergeordnet sind.

Die **Hermaphroditen** der griechischen Mythologie vereinen Merkmale des Hermes und der Aphrodite oder präziser: Hermaphroditos ist der »Sohn« des Hermes und der Aphrodite, die formale Ausprägung, die menschliche oder vermenschlichte Erscheinungsform der Doppelgeschlechtlichkeit, insbesondere in der Skulptur.

Marie Delcourt (1958) sieht auch im Hermaphroditen ein »exemple privilégié de mythe pur«.[5] Der Hermaphrodit der Antike hat sein Vorbild keineswegs in biologischen Zwittern – diese wurden nach der Geburt häufig getötet. (Busst, 1967)

manifest themselves in a plurality which it is almost impossible to survey. This often leads to the development of hypertrophic pluralistic mythologies, sumptuous realms of the gods, and a richly populated heaven full of saints. Last but not least, existence, thought and action in the present century are being increasingly shaped by pluralistic systems.

1.3. Terms, Definitions

The question of synthesizing man and woman in a single living being has evidently occupied people's minds for thousands of years: the unification of the two beings, usually as representatives of »principles«, results in what might be described as supernatural creatures, special beings, which are though not meant to exist only in myths and fantasies. Two chief terms have developed to describe this synthesis: **androgynes** and **hermaphrodites**.

Androgynes are two-sexed beings, »men-women« (or »gynandros«, »women-men«), that is to say beings which unite male and female characteristics, often with unequal intensity. (Aurnhammer, 1986) In addition, »androgyny« is intended to refer to the basic and integral unification of differing or opposed entities, and thus, in a broader sense, not merely to the synthesis of male and female.[3]

Andrea Raehs (1990) takes the view that »in the modern use of the term ... when the specifically defined sexes are merged, a new, third quality is expected which goes beyond the potencies of the two qualities which can be experienced empirically«.

Raehs attempts to achieve a demarcation between androgyne and hermaphrodite. For her an androgyne is »an internalized hermaphrodite« who must remain an »abstract concept«, whereas a hermaphrodite is an »apprehensible phenomenon«, can best »be represented by being depicted as a two-sexed being« and is related »to physical factors«. The term »androgyne« can be regarded as an idealized form of the hermaphrodite, but must certainly not be defined as an »abstract idea« which is »reserved for the pure world of the spirit«. (Raehs, 1990)

Achim Aurnhammer (1938) gives a practicable definition: »Androgyny is intended here to refer to any relationship between two complementary elements which were one, are one, or want to be one, provided that the complementarity is sexually discernible.« This last part of the sentence will only have limited validity when the second part of the present study is reached, as that part will deal specifically with androgynous architecture. In general, the matter must be understood as meaning that there is certainly no liquidation of sexuality, even though sexlessness must be mentioned as being a boundary problem of androgyny. »Androgyny does not mean the elimination of sexuality in a neutral area located above sexuality, but represents a liberation of the individual from his or her cultural shackles.« (Ehmann, 1976)

Ernst Silbermayr also emphasizes (1988) »that androgyny ... does not mean sexual neutrality, but rather the freedom to search for or to find one's sexual identity independently of culturally conditioned stereotypes«.

The term »androgyny« cannot be precisely delimited from other terms adjoining it. In general, though, it will tend rather to be found in an idealized form, in a spiritual conception, in religious-mystical ideas, and in psychological and sociological linguistic usage.

Gaston Bachelard characterized the nature of androgyny in *La Poetique de la rêverie* (1960): »Qui parle d'androgiénéité, frôle, avec un double antenne, les profondeurs de son propre inconscient.«[4]

Sometimes »androgyny« is also used as a generic term, to which hermaphroditism and bisexuality are subordinate.

The **hermaphrodites** of Greek mythology united characteristics of both Hermes and Aphrodite; or, to be more precise, Hermaphroditos was the »son« of Hermes and Aphrodite, and was, as it were, the formal shape – the human or humanized outward form – of a two-sexed nature, particularly in sculpture.

Marie Delcourt (1958) also regards a hermaphrodite as an »exemple privilégié de mythe pur«.[5] The hermaphrodite of classical antiquity was certainly not modelled on two-sexed biological beings – these were often killed after birth. (Busst, 1967)

The expression »hermaphrodite« tends rather to refer to the material, physical side of a two-sexed nature. Particularly in medical and biological usage, »hermaphrodite« is the more common term. In the German language, there is also the expression »**Zwitter**«, which refers almost exclusively to biology. However, »**Zwitter**« is also a name from older German usage, when it is usually identical in meaning with the notion of hermaphrodite.

Der Begriff »Hermaphrodit« bezeichnet eher die materielle, physische Seite der Doppelge-schlechtlichkeit. Vor allem im medizinischen und biologischen Sprachgebrauch ist der Termi-nus Hermaphrodit geläufiger. Er wird noch durch den Ausdruck **Zwitter** ergänzt, der sich fast ausschließlich auf das Biologische bezieht. Jedoch ist Zwitter auch eine Bezeichnung aus dem älteren deutschen Sprachgebrauch und dann meist identisch mit dem Begriff des Hermaphro-diten.

Ein selten gebrauchter älterer deutscher Ausdruck bezeichnet die Androgyne oder Herm-aphroditen als **Mischwesen**.

Die noch darzustellende Tatsache, daß bei vielen Menschen das somatische, biologische Geschlecht nicht mit dem psychologischen übereinstimmt, führt zu einer Fülle von Phänome-nen und Problemen. Wenn dieses Gefühl so weit geht, daß man glaubt, dem anderen Ge-schlecht anzugehören, weil man mit dem eigenen nicht zufrieden ist, spricht man von **Trans-sexualismus**. »Transsexuelle haben die innere Gewißheit, dem Geschlecht anzugehören, das ihnen körperlich nicht von Geburt an gegeben ist.« (Silbermayr, 1988)

Sie haben meist den unbedingten und heftigen Wunsch, sich in das andere Geschlecht zu verwandeln und werden versuchen, im Rahmen der gesellschaftlichen und medizinischen Be-dingungen dieses Bedürfnis zu befriedigen.

Im Unterschied dazu bedeutet der **Transvestismus**[6] nur eine temporäre, eine partielle oder eine simulierte Verwandlung in das andere Geschlecht durch die Kleidung.

Es ist also zu unterscheiden zwischen einer »passageren Übernahme gegengeschlechtli-cher Verhaltensweisen und der Annahme einer gegengeschlechtlichen Identität.« (Ehmann, 1976). Scharfe Grenzlinien zwischen Transsexualität und Transvestismus werden aber kaum zu ziehen sein.

Bisweilen gibt es auch eine fehlende Übereinstimmung zwischen den einzelnen Erschei-nungen des somatischen Geschlechtes, etwa wenn die äußeren Geschlechtsorgane nicht ein-deutig sind oder wenn eine Diskrepanz zwischen primären und sekundären Geschlechtsmerk-malen, häufig in der Pubertät, sich bemerkbar macht. Man spricht dann von **Intersexualität**, wobei dieser Begriff häufig mit Pseudohermaphroditismus (Scheinzwittrigkeit) gleichgesetzt wird. Alle diese Phänomene hängen mehr oder weniger stark mit der Androgynie zusam-men.

Nicht sehr brauchbar, obgleich in der Literatur häufig verwendet, ist die Bezeichnung **bi-sexuell**. Sie hat sehr oft die Bedeutung von androgyn, womit auf die Präsenz sowohl männ-licher als auch weiblicher Merkmale verwiesen wird. Heute bezeichnet dieser Begriff meist Personen, die zugleich homosexuell und heterosexuell veranlagt sind.[7]

2. Einheit – Teilung – Vereinigung

2.1. Platon

In Platons **Gastmahl** ist – dem Aristophanes in den Mund gelegt – von einem »dritten Ge-schlecht« die Rede, von mythischen Figuren, die männlich und weiblich zugleich waren, so daß sie die Kraft der Sonne (Ganzmänner), der Erde (Ganzweiber) und des Mondes (Mann-weiblich) besaßen:

»Früher nämlich war unsere Natur nicht dieselbe wie jetzt, sondern anderer Art. Anfangs gab es bei den Menschen drei Geschlechter, nicht wie jetzt nur zwei, ein männliches und ein weibliches: Es gab ein drittes noch dazu, das die beiden in sich vereinigte; sein Name ist noch übrig, es selbst ist verschwunden. Mannweiblich war es und hatte Gestalt und Name von bei-den, Männlichem und Weiblichem, zu einem einzigen vereinigt. ... Sie waren nun gewaltig an Kraft und Stärke und wollten hoch hinaus; ja sie wagten sich auch an die Götter ... daß sie sich einen Zugang zum Himmel bahnen wollten, um die Götter anzugreifen, das gilt von ihnen. Zeus nun und die anderen Götter hielten Rat, was sie mit ihnen anfangen sollten, und waren in Verlegenheit. ... Endlich hatte Zeus mit Mühe etwas ausgesonnen und sagte: ›Ich glaube, ein Mittel zu haben, wie es noch weiter Menschen geben kann und sie doch von ihrem wüsten Wesen lassen müssen – wenn sie nämlich schwächer werden. Ich will sie auseinanderschnei-den, jeden in zwei Teile‹ ... Sprach's und zerschnitt die Menschen in zwei Hälften, wie man Bir-nen zerschneidet, um sie einzumachen, oder wie man Eier mit einem Haar zerschneidet. ... Nachdem nun die Natur entzweigeschnitten war, ging sehnsüchtig jede Hälfte ihrer anderen Hälfte nach, und sie umfingen sich mit den Armen und schlangen sich ineinander, um über

Another older German expression, rarely used, refers to androgynes or hermaphrodites as »**Mischwesen**« (mixed beings).

There will follow a description of the fact that, with many people, their somatic, biological sex does not accord with their psychological sex. This results in an abundance of phenomena and problems. If this feeling reaches the stage where the person feels that he or she is a member of the other sex because he or she is not content with his or her own sex, the term employed is **transsexualism**. »Transsexuals are possessed of an inward certainty that they belong to the sex which is not the sex physically given to them from birth onwards.« (Silbermayr, 1988)

They usually have an absolute and violent desire to become a member of the opposite sex, and they attempt to satisfy this need on the basis of the prevailing social and medical circumstances.

In contrast to this, **transvestism**[6] signifies only a temporary, partial or simulated change into the other sex by means of clothing.

Thus a distinction must be drawn between a »temporary adoption of modes of behaviour belonging to the opposite sex, on the one hand, and the assumption of the identity of the opposite sex, on the other« (Ehmann, 1976). However, it will hardly be possible to draw sharp distinctions between transsexuality and transvestism.

Sometimes the individual phenomena of somatic sex do not accord with one another, such as when the external sexual organs are unclear or – as is often the case in puberty – a noticeable discrepancy arises between the primary and secondary sexual characteristics. The term then employed is **intersexuality**, and this concept is often equated with pseudohermaphroditism. All these phenomena are more or less strongly related to androgyny.

The term **bisexual** is not really very suitable, although frequently employed in literature. It very often refers to androgyny, that is to say the presence of both male and female characteristics, but is today usually used of persons of both homosexual and heterosexual disposition.[7]

2. Unity – Division – Unification

2.1. Plato

The **Symposium** of Plato includes a reference – put into the mouth of Aristophanes – to a »third sex«, to mythical figures which were male and female at the same time, so that they possessed the strength of the sun (all-men), the earth (all-women) and the moon (male-female):

»Our original nature was not as it is now, but quite different. For one thing there were three sexes, rather than two (male and female) we have now. The third sex was a combination of these two. Its name has survived, though the phenomenon itself has disappeared. This single combination, comprising both male and female ... They were remarkable for their strength and vigour, and their ambition led them, to make an assault upon the gods. ... they tried to make a way up to heaven, to attack the gods. ... In the end Zeus, after long and painful thought, came up with a suggestion. ›I think I have an idea. Men could go on existing, but behave less disgracefully, if we made them weaker. I'm going to cut each of them in two. ... So he started cutting them in two, like someone slicing vegetables for pickling, or slicing eggs with a wire. ... When man's natural form was split in two, each half went round looking for its other half. They put their arms round one another, and embraced each other, in their desire to grow together again. ... That is why we have this innate love of one another. It brings us back to our original state, trying to reunite us and restore us to our true human form. Each of us is a mere fragment of a man (like half a tally-stick); we've been split in two, like filleted plaice. ... And the name of this desire and pursuit of completeness is Eros, or love.« (Plato, 1989)

From that time onwards, mankind strove after its lost half. Thus this is a description of one of the basic models: mankind's originally monistic nature is divided up, but seeks its original unity. Here we encounter the androgynous being in its two-sexed nature, which represents origin and perfection simultaneously.

dem Begehren zusammenzuwachsen. ... Seit so alter Zeit also ist die Liebe zueinander den Menschen eingepflanzt: Sie stellt die ursprüngliche Natur wieder her und versucht, aus zweien eins zu machen und die menschliche Natur zu heilen. Jeder von uns ist also das Gegenstück eines Menschen, da wir ja, zerschnitten wie die Schollen, aus einem zwei geworden sind. ... Und das Begehren und der Drang nach dem Ganzen, das heißt Eros.« (Platon, 1960)

Von nun an streben die Menschen nach ihrer verlorenen Hälfte. Damit ist eines der Grundmodelle dargestellt: Die ursprünglich monistische Wesenheit des Menschen wird zerteilt, sucht aber die originäre Einheit. Das androgyne Wesen begegnet uns hier in seiner Doppelgeschlechtlichkeit, die gleichzeitig Ursprung und Vollkommenheit darstellt.

2.2. Das Ur-Eine. Die Vollkommenheit. Das Ei

Wider alle Vorstellungsgabe schildert Platon die ursprünglichen androgynen Wesen als kugelförmig. Damit soll die Vollkommenheit der Urwesen charakterisiert werden, gelten doch **Kreis** und **Kugel** seit urdenklichen Zeiten als Metaphern für die absolute Vollendung in der Mikro- und Makrowelt: Der gesamte Kosmos, Sonne und Mond, das Heilige und Göttliche, Ursprung und Urgrund des Seienden sind in Kreis und Kugel vollständig repräsentiert. »Der mütterliche Urgrund der Welt« (Bachofen, 1954) ist in der Kugel, im Runden ganz allgemein gegenwärtig.

»Das Runde enthält als Kalebasse die Ureltern. In Ägypten wie in Neuseeland, in Griechenland ebenso wie in Afrika und Indien liegen die Ureltern in Kohabitation als Himmel und Erde aufeinander ... so lange noch nichts zwischen sie getreten ist und aus der Ureinheit die Zweiheit geschaffen hat. Dies Gegensatzerhaltende ist als mann-weiblich der große Hermaphrodit, das anfängliche Schöpferische, der Purusha Indiens, der die Pole in sich verbindet.« (Neumann, 1949)

Neben Kreis und Kugel gibt es einen anderen Topos der Vollkommenheit, das **Ei**, und es ist verständlich, daß es in den Mythen als Element des Ursprungs interpretiert wird. Es gilt ähnlich wie die Kugel als die ursprüngliche Form des Kosmos, in der die Einheit von Himmel und Erde präsent ist, doch wird es schon am Beginn der Zeiten einer Spaltung unterworfen.[8]

Daß auch das Symbol der Vollkommenheit und Geschlossenheit, das Ei, in einer Polarisierung gesehen werden kann, interpretiert **Johann Jakob Bachofen** (1815–1887) an Hand eines Grabbildes in der Villa Pamfilia in Rom: Fünf Jünglinge umstehen einen Tisch, auf dem drei Eier liegen. »Sie sind aber nicht einfarbig, sondern der Länge nach geteilt, in der oberen Hälfte weiß, in der unteren dunkel bemalt ... Der Wechsel der hellen und der dunklen Farbe drückt den steten Übergang von Finsternis zum Licht, von Tod zum Leben aus ... Symbol ... des Eies, das Leben und Tod in sich schließt, sie beide zu einer untrennbaren Einheit verbindet ... aus den beiden Hälften des Eies sind Himmel und Erde hervorgegangen.« (Bachofen, 1954) Bei der Entsprechung der Eihälften zum Weiblichen und Männlichen ist die schwarze Hälfte der Erde, dem »Weiblich-Stofflichen« und die weiße Hälfte dem Himmel, dem »Männlich-Unkörperlichen« zugeordnet.

Die geometrische Entsprechung des Eies in der Architektur ist das Ellipsoid und in der zweidimensionalen Projektion die Ellipse. Zum Unterschied vom Kreis begegnet uns die Ellipse in der historischen Architektur relativ selten. In der Barockarchitektur bedeutet die elliptische Kuppel eine Dynamisierung des Zentralbaus, eine Loslösung von der in sich ruhenden Vollkommenheit der traditionellen Kuppel. Auf der Suche nach brauchbaren Metaphern und formalen Bereicherungen in der Architektur unseres Jahrhunderts gewinnen Ellipse und Ei eine neue Bedeutungsdimension, wenngleich es schwer fällt, überzeugende Interpretationen zu artikulieren.

Im Werk von **Frederick (Friedrich) Kiesler** (1890–1965) tritt wiederholt die Idee des Eies auf, vor allem bei den Entwürfen für eine »Endless Architecture«. Michael Sgan Cohen (1988) deutet Kieslers Architektur und findet eine direkte Beziehung zwischen dem Ei und dem Mutterschoß: »Es ist auch ganz leicht, in der Eiform und der runden Hülle, die das ›Endless House‹ ausmacht, eine Art Mutterschoß zu sehen, in dem Leben unter äußerst gastlichen, mütterlichen Bedingungen geformt wird. In diesem Sinne drückt Kieslers obsessiver Bezug zum eiförmigen ›Endless‹ den ›primordial‹ weiblichen Archetypus aus.«

Eine aufschlußreiche Zeichnung aus dem Jahre 1959 zum *Endless House* scheint diese These zu bekräftigen: Ganz deutlich bildet sich aus den dichten Strichlagen die äußere Form des Eies, aber gleichzeitig ist es eine offene Höhle, in deren Innerem sich ein Turm mit einem Eingangstor krümmt. Die Eiform im Querschnitt und der Kreis im Grundriß sind die formalen

2.2. The Original Unity. Perfection. The Egg

Plato runs contrary to all power of imagination in describing the original androgynous beings as spherical. This is intended to characterize the perfection of the original beings, as the **circle** and the **sphere** have, since time immemorial, been regarded as metaphors for absolute perfection in both microcosm and macrocosm: the entire cosmos, sun and moon, holiness and divinity, the origin and source of existence, are completely represented in circle and sphere. »The maternal source of the world« (Bachofen, 1954) is, in a very general sense, present in the sphere, in roundness.

»Roundness, in the form of a calabash, contains ancestors. In Egypt, New Zealand and Greece, as well as in Africa and India, ancestors lie on top of one another in cohabitation like the sky and the earth ... so long as nothing has yet come between them and created duality out of the original unity. This being that maintains the opposites is, when it is male-female, the great hermaphrodite, the originally creative being, the Purusha of India which combines the poles within itself.« (Neumann, 1949)

Apart from the circle and the sphere, there is also another topos of perfection, namely the egg. It is understandable that, in myths, the egg is interpreted as the element that constitutes the origin. Like the sphere, it is regarded as the original form of the cosmos, the form in which the unity of sky and earth is present, but it is subjected to a division at the very beginning of time.[8]

Johann Jakob Bachofen (1815–1887) uses the example of an image on a tomb in the Vila Pamfilia in Rome to argue that an egg, the symbol of perfection and self-containment, can also be considered as a polarization: in that image, five youths are standing around a table upon which there are three eggs. »They are not solid in color, but divided lengthwise, white above and dark below. ... The alternation of light and dark color expresses the continuous passage from darkness to light, from death to life.« The egg »encompasses life and death, binding them into an inseparable unity ... Heaven and earth are the product of the two halves of the egg.« (Bachofen, 1967) As regards the correspondence of the two halves of the egg to feminity and masculinity, the black half is allocated to the earth, which is the »female-material element«, and the white half allocated to the heaven, the »male-incorporeal element«.

The geometrical equivalent of the egg in architecture is the ellipsoid, and in the two-dimensional projection it is the ellipse. In contrast to the circle, the ellipse is encountered relatively rarely in historical architecture. In Baroque architecture, an elliptical dome means that the central planned building is made dynamic and that there is a movement away from the idea of the static perfection of the traditional dome. The ellipse and the egg gain a new dimension of meaning in the search for suitable metaphors and formal enrichments in the architecture of the twentieth century, even though it is hard to articulate any convincing interpretations.

The idea of the egg occurs repeatedly in the work of **Frederick (Friedrich) Kiesler** (1890 to 1965), particularly in the designs for an »Endless Architecture«. Michael Sgan Cohen (1988) interpreted Kiesler's architecture and found in it a direct relationship between the egg and the womb: »It is very easy to regard the egg shape, and also the round covering which constitutes the ›Endless House‹, as a kind of womb in which life is formed under extremely hospitable, maternal circumstances. Looked at in this way, Kiesler's obsessive relationship with oviform endlessness expresses the primordially feminine archetype.«

An illuminating drawing on the subject of the *Endless House*, dating from 1959, seems to endorse this proposition: the external shape of the egg is clearly formed from the compact lines, but at the same time it is an open cave inside which there is a crooked tower with an entrance gate. The egg shape seen in the cross-section, and the circle found in the ground plan, are the factors which formally determine the design for the *Endless Theatre* dating from 1923. The endlessness in question is to be defined as meaning that the body is hermetically enclosed within itself, thus has no beginning and no end, and displays its unlimited infinity in a perfect continuum.

Despite the additional architectural elements, the oviform shape is again clearly discernible in the sketch for an *Endless House*, dating from 1958, even though Kiesler does not confirm that that shape is present: »The continuous, flowing shell structure of the ›Endless House‹ is not an eccentric sculptural idea, neither is it an imitation of an egg. The spherical form is derived from the social dynamics produced by the two or three generations living under one roof.« (Kiesler, 1988)

Determinanten des Entwurfs für das *Endless Theater* aus dem Jahre 1923. Die »Endlessness« ist so zu definieren, daß der Körper in sich hermetisch geschlossen ist, somit keinen Anfang und kein Ende kennt und in einem vollendeten Kontinuum seine grenzenlose Unendlichkeit darstellt.

Auch die Skizze zu einem *Endless House* von 1958 läßt, unbeschadet der ergänzenden architektonischen Elemente, die Eiform deutlich erkennen, wenngleich wir sie bei Kiesler nicht bestätigt finden: »Die fortlaufende, fließende Schalenkonstruktion des Endlosen Hauses ist keine verstiegene Skulpturidee, noch ist sie die Nachahmung eines Eies. Die kugelige Gestalt leitet sich von der sozialen Dynamik der zwei oder drei Generationen ab, die unter einem Dach leben.« (Kiesler, 1988)

Besondere Bedeutung kommt den Arbeiten des japanischen Architekten **Tadao Ando** (geb. 1941) zu. Sein Formenvokabular ist zweifellos auf die geistigen Traditionen Japans gestützt. Der buddhistische Wassertempel in Tsuna, Hyogo, (1991) begnügt sich im Grundriß mit einem einfachen geometrischen Vokabular, die formale Dominanz bildet ein elliptisches Wasserbecken, das die Idee des Lotos repräsentiert. Die Halle ist gleichsam in dieses Wasserbecken abgesenkt. Zum Wettbewerb für einen Kongreßpalast in Nara (1992) entwirft Ando die Haupthalle in Form einer Ellipse, eine zweite schließt sich an, sie dient der Überdachung des Stiegenplatzes. Tadao Andos Projekt für die alte Stadthalle in Osaka aus dem Jahre 1918 geht von der Grundform des Ellipsoides aus, das in den historischen Bau implantiert wird. Andos Bezeichnung *Urban Egg* ist ein deutlicher Hinweis dafür, daß Ei und Ellipsoid als anonyme morphologische Elemente gelten können.[9]

Im Gegensatz dazu ist das »Ei«, das **Gustav Peichl** (geb. 1928) und **Rudolf F. Weber** (geb. 1933) entworfen haben, von zwei langgestreckten Baukörpern schützend umgeben: Bei der Ganztagshauptschule in Wien-Floridsdorf nimmt der elliptische Bau, durch Brücke und Gänge erschlossen, Bibliothek, Verwaltung und Pausenhalle auf.

Im Werk von **Heinz Tesar** (geb. 1939) stoßen wir einige Male auf die Idee des Eies in der Gestalt der Ellipse. Das Verwaltungsgebäude für Schömer in Klosterneuburg bei Wien (1988) birgt im Inneren eine feierliche Treppenhalle in Ellipsenform. Bei der evangelischen Kirche in Klosterneuburg (1993–1995) öffnet sich das Ei, empfängt gastlich den Eintretenden, der sich sorglich umhüllt fühlt, die Eierschale ist lediglich durch rhytmisch angeordnete Fenster kleinteilig aufgebrochen.

Die Faszination des Eies (und dessen Abstraktion, der Ellipse) in unserem Jahrhundert läßt sich vielleicht daraus erklären, daß eine Epoche der vermeintlichen Wirrnis und Zersplitterung, der Pluralität und Widersprüchlichkeit die Sehnsucht nach großer Vollkommenheit entstehen läßt und so den uralten Symbolen und Formen Aktualität verleiht.

2.3. Die Teilung des »Einen«. Parthenogenese. Schöpfung aus der Einheit

In Bachofens Beschreibung der drei Eier (vgl. Kap. 2.2) wird deutlich, wie sensibel die Vollkommenheit des »Einen« ist, wie sehr sie unweigerlich zur Zweiheit tendiert, das Wesen der Trennung latent in sich bergend. So unterliegt auch die Perfektion des Eies der Teilung: »In Indochina begegnet uns ein **Weltenei**, dem ... das erste menschliche Wesen ... entschlüpft und dabei die Schalen in Himmel und Erde teilt. ...

In Melanesien ist entweder die Rede von einer gespaltenen Kokosnuß oder wiederum vom kosmischen Ei, das der Schöpfung zugrunde liegt.«[10] (Raehs, 1990)

In vielen Religionen und Mythen hat das Thema der Trennung von Himmel und Erde eine große Bedeutung und ist ein wichtiger Teil der Weltschöpfungsmythen. Direkt oder indirekt ist damit ausgesagt, daß Himmel und Erde ursprünglich eine Einheit bildeten – oder zumindest einander sehr nahe waren.

Das Prinzip einer ursprünglichen Einheit des Menschengeschlechts und dessen spätere Spaltung und Trennung wird auf die Kosmogonien übertragen. Wenn man dazu bedenkt, daß Himmel und Erde in nahezu allen Mythen geschlechtlich differenziert sind (meist ist der Himmel männlich und die Erde weiblich gedacht), so scheint die Dichothomie der Geschlechter und der Glaube an eine ursprüngliche Einheit in großartigen kosmischen Metaphern dargestellt.

Diese Analogie wird in jenen Mythen besonders deutlich, in denen eine Person gespalten wird – ähnlich wie in Platons mythischer Erzählung – und daraus Himmel und Erde entstehen.

3. Heinz Tesar, evangelische Kirche in Klosterneuburg, Niederösterreich, 1993–1995.
4. Gustav Peichl und Rudolf E. Weber, Ganztagsschule in Wien-Floridsdorf, 1996.
5. Tadao Ando, *Urban-Egg*, Osaka, 1988.
6. Tadao Ando, Wassertempel in Tsuna, Hyogo, Japan, 1991.
7. Tadao Ando, Kongreßpalast in Nara, 1992.

3. Heinz Tesar, evangelical church in Klosterneuburg, Lower Austria, 1993–1995.
4. Gustav Peichl and Rudolf E. Weber, all-day elementary school in Floridsdorf, Vienna, 1996.
5. Tadao Ando, *Urban-Egg*, Osaka, 1988.
6. Tadao Ando, water temple in Tsuna, Hyogo, Japan, 1991.
7. Tadao Ando, congress palace in Nara, 1992.

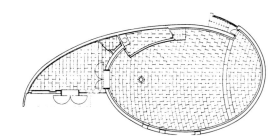

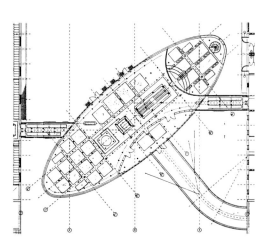

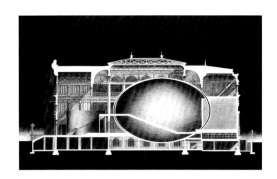

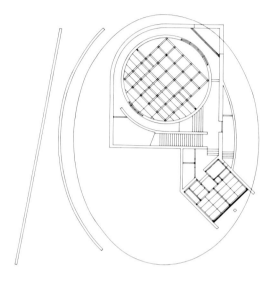

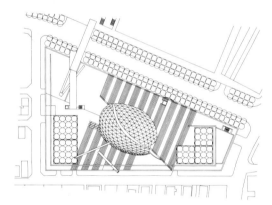

The work of the Japanese architect **Tadao Ando** (born 1941) is of particular importance. His vocabulary of shapes is undoubtedly based on Japan's spiritual traditions. The ground plan of Tsuna, the Buddhist water temple in Tsuna, Hyogo (1991), is content to stay with a simple geometrical vocabulary, and the formal dominance is produced by an elliptical water basin representing the idea of the lotus. The main temple hall is set down, as it were, inside this water basin. Ando designed the elliptically-shaped main hall as his entry for a competition for a congress palace in Nara (1992), and it is adjoined by a second hall which serves as a roof over the square where the staircase is. Tadao Ando's project for the old town hall in Osaka, which dates from 1918, proceeds from the basic shape of the ellipsoid which is to be implanted into the historical building. Ando calls this an *Urban Egg*, a clear indication that the egg and the ellipsoid can be regarded as anonymous morphological elements.[9]

In contrast to this, the »egg« designed by **Gustav Peichl** (born 1928) and **Rudolf F. Weber** (geb. 1933) is protectively surrounded by two elongated structures: in the all-day elementary school in Floridsdorf, Vienna, the elliptical structure, which is made accessible by bridges and corridors, contains the library, offices and students' common room.

We meet, several times, with the idea of an egg in the form of an ellipse in the works of **Heinz Tesar** (born 1939). The interior of the office building of the Schömer company (1988) in Klosterneuburg near Vienna harbours an elliptically shaped hall with a staircase. In the Evangelical church (1993–1995) in Klosterneuburg, the egg opens, hospitably taking in the entering visitor who feels that he is being caringly enveloped, and the rhythmically located windows provide only a slight variation on the eggshell shape.

The explanation for the fascination that flows from the egg (and its abstraction, the ellipse) in the present century may perhaps be that an epoch of what is thought to be chaos, fragmentation, plurality and contradiction gives rise to a longing for great perfection, thus lending a topical significance to the age-old symbols and forms.

2.3. The Division of the »One«. Parthenogenesis. Creation out of Unity

Bachofen's description of the three eggs (see chapter 2.2) makes it clear that the perfectness of the »one« is a sensitive matter which unavoidably tends towards duality and latently harbours within itself the nature of separation. Thus the perfection of the egg is also subject to division: »In Indochina we encounter a **cosmic egg** from which ... the first human being ... escapes, dividing the eggshells into heaven and earth. ...

In Melanesia, reference is made either to a split coconut or, once again, to a cosmic egg upon which the universe is based.«[10] (Raehs, 1990)

The separation of heaven and earth is a matter of great significance in many religions and myths, and is an important part of the myths of the world's creation. Either directly or indirectly, this expresses the idea that heaven and earth were originally one unit – or were at least very close to one another.

The principle that the human race was originally a single unity and later became split up and divided is transferred to the cosmogonies. If it is also remembered that heaven and earth are of different sexes in nearly all the myths (usually, heaven is male and the earth female), the dichotomy of the sexes, and the belief in an original unity, appear to be depicted in magnificent cosmic metaphors.

This analogy becomes especially clear in the myths in which a person is split – similarly to what occurs in Plato's mystic story – and the result gives rise to heaven and earth.

In the case of the Babylonians, »Marduk splits Tiâmat, the chaotic original being, in two, creating heaven and earth from the two parts. With the Maoris, the two parents are torn apart, and the two halves form heaven and earth.« (Staudacher, 1942)

In the mythology of Tonga in Africa, the first two humans were created from a single unity: »In the beginning there was a great worm. It was cut in two by a messenger from heaven. The two parts were the first human beings.« (Eliade, 1962)

Finally, the Biblical history of creation includes, in Genesis, i, 6–8, a myth of separation, with God separating light and darkness, earth and water.

Splitting, separation, division, cutting one person – the original unity – into two: that is one of the two mythical formulations explaining the creation of duality and plurality, while the other formulation postulates self-generating beings, with the original pair arising from a single being, which was similar to a human or animal. A logical consequence is that the chief constituents,

Bei den Babyloniern »spaltet Marduk das chaotische Urwesen Tiâmat und schafft aus den beiden Teilen Himmel und Erde. Bei den Maoris wird das Elternpaar auseinandergerissen, die beiden Hälften bilden Himmel und Erde«. (Staudacher, 1942)

In der Mythologie der afrikanischen Tonga entstehen die beiden ersten Menschen aus einer Einheit: »Im Anfang war ein großer Wurm. Dieser wurde von einem Boten des Himmels entzweigeschnitten. Die beiden Stücke waren die ersten Menschen.« (Eliade, 1962)

Schließlich enthält auch der biblische Schöpfungsbericht nach Gen . I, 6–8 einen Trennungsmythos, wenn Gott das Licht und die Finsternis, die Erde und das Wasser voneinander trennt.

Die Spaltung, Trennung, Teilung, das Auseinanderschneiden einer Person, des Ur-Einen, ist der eine mythische Ansatz, der die Entstehung der Zweiheit und Vielheit erklärt, der andere postuliert **selbstzeugende Wesen**, das Ur-Paar entsteht aus einer einzigen Gestalt, mensch- oder tierähnlich. Es ist eine logische Konsequenz, daß die wesentlichen Konstituenten, vor allem das Weibliche und das Männliche, in irgendeiner Form in diesem Ur-Einen vorhanden sein müssen. Römer (1903) ist der Meinung, »daß wirklich in fast jeder Religion der höchste Gott, oder der einzige Gott bestimmt androgynisch gedacht und abgebildet wurde.«

Allerdings geben die realen gesellschaftlichen Strukturen den Ausschlag, ob die Gottheit weiblich oder männlich definiert wird, und so ist es auch verständlich, daß etwa in den patriarchaischen Hochkulturen die männlichen Götter oder ein männlicher Gott dominieren.

In der **ägyptischen Mythologie** nimmt der Gedanke des Ur-Einen einen wichtigen Platz ein. »Die Zeit vor der Weltschöpfung wird als eine Art Un-Zeit beschrieben, in der es noch nicht zwei Dinge gab, d. h. erst mit der ordnenden Teilung bzw. Trennung der chaotischen Einheitsmaterie setzt die Schöpfung mit den Lebensqualitäten Licht und Zeitablauf ein.« (Westendorf, 1986)

Der Urgott ist Atum, in ihm ist die Zweiheit von vornherein angelegt. »Er schuf das erste geschlechtlich differenzierte Götterpaar Schu und Tefnut. Die Pyramidentexte schildern, wie Atum die aus seinem Samen entstandenen Kinder ... aushustet bzw. ausspeit. ... Einen Gott mit derartigen Qualitäten nennen die Texte Vater und Mutter, was besagen will, daß beide Schöpfungsprinzipien, das Zeugen und das Gebären, in einer Gottheit vereinigt sind.« (Westendorf, 1986) Atum ist gleichwohl ein männlicher Gott, obwohl Empfängnis und Geburt durch seinen Mund erfolgen.

»Der ägyptische Sonnengott Horus erliegt ... jeden Abend im Kampf gegen seinen Bruder Seth, ist aber am nächsten Morgen wieder neugeboren von seiner Mutter Hathor, in welcher er sich selbst zeugt.« (Lurker, 1958)

Nach ägyptischer Auffassung ist aber auch die Fruchtbarkeit der Erdmutter und der Großen Mutter derart intensiv, daß sie, vor allem als Mutter am Anfang des menschlichen und göttlichen Seins, auf den männlichen Partner verzichten kann. Der Gedanke der **Parthenogenese** begegnet uns hier: Die Göttin ist selbstzeugend. »Sie wurde zugleich als Mutter und Tochter betrachtet, die ihren Begatter erschuf, und wurde oft als androgynes Wesen gedacht und manchmal auch dargestellt.« (Giedion, 1964)

Zu den selbstzeugenden Göttinnen gehört Neith. Auch Isis wird eine Empfängnis als Werk eigener Kraft zugeschrieben, und in der Totengeschichte des Isis-Schauspiels sagt sie von sich selbst: »Ich machte mich zum Manne, obwohl ich eine Frau war um Deinen (Osiris) Namen auf Erden leben zu lassen.« Ähnliches gilt für Hathor, in deren Pluralität der Fähigkeiten auch die Eigenschaft enthalten ist, allein Kinder zu erzeugen.

Auch die **griechische Mythologie** kennt das Thema der Selbstzeugung. Der Vorgang des Empfangens und Gebärens durch ein Wesen, ohne Zutun eines Partners, erfährt eigenartige Varianten.

Gaia, die Erde, gebiert aus sich heraus Uranos, den männlichen Himmel, aber auch das Meer, ohne Eros, ohne Begattung. (Kerenyi, 1951) »Das große Gefäß zeugt in sich seinen eigenen Samen, es ist urzeugerisch, parthenogenetisch, und braucht das Männliche nur als Verbreiter des Samens, welcher der weiblichen Erde entstammt.« (Neumann, 1956)

Hera gebiert mehrere Gottheiten parthenogen: Ares, Eris, Hephaistos, Hebe sind ohne männliche Teilnahme entstanden. Zeus, der dies nicht glauben will, setzt sie auf einen Folterstuhl und zwingt sie, zu schwören, daß sie die Wahrheit gesagt habe.

Kybele ist eine androgyne Göttin. Als ihre männlichen Organe abgetrennt werden, entsteht daraus ein Baum. Die Früchte dieses Baumes ißt die Jungfrau Nana, woraufhin sie schwanger wird und Attis gebiert. Aber Kybele, die nun in Gestalt des Hermaphroditen Agdistis auftritt, verliebt sich in Attis und macht ihn wahnsinnig vor Liebe.

particularly the female and male elements, must, in some form or other, be present in this original unity. Römer (1903) takes the view »that almost every religion actually thought of, and depicted, the highest god, or the one god, as being definitely androgynous.«

However, it is the actual social structures that determine whether the deity is defined as being female or male, and this makes it understandable why, in the very advanced patriarchal civilizations for example, male gods, or a male god, dominate.

The idea of original unity plays an important part in **Egyptian mythology**. »The time before the creation of the world is described as a kind of non-time, in which there were not yet two things, so that creation, along with light and the passage of time which are properties of life, did not begin until the chaotic material of unity was ordered by being divided or separated.« (Westendorf, 1986)

The original god was Atum, in whom duality applied from the start. »He created Shu and Tefnut, the first sexually differentiated pair of gods. The pyramid texts describe Atum ... coughing out, or spitting out, the children created from his seed ... A god possessing such qualities is referred to in the texts as father and mother, which denotes that both principles of creation, begetting and giving birth, are combined in a single deity.« (Westendorf, 1986) Atum is nevertheless a male god, although conception and birth take place through his mouth.

»Horus, the Egyptian sun god, died ... every evening in the battle against his brother Seth, but the next morning his mother Hathor gave him new birth, and in her he generated himself.« (Lurker, 1958)

However, according to the Egyptian interpretation, the fertility of the earth mother and of the Great Mother is also so intense that– particularly in her capacity as a mother at the beginning of human and divine existence – she can dispense with a male partner. Here we encounter the idea of **parthenogenesis**: the goddess is self-generating. »She was considered the daughter and mother who created her begetter, and was often thought of and indeed sometimes represented as an androgynous being.« (Giedion, 1964)

Neith is one of the self-generating goddesses. Conception is also attributed to Isis as being the work of her own power and, in the story of the dead in the Isis stage play, she says of herself: »I made myself into a man, although I was a woman, in order to let your (Osiris) name live on earth.« Something similar applies to Hathor, the plurality of whose abilities also includes the property of generating children of her own accord.

Greek mythology also includes the topic of self-generation. There are some peculiar variations on the theme of the process by which a being conceives and gives birth without the assistance of a partner.

Gaia, the earth, gives birth, of her own accord, to Uranos, the male sky, and also to the sea, and does it without Eros, without any copulation. (Kerenyi, 1951) »The great vessel generates its own seed within itself. It generates spontaneously, it is parthenogenetic, and it requires the male only as a disseminator of the seed which derives from the female earth.« (Neumann, 1955)

Hera gives birth to several deities parthenogenetically: Ares, Eris, Hephaistos and Hebe came into being without any male involvement. Zeus, who did not want to believe this, placed her on a torture chair and forced her to swear that she had told the truth.

Kybele was an androgynous goddess. When her male organs were separated from her, they turned into a tree. The fruit of this tree was eaten by the virgin Nana, whereupon she became pregnant and gave birth to Attis. But Kybele, who now appeared in the shape of the Hermaphrodite Agdistis, fell in love with Attis and made him mad with love.

There was also a kind of self-generation with men. »Orphic cosmogony described ... Dionysos ... as a self-generating deity (protogonos) with a tail-like penis with which he fertilized his own anus.« (Bornemann, 1975) The Greek god Mise was thought of as a female two-sexed being – with breasts, a vagina and a penis above the anus, so that it could fertilize itself.

According to some later mythological ideas, Zeus, the father of the gods, also produced divine beings without a woman's assistance: Zeus' head was the seat of Metis, which was the divine mind, and from that head there issued Pallas Athene, the goddess of wisdom and peace, equipped with helmet and breastplate. Athene for her part gave virgin birth to Heracles.

The idea of parthenogenesis, of virgin birth, can be regarded as a symptom of androgynous tendencies, given that it is an attempt to eliminate the duality, the differentiation between the sexes, which is necessary in generation, and to do so by making a single being capable of

Auch bei Männern gibt es eine Art der Selbstzeugung. »Die orphische Kosmogonie beschreibt ... Dionysos ... als selbstzeugende Gottheit (protogonos) mit einem schwanzartigen Penis, mit dem er seinen eigenen After befruchtet.« (Bornemann, 1975) Das griechische Gottwesen Mise wurde als weiblich doppelgeschlechtlich aufgefaßt – mit Brüsten, einer Scheide und einem Penis über dem After, so daß es sich selbst befruchten konnte.

Nach späteren mythologischen Vorstellungen bringt auch der Göttervater Zeus göttliche Wesen ohne Zutun einer Frau hervor: Das Haupt des Zeus ist der Sitz der Metis, des göttlichen Denkens, und aus ihm entspringt, mit Helm und Brustpanzer ausgestattet, Pallas Athene, die Göttin der Weisheit und des Friedens. Athena ihrerseits bringt den Herakles jungfräulich zur Welt.

Der Gedanke der Parthenogenese, der Jungfernzeugung, kann als ein Symptom androgyner Tendenzen angesehen werden, handelt es sich doch dabei um den Versuch, die notwendige Zwei-Wesenheit bei der Zeugung, die Geschlechterdifferenzierung, dadurch aufzuheben, daß ein einziges Wesen zur Fortpflanzung fähig ist. Dieses einzige Wesen kann auch, wie oben erwähnt, männliche Charakteristika aufweisen, im allgemeinen aber sind es die Jungfrauen, die virginen Mütter, die als alleinige Urheber des Lebens angesehen werden.

Das im christlichen Kulturkreis geläufigste Beispiel ist die **Jungfrau Maria,** wobei es sich allerdings nicht um eine völlig partnerlose Zeugung handelt, sondern der Heilige Geist als Bewirker der Parthenogenese angesehen wird. Beim Laterankonzil 649 wurde die Jungfernschaft Mariens dogmatisch festgeschrieben.

Die Kinder der Parthenogenese, aus einer Jungfrau geboren, sind ihrerseits wieder Götter oder gottähnliche Wesen: Christus und Buddha, Quetzalcoatl und Huitzliopochtli, Montezuma und Dschingis-Khan. (Galahad, 1932) »Dschingis-Khan führte seinen Stammbaum auf eine Jungfrau zurück, deren Gravität vom Mond verursacht wurde.« Der Glaube an eine Fruchtbarkeit ohne Zutun des Mannes lebte noch bis in die Neuzeit fort, so etwa bei den Ureinwohnern Australiens, die die Kausalität zwischen Geschlechtsakt und Fortpflanzung nicht kannten.

Die Parthenogenese vollzieht sich nicht immer konsequent: Ist es in der christlichen Theologie der Heilige Geist, der die Empfängnis Mariens bewirkt, so ist es in der ägyptischen Mythologie der »Ka«, der die Verbindung zwischen dem Vater und dem Sohn darstellt. (Aurnhammer, 1986)

Aus dem asiatischen Kulturbereich kennen wir mythische Beispiele einer Art von Parthenogenese, die unter Beihilfe, aber ohne männliche Wesen abläuft. »So wird eine mongolische Prinzessin durch ein Nordlicht gravid, eine japanische Göttin durch den Genuß einer Kirsche; Lotosblumen schwängern die Fürstinnen von China. Die Shang-Dynastie führt sich auf Prinzessin Kien-Ti zurück, der ein Schwalbenei in den Mund fiel, und die Mandschu stammen von einem Mädchen und einer roten Frucht ab.« (Galahad, 1932)

In den brasilianischen Volkssagen und Mythen begegnen wir dem Wesen Korupira, der/die gleichzeitig »Herr« und »Mutter« ist, ein Schutzgeist der Wälder und des Wildes und die oberste Gottheit.

Bei den Monumbos in Afrika ist das erste Wesen eine Frau: »Denn plötzlich ... erschien ... eine Frau ... sie befruchtete sich selbst mit der großen Zehe und gebar zwei Söhne.« (Winthuis, 1931)

Bei den in Amerika lebenden Zuñi hat der bisexuelle Hochgott Awonawilona (»Er-Sie«) den Himmelsvater und die Erdmutter aus zwei Bällen seiner eigenen Haut angefertigt. (Lurker, 1958)

Bei den australischen Kurnai ist Mungan das höchste Wesen, es ist zugleich zeugendes und gebärendes Prinzip.

Diese Beispiele aus einem reichen ethnologischen Fundus sollen die Parthenogenese und deren Varianten als ein Phänomen im Bereiche der Androgynie dokumentieren.

Das Symbol des **Uroboros** kann androgyn-parthenogenetisch gedeutet werden. Der Drache oder die Schlange beißt sich selbst in den Schwanz und bildet dabei einen vollkommenen Kreis. Der Uroboros »tötet sich selbst, heiratet sich selbst und befruchtet sich selbst. Er ist Mann und Frau, zeugend und empfangend, verschlingend und gebärend, aktiv und passiv, oben und unten zugleich.« (Neumann, 1949)

Das eigenartige Symbol des Uroboros unterliegt einer Vielzahl von Deutungen und tritt in zahlreichen Kulturen in verschiedenen Varianten auf. Seine Faszination besteht wohl darin, daß ein Wesen von sich selbst aus die Vollkommenheit des Kreises bilden kann. Damit ist es gleichsam das Gegenmodell zu all den Vorstellungen, bei denen erst aus der Zweiheit unter gewissen Voraussetzungen die vollkommene Einheit gebildet werden kann.

8. Uroboros aus Griechenland, 3. Jh. v. Chr.

8. Uroboros from Greece, 3rd cent. BC.

propagation. As mentioned above, this single being can also possess male characteristics, but in general it is the virgin mothers who are regarded as the sole originators of life.

The commonest example in the Christian cultural complex is the **Virgin Mary**, although this act of generation was not performed entirely without a partner, as the Holy Ghost is regarded as the occasioner of parthogenesis. Mary's virginity was dogmatically laid down at the Lateran Council of 649.

The children of parthenogenesis, born of a virgin, are themselves gods or godlike beings: Christ and Buddha, Quetzalcoatl and Huitzliopochtli, Montezuma and Genghis Khan. (Galahad, 1932) »Genghis Khan traced his family tree back to a virgin whose pregnancy was caused by the moon.« The belief in fertility without a man's assistance continued until modern times, an example being the Australian aborigines, who did not recognize the causal relationship between coitus and propagation.

Parthenogenesis does not always take place logically: in Christian theology, it is the Holy Ghost that occasions the Virgin Mary's conception, while in Egyptian mythology the link between father and son is represented by »Ka«. (Aurnhammer, 1986)

In the Asian cultural area there are mythical examples of a kind of parthenogenesis which takes place with some assistance, but without any male beings. »Thus a Mongolian princess became pregnant by northern lights, and a Japanese princess by eating a cherry; lotus blossoms impregnated the princesses of China. The Shang dynasty traced itself back to Princess Kien-Ti, into whose mouth a swallow's egg fell, and the Mandshu were descended from a girl and a red fruit.« (Galahad, 1932)

In Brazilian folk legends and myths the being called Korupira is encountered, who is at the same time both »lord« and »mother«. Korupira is a guardian spirit of the forests and game animals, and is also the highest deity.

For the Monumbos in Africa, the first being was a woman: »For suddenly ... a woman ... appeared ... she fecundated herself with her big toe and gave birth to two sons.« (Winthuis, 1931)

In the case of the Zuñi who live in America, the bisexual high god Awonawilona (»He-She«) created the father of heaven and the mother of earth from two balls of his/her own skin.« (Lurker, 1958)

For the Australian Kurnai, Mungan is the supreme being, and represents at once both the begetting and the birth-giving principle.

These examples from the abundant ethnological records are intended to document parthenogenesis and its variants as a phenomenon within the field of androgyny.

The symbol of **Uroboros** can be interpreted in an androgynous-parthenogenetic sense. A dragon or snake bites itself in its own tail, forming a perfect circle. The Uroboros »kills itself, marries itself and fertilizes itself. It is man and woman, begetting and conceiving, devouring and giving birth, being active and passive, above and below, all at once.« (Neumann, 1949)

The peculiar symbol of the Uroboros is subject to a great number of interpretations and occurs in numerous cultures in different variations. Its fascination probably lies in the fact that a being can, of its own accord, form the perfection which is a circle. This means that it is practically the opposite of all the notions according to which perfect unity can, with certain conditions being fulfilled, be formed only from duality.

This symbol of the snake which forms a ring was still current in the alchemy of the late medieval period. Snakes have since time immemorial been part of a rich symbolic area of meaning. One possible interpretation – to be found in the works of Kafka, for example – lies in the longing for perfection, for oneness in sexuality, for what might be described as an autistic self-sufficiency.

The Uroboros is also seen in relation to the multi-layered being which is the **Gorgo**. »There is a uroborically male-female emphasis about the Gorgo, as is indicated not only by the bristling tusks of her mouth-womb, but also by her extended tongue which – in contrast to her female lips – always has a phallic character ... wherever the female appears as a dreadful figure, she is also the uroboric snake-woman, the woman with the phallus, the unity of giving birth and begetting, of life and death. This is why the Gorgo has all the male attributes: the snake, the tooth, the boar's tusks, the extended tongue, and sometimes even a beard.« (Neumann, 1955)

»Uniparental propagation« is found only sporadically in the real world of natural science: in protozoans which multiply by dividing up, in insects, fish and numerous plants. In humans, a unicellular twin might be regarded as a uniparental phenomenon. (Bischof, 1980)

Dieses Symbol der Schlange, die einen Ring bildet, ist noch in der Alchemie des späten Mittelalters gebräuchlich. Die Schlange wird von jeher in ein reiches symbolisches Bedeutungsfeld einbezogen. Eine der möglichen Deutungen – wir finden sie etwa bei Kafka – liegt in der Sehnsucht nach Vollkommenheit, nach der Einheit des Geschlechtlichen, nach einem gleichsam autistischen Selbstgenügen.

Der Uroboros wird auch mit dem vielschichtigen Wesen der **Gorgo** in Zusammenhang gebracht. »Die uroborisch mann-weibliche Betonung der Gorgo geht nicht nur aus den starrenden Hauern ihres Maul-Schoßes hervor, sondern ebenso aus der herausgestreckten Zunge, welche – im Gegensatz zu den weiblichen Lippen – immer phallischen Charakter besitzt ... wo das Weibliche als furchtbar auftritt, ist es auch die uroborische Schlangenfrau, das Weib mit dem Phallus, die Einheit von Gebärendem und Zeugendem, von Leben und Tod. Deshalb ist die Gorgo mit allen männlichen Attributen ausgestattet, der Schlange, dem Zahn, den Eberhauern, der hervorgestreckten Zunge und manchmal sogar mit dem Bart.« (Neumann, 1956)

Im realen Bereich der Naturwissenschaft finden wir nur sporadisch eine »uniparentale Fortpflanzung« bei Einzellern, die sich durch Teilung vermehren, bei Insekten, bei Fischen, bei zahlreichen Pflanzen. Beim Menschen könnte der einzellige Zwilling als uniparentales Phänomen angesehen werden. (Bischof, 1980)

2.4. Schöpfung aus der Zweiheit

Viel häufiger als die unmittelbare Schöpfung aus der Einheit finden wir mythische Welterklärungen aus dem Prinzip der Zweiheit des Seienden.

In zahlreichen frühen Kulturen nimmt die Frau, die Mutter, die dominierende Stellung ein. Aus der Bedeutung der Fruchtbarkeit – auch übertragen auf Tier und Pflanze – und der Geburt ist wohl in erster Linie die Grundlage der frühen matriarchalischen Gesellschaft zu erklären.

Das »Mysterium der Geburt« hat den Menschen seit urdenklichen Zeiten bewegt, und es wurde selbstverständlich in den magisch kultischen Bereich einbezogen.

Für die Epoche des Paläolithikums (Altsteinzeit, ca. 3 Millionen v. Chr. bis 10 000 v. Chr.) sind die sogenannten **Venus-Figuren** charakteristisch, die zweifellos weibliche Fruchtbarkeitsidole darstellen, wie etwa die Venus von Willendorf aus Niederösterreich. Für die primitive Vorstellungskraft waren die weibliche Figur mit besonders betonten femininen Attributen und der Phallus die beiden Pole schöpferischer Lebensenergie – der eine rezeptiv, der andere als zeugende Kraft. Beide werden als vollkommene Einheit im Mysterium der Geburt begriffen. Die Geschlechtsteile stellt man sich als mit generativer Macht begabt vor, wodurch sie zu Symbolen der Fruchtbarkeit und der Fortpflanzung wurden. Bei dem komplexen Geburtsvorgang stellt die Empfängnis den Anfang dar: » ... Dies setzt eine Vereinigung der aktiven und passiven Elemente voraus, Mann und Weib vereinigen sich in einer sakralen Verschmelzung, um die Nachkommenschaft zu zeugen.« (James, 1957)

Die Frage nach der Entstehung, nach der **Zeugung** der Welt findet demnach in zahlreichen frühen Kulturen eine naheliegende Antwort: Die **Kosmogenese** läuft analog zur **Anthropogenese** ab, die Erzeugung der Welt ist ein paralleler Prozeß zur Erzeugung neuen menschlichen Lebens und wird durch die Vereinigung gegensätzlicher Prinzipien, im allgemeinen weiblicher und männlicher, bewerkstelligt.

Naheliegend ist es, daß **der** Himmel das männliche und **die** Erde das mütterliche Prinzip repräsentieren. Die Akzentverteilung ist in den einzelnen Mythen unterschiedlich, das äquivalent-partnerschaftliche Prinzip stellt zwar oft den Ausgangspunkt der Kosmogonien dar, doch bilden sich sehr bald mythische Hierarchien heraus. In den frühen matriarchalischen Kulturen übernimmt die Muttergottheit die führende Position, aber häufiger ist es der Mann, der die patriachalische Führungsrolle beansprucht.

Der Geschlechtsakt bei Göttern und Menschen wird austauschbar. »Menschen vollziehen die Vereinigung der Götter nach: Das ist die alte Idee von der heiligen Heirat, dem **hierós gamós.** ... Nach in Indien sehr alter begründeter Ansicht entstehen die Wesen aus der Verbindung von Natur/Materie und Seele. Die abstrakte Form der Materie ist dann mit der Göttin, die höchste Seele mit dem Gott gleichgesetzt worden: Und in der Vereinigung der beiden hebt sich der Gegensatz zwischen Seele und Materie auf.« (Gutschow, Pieper, 1981)

2.4. Creation out of Duality

Mythical interpretations of the world which arise from the principle of the duality of existence are found much more frequently than theories of direct creation out of oneness.

The woman, the mother, occupies the dominant position in numerous early cultures. The basis for early matriarchal societies is probably explained first and foremost by the significance of fertility – which was also transferred to animals and plants – and of birth.

The mystery of birth has exercised human minds since time immemorial, and was of course also part of the magic-cultic sphere.

The so-called **Venus figures** are characteristic of the palaeolithic period (Old Stone Age, from ca. 3 million BC to 10,000 BC). They undoubtedly depict female fertility idols, an example being Venus of Willendorf in Lower Austria. The female figure with its strongly emphasized feminine attributes, and the phallus, were – to the primitive imagination – the two poles of creative living energy, the first being receptive, and the other the generating force. They were understood as both being combined in perfect unity in the mystery of birth. The sexual organs were thought of as being endowed with generative power, and this meant that they became symbols of fertility and propagation. In the complex process of birth, conception was the beginning: »...This made it necessary to unite the active and passive elements, and man and woman were united in a sacred fusion in order to generate their progeny.« (James, 1957)

The question of the creation, the **generation**, of the world accordingly finds an obvious answer in numerous early cultures: **cosmogenesis** proceeds in analogous fashion to **anthropogenesis**, the creation of the world runs in parallel to the creation of new human life, and is effected by uniting opposing – generally female and male – principles.

It is natural that the sky represents the male principle and the earth the maternal. The allocation of emphasis differs in the individual myths. The principle of equivalent partners is often the starting point of cosmogonies, but mythical hierarchies very soon develop. In early matriarchal cultures, the maternal deity takes over the leading position, but it is more frequently the man who occupies the leading rôle of patriarch.

The sex act in gods and humans becomes interchangeable. »Humans copy the unification of the gods: this is the old idea of holy marriage, of **hierós gamós**. ... According to a view which was established a very long time ago in India, beings were created out of the combination of nature/material on the one hand and soul on the other. The abstract form of material was then equated with the female goddess, and the supreme soul with the male god: and, in the union of the two, the contrast between soul and material was eliminated.« (Gutschow, Pieper, 1981)

2.5. Criteria Distinguishing Women and Men. Sexual Identity

A precondition in an androgyne is that the sexual characteristics by no means disappear, but remain discernible.

Thus there first arises the question, not so very easy to answer, of how these characteristics are to be described and what we are to understand by »woman« and »man«.

When two-sexed malformations are left out of account, there is no doubt about which sex is to be allocated to a human being from a medical and biological point of view if the differentiation is restricted to the genital area, to the **primary sexual characteristics**, and thus to the external and internal sexual organs and to the organs of reproduction.

This determination is rightly regarded as not being sufficiently expressive of the **nature** of man and woman, and this is why there is a broadly-based discussion of the extent to which **psychological sex** and the circumstances of social history, particularly education, can modify or reinforce biological sex. Let us start with the biological facts.

We should bear in mind that the particular biological sex of a human being has been decided from conception onwards. »One phase of embryonic development is of particular interest: it is the time from conception up to the point when the gonadal system begins to be differentiated. Until that point, both sexes have the same appearance, and the embryo is a ›morphologically neutral foetus‹ which is able to develop further in either one direction or the other. ... The differentiation of the gonadal system does not begin until after the sixth week of pregnancy if testicles are to result from it, and about another six weeks later if an ovary is to be formed.« (Ehrmann, 1976)

2.5. Kriterien Frau/Mann. Geschlechtsidentität

Voraussetzung des Androgynen ist es, daß die Geschlechtscharakteristika keineswegs zum Verschwinden gebracht werden, sondern erkennbar bleiben.

Es stellt sich also zunächst die nicht so leicht zu beantwortende Frage, wie diese Charakteristika zu beschreiben sind, was wir unter »Frau« und »Mann« zu verstehen haben.

Lassen wir zwitterartige Mißbildungen außer acht, so besteht auf dem medizinisch-biologischen Sektor kein Zweifel über die geschlechtliche Zuordnung eines Menschen, wenn wir die Differenzierung auf den genitalen Bereich, auf die **primären Geschlechtsmerkmale**, somit auf die Geschlechtsorgane (äußere und innere) bzw. auf die Fortpflanzungsorgane beschränken.

Mit Recht wird diese Determinierung als zu wenig aussagekräftig für das **Wesen** von Mann und Frau angesehen, und auf breiter Basis wird daher die Frage diskutiert, inwieweit das **psychologische Geschlecht** und die kulturhistorischen Randbedingungen, insbesondere die Erziehung, das biologische Geschlecht modifizieren oder verfestigen können. Gehen wir zunächst von den biologischen Fakten aus.

Wir sollten vor Augen haben, daß die Entscheidung zu jeweils einer biologischen Geschlechtszugehörigkeit von der Empfängnis weg vorgegeben ist. »Eine Phase der **embryonalen Entwicklung** verdient besonderes Interesse, und zwar die Zeit von der Konzeption bis zum Beginn der Ausdifferenzierung der Keimdrüsenanlage: Bis zu diesem Punkt nämlich zeigt sich bei beiden Geschlechtern das gleiche Erscheinungsbild, handelt es sich bei dem Embryo um einen ›morphologisch neutralen Keimling‹ mit der Fähigkeit, sich in die eine oder andere Richtung weiterzuentwickeln. ... Erst nach der sechsten Schwangerschaftswoche setzt die Differenzierung der Keimdrüsenanlage ein, wenn daraus Hoden resultieren sollen, und etwa weitere sechs Wochen später, wenn sich ein Eierstock bilden soll.« (Ehmann, 1976)

Könnten wir vielleicht von einer **Neutrality-at-birth**-Theorie ausgehen, von einer psychosexuellen Neutralität zum Zeitpunkt der Geburt? Welchen Einfluß aber haben bereits die hormonalen Prozesse während der Schwangerschaft?

Es erscheint plausibel, sowohl die prä- als auch die postnatalen Faktoren bei der Geschlechterzuordnung zu berücksichtigen. Unmittelbar nach der **Geburt** setzt jedenfalls die rollenspezifische Konditionierung nach männlichen oder weiblichen Verhaltensweisen durch die Umwelt, vor allem durch die elterliche Erziehung, ein. »Die Entwicklung der Geschlechterkonstanz, also das Wissen um die Unveränderlichkeit ... des biologischen Geschlechts ... ist im allgemeinen im Alter von ca. 7 Jahren abgeschlossen.« (Bierhoff-Alfermann, 1977)

Bestimmend bleiben selbstverständlich die **primären Geschlechtsmerkmale**. Bei den **sekundären Geschlechtsmerkmalen** ist die Differenzierung nach männlich/weiblich weitgehend gegeben, aber nicht absolut eindeutig: Die Ausbildung der Milchdrüsen und die Entwicklung der Brust ist zwar der Frau vorbehalten, die Zuordnung der Behaarung ist jedoch nicht mehr ganz eindeutig, denn es gibt auf der einen Seite bartlose Männer und auf der anderen den Frauenbart. Ähnliches gilt für die Stimmlage der Sprache, aber auch des Gesanges: Kontertenöre haben eine Sopranstimme, während Alt-Sängerinnen in der Stimmlage unter der des Mannes liegen können. Vor allem hormonelle Einflüsse verändern signifikant die sekundären Geschlechtsmerkmale.

Den Übergang von den sekundären zu den **tertiären Geschlechtsmerkmalen**, und diesen unterschiedlich zugeordnet, bilden Körpergröße, Knochenbau sowie Herz- und Atemtätigkeit. Auch hier ist die Zuordnung keineswegs eindeutig.[11]

Als weitere Geschlechtsunterschiede werden der frühere Wachstumsabschluß der Frau, die ausgeprägte Entwicklung des Unterhautfettgewebes und die unterschiedlichen Proportionen des Körperbaus (Hüften, Becken, Schultern) angegeben. Verallgemeinerungen sind nicht möglich, aber immerhin lassen sich einige statistische Durchschnittswerte angeben: Männer sind im Durchschnitt 5 bis 10% größer, ihre Muskulatur macht 42% des Körpergewichtes aus, bei den Frauen 36%, das Fettdepot des Mannes liegt bei 18%, das der Frau bei 28%.[12]

Eindeutig zu den tertiären Geschlechtsmerkmalen sind die psychischen und die psychosozialen Faktoren zu zählen. Dabei relativiert sich die Zuordnung vollends, wenn wir uns vom konservativen Rollenschema distanzieren.

Es ist im einzelnen schwierig festzustellen, ob die tertiären Geschlechtsmerkmale zwingend aus den primären (eventuell sekundären) abgeleitet werden können, oder ob sie nicht vielmehr kulturhistorische, politische und soziale Phänomene darstellen.

Might we perhaps proceed on the basis of a **neutrality-at-birth** theory, of a psychosexual neutrality at the time of birth? But what influence do hormonal processes have as early as the pregnancy stage?

It appears plausible that both pre- and post-natal factors should be taken into account when it comes to allocating the child to one of the two sexes. Whatever the case, the environment, in particular the parental upbringing, begins, immediately after birth, to condition the child in accordance with a specific rôle, in accordance with either male or female modes of behaviour. »The development of sexual constancy, the knowledge of the unchangeability ... of the biological sex ... is generally completed at the age of about seven years.« (Bierhoff-Alfermann, 1977)

The **primary sexual characteristics** are of course the chief determinant factor. In the **secondary sexual characteristics**, the differentiation between male and female is largely present, but is not absolutely clear-cut: it is true that the formation of the lacteal glands and the development of the breast occur only in women, but the allocation of hairiness to one sex or the other is not entirely definite, as beardless men exist, as do women with beards. Something similar applies to the register of the voice in speech, and also in song: countertenors have a soprano voice, whereas the register of female contralto singers can be below that of the male voice. Hormonal influences, in particular, significantly change the secondary sexual characteristics.

Body height, bone structure, and cardiac and respiratory activity, form the transition from the secondary to the **tertiary sexual characteristics**, and are assigned to them in different ways. Here too, allocation is by no means definite.[11]

The earlier completion of growth in women, the pronounced development of subcutaneous fatty tissue, and the differing proportions in the structure of the body (hips, pelvis, shoulders), are stated as being additional differences between the sexes. No generalizations are possible, but some statistical averages can nevertheless be given: men are 5–10% taller on average, their muscles make up 42% of the body weight while the figure for women is 36%, and the fat deposit is 18% with men and 28% with women.[12]

The mental and psychosocial factors must definitely be reckoned among the tertiary sexual characteristics. But the allocation becomes entirely relative if we disassociate ourselves from the traditionally accepted system of rôles.

It is difficult to determine, in detail, whether the tertiary sexual characteristics can be conclusively derived from the primary (and possibly the secondary) characteristics, or whether they are not, instead, phenomena resulting from politics, society and cultural history.

The **structure of the body**, and the **division of labour**, may provide some initial pointers to a specific distinction between man and woman. J. J. Sulzer (1794) takes the view that men are born to carry out hard and laborious tasks, and that there is a feeling »that more tender limbs which have something soft about them are part of female beauty, and that stronger limbs which indicate something lasting and more bold are part of male beauty.«

Annette Degenhardt and Hans Martin Trautner (1979) make a distinction based on those features which are typical of the particular sex, and those which are specific to it. The former are those which are observed relatively frequently or intensively in a particular sex; they vary markedly more strongly between the two sexes than they do within one and the same sex. The latter occur exclusively in only one of the sexes, and are usually genetic and morphological features.

According to Degenhardt/Trautner, **the rôle played by the particular sex** is characterized by »the behavioural characteristics – attitudes, interests, abilities, motives, modes of behaviour – which, for the phenotypically male or female sex, are regarded as appropriate or are expected or prescribed by the culture.«

Dorothee Bierhoff-Alfermann (1977) proposes a plausible terminological differentiation: the designations employed for biological sex should be **male** and **female**, but »if what we mean by it is the associated characteristics which are taken on by, and are typical of, the particular sex, the terms used should be **masculine** and **feminine**«, and the reference should be to »psychological sex«, and this expresses the idea that the two need not necessarily coincide.

By way of another terminological differentiation, a distinction might be made between **sexus** as a biological factor, and **genus** as a factor determined by social culture.

This differentiation corresponds approximately to one found in American usage and employed mainly by Sandra Lipsitz Bem (1993), who also distinguishes between the terms **sex** and **gender**.[13]

Körperbau und **Arbeitsteilung** mögen Ansätze zu einer Spezifikation nach Mann und Frau liefern. J. J. Sulzer (1794) meint, daß der Mann zu schweren und mühsamen Verrichtungen geboren sei, man hat das Gefühl »daß zartere Gliedmaßen, die etwas Weichliches haben, zur weiblichen, und stärkere, etwas Dauerhaftes und Kühneres anzeigende zur männlichen Schönheit gehören.«

Annette Degenhardt und Hans Martin Trautner (1979) unterscheiden nach geschlechtstypischen und geschlechtsspezifischen Merkmalen. Erstere sind jene, die relativ häufig oder intensiv bei einem Geschlecht beobachtet werden, sie variieren zwischen den Geschlechtern deutlich stärker als innerhalb eines Geschlechtes. Letztere kommen ausschließlich bei einem Geschlecht vor, es sind in der Regel genetische und morphologische Merkmale.

Die **Geschlechtsrolle** charakterisieren nach Degenhardt/Trautner »die für das phänotypisch männliche bzw. weibliche Geschlecht als angemessen betrachteten, kulturell erwarteten oder vorgeschriebenen Verhaltensmerkmale (Einstellungen, Interessen, Fähigkeiten, Motive, Verhaltensweisen)«.

Dorothee Bierhoff-Alfermann (1977) schlägt eine plausible terminologische Differenzierung vor: Das biologische Geschlecht soll als **männlich** und **weiblich** bezeichnet werden, aber es soll, »wenn wir die damit verbundenen geschlechtstypisch angenommenen Charakteristika meinen, von **maskulin** und **feminin**« gesprochen werden, vom »psychologischen Geschlecht«, und damit ist ausgedrückt, daß beides nicht notwendig zusammenfallen muß.

Eine weitere terminologische Differenzierung könnte zwischen **Sexus** als biologischem und **Genus** als sozio-kulturell determiniertem Geschlecht unterscheiden.

Diese Differenzierung entspricht in etwa jener nach **sex** und **gender**,[13] der wir im Amerikanischen begegnen, praktiziert vor allem von Sandra Lipsitz Bem (1993).

Wenn wir bei Philosophen und Wissenschaftlern anfragen, bekommen wir sehr unterschiedliche Antworten zur Definition des Männlichen und Weiblichen.

Wilhelm v. Humboldt (1767–1835) geht von einer faszinierenden, poetisch-philosophischen Erläuterung des Weiblichen aus, die nicht nur charakteristisch für seine Zeit ist, sondern zweifellos bis in unsere Gegenwart weiterwirkt, gleichwohl aber als verbindliche Definition nicht geeignet ist. Für Humboldt (1960) manifestiert sich das Männliche im Zeugenden, das Weibliche im Empfangenden. Es sind »verschiedene, ungleichartige Principien« die keineswegs allein auf die »Körperwelt« beschränkt sind, sondern auch im Geistigen ihre Bedeutung haben. »Indem nun das Männliche angestrengte Energie, alles Weibliche beharrliche Ausdauer besitzt, bildet die unaufhörliche Wechselwirkung von beiden die unbeschränkte Kraft der Natur, deren Anstrengung nie ermattet, und deren Ruhe nie in Unthätigkeit ausartet.«

»Alles Männliche ... ist mehr aufklärend, das Weibliche ist mehr rührend. Das eine gewährt mehr Licht, das andere mehr Wärme.« Das Männliche ist mit »Kraft« ausgestattet, das Weibliche hingegen mit »Stoff«. Die Anlagen zwischen beiden Geschlechtern sind aber so verteilt, daß es möglich wird, das »unermeßliche Ganze« zu bilden.

Bei **Sigmund Freud** (1856–1939) gibt es keine vollständige geschlechtliche Abgrenzung der Person. Vor allem Penisneid und Kastrationskomplex verwischen die Grenzen. »Wenn das kleine Weib bei ihrem ersten Wunsch beharrt, ein ›Bub‹ zu werden, so wird sie im extremen Fall als manifeste Homosexuelle enden, sonst in ihrer späteren Lebensführung ausgeprägt männliche Züge zum Ausdruck bringen, einen männlichen Beruf wählen und dgl.« (Freud, 1972)

»Nach Sigmund Freud bewirken die Entdeckung des Penis beim Jungen und die Entdeckung der Penislosigkeit beim Mädchen die Differenzierung der Geschlechter.« (Silbermayr, 1988)

Dieser Aussage kann nicht vorbehaltlos zugestimmt werden. »Heute besteht weitgehend Einigkeit darüber, daß das Geschlecht des Menschen sowohl durch biologische als auch durch soziale Faktoren bestimmt wird, die miteinander in einem überaus komplexen und kommunikativen Verhältnis stehen.« (Bock, 1988)

»Weitgehend Konsens herrscht darüber, daß die Entwicklung der Geschlechtsidentität und des geschlechtstypischen Verhaltens von mehreren Variablengruppen abhängig ist: biologischen Faktoren, der Morphologie der äußeren Genitalien, dem Zuweisungsgeschlecht und den allgemeinen Umweltbedingungen«. (Ehmann, 1976)

So gesehen ist keineswegs »die Anatomie das Schicksal« (Freud), vielmehr ist sie nur einer der Parameter in einer komplexen Definition des Geschlechtsspezifischen.

Irenäus Eibl-Eibesfeldt (geb. 1928) (1984) versucht aus der Ethologie der Naturvölker und der naiven Völker typische Charakteristika herauszuarbeiten, die für unsere Gegenwart wohl nur sehr beschränkte Gültigkeit haben.

When we make the works of philosophers and scientists the object of our inquiries, we obtain widely differing answers defining what is male and what is female.

Wilhelm von Humboldt (1767–1835) proceeds on the basis of a fascinating, poetic and philosophical explanation of femininity. That explanation is not merely characteristic of his times, but undoubtedly also continues to have its effect at the present time, although it is not suitable as a binding definition. To Humboldt (1960), masculinity manifests itself in the act of begetting, and femininity in that of conceiving. These are »different, divergent principles« which are by no means limited solely to the »material world«, but also have significance in the spiritual realm. »Given that masculinity possesses strenuous energy, while everything feminine has a steadfast persistence, the incessant interaction between the two forms the unlimited power of nature, whose exertion never grows weary and whose tranquillity never degenerates into inactivity.«

»Everything male ... tends to be elucidating, while femininity tends to be affecting. The former provides more light, the latter more warmth.« Masculinity is equipped with »force«, whereas femininity is endowed with »matter«. But the abilities are distributed among the two sexes in such a way that it becomes possible to form the »immeasurable whole«.

In the view of **Sigmund Freud** (1856–1939), a human being cannot be entirely demarcated sexually. It is particularly penis envy and the castration complex that blur the borderlines. »If a little girl insists on her initial wish to become a ›boy‹, then in the extreme case she will end up a manifest homosexual; in lesser cases, she will display distinctly male characteristics in her later way of life, and will choose a man's career and the like.« (Freud, 1972)

»According to Sigmund Freud, the discovery of the penis in the case of boys, and the discovery of the absence of a penis in the case of girls, brings about the differentiation between the sexes.« (Silbermayr, 1988)

It is not possible to agreed unreservedly with this statement. »Today it is largely agreed that the sex of a human being is determined by both biological and social factors, which have an extremely complex and communicative relationship with one another.« (Bock, 1988)

»There is a large degree of consensus that the development of sexual identity and of behaviour typical of the particular sex is dependent on several groups of variables: biological factors, the morphology of the external genitals, the sex allocated to the particular person, and the general environmental circumstances.« (Ehmann, 1976)

Looked at in this way, it is by no means the case that »anatomy is fate« (Freud); instead, anatomy is only one of the parameters in a complex definition of the specific features of one sex or the other.

Irenäus Eibl-Eibesfeldt (born 1928) tried (1984) to extract, from the ethology of primitive and naive races, some typical characteristics which probably have only very limited applicability to our present-day circumstances.

For example, the observation that women in primitive races breast-feed for three years, and, if there is a large number of children, therefore remain confined and in need of protection for a long time, is – at least in the Western world – hardly of any significance today. In the same way, »hunting for big game and defending the group« is not a relevant »male activity« in our society.

On the other hand, some specific properties have been convincingly proved by experiment, and they can, with some reservations, be accepted by way of a certain generalization. One of them is the observation that boys turn out to be more aggressive at a very early age, whereas girls present themselves as more helpful. But the extent to which these properties can ultimately be once again traced back to the primary, that is to say the genital, differentiation between the sexes is still an unresolved question. The observation that girls are more timid, do not go so far away from their mothers, are more talented verbally, and other matters besides, may point to their potential maternal rôle.

Eibl-Eibesfeldt cites certain differences during adolescence which are specific features of one or other of the sexes, but increasing scepticism must be expressed regarding those differences, as the influence of the social surroundings is undoubtedly beginning to grow rapidly.

Margaret Mead (1901–1978) repeatedly asks how the sexes are differentiated and tries, on the basis of her ethnological research material, to arrive at an approach to certain answers, but she does not come to any convincing conclusions. »We know of no culture that has said, articulately, that there is no difference between men and women except in the way they con-tribute to the creation of the next generation; that otherwise in all respects they

So hat zum Beispiel die Feststellung, daß Frauen bei Naturvölkern drei Jahre lang stillen und bei großer Kinderzahl daher lange Zeit konfiniert und schutzbedürftig sind, heute kaum noch eine Bedeutung, zumindest in der westlichen Welt. Ebenso ist »das Jagen auf Großwild und die Verteidigung der Gruppe« in unserer Gesellschaft keine relevante »männliche Tätigkeit«.

Bestimmte Eigenschaften hingegen, die experimentell glaubwürdig nachgewiesen sind, werden in einer gewissen Verallgemeinerung mit Vorbehalten akzeptiert werden können, so etwa die Beobachtung, daß sich Knaben schon sehr früh als aggressiver erweisen, während sich Mädchen als hilfsbereiter darstellen. Inwieweit aber diese Eigenschaften letzlich doch wieder auf die primäre, also genitale Geschlechtsdifferenzierung zurückgeführt werden können, ist nach wie vor eine ungeklärte Frage. Auch die Beobachtung, daß Mädchen ängstlicher sind, sich weniger weit von der Mutter entfernen, verbal begabter sind und anderes mehr, kann auf die potentielle mütterliche Rolle verweisen.

Die geschlechtsspezifischen Unterschiede in der Adoleszenz, wie sie Eibl-Eibesfeldt zitiert, sind mit zunehmender Skepsis zu registrieren, da zweifellos der Einfluß des sozialen Umfelds rasch zu wachsen beginnt.

Margaret Mead (1901–1978) stellt wiederholt die Frage nach der Differenzierung der Geschlechter und versucht, sich auf der Basis ihres ethnologischen Forschungsmaterials bestimmten Antworten anzunähern, ohne jedoch zu überzeugenden Schlußfolgerungen zu gelangen. »Wir kennen keine Kultur, die ausdrücklich behauptet, der Unterschied zwischen Mann und Frau bestehe lediglich in der Form, in der beide Geschlechter zur Erzeugung der Nachkommenschaft beitragen, im übrigen aber seien beide nur menschliche Wesen mit verschiedenen Anlagen, von denen keine einem Geschlecht ausschließlich zugesprochen werden kann.« Die Tatsache, daß es geschlechtsspezifische Zuordnungen bisher in allen Gesellschaftsformen gegeben hat, ist kein überzeugendes Argument für die mögliche Objektivierung und Generalisierung von Geschlechterrollen. »Da Männer und Frauen in allen Gesellschaftsformen einen großen Überbau sozial bedingter Geschlechtsunterschiede errichtet haben, der offensichtlich nicht für die ganze Menschheit gültig sein kann ... fragt es sich also, ob solche Überbauten unbedingt errichtet werden müssen?« (Mead, 1975)

Der Zwang zu einem solchen Überbau kann nach Mead aus zwei Komponenten motiviert werden: aus der »biologischen Säugetiernatur« und aus der »gesellschaftlichen Bequemlichkeit«. »Sind nicht die geschlechtlichen Unterschiede überaus wertvoll, eine der Kraftquellen unserer menschlichen Natur ...?« Die Frage, »welche positiven Möglichkeiten liegen in den Geschlechtsunterschieden?«, wird nicht klar beantwortet, sondern immer wieder direkt oder indirekt auf die biologischen Unterschiede des »Säugetieres« zurückgeführt. So wird zum Beispiel die ganz unterschiedliche Bedeutung des Stillens bei Knaben und bei Mädchen sehr hoch eingeschätzt. »Aufnehmen ist für das männliche Wesen nicht dasselbe wie für das weibliche.«

Das Bekenntnis zu einem prinzipiellen Unterschied zwischen dem Männlichen und dem Weiblichen über das Biologische hinaus ist nicht überzeugend, wenn es nicht präzisiert werden kann.

Die Unterscheidung nach tradierten Rollenmustern einerseits und sinnvollen und logischen geschlechtsspezifischen Zuordnungen andererseits ist nach wie vor eine unbeantwortete Streitfrage. Gewisse Verhaltensweisen, Eigenschaften und soziale Bezüge lassen sich wohl aus den primären Geschlechtsmerkmalen und deren Funktionen ableiten wie etwa die Begriffskette: Schwangerschaft – Mütterlichkeit – Schutz – Behütung – Uterus – Höhle – Behausung oder, im maskulinen Bereich, Phallus – Mast – Turm – Waffe.

Die weitere Extrapolation in tertiäre Geschlechtsmerkmale, wonach etwa das Weibliche mit dem Friedlichen oder mit Schwäche und das Männliche mit dem Kämpferischen oder mit Kraft gleichzusetzen wäre, ist schon äußerst fragwürdig. Trotzdem haben sich auch in unserer heutigen – nach wie vor patriarchalischen – Gesellschaft prädikative Zuordnungen erhalten, die im Bewußtsein der Menschen zutiefst verwurzelt sind. Am schwierigsten dürfte es sein, das Weibliche und Männliche an **kulturhistorischen Phänomenen** festzumachen. Die Bekleidung ist wohl bei nahezu allen Völkern ein Unterscheidungsmerkmal und vom rituellen und erotischen Kleidertausch wird noch zu sprechen sein. Aber es gibt keine generalisierenden Zuordnungen wie etwa den Mann zur Hose und die Frau zum Rock. Ähnliches gilt für die Haartracht: Lange Haare für Frauen und kurze für Männer kann nur für lokal und historisch abgegrenzte, relativ kleine Kulturkreise gelten – wie die Gegenwart deutlich beweist. Ebenso kann das Schminken oder die Körperbemalung keineswegs als typisch weibliches Charakteristikum an-

are simply human beings with varying gifts, no one of which can be exclusively assigned to either sex.«

The fact that specific allocations to one sex or the other have so far occurred in all forms of society is not a convincing argument in favour of the idea that the rôles of the sexes might be objectivized and generalized. »Because men and women have always in all societies built a great superstructure of socially defined sex differences that obviously cannot be true for all humanity – or the people just over the mountain would not be able to do it all in the exactly opposite fashion – must some such superstructures be built?« (Mead, 1975)

According to Mead, the compulsion to erect such a superstructure can be motivated by two factors: one is the »biological nature of the mammal«, and the other is »social convenience«. »Are not sex differences exceedingly valuable, one of the resources of our human nature...?« The question: »what positive opportunities are to be found in the differences between the sexes?« is not given a clear answer, but is repeatedly traced back, either directly or indirectly, to the biological differences to be found in »mammals«. Thus, for example, great importance is attached to the difference between breast-feeding for boys and for girls: »Receiving is not the same for a male being as it is for a female.«

The allegation that there is, over and above biological matters, a basic difference between masculinity and femininity is not convincing unless it can be precisely defined.

A distinction in accordance with traditional rôles on the one hand, and appropriate and logical specific allocations to one of the two sexes on the other, is a disputed question, as yet unresolved. Certain modes of behaviour, qualities and social relationships can though be derived from the primary sexual characteristics and their functions. Examples are the following chain of concepts: pregnancy – maternity – protection – shielding – uterus – cave – dwelling, or, in the male realm: phallus – mast – tower – weapon.

A further extrapolation into tertiary sexual characteristics, in which femininity is equated with peacefulness or weakness, and masculinity with pugnacity or with strength, is an extremely dubious matter. Allocations based on certain notions have nevertheless survived in our modern society, which is still patriarchal, and are very deeply rooted in human consciousness. What is probably most difficult of all is to determine femininity and masculinity on the basis of the **phenomena of cultural history**. Clothing is probably a differentiating feature in nearly all peoples, and reference to ritual and erotic exchanges of clothes will be made below. But there are no generalizing allocations, such as that of allocating men to trousers and women to skirts. Something similar applies to hairstyles: long hair for women and short hair for men can, as modern times clearly show, only be applicable to relatively small cultural complexes which are locally and historically demarcated. In the same way, makeup, or paint on the body, can by no means be regarded as a typically feminine characteristic. **Cultural** history shows that men have changed the appearance of their face again and again, not merely for magical and cultic reasons, but also out of erotic motives. In the Rococo period it was still customary for men not only to wear a splendid wig, but also to have their lips and cheeks heavily made up.

According to Bierhoff-Alfermann (1977), the **psychological identity of the sexes** is to a large extent **socially defined** and is thus – in contrast to the biological sex – capable of being changed.

John Money (1975) understands sexual identity as meaning »persistently sensing one's own individuality, one's own behaviour, and one's own kinds of experience, as being clearly and unrestrictedly male, clearly and unrestrictedly female, or to a greater or lesser degree ambivalent.«

»The programme of psychosexual differentiation proceeds according to an interactive model and is not governed solely by disposition or environment.« When a person's sex has been biologically determined, this does not in any way mean that his or her personal sexual identity, or the articulation of his or her »psychological sex«, has been completed.

The differentiation of sexual identity, starting from the chromosomes and continuing up to sexual identity in adulthood, proceeds according to a very complicated »electric circuit«.

Social influences, the circumstances of society, and the background of social history, play a determinant part in forming this psychological sexuality. Becker/Schmidt/Knapp (1989) try to indicate two tendencies where »sexual identity« is concerned. »... the more a person's disposition is limited to questions of consciousness (cognitivism), and the more strongly it is concentrated on behaviour (behaviourism), the more unbroken and one-dimensional is the resultant notion of sexual identity.«

gesehen werden. Die Kulturgeschichte zeigt, daß immer wieder die Männer ihr Gesicht verändert haben, nicht nur aus magisch-kultischen Gründen, sondern auch mit erotischen Motivationen. Noch in der Rokokozeit war es üblich, daß die Männer nicht nur mit einer prächtigen Perücke ausgestattet waren, sondern auch Lippen und Wangen intensiv schminkten.

Nach Bierhoff-Alfermann (1977) ist die **psychologische Geschlechteridentität** weitgehend **sozial definiert** und damit, zum Unterschied vom biologischen Geschlecht, auch veränderbar.

John Money (1975) versteht unter Geschlechtsidentität die »überdauernde Erfahrung der eigenen Individualität, des eigenen Verhaltens und der eigenen Erlebnisweisen als eindeutig und uneingeschränkt männlich, als eindeutig und uneingeschränkt weiblich oder als im größerem bzw. kleinerem Grad ambivalent.«

»Das Programm der psychosexuellen Differenzierung verläuft nach einem Interaktionsmodell und wird nicht ausschließlich durch Anlage oder Umwelt bestimmt.« Mit der biologischen Festlegung des Geschlechts ist die personale Geschlechtsidentität, die Artikulation des »psychologischen Geschlechts« keineswegs abgeschlossen.

Die Differenzierung der Geschlechtsidentität, ausgehend von den Chromosomen bis zur Geschlechtsidentität im Erwachsenenalter, verläuft nach einem überaus komplizierten »Schaltkreis«.

An der Bildung dieser psychologischen Geschlechtlichkeit sind die sozialen Einflüsse, die gesellschaftlichen Konstellationen, die kulturhistorischen Hintergründe wesenhaft beteiligt. Becker/Schmidt/Knapp (1989) versuchen im Hinblick auf die »Geschlechtsidentität« zwei Tendenzen aufzuzeigen. » ... je mehr ein Ansatz sich auf Fragen des Bewußtseins beschränkt (Kognitivismus), und je stärker er sich auf Verhalten konzentriert (Behaviourismus), desto ungebrochener und eindimensionaler ist die Vorstellung von Geschlechtsidentität, die dabei herauskommt.«

Mit Recht warnt der Theologe **Leonardo Boff** (geb. 1938) vor der »Verkürzung der geschlechtlichen Bestimmungen auf eine rein genitale und biologische Gegebenheit«, die er als »eines der bösartigsten Laster unserer eindimensionalen Kultur« ansieht. Gleichzeitig polemisiert Boff gegen die Kategorisierungen außerhalb der geschlechtlichen Merkmale. Der Schlußfolgerung hingegen kann vorbehaltlos zugestimmt werden: »Das Weibliche und das Männliche sind keine Akzidentien der menschlichen Natur, sondern Wesensbestimmungen, die jede von beiden auf spezifische Weise zugleich männlich und weiblich sein lassen.« (Boff, 1985)

Regine Gildemeister (1990) weist kritisch darauf hin, daß die strikt binäre Geschlechterzuordnung in unserer Gesellschaft letztlich doch wieder an den Genitalien festgemacht wird und daß diese gleichsam zu »kulturellen Genitalien« werden.

Die Frage nach dem Ausmaß der Ähnlichkeit oder Unähnlichkeit der Geschlechter bleibt im Grundsätzlichen nach wie vor unbeantwortet. Absolut unbestritten muß lediglich die Tatsache der biologischen Differenzierung im genitalen Bereich bleiben, daß nur Frauen Kinder gebären, Männer hingegen nur zeugen können. Aussagen, die darüber hinausgehen, wie etwa die hormonale Ausstattung, die größere Muskelkraft und die höhere Aggressivität bei Männern relativieren sich zusehends in unserer Gesellschaft. Auch die Zuordnung von Jagd und Krieg zum Manne und von Bemutterung an die Frau (Badinter, 1991) muß in der heutigen Gesellschaft, zumindest in der Generalisierung, ernsthaft in Frage gestellt werden.

So kritikwürdig es zweifellos ist, vom Biologischen, ja vom Genitalen auszugehen, dürfte darin doch die einzig tragfähige Basis liegen. Allerdings sind direkte Ableitungen aus den biologischen Tatsachen möglich, die dann weit in psychologische Aussagen hineinreichen. Eine der größten Hürden in unserer Zeit besteht darin, das Geschlechtsspezifische vom Fortpflanzungsgedanken zu trennen. Dies gilt vor allem für die Frau. Wenn etwa das Schützende, Bergende, Bewahrende als weibliche Spezifika angesehen werden, dann sind es Eigenschaften, die unmittelbar oder mittelbar aus der mütterlichen Funktion abzuleiten sind.

Aus den vorangegangenen Ausführungen geht deutlich hervor, daß es heute kaum mehr möglich ist, das Weibliche und das Männliche jenseits des Biologischen schlüssig zu definieren. Könnte daraus ein Plädoyer für den androgynen Menschen abgeleitet werden?

Nach den Schriften zur Androgynie in den siebziger Jahren hat Sandra Lipsitz Bem (1993) sich mit den »Lenses of Gender« auseinandergesetzt und geht von folgenden drei »Lenses« aus: »the gender polarziation, androcentrism and biological essentialism. ...These three gender lenses provide of how biology, culture, and the individual psyche all interact in historical context to systemically reproduce male power.«[14] Die »gender polarisation« umfaßt die exklusive Festlegung von nur zwei »skripts for being male and female«, von denen nicht abgewichen werden kann. Der »androcentrism« sieht den Mann als die menschliche Norm an, die

9. Prähistorische Figurine vom Trasimenischen See, Italien.
10. Prähistorische Figurine aus Mauern, Bavaria.
11. Prähistorische Figurine aus dem Jordantal, Palästina.

9. Prehistoric figurine from Lake Trasimeno, Italy.
10. Prehistoric figurine from Mauern, Bavaria.
11. Prehistoric figurine from the Jordan valley, Palestine.

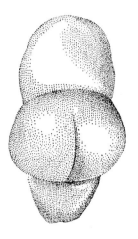

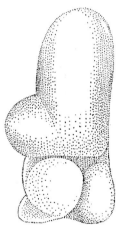

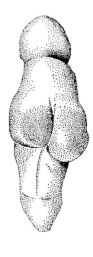

The theologian **Leonardo Boff** (born 1938) rightly warns against »reducing sexual matters to nothing but genital and biological factors«. He regards such a reduction as »one of the most malignant vices of our one-dimensional culture«. At the same time Boff also polemicizes against categorizations which are unrelated to sexual characteristics. His conclusion, on the other hand, can be unreservedly concurred with: »Femininity and masculinity are not accidents of human nature, but factors which determine a being and which allow both femininity and masculinity to be – in a specific way – both masculine and feminine at the same time.« (Boff, 1985)

Regine Gildemeister (1990) draws critical attention to the fact that the strictly binary allocation of sex in our society is ultimately once again fixed to the genitals and that these become what might be described as »cultural genitals«.

The question of the extent to which the sexes resemble or do not resemble one another still remains basically unanswered. All that must remain absolutely undisputed is the fact of biological differentiation in the genital area, the fact that only women give birth to children, whereas men can only beget them. Statements that go beyond this, such as those relating to the hormonal equipment and to greater muscular strength and heightened aggressiveness in men, are undergoing rapid modification in our society. The attribution of hunting and wars to men, and of mothering to women, (Badinter, 1991) must be seriously questioned in today's society, at least when regarded as a generalization.

Although the idea of proceeding on the basis of biological, indeed of genital, matters undoubtedly deserves to be criticized, it is probably the only sound basis to go on. However, it is possible, from the biological facts, to make direct deductions which then go far into the realm of psychological statements. One of the greatest obstacles of our times lies in separating specifically sexual matters from the idea of propagation. This applies in particular to women. If protectiveness, sheltering and preservation are regarded as specifically female features, they are properties which are directly or indirectly derivable from the maternal function.

It is clear from the above remarks that it is today hardly possible any longer to give a conclusive definition of femininity and masculinity in matters over and above the biological. Could an argument in favour of an androgynous human being be derived from this?

After writing about androgyny in the 1970s, Sandra Lipsitz Bem critically examined the »lenses of gender« (1993) and assumed the following three »lenses«: »gender polarization, androcentrism and biological essentialism«. »These three gender lenses provide the manner in which biology, culture and the individual psyche all interact in historical context to systemically reproduce male power. ...Gender polarization« comprises the exclusive definition of only two »scripts for being: male and female«, from which it is not possible to deviate. »Androcentrism« regards the man as the human norm, while the woman is always the different one. »Biological essentialism« provides the so-called scientific foundations for these ways of looking at things, and here it is not facts but interpretations that decide matters.

3. Non-Christian Myths – Religions – Philosophies

3.1. Prehistory

We are exclusively dependent on artistic finds here, so that there is a certain breadth of interpretation, which does though seem perfectly justifiable.

One specific form of androgyny lies in interpreting prehistoric sculptural works in terms of differing dimensions. The question of whether small **statuettes dating from earliest history** (Aurignacien, Magdalénien, etc.) should be interpreted as female figures on the one hand, and as phallic depictions on the other, is though not undisputed. (Giedion, 1964) A clay idol found in the former Yugoslavia is considerably more obvious: despite the abstraction, the breasts and a penis with testicles are clearly discernible. The interpretation of an idol from Italy, in the form of a woman, may also be doubted, because the head section, which tapers to a point, might also be identified as a phallus. This interpretation is supported by a find from Gravettien in the Ukraine (ca. 11000 BC): this idol in the form of a woman has a clearly phallic character. If we compare this figure with certain works from the contemporary art scene, we see that *Fillette* by Louise Bourgeois and *Chaussure* by Yves Tanguy display a very similar subject matter. (Cf. chap. 6.2)

Frau ist jeweils das Andere. Der »biological essentialism« liefert die sogenannten wissenschaftlichen Grundlagen für diese Sichtweisen, wobei nicht die Fakten, sondern die Interpretationen entscheiden.

3. Außerchristliche Mythen – Religionen – Philosophien

3.1. Prähistorie

Da wir ausschließlich auf bildnerische Funde angewiesen sind, ergibt sich eine gewisse Interpretationsbreite, die aber durchaus vertretbar erscheint.

Eine spezifische Form der Androgynität liegt in der unterschiedlichen maßstäblichen Interpretation von bildnerischen Arbeiten, die wir in der Prähistorie finden. Die Deutung von kleinen **Statuetten aus der Urgeschichte** (Aurignacien, Magdalénien u. a.) als weibliche Figuren einerseits und als Phallusdarstellungen andererseits ist allerdings nicht unumstritten. (Giedeon, 1964) Wesentlich eindeutiger präsentiert sich ein Tonidol, das im ehemaligen Jugoslawien gefunden wurde: Trotz der Abstraktion sind die Brüste und ein Penis mit Hoden deutlich zu erkennen. Auch die Interpretation eines Frauenidols aus Italien kann angezweifelt werden, denn in der spitz zulaufenden Kopfpartie könnte man ebenso einen Phallus erkennen. Diese Deutung wird unterstützt durch einen Fund aus der Ukraine aus dem Gravettien (ca. 11 000 v. Chr.): Das Frauenidol hat eindeutig phallischen Charakter. Vergleichen wir die »Figur« mit Arbeiten aus der zeitgenössischen Kunstszene, so weisen etwa die *Fillette* von Louise Bourgeois oder die *Chaussure* von Yves Tanguy eine ganz ähnliche Thematik auf. (Vgl. Kap. 6.2.)

Bei einer Kleinplastik aus Pembrokeshire (Wales) verweist die Andeutung des Vulva-Dreiecks auf eine weibliche Figur mit kräftigen Oberschenkeln, diese sind aber gleichzeitig die Hoden eines erigierten Penis. (Giedion, 1964)

In den prähistorischen **Lochstäben**, meist leicht gekrümmte Knochenstäbe mit einer Bohrung, könnte man eine Kombination des Männlichen und des Weiblichen sehen. Diese These scheint besonders plausibel beim Lochstab aus der Gorge d'Enfer (Dordogne): Ein gabelförmiges Element (das überraschend an Walter Pichlers *Skulptur im Organzakleid* erinnert) stellt deutlich zwei Phalli dar, die große Perforation ist aber zweifellos ein Vulvasymbol. Die morphologische Parallele zu den Y-Gebilden der Androgyn-Vorstellungen des 17. Jahrhunderts ist ein weiteres Kriterium für eine archetypische Symbolik des Mann-Weiblichen.

Giedion deutet das ägyptische **Henkelkreuz** als ein androgynes Symbol: »Das Lebenszeichen dürfte in seinen Bestandteilen den prähistorischen Fruchtbarkeitssymbolen, der Vulva und dem Phallus, am nächsten verwandt sein. Sein Oberteil gleicht der herzförmigen Form, die dem Vulvasymbol im Aurignacien gegeben wurde, und die hier mit einer Abstraktion eines Phallus verbunden erscheint, ein Symbol des Androgynen, ewig sich erneuernder Zeugung, eine Verbindung von Männlichem und Weiblichem, der eine besonders magische Kraft innewohnt.« (Giedion, 1964) In diesem Zusammenhang kann auf die Darstellung des androgynen Ardanari Iswara aus der indischen Ikonographie verwiesen werden, bei dem die männlichen und weiblichen Geschlechtsteile durch ein liegendes Henkelkreuz dargestellt werden.[15]

3.2. Naive Völker

Die Androgynie-Vorstellungen naiver Völker sind zumeist direkt verknüpft mit den Mythologien, insbesondere auch mit den Kosmogonien.

Aber auch der Alltag wird immer wieder in den Kreis einer magischen Symbolik miteinbezogen. Für **Josef Winthuis** ist die Vorstellungswelt primitiver Völker vor allem auf dem Zweigeschlechter-Gedanken aufgebaut. Die Präsenz beider Geschlechter im Menschen, oder die verschiedenen Methoden der Austauschbarkeit des Geschlechtes werden an einem reichhaltigen ethnologischen Befund dargestellt.

Nach Winthuis ist die Subinzision[16] von der Idee der Doppelgeschlechtigkeit geprägt.

» ... zu seiner männlichen Natur soll der junge Mann die weibliche und zu seiner weiblichen Natur soll das Mädchen die männliche erhalten, die ... Initianden sollen durch die Kulte die ursprüngliche Doppelgeschlechtigkeit wiedererlangen.« (Winthuis 1931)

Die Initiationsrituale der Aranda in Australien erscheinen uns von einer schmerzhaften Grausamkeit. Nach Winthuis ist das Ziel die »Verwandlung des Mysten in das Urtotemwesen. Um

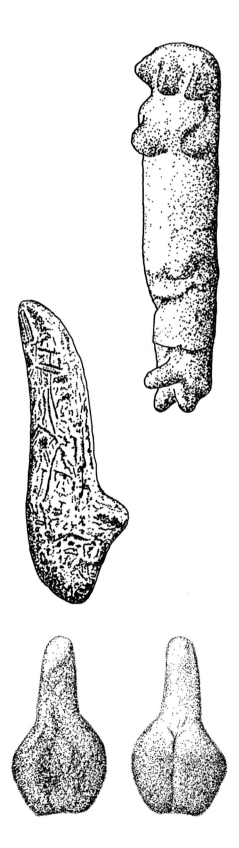

In a small sculpture from Pembrokeshire (Wales), the outline of the vulval triangle points to a female figure with powerful thighs, but the latter are at the same time the testicles of an erect penis. (Giedion, 1964)

The prehistoric **holed rods**, which are usually slightly curved rods of bone with a borehole, might be regarded as a combination of masculinity and femininity. This theory appears especially plausible in the case of the holed rod from the Gorge d'Enfer (Dordogne): a fork-shaped element (which is surprisingly reminiscent of Walter Pichler's *Skulptur im Organzakleid* (*Sculpture in organza dress*) clearly depicts two phalli, while the large perforation is doubtless a vulval symbol. The morphological parallel with the Y-shapes given to androgynous concepts in the 17th century is a further criterion for an archetypal symbolism of combined masculinity and femininity.

Giedion interprets the Egyptian **cross with handles** as an androgynous symbol: »The components of this symbol of life are probably most closely related to the vulva and the phallus, which are the prehistoric symbols of fertility. Its upper part resembles the heart shape which was given to the vulval symbol in Aurignac and which here appears to be associated with an abstracted phallus; this shape seems to be a symbol of androgyny, of eternally self-renewing generation, a combination which embraces both male and female and possesses a particularly magical force.« (Giedion, 1964) Reference may be made in this connection to the androgynous Ardanari Iswara which occurs in Indian iconography and in which the male and female sexual organs are represented by a horizontal cross with handles.[14]

3.2. Naive races

The androgynous notions possessed by naive races are usually directly linked to mythologies, and in particular also to cosmogonies.

But everyday life, again and again, is also included within the circle of magical symbolism. **Josef Winthuis** takes the view that primitive peoples base their world of ideas mainly on the notion of two sexes. The presence of both sexes in humans, or the various methods by which the sexes can be exchanged, are depicted in abundant ethnological findings.

According to Winthuis, subincision[15] is characterized by the idea of a two-sexed nature. »... the intention is that a young man will obtain a female nature in addition to his male nature, and that a girl will receive a male nature as well as her female one. The cults are meant to restore to the ... initiates their original two-sexed nature.« (Winthuis, 1931)

The initiation rites of the Aranda people in Australia appear to us to be painfully cruel. According to Winthuis, the aim is »that the person being initiated into the mystery should be transformed into the original totemic being. However, in order to take part in this transformation, the person must himself be a two-sexed being ... One of his teeth is knocked out, because the gap in the row of teeth signifies the vulva. He is subincised, that is to say his phallus is cut open from underneath and in this way the vagina is attached.« Some other Australian tribes also symbolically give the neophyte a female sexual organ. One is not a sexually mature man unless one accustoms oneself to the fact that the other sex also exists.

To Winthuis, »everything that runs in straight lines in the thinking of primitive man ... signifies the membrum virile, the phallus; everything round or sickle-shaped is the membrum muliebre, the vagina«. This simplification reminds us of Freud's simple statements about dream symbolism and has caused Winthuis, in similar fashion to Sigmund Freud, to be not unjustifiably accused of pansexualism.

According to Thiel, numerous symptoms of androgyny can be seen in the religions of Africa, particularly when the myths concerning the dawn of time are considered. »In those myths, the god Amma is united with the earth, after the god has hewn away the termite hill which is the male principle of the earth.« (Thiel, 1986)

The tendency »to eliminate the contrast between man and woman in order to restore the original condition« is repeatedly seen in Africa. (Baumann, 1986)

Circumcision is common among some African tribes and is related, here too, to the idea of androgyny.

The Bambara people practice »circumcision« and »subincision«, the latter being an incision into the under side of the penis. »It is partly done as a trial of courage in the puberty rites, but it is also an imitation of the vagina. The menstruation-like bleedings from the wound, which is opened on certain occasions, are intended to cleanse, as well as to ward off dangers.« (Raehs, 1990)

12. Hermaphroditisches Idol aus dem ehem. Jugoslawien, Bronzezeit.
13. Hermaphroditisches Idol aus der Ukraine, um 12 000 v. Chr.
14, 15. Hermaphroditisches Idol aus Pembrokeshire, England.
16. Sitzfigur der Dogon, Afrika.
17. Lochstab aus der Gorge d'Enfer, Dordogne, Frankreich.

12. Hermaphroditic idol from former Jugoslavia, Bronce Age.
13. Hermaphroditic idol from the Ukraine, ca. 12 000 BC.
14, 15. Hermaphroditic idol from Pembrokeshire, England.
16. Sitting figure of the Dogon, Africa.
17. Roled rod from the Gorge d'Enfer, Dordogne, France.

jedoch dieser Verwandlung teilhaftig zu werden, muß der Mensch selbst ein doppelgeschlech-tiges Wesen sein ... Es wird ihm ein Zahn ausgeschlagen, denn die Lücke in der Zahnreihe be-deutet die Vulva. Er wird subinzidiert, d. h. der Phallus wird ihm von unten her aufgeschnitten und so die Vagina angebracht.« Auch bei anderen australischen Stämmen wird dem Neophy-ten symbolisch ein weibliches Sexualorgan verliehen. Man wird kein geschlechtsreifer Mann, wenn man sich nicht mit der Koexistenz des anderen Geschlechtes vertraut macht.

Für Winthuis bedeutet »alles Geradlinige im Denken des Primitiven ... das membrum virile, den Phallus: alles Runde, Sichelförmige das membrum muliebre, die Vagina«. Diese Simplifika-tion erinnert an die einfachen Aussagen Freuds zur Traumsymbolik und hat Winthuis, ähnlich wie Sigmund Freud, den nicht unberechtigten Vorwurf des Pansexualismus eingebracht.

Nach Thiel lassen sich in den Religionen **Afrikas** zahlreiche Symptome des Androgynen aufzeigen, vor allem wenn man die Urzeitmythen betrachtet, »wo sich Gott Amma und die Erde vereinigen, nachdem Gott das männliche Prinzip der Erde, den Termitenhügel abgeschla-gen hat«. (Thiel, 1986)

In Afrika zeigt sich immer wieder die Tendenz »den Gegensatz Mann-Frau aufzuheben, um den Urzustand wieder herzustellen«. (Baumann, 1986)

Die **Beschneidung** ist auch einigen afrikanischen Stämmen geläufig und steht auch hier mit der Idee der Androgynie in Verbindung.

Bei den Bambara gibt es die »Circumsion« und »Subincision«, das Einschneiden an der Un-terseite des Penis, »was zum einen als Mutprobe bei den Mannbarkeitsriten geschieht, es hat aber auch die Bedeutung einer Vagina-Imitation. Die menstruationsähnlichen Blutungen aus der Wunde, die zu bestimmten Anlässen geöffnet wird, sollen reinigen und Gefahren abwen-den«. (Raehs, 1990)

Geza Roheim (1970) interpretiert den Ritus der »Circumcision« und »Subincision« als »ein Vorgehen, das die ›phallische Mutter‹ durch den ›Vater mit Vagina‹ ersetzen soll«.

Bei den Dogon erfährt die Beschneidung der Jugendlichen – Mädchen und Jungen – eine wesentlich andere Deutung: Man nimmt an, daß jeder Mensch mit zwei Seelen geboren wird, einer männlichen und einer weiblichen. (Raehs, 1990) »Der Knabe ist weiblich in seiner Vor-haut, das Mädchen ist männlich in seiner Klitoris«. Damit ist zwar die Erkenntnis der Doppel-geschlechtlichkeit ausgesprochen, bei der Beschneidung aber werden, zum Unterschied von zahlreichen gegenteiligen Ritualen bei anderen Stämmen, die Kennzeichen des anderen Geschlechtes entfernt. Erst durch die Beschneidung wird der Mensch eindeutig einem Ge-schlecht zugeordnet. Damit wird der androgyne Charakter des Menschen aufgehoben.

Die **Bildnerei der Afrikaner** liefert zahlreiche Beispiele dafür, daß zumindest ansatzweise die Androgynie eine wichtige Rolle spielt: Da gibt es Masken in Doppelkopfformen Mann/Frau und Skulpturen, die mit Brüsten und Penis ausgestattet sind, ganz im Sinne der europäischen Hermaphroditen, etwa der Antike. Bei den Holzfiguren der Yorubas in Nigeria deutet Neumann die Brüste der Frauen als phallische Symbole. »Die in Afrika künstlich herbeigeführte schlaffe Hängebrust wird hier zu einer plastisch-phallischen Wirklichkeit gesteigert, aus welcher die zeugerische Kraft des Lebens in das empfangende Kind einströmt. Dabei wird, wie selten, die archetypische Symbolik des empfangenden Mundes der zeugerischen Brust gegenüber in ih-rer echten und völlig unperversen Bedeutung sichtbar.« (Neumann, 1956)

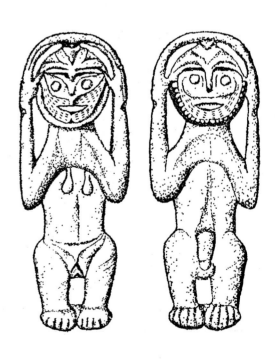

Das Motiv der phallischen Brüste, die gleichsam eine Hypertrophierung der Fruchtbarkeit darstellen, ist keineswegs auf den afrikanischen Raum beschränkt. So wird etwa auf **Bali** die Göttin Hati mit weit vorstehenden Brüsten dargestellt, die Neumann ebenfalls als phallische Darstellung deutet.

Die Gültigkeit dieses Themas für unsere Gegenwart soll ein Vorgriff auf die Kunst des 20. Jahrhunderts bekräftigen. Die amerikanische Künstlerin **Louise Bourgeois** (geb. 1911) model-liert 1971/72 eine *Trani-Episode*: Es sind phallische Brüste, gleichzeitig aber auch Körper, die übereinander gestürzt sind.

Einer anderen Version androgyner Darstellungen begegnen wir in **Ozeanien**: Hier wurden Figuren gefunden, die auf der einen Seite einen Mann, auf der anderen Seite eine Frau zeigen.

3.3. Ägypten

Im Kapitel 2.3 wird das Prinzip der Teilung des Ur-Einen durch Beispiele aus der ägyptischen Mythologie erläutert. Dabei zeigt sich, daß die Mehrzahl der Ur-Götter/Göttinnen androgyner oder selbstzeugender Natur ist, wie etwa Atum, Hathor, Neith und Isis.

Geza Roheim (1970) interprets the rite of »circumcision« and »subincision« as being »a procedure intended to replace the ›phallic mother‹ by the ›father with a vagina‹«.

The Dogon people interpret the circumcision of young people – both girls and boys – in a very different way: it is assumed that each person is born with two souls, one male and one female. (Raehs, 1990) »A boy is female in his foreskin, and a girl is male in her clitoris.« It is true that this expresses the recognition of a two-sexed nature, but the distinguishing features of the other sex are removed in circumcision, and this differs from numerous opposite rituals performed by other tribes. Not until circumcision is a person definitely assigned to one or other of the sexes. This eliminates the person's androgynous character.

African sculpture provides numerous examples of how androgyny plays an important part, at least as a tendency. There are double-headed man-woman masks, and sculptures having breasts and a penis, very much like the European hermaphrodites, for example those of classical antiquity. The breasts of the women in the wooden figures made by the Yorubas in Nigeria are interpreted by Neumann as being phallic symbols. »The hanging breasts, artificially induced in Africa, are here exaggerated to produce a phallic form, from which the generative force of life pours into the receiving child. Here the archetypal symbolism of the receiving mouth in relation to the engendering breast is particularly apparent in its authentic and utterly unperverse form.« (Neumann, 1955)

The motive of the phallic breasts, which depict what might be described as a hypertrophy of fertility, is by no means limited to Africa. In **Bali,** for example, the goddess Hati is depicted with breasts protruding far forwards, and Neumann interprets these too as being phallic representations.

A jump ahead to 20th-century art may support the notion that this topic is applicable to the present day. The American artist **Louise Bourgeois** (born 1911) fashioned a *Trani episode* in 1971/72: it has phallic breasts, which are though at the same time also bodies which have fallen over one another.

Another version of androgynous depictions is to be found in Oceania. Figures were found here which depict a man on one side and a woman on the other.

3.3. Egypt

The principle of the division of the original unity is explained in chapter 2.3 by means of examples from Egyptian mythology. It is seen there that most of the original gods/goddesses are of an androgynous or self-generating nature, examples being Atum, Hathor, Neith and Isis.

The Pharaoh Eje was depicted as a god of the Nile, and has long, narrow, breasts which are strangely eccentrically positioned. »The fertility-giving power of the Nile waters was symbolized by Nile gods with deeply pendulous breasts. The Pharaohs ... caused themselves to be revered as Nile gods with female breasts.« (Weiler, 1991) Conversely, the perfection of the goddesses was also intended to be depicted, and that perfection was only achieved when female and male characteristics were present simultaneously: the phallus, being the creative original power of nature, was added to the female body.

The Egyptian god Min was undoubtedly a fertility idol. Its depictions have both male and female symbols, so that it can be regarded as an androgynous being, even though it is depicted ithyphallically in later representations.

Sigmund Freud repeatedly considers the question of what he refers to as bisexuality in mythology. »Most of the depictions of Mut, the Egyptian goddess with a vulture's head, ... were phallically formed; her body, which her breasts showed to be female, also had a male member in an erect state ...«

18. Mutter mit Kind, Yoruba, Nigeria.
19, 20. Doppelgeschlechtliche Kreidefigur, Ozeanien. Vorder- und Rückseite.
21. Göttin Rati, Bali, 19. Jh.
22. Louise Bourgeois, *Trani-Episode*, 1971.

18. Mother with child, Yoruba, Nigeria.
19, 20. Bisexual chalk figure, Oceania. Front and back.
21. Goddess Rati, Bali, 19. cent.
22. Louise Bourgeois, *Trani-Episode*, 1971.

3.4. Greece. Rome

The concept of the hermaphrodite stems directly from the Greek world of myth. Hermaphroditos was the child of Hermes and Aphrodite, and united within himself his parents' beauty.
»... Eros, dream and water – it was the last of these three elements that shaped his existence were united in his (Hermaphroditos') person: when Hermaphroditos, while on one of his hunting expeditions in the country of the Carers, was about to refresh himself at a spring, Salmacis, the nymph of that pool, fell in love with the handsome Hermaphroditos and, when her love

Der Pharao Eje wird als Nilgott dargestellt und ist mit merkwürdig exentrisch positionierten, langen, schmalen Brüsten ausgestattet. »Die Fruchtbarkeit spendende Kraft des Nilwassers wird durch **Nilgötter** mit tief herabhängenden Brüsten symbolisiert. Die Pharaonen ... lassen sich als Nilgötter mit weiblichen Brüsten verehren.« (Weiler, 1991) Umgekehrt sollen auch die Göttinnen in ihrer Vollkommenheit dargestellt werden, die erst dann erreicht ist, wenn Weibliches und Männliches gleichzeitig vorhanden ist: Dem weiblichen Körper wird der Phallus als schöpferische Urkraft der Natur hinzugefügt.

Der ägyptische Gott Min ist zweifellos ein Fruchtbarkeitsidol, seine Darstellungen zeigen männliche und weibliche Symbole, so daß er als ein androgynes Wesen angesehen werden kann, unbeschadet der Tatsache, daß er in späteren Darstellungen ithyphallisch gezeigt wird.

Sigmund Freud geht wiederholt, wie er es nennt, auf die Bisexualität in der Mythologie ein. »Die geierköpfig gebildete Göttin Mut der Ägypter ... wurde in den meisten Darstellungen phallisch gebildet; ihr durch die Brüste als weiblich gekennzeichneter Körper trug auch ein männliches Glied im Zustande der Erektion ...«

3.4. Griechenland. Rom

Der Begriff des **Hermaphroditen** stammt unmittelbar aus der griechischen Sagenwelt. Hermaphroditos ist das Kind des Hermes und der Aphrodite, und er vereinigt in sich die Schönheit der Eltern. » ... in seiner (Hermaphroditos) Person vereinigen sich Eros, Traum und das Element Wasser, das seine Existenz prägt: Als er sich auf einem seiner Jagdzüge im Lande der Carer an einer Quelle laben wollte, verliebte sich Salmacis, die Nymphe jenes Gewässers, in den schönen Hermaphroditos und beschwor, als sie auf keine Gegenliebe stieß, die Götter, beider Leiber auf ewig zu einem werden zu lassen. Die Götter erfüllten diesen Wunsch...« (Hoffmann, 1987) Und jeder Sterbliche, der fürderhin in den Gewässern badet, wird zum Hermaphroditen.

In der Sage von Hermaphroditos und Salmacis spielt sich der umgekehrte Vorgang wie bei Platon ab: Nicht das ursprüngliche Eine wird geteilt, sondern das Zweifache verschmilzt zu einer neuen Einheit.

Es ist erstaunlich, wie sehr dieses Thema, über die Antike hinaus, zu bildnerischen Darstellungen angeregt hat, besonderes Interesse findet es im 16.–18.Jahrhundert. In einem Holzschnitt von **Virgil Solis** (1514–1562) ist die Szene am Bach mit Hermaphroditos und Salmacis dargestellt, im Hintergrund steht ein Hermaphrodit, ein zusammengewachsenes Wesen mit zwei Köpfen.

Hendrick Goltzius (1558–1617) zeigt den Moment, da Salmacis ihre Liebeswerbung beginnt, die von Hermaphroditos abgewehrt wird.

Zurück in die Antike: Wir finden ganz selten Darstellungen der Legende von Hermaphroditos und Salmacis, dafür aber eine Fülle von vorwiegend plastischen Gestaltungen hermaphroditischer Wesen, deren Interpretation als Götter umstritten ist.

Zahlreiche Skulpturen sind noch erhalten. Die Hermaphroditen sind nahezu alle nach dem gleichen Schema gestaltet: zumindest im Oberkörper, meist aber in der ganzen Figur durchaus feminin konzipiert, jedoch mit einem Penis ausgestattet. Der Zusammenhang mit der beliebten und in der Antike tolerierten Päderastie[17] ist nicht zu leugnen. »Die Kunst der Hellenen zeigt von ihren frühesten Anfängen an ... die größtmögliche Annäherung der Geschlechtsmerkmale, ein Schönheitsideal, das die Einordnung des weiblichen in die Größenmaße des männlichen Körpers anstrebt. Manche Kunstforscher ... haben behauptet, die griechischen Frauenfiguren seien ›Männer mit weiblichen Gesichtern und Genitalien‹« (Bornemann, 1975) Doch auch die umgekehrte These ist akzeptabel: daß es sich um typische Frauenfiguren mit einem applizierten männlichen Geschlechtsorgan handelt.

Hannelore Gauster (1985) vermutet, daß im Hellenismus eine neue Bewertung der Frau Platz greift und damit auch die weiblichen Merkmale bei den Hermaphroditendarstellungen deutlicher werden. Auch die Idee der Fruchtbarkeit mag nicht ohne Einfluß auf die Darstellungen geblieben sein.

Johann Joachim Winckelmann (1717–1768) geht wiederholt auf den antiken Typus des Androgynen ein: »Der höchste Begriff jugendlicher Schönheit wurde den Figuren des Bakchus und Apollo zugeeignet. Diese Gottheiten zeigen uns vermöge der ihnen von den Dichtern gegebenen Vereinigung beider Geschlechter in ihren auf uns gekommenen Abbildungen eine vermischte und zweideutige Natur, welche sich durch die Völligkeit und stärkere Ausschweifung

was not requited, besought the gods to make their two bodies eternally one. The gods fulfilled this wish...« (Hoffmann, 1987) And any mortal bathing in the pool from that time on became a hermaphrodite.

The process occurring in the myth of Hermaphroditos and Salmacis is the reverse of that in Plato: instead of the original unity being divided, it is the duality that merges into a new unity.

It is astonishing to note the extent to which this topic has stimulated works of sculpture at other times than in classical antiquity. It met with particular interest in the 16th to 18th centuries. The scene with Hermaphroditos and Salmacis by the stream is depicted in a woodcut by **Virgil Solis** (1514–1562); in the background there stands a hermaphrodite, an accreted being with two heads.

Hendrick Goltzius (1558–1617) shows the moment when Salmacis begins to woo Hermaphroditos, who wards her off.

Returning to classical times, we very rarely find depictions of the legend of Hermaphroditos and Salmacis, but on the other hand there is an abundance of mainly sculptured figures of hermaphroditical beings. It is a moot point whether they should be interpreted as gods.

Numerous sculptures still survive. Nearly all the hermaphrodites are designed to the same scheme: at least the upper body, and usually the entire figure, is conceived of as entirely feminine, but the figure has a penis. There is an undeniable link with paederasty which was popular, and was tolerated in antiquity.[16] »The art of the Hellenes, from its earliest beginnings, ... shows the greatest possible approach to one another of the characteristics of the two sexes.

der Hüften und durch die zarten und rundlichen Glieder dem Körper der Verschnittenen und Weiber annähert.« (Winckelmann, 1829)

In seinen Abhandlungen zur Kunst findet Winckelmann die antiken Statuen »von so seltener Schönheit, daß die Gesichtszüge den Unterschied des Geschlechts fast vergessen lassen«. (Winckelmann, 1965) Die antiken Statuen bestätigen, was Winckelmann formulierte: die An-näherung der Göttergestalten an die Figur der Frauen und somit eine gleichsam latente An-drogynie.

Im Museum of Fine Arts in Boston gibt es einen androgynen Eros, der gleich einem Engel zu fliegen scheint. Er ähnelt dem im folgenden erwähnten Eros aus dem Kunsthistorischen Museum in Wien. Besonders beliebt waren die liegenden Hermaphroditen, das Haupt auf den Arm abgestützt. Sie bieten sich dem Betrachter zunächst als Frauenfigur dar, erst bei näherem Hinsehen von der anderen Seite erkennt man einen kleinen Penis. Im Museo Nazionale Ro-mano und im Thermenmuseum in Rom finden wir charakteristische Beispiele.

Vermutlich aus Carnuntum stammt die eher naive Statuette eines Hermaphroditen (Flei-scher, 1967), die im Museum Carnuntinum (Deutsch-Altenburg, Niederösterreich) ausgestellt ist. Das Kunsthistorische Museum in Wien verfügt über die schöne Figur eines geflügelten Hermaphroditen, der vom Boden abzuheben scheint.

Ein ähnliches Motiv finden wir auf einem Lekythos:[18] Das geflügelte, leicht schwebende Wesen hat einen eher männlichen Körperbau, jedoch einen eindeutig weiblichen Kopf. In den Händen hält es einen Fächer und einen Kranz, zu seinen Füßen flattert eine Gans auf.

Eine beträchtliche Anzahl der antiken Götter ist durch ihre permanente oder temporäre Doppelgeschlechtlichkeit charakterisiert, allen voran Dionysos/Bacchus. »Platon nennt Diony-sos androgynos, weil er den Beischlaf als Mann ausführte, sich aber auch anal als Frau ge-brauchen ließ. Als pseudanor, ›den man fälschlich für einen Mann hält‹, verehrte man ihn in Makedonien. Der makedonische König Argaios setzt ihm ein Denkmal, auf dem er als dicker Mann mit großem Bauch und prallen Frauenbrüsten, jedoch mit erigiertem Penis zu sehen war ... « »Das Motiv des als Frau verkleideten Mannes taucht in fast allen ihm gewidmeten Festen auf ...« (Bornemann, 1975)

In der Charakterisierung **Wilhelm v. Humboldts** wird die Weiblichkeit des Bacchus in anti-ken Darstellungen angesprochen: » ... seine Hüften sind weiblich ausgeschweift und der gan-ze Bau seiner Glieder ist voller und runder, er nähert sich der Gränze der Weiblichkeit ...« (Humboldt, 1960)

This is an ideal of beauty which aims to incorporate the female body within the dimensions of the male. Some art researchers ... have alleged that the Greek women figures are ›men with female faces and genitals‹.« (Bornemann, 1975) But the reverse proposition is also acceptable, namely that these are typical female figures with a male sexual organ attached.

Hannelore Gauster (1985) surmises that a new assessment of women was gaining ground in Hellenism and that female characteristics were thus becoming more marked in depictions of hermaphrodites. The idea of fertility may also have had an influence on the representations.

Johann Joachim Winckelmann (1717–1768) repeatedly considers the classical type of the androgyne: »The concept of supreme youthful beauty was attributed to the figures of Bacchus and Apollo. Thanks to that unification of the two sexes which the poets gave to Bacchus and Apollo, these deities, in the depictions of them which have come down to us, display a mixed and ambiguous nature which approximates to the bodies of eunuchs and women, due to the fullness and greater curvature of the hips and to the delicate, plump limbs.« (Winckelmann, 1829)

In his treatises on art, Winckelmann regards the classical statues as »of such rare beauty that the facial features almost cause the difference between the sexes to be forgotten.« (Winckelmann, 1965) The classical statues confirm what Winckelmann was enunciating: the shapes of the deities approximate to women's figures, thus displaying what might be described as a latent androgyny.

In the Museum of Fine Arts in Boston there is an androgynous Eros who seems to be flying like an angel. He resembles the Eros, mentioned below, in the Kunsthistorisches Museum in Vienna. The recumbent hermaphrodites, with their head resting on their arm, were especially popular. At first they appear to the onlooker to be female figures, and only when he looks more closely from the other side does he discern a small penis. Characteristic examples are to be found in the Museo Nazionale Romano and in the museum at the thermal springs in Rome.

The rather naive statuette of a hermaphrodite which is on display at the Museum Carnuntinum (Deutsch-Altenburg, Lower Austria) probably derives from Carnuntum (Fleischer, 1967). The Kunsthistorisches Museum in Vienna possesses the fine figure of a winged hermaphrodite who seems to be taking off from the ground.

A similar motive is to be found on a narrow-necked vase:[18] this winged, slightly swaying being has a body structure which is rather male than female, but a clearly female head. It is holding a fan and a garland in its hands, and at its feet a goose is fluttering up.

A considerable number of the gods of antiquity, chief among them Dionysos/Bacchus, are characterized by a permanently or temporarily two-sexed nature. »Plato describes Dionysos as androgynous because he performed coitus as a man, but also allowed himself to be used anally as a woman. He was revered in Macedonia as a pseudanor ›who was wrongly thought to be a man‹. King Argaios of Macedonia built a monument to him on which he appeared as a fat man with a large belly and plump female breasts, but an erect penis ...« »The motive of a man disguised as a woman appears in almost all the festivals dedicated to Dionysos ...« (Bornemann, 1975)

Wilhelm von Humboldt's description refers to the feminine appearance of Bacchus in classical portrayals: »... his hips curve in a female manner, and the entire structure of his limbs is fuller and rounder; he approaches the border with femininity ...« (Humboldt, 1960)

The »great god Pan«, guardian of shepherds and companion of Bacchus, is sometimes interpreted as androgynous, and so too is Trophonius, the legendary constructor of the temple in Delphi and the healing god of the Boeotians.

Priapos was the god of generation and fertility. He was usually depicted with a large erect member and was also regarded as the god of carnal appetite and lechery. But androgynous properties were also attributed to him.

»Konisalos was a two-sexed Attic deity, similar to Orthanes and Tychon, who were always depicted ithyphallically, that is to say with an erect member, but at the same time also with women's breasts...« (Bornemann, 1975) »Aphroditos was the Aphrodite of homosexuals. His temples stood in Pamphylia and Cyprus. He was bearded, but wore women's clothes. His worshippers also wore women's clothes during public worship.« (Bornemann, 1975)

The festival of »Venus barbata«, the bearded Venus, who also had a male nature, was celebrated in Cyprus. She was served by women wearing men's clothes and by men wearing women's clothes. (Bertholet, 1934)

The hermetic philosophy of the late classical period provides the link with Christian gnosis. The subject of androgyny is touched upon in a dialogue between Hermes Trismegistos and Asklepius.

Der »große Gott Pan«, Beschützer der Hirten, Begleiter des Bacchus, wird bisweilen androgyn interpretiert, ebenso Trophonius, der sagenhafte Erbauer des Tempels in Delphi und Heilgott der Böotier.

Priapos ist der Gott der Zeugung und der Fruchtbarkeit, er wird meist mit großem erigiertem Glied dargestellt und gilt auch als Gott der Begierde und Lüsternheit. Doch werden ihm auch androgyne Eigenschaften zugeschrieben.

»Konisalos war eine doppelgeschlechtliche attische Gottheit, ähnlich dem Orthanes und dem Tychon, die stets ithyphallisch, d.h. mit erigiertem Glied, gleichzeitig aber auch mit Frauenbrüsten dargestellt, wurden ... « (Bornemann, 1975) »Aphroditos war die Aphrodite der Homosexuellen. Seine Heiligtümer standen in Pamphilien und auf Zypern. Er war bärtig, trug aber weibliche Kleidung. Auch seine Anbeter trugen beim Gottesdienst Frauenkleidung.« (Bornemann, 1975)

Auf Zypern wird das Fest der »Venus barbata«, der bärtigen Venus gefeiert, die auch männlicher Natur war. Frauen dienten ihr in Männerkleidung und Männer in Frauenkleidung. (Bertholet, 1934)

Die hermetische Philosophie der Spätantike stellt die Verbindung zur christlichen Gnosis dar. In einem Dialog zwischen Hermes Trismegistos und Asklepius wird das Thema der Androgynie angeschnitten.

» – Gott hat keinen Namen oder vielmehr er hat deren alle, denn er ist der Eine und das Ganze, endlos erfüllt mit der Fruchtbarkeit der beiden Geschlechter, er gebiert ständig alles das, was er zu zeugen beabsichtigt. – Wie, du sagst, Trismegistos, daß Gott die zwei Geschlechter hat? – Ja, Asklepius, und nicht nur Gott allein, sondern alles beseelte und pflanzliche Sein.«

3.5. Indien

Das Thema der Androgynie wird im **Hinduismus** auf breiter Ebene aufgerollt. Ähnlich wie in Platons Erzählung von der ursprünglichen Ungeteiltheit des Menschen weiß auch eine hinduistische Mythe zu berichten, »daß es eine Zeit gab, in der die erzeugten (emanierten) Geschöpfe sich nicht vermehrten, und die Welt drohte, wieder in ihren Urzustand zurückzufallen. Da zweiteilte sich der Gott, der mit Shiva identifiziert wird, nahm mit der rechten Körperhälfte die Gestalt eines Mannes und mit der linken die einer Frau an. Mit diesem androgynen Körper zeugte Shiva dann die mannigfaltigen Geschöpfe.« (Schleberger, 1986)

In einer Fußnote zu »Jenseits des Lustprinzips« von Sigmund Freud (1978) ist eine der mythologischen Wurzeln der Androgynie nach Heinrich Gomperz (1993) zitiert, und zwar aus den Upanishaden: » ... darum hat er (der Atman, das Selbst oder das Ich) keine Freude, wenn er allein ist. Da begehrte er nach einem Zweiten. Nämlich er war so groß wie ein Weib und ein Mann, wenn sie sich umschlungen halten. Dieses sein Selbst zerfällt er in zwei Teile: daraus entstanden Gatte und Gattin. ...«

Die Ähnlichkeit mit dem platonischen Androgyn-Mythos ist auch in dieser Erzählung offenkundig. Die Zweiteilung, auf die sich die Welt und ihre Phänomene gründen, wird in der Vereinigung von Gott und Göttin, von Mann und Weib aufgehoben.

Dieses Prinzip konkretisiert sich in der Darstellung von Shiva und Shakti. Wohl gibt es auch zahlreiche Einzeldarstellungen von Shiva, aber Shakti ist sozusagen der schöpferische Teil Shivas und somit Anlaß zu androgynen Vorstellungen. Die rechte Hälfte der Darstellungen zeigt den (erigierten) Phallus, die gerade Hüfte, die flache Brust und die männliche Figur, manchmal die Attribute Dreizack und Rad, während die linke Seite das halbe Schamdreieck (selten die Vulva), eine ausschwingende Hüfte, üppige Brust und weibliche Haartracht aufweisen, dazu kommen bisweilen die Attribute Spiegel und Lotus. Das Gesicht ist symmetrisch und kann männlich oder weiblich interpretiert werden.

Die Darstellungen des **Ardhanarishvara** folgen diesem Prinzip. Schon im 3. Jahrhundert waren diese Götterbilder zur Verehrung aufgestellt wie ein Beispiel aus Mathura zeigt.

Aus dem 11.–13. Jahrhundert sind schöne und anmutige Figuren erhalten, die ganz im Gegensatz zu den ebenfalls vertikal geteilten Androgyndarstellungen im Europa des 16. und 17. Jahrhunderts uns durchaus als eine integrale Person gegenüberstehen.

Neben diesen zweigeschlechtlichen Figuren ist es aber vor allem die **Linga/Yoni**[19]-Darstellung der indischen Kunst, in der das wohl eindrucksvollste und deutlichste Symbol einer Vereinigung, einer Synthese, ja Identität gezeigt wird: Der Linga-Pfahl, das Zeichen Shivas als Phal-

30. Ardanarishvara, 3. Jh.
31. Ardanarishvara, 11. Jh.

30. Ardanarishvara, 3rd cent.
31. Ardanarishvara, 11th cent.

»›God has no name, or rather he has all the names, because he is the one and all, infinitely filled with the fertility of the two sexes. He constantly gives birth to everything which he intends to beget.‹ ›What, are you saying, Trismegistos, that God has the two sexes?‹ ›Yes, Asklepius, and so does not only God, but all animate and vegetable creation.‹«

3.5. India

The subject of androgyny is dealt with extensively in **Hinduism**. A Hinduistic myth – in similar fashion to Plato's tale of the originally undivided nature of human beings – relates »that there was a time when the generated (emanated) creatures were not multiplying, and the world was threatening to fall back into its original state. Then the god who is identified with Shiva divided himself into two, with the right half of his body taking on the shape of a man and the left half that of a woman. Shiva then used this androgynous body to generate the different creatures.« (Schleberger, 1986)

In a footnote to »Beyond the Pleasure Principle« by Sigmund Freud (1978), one of the mythological roots of androgyny, taken from the Upanishads, is quoted on the authority of Heinrich Gomperz (1993): »... this was why he (the atman, the self or the ego) experienced no joy when he was alone. He desired a second being. He was as large as a woman and a man when they are embracing. He divided this self of his into two parts: a husband and wife were created from this ...«

The similarity with the Platonic myth of androgyny is evident from this story too. That division into two upon which the world and its phenomena are based is eliminated in the unification of god and goddess, of man and woman.

This principle is specifically seen in the portrayal of Shiva and Shakti. It is true that there are also numerous depictions of Shiva appearing on his own, but Shakti may be described as being the creative part of Shiva and thus gives rise to androgynous notions. The right half of the depictions shows the (erect) phallus, the straight hip, the flat chest and the male figure, and sometimes the trident and wheel as attributes, whereas the left side shows half the pubic triangle (rarely the vulva), a hip which curves outwards, an opulent breast and a feminine hairstyle. A mirror and a lotus, two attributes, are sometimes also found. The face is symmetrical and can be interpreted as either male or female.

The depictions of **Ardhanarishvara** follow this principle. These images of deities were set up for purposes of reverence as long ago as the 3rd century, as an example from Mathura shows.

Beautiful and graceful figures survive from the 11th to 13th centuries. They present a perfectly integral person to the onlooker, and this contrasts them with the androgynous depictions which are found in 16th- and 17th-century Europe and are also divided vertically.

However, in addition to these two-sexed figures, the most impressive and obvious symbol of a unification, a synthesis, an identity, is probably seen first and foremost in the **linga/yoni**[18] depiction of Indian art: the pole which is the linga, Shiva's sign employed as a phallic symbol, plunges into a round bowl, the yoni, which usually stands on a base or pedestal and is the symbol of female receiving. »... the characteristic male and female features appear in a unity which precedes the later division. The myth also tells of this starting point. Shiva was inseparably linked to Shakti; the latter, the goddess who is incarnated in all the manifestations such as Parvati, Uma and Durga, is there regarded as activity, as the god's power to act, and thus as the first stage in the process of development to form the world. ...« (Gutschow, Pieper, 1981)

»It is noteworthy that, for a Hindu, linga and yoni usually no longer evoke any erotic associations; they have become widespread symbols whose real meaning is known but only rarely still thought of.« (Glasenapp, 1922)

The Indian cultural complex is impressively universal in displaying the original unity of religion, sexuality, architecture and everyday life. One example may be cited: »In India, lighting a fire is an action which is interpreted in an entirely sexual way, the rod-shaped pramantha« (the word is related to »Prometheus«) »being the phallus, and the bored piece of wood underneath it being the female vulva: the fire which is achieved by boring is Agni, the heavenly son, the shining tongue of the gods.« (Galahad, 1932)

The countless portrayals of copulating couples in what, to a Westerner, are »obscene« positions are abundantly in evidence on the outside of the large Indian temples. They teach us that an entirely different attitude towards sexuality, an attitude which Westerners find it hard to comprehend, prevails in Indian and Asian countries outside the Islamic cultural complex.

lussymbol taucht in eine runde, meist auf einem Fuß oder Sockel stehende Schale, die Yoni, als Symbol des Weiblich-Empfangenden ein. » ... männliches und weibliches Merkmal erscheinen in einer Einheit, die der späteren Aufteilung vorangeht. Vom gleichen Ausgangspunkt erzählt auch der Mythos. Shiva ist untrennbar mit der Shakti verbunden; sie, die Göttin, die sich in all den Manifestationen wie Parvati, Uma, Durga inkarniert, gilt da als Aktivität, Handlungskraft des Gottes, und so als erste Stufe im Prozeß der Entwicklung zur Welt ... « (Gutschow, Pieper, 1981)

«Beachtenswert ist, daß Linga und Yoni für den Hindu zumeist keinerlei erotische Assoziationen mehr hervorrufen; sie sind zu allgemein verbreiteten Sinnbildern geworden, deren eigentliche Bedeutung man wohl kennt, an die man aber nur selten noch denkt.« (Glasenapp, 1922)

Der indische Kulturkreis zeigt in einer beeindruckenden Universalität die ursprüngliche Einheit von Religion, Sexualität, Architektur und Alltag. Ein Beispiel dafür soll zitiert werden: »In Indien ist das Feuer bereiten eine völlig sexuell gefaßte Handlung, mit dem stabförmigen Pramantha« (Wortverwandtschaft zu Prometheus!) »als Phallus, dem darunterliegenden gebohrtem Holzstück als weibliche Vulva: Das erbohrte Feuer ist der himmlische Sohn Agni, die glänzende Zunge der Götter.« (Galahad, 1932)

Die zahllosen Darstellungen kopulierender Paare in für den westlichen Menschen »obszönen« Stellungen entfalten sich üppig an der Außenseite der großen indischen Tempel. Sie lehren uns, daß in den indischen und asiatischen Ländern, außerhalb des islamischen Kulturbereichs, eine völlig andere und für den westlichen Menschen nur schwer nachvollziehbare Einstellung zur Sexualität vorherrscht.

3.6. Andere Religionen

Die prägnanteste Ausbildung dualistischer Systeme finden wir in den **altpersischen Religionen**. Obwohl der Manichäismus vom Christentum verworfen wurde, kann kein Zweifel darüber bestehen, daß schon das frühe Christentum zahlreiche Motive der persischen Religionen aufgenommen hat.

In der iranischen Lehre des Zarathustra ist Ahura-Mazda oder Ormuzd das Prinzip des Lichtes, der Wahrheit, sein Widerpart Angramanyu oder Ahriman, das Prinzip des Bösen, der Lüge, des Dunklen. Beide Urgeister haben Schöpfer-Qualitäten und stehen einander gleichwertig gegenüber – sie stehen aber auch in einem unentwegtem Kampf. Hervorgegangen sind sie aus der androgynen Einheit des Zeitengottes Zurvan akarana. (Wehr, 1964)

»Die Welt als Ganzes ist somit zweigeteilt in eine geistige und eine leibliche Hälfte. Es besteht ein zwiefacher Dualismus, der von Gut und Böse und der von Geist und Leib « (Lommel, 1966) Der Mensch hat die Aufgabe, sich an die Seite des Guten zu stellen, und so könnte eine neue Einheit entstehen: Die Welt wird vom Bösen erlöst, der Dualismus von Geist und Körper ist aufgehoben, die geistige und leibliche Welt sind eins geworden, der Himmel ist zur Erde herniedergestiegen. Die große Ureinheit ist wiederhergestellt.

In den alten Religionen **Chinas** ist »P'anku ... der chinesische Urmensch, der aus seinem Riesenkörper die Welt hervorgehen läßt«. (Wehr, 1964) Sonnengottheit und Himmelsgottheit wurden nicht streng auseinandergehalten, der Himmel wird durch das Sonnenbild, die durchbohrte Nephritscheibe dargestellt: ein universelles, optisches Symbol.

Im **germanischen Mythos** der Snorra-Edda ist von dem Urriesen Ymir oder Örgelmir die Rede. Seine Androgynität tut sich darin kund, daß während des Schlafes seiner Achselhöhle Mann und Frau entwachsen. Freya, Fricka oder Friggo begegnen uns mit deutlichen androgynen Zügen, und der Gott Tuisto ist ein Hermaphrodit.

Loki (auch Loptr) nimmt eine merkwürdige Stellung ein. Oft als boshaft und abgefeimt beschrieben, ist er doch von schönem Aussehen. Er besitzt die Fähigkeit, seine Gestalt und auch sein Geschlecht zu wechseln. Loki wird zum Weib, zur Magd. Und durch das Verzehren eines Hexenherzens wird er schwanger. »Schwangerschaft bei Männern infolge des Essens von Tierfleisch ist in Eurasien als Märchenmotiv bekannt. An die Möglichkeit einer durch Hexen bewirkten Geschlechtsverwandlung hat man noch im Mittelalter geglaubt.« (Bleibtreu-Ehrenberg, 1970)

Die Fähigkeit zum Gestaltwechsel ist freilich nur eine Vorstufe zur Androgynie, die ja eine permanente Doppelgeschlechtlichkeit bedeutet.[20]

Die Idee androgyner mythologischer Wesen taucht sporadisch auch in der **Gegenwart** auf. Für **Niki de Saint Phalle** (geb. 1930) ist der Teufel ein gehörntes und geflügeltes Wesen mit

32. Linga/Yoni aus Pashupatinath, Nepal, 18. Jh.

32. Linga/yoni from Pashupatinath, Nepal, 18th cent.

3.6. Other Religions

It is in the **Old Persian religions** that dualistic systems are developed in the most incisive way. Although Manichaeism was rejected by Christianity, there can be no doubt that early Christianity adopted numerous motives from the Persian religions.

In the Iranian doctrine of Zarathustra, Ahura-Mazda or Ormuzd is the principle of light and truth, while its adversary Angramanyu or Ahriman is the principle of evil, of untruth, of darkness. Both these original spirits are creators and are evenly matched in their opposition to one another – but they also conduct an incessant struggle with one another. They derived from Zurvan akarana, the god of time who was an androgynous unity. (Wehr, 1964)

»The world as a whole is thus divided into one spiritual and one physical half. There is a twofold dualism: that of good and evil, and that of spirit and body.« (Lommel, 1966) It is the duty of mankind to take the side of good, and this might lead to a new unity in which the world is delivered from evil, the dualism of spirit and body is eliminated, the spiritual and physical worlds become one, and the sky descends to earth. The great original unity has been restored.

In the old religions of **China**, »P'anku is ... the Chinese original man, who causes the world to spring from his giant body.« The deity of the sun and that of the sky were not strictly distinguished (Wehr, 1964), and the sky is depicted by the image of the sun, which is a disc of nephrite with a hole through it: this is a universal, optical symbol.

The **Germanic myth** of Snorra-Edda tells of Ymir or Örgelmir, the original giant. His androgyny becomes apparent from the fact that man and woman grow out of his axilla while he is asleep. Freya, Fricka or Friggo appear with clearly androgynous features, and the god Tuisto is a hermaphrodite.

Loki (also Loptr) is a strange figure. Although often described as wicked and crafty, he looks beautiful. He has the ability to change his shape and also his sex. Loki turns into a woman, a maid, and he becomes pregnant by eating a witch's heart. »A motive occurring in fairy tales in Eurasia is that men can become pregnant through eating the meat of animals. It was still believed in the Middle Ages that witches might change a person's sex.« (Bleibtreu-Ehrenberg, 1970)

The ability to change one's shape is admittedly only a preliminary stage on the way towards androgyny, as the latter signifies a permanently two-sexed nature.[19]

The idea of androgynous mythological beings also sporadically arises in **modern times**. To **Niki de Saint Phalle** (born 1930), the devil is a horned and winged being with a threefold penis, but with broad hips and a woman's breasts: this is how he appears in the fantastical »Tarot« garden near Rome.

Viktor Brauner (1903–1966) had parthenogenesis in mind when he was drawing a *Selbstbefruchtende Mutterfigur* (*Self-Fertilizing Mother Figure*) in 1961. (Cf. chap. 6.2.)

These few quotations are intended to show that it would be wrong to believe that the topic of androgyny found acceptance only in early, primitive and classical myths. Instead, »... it must be assumed that a knowledge of the male-female wholeness of mankind appears in religious traditions dating from all the eras of history.« (Wehr, 1980)

4. Christianity. Judaism

4.1. God's Sex. Adam

The Christian God of the Old Testament, the Jewish God of Holy Writ, plainly encounters us in the shape of a man, a father, a ruler. This allocation of a specific sex undoubtedly implies a need for anthropomorphism, so that the workings of God can be made plausible. But if God is really perfect, he cannot be content with the characteristics of only one of the sexes: would he therefore not have to be an **androgynous God**? The grammatical gender of the expression »Jehovah« or »Yahweh«, which was only later replaced by »the Lord«, is certainly in dispute. But it is easy to understand that, in the patriarchal structure of the Old and New Testaments, God could only be defined as a man. On the basis, in many cases, of the feminist movement, and in remembering the great prehistoric goddesses, repeated attempts are made to postulate the femininity, the feminine portions, in short, the androgyny of God, but this undertaking has few prospects of success.

einem dreifachen Penis, aber mit breiten Hüften und Frauenbrüsten: So steht er im phantastischen »Tarot«-Garten in der Nähe Roms.

Viktor Brauner (1903–1966) erinnert sich der Parthenogenese, wenn er (1961) eine *Selbstbefruchtende Mutterfigur* zeichnet. (Vgl. Kap. 6.2.)

Diese wenigen Zitate sollen zeigen, daß es falsch wäre zu glauben, das Thema der Androgynie habe lediglich in den frühen, den primitiven und den antiken Mythten Eingang gefunden Vielmehr »... ist davon auszugehen, daß das Wissen um die männlich-weibliche Ganzheit des Menschen zu allen Zeiten in den religiösen Überlieferungen auftaucht«. (Wehr, 1980)

4. Christentum, Judentum

4.1. Geschlecht Gottes. Adam

Der alttestamentarische christliche Gott, der jüdische Gott der heiligen Schrift tritt uns eindeutig als Mann, Vater, Herrscher entgegen. In dieser geschlechtlichen Zuordnung liegt zweifellos eine notwendige Anthropomorphisierung, um das Wirken des Gottes plausibel zu machen. Wenn aber Gott tatsächlich vollkommen ist, kann er sich mit den Merkmalen nur eines Geschlechtes nicht zufriedengeben: Müßte er demnach nicht ein **androgyner Gott** sein? Der Ausdruck »Jehova« oder »Jahve«, der erst später durch »der Herr« ersetzt wurde, hat einen durchaus umstrittenen Genus. Es ist aber leicht verständlich, daß Gott in der patriarchalischen Struktur des Alten wie des Neuen Testamentes nur als Mann definiert werden konnte. Vielfach ausgehend von der Frauenbewegung und in Erinnerung an die großen, prähistorischen Göttinnen wird immer wieder versucht, die Weiblichkeit Gottes, die weiblichen Anteile, kurzum: die Androgynie Gottes zu postulieren, ein nicht sehr aussichtsreiches Unterfangen.

Um die »Androgynität Gottes« ist Kurt Lüthi (1996) bemüht. Er gibt zu, daß der Begriff der »Androgynität« in der Bibel nicht zu finden ist, und so bedarf es schon einiger sehr spektakulativer Ansätze, um in den patriarchalischen Gottesvorstellungen der Bibel auch einige »weibliche« Züge zu entdecken, die man mit einem Begriff der Androgynie, mühsam genug, verknüpfen kann. So müssen die alten Muttergottheiten und deren spärliche Traditionen zitiert werden, wenn latent Weibliches aufgezeigt werden soll. Lediglich in der Idee der »Sophia«, der Weisheit als weibliches Wesen und als Partnerin Jahwes, später Christi, mag das Weibliche einen gewissen Stellenwert bekommen haben. (Vgl. Kap. 4. 4.) Lüthi zitiert u. a. die »Vogelmutter-Symbolik«: So wird etwa Jahwe »mit der Adlermutter verglichen, die ihre Jungen das Fliegen lehrt.« Oder: »Jahwe wird mit der Henne verglichen, die ihre Jungen unter ihren Flügeln birgt und schützt.« (Lüthi, 1994)

»Gott als Weisheit« ist auch U. R. Mollenkott (1985) ein wesentliches Argument für die Präsenz des Weiblichen im jüdischen und christlichen Schrifttum. Sie zitiert noch andere Charakteristika, die den weiblichen Charakter Gottes belegen sollen und entdeckt in der Bibel unter anderem die Gottheit als »gebärende Frau«, »stillende Mutter«, »Geburtshelferin«, »Bärenmutter«, »Haushälterin«, »Geliebte«, »Bäckerin« und »Adlermutter«.

So verständlich die Anthropomorphisierungen Gottes auch sein mögen, könnte doch eher jener theologischen Auffassung zugestimmt werden, wonach der vollkommene christliche Gott jenseits einer geschlechtlichen Zuordnung zu finden ist, ohne an seiner Personalität Schaden zu nehmen.

Gott selbst nimmt sich von den ewigen Teilungsprozessen nicht aus: Zunächst schafft er, der sich in seiner Vollkommenheit doch selbst genügen sollte, ein »Ebenbild«: den Menschen, den Mann Adam. Doch damit nicht genug: Auch dieses Wesen wird geteilt, und die »bessere Hälfte« entsteigt der Lende Adams, womit offenkundig die Teilung der Menschheit für alle Ewigkeit festgelegt ist.

Sehen wir Gott als androgyn an, dann muß das Ebenbild Gottes ähnliche Eigenschaften aufweisen: Adam ist als männlich und weiblich erschaffen worden. Ungeachtet der Tatsache, daß in der alttestamentarischen patriarchalischen Gesellschaft Gott als männlich dargestellt wird, gibt es doch auch Indizien dafür, daß Adam als Ebenbild Gottes in einer Einheit von »männlich« und »weiblich« erschaffen wird. Eine andere Leseart der Erschaffung des Menschen (Gen. 1,27) lautet: »Und Gott schuf **den** Menschen ... er schuf **ihn** männlich und weiblich.« Und später (Gen. 2,21–24) finden wir die Verheißung, daß eine neue Einheit zwischen den Menschen möglich sein wird: »Darum wird der Mann seinen Vater und seine Mutter verlassen und an seinem Weibe hangen und sie werden sein ein Fleisch.«

Kurt Lüthi endeavours to point out the »androgynity of God« (1994–1996). He admits that the concept of androgyny is not to be found in the Bible, so that some very speculative attempts are required in order to discover, in the patriarchal ideas of God in the Bible, any female traits which might, with considerable difficulty, be linked with some concept of androgyny. Thus the old matriarchal deities and their scanty tradition have to be cited if anything latently feminine is to be pointed out. It is only in the idea of »Sophia«, of wisdom as a female being and as the female partner of Yahweh and later of Christ, that femininity may have obtained a certain ranking. (cf. chap. 4.4.) The matters cited by Lüthi include the »symbolism of the bird as mother«. For example, Yahweh is compared »with the mother eagle who teaches her young to fly.« Or: »Yahweh is compared with the ›hen who shelters and protects her young under her wings‹.« (Lüthi, 1994)

It is also the view of U. R. Mollenkott (1985) that »God as wisdom« is an essential argument for the presence of the female in Jewish and Christian literature. She also cites other characteristics intended to prove the female character of God, and discovers that the references to the deity in the Bible include »birth-giving woman«, »suckling mother«, »midwife«, »mother bear«, »female housekeeper«, »female loved one«, »baker woman« and »mother eagle«.

However understandable the anthropomorphisms of God may be, the tendency might rather be to agree with the theological interpretation which states that the perfect Christian God stands over and above any allocation to a particular sex, without his personality being damaged thereby.

God does not exclude himself from the eternal processes of division: he, who in his perfection should be sufficient unto himself, starts by creating an »image«: this is a human being, the man Adam. But this is not enough: this being is itself divided, the »better half« emerges from Adam's loins, and the division of mankind is thereby evidently laid down for all eternity.

If we regard God as androgynous, then God's image must also have similar properties: Adam was created as both male and female. Although God is represented as male in the patriarchal society of the Old Testament, there are also some indications that Adam was created in God's image in a unity of »male« and »female«. A different reading of the creation of man (Genesis, i, 27) is as follows: »And God created man ... he created him male and female.« And later (Genesis, ii, 21–24), we find a promise that a new unity among men will be possible: »This is why a man will leave his father and his mother and be united with his wife, and the two will become one flesh.«

Thus, in this interpretation, man, Adam the first man, is seen as a being whose sex has not yet been specified. This would mean that the original man was an androgyne.

»It is generally true of hermaphrodites that they cannot beget of their own accord, without any seed or external matter: God is said to have originally created Adam as a male-female. But because he could not beget of his own accord, the woman was separated from him, and after that, it is said, he begat by conjunction.« (Bracesco, 1544, Aurnhammer, 1986) Another interpretation regards Adam as the one, the only, the undivided, the image of God, and he is not divided until he is asleep.

»Thus, before a human being is divided into man and woman, his body and soul are still ›one, although they are in a different state‹. ... After division, the body receives a life of its own, as it is a particular being. This division into man and woman is caused because the original human being does not connect the world, life or material things ... with his origin. ... A need arises in the human being to be reunited with the one to whom he feels that he belongs ... all his senses are directed at cancelling the separation so that he can unite himself with his other part.« (Weinreb, 1948)

This thesis concerning an androgynous Adam met with scant approval in the orthodox doctrine of the Catholic church. One exception was Pope Innocent I, whose pontificate lasted from 402–417. He clearly took the view that Adam was created as a two-sexed being. (Neugebauer, 1908)

There is some very revealing information in Jewish religious literature. In the **Kabbala**, the myth of creation is interpreted in a clearly androgynous way. The *Book of Brightness* (Sefar ha Sohar) states: »Rabbi Aba said: The first human being consisted of male and female, and it is said: ›And God spoke: Let us make a human being in our own image!‹ Thus, after this, male and female were created in one, and did not separate until later.« (Müller, 1932) And in another passage: »When they (male and female) are united, they look like one body. From this we learn that a male by himself only appears like a part of a body, and the same applies to a female by herself.« (Wehr, 1986)

33. Viktor Brauner, *Selbstbefruchtende Mutterfigur*, 1961.

33. Viktor Brauner, *Self-Fertilizing Mother Figure*, 1961.

In dieser Interpretation wird also der Mensch, der erste Mensch Adam, als ein Wesen gesehen, dessen geschlechtliche Spezifikation noch nicht vollzogen ist: Der Urmensch wäre demnach ein Androgyn.

»Im allgemeinen gilt für Hermaphroditen, daß sie nicht durch sich selbst und ohne Samen oder äußere Materie zeugen können: Gott soll Adam am Anfang mannweiblich geschaffen haben. Weil er aber in sich selbst nicht zeugen konnte, ist von ihm die Frau getrennt worden, danach habe er durch Konjunktion gezeugt.« (Bracesco, 1544, Aurnhammer, 1986) Eine weitere Deutung sieht Adam als den Einen, Einzigen und Ungeteilten, als Ebenbild Gottes, und er wird erst im Schlafe geteilt.

»Im Menschen vor der Teilung in Mann und Weib sind daher Leib und Seele noch ›eins‹ obwohl in einem anderen Zustand. ... Nach der Teilung erhält der Leib, als ein besonderes Wesen, ein eigenes Leben. Diese Teilung in Mann und Frau wird verursacht, weil der ursprüngliche Mensch die Welt, das Leben, das Materielle ... nicht mit dem Ursprung verbindet ... Im Menschen entsteht das Bedürfnis wieder eins zu werden mit demjenigen, das er als zu sich gehörend fühlt ... alle seine Sinne sind darauf gerichtet, die Trennung rückgängig zu machen, um sich mit dem anderen Teil zu vereinigen.« (Weinreb, 1948)

In der orthodoxen Lehre der katholischen Kirche hat die These von einem androgynen Adam wenig Anklang gefunden. Eine Ausnahme bildet Papst Innozenz I. (Pontifikat 402–417). Er vertritt eindeutig die Ansicht, daß Adam als doppelgeschlechtliches Wesen erschaffen wurde. (Neugebauer, 1908)

In der jüdischen religiösen Literatur finden wir einige sehr aufschlußreiche Hinweise. In der **Kabbala** wird der Schöpfungsmythos eindeutig androgyn interpretiert. Im *Buch des Glanzes* (Sefar ha Sohar) heißt es: »Rabbi Aba sagte: ›Der erste Mensch bestand aus Männlichem und Weiblichem, wie es heißt‹: ›Und es sprach Gott: Lasset uns einen Menschen machen in unserem Gleichnis!‹ Hiernach wurden also Männlich und Weiblich in Einem geschaffen und trennten sich erst später.« (Müller, 1932) Und an anderer Stelle: »Wenn sie (das Männliche und das Weibliche) sich vereinigen, dann sehen sie aus wie ein Körper. Daraus lernen wir: das Männliche allein erscheint nur wie ein Teil eines Körpers, ebenso auch das Weibliche.« (Wehr, 1986)

Bei **Samuel Bar Nachman** finden wir eine Erzählung, die eine genaue Parallele zu einer Darstellung auf einer Medaille aus der Renaissance des **Marcantonio Passeri** (vgl. Kap. 6.1.) darstellt: Der Mensch hat zwei Gesichter und ist am Rücken aneinandergewachsen, solange, bis Gott ihn in zwei Hälften zersägt. »Erinnern wir uns auch daran, daß mehrere Midrashim (eine gnostische Sekte) Adam als Androgyn vorstellten. Nach Bereshit rabba waren Adam und Eva Rücken an Rücken gemacht, an den Schultern zusammengehängt: Dann trennte sie Gott durch einen Beilschlag und teilte sie in zwei ... Adam war der Mann an der rechten Seite und die Frau an der linken Seite.« (Eliade, 1962)

Um 1180 schreibt der jüdische Philosoph **Moses Maimonides** (1135–1204): »Adam und Eva sind zusammen erschaffen worden, vereinigt mit ihrem Rücken; diesen doppelten Menschen teilte Gott und nahm die Hälfte, welche Eva war und dieselbe ward der anderen Hälfte (Adam) gegeben als Gefährten.« (Lurker, 1958)

4.2. Trinität. Quaternität

Nach der Schöpfung des Menschen entäußert sich der christliche Gott noch ein zweites Mal seiner selbst und verzichtet auf die bedingungslose Einheit: In der Schaffung seines eigenen Sohnes, die nach christlicher Theologie ohne Zutun eines irdischen Mannes erfolgt. Diese Duplizierung ist aber auch gleichzeitig ein Weg zur Einheit, denn **Christus** ist es, der die Dualität von Gott und Mensch in sich selbst auflöst, ist er doch Gott und Mensch zugleich. Diese elementare theologische Frage der »consubstantialem patris« wird Generationen von Theologen beschäftigen und das Christentum vorübergehend in ein Schisma führen.

Der »Spaltung« Gottes in der Schaffung seines Sohnes wird ein weiterer Aspekt hinzugefügt: Gemeinsam mit dem Heiligen Geist ist die **Trinität** ein zentrales christliches Glaubensproblem. Die unüberbrückbare Divergenz von Monismus, Dualismus und Pluralismus des göttlichen Wesens wird mit dem Hinweis auf »unergründbare Glaubensgeheimnisse« dem rationalen Denken entzogen. Nicht unerwähnt soll die fallweise Erweiterung der Trinität auf eine **Quaternität** bleiben, für die vor allem die Ikonologie ein reiches Material liefert: Die Trinität wird zusammen mit Maria (als Himmelskönigin) dargestellt, in gleichwertiger, oft sogar bedeutender

In **Samuel Bar Nachman**, we find a story which is an exact parallel to a depiction on a medal by **Marcantonio Passeri** dating from the Renaissance (cf. chapter 7.1.): the human being has two faces and a coalesced dorsum until God saws him into two halves. »Let us remember that several midrashim (a gnostic sect) represented Adam as androgynous. According to Bereshit rabba, Adam and Eve were created back to back, being joined at the shoulders. Then God separated them by the stroke of an axe and divided them into two. ... Adam was the man on the right-hand side and the woman was on the left.« (Eliade, 1962)

The Jewish philosopher **Moses Maimonides** (1135–1204) wrote the following in ca. 1180: »Adam and Eve were created together, being joined at their backs; God divided this double human being and took the half which was Eve, who was given to the other half (Adam) as his companion.« (Lurker, 1958)

4.2. Trinity. Quaternity

After man's creation, the Christian God parted with himself a second time, and dispensed with unconditional unity by creating his own son. According to Christian theology, that creation took place without the agency of an earthly man. But this duplication was itself at the same time a path to unity, because it is **Christ** who resolved within himself the duality of God and man, as he was at once both God and man. This elemental theological question of »consubstantialem patris« was to keep generations of theologians occupied and brought about a temporary schism in Christianity.

A further aspect was added to the matter of God's being divided when creating his son. Together with the Holy Ghost, the **Trinity** is a central problem of Christian belief. The irreconcilable divergency between monism, dualism and pluralism in the divine being is removed from the reach of rational thought when reference is made to »unfathomable mysteries of belief«. Mention should also be made of the occasional expansion of the Trinity into a **Quaternity**, a notion for which iconology, in particular, provides abundant material. The Trinity is depicted along with the Virgin Mary as the Queen of Heaven, and her position in the composition of the painting is equivalent to, and sometimes in fact more significant than, that of the other three elements. The fourfold archetype which is familiar to us from many other religions thus obtained a dominant position in Christianity (as did the Evangelists, the church doctrines, and so on)[21] (Jung, 1948, 1972, Feuerstein, 1966)

4.3. Christ

There can be no doubt that Christ was male, and it is not easy to derive from Holy Writ any androgynous characteristics of Christ.

In orthodox theology, Christ is only part of the great totality: only in union with the Father and the Spirit is he the perfection of the deity. A speculative attempt is to be found in the link with Adam: if the »old« Adam is interpreted as an androgynous being, it is understandable that the »new« Adam, that is to say Christ, may have androgynous properties. »Neither the eternal male nor the eternal female is embodied in the new Adam; instead, he is characterized by the cult of androgyny. He combines female virginhood with male youthfulness.« (Koepgen, 1939)

Although Christ was physically a man and his male characteristics are very clearly marked, the female traits cannot be overlooked: »He was accompanied by women, he was sensitive and wept when he was sad ... there was a feminine feeling about his death, and his voluntary surrender to expiatory death was feminine in character ... this was the consummation of the male-femaleness which became visible in Christ.« (Koepgen, 1939)

»The tension and antagonistic struggle to be found in sexual matters is compensated in Jesus by an androgynous unity. The Church has taken this characteristic over from him as a heritage: the Church is androgynous.«

We can find somewhat more such material outside Catholic orthodoxy, in **gnostic and apocryphal** writings. For example, in the gospel of St. Thomas, which is not recognized by the Church, we read a noteworthy saying of Christ's: »If you create two in one, and if you form into a single whole the inside as the outside, the outside as the inside, what is above and what is below, male and female, so that the man is not male and the woman is not female ... you will have the kingdom.« (Exner, 1979, Paulsen, 1979)

Position in der Bildkomposition. Der Archetypus der Vierzahl, der uns aus vielen anderen Religionen geläufig ist, hat damit auch im Christentum (neben Evangelisten, Kirchenlehren usw.) eine dominante Position bekommen.[21] (Jung, 1948, 1972, Feuerstein, 1966)

4.3. Christus

Es kann kein Zweifel darüber bestehen, daß Christus männlicher Natur ist, und es fällt nicht leicht, androgyne Züge Christi aus der Heiligen Schrift abzuleiten.

In der orthodoxen Theologie ist Christus nur ein Teil der großen Gesamtheit: Erst mit dem Vater und mit dem Geiste wird er zur Vollkommenheit der Gottheit. Einen spekulativen Ansatz finden wir in der Verbindung mit Adam: Wenn der »alte« Adam als ein androgynes Wesen interpretiert wird, dann ist es verständlich, daß auch der »neue« Adam, eben Christus, androgyne Eigenschaften haben kann. »Im neuen Adam verkörpert sich weder das ewig Männliche noch das ewig Weibliche, sondern der Kultus der Androgyne ist ihm eigen: Er verbindet das Jungfräuliche mit dem Jünglinghaften.« (Koepgen, 1939)

Wenngleich Christus physisch Mann war und die männlichen Züge sehr deutlich ausgeprägt sind, können die weiblichen nicht übersehen werden: »Er hat Frauen in seinem Geleit, er ist empfindsam und weint, wenn er traurig ist ... er stirbt mit weiblichem Gefühl, und weiblich ist seine freiwillige Hingabe zum Opfertod ... Vollzug der in Christus sichtbar gewordenen Mannweiblichkeit.« (Koepgen, 1939)

»Die Spannung und der gegensätzliche Kampf des Geschlechtlichen ist in Jesus durch eine androgyne Einheit ausgeglichen. Und das hat die Kirche als Erbe von ihm übernommen: Sie ist androgyn.«

Etwas fündiger werden wir jenseits der katholischen Orthodoxie, in **gnostischen und apokryphen** Schriften. So lesen wir etwa im Thomas-Evangelium, das von der Kirche nicht anerkannt wird, einen bemerkenswerten Ausspruch Christi: »Wenn Ihr zwei in eines schafft und das Innere als das Äußere und das Äußere als das Innere und das Oben wie das Unten und das Männliche wie das Weibliche in ein einziges, so daß der Mann nicht männlich und das Weib nicht weiblich ist ... so werdet Ihr das Reich haben.« (Exner, 1979, Paulsen, 1979)

4.4. Vermählung

Die Idee einer neuen Vereinigung der getrennten, gespaltenen Menschenwesen ist eines der Grundmotive der Androgynie und wird schon in Platons Gleichnis angesprochen. Als eine ideale Methode wird immer wieder die fixe Partnerschaft, institutionalisiert als **Ehe**, angesehen. In der Bibel heißt es: »Sie werden sein ein Fleisch« – »duo in carne una«.[22]

Der Weg von der Zweiheit zur Einheit und somit zur Vollkommenheit hat im Christentum eine bedeutsame Position im Gedanken der bräutlichen Vermählung gefunden. Die sakramentale Vereinigung in der katholischen Ehe unterstreicht die Bedeutung der geschlechtlichen Vereinigung. Dies geht aus dem katholischen Eherecht hervor, da die Bestätigung der Unauflöslichkeit erst durch die consumatio, durch den geschlechtlichen Vollzug gegeben ist.

Aus der Analogie der Ehe zur Vermählung Christi mit der Kirche, aber auch aus dem Verständnis des »duo in carne una« mag die mit Recht viel kritisierte Unauflöslichkeit der katholischen Ehe verständlich werden: Es bildet sich eine neue Einheit in der Weise, daß eine nochmalige Spaltung erst durch den Tod erfolgen kann.

Erstaunliche Formulierungen zur Partnerschaft Mann-Frau findet **Hildegard von Bingen** (1098–1179) in einer mittelalterlich-patriarchischen Welt: »Gott gab dem Mann eine Gehülfin in der Gestalt des Weibes, gleichsam einer Spiegelgestalt, in der das ganze Menschengeschlecht latent vorhanden war ... Mann und Frau sind auf eine solche Weise miteinander vermischt, daß einer das Werk des anderen ist. Ohne die Frau könnte der Mann nicht Mann heißen, ohne Mann könnte die Frau nicht Frau genannt werden. So ist die Frau das Werk des Mannes, der Mann ist ein Anblick voller Trost für die Frau und keiner vermöchte es, hinfort ohne den anderen zu leben. Der Mann ist dabei ein Hinweis auf die Gottheit, die Frau auf die Menschheit des Sohnes Gottes. Und so sitzt der Mensch auf dem Richterstuhl der Welt. Er beherrscht die gesamte Schöpfung.« (Schipperges, 1965)

Die Wertschätzung der Ehe findet vor allem in der theologischen Artikulation bei **Emanuel Swedenborg** (1689–1772) ihren Niederschlag. Swedenborg geht, ähnlich wie Böhme und die

4.4. Marriage

The idea that human beings, who are divided and split, are to be reunited is one of the basic motives of androgyny and is referred to in Plato's allegory. A fixed partnership, institutionalized as **marriage**, is repeatedly regarded as an ideal method. The Bible says: »They will be one flesh« – »duo in carne una«.[21]

The path from duality to unity, and thus to perfection, has attained an important position in Christianity in the idea of a bridal wedding. Sacramental unification in Catholic marriage emphasizes the significance of sexual unification. This is to be seen from Catholic marriage law, as indissolubility is not confirmed until the consumatio, the sexual consummation, takes place.

The indissolubility of Catholic marriage has rightly been much criticized, but it may become understandable by drawing an analogy between marriage on the one hand and Christ's being wedded to the Church on the other, as well as by comprehending the meaning of »duo in carne una«: a new unity is formed because another division can only be brought about by death.

Hildegard von Bingen (1096–1179) derived, from the patriarchal medieval world, some astonishing statements concerning the partnership of man and woman: »God gave the man a helper in the shape of the woman, who was a kind of mirror figure in whom the entire human race was latently present. ... Man and woman are blended with one another in such a way that the one is the work of the other. The man could not be called a man without the woman, and the woman could not be described as a woman without the man. Thus the woman is the work of the man, the man is a very consoling sight for the woman, and neither would be able to live without the other from that time on. Here, the man points to the deity of the son of God, and the woman to that son's humanity. Thus it is that a human being sits on the world's judgement seat. He rules over all creation.« (Schipperges, 1965)

The esteem in which marriage was held was articulated theologically by **Emanuel Swedenborg** (1689–1772). In similar fashion to Böhme and the theosophists, Swedenborg proceeds on the basis of an androgynous original human being. Although man and woman are two beings, they combine to form one person, one unity, which also includes the spiritual and mental parts. Thus it is only logical that marriage continues even after death, and the ideal matrimonial community may only be attainable in heaven.

Among the innumerable eulogies concerning marriage – or, to put it better, concerning unceasing or even eternal partnerships –, *Lucinde* by **Friedrich Wilhelm Schlegel** (1772–1829) will be quoted, as it articulates with particular clarity the idea of a new and eternal unity. »I can no longer say ›my love‹ or ›your love‹; both are equal and are a perfect unity, with just as much love given as taken. It is marriage, the eternal unity and conjunction of our minds ...« (Schlegel, 1985)[22]

The comparison with marriage gives the idea of androgyny an acceptable position in the field of Christianity. It is initially Christ himself who weds the Church. The »ecclesia« is feminine and is iconographically depicted as such. The **church as Christ's bride**, forming a unity with him, is the »corpus christi mysticum«, a holy entity.

Just as the Church is »Christ's bride«, a nun in a convent is also wedded to Christ and is absorbed in him. The investiture ceremony is very similar to a marriage ritual.

The doctrine of heavenly and holy wisdom, of **Hagia Sophia**, has been recognized in different ways in Christianity. That wisdom is the female partner of heaven or of Christ. It exists side by side with the Virgin Mary, or even becomes identical with her: the Virgin Mary is sometimes an incarnation of Sophia.

Felix Christ (1970) shows »that Jesus, as early as the synoptic tradition, appears not merely as a vehicle of wisdom, but as wisdom itself«. Jesus becomes identical with Sophia – incidentally, »Weisheit«, the word for »wisdom« in the German language, is also feminine – and once again gains some feminine attributes. »... this last androgynous unity of Christ, consisting in his eternal coexistence with Sophia, is the reason for the peculiar multiformity of expression in the religious experience of »unio«: unification with Christ can in each case be described so that Christ appears as either the bridegroom or the bride. He is the bridegroom when he is the husband of Sophia, who is the heavenly image of God; he is the bride when he is the notion of heaven itself, wedded to the soul. ... But the decisive factor is that this marriage of Christ and Sophia takes place not in an aeon far away from humans, but in man.« (Benz, 1970)

The whole significance of the idea of the wedding is emphasized in the Gospel of St. John in the New Testament: Christ performs his first miracle and turns water into wine at the wedding

Theosophen, vom androgynen Urmenschen aus. Mann und Frau sind zwar zwei Wesen, aber sie bilden zusammen eine Person, eine Einheit, die auch das Seelische und Geistige miteinbezieht. So ist es nur logisch, daß die Ehe sogar nach dem Tode weiterbesteht, die ideale eheliche Gemeinschaft ist vielleicht erst im Himmel erreichbar.

Aus den zahllosen Lobpreisungen der Ehe – oder besser der immerwährenden oder gar ewigen Partnerschaften – soll die *Lucinde* von **Friedrich Wilhelm Schlegel** (1772–1829) zitiert werden, da hier der Gedanke einer neuen, ewigen Einheit besonders deutlich artikuliert wird. »Ich kann nicht mehr sagen, meine Liebe oder Deine Liebe, beide sind sich gleich und vollkommen eins, so viel Liebe als Gegenliebe. Es ist Ehe, ewige Einheit und Verbindung unserer Geister ...« (Schlegel, 1985)[23]

Mit dem Ehevergleich gewinnt die Idee des Androgynen eine akzeptable Position im Bereich des Christentums. Zunächst ist es Christus selbst, der sich mit der Kirche vermählt, die »ecclesia« ist weiblich und wird auch ikonographisch so dargestellt. Die **Kirche als Braut Christi** und mit ihm eine Einheit bildend ist der »corpus christi mysticum« als heilige Wesenheit.

Wie die Kirche die »Braut Christi« ist, so wird auch die Nonne im Kloster mit Christus vermählt und geht in ihm auf. Das Einkleidungszeremoniell ist sehr ähnlich einem Trauungsritual.

Unterschiedliche Anerkennung hat im Christentum die Lehre von der himmlischen und heiligen Weisheit, der **Hagia Sophia** gefunden. Sie ist die Partnerin des Himmels oder die Partnerin Christi. Sie besteht neben Maria – oder wird sogar mit ihr identisch, Maria ist bisweilen eine Inkarnation der Sophia.

Felix Christ (1970) weist nach, »daß Jesus schon in der synoptischen Tradition nicht nur als Träger der Weisheit, sondern als die Weisheit selbst erscheint«. Jesus wird identisch mit der Sophia – **die** Weisheit auch im Deutschen – und gewinnt einmal mehr feminine Attribute. » ... diese letzte androgyne Einheit Christi, die in seinem ewigen Zusammensein mit der Sophia besteht, ist der Grund für die eigentümliche Vielgestaltigkeit des Ausdrucks in der religiösen Erfahrung der unio: Die Einigung mit ihm kann jeweils so beschrieben werden, daß Christus als der Bräutigam oder als die Braut erscheint. Bräutigam ist er als der Gemahl der Sophia, des himmlischen Gottebenbildes; Braut ist er als das himmlische Bild selbst, das sich mit der Seele vermählt. ... Entscheidend aber ist, daß sich diese Ehe zwischen Christus und Sophia nicht in einem menschenfernen Aeon vollzieht, sondern im Menschen.« (Benz, 1970)

Der Gedanke der Hochzeit wird im neuen Testament, im Evangelium des Johannes, in seiner ganzen Bedeutung hervorgehoben: Christus wirkt sein erstes Wunder und verwandelt Wasser in Wein bei der Hochzeit zu Kana. Es ist jedoch mehr als eine freundliche Episode: Ordnen wir dem Monde das Wasser und der Sonne den Wein zu, dann durchdringen die Kräfte einander, eine »conjunctio« wie es viel später die Alchimie dargestellt hat. »Die gleichen Kräfte sind es, die überströmen zwischen Sonne und Mond, Maria-Sophia und Christus, Mann und Frau, Wasser und Wein. Aus der Vereinigung von Sonnenhaftem und Mondhaftem, Männlichem und Weiblichem, wird der mann-weibliche, der urbildliche ganze Mensch, verklärt nach Geist, Leib und Seele.« (Schult, 1965) [24]

In der katholischen **Osterliturgie** finden wir ein eigenartiges Ritual, das eine überraschende Parallele zu den hinduistischen Linga/Yoni-Darstellungen aufweist. In drei Etappen, unter Absingen der Worte »lumen Christi« wird der Pfahl der Osternachtskerze – er repräsentiert Christus – in das Becken mit dem geheiligten Taufwasser eingetaucht, ein latentes Vermählungsritual.

4.5. Nikolaus von Kues: Coincidentia oppositorum

Das Bewußtsein von den Gegensätzlichkeiten in der Welt des Seienden beschäftigt die christlichen Denker bereits im 15. Jahrhundert. Die wichtigsten Aussagen hierzu liefert **Nikolaus von Kues** (1401–1464). Die **coincidentia oppositorum**, der Zusammenfall der Gegensätze, ist ein zentrales Thema seiner Theologie.

Zu den wichtigsten Gegensatzpaaren zählen das Endliche und das Unendliche, das Wissen und das Nichtwissen. Bei Nikolaus von Kues finden wir darüber zahlreiche spekulativ-theologische Überlegungen.

»Das Unendliche der Gottheit ist zwar nicht durch Verstandeswissen, wohl aber im Nichtwissen des Verstandes durch Vernunft berührbar. Dieses Nichtwissen ist nicht das leere Nicht-

in Cana. But this is more than an amicable episode. If we attribute water to the moon and wine to the sun, then the forces penetrate one another in a »conjunctio« like that represented by alchemy at a much later date. »These are the same forces as those which flow between sun and moon, between Maria-Sophia and Christ, man and woman, water and wine. The male-female, the prototypical entire human being, is transfigured in mind, body and soul as a result of the union of the solar and the lunar, the male and the female.(Schult, 1965)[23]

The Catholic **Easter liturgy** includes a peculiar ritual displaying a surprising parallel with the linga/yoni depictions of Hinduism. In three stages, while the words »lumen Christi« are sung, the rod of the Easter Eve candle, representing Christ, is dipped into the basin containing the consecrated baptismal water: this is a latent marriage ritual.

4.5. Nicholas of Cusa: Coincidentia Oppositorum

An awareness of the antagonisms present in the world of existence occupied the minds of Christian thinkers as early as the 15th century. The most important statements here were made by **Nicholas of Cusa** (1401–1464). The **coincidentia oppositorum**, the coincidence of opposites, is a central topic of his theology.

The important pairs of opposites include the finite and the infinite, knowledge and ignorance. The works of Nicholas of Cusa contain numerous speculative theological reflections on these matters.

The infinity of the deity cannot be touched by intellectual knowledge, but it can be touched by reason in the ignorance of the intellect. This ignorance is not the empty ignorance which does not know that it knows nothing, or which indifferently neglects the things which it cannot know. Instead, it is the knowing ignorance (docta ignorantia), which develops by thinking and can be fulfilled.

A different logic is required for this purpose. When intellectual thinking fails, a kind of thinking arises where contrasts and contradictions – which, in the world of the finite, either tie things down because of the existing differences or destroy them because of the absurdity – no longer separate things in objectivity, but coincide in an absence of objectivity (coincidentia oppositorum). (Jaspers, 1987)

»Coincidentia oppositorum is a form of ignorance. It rebuffs the intellect, which rejects it as absurd. It demands a different way of thinking which, although it uses the intellect as a tool at every step of the way, is no longer understood by the intellect.«

The place where God »is found unveiled ... is surrounded by the coincidence of contradictions. ... Beyond the wall where contradictions coincide, God can be seen.« (Jaspers, 1987)

Apart from theological subjects, Nicholas of Cusa dealt with many scientific, and particularly mathematical, problems which gave occasion for various speculations which were pursued at the beginning of modern times. Nicholas of Cusa referred to the polygon and the circle as an example of the coincidentia oppositorum. »The square and the circle are particular finite figures. They contrast with one another and cannot coincide. If I now replace the square (the rectangle) by a regular pentagon, a regular hexagon, ... a regular figure with n sides, that is to say by polygons having more and more angles, the polygon will never coincide with the circle. But if the number of angles becomes infinite, the infinite polygon ... is identical to the circle.« (Jaspers, 1987)

God is incomprehensibly comprehended by the coincidence of the opposites. His infinite abundance is expressed by the infinite varieties, which again all become one in the coincidence of the opposites.

Existence and non-existence, the largest and the smallest, being and being able to be, past, present and future – all coincide.

This is the magnificent conclusion arrived at by Nicholas of Cusa: »No association is more wonderful and sublime than the love joining the infinite to the finite, the creature to the creator.« (Kues, 1984)

It is understandable that this 15th-century theologian did not deal with coincidentia as it relates to the differentiation between the sexes, but elevated it in a far-seeing spiritual way. The »mysterium coniunctis«, on the other hand, refers to a mystery of becoming one, where what has been separated and divided finds its way to one another in a loving meeting. This is seen at its most convincing in the unification of man and woman into a **felix coniunctio**.

wissen, das nicht weiß, daß es nichts weiß, oder das gleichgültig liegen läßt, was es nicht wissen kann. Es ist vielmehr das wissende Nichtwissen (docta ignorantia), das sich denkend entfaltet und sich erfüllen läßt.

Dazu braucht es eine andere Logik. Im Scheitern des Verstandesdenkens entspringt ein Denken, für das Gegensätze und Widersprüche, die in der Welt des Endlichen entweder an das Unterschiedene fesseln oder im Absurden zerstören, nicht mehr im Gegenständlichen trennen, sondern im Gegenstandslosen zusammenfallen (coincidentia oppositorum).« (Jaspers, 1987)

»Die coincidentia oppositorum ist eine Form des Nichtwissens. Sie brüskiert den Verstand, der sie als für ihn absurd verwirft. Sie fordert ein anderes Denken, das zwar in jedem Schritt sich des Verstandes als Mittel bedient, das aber der Verstand als solches nicht mehr versteht.«

Der Ort, an dem man Gott »unverhüllt findet ... ist umgeben vom Zusammenfall der Widersprüche. ... Jenseits der Mauer des Zusammenfalls der Widersprüche kann man Gott schauen.« (Jaspers, 1987)

Über theologische Themen hinaus beschäftigt sich Nikolaus von Kues mit naturwissenschaftlichen, insbesondere mathematischen Problemen, die Anlaß zu mancherlei Spekulationen zu Beginn der Neuzeit bieten. Als Beispiel der coincidentia oppositorum nennt er Vieleck und Kreis. »Das Quadrat und der Kreis sind bestimmte endliche Figuren. Sie sind Gegensätze, können nicht zusammenfallen. Wenn ich nun das Quadrat (das Viereck) durch ein regelmäßiges 5-eck, 6-eck, ... n-Eck ersetze, also durch Polygone mit immer mehr Ecken, so wird das Polygon nie mit dem Kreis zusammenfallen. Werden aber die Ecken unendlich an Zahl, so ist ... das unendliche Vieleck identisch mit dem Kreis. (Jaspers, 1987)

Gott wird unbegreiflich begriffen durch den Zusammenfall der Gegensätze. Seine unendliche Fülle ist durch die unendlichen Verschiedenheiten, die wieder eins werden in dem Zusammenfall der Gegensätze, ausgedrückt.

Sein und Nichtsein, Größtes und Kleinstes, Sein und Seinkönnen, Vergangenheit, Gegenwart und Zukunft, alle fallen zusammen.

Und die großartige Schlußfolgerung, zu der Nikolaus von Kues kommt: »Keine Verknüpfung ist wunderbarer und erhabener, als die Liebe zwischen dem Unendlichen und dem Endlichen, die zwischen Geschöpf und Schöpfer.« (Kues, 1984)

Aus der Sicht des Theologen des 15. Jahrhunderts ist es verständlich, daß die coincidentia nicht im Bereich der Geschlechterdifferenzierung abgehandelt wird, sondern eine weitblickende spirituelle Überhöhung erfährt. Das »mysterium coniunctis« hingegen meint ein Geheimnis der Einswerdung, bei der das Getrennte und Geschiedene in liebender Vereinigung zueinanderfindet – am überzeugendsten sichtbar in der Vereinigung von Mann und Frau zu einer **felix coniunctio**.

Die coincidentia oppositorum beschäftigt auch noch das 17. Jahrhundert, und in einer Darstellung des **Michael Maier** aus dem Jahre 1618 werden Mann und Frau in die Harmonie geometrischer Figuren einbezogen.

4.6. Theosophie. (Geheim-)Lehren des 16. bis 18. Jahrhunderts

In den folgenden Jahrhunderten wird – vielfach in der Nachfolge des Nikolaus von Kues – die Frage nach der großen Einheit alles Seienden nicht verstummen und Theologen wie Philosophen suchen nach einer gültigen Antwort.

Die **Theosophen** des 17. Jahrhunderts glauben, eine sehr spezifische Antwort gefunden zu haben, und es ist bemerkenswert, daß in ihrem Denken die Androgynie eine nicht unwichtige Rolle spielt. Der bedeutendste Theosoph ist **Jakob Böhme** (1575–1624). Er versucht, das Mißverständnis der Manichäer aufzuklären: »Der heiligen Welt Gott und der finsteren Welt Gott sind nicht zween Götter. Es ist ein **einiger** Gott. Er ist selber **alles** Wesen.« (Wehr, 1980)

Die Frage nach dem Bösen wird in der Weise beantwortet, daß das negative Prinzip in Gott selbst verlegt wird. Diese riskante theologische Spekulation ist einer der Wege, die Böhme auf den großen Gedanken der Einheit des Seienden zuführt. Bedeutsam an Böhme ist jedoch, daß er in seinem Menschenbild von einer androgynen, »das männliche und das weibliche Prinzip umfassenden Ganzheit des Menschen« spricht. Auch Böhme beruft sich dabei auf die vieldeutige Stelle des Schöpfungsberichtes in der Genesis, die von Martin Buber so übersetzt wird: »Gott schuf den Menschen in seinem Bilde. Im Bilde Gottes schuf er ihn, **männlich-weiblich** schuf er sie.« (Wehr, 1980) (Vgl. Kap. 4.1 u. 4.4.)

34. Michael Maier, Abbildung aus *Atlanta fugiens*, Oppenheim 1618.

34. Michael Maier, illustration from *Atlanta fugiens*, Oppenheim 1618.

Coincidentia oppositorum also occupied men's minds in the 17th century, and a depiction by **Michael Maier** dating from 1618 shows man and woman being included in the harmony of geometrical figures.

4.6. Theosophy. (Secret) Doctrines of the 16th to 18th Centuries

The question of the great oneness of all existence continued to be asked in the centuries that followed, often by following up the work of Nicholas of Cusa. Theologians and philosophers sought a valid answer.

The 17th-century **theosophists** believed that they had found a very specific answer, and it is noteworthy that androgyny plays an important part in their thinking. The most significant theosophist was **Jakob Böhme** (1575–1624). He tried to correct the misunderstanding of the Manichaeans: »The god of the holy world and the god of the sinister world are not two gods. He is one God. He is himself **all** that exists.« (Wehr, 1980) (Cf. chap. 4.1 and 4.4.)

The question of evil was answered by transferring the negative principle to God himself. This risky theological speculation was one of the paths which led Böhme to the great idea of the unity of existence. But what is significant about Böhme is that he referred, in his conception of mankind, to an androgynous »totality of mankind which embraces both the male and the female principle«. Böhme also cites that equivocal passage in the history of creation in Genesis which was translated by Martin Buber as follows: »God created man in his own image. He created him in the image of God; he created them male-female.« (Wehr, 1980)

»There is a mystery at the centre of Böhme's conception of mankind: it is the mystery of the androgynous totality of mankind, a totality which embraces both the male and the female principle. Although Böhme, in his thinking, was carried away by the intellectual parade of ideas, his contribution on the question of androgyny cannot be isolated from the rest of the history of thought.« (Wehr, 1980)

However, official theology has never recognized this interpretation. On this subject Wehr writes: »Although rabbinical Judaism and official ecclesiastical theology emphatically rejected

»Im Mittelpunkt des Böhmeschen Menschenbildes steht ein Geheimnis. Es ist das Mysterium von der androgynen, das männliche und das weibliche Prinzip umfassenden Ganzheit des Menschen. Wenngleich sich Böhmes Denken an der geistigen Schau entzündet hat, so ist doch sein Beitrag zur Androgyn-Frage aus der übrigen Geistesgeschichte nicht zu isolieren.« (Wehr, 1980)

Von der offiziellen Theologie ist diese Interpretation jedoch nie anerkannt worden. Wehr schreibt dazu: »Trotz der nachdrücklichen Ablehnung der erwähnten Androgyn-Vorstellung durch das rabbinische Judentum und durch die offizielle kirchliche Theologie hat gerade dieser kühne Gedanke immer wieder die Menschen zu allerlei Spekulationen beflügelt. Der russische Philosoph und Böhme-Verehrer Nikolaj Berdjajew kommt zu dem Schluß: ›Der Mythus vom Androgynen ist der einzige große anthropologische Mythus, auf dem die anthropologische Metaphysik aufgebaut werden kann.‹ Es ist daher kein Zufall, wenn die Schau des männlich-weiblichen Menschen vor allem seit den Tagen Böhmes nachhaltigen Einfluß auf die europäische Geistesgeschichte ausgeübt hat. Bei Böhme ist es die Sehnsucht nach der Wiederherstellung des Urstandes, den der Mensch vor dem tragischen Fall gehabt haben soll. Es ist das Verlangen, den Menschen in seiner ursprünglichen Größe und Schönheit erneuert zu sehen. Kennzeichnend für diese Erneuerung ist es, daß die menschliche Leiblichkeit prinzipiell einbezogen wird.« (Wehr, 1980) In Böhmes Genesis-Auslegung »Mysterium magnum« heißt es: »Adam war ein Mann und auch ein Weib, und doch deren keines, sondern eine Jungfrau voller Keuschheit, Zucht und Reinigkeit als Bild Gottes: er hatte beyde Tincturen vom Feuer und Lichte in sich, in welcher Conjunction die eigene Liebe, als das Jungfräuliche Centrum stund ...« (Böhme, 1958)

»Darum ward Christus von einer Jungfrau geboren, daß Er die weibliche Tinctur wieder heiligte, und in die männliche Tinctur wandelte, daß der Mann und das Weib wieder ein Bild Gottes würden, und nicht mehr Mann und Weib waren, sondern männliche Jungfrauen, wie Christus war.« (Böhme, 1958)

Der androgyne Urmensch erhebt sich gegen Gott und wird geteilt in Adam und Eva – die Analogie zur Teilung des Menschen bei Platon. Und auf die Frage, wie der Urzustand wiederhergestellt werden könne, antwortet Böhme: »Als Christus am Kreuze unser jungfräulich Bild wieder erlösete vom Manne und Weibe und mit seinem himmlischn Blute in göttlicher Liebe tingierete, als er dies vollbracht hatte, so sprach er: ›Es ist vollbracht ...‹ Christus wandte Adam in seinem Schlaf von der Eitelkeit (d. h. Vergänglichkeit) und vom Mann und Weibe wieder um in das englische Bild. Groß und wunderlich sind diese Geheimnisse, welche die Welt nicht ergreifen mag.« (Wehr, 1980)

Der Ausdruck »Tinctur« stammt aus der Alchemie und bezeichnet einen Wandlungsvorgang. In der »Temperatur« des androgynen Menschen durchdringen sich die männliche Feuer- und die weibliche Licht-Tinctur in einer vollkommenen Einheit.[25] (Baader, 1991)

In der Nachfolge Jacob Böhmes hat die Idee des androgynen Adams bei **Franz von Baader** (1765–1841) einen festen Platz. Für Baader gilt die Einsicht, daß »ohne den Begriff der Androgynie der Zentralbegriff der Religion, nämlich jener des Bildes Gottes unverstanden bleibt ...« (Baader, 1966) Wie Adam ist aber auch Maria ein androgynes Wesen und auch Christus als der neue Adam. Baader distanziert jedoch den Androgyn von den heidnischen Darstellungen des Hermaphroditen, bei dem die »Integrität der menschlichen Natur in Mann und Weib« pervertiert erscheint. Für Baader ist die »höhere Bedeutung der Geschlechtsliebe ... folglich keine geringere, als daß sie dem Manne wie dem Weibe behilflich sein soll, sich zum ganzen Menschenbild zu ergänzen, d. i. zum ursprünglichen Gottesbild.« (Baader, 1966)[25]

Franz von Baader hat einen bedeutenden Einfluß auf den russischen Religionsphilosophen **Wladimir Solowjew** (1853–1900) ausgeübt. Er ging von der Idee einer »All-Einheit« aus, die durch die göttliche All-Weisheit, die »Sophia« vorherbestimmt ist.

Es besteht kein Zweifel, daß sie als ein weibliches Prinzip gedacht war. »Die heilige Sophia war für unsere Vorfahren, die durch die Erscheinungen der niederen Welt verhüllte himmlische Wesenheit ... die zukünftige und endgültige Erscheinungsform der Gottheit« (Solowjew, 1994) (Vgl. Kap. 4.1 u. 4.4.)

Solowjew sieht die »wesenhafte Einheit des menschlichen Seins im Mann, Weib und Gesellschaft«, und es gibt im Grunde nur ein einziges menschliches Wesen ... die inkarnierte Sophia, deren zentrale und vollkommen personenhafte Äußerung Jesus Christus ist, die weibliche Ergänzung: die heilige Jungfrau; und die universelle Erweiterung: die Kirche.« (Solowjew, 1994) (Vgl. Kap. 4.1 u. 4.4.)

35. *Coniunctio sive Coitus*, Deutschland, 1550.
36. Hermaphrodit aus der *Aurora Consurgens*, Schweiz, spätes 15. Jh.

35. *Coniunctio sive Coitus*, Germany, 1550.
36. Hermaphrodite from the *Aurora Consurgens*, Switzerland, late 15th cent.

56

the above-mentioned conception of androgyny, it is precisely this bold notion that has repeatedly spurred people into all kinds of speculations. Nikolay Berdyayev, a Russian philosopher and admirer of Böhme, comes to the following conclusion: ›The myth of androgyny is the only great anthropological myth upon which anthropological metaphysics can be based.‹ It is therefore no mere chance that the notion of the male-female human being has had an enduring influence on the history of European thought ever since the days of Böhme. In the view of Böhme, this is a longing for the restoration of the original state in which man is supposed to have been before his tragic fall. It is a yearning to see man restored to his original greatness and beauty. A characteristic feature of this restoration is that human physicality is to be included as a matter of principle.« (Wehr, 1980) »Mysterium magnum«, which is Böhme's interpretation of Genesis, states: »Adam was a man and also a woman, and was nevertheless neither of them, but rather a virgin full of chastity, decency and purity in the image of God: he had within himself the tinctures of both fire and light, and it was in this conjunction that his own love stood as the virginal centre. ...« (Böhme, 1958)

»This was why Christ was born of a virgin, so that he would once again sanctify the female tincture and transform it into the male tincture, so that the man and the woman would once again become an image of God, and would no longer be man and woman, but male virgins like Christ.« (Böhme, 1958)

The androgynous original human being rebelled against God and was divided into Adam and Eve: this is the analogy to the division of humankind found in Plato. Böhme gives the following answer to the question of how the original state can be restored: »When Christ was on the Cross, he once again released our virginal image from the notion of man and woman, and transformed it with his heavenly blood in divine love. When he had finished this, he said: ›It is finished‹. ... Christ turned the sleeping Adam away from vanity (that is to say transitoriness) and from man and woman, and transformed him back into the angelic image. These mysteries, which the world does not wish to grasp, are great and strange.« (Wehr, 1980)

The expression »tincture« derives from alchemy and refers to a process of transformation. The male tincture of fire, and the female tincture of light, penetrate one another in perfect unity in the »temperature« of the androgynous human being. (Baader, 1991)

As regards the works following up the ideas of Jakob Böhme, the notion of an androgynous Adam plays a definite part in the writings of **Franz von Baader** (1765–1841). Baader regarded it as right to realize that »the central concept of religion, namely that of the image of God, cannot be understood without the notion of androgyny ...« (Baader, 1966) Adam and the Virgin Mary are both androgynous beings, and so too is Christ, the new Adam. But Baader disassociates androgynes from the heathen representations of hermaphrodites, in whom the »integrity of human nature« appears to be perverted »in man and woman«. To Baader, the »higher significance of sexual love ... therefore consists in no less than in helping both man and woman to complement one another in achieving the complete image of a human being, that is to say the original image of God.« (Baader, 1966)[24]

Franz von Baader had a considerable influence on **Vladimir Solovyev**, the Russian philosopher of religion (1853–1900). He proceeded from the idea of an »all-unity« which is predetermined by divine all-wisdom, by »Sophia«.

There is no doubt that this all-wisdom was thought of as a female principle. »To our ancestors, the holy Sophia was the heavenly essence which was veiled by the phenomena of the world below ... and was the future and final manifestation of the deity« (Solovyev, 1994) Solovyev sees the »intrinsic unity of human existence as consisting in man, woman and society«, and there is basically only one human being, namely »the incarnate Sophia, whose central and entirely personal manifestation is Jesus Christ; the female complement is the Blessed Virgin; and the universal extension is the Church.« (Solovyev, 1994) (Cf. chap. 4.1 and 4.4.) In this way Solovyev constructs what might be called a new Trinity, in which two of the beings are female in nature: apart from Christ, it is the Virgin Mary and the Church that unite all mankind. But all these three persons are ultimately Sophia, who is divine wisdom. (Solovyev, 1994) According to Solovyev, all-unity can be restored by uniting God with the world, if man proves his worth as a mediator. It is not surprising that the idea of androgyny plays an important part in this longing for a great unity.

The idea of androgyny is described not only by Solovyev, but also in the works of **Nikolay Berdyayev** (1874–1948), the Russian philosopher.

Pansophy, although it is not part of the immediate succession to theosophy, also displays numerous parallels with the ideas and statements of Jakob Böhme. **Johann Amos Comenius**

Damit errichtet Solowjew gleichsam eine neue Trinität, in der zwei Wesen weiblicher Natur sind: Neben Christus sind es Maria und die Kirche, die die Menschheit vereinen. Alle drei Personen sind aber letztlich die Sophia, eine göttliche Weisheit. (Solowjew, 1994) Durch die Vereinigung von Gott und der Welt könne die All-Einheit wiederhergestellt werden, wenn der Mensch sich als Vermittler bewährt. Es ist nicht verwunderlich, wenn in dieser Sehnsucht nach einer großen Einheit auch der Gedanke der Androgynie eine wichtige Rolle spielt.

Neben Solowjew hat auch der russische Philosoph **Nikolai Berdjajew** (1874–1948) in seinem Werk die Idee der Androgynie dargestellt.

Wenngleich auch nicht zur unmittelbaren Nachfolge der Theosophie zu rechnen, weist die **Pansophie** zahlreiche Parallelen zu den Ideen und Aussagen Jakob Böhmes auf. Der tschechische Philosoph und Pädagoge **Johann Amos Comenius** (1592–1670) interpretiert die Schöpfung als ein weltgeschichtliches Geschehen, an dem der Mensch im Auftrag Gottes mitzuwirken habe. Voraussetzung dafür sei die Einsicht, die universelle Bildung, die daher allen Menschen zugänglich sein müsse. In der *Pansophia prodromus* (*Vorbote der Allweisheit*) von 1639 versucht Comenius die große Synthese des Wissens von Gott und der Welt zu erläutern und zeigt damit einen weiteren Gesichtspunkt der coincidentia.

Die **Alchimie** bietet ein reiches Entfaltungsfeld für die Idee der Androgynie, geht es doch immer wieder darum, zu trennen und zu vereinigen in der Weise, daß neue Elemente, neue Wesenheiten entstehen. Die Metalle werden den Planeten zugeordnet, und diese wiederum sind männlich oder weiblich. Erhitzt der Alchimist Zinn und Kupfer in einem Schmelztiegel, so werden gleichzeitig die Gottheiten Jupiter und Venus in einer mystischen Ehe vereinigt. Das Gold wird der Sol/Sonne, also dem Männlichen, zugeordnet, das Silber der Luna/Mond, dem Weiblichen. Die Synthese finden wir im Quecksilber des Mercurius: Er ist hermaphroditischer Natur. Im *Buch der Heiligen Dreifaltigkeit* ist dieses androgyne Wesen abgebildet: Die Teilung des doppelköpfigen Wesens ist vertikal, und wieder ist dem Mann die rechte Seite vorbehalten. (Aurnhammer, 1986)

Die Alchimie setzt sich mit dem Wandel, mit der Umwandlung auseinander, die sich vor allem in den chemischen Substanzen manifestiert. Darin liegt eine weitere Affinität zur Androgynie. Denn eine der tragenden Grundideen des Androgynen ist der Glaube an den Wandel, an die Verwandlung nicht nur der Dinge, der Welt, sondern auch des Menschen. Dieser Wandel wird im mythischen Bereich durch die Götter persönlich vollzogen, oder er wird durch magische Einwirkung wie in Ovids *Metamorphosen* dargestellt, bewirkt.

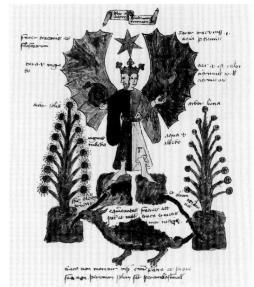

In der alchimistischen Praxis wird der Hermaphrodit zum Symbol der Vereinigung der Gegensätze. Ziel dieser Forschung war es, die ›prima materia‹ zu finden. »Um die Vereinigung der Gegensätze, die ›conjunctio oppositorum‹ bei den Versuchen zu bewirken, sollten jene von einem Mann gemeinsam mit einer Frau ausgeführt werden.« (Raehs, 1990)

Die Alchimie hat sich auch in einer üppigen bildnerischen Symbolwelt zum Thema des Androgynen geäußert. Die zahlreichen Rebis-Illustrationen (aus res binae, doppelte Sache) sind »fast alle auf ein gemeinsames ikonographisches Muster zurückzuführen ... eine meist frontal abgebildete doppelköpfige, zweibeinige menschliche Gestalt, häufig geflügelt, deren heraldische rechte Hälfte männlich und heraldische linke Hälfte weiblich ist.« (Aurnhammer, 1986)

Bernard Salomon (1506/10–1561) stellt seine Hermaphroditendarstellung in das Spannungsfeld von Mythologie und Bibel: Ein Satyr und Moses flankieren das androgyne Wesen. Des weiteren ist nochmals **Michael Maier** zu zitieren. Im »Symbola aurea« von 1617 zeigt der Bischof Albertus Magnus auf einen Androgyn: »Omnes concordant in uno, qui est bifidus.« Einige Darstellungen der Alchimie weisen noch ein interessantes Symbol auf: Der männliche Teil der Figur hält ein Y-förmiges Element in der Hand. Es ist ein Symbol der Einheit und der Zweiheit zugleich, der Synthese und der Spaltung. Es kann aber auch als Präsenz des Männlichen und des Weiblichen zugleich gesehen werden und in einer Distanz von Jahrtausenden scheint es diese Deutungsmöglichkeit zu erlauben: Noch einmal sollen der Lochstab aus der Gorge d'Enfer und das Bettobjekt von Walter Pichler erwähnt werden.

Die Form des Y begegnet uns im primitiven Gabelstock, der magisch-mythische Bedeutung hat. In einer bretonischen Sage (Ganger, 1988) schützt er den Bauern und seine Frau vor bösen Geistern. Das Y steht bei Pythagoras als Zeichen für den Scheideweg zwischen Tugend und Laster. Auch die Wünschelrute hat die Form des Y. Die Wandsäulen am Westportal von St. Stephan haben ein Y-Profil, Zeichen des griechischen Eros.

Ein weiteres Beispiel der Einbindung des Androgyn in die üppige Symbolik der Alchimie finden wir im *Rosarium philosophorum* in Frankfurt um 1550. Ein doppelköpfiges Wesen ist von Schlangen, einem Pelikan und einem Löwen umgeben. Aus der Erde wächst der Sonnenbaum.

(1592–1670), the Czech philosopher and pedagogue, interpreted creation as a set of events which occurs in the history of the world and in which man must play a part at God's behest. A precondition for this lies in comprehension, in universal education, which must therefore be available to all mankind. In his **Pansophia prodromus** (Harbinger of All-Wisdom) dated 1639, Comenius attempts to explain the great synthesis of the knowledge of God and the world, thus displaying another aspect of coincidentia.

Alchemy provided an abundant field for developing the idea of androgyny, as it deals repeatedly with the question of separating and uniting things so that new elements and new substances come into being. The metals are assigned to the planets, and the latter in turn are male or female. When the alchemist heats tin and copper in a melting crucible, the two deities Jupiter and Venus are simultaneously united in a mystic marriage. Gold is allocated to sol/the sun, that is to say to masculinity, and silver to luna/the moon, which is femininity. The synthesis is to be found in the quicksilver of Mercury, who is hermaphroditic in nature. This androgynous being is depicted in the *Book of the Holy Trinity*: this two-headed creature is divided vertically, and once again the right-hand side is reserved for the man. (Aurnhammer, 1986)

Alchemy deals with change and transformation, which is chiefly manifested in the chemical substances. A further affinity with androgyny is to be found here, because one of the basic ideas of androgyny is the belief in the transformation not only of things and the world, but also of human beings. In the mythical realm, the gods personally carry out this transformation, or else it is caused by magical effects as in Ovid's Metamorphoses.

In the practice of alchemy, the hermaphrodite became a symbol for the unification of opposites. The aim of this research was to find the »prima materia«. »In order to bring about the unification of opposites, the ›conjunctio oppositorum‹, in the experiments, they were to be performed jointly by a man and a woman.« (Raehs, 1990)

Alchemy also expressed itself on the subject of androgyny in a world of profuse pictorial symbols. Almost all the numerous Rebis illustrations (from res binae, a double affair) »can be traced back to a common iconographic pattern ... a double-headed, two-legged human shape, usually depicted frontally, and often having wings; its heraldic right half is male and its heraldic left half is female.« (Aurnhammer, 1986)

Bernard Salomon (1506/10–1561) places his representation of the hermaphrodite amidst the energy forces of mythology and the Bible: the androgynous being is flanked by a satyr and by Moses. **Michael Maier** should be cited again here: in the »Symbola aurea« of 1617, the bishop Albertus Magnus is seen pointing to an androgyne: »Omnes concordant in uno, qui est bifidus.«

In der *Aurora Consurgens* ist der Hermaphrodit nackt dargestellt und sehr eigenartig zusammengewachsen: die Geschlechtspartie des Mannes mit dem Gesäß der Frau.

Die »materia prima« wird häufig als zerteilt angesehen, und die Vereinigung ist anzustreben, sie ist auch die Vereinigung des Männlichen und des Weiblichen: das matrimonium, die conjunctio, der coitus. Die Verbindung von Luna und Sol wird sehr real durch ein kopulierendes Paar dargestellt.

Unbeschadet der vielfach am »Heidnischen« orientierten Geistigkeit der Alchimie ist sie gleichwohl eingebunden in das christliche Weltbild. Der gedankliche Zusammenhang zwischen Christus und der Doppelgeschlechtlichkeit findet bei den Alchimisten eine assoziative Verbindung: »Als Lapis philosophorum galt u. a. der Hermaphrodit, in dem die Vereinigung der Gegensätze erreicht ist und der in Parallele zu Christus gesetzt wurde, in dem Männliches und Weibliches aufgehoben sind, in dem Anfang und Ende, Gott und Mensch zusammenfallen.« (Lurker, 1958)

Die Wirkung der Alchemie reicht bis ins 19. Jahrhundert, und nach Eliade (1962) war die »Alchimie eine der Quellen der deutschen Romantik und wirksam für die neuerliche Aktualisierung des Androgynen ... der Androgyn war der vollkommene Mensch der Zukunft.«

Aus den zahlreichen (Geheim-) Lehren, die in der Zeit vom 16. bis zum 18. Jahrhundert Bedeutung hatten, soll nur noch eine zitiert werden, die der **Rosenkreuzer**, bei denen das Thema einer großen geistigen Einheit verschlüsselt und latent abgehandelt wird. Die Rosenkreuzer weisen sowohl zur Pansophie als auch zur Freimaurerei – wenngleich wechselvolle – Bezüge auf. **Johann Valentin Andreae** (1586–1654) ist einer der wichtigen Autoren für die Formulierung der Rosenkreuzer-Idee. Seine Schrift *Christianopolis* enthält Illustrationen, über die im Kapitel 9.4.1 noch zu berichten sein wird.

Noch im 20. Jahrhundert finden sich in der Anthroposophie von **Rudolf Steiner** (1861 bis 1925) Rudimente der Lehren des 16.–18. Jahrhunderts, vor allem auch der Rosenkreuzer. (Wehr, 1964). In Rudolf Steiners Anthroposophie ist auch die Idee der Androgynie eingebettet, obgleich wir keine präzisen Aussagen herauslesen können. Verständlicherweise ist es bei Steiner ein geistig-seelischer Vorgang, wenn er von der Ganzwerdung des Menschen schreibt: »Die männliche Seele im weiblichen Leibe und die weibliche Seele im männlichen Leibe werden beide wieder zweigeschlechtlich durch die Befruchtung mit dem Geist. So sind Mann und Weib in der äußeren Gestalt verschieden; im Inneren schließt sich bei beiden die seelische Einseitigkeit zu einer harmonischen Ganzheit zusammen.« (Wehr, 1986)

4.7. Ikonographie

So spärlich die Zeugnisse einer androgynen Interpretation in der christlichen Theologie sind, so häufig finden wir in der Ikonographie **Feminisierungen Christi** und der Heiligen, die dadurch zu androgynen Wesen werden.

Mannweibliche Gekreuzigte finden wir sehr selten. Bei den afrikanischen Völkern lassen sich, aus den vorchristlichen Traditionen verständlich, solche Darstellungen nachweisen. Weibliche Darstellungen Christi gibt es bis ins 18. Jahrhundert, wobei die so häufige ikonographische Feminisierung jenseits der geschlechtlichen Fixierungen liegen mag.

Eine der merkwürdigsten Darstellungen der Madonna mit dem Kind hat um 1527 **Jan Gossaert** (1482–1532), genannt **Mabuse**, geschaffen. Das Jesuskind, deutlich als Knabe erkennbar, ist mit kleinen, prallen Brüsten ausgestattet, die rechte Hand Mariens umfaßt die Brust, als wollte sie die Milch herauspressen. »Die Amor Dei, die Liebe Gottes, wird mit der Liebesgöttin Venus in Verbindung gebracht, aber auch mit der caritas, aus deren Brüsten die Milch hervorsprießt als Symbol der alles nährenden Liebe.« (Orchard, 1992)

Christus als Gott-Mensch muß alle positiven Eigenschaften in seiner Person vereinen. So verlangt vor allem die Renaissance, daß er auch von anmutiger Schönheit, von Milde und Güte geprägt sein müsse, von Eigenschaften also, die vor allem dem weiblichen Geschlechte zugesprochen werden. Demnach ist es verständlich, daß Christus mit einem durchaus weiblichen Habitus dargestellt wird. Christus wird aber darüber hinaus auch als Braut und als Mutter interpretiert, die daher mit Brüsten ausgestattet sein kann.

Zu den wenigen ikonographischen Zeugnissen zählt eine anonyme deutsche Zeichnung von 1657, in der Christus als weiblicher Richter über Islam und Heidentum dargestellt ist. (Orchard, 1992)

Der Gedanke eines »mütterlichen« Jesus entspringt keineswegs feministischen Wunschvorstellungen, sondern reicht theologisch weit zurück, zumindest bis ins 13. und 14. Jahrhundert,

41. Christus als Richter über Islam und Heidentum, Deutschland, 1657.
42. Jan Gossaert, genannt Mabuse, Maria mit dem Christuskind, Breda, um 1520.

41. Christus judging Islam and paganism, Germany, 1657.
42. Jan Gossaert, known as Mabuse, Maria with infant Jesus, Breda, ca. 1520.

Some depictions of alchemy include an interesting symbol: the male part of the figure is holding a Y-shaped element in his hand. This is a symbol of unity and duality at the same time, of synthesis and division. It may though also be regarded as the simultaneous presence of both male and female, and at a distance of thousands of years it seems to permit this possible interpretation. The holed stick of the Gorge d'Enfer, and the sexual object depicted by Walter Pichler, may again be mentioned.

The Y-shape is encountered in the primitive forked stick, which has a magical-mythical significance. There is a Breton legend (Ganger, 1988) in which it protects the farmer and his wife from evil spirits. In Pythagoras' works, the Y is a symbol of the place where virtue and vice part. A divining rod also has a Y-shape. The columns in the wall at the western portal of St. Stephan have a Y-shaped outline, the symbol of the Greek Eros.

Another example of how the androgyne is included within the profuse symbolism of alchemy is to be found in the *Rosarium philosophorum* in Frankfurt (ca. 1550). A two-headed being is surrounded by snakes, a pelican and a lion. The sun-tree is growing out of the earth.

In the *Aurora Consurgens*, the hermaphrodite is depicted in the nude and with a very peculiar accretion: a man's sexual organ and a woman's buttocks.

The »materia prima« is often regarded as being split up, and its unification is aimed at. This is also the unification of male and female: matrimonium, conjunctio, coitus. The combination of luna and sol is very realistically depicted by a copulating couple.

Although the intellectual aspects of alchemy are frequently based on heathen notions, it is nevertheless part of the Christian conception of the world. The alchemists give an associative connection to the conceptual link between Christ and a two-sexed nature: »The hermaphrodite was one of the creatures regarded as a lapis philosophorum. In him, opposites are united, and he is seen in parallel with Christ, in whom male and female are eliminated and the beginning and the end coincide, as do God and man.« (Lurker, 1958)

The effects of alchemy continued into the 19th century. According to Eliade (1962), »alchemy was one of the sources of German romanticism, and had an effect on the topical significance once again attached to androgyny ... the androgyne was the perfect human being of the future.«

Of the numerous (secret) doctrines which played a part from the 16th to the 18th century, only one will be mentioned here: it is that of the **Rosicrucians**, who deal, in a coded and latent manner, with the topic of a great spiritual unity. The Rosicrucians are related – albeit in an inconstant way – to both pansophy and Freemasonry. **Johann Valentin Andreae** (1586–1654) is an important author on the subject of enunciating the Rosicrucian idea. His work entitled *Christianopolis* contains illustrations which will be referred to in chapter 9.4.1.

Rudiments of the doctrines of the 16th to 18th centuries, particularly the Rosicrucian doctrine, are still found in the 20th century in the Anthroposophy of **Rudolf Steiner** (1861–1925). (Wehr, 1964) The idea of androgyny is embedded in Rudolf Steiner's anthroposophy, although we cannot gather any precise statements from it. When Steiner writes of man's attaining wholeness, he sees it, understandably enough, as an intellectual and psychological process: »The male soul in the female body, and the female soul in the male body, both become two-sexed again when they are fertilized by the spirit. Thus man and woman are different in their outward shape; on the inside, the psychological one-sidedness of each of them is combined into a harmonious whole.« (Wehr, 1986)

4.7. Iconography

Christian theology contains scant evidence of any androgynous interpretations, but on the other hand **feminizations of Christ** and the Saints, who thereby become androgynous beings, are often found in iconography.

Male-female depictions of the crucified Christ are very rare. Such representations are found among the African nations, and they are to be explained by pre-Christian traditions. Female depictions of Christ continue into the 18th century, and the frequent iconographical feminization may go beyond any prescription of one sex or the other.

One of the strangest depictions of Madonna and Child was created in ca. 1527 by **Jan Gossaert**, known as **Mabuse** (1482–1532). The Christ-child, clearly identifiable as male, has small, firm breasts, and the Virgin Mary's right hand is clasping the breast as if she wanted to press milk out of it. »Amor Dei, the love of God, is associated with Venus the goddess of love, and

(Bynum, 1982) und wurde vor allem von den Zisterziensern vertreten. Schon vor den Zisterziensern war es der Benediktiner **Anselm von Canterbury** (gest. 1109), der Jesus mütterliche Aspekte zuschrieb: Er belebt von Neuem die Seele an seiner Brust, ja mehr, er schenkt ein zweites Mal das Leben durch die Einmaligkeit seiner bewundernswerten Liebe. (Bynum, 1982)

Der Zisterzienser-Abt Guerric von Igny artikuliert noch anschaulicher das Mütterliche in Jesus: »Der Bräutigam (Christus) hat Brüste, damit nicht vermißt werde irgendeine der Pflichten und Ansprüche der liebenden Güte ... Er ist auch eine Mutter in der Milde der Empfindungen, und er ist eine Nährmutter ... « (Bynum, 1902)

Der Wunsch, Christus als androgynes Wesen oder gar eine Frau gekreuzigt abzubilden, wird von der Kirche begreiflicherweise nicht toleriert. Die Idee fasziniert aber offenkundig derart, daß immer wieder ein Vorwand gefunden wird, eine **gekreuzigte Frau** darzustellen. Dazu gibt es einige interessante Vorbilder aus den Vitae der Heiligen. Eine in einigen Alpenregionen populäre Legende wird zum Vorwand genommen, um eine bärtige Frau am Kreuze zu zeigen, die heilige Ludegardis, volkstümlich heilige Kümmernis genannt. Damit sie der Heirat mit einem ungeliebten Mann entgehen kann, verwandelt Gott sie und läßt ihr einen Bart wachsen. Der erboste Vater läßt sie jedoch kreuzigen. Überraschenderweise finden wir ein gleichsam androgynes Wesen ans Kreuz geschlagen. Das Augustinerkloster in Rattenberg, Tirol, bewahrt ein solches Bild auf: Gott Vater blickt wohlgefällig auf einen bärtigen, gekreuzigten Menschen, der keinesfalls Christus sein kann. Vielmehr ist es die heilige Kümmernis der Legende.

Nach anderen Legenden wurde der heiligen Wilgefortis im 11. Jahrhundert dieses Schicksal zuteil, sie wird als Sankt Entkommer verehrt. Auf Sizilien finden wir eine ans Kreuz geschlagene Heilige, aber es ist gleichzeitig der feminisierte Christus.

Darstellungen gekreuzigter Frauen kommen wiederholt in der neueren Kunst vor. Allzu leichtfertig können diese Bilder als obszöne Blasphemie interpretiert werden. **Felicien Rops** (1833 bis 1898) stellt in einigen Radierungen die *Versuchung des heiligen Antonius* dar. (Orlan, 1959) Der gepeinigte Heilige sieht eine üppige, verführerisch lächelnde Frau gekreuzigt, der zerschundene Körper Christi scheint vom Kreuze zu stürzen und die Kreuzesinschrift lautet »Eros«.

Die britischen Pop-Künstler **Pierre et Gilles** schlagen eine *Betrübte Heilige* im üppigen Brautkleid und mit der Krone auf dem Haupt ans Kreuz. In der erotischen Photographie wird dieses Motiv schon um die Jahrhundertwende verwendet, die Photographen müssen anonym bleiben.

Wesen, die latent androgyn erscheinen, begegnen uns in großer Zahl in der **Malerei der Renaissance**. Zumindest in den Physiognomien, häufig aber auch im Körperbau werden männliche und weibliche Heilige bisweilen nahezu austauschbar. Der (junge) Johannes der Täufer wird meist bartlos dargestellt, oft mit langem, gewelltem Haar. **Leonardo da Vinci** (1452–1519) stattet ihn in der Darstellung im Louvre mit der traditionellen »ecce homo« Handgeste aus, aber sein liebliches Antlitz hat weiche, feminine Züge. Der Vergleich mit der »Mona Lisa« liegt nahe, und wir könnten das reziproke Phänomen feststellen: Der Mona Lisa wurden maskuline Züge zugeordnet, dem Johannes feminine, beide nähern sich somit einer androgynen Gestalt. Die Engels- und Madonnendarstellungen bei Leonardo, ja selbst der Habitus der Leda, zeigen überraschende Verwandtschaften zu den Heiligendarstellungen.

Das Lächeln des Johannes » ... ist nicht sanft, nicht gottergeben oder fromm. Es hat ... etwas Verführerisches, das an anderes als die strenge Askese des Heiligen denken läßt ... so daß diese Figur in ihrer Vieldeutigkeit den ... klassischen Gedanken göttlicher Androgynität wiederaufgreift ... Das vieldeutige wissende Lächeln ... bedeutet ... im cusanischen Sinne eine ›coincidentia oppositorum‹«. (Raehs, 1990)

Die verblüffende Ähnlichkeit zwischen dem Bacchus der Leonardo-Schule und Johannes dem Täufer von Leonardo kommt nicht von ungefähr: Tatsächlich war der Bacchus ursprünglich ein Johannes, der Kreuzstab wurde erst im 17. Jahrhundert in einen Thyrsos umgewandelt. Somit geht der Johannes mit den deutlich femininen Zügen auf die eindeutig androgyne Figur des Bacchus zurück. Diese Ähnlichkeiten sind nicht nur ikonographischer Natur, vielmehr gibt es theologische Spekulationen, die Bacchus gleichsam als Vorläufer Johannes des Täufers und somit auch als Indikator Christi ansehen.[26]

Aus der Schule Leonardos, von **Marco d'Oggione** (1475–1530), besitzt die Galleria Borghese in Rom ein anmutiges »Portrait« mit dem leonardesken Lächeln in den Mundwinkeln und langem, lockigem Haar: An der segnenden Hand erkennen wir Christus als Salvator Mundi.

Die Darstellungen bei **Raffael** (1483–1520) scheinen zunächst kaum vom Thema der Androgynie geprägt zu sein, obwohl etwa ein Bild des bartlosen Christus im Museum in Brescia zweifellos feminine Züge aufweist.

also with caritas from whose breasts milk shoots forth as a symbol of the love that nourishes everything.« (Orchard, 1992)

Christ as God made man must unite all positive qualities within himself. Thus the Renaissance, in particular, requires that he must also be characterized by graceful beauty, by mildness and goodness, that is to say by qualities mainly attributed to the female sex. It is thus understandable that Christ is depicted as having an entirely feminine deportment. In addition, Christ is also interpreted as a bride and mother, who can accordingly have breasts.

One of the few pieces of iconographic evidence is an anonymous German drawing dating from 1657, in which Christ is depicted as a female judge of Islam and paganism. (Orchard, 1992)

The idea of a »maternal« Jesus does not arise from feminist wishful thinking. Instead, it dates back a long way into the history of theology, at least to the 13th and 14th centuries (Bynum, 1982), and was propounded mainly by the Cistercians. It was the Benedictine monk Anselm of Canterbury (died 1109) who, before the Cistercians, attributed maternal characteristics to Jesus: according to Anselm, Jesus endues the soul at his breast with new life; indeed, he gives life a second time, thanks to the uniqueness of his admirable love. (Bynum, 1982)

The Cistercian abbot Guerric von Igny described the maternal features of Jesus still more vividly: »Christ the bridegroom is provided with breasts so that not one of the duties and demands of loving goodness may be omitted. ... He is also a mother in respect of the mildness of his feelings, and he is a fostering mother. ...« (Bynum, 1902)

The Church, understandably enough, does not tolerate any desire to depict Christ as an androgynous being or even as a woman. But the idea is evidently so fascinating that pretexts for depicting a **crucified woman** are repeatedly found. There are some interesting examples of this in the lives of the Saints. A popular legend in some Alpine regions is taken as a pretext for depicting a bearded woman hanging on a cross. This is St. Ludegardis, popularly known as Saint of Sorrows. To enable her to escape having to marry a man whom she did not love, God transformed her and caused her to grow a beard – but her irate father ordered her to be crucified. Surprisingly enough, a kind of androgynous being, nailed to the cross, does occur. Such an image is preserved in the Augustinian monastery in Rattenberg, Tyrol: God the Father is seen looking with satisfaction upon a bearded, crucified person, who cannot under any circumstances be Christ. Instead, it is the legendary Saint of Sorrows.

According to some other legends, St. Wilgefortis met this fate in the 11th century, and she is revered as a Saint Escaper. A female saint is to be found nailed to the Cross in Sicily, but this is at the same time Christ feminized.

Depictions of crucified women repeatedly occur in more modern art. It is all too easy thoughtlessly to interpret these images as being an obscene blasphemy. The *Versuchung des heiligen Antonius* (*Temptation of St. Anthony*) was depicted by **Felicien Rops** (1833–1898) in some of his etchings. (Orlan, 1959) The distressed saint sees a voluptuous woman with a seductive smile being crucified, the bruised body of Christ seems to be falling from the Cross, and the inscription on the Cross reads »Eros«.

The British pop artists **Pierre et Gilles** depicted a *Distressed Female Saint* nailed to the Cross. She was wearing an elaborate bridal dress, with a crown on her head. This motif was employed in erotic photography as early as the turn of the century, but the photographers must remain anonymous.

A large number of beings with latently androgynous features are to be found in Renaissance painting. The male and female saints are sometimes almost interchangeable, at any rate in their physiognomy, but often also in their anatomy. The (young) John the Baptist is always depicted as beardless, and often with long, wavy hair. In the representation in the Louvre, **Leonardo da Vinci** (1452–1519) gave him the traditional »ecce homo« manual gesture, but his delightful face is of a soft, feminine smoothness. It is natural to draw a comparison with the »Mona Lisa«, and we might also observe the reciprocal phenomenon: the Mona Lisa was given masculine features, John the Baptist feminine ones, and thus both of them come close to being an androgynous figure. Leonardo's representations of angels and the Madonna, and even the deportment of Leda, all show surprising resemblances to the depictions of saints.

John's smile »... is not gentle, pious or resigned to God's will. There is ... something seductive about it, something which gives rise to thoughts other than those of a saint's strict asceticism ... so that the equivocal nature of this figure revives the ... classical notion of divine androgyny... The ambiguous, knowing smile ... signifies ... a ›coincidentia oppositorum‹ in Cusa's sense.« (Raehs, 1990)

Bolsena (1980) versucht in einer ausführlichen Studie darzulegen, daß die »Iconologia bisessuale« als ein »segreto di Raffaello e del Rinascimento« angesehen werden kann. In seinen Analysen geht Bolsena von der Freudschen Sexualsymbolik des Männlichen und Weiblichen aus und versucht darzulegen, daß sich im Werk von Raffael, äußerst verborgen allerdings, diese Symbolsprachen überlagern und somit von einer »Bisexualität« gesprochen werden kann. Die sehr breit gestreuten Spekulationen und Interpretationen sind sicherlich kritisch zu sehen, vor allem dann, wenn Bolsena Christus mit Eros und Maria mit Venus, allgemein mit einer antiken Göttin, vergleicht. Nur schwer folgen läßt sich den Projektionen Bolsenas, wenn er nicht nur in der Mandorla das Vulvazeichen sieht, sondern auch in den Madonnengestalten Raffaels, in Emblemen und Akzessoirs phallische Elemente erkennt und daraus die Bisexualität, den Hermaphroditismus ableitet. Die Interpretationen Bolsenas dürfen nicht unwidersprochen bleiben: Das Auftauchen von weiblichen und männlichen Symbolen in einem Bild ist noch nicht als hermaphroditisches Kriterium anzusehen. Davon kann man erst dann sprechen, wenn es tatsächlich zu einer »coincidentia« kommt.

Besonders eindrucksvoll sind die femininen Züge bei den Darstellungen des **heiligen Sebastian**. Er wird immer bartlos dargestellt, und damit entfällt eines der entscheidenden geschlechtlichen Unterscheidungsmerkmale in der christlichen Ikonographie, insbesondere der Renaissance.

Ähnlich wie der Pfeil des Engels bei den Darstellungen der heiligen Theresia werden auch die Pfeile, mit denen der heilige Sebastian durchbohrt wird, mit Cupido/Amor in Verbindung gebracht: Sie entzünden die Liebe im Leiden – die Liebe zu Gott. Beim heiligen Sebastian wird scheinbar nicht das Weibliche penetriert, sondern das Männliche – wenn Sebastian nicht auch weibliche Züge hätte. Die Schönheit und Anmut, die Nacktheit des heiligen Sebastian, hat oft genug die Klosterschwestern zu »sündhaften Gedanken« verleitet, so daß die Darstellungen manchmal entfernt werden mußten. (Vgl. Kap. 9.2.1.)

Die Engel sind – aus dem patriarchalischen Hintergrund der Bibel heraus durchaus verständlich – männlichen Geschlechtes, und bei den gestürzten Engeln, den Teufeln, sowie bei den Erzengeln gab es wohl keinen Zweifel über deren Geschlecht. Die Ikonographie – und die Vorstellungen gehen dabei weit über die Bibel hinaus – weist aber die Engel als Wesen mit durchaus femininen Zügen auf: oft wallendes, blondes Haar, ein zarter Gesichtsschnitt und weiche Gestik sind Symptome für die Annäherung an das Weibliche. Es dürfen also mit Recht die Engel als androgyn oder aber als geschlechtslose Wesen bezeichnet werden.

Es ist nicht ganz einfach, doppelgeschlechtliche und ungeschlechtliche Wesen voneinander abzugrenzen. Hinweise auf eine Geschlechtszuordnung sind allerdings bereits aus der Physiognomie abzulesen. Wenn wir die Engel als geschlechtslos ansprechen, würden wir ihrer Bedeutung als vollkommene Wesen nicht gerecht werden, da die Vollkommenheit mit der Idee des Doppelgeschlechtlichen zusammenhängt.

Auf das Werk von **Aubrey Vincent Beardsley** (1872–1898) wird noch ausführlich einzugehen sein. Im Zusammenhang mit der Effeminierung Christi ist eine seltsame Darstellung vorwegnehmend zu zitieren, das Blatt *The Kiss of Judas* von 1893.

Ein Wesen, gleichzeitig Embryo, Kind und Mann, küßt Jesus die Hand. Dieser aber ist eine jener Figuren, wie Beardsley sie immer wieder darstellt: mit erotischer Gestalt, Frauengesicht, üppigem schwarzem Haar und schwarzem Kleid, lasziv hingegossen an einem Ölbaum. (Mattenklott, 1970)

Den zahlreichen femininen Heiligengestalten stehen ganz wenige maskuline Interpretationen **Mariens** gegenüber. Zwar ist sie die aus sich selbst heraus autonom Gebärende und benötigt demnach auch männliche Eigenschaften, von wenigen Ausnahmen abgesehen, begegnen wir jedoch kaum einer Virilisierung Mariens.

5. Reversibilität. Geschlechtswechsel

5.1. Geschlechtswandel – mythisch, magisch, kultisch, ethnisch

Das Thema des »Wandels«, der Modifikation des Geschlechtes, insbesondere des biologischen Geschlechtes, wurde in den vorhergehenden Kapiteln wiederholt angesprochen. Aus der menschlichen Erfahrung der Eindeutigkeit des biologischen Geschlechtes einerseits, und aus dem Wunsch nach Veränderung dieses Geschlechtes andererseits erwachsen die zahlreichen Mythen, Vorstellungen und Praktiken des sexuellen Wandels, der sich entweder

47. Leonardo da Vinci, Johannes der Täufer, um 1513/1516.
48. Schule Leonardo da Vinci, Bacchus/Johannes der Täufer um 1513/1516.
49. Aubrey Vincent Beardsley, *The Kiss of Judas*, 1893.

47. Leonardo da Vinci, John the Baptist, ca. 1513/1516.
48. School of Leonardo da Vinci, Bacchus/John the Baptist, ca. 1513/1516.
49. Aubrey Vincent Beardsley, *The Kiss of Judas*, 1893.

THE KISS OF JVDAS

The startling similarity between the Bacchus of the Leonardo school and Leonardo's John the Baptist is no mere chance: Bacchus really was a John originally, and the cross-staff was not transformed into a thyrsus until the 17th century. Thus the John with the markedly feminine features derives from the clearly androgynous figure of Bacchus. These similarities are not merely iconographic in nature. Instead, there are theological speculations which regard Bacchus as a kind of forerunner of John the Baptist and thus as a pointer towards Christ.[25]

In the Galleria Borghese in Rome there is a charming »Portrait« by **Marco d'Oggione** (1475 to 1530). This is a work of the Leonardo school. The corners of the mouth have a Leonardo-like smile, and the hair is long and curly. The blessing hand reveals that this is Christ as Salvator Mundi.

At a first glance, the depictions by **Raphael** (1483–1520) scarcely seem to show any androgynous characteristics, although a picture of the beardless Christ in the museum in Brescia is an example which undoubtedly has some feminine features.

In a detailed study (1980), Bolsena tries to demonstrate that the »iconologia bisessuale« may be regarded as a »segreto di Raffaello e del Rinascimento«. Bolsena bases his analyses on Freudian male and female sexual symbolism, and attempts to show that these symbolic languages are, albeit in an extremely concealed way, superimposed on one another in Raphael's works, so that it is possible to speak of »bisexuality«. It is certainly necessary to take a critical view of these very widely dispersed speculations and interpretations, especially when Bolsena compares Christ with Eros and the Virgin Mary not only with Venus, but also, in general terms, with a classical goddess. It is difficult to follow Bolsena's projections when he not only regards the mandorla as a vulval symbol, but also detects phallic elements in the emblems and accessories in the Madonna depictions by Raphael, and derives from this the notion of bisexuality, of hermaphroditism. Bolsena's interpretations must not go unopposed: the occurrence of female and male symbols in one and the same picture is not in itself to be regarded as a hermaphroditic criterion. That criterion only arises if there really is a »coincidentia«.

The feminine features in representations of **St. Sebastian** are particularly impressive. He is always depicted without a beard, and this means the elimination of one of the basic characteristics distinguishing the sexes in Christian iconography, particularly in the Renaissance.

Like the angel's arrow in depictions of St. Theresa, the arrows with which St. Sebastian is transfixed are associated with Cupido/Amor: they arouse love in suffering – the love of God. In the case of St. Sebastian, it is ostensibly not the female that is being penetrated, but the male – were it not the case that Sebastian also has feminine characteristics. The beauty, grace and nudity of St. Sebastian have, often enough, tempted nuns to think »sinful thoughts«, so that the pictures sometimes had to be removed. (Cf. chap. 9.2.)

Given the patriarchal background of the Bible, it is understandable that **angels** are male, and there was probably no doubt about the sex either of the fallen angels, that is to say the devils, or of the archangels. But iconography – and the ideas here go far beyond the Bible – displays the angels as beings with characteristics that are certainly feminine: hair that is often blond and flowing, delicate facial features, and gentle gestures – these are symptoms of an approach towards femininity. Angels may therefore rightly be described as androgynous or as sexless beings.

It is not so easy to draw a distinction between two-sexed beings and sexless beings. But the physiognomy of a depiction gives some indication of the sex which is to be assigned to it. If we regarded angels as sexless, we would not do justice to their significance as perfect beings, because perfection is related to the idea of a two-sexed nature.

The works of **Aubrey Vincent Beardsley** (1872–1898) will be dealt with in detail below. In connection with the effemination of Christ, anticipatory mention should be made of a curious picture, the sheet entitled *The Kiss of Judas* (1893).

A being which is at the same time an embryo, a child and a man is kissing Jesus's hand. But Jesus is one of the figures repeatedly found in Beardsley's works: an erotic person with a woman's face, luxuriant black hair and a black dress, relaxing against an olive tree. (Mattenklott, 1970)

By contrast with the numerous feminine depictions of saints, there are only a very few masculine interpretations of the **Virgin Mary**. Although she gives birth autonomously out of her own-self and accordingly also requires male properties, there is hardly a single depiction of a virile Virgin Mary, apart from a few exceptions.[23]

in der Richtung Androgynie, Hermaphroditismus oder zum konträren Geschlecht hin bewegt.

Die Flexibilität der frühen Gottheiten im Hinblick auf ihr Geschlecht wurde schon erörtert. Über die Teilungs- und Schöpfungsmythen hinausgehend, wird von merkwürdigen Wandlungen des Geschlechts berichtet.

Die griechische Sage erzählt ein schönes Beispiel der **Geschlechtsumwandlung**: »... Leukippos ... war ursprünglich ein Mädchen, das Leukippe hieß. Da sie sich in ein anderes Mädchen verliebt hatte, flehte sie die Göttin Leto (Latona) um einen Penis an. Die Statue des Leukippos trug deshalb Mädchenkleidung, besaß aber einen meist erigierten Penis.« (Bornemann, 1975)

Ovid beschreibt in seinen *Metamorphosen* eine wunderbare Geschlechtsumwandlung: Ein Mann namens Igdus wollte nur einen Sohn als Nachkommen akzeptieren, doch seine Frau gebiert eine Tochter. Um sie vor dem Tode zu schützen, wird sie wie ein Knabe aufgezogen und Iphis genannt. Sie soll mit der schönen Janthe vermählt werden, die Hochzeit kann nicht mehr länger hinausgeschoben werden, und die Mutter der Iphis fleht um ein Wunder. Und als beide den Tempel verlassen, ist Iphis in einen Mann verwandelt: »... es wachsen die Kräfte, die Züge sind sichtlich kühner geworden und kürzer das Maß der entbundenen Haare, größeres Feuer ist da, als das Mädchen besessen. Denn du bist, eben noch Weib, ein Mann.« (Ovid, 1989)

Merkwürdige Wandlungen widerfahren auch **Teiresias**, dem blinden Seher. Seine Blindheit rührt daher, daß er Athene nackt im Bade gesehen hat. Ehe er blind wird, beobachtet er Schlangen, die sich paaren. Sie greifen ihn an, und er tötet das Weibchen. Daraufhin wird er in eine Frau verwandelt. Sieben Jahre später tötet er eine männliche Schlange und wird wieder zum Manne. Nach einer anderen Version verwandelt ihn Aphrodite in eine alte Frau, weil er ihr den Preis der Schönheit nicht zuerkannt hat.

Zu den ethnologischen Merkwürdigkeiten zählt der **Geschlechtswandel**, der sich freilich nur in äußeren Eigenschaften, nicht in biologischen Veränderungen manifestieren kann. Hermann Baumann (1986) geht ausführlich auf diese Phänomene ein. Als Prinzip einer vorwiegend kultisch motivierten Modifikation des Geschlechtes kann es angesehen werden, daß »ein weiblich erscheinender Knabe ... systematisch als Frau erzogen« wird. Er »gewinnt dadurch gleichzeitig den Ruf einer besonderen magisch oder religiös gezeichneten Wirkungsmächtigkeit.« »Der umgekehrte Fall, wo Mädchen ... als Männer erzogen werden, ist weitaus seltener festzustellen.«

An äußeren Attributen des Geschlechtswandels gibt es nur wenige: In erster Linie ist es die Kleidung, es handelt sich also um eine Art Transvestismus. Zusätzlich unterscheidet man sich vom anderen Geschlecht durch die Haartracht.

Wesentlich komplexer sind die Verhaltensweisen, die sich denen einer Frau weitgehend anpassen müssen, und im Extremfall heiratet ein solcher »Weibmann« einen Mann, wodurch de facto der Sachverhalt der Homosexualität gegeben ist.

Margaret Mead (1975) beschreibt den Geschlechtswandel bei einigen amerikanischen Indianerstämmen. Bei ihnen »... war der ›Berdache‹ der Mann, der sich wie eine Frau kleidete und lebte, eine anerkannte soziale Institution und bildete ein Gegengewicht zu der übertriebenen Betonung der Tapferkeit und Kühnheit der Männer«.

»Eine besonders extreme Form der Initiation stellt der Ritus der Couvade dar. Es ist dies eine Form des Schwangerschaftstransvestismus und beruht auf der Zwangsvorstellung von Männern, daß sie schwanger sind. Diese Schwangerschaft wird bis zur Geburt und dem sogenannten ›Wochenbett‹ von diesen Männern durchgelebt.« (Silbermayr, 1988)

Ein eigenartiges Phänomen des Geschlechtswandels sehen wir in den männlichen Priesterinnen, die in Indonesien, vor allem in Celebes, im Toraja-Land, zu finden waren. Die Männer sind von ihrer Aufgabe derart überzeugt, daß sie sich vollkommen wie Frauen verhalten und auch von der Gesellschaft als solche anerkannt werden. (Winthuis, 1931)

Überraschend ist es, daß es in Nordalbanien und im Kosovo bis in jüngste Zeit hinein die »geschworenen Jungfrauen« gab. Eine Frau konnte das feierliche Gelübde der Enthaltsamkeit ablegen und wie ein Mann leben, sie durfte Waffen tragen – eine besondere Auszeichnung – und manche haben angeblich Frauen geheiratet. (Dekker, v. d. Pol 1990)

Bei den arktischen Eskimos ist, eingebunden in den Kult, ein Geschlechtswechsel möglich. »Weibliche« Medizinmänner gibt es bei den Dajak auf Borneo und den Patagoniern in Südamerika. Bei den arabischen Stämmen im Süd-Irak können Mädchen unter gewissen Voraussetzungen das Leben eines Mannes führen; in einer Pueblo-Kultur westlich von Neu-Mexiko können sowohl Knaben als auch Mädchen ihr Geschlecht wechseln, aber nur bis zum Tode.

5. Reversibility. Change of Sex

5.1. Modification of Sex – Mythical, Magical, Cultic, Ethnic

The subject of »change«, of the modification of sex, particularly biological sex, has been repeatedly referred to in the preceding chapters. The numerous myths, ideas and practices relating to sexual modification – a modification in the direction either of androgyny, hermaphroditism or the opposite sex – result, on the one hand, from the human experience that biological sex is unambiguous and, on the other, from the wish to change that sex.

The flexibility of the early deities where their sex is concerned has already been discussed. Apart from the myths of division and creation, there are also accounts of strange changes of sex.

Greek mythology tells of a fine example of a **sex change**: »... Leukippos ... was originally a girl called Leukippe. She had fallen in love with another girl, and she therefore besought the goddess Leto (Latona) to give her a penis. This was why the statue of Leukippos had a girl's clothes but possessed a penis which was usually erect.« (Bornemann, 1975)

Ovid describes a miraculous sex change in his *Metamorphoses*: a man named Igdus wants to accept only a son as his successor, but his wife gives birth to a daughter. In order to protect her from death, she is brought up like a boy and given the name Iphis. She is to be married to the beautiful Janthe, the wedding can be postponed no longer, and Iphis's mother prays for a miracle. And when the two of them leave the temple, Iphis has been transformed into a man: »... with longer strides / Than usual, her checks of darker hue, / Her features firmer, limbs more powerful, / Her hanging tresses shorter and her strength / Greater than woman's wont. She who had been / A girl a moment past was now a boy.« (Ovid, 1992)

Strange changes also befell **Teiresias**, the blind seer. The cause of his blindness was that he had seen Athene naked in her bath. Before he went blind, he observed some snakes mating. They attacked him, and he killed the female. He was thereupon transformed into a woman. Seven years later, he killed a male snake and was turned back into a man. According to another version, Aphrodite turned him into an old woman because he did not award her the prize for beauty.

One ethnological peculiarity is **sexual modification**. It can though only manifest itself in external characteristics, and not in any biological changes. Hermann Baumann (1986) goes into these phenomena in detail. The fact that »a boy who has a feminine appearance is ... systematically brought up as a woman« can be regarded as the basic principle of a sexual modification whose motivation is chiefly cultic. The boy »thereby at the same time acquires a reputation for having a particular efficacy characterized by magic or religion.« »The reverse case, where girls ... are brought up as men, is much more rarely encountered.«

Sexual modification has only a few external attributes. This is primarily a matter of clothing, so that it is a kind of transvestism. In addition, the hairstyle distinguishes the person from the other sex.

What is considerably more complicated is the behavioural patterns, which must largely adapt themselves to those of a woman. In extreme cases, a »female man« such as this marries a man, resulting in a case of de facto homosexuality.

Margaret Mead (1975) describes the sexual modification which occurs in some American Indian tribes. In those tribes, »... the ›Berdache‹, the man who lived and dressed like a woman, was a recognized social institution and formed a counterpoise to the excessive emphasis attached to bravery and boldness in men«.

»The ritual of couvade is a particularly extreme form of initiation. It is a form of transvestism in pregnancy, and is based on some men's obsessive idea that they are pregnant. These men live through this pregnancy until the time of birth and childbed.« (Silbermayr, 1988)

A strange case of sexual modification is to be seen in the male priestesses who were to be found in Indonesia, particularly in Celebes, in the Toraja country. These men were so convinced of their function that they behaved entirely like women and were also recognized as such by society. (Winthuis, 1931)

One surprising fact is that, until recently, there were »sworn virgins« living in northern Albania and in Kosovo. A woman was able to take a solemn vow of abstinence and live like a man; she was allowed to carry weapons – a particular distinction – and some of them are alleged to have married other women. (Dekker, v. d. Pol, 1990)

A sex change linked to a particular cult can occur among the Arctic Eskimos. The Dajak in Borneo have »female« medicine men, as do the Patagonians in South America. Among the Arab

5.2. Transvestismus

Transvestismus finden wir – mit unterschiedlicher Motivation – bei zahlreichen Völkern. In den frühen Kulturen und bei primitiven Völkern ist der Kleidertausch zumeist in **kultische Bezüge** eingebettet, wird oft ritualisiert und mit magischen Bedeutungen ausgestattet. Der Transvestismus ist die einfachste Möglichkeit, sich in das andere Geschlecht zu verwandeln, das temporär oder permanent angeeignet wird.

Peter Gorsen (1987) versucht das Wesen des Transvestismus aufzuzeigen: »Das phänomenologische Besondere seines Verhaltens ist, daß der Transvestit, im Unterschied zum Homosexuellen mit transvestitischen Neigungen, dem antagonistischem Geschlecht (wenn auch nicht immer wirklich, so tendenziell) zugewandt bleibt ... Der den transvestitischen Menschen mehr oder weniger zwanghaft bestimmende Wunsch bedeutet doch, in Kleidung und Benehmen das entgegengesetzte Geschlecht: das eigene durch das andere und als das andere darstellen zu müssen.«

Der Transvestismus als sexuelle Praktik, als kultischer Vollzug, Wunscherfüllung oder Symbol darf nicht verwechselt werden mit spaßhaften Verkleidungen im Karneval oder in Kabaretts, obwohl sich auch darin zweifellos die verdeckten Wünsche nach dem Geschlechtswandel zu Wort melden.

In den **Mythologien**, den Sagenwelten vieler Völker stellt die Praktik des Kleidertausches, welche meist mit einer reichen Symbolik ausgestattet ist, eine realistische Stufe zum Geschlechtswandel dar. So berichtet die griechische Mythologie über einen eigenartigen Tausch der Geschlechterrollen. Herakles unterzieht sich einer mehr oder weniger freiwilligen Knechtschaft bei der Königin von Lydien, Omphale, der Gemahlin des Berggottes Tmolus. Wenn er bei ihr verweilt, muß er in Omphales Kleidern weibliche Arbeiten verrichten und am Spinnrocken sitzen, während Omphale das Löwenfell umhängt und die Keule schultert. Unter anderen hat **Bartholomäus Spranger** (1546–1611) diese Szene dargestellt. Nach einer anderen Version haben Herakles und Omphale zum Scherze ihre Kleider getauscht, wodurch Pan, der sich Omphale nähern wollte, getäuscht wurde. Aus Rache verbreitet er das Gerücht, daß der Kleidertausch des Herakles eine perverse Gewohnheit sei. (Ranke-Graves, 1960)

Der Kleidertausch mit kultischen Anklängen hat auch im realen Leben des Menschen in der Antike seine Bedeutung. »Zu den feinsten Zügen lykischer Gynaikokratie gehört jene ungeschriebene, unbeschreiblich rein empfundene Sitte, daß Männer Weiberkleider trugen, wenn sie trauerten ... Nur durch weibliche Mimikry, ... kann er teilnehmen am Schicksal des Menschengeschlechts.« (Galahad, 1932)

Neben den mythologischen Berichten über Götter, die sich verkleiden, hat es in der Antike auch außerhalb des Rituellen einen Transvestismus gegeben. So wird von Caligula berichtet, daß er sich in seidene Frauengewänder gehüllt und Damenschuhe getragen habe.

Der Tranvestismus war offenkundig auch in biblischen Zeiten bekannt, aber nicht geduldet. Im 5. Buch Moses, *Deuteronium* 22.5 heißt es: »Ein Weib soll nicht Männertracht tragen, und ein Mann soll nicht Frauenkleider anziehen, denn ein Greuel ist dem Herrn, deinem Gott, ein jeder, der solches tut.«

Dieses Verbot richtet sich vor allem gegen die Kulttransvestition im Dienste der kanaanitischen Göttin Astarte, sexuelle Motive mögen jedoch auch eine Rolle gespielt haben. Das biblische Verbot wirkt noch weit in die Rechtsprechung des Mittelalters, ja der Neuzeit hinein, nach der Transvestiten mit hohen Strafen zu rechnen hatten.

Der Transvestismus war sicherlich im 4. Jahrhundert in Karthargo noch gebräuchlich sowie in Mesopotamien, dem vorchristlichen Ägypten, allgemein in Südostasien. Man könnte ihn als Rest einer kultischen Institution ansehen. (Bleibtreu-Ehrenberg, 1970)

Rudimente eines magisch kultischen Kleiderwechsels finden wir noch im Brauchtum. Ein Motiv für den oft nur angedeuteten Kleiderwechsel ist der Wunsch nach einer guten Geburt und nach dem Schutz des Kindes. Hier tritt der viel seltenere Fall auf, daß eine Frau Männerkleider anlegt. Im Schweizer Bernbiet legt sich die Frau bei der Geburt die Soldatenuniform des Mannes an. In Waidhofen a. d. Ybbs, Niederösterreich, war es Brauch, daß die Wöchnerin 40 Tage lang ein männliches Kleidungsstück trug. Auch die Neugeborenen selbst wurden in Kleidungsstücke des anderen Geschlechtes eingewickelt. (Scholze, 1948) Auf diese Weise sollten die bösen Dämonen getäuscht werden oder die positiven Eigenschaften des anderen Geschlechtes auf das Kind übergehen.[27]

Im **Schamanismus** verschiedener Völker und Frühzeit-Religionen spielt der Transvestismus (die Transvestition) eine nicht unbedeutende Rolle. Die Phänomene wurden bereits beschrie-

50. Bartholomäus Spranger, *Herkules und Omphale*, um 1610.

50. Bartholomäus Spranger, *Herkules and Omphale*, ca. 1610.

tribes of southern Iraq, girls can under certain conditions lead the lives of men; there is a Pueblo culture to the west of New Mexico where boys and girls can both change their sex, but only until they die.

5.2. Transvestism

Transvestism is to be found in numerous peoples, with differing motivations. In early cultures and among primitive peoples, the exchange of clothes is usually tied in with **cultic matters**, and is often ritualized and given magical meanings. Transvestism is the simplest way of adopting the opposite sex, which is acquired temporarily or permanently.

Peter Gorsen tried (1987) to describe the nature of transvestism: »The particular phenomenological feature of a transvestite's behaviour, as opposed to that of a homosexual with tranvestite leanings, is that he continues to incline towards the opposite sex, and if he does not always do so in reality, the tendency is still there. ... The wish which, more or less obsessively, dominates a transvestite relates to the clothes and behaviour of the opposite sex: it means that he has to replace his own sex by the other sex and depict it as the other sex.«

Transvestism as a sexual practice, a ritual performance, a wish fulfilment, or a symbol, must not be confused with the comical disguises worn at carnival time or in cabaret acts, even though hidden desires for sexual modification unquestionably make their presence felt at such times too.

Mythologies, which are the worlds of legend to be found in many nations, employ the practice of exchanging clothes. This is usually accompanied by a rich symbolism, and is a realistic step on the way towards sexual modification. Greek mythology tells the story of a curious exchange of sexual rôles. Heracles submits to a more or less voluntary period of servitude under Omphale, who is Queen of Lydia and the wife of the mountain god Tmolus. While on her premises, he has to wear Omphale's clothes, perform female tasks and sit at the distaff, while Omphale wraps the lion's skin around herself and puts the club over her shoulder. Those who have depicted this scene include Bartholomäus Spranger (1546–1611).

According to another version, Heracles and Omphale exchange their clothes as a jest, thereby deceiving Pan who had intended to make advances towards Omphale. In revenge, he spreads the rumour that Heracles's exchanging of clothes is a perverted habit. (Ranke-Graves, 1960)

Exchanging clothes, accompanied by suggestions of ritualism, was also a significant factor in the real life of people in classical times. »One of the finest characteristics of Lycian gynaecocracy was the unwritten custom, experienced with indescribable purity, by which men wore women's clothes when they were mourning. ... Only by female mimicry ... could a man share in the fate of the human race.« (Galahad, 1932)

Apart from the tales which the myths tell of gods disguising themselves, a kind of transvestism which lay outside the realm of ritual also existed in classical times. Thus accounts of Caligula state that he wrapped himself in silken women's garments and wore ladies' shoes.

Transvestism was evidently also known in Biblical times, but was not tolerated. *Deuteronomy*, 22, 5, states: »No woman shall wear an article of men's clothing, nor shall a man put on woman's dress; for those who do these things are abominable to the Lord your God.«

This prohibition is chiefly directed against ritual transvestism in the service of the Canaanite goddess Astarte, although sexual motives may also have played their part. The Biblical prohibition continued to have an effect on jurisdiction until well into medieval and even modern times. According to that jurisdiction, transvestites had to reckon with severe penalties.

Transvestism was certainly still customary in Carthage in the 4th century, and also in Mesopotamia, in pre-Christian Egypt, and in south-east Asia generally. It might be regarded as a survival of a cultic institution. (Bleibtreu-Ehrenberg, 1970)

Rudiments of a magical, ritual exchange of clothes are to be found in human customs. The exchange of clothes is often only hinted at, and one motive for it is the desire that there should be a good childbirth and that the child should be protected. Here, something much rarer occurs: a woman puts on a man's clothes. In Bernbiet in Switzerland, a woman puts on a man's soldier's uniform when giving birth. In Waidhofen an der Ybbs, Lower Austria, there was a custom that a woman in childbed wore a man's garment for forty days. The newborn babies were themselves wrapped in garments of the opposite sex. (Scholze, 1948) The intention was to mislead the evil demons or to transfer to the child the positive properties of the other sex.[26]

ben: Mit dem Wechsel der Kleider soll auch ein weitgehender Wandel der Persönlichkeit erreicht werden. Man will sich mit geistigen, göttlichen, außerweltlichen, jenseitigen Wesen vollständig identifizieren, wobei die eigene Persönlichkeit, meist nur temporär, weitgehend aufgegeben wird und der Schamane in vielerlei Arten der »Besessenheit« gerät.

Nach Bleibtreu-Ehrenberg (1970) sind es meist jüngere Männer, die das Verlangen haben – auf Befehl der Geister – weibliche Kleider anzulegen, wobei der Schamane auch die soziale, ja sexuelle Rolle des anderen Geschlechtes übernimmt und »Geistergatte« wird, aber sich auch mit einem Manne vermählt. In Mythen wird berichtet, daß solche »Frauen« sogar Kinder geboren haben.

Die Zuñi in Nordamerika kennen den rituellen, transvestitischen Geschlechtswandel, und ihr Schöpfergott wird als »Er-Sie« bezeichnet. Auch die Navaho-Indianer, welche in der Nähe der Zuñi leben, praktizieren den Transvestismus. Das Geschlecht kann von der Geburt an oder erst später gewechselt werden, und Heiraten sind möglich.

In unserem Kulturkreis – in den Alpenregionen – war es vor noch nicht allzulanger Zeit üblich, daß die männlichen Kinder, sobald sie gehen konnten, mit Röckchen ausgestattet wurden. Die begehrten »ersten Hosen« erhielten die Buben oft erst mit dem Schuleintritt, also knapp vor jenem Alter, in dem sich das Bewußtsein des spezifischen Geschlechtes entwickelt.

Vor allem in einer explizit patriarchalischen Gesellschaft sind Frauen oft dazu genötigt, Männerkleidung anzulegen, um ihre taktischen Ziele zu erreichen oder um vor Verfolgern sicher zu sein. Auch dieser **strategische Transvestismus** kann nur als eine Randzone der Androgynie angesehen werden.

Wie bei so vielen erotischen Praktiken ist es auch beim Transvestismus nicht gelungen, ihn, zum Unterschied von vielen anderen Völkern, in das religiöse System des **Christentums** zu integrieren.

Eine Ausnahme bilden hier, ähnlich wie bei den weiblichen Gekreuzigten, die **Heiligenlegenden**. So wird etwa berichtet, daß die heilige Thekla ihren Verlobten verließ und in Männerkleidung dem heiligen Paulus folgte. Die heilige Margaretha flüchtete in der Hochzeitsnacht in Männerkleidern und wurde der Mönch Pelagius. Die heilige Eugenia schloß sich einem Männerorden an und brachte es sogar zur Würde des Abtes. Die heilige Anna schließlich begab sich als Mann in ein Kloster und wurde dort für einen Eunuchen gehalten. Die Heiligen Perpetua, Apollinaris, Euphrosyne, Anastasia, Patricia trugen – zumindest zeitweise, oft in kritischen Situationen – Männerkleidung. (Garber, 1993)

In den Bereich der Legende wird die Erzählung von der Päpstin Johanna verwiesen. Im 9. Jahrhundert soll sie ihr Pontifikat ausgeübt haben, und erst durch ihre Niederkunft, während einer Prozession, wurde sie als Frau erkannt.[28]

5.3. Kämpfer(innen), Herrscher(innen)

Die Königin **Hatschepsut** nimmt eine einmalige Sonderstellung unter den ägyptischen Herrschern ein. In der Reihe der mächtigen Pharaonen ist sie gleichsam zu einem Rollentausch genötigt und wird so zu einer androgynen Herrscherin. Sie ist mit einem künstlichen Bart ausgestattet (der allerdings auch bei männlichen Herrschern verwendet wurde) und wird auch im Tal der Könige bestattet. Sie regiert eigentlich nicht als Frau, sondern nur Kraft ihrer angenommenen Rolle als Mann.

Die **Amazonen** sind nicht direkt als androgyne Wesen anzusehen, aber ihr grimmiger und kriegerischer Charakter rückt sie in die Nähe der antiken Kämpfer. Nach Biedermann (1987) »kommt die Amazone dem alten Mythenbild des androgynen Doppelwesens nahe ... es ist ein Sehnsuchtssymbol der verlorengegangenen Vollkommenheit vor der Aufspaltung in männlich und weiblich, der ursprünglichen Harmonie mit Welt und Überwelt«. Um besser mit Pfeil und Bogen hantieren zu können, haben die Amazonen einen Busen abgeschnitten. Die nur einseitige Brust erinnert an die androgynen Shiva-Darstellungen des Hinduismus.

Für die Darstellung von kämpferischen Frauen in Rüstungen oder mit Helmen bieten, über die Amazonen hinaus, die Mythologie und die Allegorie zahlreiche Vorwände.

Minerva als Siegerin über die Unwissenheit wird von **Bartholomäus Spranger** in einem Bild dargestellt, das die Göttin mit einem Helm und einer Art Panzer zeigt, der der Körperform genau angepaßt ist, aber die Brüste kokett frei läßt.

Auch der höfischen Gesellschaft des Mittelalters waren die Verkleidungen in ein anderes Geschlecht durchaus geläufig. Aus Berichten des 14. Jahrhunderts geht hervor, daß adelige

51. Vincent Vignon, *Jeanne d'Arc*.
52. Bartholomäus Spranger, Minerva als Siegerin über die Unwissenheit, 1591.

51. Vincent Vignon, *Jeanne d'Arc*.
52. Bartholomäus Spranger, Minerva as victress over the ignorance, 1591.

Transvestism has a significant part to play in the **shamanism** of various peoples and early religions. These phenomena have already been described: the exchange of clothes is also intended to bring about a considerable change in personality. The aim is to identify oneself entirely with spiritual, divine, supernatural, other-worldly beings; one's own personality – usually only temporarily – is largely abandoned, and the shaman enters into various states of »possession by spirits«.

According to Bleibtreu-Ehrenberg (1970), it is usually younger men who – at the spirits' command – have a longing to put on women's clothes, with the shaman also taking on the social and even the sexual rôle of the opposite sex, thus becoming a »spiritual consort«. But the shaman can also marry a man. Myths relate that such »women« even gave birth to children.

The North American Zuñi are familiar with ritual, tranvestite sex-change, and their creator-god is known as »he-she«. The Navaho Indians, who live nearby, also practise transvestism. Sex changes can be made from birth, and marriages are possible.

Frauen sich als Ritter verkleideten und als Männer an Turnieren teilnahmen. Viele Frauen gingen sogar noch einen Schritt weiter und waren in ihrer Verkleidung als Soldaten oder als Matrosen aktiv.

Das bekannteste Beispiel für die heroische Ausprägung der gerüsteten Frau liefert die kämpferische **Jeanne d'Arc** (1410–1431). Von einer geheiligt patriotischen Mission erfüllt und der Jungfräulichkeit ergeben, zieht sie in den Kampf gegen die Engländer. Die Faszination dieser Gestalt beruht nicht zuletzt auf der androgynen Wirkung, die eine Frau in einer Rüstung erzielt, welche eine extreme Ausformung männlicher Bekleidung darstellt.

Die Verkleidung als Soldat, als Kämpfer, ist oft das Motiv für die pragmatische Seite des Transvestismus.

Rudolf Dekker und Lotte van den Pol (1990) weisen allein in den Niederlanden für die Zeit vom 16.–19. Jahrhundert 120 Fälle von Rollenwechsel durch Verkleidung nach. Der kämpferische Geist war beispielsweise bei **Christine de Meyrak** oder **Anna Bonney** ausschlaggebend. Regentinnen sahen sich genötigt, ihre Tapferkeit zu dokumentieren. **Elisabeth I.** (1533–1603) tritt als Amazonenkönigin auf, aber in einem Stich von Thomas Cecill ist sie gleichzeitig der tugendhafte heilige Georg, obgleich im Hintergrund Feldlager und Kriegsschiffe zu erkennen sind. In ihrer Ansprache an die Truppen hebt sie ihre männliche Kraft hervor: »Ich weiß, daß ich nur den schwachen Körper einer Frau habe, doch das Herz und den Mut eines Königs.« (Orchard, 1992)

Das **Frauenhaar,** das aus dem Helm hervorquillt oder bei dessen Abnahme über die Schultern wallt, scheint von besonderem erotischen Reiz zu sein, eine Tatsache, die auch heute in der Werbung bisweilen eingesetzt wird.

Herrscher in Frauenkleidern bilden eine Ausnahme. Der französische König **Franz I.** (1494 bis 1547) wird von **Niccola da Modena** (1454–1515) in seiner ganzen Machtfülle dargestellt: Nicht nur die Götter, sondern auch die Göttinnen leihen dem Herrscher ihre Attribute: Er ist mit wallenden Frauengewändern angetan.

In the Alpine regions of our own cultural complex, it was until not so very long ago customary for the male children to be fitted out with skirts as soon as they could walk. The boys were often only given their longed-for first trousers when they started school, that is to say shortly before the age when the awareness of belonging to a particular sex is developed.

It is chiefly in an explicitly patriarchal society that women are often compelled to put on men's clothes in order to achieve their tactical goals or to be safe from pursuers. This **strategic transvestism** can only be regarded as a marginal area of androgyny.

As is the case with so many erotic practices, success has not been achieved in integrating transvestism into the religious **system of Christianity**, although many nations have incorporated it into their religions.

Like the females who were crucified, an exception to this is the **legends of the Saints**. For example, it is related that St. Thecla left the man to whom she was betrothed and, wearing man's attire, followed St. Paul. St. Margaret fled in men's clothes on her wedding night and turned into the monk Pelagius. St. Eugenia joined a men's order and even attained the rank of abbot. Finally, St. Anna, in the guise of a man, entered a monastery, where she was thought to be a eunuch. Saints Perpetua, Apollinaris, Euphrosyne, Anastasia and Patricia all wore men's clothes, at any rate from time to time, often in critical situations. (Garber, 1993)

The tale of Pope Joan is assigned to the realm of legend. She is said to have held her pontificate in the 9th century, and the fact that she was a woman was only detected when she was brought to bed of a child during a procession.[27]

5.3. Male and Female Warriors – Male and Female Rulers

Queen **Hatshepsut** has a unique and special place among the Egyptian rulers. As one of the succession of mighty Pharaohs, she was compelled to perform a kind of exchange of rôles, and thus became an androgynous female ruler. She had an artificial beard (a feature which was though also employed with male rulers), and is buried in the Valley of the Kings. She did not really rule as a woman, but only by virtue of her assumed rôle as a man.

The **Amazons** are not to be regarded as androgynous beings pure and simple, but their fierce and warlike character makes them closely related to the male warriors of classical antiquity. According to Biedermann (1987), »the concept of an Amazon comes close to the old mythical image of an androgynous dual being ... this is a symbol of the longing for lost perfection, a perfection which existed before the division into male and female and consisted in the original harmony with this world and the supernatural world«. The Amazons used to cut off one of their breasts, the better to be able to handle their bows and arrows. The breast on only one side of the body is reminiscent of the androgynous Shiva depictions in Hinduism.

Mythology and allegory provide numerous pretexts, not only in the case of the Amazons, for depicting warlike women wearing armour or helmets.

Bartholomäus Spranger depicts Minerva triumphing over ignorance in a picture which displays the goddess in a helmet and a kind of suit of armour, which fits her body exactly but coquettishly leaves her breasts bare.

In the courtly society of the medieval period, it was common for people to dress up as the opposite sex. Accounts from the 14th century relate that noblewomen dressed up as knights and took part in tournaments as men. Many women went still further and, in their disguise, became active as soldiers or sailors.

The best-known example of a woman in armour taking on a heroic rôle is the warlike **Joan of Arc** (1410–1431). Inspired by a sanctified patriotic mission, and dedicated to virginity, she went into battle against the English. Not the least fascinating aspect of this figure is the androgynous effect produced by a woman wearing a suit of armour, which constitutes male clothing taken to the extreme.

Dressing up as a soldier, a warrior, is often the motive for the pragmatic aspects of transvestism.

Rudolf Dekker and Lotte van den Pol (1990) have demonstrated that 120 cases of rôle reversal by wearing disguise occurred between the 16th and 19th centuries in the Netherlands alone. For example, the warlike spirit was the decisive factor for both **Christine de Meyrak** and **Anna Bonney**. Female rulers felt compelled to document their bravery. **Elizabeth I** presented herself as the Queen of the Amazons, but in an engraving by Thomas Cecill she also appears as the virtuous St. George, even though a military encampment and warships are to be seen in the background.

5.4. Erotisch. 20. Jahrhundert

Es kann kein Zweifel darüber bestehen, daß die hermaphroditische Erscheinungsform des menschlichen Körpers dazu imstande ist, sexuelle Appelle auszulösen. In der Kunst und neuerdings auch in der Werbung hat das Androgyne einen beachtlichen Stellenwert erhalten, der von einer erotischen Rezeption nicht mehr abzukoppeln ist. Dabei reicht die Spannweite vom unterschwel!ig erotischen Reiz bis zur Grenze der Obsession, der Zwanghaftigkeit.

Der heutige »echte« Transvestismus ist zweifellos auch erotischen Ursprungs, darf aber mit dem Begriff »Perversion« nicht leichtfertig abgeurteilt werden. Es handelt sich um eine atypische Verhaltensweise, der verschiedene psychische Motive zugrunde liegen. In erster Linie ist es wohl die Unzufriedenheit mit dem eigenen Geschlecht, eine erste Stufe der Geschlechtsumwandlung. Transvestismus finden wir heute hauptsächlich bei Männern, und es ist auffällig, daß sie zu Hypertrophien in Kleidung, Schmuck, Kopfputz und Kosmetik neigen.

Aus dem 15. Jahrhundert wird berichtet, daß in Frankreich sowohl Männer als auch Frauen die Kleidung des anderen Geschlechtes wählen. Keineswegs handelt es sich dabei um Karnevalsscherze, sondern vielmehr um einen »erotischen Zeitvertreib«.

Der Tausch der Geschlechterrollen, der meist in Verbindung mit dem Transvestismus steht, entwickelt sich in der Renaissance zu einer geläufigen Praxis. Zahlreiche literarische Zeugnisse lassen darauf schließen, daß sich dieser Usus vor allem an den italienischen Fürstenhöfen großer Beliebtheit erfreute. Dabei kann es sich keineswegs allein um höfische Launen gehandelt haben, sondern auch um das tief verborgene Bedürfnis der Auseinandersetzung mit der Doppelgeschlechtlichkeit.

Die Unterweisung, die die Dirne Nanna ihrer Tochter Pippa in Aretinos »Gesprächen« zuteil werden läßt, belegt die Tatsache, daß der Kleidertausch auch erotische Motive hatte. Lange vor der Legitimierung der Frauenhose sind Prostituierte in Männerkleidern aufgetreten. Ansätze zum Transvestismus des Mannes können wir etwa bei **Charles Baudelaire** (1821–1867) (nach der Biographie Sartres, 1949) feststellen: gefärbtes Haar, weibliche Fingernägel, Tragen von rosa Handschuhen und langen Locken, eine Vorliebe für weibliche Kleidung überhaupt. In der höfischen Welt des 18. Jahrhunderts wäre Baudelaire damit kaum aufgefallen, in unserem Jahrhundert jedoch würde er sich dem Vorwurf der Perversion aussetzen.

Begreiflicherweise stößt das offene Bekenntnis zum Transvestismus – und es wird sinnfälliger als etwa das zur Homosexualität – auf gesellschaftliche Diskriminierung. Dennoch gibt es zahlreiche Beispiele dafür, daß die Tendenz zur Transsexualität allein mit dem Medium des Transvestismus abgefangen werden kann.

Lothar Berfelde (geb. 1928), lebt seit dem 13. Lebensjahr als Transvestit und nennt sich **Charlotte von Mahlsdorf**. »Ich habe mich immer als Frau gefühlt, hatte aber nie das Bedürfnis, mich umoperieren zu lassen.« Offenkundig ist der Transvestismus ein vollwertiger Ersatz

She emphasized her masculine power in an address to the troops: »I know that I only have the weak body of a woman, but I have the heart and courage of a king.« (Orchard, 1992)

Women's hair, which flows forth from underneath the helmet or undulates over the shoulders when the helmet is removed, seems to exude a particular erotic attraction. Modern-day advertising sometimes makes use of this attraction.

Rulers in women's clothes are an exception. **Niccola da Modena** (1454–1515) depicted the French King **François I** (1494–1547) in his full authority. Not only the gods, but also the goddesses, lend the ruler their attributes: he is dressed in flowing women's garments.

5.4. Eroticism. Twentieth Century

There can be no doubt that the human body, in its hermaphroditic form, is able to produce a sexual appeal. Androgyny has, in art and more recently also in advertising, achieved a notable importance which can no longer be detached from the idea of erotic acceptance. This can extend all the way from a subliminal erotic attraction to the verge of a compulsive obsession.

Today's »genuine« transvestism is undoubtedly also erotic in origin, but must not be too hastily condemned by terming it perversion. It is an atypical mode of behaviour based on various psychological motives. It is probably primarily a dissatisfaction with one's own sex, a first stage towards a sex change. Transvestism is today found mostly in men, and it is noticeable that they tend towards hypertrophies in their clothes, their jewellery, their cosmetics, and the decorations on their heads.

A 15th-century account relates that men and women in France both used to choose for themselves the clothing of the opposite sex. These were not merely jests employed at carnival time, but an »erotic pastime«.

The reversal of the rôles played by the sexes is usually related to transvestism, and developed into a common practice in the Renaissance period. An abundance of literary evidence gives rise to the conclusion that this custom was particularly popular at the Italian princes' courts. This was by no means merely a matter of courtly whims; rather, it expressed a deeply concealed need to come to grips with the question of a two-sexed nature.

The instructions which Nanna the prostitute gives her daughter Pippa in Aretino's »Conversations« are evidence of the fact that there were also erotic motives for the switching of clothes. Prostitutes appeared in men's clothes long before trousers for women were legitimized. Tendencies towards transvestism in a man are to be observed in, for example, the behaviour of **Charles Baudelaire** (1821–1867): dyed hair, feminine-looking fingernails, pink gloves, long curly hair, and a general preference for female clothing. (This is according to the biography by Sartre, 1949) This would hardly have made Baudelaire a conspicuous figure in the court world of the 18th century, but in the 20th century he would have been accused of perversion.

Anyone openly declaring that he or she is a transvestite – and such a declaration is more striking than, for example, an open declaration of homosexuality – will, understandably enough, meet with social discrimination. Despite this, there are numerous examples showing that a tendency towards transsexualism can only be thwarted by the medium of transvestism.

Lothar Berfelde, born in 1928, has lived as a transvestite since he was twelve years old, and calls himself **Charlotte von Mahlsdorf**. »I have always felt like a woman, but have never had any need for a sex-change operation.« Transvestism is evidently a perfect substitute for transsexual intentions. Charlotte von Mahlsdorf has set down her story in the book *Ich bin meine eigene Frau* (*I am my own wife*). Rosa von Praunheim, himself a male transsexual, filmed the life of this male woman in 1992.

It is relatively rare for anyone to deal with his or her own transvestism in a personal and artistic way. One example is the French photographer **Pierre Molinier** (1900–1976), who repeatedly photographed himself in an erotic and transvestite pose. At the same time he developed a noteworthy system of combinations, which resulted in the complete effacement of any sexual identity. As a man, he transformed himself into a woman by temporarily eliminating the penis, and then »artificially« converted himself back into a man by putting on the Godmiche, the artificial penis. The series called »Le chaman« displays those varieties of hermaphroditism for which social history provides evidence. In one case the upper part of the body is largely male, although the budding breasts are outlined, while the abdomen is female; and in another picture a woman's breast is feigned, and the abdomen has an artificial penis.

56. Man Ray, Marcel Duchamp als »Rrose Sélavy«, 1924.
57. Chris Makos, Andy Warhol als Frau.
58. Charlotte von Mahlsdorf, 1990.

56. Man Ray, Marcel Duchamp as »Rrose Sélavy«, 1924.
57. Chris Makos, Andy Warhol as a woman.
58. Charlotte von Mahlsdorf, 1990.

für transsexuelle Intentionen. Charlotte von Mahlsdorf hat ihre Geschichte in dem Buch *Ich bin meine eigene Frau* niedergelegt. Rosa von Praunheim, selbst männlicher Transsexueller, hat 1992 das Leben der Mann/Frau verfilmt.

Die persönlich-künstlerische Bewältigung des Tranvestismus tritt uns relativ selten entgegen. Als Beispiel soll der französische Photograph **Pierre Molinier** (1900–1976) genannt werden, der sich selbst immer wieder in einer erotisch-transvestistischen Pose ablichtet. Dabei entwickelt er eine bemerkenswerte Kombinatorik, die zu einer völligen Verwischung der sexuellen Identität führt. Als Mann verwandelt er sich in eine Frau (temporäres Eliminieren des Penis), um sich sodann wieder »künstlich« in einen Mann zu verwandeln (Umhängen des Godmiche, des künstlichen Penis). Die Serie »Le chaman« zeigt die auch kulturhistorisch belegten Varianten des Hermaphroditismus: Einmal bleibt der Oberkörper weitgehend männlich, jedoch werden die Brustknospen markiert, der Unterleib ist weiblich, das andere Mal wird eine Frauenbrust vorgetäuscht, der Unterleib ist mit einem künstlichen Penis ausgestattet.

Wenn Künstler die Kleider des anderen Geschlechtes anlegen, dürfen wir annehmen, daß es sich um mehr als einen bloßen Verkleidungsscherz handelt: Es ist eine persönliche Aussage zur Wandelbarkeit des Menschen, zur Relativierung der Geschlechterrollen. **Marcel Duchamp** (1897–1968) verkleidet sich, nennt sich »Rrose Sélavy (offenkundig ein Wortspiel mit »c'est la vie«) und läßt sich von Man Ray photographieren. Chris Makos photographiert eine aparte junge Dame: In Wahrheit ist es **Andy Warhol** (1927–1987) in einer seiner vielen visuellen Verwandlungen.

5.5. Theater, Revue, Film

5.5.1. Motive

Die programmatischen Motive für einen Geschlechtertausch in den darstellenden Künsten stellen sich in den einzelnen Kulturen sehr unterschiedlich dar. Am häufigsten treffen wir **Tabuisierungen** für das Auftreten von Frauen im Theater an. Schon im antiken Theater trugen Männer Frauenmasken. Die mittelalterlichen Mysterienspiele, die meist in Kirchen stattfanden, mußten ohne Frauen auskommen. Auch bei den Theateraufführungen in den Mönchsklöstern standen keine Frauen zur Verfügung, so daß die Frauenrollen von Männern gespielt wurden. Die Theater im italienischen Kirchenstaat mußten bis zum 18. Jahrhundert ohne weibliche Mimen auskommen. Im japanischen No- und Kabuki-Theater ist es selbstverständlich, daß der Mann, mit einer Frauenmaske ausgestattet, die weibliche Rolle übernimmt.

Das Theater bietet darüber hinaus von jeher ein reiches Entfaltungsfeld für den Tausch der Geschlechter- »Rollen«, nun im wahrsten Sinne des Wortes. Allerdings muß es sich keineswegs immer um androgyne Phänomene handeln. Der Rollentausch im Theater ist dem Transvestismus verwandt, und auch dieser kann nur als ein androgynes Randphänomen angesehen werden. Wenn wir jedoch davon ausgehen, daß der Schauspieler zwar nicht gleichzeitig, aber knapp hintereinander die Identität von Mann und Frau repräsentiert, so mag die Darstellung im Zusammenhang mit dieser Arbeit durchaus gerechtfertigt erscheinen.

5.5.2. Theater: Mann als Frau

Die barocke Musik- und Theaterpraxis kennt eine uns heute grausam erscheinende Geschlechtermodifikation: die **Kastratensänger.** Sangesbegabte Knaben wurden entmannt, um ihre Sopranstimme zu erhalten und ihnen somit weitere Auftrittsmöglichkeiten für Frauenrollen im höfischen Theater zu sichern. Die Motivation für die römischen Kastraten des 17. und 18. Jahrhunderts entspringt zunächst der bereits erwähnten Tatsache, daß im Kirchenstaat das Auftreten von Frauen im Theater verboten war. »In den Kastraten erfüllten sich die hermaphroditischen Wunschträume des Barock. Die Suche nach dem Stein der Weisen, die das spekulative Denken dieser Zeit beschäftigt, ist die Suche nach einem mythischen Symbol, das zur Hälfte männlich, zur Hälfte weiblich ist. In den Kastraten schien dieses Ideal gefunden.« (Ortkemper, 1993)

Die Kastraten haben keineswegs nur Frauenrollen gespielt, vielmehr gab es zahlreiche Männerrollen vor allem von jugendlichen Helden oder von Figuren der antiken Mythologie, die mit Sopranstimme gesungen wurden. Es hat sich offenbar nicht um völlig effeminierte Männer gehandelt, sondern die Bühnenfiguren behielten auch einige männliche Eigenschaften. In ei-

When artists put on the clothes of the opposite sex, we may assume that this is more than the mere jest of adopting a disguise: it is a personal statement on the changeability of humankind, on the relativization of the rôles played by the sexes. **Marcel Duchamp** (1897–1968) dressed up as a woman, called himself »Rrose Sélavy« (evidently a pun on »c'est la vie«), and had himself photographed by Man Ray. Chris Makos photographed a striking young woman: this was in fact **Andy Warhol** (1927–1987) in one of his many visual transformations.

5.5. Theatre, Revue, Film

5.5.1. Motives

The planned motives for adopting the opposite sex in the performing arts differ very widely from one culture to another. The most common feature is that the appearance of women on stage is placed under a **taboo**. Men wore women's masks in the theatre in classical antiquity. The medieval mystery plays, which were usually performed in churches, had to make do without women. Neither were there any women available for theatrical performances in monasteries, so that the women's parts were played by men. Until the 18th century, theatres in the Italian Papal States had to manage without actresses. In the Japanese No and Kabuki theatre, it goes without saying that the woman's part is played by a man wearing a female mask.

In addition, theatre has always provided a rich field for working on the matter of switching the rôles played by the sexes, with the word »rôle« here being used in its truest sense. But these need not always be androgynous phenomena. The switching of rôles in the theatre is related to transvestism, and it can only be regarded as a marginal androgynous phenomenon. However, although it is true that an actor does not portray a man and a woman as being identical with one another both at the same time, he does portray first a man and shortly thereafter a woman. If we proceed on this basis, a description of this matter in the context of the present work may seem to be perfectly justified.

5.5.2.. Theatre: Man as Woman

In the Baroque period, music and the theatre employed a sexual modification which appears inhuman to us today. The reference is to the **castrato singers**. Talented boy singers were castrated in order to preserve their soprano voices, thus enabling them to continue to play women's parts at the court theatre. The initial motive for producing the Roman castrati of the 17th and 18th centuries lay in the above-mentioned fact that women were banned from appearing on stage in the Papal States. »The hermaphroditic pipe-dreams of the Baroque period met with fulfilment in the castrati. The search for the philosopher's stone was a subject of speculative thinking at that period. It was a search for a mythical symbol which is half male and half female. It seemed that, in the castrati, this ideal had been found.« (Ortkemper, 1993)

The castrati did not only play women's parts. There were numerous men's parts, chiefly youthful heroes or figures from classical mythology, which were sung in a soprano voice. The theatrical rôles were evidently not those of entirely effeminate men; the characters did retain some masculine qualities. In an account dating from 1902, Francois Raguenet, a Papal Secretary of State living in Rome, wrote that »...castrati can play any part they want to, whether it is that of a man or a woman... Their voice is as gentle as a woman's, but much stronger. They are normally taller than women, and this makes them look more majestic.« (Ortkemper, 1993)

But in the opera of the Baroque period, a reverse »switching of the sexes« was also possible: male rôles were sung by women. The double switch occurred when an opera by Händel was performed in London in 1741: Achilles was played by a woman, while the rôle of Odysseus was sung by a castrato with a soprano voice.

One castrato has gone down in the history of music. This is Carlo Broschi, known as **Farinelli**, born in Apulia in 1705. His career took him to Rome, Naples, Venice, Vienna, Munich, London, Paris and Madrid. Gerard Corblau made a film on the subject of this singer, with Stefano Dionisi in the title rôle. This biographical film is very loosely based on the singer's real life. No singer's voice today has the register and volume of a castrato's, and for this reason a computer-generated voice was dubbed on. The director of the film refers to the singer's »inner androgyny« and takes the view that »people's fascination with castrato singing pointed to a kind of

nem Bericht aus dem Jahre 1902 schreibt Francois Raguenet, in Rom lebender Kardinals-sekretär, daß » ... Kastraten jede Rolle spielen können, die sie wollen, gleich ob einen Mann oder eine Frau ... ihre Stimme ist so weich wie die einer Frau, aber dabei ist sie viel stärker, sie sind normalerweise größer als Frauen, und sie sehen deshalb majestätischer aus.« (Ortkemper, 1993)

In der Opernpraxis des Barocktheaters war aber auch der umgekehrte »Geschlechter-tausch« möglich: Männliche Rollen wurden von Frauen gesungen. Der doppelte Tausch hat sich wohl bei der Aufführung der Händel-Oper im Jahre 1741 in London abgespielt: Der Achill wurde von einer Frau dargestellt, Odysseus hingegen von einem Kastraten mit Sopranstimme gesungen.

Ein Kastrat ist in die Musikgeschichte eingegangen: Carlo Broschi, genannt **Farinelli,** 1705 in Apulien geboren. Seine Karriere führte nach Rom, Neapel, Venedig, Wien, München, Lon-don, Paris, Madrid. Gerard Corbiau hat dem Sänger einen Film mit Stefano Dionisi in der Titel-rolle gewidmet – in sehr freier biographischer Interpretation. Da die Stimmlage und das Stimm-volumen der Kastraten heute keinem Sänger mehr zu eigen ist, wurde eine computergene-rierte Stimme unterlegt. Der Regisseur des Filmes spricht von der »inneren Androgynität« des Sängers und glaubt, »daß die Faszination am Gesang des Kastraten auf eine Art erwünschter, universeller Harmonisierung zwischen den Geschlechtern, Mann und Frau und sogar Kind ver-wies. Ihre Stimme war all das, untrennbar und wunderbar, die Stimme Gottes oder die der En-gel ... die Verkörperung der ursprünglichen Einheit, nach der wir uns alle sehnen ...« (Filmla-den, 1995)

Das sexuelle Bezugsfeld der Kastraten ist wohl nicht ganz eindeutig zu klären. Bei den Frauen genossen sie ihre Gunst nicht zuletzt deshalb, weil sie zwar coitusfähig, aber zeu-gungsunfähig waren. Doch liebten die Frauen wohl auch das Weibliche an ihnen und konnten somit ihre lesbischen Intentionen befriedigen, ohne den harten Strafen der damaligen Zeit aus-gesetzt zu sein. Umgekehrt jedoch verliebten sich die Männer in die Weiblichkeit der Kastraten und begaben sich damit an die Grenze der Homosexualität. Wie auch immer das sexuelle Spektrum interpretiert werden mag, deutet alles darauf hin, daß es sich hier um eine Faszina-tion handelt, die durch die Androgynität der Sänger hervorgerufen wird. Die Kastraten waren auf der Bühne dermaßen beliebt, daß man außerhalb des Kirchenstaates bisweilen weibliche Schauspieler als Kastraten ausgab, also eine Frau sich als Mann gebärdete, der sich wie eine Frau aufführte – ein weiterer überaus merkwürdiger Beitrag zur Verwirrung oder besser zur Aufhebung der Geschlechtergrenzen.

Die Methode der Kastration wird selbstverständlich heute nicht mehr angewendet, aber die Faszination, die Männer mit Sopranstimmen auslösen konnten, hat sich offenbar gehalten. Es gibt nach wie vor einige »Contratenöre« oder **Countertenöre,** deren Stimmlage sich im So-pranbereich bewegt. Nach einer Aufführung mit dem Contratenor Jochen Kowalski äußert sich ein Zuhörer: »Es ist eine wunderbare Stimme, das Weibliche und das Männliche ist im Sänger vereint!«

5.5.3. Theater: Frau als Mann – Die Hosenrolle

Viel häufiger begegnen wir im 19. und 20. Jahrhundert dem Phänomen, daß Männer von Frauen dargestellt werden. Die **Hosenrolle** gehört längst zum gängigen Repertoire des Thea-ters. Für die Darstellung eines Mannes durch eine Frau gibt es im Theater zunächst auch prak-tische Motive: Wenn für einen Mann oder Jüngling eine hohe Stimmlage gefordert wird, kann diese nur von einer weiblichen Stimme erbracht werden. Der Cherubin in Mozarts Figaros Hochzeit und Der Rosenkavalier in der gleichnamigen Oper von Richard Strauss sind die schönsten Beispiele von Hosenrollen auf der Opernbühne.

Bei manchen Rollen bleibt die Geschlechterzuordnung offen. Ist die »Jugend« in Raimunds Bauer als Millionär nun männlicher oder weiblicher Natur? Betrachten wir die legendäre **The-rese Krones** (1801–1830) in ihrer Glanzrolle, dann erinnert sie an die Show-Darbietungen der Gegenwart: Sie trägt einen sehr feminin aussehenden Männeranzug mit einem Zylinder und nähert sich damit der Androgynie.

Alfred Holtmont (1925) sieht in der Hosenrolle wesentlich mehr als nur die praktische Forde-rung des Theaters, Knaben und junge Männer überzeugend darzustellen. Impliziert ist auch der Wunsch nach geschlechtlicher Verwandlung, und es handelt sich meist um »dichterisch entworfene Androgyne«, um die »Idee eines Zusammenfließens der Geschlechter in ein dop-

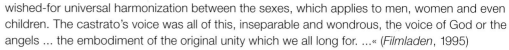

wished-for universal harmonization between the sexes, which applies to men, women and even children. The castrato's voice was all of this, inseparable and wondrous, the voice of God or the angels ... the embodiment of the original unity which we all long for. ...« (*Filmladen*, 1995)

The castrati's sexual field of reference probably cannot be clearly defined. Not the least reason why they found favour with women was that they were capable of coitus but not of procreation. But women probably also loved the castrati's female characteristics and were thus able to satisfy their lesbian intentions without being subject to the severe penalties imposed at that period. However, in the reverse situation, men fell in love with the castrati's femininity and thus betook themselves to the border with homosexuality. However the sexual spectrum may be interpreted, everything points to the fascination exercised by an androgynous being. Castrati were so popular on stage that, outside the Papal States, actresses were sometimes passed off as castrati, so that a woman was pretending to be a man behaving like a woman. This was another very strange contribution towards confusing or, to put it better, eliminating the borders between the sexes.

Castration is of course no longer employed today, but the fascination which could be exercised by men with soprano voices has evidently been preserved. There are still some **counter-tenors** whose register lies in the soprano range. After a performance by the counter-tenor Jochen Kowalski, one listener said: »It is a wonderful voice: femininity and masculinity are combined within a single singer!«

5.5.3. Theatre: Women as Men – Breeches Part

A much more common phenomenon in the 19th and 20th centuries is that of men's parts being played by women. **Breeches-parts** have long been part of the established theatrical repertoire. In the theatre, the idea of a woman playing a man's part also starts from practical considerations. If a high vocal register is required for a man or a youth, only a female voice is capable of it. The cherub in Mozart's *Marriage of Figaro,* and *Der Rosenkavalier* by Richard Strauss, are the finest examples of breeches-parts in opera.

The sex to be assigned to certain rôles remains an open question. Is Youth in Raimund's *Peasant as Millionaire* male or a female? If we consider the legendary **Therese Krones** (1801 to 1830) in her star rôle, she reminds us of today's show-business performances. She wears a very feminine-looking man's suit with a top hat, and thus comes close to being androgynous.

Alfred Holtmont (1925) takes the view that breeches-parts are something much more than merely the practical theatrical necessity of presenting boys and young men convincingly. They also imply a wish for sexual transformation, and they are usually »poetically designed androgynes« representing the »idea of the sexes coalescing into a two-sexed being which begets and gives birth of its own accord like a hermaphrodite, or seems to be infertile like an androgyne.« Holtmont reminds us that »the hierodules who prostituted themselves in women's clothes, and the virago who was a warrior in the service of the god of procreation, are on the same level as the castrati of the older operas and the actresses playing men's parts in the theatre.« To Holtmont, the »history of the breeches-part is ... the history of emancipation from symbolic women's clothing, and is not the history of the negation of everything female. ...«

The possibility of developing a kind of dual sexuality in the theatre was described in great detail by Rosa von Braunschweig in an article about Anne Marie Stögemann, who calls herself **Felicita von Vestvali**: (Braunschweig, 1903) In accordance with the terminology of those times, she was called a pederast, but was by no means a hermaphrodite in biological terms. She was an actress in Leipzig, but soon became a much-praised performer on numerous European and American stages: she was an enthusiastically acclaimed singer with a sonorous alto voice. But very soon she was playing men's parts, such as Romeo, Figaro in *The Barber of Seville*, and finally Hamlet. This placed her at the beginning of a long series of attempts by the modern theatre to have women play the parts of thoroughly male characters.

The French actress **Mademoiselle Maupin** was evidently in a similar situation. Acting and the theatre were her passion. She was as brave and decisive as a man, and was very fond of friendly relationships with women.

Honoré de Balzac (1799–1850) tells, in *Sarrasine*, the story of a young man who has great success as a female singer called »Zambinella«.

Oscar Wilde (1854–1900) played the part of Salome, and we cannot judge how far, for today's taste, he lapsed into the ridiculous.

pelgeschlechtliches Wesen, das aus sich selbst zeugt und gebärt wie das Hermaphroditische, oder unfruchtbar anmutet, wie das Androgynische«. Holtmont erinnert daran, daß die »in Frauengewändern sich prostituierenden Hierodulen und die im Dienst der Zeugungsgottheit kriegerische Männin mit dem Kastraten der älteren Oper und der Männerspielerin des Schauspieles eine gemeinsame Linie bildet«. Für Holtmont ist die »Geschichte der Hosenrolle ... die Geschichte der Emanzipation von der symbolhaften weiblichen Kleidung und nicht die Geschichte der Verneinung alles Weiblichen ...«

Die Entfaltungsmöglichkeit einer Art Doppelgeschlechtlichkeit auf dem Theater beschreibt Rosa von Braunschweig sehr ausführlich in einem Beitrag über Anne Marie Stögemann, die sich **Felicita von Vestvali** nennt (Braunschweig, 1903). Sie wird, entsprechend der damaligen Terminologie, als »Urning« bezeichnet, war biologisch gesehen jedoch keineswegs ein »Zwitter«. In jLeipzig wurde sie Schauspielerin, bald aber auf zahlreichen europäischen und amerikanischen Bühnen eine gefeierte Darstellerin, eine umjubelte Sängerin mit sonorer Alt-Stimme. Sehr bald aber stellte sie auch männliche Rollen dar, den Romeo, den Figaro in *Der Barbier von Sevilla* und schließlich den Hamlet. Damit steht sie am Anfang einer langen Serie von Versuchen, auch durchaus männliche Charaktere im heutigen Theater durch Frauen darstellen zu lassen.

Eine ähnliche Position hatte offenbar **Mademoiselle Maupin** inne, eine französische Schauspielerin. Theater und Schauspiel waren ihre Leidenschaft, sie war von »männlicher« Tapferkeit und Entschlossenheit und Frauenfreundschaften sehr zugetan.

Honoré de Balzac (1799–1850) erzählt in *Sarrasine* die Geschichte eines jungen Mannes, der als Sängerin »Zambinella« überaus erflogreich ist.

Oscar Wilde (1854–1900) hat die Salome gespielt, und wir vermögen nicht zu beurteilen, inwieweit er für den heutigen Geschmack ins Lächerliche abgeglitten ist.

Eine seltsame Anziehungskraft auf weibliche Schauspieler scheint Shakespeares Hamlet zu haben. Unter den bedeutenden Schauspielerinnen war es keine geringere als die große **Sarah Bernhardt** (1844–1923), die den Hamlet dargestellt hat. Die später als Volksschauspielerin prädikatierte **Adele Sandrock** (1864–1937) hat in ihrer Glanzzeit den Hamlet gespielt, wobei ihre tiefe Altstimme dieser Rolle sicherlich Glaubwürdigkeit verliehen hat. Auch in der neusten Theaterpraxis wird die Rolle des Hamlet bisweilen mit einer Frau besetzt, so etwa in einer Inszenierung von **George Tabori** (geb. 1914) im Jahre 1990. Damit nicht genug, läßt Tabori den Diktator Stalin 1988 durch eine Frau darstellen. Die Darstellung des Todes fallweise als Mann oder Frau könnte als Hinweis auf dessen androgynen Charakter dienen. Der Tod – La morte – ist im französischen weiblich, und so wird er auch dargestellt, etwa in Cocteaus Film *Orphée*. In der japanischen Version des Musicals *Elisabeth* werden alle männlichen Rollen, auch der Tod, von Frauen dargestellt.

Den umgekehrten Effekt des Kastraten bewirkt die weibliche Alt-Stimme, die in die Stimmlage des Mannes vordringt. Die Faszination, die in den vierziger Jahren vom Timbre der Altstimme der schwedischen Sängerin **Zarah Leander** (1907–1981) ausging, ist zweifellos durch den androgynen Charakter bedingt, der allerdings vor allem bei Männern Anklang fand. Es ist symptomatisch, daß die szenische Darstellung Zarah Leanders 1989/90 durch einen Mann (Armand, recte Franz Fischer) erfolgte, also wieder eine Art Theater-Transvestismus darstellte.

Von der Hosenrolle deutlich zu unterscheiden sind **Verkleidungsrollen**, bei denen nur temporär aus dramarturgischen Gründen eine Frau sich als Mann verkleidet (aber viel seltener umgekehrt). *Fidelio* in Beethovens Oper ist das klassische seriöse Beispiel dafür.

Die Verwechslungs- und Täuschungskomödien sind seit Jahrhunderten beliebt und stellen auch für den Film eine unerschöpfliche Quelle der Komik dar. Wenn auch die Thematik des Tranvestismus ins Komische transferiert wird, mögen doch noch die Rudimente androgyner Tendenzen durchschimmern.

5.5.4. Revue. Show

Die **Musikrevue** erlebte in den USA am Anfang dieses Jahrhunderts und dann wieder in den zwanziger Jahren einen Höhepunkt. Ein spezifischer Typus von Tänzerinnen hat sich bis heute erhalten: Es sind gleichsam umgekehrte Hermaphroditen. Der Oberkörper der Frauen ist mit männlichen Attributen ausgestattet: Ein hoher Zylinder oder eine Melone und ein Herren-Jacket stehen in einem spannungsreichen Gegensatz zur weiblichen Erotik der schlanken, fast nackten Beine, häufig mit Strapsen den Sexappeal unterstreichend. Oft sind die Tänzerinnen aber auch mit Hosen bekleidet. Bemerkenswert ist, daß die Frauen gleichsam in einem diszi-

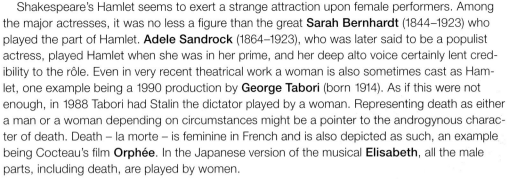

63. Oskar Wilde als Salome, um 1890.
64. Sarah Bernhardt als Hamlet, um 1880.
65. Tanzduo Cherry und June Blossom, um 1930.

63. Oskar Wilde as Salome, ca. 1890.
64. Sarah Bernhardt as Hamlet, ca. 1880.
65. Dancing duo Cherry and June Blossom,
ca. 1930.

Shakespeare's Hamlet seems to exert a strange attraction upon female performers. Among the major actresses, it was no less a figure than the great **Sarah Bernhardt** (1844–1923) who played the part of Hamlet. **Adele Sandrock** (1864–1923), who was later said to be a populist actress, played Hamlet when she was in her prime, and her deep alto voice certainly lent credibility to the rôle. Even in very recent theatrical work a woman is also sometimes cast as Hamlet, one example being a 1990 production by **George Tabori** (born 1914). As if this were not enough, in 1988 Tabori had Stalin the dictator played by a woman. Representing death as either a man or a woman depending on circumstances might be a pointer to the androgynous character of death. Death – la morte – is feminine in French and is also depicted as such, an example being Cocteau's film **Orphée**. In the Japanese version of the musical **Elisabeth**, all the male parts, including death, are played by women.

The female alto voice which penetrates into the male register produces a reverse castrato effect. The fascination which, in the 1940s, emanated from the timbre of the alto voice of the Swedish singer **Zarah Leander** (1907–1981) was doubtless conditioned by its androgynous character which, however, found favour mostly with men. It is symptomatic that, in 1989/90, the part of Zarah Leander was played in the theatre by a man (Armand, real name Franz Fischer), so that this was another kind of theatrical trasvestitism.

A clear distinction must be drawn between breeches-parts and and cover parts in which a woman dresses up as a man (or, much less commonly, a man as a woman) only temporarily, for dramatic reasons. **Fidelio** in Beethoven's opera is the classical serious example of this.

Comedies of deception and mistaken identity have been popular for centuries, and are also an inexhaustible source of humour in film. Even though the subject of transvestism is transferred to the field of comedy, the rudiments of androgynous tendencies may still show through, if only faintly.

5.5.4. Revues. Shows

Musical revues experienced a peak period in the USA at the beginning of the 20th century, and another in the 1920s. Female dancers of a specific type are still found at the present day. They might be called hermaphrodites in reverse. The upper part of the women's bodies is given male attributes: a tall top hat or a bowler, and a man's jacket, are seen in an exciting contrast with the female eroticism of the slender, almost naked legs, where suspender belts frequently emphasize the sex appeal. But the female dancers often also wear trousers. It is noteworthy that the women appear in a kind of well-disciplined collective, whereas their partner is the dominant individual who directs the troupe of girls.

The top hat plays an astonishingly dominant part. It was of course an elegant male garment and, like many items of male headgear, its function was to make the man appear taller, more dignified and more impressive. The shape given to such male headgear as the »sailor's hat of Freudenstadt« or the »papal tiara« makes it natural to suppose that male »tallness« can certainly also be transferred to the phallic principle. The usurpation of the top hat in countless films and revues might accordingly be regarded as the simple appropriation of the phallic principle. It is permissible to draw a comparison with the sculpture called *Fillette* (*The Little Girl*) by Louise Bourgeois, and also to see an association with archaic bisexual figurines and anthropophallic depictions.

Marlene Dietrich and **Betty Grable** are among the most prominent female wearers of top hats. The legendary **Josephine Baker** (1906–1975) also sometimes appeared in men's clothes. Apart from the fascination of the exotic skin colour somewhere between black and white, there was also that of the indeterminate area somewhere between a man and a woman.

Michael Jackson (born 1958) is doubtless one of the most fascinating male »androgynes« in the music scene of the 1980s and 1990s. The press repeatedly refers to Jackson as a sort of two-sexed being, and describes him as »the perfectly androgynous sex symbol«. According to press reports, his present appearance (1997) is the result of, among other things, a number of cosmetic operations. **Jeff Koons** (born 1955), the American sculptor of kitsch, pop art and realism, has produced a significant depiction in which he pays particular attention to emphasizing Jackson's feminine character.

On the musical, theatrical and show-business scene of today, there are other names which are also apostrophized as being androgynous types: David Bowie, Grace Jones, Laurie Anderson, Boy George, Amanda Lear, Mick Jagger and Annie Lennox, to name but a few.

The **drag queens** are one variety of transvestism on the fringe of the show-business scene. They are men, usually homosexual, who appear in women's clothes and imitate or satirize female

Tanz-Duo Cherry und June Blossom

pliniertem Kollektiv auftreten, während der Partner als dominate Einzelperson die Girltruppe dirigiert.

Der Zylinder spielt eine erstaunlich dominante Rolle. Natürlich war er das elegante männliche Kleidungsstück und hatte, wie so viele männliche Kopfbedeckungen, die Aufgabe, den Mann größer, würdiger, feierlicher erscheinen zu lassen. Die Ausformung mancher Kopfbedeckungen wie etwa der »Schifferhut von Freudenstadt« oder die »päpstliche Tiara« legt die Vermutung nahe, daß die männliche »Größe« durchaus auch auf das phallische Prinzip übertragbar ist. Demnach könnte die Usurpation des Zylinders in den zahllosen Film- und Revueszenarien als eine einfache Aneignung des Phallischen gesehen werden. Der Vergleich mit der Skulptur *Fillette (Das kleine Mädchen)* – von Louise Bourgeois ist zulässig, ebenso die Assoziation zu den archaischen »bisexuellen« Figurinen und den anthropophallischen Darstellungen.

Marlene Dietrich und **Betty Grable** zählen zu den prominentesten Zylinderträgerinnen. Auch die legendäre **Josephine Baker** (1906–1975) tritt bisweilen in Männerkleidern auf, und zu der Faszination der exotischen Hautfarbe zwischen schwarz und weiß kommt noch jene des Unentschiedenseins zwischen Mann und Frau.

Zu den faszinierendsten »Androgynen« männlicher Natur in der Musikszene der achtziger und neunziger Jahre zählt zweifellos **Michael Jackson** (geb. 1958). Auch die Presse apostrophiert Jackson wiederholt als ein quasi beidgeschlechtliches Wesen und bezeichnet ihn als »das perfekt androgyne Sexsymbol«. Pressemeldungen zufolge ist das heutige (1997) Aussehen nicht zuletzt eine Folge von kosmetischen Operationen. **Jeff Koons** (geb 1955), der amerikanische Kitsch-Pop-Realismus-Plastiker hat in einer signifikanten Darstellung den femininen Charakter Jacksons besonders deutlich herausgearbeitet.

In der heutigen Musik-, Theater- und Show-Business-Szene werden auch noch andere Namen als androgyne Typen apostrophiert: David Bowie, Grace Jones, Laurie Anderson, Boy George, Amanda Lear, Mick Jagger, Annie Lennox, um nur einige zu nennen.

Eine Spielart des Transvestismus am Rande der Show-Szene sind die **drag queens,** meist homosexuelle Männer, die in Frauenkleidern auftreten, weibliches Verhalten nachahmen oder persiflieren. Mit Transvestismus in seiner klinischen Bedeutung hat das nichts zu tun. Im Gegensatz zur latenten Androgynie ist die **Transvestie-** oder **Travestie-Show** heute zu einem gängigen Typus der Unterhaltungsszene geworden, und es fällt schwer, hinter dem Klamauk die elementaren Anliegen der Verwandlung zu erkennen.

5.5.5. Film: Frau als Mann

Vielfach behält die Frau im Film ihren weiblichen Charakter und wird lediglich durch transvestitische Embleme an die Grenze des Androgynen herangeführt. **Marlene Dietrich** (1901–1992) – auch im Privatleben als Hosenträgerin oft kritisiert – hat in der unsterblichen Rolle in *Der blaue Engel* ein Vorbild für diese Diskrepanz in der Bekleidung geliefert, die bis heute an Faszination offenbar nichts verloren hat.

Josef von Sternberg (1894–1969) dreht 1931 mit Marlene Dietrich auch den Film *Morocco*. Der große Star wird gleichzeitig mit männlichen und weiblichen Zügen ausgestattet und erhält dadurch einen androgynen Charakter. »Es war die Intelligenzia hier und in Übersee, die das Androgyne an Marlene mochte – nicht das große Publikum.« (Sichtermann, 1991)

Ein anderer großer Star aus der Frühzeit des Films, **Greta Garbo** (1905–1990) zeigt sich in Männerkleidern: In *Königin Christine* (USA 1933, Rouben Mamoulian) wird einmal mehr der Grenzübergang der Geschlechter deutlich.

Wie im Theater war auch im Film die Rolle des Hamlet für die Darstellung durch eine Frau prädestiniert. Eine Hamlet-Inszenierung aus dem Jahre 1920 (Regie: Svend Gade, Heinz Schall) findet einen seltsamen Vorwand, um Hamlet durch eine Frau – die bedeutende Schauspielerin **Asta Nielsen** (1881–1972) – darstellen zu lassen. Die dänische Königin bringt ein Mädchen zur Welt – da kommt die Nachricht vom Tod ihres Mannes. Die Dynastie muß aber gerettet werden – also wird das Kind zum Knaben erklärt. Als der König überraschend zurückkehrt, behält die Tochter trotzdem nach außen ihr männliches Geschlecht.

Die Faszination, die die kriegerische Frau auslöst, kommt in zahlreichen Filmen über **Jeanne d'Arc** zum Ausdruck. Zu den bekanntesten Werken zählt **Carl Theodor Dreyers** (1889–1968) Film *Passion de Jeanne d'Arc* aus dem Jahre 1928.

Die **Amazonen** und Jeanne d'Arc – die bewaffneten, kämpferischen Frauen – finden zeitgenössische Interpretationen im modernen Action-Film, insbesondere amerikanischer Prove-

66. Asta Nielsen als Hamlet in dem gleichnamigen
Film, 1920.
67. Jeff Koons, *Michael Jackson and Bubbles*,
1988.
68, Marlene Dietrich als Lola in *Der blaue Engel*,
1930.

66. Asta Nielsen as Hamlet in the film of the same
name, 1920.
67. Jeff Koons, *Michael Jackson and Bubbles*,
1988.
68, Marlene Dietrich as Lola in *The Blue Angel*,
1930.

behaviour. This has nothing to do with transvestism in the clinical sense. In contrast to androgyny, transvesty or travesty shows have today become a common feature of the entertainment scene, and it is hard to detect, behind the slapstick, any elemental desires for transformation.

5.5.5. Film: Women as Men

Women often retain their female character in film, and it is only transvestite emblems that take them to the verge of androgyny. **Marlene Dietrich** (1901–1992), who has also often been criticized for wearing trousers in her private life, gave a precedent for this discrepancy in clothing in the immortal rôle she played in *The Blue Angel.* That discrepancy has evidently lost none of its fascination even today.

Josef von Sternberg (1894–1969) also made, in 1931, the film called *Morocco*, with Marlene Dietrich in it. The great star was provided with both male and female characteristics simultaneously, thus giving her an androgynous character. »Both inside and outside Germany, it was the intelligentsia, and not the public at large, that had a liking for Marlene's androgyny.« (Sichtermann, 1991)

Greta Garbo (1905–1990) was another great star from the early period of film who appeared men's clothes. The border between the sexes is plainly crossed in the film called *Queen Christine* (USA, Rouben Mamoulian, 1933).

As was the case in the theatre, the part of Hamlet was predestined to be played by a woman in a film too. In a film of Hamlet dating from 1920 (directors: Svend Gade, Heinz Schall), a strange pretext was found for having Hamlet played by a woman, namely **Asta Nielsen** (1881 to 1972), the eminent actress. The Queen of Denmark gives birth to a girl, and then the news arrives that her husband has died. But the dynasty has to be saved, and so the baby is declared to be a boy. When the king surprisingly returns, the daughter nevertheless retains the outward appearance of being of the male sex.

Fascination with warlike women is expressed in numerous films about **Joan of Arc**. One of the best-known productions is the film *Passion de Jeanne d'Arc* by **Carl Theodor Dreyer** (1889–1969), dating from 1928.

The **Amazons** and Joan of Arc – armed, belligerent women – are given contemporary interpretations in modern action films, especially those of American origin. However, this is sometimes much more than a matter of suggestive aggressiveness with rôles reversed: it may also relate to the conflict-ridden dispute between male and female. Georg Seeßlen analyzed (1990) the film called Blue Steel (Kathryn Bigelow, 1989), and pointed out the deeper connections:

nienz. Es geht jedoch bisweilen um weit mehr als um die pikante Aggression im Rollentausch, es kann auch um die konfliktgeladene Auseinandersetzung zwischen dem Männlichen und dem Weiblichen gehen. Georg Seeßlen (1990) analysiert den Film *Blue Steel* (Kathryn Bigelow, 1989) und verweist auf die tieferen Zusammenhänge: »Diese Versöhnung des weiblichen Chaos mit der männlichen Ordnung und gleichzeitig, anders herum, der weiblichen Vernunft mit der männlichen Barbarei, kann auf zwei mythische Traditionen zurückgreifen: die ›androgyne Frau‹ und die ›Amazone‹. In den klassischen Mythen müssen solche Frauengestalten entweder sterben, oder sie werden entwaffnet und wieder in ihre Rolle als ›richtige‹ Frau gefesselt.«[29]

5.5.6 Film: Mann als Frau

Auch Männer in Frauenrollen werden im Film eingesetzt. **Dustin Hoffman** (geb. 1937) spielt die *Tootsie* in dem gleichamigen Film von Sydney Pollack: einen Mann, der sich als Frau verkleidet, um Karriere als Schauspielerin zu machen. Wenn auch der Film komödiantische Züge aufweist, stellt er doch ein ernstes Problem dar, das der Drehbuchautor Murray Schisgal wie folgt skizziert: »Die geschlechtliche Identität ist heute ein aktuelles Thema geworden. Was die Reinheit der eigenen sexuellen Impulse betrifft, so herrscht heute höchste Verwirrung.« (Seeßlen, 1990)

5.5.7. Film: Androgyne, Transsexuelle

Die Verfilmung des Romans *Tod in Venedig* von **Thomas Mann** (1875–1955) (Italien 1970, R. L. Visconti) führt einen anderen Grenzübergang, den zu einer Art Päderastie vor Augen: Der Komponist Gustav von Aschenbach[30] (Dirk Bogarde) verliebt sich in den polnischen Knaben Tadzio (Björn Andresen), dessen feminine Züge auf einen androgynen Charakter verweisen. Darauf auch deutet der »Matrosenanzug« hin, den Tadzio trägt, ein einstmals beliebtes Kinderkleidungsstück, das von Knaben und Mädchen getragen wurde.

In einer Buntstiftzeichnung phantasiert **Pierre Klossowski** (geb. 1905) von der »Réalisation invraisemblable de l'entente de Tadzio et Aschenbach«[30]. Tadzio ist halb angelehnt am Oberschenkel Aschenbachs, Gesichter und Hände sind einander zugewandt. Merkwürdig dabei ist, daß eine Falte im Höschen Tadzios eine Vulva erahnen läßt und damit den androgynen Charakter des Knaben eindeutig unterstreicht.

Der Roman *Orlando* von **Virginia Woolf** (1881–1942) konnte einer Verfilmung nicht entgehen. In einer ambitionierten Regie hat Sally Potter 1992 das Thema der doppelten Existenz Orlandos auf die Leinwand gebracht. Orlando wird »betörend androgyn gespielt von Tilda Swinton ... voller Witz und Poesie« (*Kölner Stadtanzeiger*), aber er/sie bleibt doch Frau, auch dort, wo sie die männliche Verwandlung darstellen soll. (Vgl. Kap. 5.7.)

Das Thema der **Transsexualität** wurde in den letzten Jahrzehnten auf breiter Ebene im Film abgehandelt. Dabei schließt das **cross-dressing** (wie es nicht ganz korrekt bezeichnet wurde) legitim an das alte Thema der Hosenrolle einerseits, der Verwechslungs- und Verkleidungskomödie andererseits an. Lange Zeit wurde dieses Thema in Theater und Kino fast ausschließlich auf komödiantischer Ebene abgehandelt, was freilich nicht ausschließt, daß Fundamente menschlicher Probleme durchschimmern. Schon 1918 dreht **Ernst Lubitsch** (1892–1947) seine Komödie *Ich möchte kein Mann sein*, die Geschichte von einem aufmüpfigen Mädchen (Ossi Oswalda), das in Männerkleidern mancherlei Abenteuer besteht.

Auf den Film *Ich bin meine eigene Frau*, der das Leben der Charlotte von Mahlsdorf zum Inhalt hat, wurde bereits in Kap. 5.4 hingewiesen.[31]

5. 6. Frauenemanzipation und Kleidung

Es ist uns heute kaum mehr bewußt, daß es noch vor hundert Jahren den Frauen faktisch verwehrt war, Männerkleidung anzulegen. Die Ausnahmen, die in Kap. 5. 3 angeführt sind, bestätigen nur die Regel. So gewinnt die »Eroberung« der männlichen Kleidung durch die Frau jenseits des Transvestismus einen emanzipatorisch-kämpferischen Charakter.

Das **Hosentragen** ist für die heutige Frau zu einer Selbstverständlichkeit geworden. Fragt man nach den Ursachen, so werden vor allem praktische Gründe des Alltags angegeben.

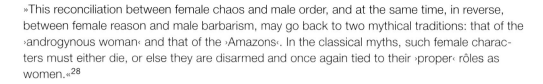

69. Dustin Hoffmann als Michael Dorsey in dem Film *Tootsie*, 1982.
70. Pierre Klossowski, *La realisation invraisem-blable de l'entente de Tadzio et Aschenbach*, 1987.

69. Dustin Hoffmann as Michael Dorsey in the film *Tootsie*, 1982.
70. Pierre Klossowski, *La realisation invraisem-blable de l'entente de Tadzio et Aschenbach*, 1987.

»This reconciliation between female chaos and male order, and at the same time, in reverse, between female reason and male barbarism, may go back to two mythical traditions: that of the ›androgynous woman‹ and that of the ›Amazons‹. In the classical myths, such female characters must either die, or else they are disarmed and once again tied to their ›proper‹ rôles as women.«[28]

5.5.6. Film: Men as Women

Men also play women's parts in films. **Dustin Hoffman** (born 1937) played *Tootsie* (directed by Sydney Pollack) in the film of the same name: a man who dresses up as a woman in order to have a career as an actress. Even though this film has its farcical side, it does depict a serious problem which Murray Schisgal, who wrote the screenplay, outlined as follows: »Sexual identity has become a topical issue today. Very great confusion prevails today where the purity of a person's own sexual impulses is concerned.« (Seeßlen, 1990)

5.5.7. Film: Androgynes, Transsexuals

The film version (R. L.. Visconti, Italy, 1970) of the novel *Death in Venice* by **Thomas Mann** (1875–1955) displays the crossing of another border: the border with a kind of pederasty. The composer Gustav von Aschenbach (Dirk Bogarde) falls in love with the Polish boy Tadzio (Björn Andresen), whose feminine features indicate an androgynous character. This is also suggested by the sailor's suit which Tadzio wears. This was once a popular children's garment worn by boys and girls.

In a drawing in crayons, **Pierre Klossowski** (born 1905) indulges in a fantasy about the »Réalisation invraisemblable de l'entente de Tadzio et Aschenbach«[29]. Tadzio is half leaning against Aschenbach's thigh, and their faces and hands are turned towards one another. A strange feature is that a fold in Tadzio's small breeches suggests a vulva, thus plainly emphasizing the boy's androgynous character.

The novel *Orlando* by **Virginia Woolf** (1881–1942) could not avoid being filmed. Sally Potter, the director (1992), ambitiously brought to the screen the matter of Orlando's double existence. Orlando is »played by Tilda Swinton as a captivatingly androgynous figure ... full of wit and poetry« (*Kölner Stadtanzeiger*, newspaper), but he/she still remains a woman, even when she is meant to portray a man's transformation. (Cf. chap. 5.7.)

The topic of transsexuality has been treated on a wide scale in films over the last few decades. **Cross-dressing** (as it was described, not quite correctly) is a legitimate link with the old topic of the breeches-part on the one hand, and the comedy of disguise and mistaken identity on the other. This topic was for a long time handled almost exclusively at the level of comedy in theatre and cinema, but this does not mean that some basic aspects of human problems also became apparent, if only faintly. It was as early as 1918 that **Ernst Lubitsch** (1892–1947) made his comedy film *Ich möchte kein Mann sein* (*I would not like to be a man*), the story of a rebellious girl (Ossi Oswalda) who, wearing men's clothes, has success in various adventures.

Reference has already been made in Chapter 5.4 to the film *I am my own wife*, whose theme is the life of Charlotte von Mahlsdorf.[30]

5.6. Women's Emancipation and Clothing

Today we are hardly still aware that a hundred years ago women were actually prevented from wearing men's clothes. The exceptions referred to in Chapter 5.3 only prove the rule. Thus the »conquest« of men's clothes by women acquires, outside the field of transvestism, an emancipatory and militant character.

For today's woman, **wearing trousers** has become a matter of course. Anyone asking for the reasons for this will be told that these are mostly of a practical everyday nature. But that is probably not the full tale of the motivation here. A look at the historical development of the usurpation of a specifically male garment permits the conclusion to be drawn that the female preference for trousers was also influenced by emancipatory impulses. (Wolter, 1994)

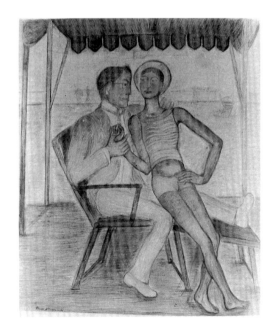

Damit dürften aber die Motive keineswegs erschöpft sein. Der Blick auf die historische Entwicklung der Usurpation eines spezifisch männlichen Kleidungsstückes läßt den Schluß zu, daß auch emanzipatorische Impulse die weibliche Vorliebe für Hosen beeinflussen. (Wolter, 1994)

Im Anschluß an die französische Revolution gab es eine kurze Phase, in der Frauen Hosen anlegen durften, eher eine »Modetorheit«, die bald eingestellt wurde: Man kann darin aber auch ein revolutionäres und emanzipatorisches Signal erblicken.

Nach 1800 kamen die weiblichen »Pantalons« auf: lockere Seidenhosen, die bis zu den Knöcheln reichten. Darüber trug man, dem konventionellen Weiblichkeitsbild folgend, ein langes, locker fallendes, einfaches Kleid.

Diese Art der Frauenbekleidung wird in der ersten Hälfte es 19. Jahrhunderts vielfach variiert und allmählich auch akzeptiert. Nicht selten war sie mit reformerischen und emanzipatorischen Intentionen verknüpft. Die Amerikanerin **Amelia Bloomer** (1818–1894) propagierte eine spezifische Form dieser Kleidung – der »Bloomerism« trug sehr energische, frauenrechtlerische Züge und rief ebenso leidenschaftliche Kritik wie Zustimmung hervor.

Das Übergreifen der Ideen Bloomers nach Europa ging nur sehr zögernd vor sich, und die zweite Hälfte des 19. Jahrhunderts war in den Reformbestrebungen nicht sehr erfolgreich. Auch die zunehmende Berufstätigkeit der Frau brachte keine wesentlichen Neuerungen.

Für die um die Mitte des 19. Jahrhunderts verstärkt einsetzende Frauenbewegung war jedoch die Beibehaltung der Frauenkleidung kein Problem. Um 1855 macht sich allerdings **Johann Baptist Reiter** (1813–1890), ein Wiener Maler des Spätbiedermeier, über *Die Emanzipierte* lustig, die er zigarrenrauchend in Männerkleidung darstellt.

Zweifellos war es eine Sensation, daß die Schriftstellerin **George Sand** (man beachte das männliche Pseudonym) recte Aurore Dupin (1804–1876), nachdem sie 1831 ihren Mann verlassen hatte, Männerkleider trug, für die damalige Gesellschaft ein Skandal.

Ihre Freude beim Anlegen der Männerkleider schildert sie so: »... ich trug einen grauen Hut und eine dicke wollene Halsbinde und sah nun ganz aus wie ein Student im ersten Jahre. Wie ich mich auf die Stiefel freute, vermag ich gar nicht zu sagen ... Mit meinen kleinen, eisenbeschlagenen Absätzen hatte ich einen festen Schritt.« (Holtmont, 1925)

Zur Zeit der frühen Emanzipationsbestrebungen, etwa bei den Suffragetten in England um 1910, war die traditionelle »frauliche« Kleidung noch eine Selbstverständlichkeit.

Wenn ein – im Bild als solcher kaum wahrnehmbarer – Hosenrock von Morin-Bloissier in *Les Modes* von 1908 als »Robe Androgyne« vorgestellt wird, fällt es jedoch schwer, das maskuline Element an der Kreation zu entdecken.

Ein wesentlicher Schritt in diese Richtung erfolgte durch die neuen **Sportarten,** die nicht mehr allein als Domäne des Mannes angesehen werden konnten. Vor allem das Radfahren brachte es mit sich, daß die Frauen allmählich den Überrock über der Hose ablegten und nun erstmalig ganz »maskulin« an die Öffentlichkeit treten durften.

Trotz mancher pragmatischer Motive ist nicht zu übersehen, daß die emanzipierte Frau des 20. Jahrhunderts kaum eine eigenständige »sportliche« Mode entwickelt, sondern die Mode des Mannes übernimmt und sich seinen Attitüden anpaßt.

Den entscheidenden Durchbruch der Frauenhose brachte der Erste Weltkrieg: In den zwanziger Jahren hatte die Männerhose kompromißlos die Frauenwelt erobert. Nicht zuletzt war es das breite Feld der notwendigen Berufstätigkeit der Frau während des Krieges, die diese Wende herbeigeführt hatte.

Die Frauenhose wird jedoch nicht nur der »arbeitenden« Unterschicht zugestanden. 1925 malt **Tamara de Lempicka** (1898–1980) die *Duchesse de la Salle:* eine Frau mit Hosen und Reitstiefeln, mit Sacco und weißem Hemd – freilich mit offenem Kragen und dem typischen »Bubikopf«, der gescheitelten, glatt anliegenden Frisur. Vielleicht verrät noch ein Detail in Lempickas Malerei den Hang zum Androgynen: Da gibt es einige Darstellungen der Kalla, jener großen Blütenform, die gleichsam als eine biologische Analogie zum Linga/Yoni-Symbol angesehen werden kann: Der große phallische Stempel der Blüte taucht tief in das umhüllende Blütenblatt ein.

5.7. Biologische Reversibilität. Transsexualismus

Immer wieder wird der – nicht ganz überzeugende – Versuch unternommen, auch im biologischen Bereich die »kleinen Unterschiede« als unbedeutend darzustellen. Es wird auf die reversible Interpretation der Genitalien bei Mann und Frau verwiesen, etwa auf die »Reziprozität von

71. Johann Baptist Reiter, *Die Emanzipierte,* um 1855.
72. Tamara de Lempicka, *Duchesse de la Salle,* 1925.

71. Johann Baptist Reiter, *The Emancipated Woman.* ca. 1855.
72. Tamara de Lempicka, *Duchesse de la Salle,* 1925.

Following the French Revolution, there was a brief phase when women were allowed to put on trousers, but this was more of the order of a piece of fashionable tomfoolery which soon came to an end. However, it was at the same time a revolutionary and emancipatory signal.

Pantaloons for women came into fashion after 1800: these were loose silk trousers reaching down to the ankles. A long, simple, loosely falling dress was worn over this to accord with the conventional feminine image.

This type of women's clothing was varied many times in the first half of the 19th century, and gradually came to be accepted. It was not infrequently linked to reformist and emancipatory intentions. **Amelia Bloomer** (1818–1894), an American, propagated a specific form of this clothing: »bloomerism« had some very energetic feminist characteristics and evoked criticism as well as approval, both of them equally passionate.

Bloomer's ideas spread to Europe only very gradually, and reformist endeavours were not very successful in the second half of the 19th century. Neither did the fact that more and more women were pursuing careers lead to any great changes.

But the retention of women's clothing did not pose a problem to the women's movement which set in with greater intensity in about the mid-19th century. Nevertheless, **Johann Baptist Reiter** (1813–1890), a Viennese painter of the late Biedermeier style, poked fun at *Die Emanzipierte* (*The Emancipated Woman*) in his work (cf. 1855) of that name. He depicted her smoking a cigar and wearing men's clothes.

A sensation undoubtedly arose when the writer **George Sand** (that is a male pseudonym), whose real name was Aurore Dupin (1804–1876), after leaving her husband in 1831, wore men's clothes, as this was regarded as scandalous in the society of those times.

This is how she described her joy at putting on men's clothes: »... I wore a grey hat and a thick woollen muffler, and now looked just like a male student in his first year. I cannot say how much I was looking forward to wearing boots ... My small, iron-tipped heels gave me a firm footfall.« (Holtmont, 1925)

At the time of the early strivings for emancipation, such as those of the suffragettes in England in around 1910, it was still regarded as self-evident that traditional female clothing should be worn.

Although a divided skirt – scarcely discernible as such in the picture – by Morin – Bloissier was presented as a »Robe Androgyne« in *Les Modes* of 1908, it is still difficult to discover a masculine element in this creation.

A considerable step in this direction resulted from the new **types of sports**, which could no longer be regarded as a male domain. One consequence of cycling, in particular, was that women gradually tended to take off the skirt over their trousers and were now permitted to appear in public in an entirely »masculine« guise.

Despite certain pragmatic motives, the fact cannot be overlooked that the emancipated 20th-century woman scarcely developed any independent »sporting« fashions of her own, but adopted men's fashions and conformed to men's attitudes.

Trousers for women achieved a decisive breakthrough as a result of World War 1. In the 1920s, the world of women had been won over by men's trousers in uncompromising style. Not the least reason for this transformation was the wide range of professional activities necessarily pursued by women during the war.

But it was not merely among the lower »working« classes that trousers for women were permitted. In 1925, **Tamara de Lempicka** (1898–1980) painted the *Duchesse de la Salle*: a woman wearing trousers, riding boots, a sports jacket and a white shirt – but with her neck open and the typical bobbed hairstyle, in which the hair was parted and lay smoothly against the scalp. There is one detail in Lempicka's paintings which may disclose an androgynous tendency: they include some depictions of the calla, a large blossom shape which may be regarded as a kind of biological analogy of the linga/yoni symbol. The large phallic pistil of the blossom plunges far into the surrounding petal.

5.7. Biological Reversibility. Transsexualism

Attempts are repeatedly made, not entirely convincingly, to depict the »small differences« as insignificant in the biological field too. Reference is made to the reversible interpretation of the genitals in men and women, an example being the »reciprocity of vagina and penis«. The secondary sexual characteristics, particularly of women, may also be assigned to the opposite

Vagina und Penis«. Auch die sekundären Geschlechtsmerkmale vor allem der Frau können dem anderen Geschlecht zugeordnet werden. Die Brüste der Frau können phallische Formen annehmen, die Oberschenkel können als Hoden gedeutet werden.

Die Unzufriedenheit mit dem eigenen Geschlecht ist eher bei der Frau als beim Mann anzutreffen, was in einer maskulinen Gesellschaft keineswegs verwunderlich ist: Nicht allein die psychische Situation ist ausschlaggebend, sondern auch die Erwartung einer besseren gesellschaftlichen Stellung.

In der Oper *Der Waffenschmied* von **Albert Lortzing** (1801–1851) drückt es die Marie in der Arie des 3. Aufzuges so aus: »Ich wollt ich wär kein Mädchen, ich wollt ich wär ein Mann«.

Auch die Literatur unseres Jahrhunderts beschäftigt sich mit dem Thema der **Geschlechts- umwandlung**. Der bedeutendste Roman zu diesem Thema ist wohl das 1928 erschienene Buch *Orlando* (1988) von **Virgina Woolf**. Ein Mann durchlebt einige Jahrhunderte – zunächst als Mann und dann als Frau. Das Buch ist eine Huldigung für ihre Freundin, die Schriftstellerin Victoria Sackville-West, genannt Vita. Sie »sollte darin ein junger Adelsherr sein ... jedoch mit einem Wechsel von einem Geschlecht zum anderen«.

Die Verwandlung Orlandos zur Frau erfolgt im Schlafe, ein Vorgang, der wiederholt in der Literatur beschrieben wird. Über eine Woche dauert Orlandos tranceartiger Schlaf. Drei Wesen: Wahrheit, Reinheit und Schamhaftigkeit (nicht ohne Ironie geschildert) umtanzen den »Herzog« und nach einem Trompeten-Tusch »Die Wahrheit« erwacht Orlando: »Er war ein Weib.«

Orlando, bereits Frau geworden, reflektiert über das, was mit ihr geschehen ist: »Und hier könnte es durch eine gewisse Zweideutigkeit ihrer Worte den Anschein haben, sie tadelte beide Geschlechter gleichermaßen, als gehörte sie keinem von ihnen an; und tatsächlich schien sie vorläufig zu schwanken; sie war ein Mann; sie war ein Weib; sie wußte die Geheimnisse, kannte die Schwächen beider: Es war höchst verwirrend und machte einen ganz wirbelig, sich in einem solchen Gemütszustand zu befinden. Die Annehmlichkeiten des Nichtwissens schienen ihr völlig versagt zu sein. Sie war eine vom Sturmwind dahingetriebene Flaumfeder. Und so ist es kein großes Wunder, wenn sie, das eine Geschlecht dem anderen gegenüberstellend und abwechselnd jedes voll der beklagenswertesten Schwächen findend und ungewiß welchem sie selbst angehörte, – wenn sie nahe daran war, aufzuschreien ...«

Die Umwandlung des Geschlechtes indes scheint niemals eine vollständige zu sein: denn begreiflicherweise bleibt in dem neuen Geschlecht etwas, sehr viel sogar, vom alten Geschlecht zurück, solchermaßen die Androgynie bestätigend.

Die Frau »Orlando« begegnet nun doch einem jungen Mann, dem Shelmerdine Esquire, mit dem sie sich verlobt, aber gleichzeitig schoß beiden »ein gräßlicher Verdacht« durch den Kopf: »Du bist ein Weib, Shel!«, rief sie. »Du bist ein Mann, Orlando!«, rief er. (Vgl. Kap. 5.5.7.)

Das Thema des Geschlechtertausches hat in den letzten Jahrzehnten erneut an Bedeutung gewonnen, der Niederschlag davon ist auch in der neueren Literatur, insbesondere der Frauenliteratur zu registrieren. Drei Autorinnen aus der ehemaligen DDR haben sich dieses Themas angenommen (Kirsch, 1980). »Sie lösen, fabulierend, die Geschlechterfixierung und das nicht nur biologische, sondern auch gesellschaftliche Koordinatensystem, das sie geschaffen hat, versuchsweise auf.« Bei **Sarah Kirsch** (geb. 1935) wird die Naturwissenschaftlerin Katharina in den Mann Max verwandelt, ohne daß ihre Beziehung zu ihrem Freund zerbricht (*Blitz aus heiterm Himmel*). In einer Erzählung **Christa Wolfs** (geb. 1929), die im Jahr 1992 spielt, ist die Frau das »Opfer« einer wissenschaftlichen Geschlechtsumwandlung in einen Mann (*Selbstversuch*). Auch bei **Irmtraud Morgner** (1933 bis 1990) verwandelt sich die Frau – Valeska – in einen Mann, aber sie bleibt von ihrem Liebhaber Rudolf akzeptiert (*Gute Botschaft der Valeska*). »Ziel der literarischen Phantasiearbeit ist die Aufhebung der ›Halbmenschen‹ Mann und Frau – nicht etwa der reale Eintausch einer neuen biologischen Geschlechtsidentität ... «

Es geht also nicht allein um eine Art des Transexualismus, bei der der unüberwindbare Wunsch besteht, dem anderen Geschlecht anzugehören, vielmehr künden die literarischen Zeugnisse davon, daß die Ambivalenz der Geschlechtszugehörigkeit durchaus eine neue Ebene des Menschsein erschließen könnte, eben die der Androgynie.

Die tatsächlichen Geschlechtsumwandlungen, die aufgrund der heutigen medizinischen Kenntnisse möglich geworden sind, können als Beispiel des Transsexualismus, kaum jedoch als androgyne Phänomene angesehen werden. Die umgewandelten Personen fühlen sich nicht beiden Geschlechtern verbunden, sondern praktizieren die volle gegengeschlechtliche Identität. Dennoch sind diese Personen ein Zeugnis dafür, daß das biologische Geschlecht und das identifikatorische, psychologische eine Divergenz aufweisen können, die im Extremfall im Transsexualismus mündet.

73. Julian (Jutta) Schutting.

sex. Women's breasts can take on phallic shapes, and the thighs may be interpreted as testicles.

Dissatisfaction with one's one sex is found more frequently among women than men, and this is not at all surprising in a male-dominated society. The decisive factor here is not merely the psychological situation, but also the expectation of a better position in society.

Marie expresses it plainly in an aria in the third act of the opera *Der Waffenschmied* (*The Armourer*) by **Albert Lortzing** (1801–1851): »I would like not to be a girl. I would like to be a man.«

The literature of the 20th century also deals with the topic of **sex change**. The most significant novel on this subject is probably *Orlando* by **Virginia Woolf**, published in 1928. A man lives though a number of centuries, first as a man and then as a woman. The book is an act of homage to Virginia Woolf's friend, the writer Victoria Sackville-West, known as Vita. »In the book, Vita was intended to be a young aristocrat ... but with a changeover from one sex to the other.«

Orlando is transformed into a woman while he is asleep, a process repeatedly described in literature. Orlando's trance-like sleep lasts for over a week. Three beings – Purity, Chastity and Modesty (they are depicted not without irony) – dance around the »Duke« and, after a fanfare of trumpets called »Truth«, Orlando awakes: »... he was a woman.«

Orlando, who has already become a woman, reflects on what has happened to her: »And here it would seem from some ambiguity in her terms that she was censuring both sexes equally, as if she belonged to neither; and indeed, for the time being, she seemed to vacillate; she was man; she was woman; she knew the secrets, shared the weaknesses of each. It was a most bewildering and whirligig state of mind to be in. The comforts of ignorance seemed utterly denied her. She was a feather blown on the gale. Thus it is no great wonder, as she pitted one sex against the other, and found each alternately full of the most deplorable infirmities, and was not sure to which she belonged – it was no great wonder that she was about to cry out ...«

However, the change of sex never seems to be complete, because something, in fact a great deal, of the old sex understandably still remains in the new sex, and this is a confirmation of androgyny.

The woman »Orlando« now does meet a young man called Shelmerdine, Esquire, to whom she becomes betrothed, but at the same time »... an awful suspicion rushed into both their minds simultaneously. ›You're a woman, Shel!‹ she cried. ›You're a mah, Orlando!‹ he cried«. (Cf. chap. 5.5.7.)

The matter of exchanging sexes has once again gained in significance over the past few decades, and this finds expression in more recent literature, especially women's literature. Three women authors from the former East Germany took up this topic. (Kirsch, 1980) »By way of an experiment, they tell stories in which they eliminate firstly the notion of being tied to a single sex, and secondly the system of coordinates, both biological and social, which that notion has created.« **Sarah Kirsch** (born 1935) converts Katharina, a scientist, into a man called Max, without her relationship with her boy friend breaking down as a result (*Blitz aus heiterm Himmel*). **Christa Wolf** (born 1929) sets her story in 1992: the woman is the »victim« of a scientific sex change in which she becomes a man (*Selbstversuch*). **Irmtraud Morgner** (1933–1990) also wrote a story in which Valeska, who is a woman, is converted into a man but continues to be accepted by Rudolf, her lover (*Gute Botschaft der Valeska*). »The aim of this imaginative literary work is to abolish men and women, those ›semi-human beings‹, and there is no notion of really obtaining a new biological sexual identity in exchange for them ...«

Thus this is not merely a kind of transsexualism in which there is an overpowering desire to belong to the opposite sex. Instead, the literary evidence proclaims that the ambivalence of the sex to which one belongs might very well open up a new level of human existence: the level of androgyny.

The real sex changes which have become possible by reason of today's medical knowledge may be regarded as an example of transsexualism, but hardly as androgynous phenomena. People who have had a sex change do not feel linked to both sexes, but exercise a complete identity with the other sex. These people are nonetheless evidence of the fact that there may be a divergency between a person's biological sex on the one hand, and the psychological sex with which the person identifies himself or herself on the other. This divergency may lead to transsexualism in extreme cases.

Only a few of the real medical sex changes enter the public arena. When the woman writer **Jutta Schutting** (born 1937) changed her sex into that of the man called **Julian Schutting**,

Von den realen medizinischen Geschlechtsumwandlungen treten nur wenige in das Licht der Öffentlichkeit. Große Beachtung, obgleich mit erstaunlicher Diskretion behandelt, fand in die Geschlechtsumwandlung der Schriftstellerin **Jutta Schutting** (geb. 1937) in den Mann **Julian Schutting.** Bereits eine Abbildung der Jutta läßt die maskulinen Tendenzen erkennen, wie so häufig bildet eine Art Transvestismus den ersten Ansatz zur Geschlechtermodifikation.

Die vielfältige Problematik mit der Gesellschaft wird nur stellenweise sichtbar. Zum Beispiel dann, wenn **Giovanna Franelli** zu den italienischen Mißwahlen 1992 antritt. Es stellte sich jedoch heraus, daß sie als Giovanni geboren wurde und erst seit einem Jahr Frau ist, womit sie gegen das Reglement verstoßen hatte.

Der Britin **Caroline Cossey,** die früher ein Mann namens Charles war, hat man die Ehe mit einem Mann verweigert, weil ihre Geburtsurkunde auf den ursprünglichen Namen Charles Cossey lautet.

In der Öffentlichkeit stieß das Leben des Amerikaners **Richard Raskind,** des erfolgreichen New Yorker Augenarztes und Tennismeisters, auf großes Interesse. Er fühlt sich durchaus als Frau, und nachts zieht er sich oft Frauenkleider an und streift durch die Straßen. Gleichwohl wird seine Freundin schwanger, und nun beschließt Richard Raskind seine Geschlechtsumwandlung. Die nunmehrige Renée Raskind lernt einen Mann kennen, der sie wieder zum Tennisspielen animiert, aber bei einem Damenturnier wird ihre androgyne Wesenheit offenkundig, und sie kämpft um ihr Frausein. Ihr Leben wurde 1986 unter dem Titel *Zweiter Aufschlag* mit Vanessa Redgrave in der Hauptrolle verfilmt.

1944 wurde in Saarbrücken **Walter Schiffels** »*Im falschen Körper*« – so der Titel des Buches – geboren. Mit großer Konsequenz, mit Intelligenz und einem offenen »Outing« hat Walter seine Umwandlung zu Waltraud betrieben: 1988, nach mehreren Operationen, wurde ihr der amtliche Name Waltraud zugestanden. (Kamprad, 1991). Waltraud Schiffels (1992) hat ihren Bericht sehr offen und literarisch klar dargestellt, aber es geht doch auch daraus hervor, daß »Reste« des Männlichen verbleiben. Schiffels bezeichnet sich sogar als »bisexuell«, und neben ihrer ständigen Freundin als Partnerin haben für sie auch Männer eine erotische Bedeutung, so daß es sogar zu einer sexuellen Begegnung kommt. Diese Persönlichkeitsstruktur hätte insofern androgyne Aspekte, als wiederholt dargelegt wurde, daß in jedem Menschen mehr oder weniger deutliche Spurenelemente des anderen Geschlechtes vorhanden sind.[32]

6. Androgynie in der Kunst der Neuzeit

6.1. Bildende Kunst: Renaissance, Manierismus, Barock, Klassizismus

In der Gegensätzlichkeit als künstlerischem Prinzip sieht Werner Hofmann (1987) eine der Quellen des **Manierismus** – oder besser der Manierismen. Die Medusa in ihrer Ambivalenz (ähnlich wie die hinduistische Kali) wird zum Symbol der Gegensätzlichkeit. »Das Kind, das Mars mit seiner Geliebten (Venus) zeugt, trägt diesen Selbstwiderspruch weiter: Harmonia est discordia concors. Diese klassische Formel wird durchaus folgerichtig auch umgekehrt in cocordia discors ... Einträchtige Zwietracht und zwieträchtige Eintracht – das besagt zweierlei: einmal, daß jedes Ding sein Gegenteil in sich trägt, und zum anderen, daß künstlerische Gebilde aus Gegensätzen zusammengefügt sind ...

Auf Plutarch zurückgreifend und Platons wie Plotins Lehre von den Gegensätzen nützend, definiert Pico delle Mirandola die Schönheit als zusammengesetztes und in sich gegensätzliches Prinzip von Mann und Frau, von Mars und Venus. In der Kunstpraxis leitet sich daraus eines der für den Manierismus kennzeichnenden Themen ab: der Androgyn.«

Das Motiv des Hermaphroditen und der Androgynie schöpft in der **Renaissance** vor allem aus dem Fundus der antiken Mythologie und aus den Schriften Platons. Eines der interessantesten Motive leitet sich aus dem schon zitierten Hermaphroditos-Salmacis-Mythos ab.

Die antike Tradition der Hermaphroditen-Darstellungen wird ziemlich genau fortgeführt. Im oberen Körperteil ist es eine Frau mit Brüsten, dargestellt mit weiblicher Physiognomie und weiblicher Frisur, der Unterleib ist zumeist knabenhaft schmal, immer aber mit einem Penis ausgestattet.

Von der Position her wird der **liegende Hermaphrodit** bevorzugt. Er garantiert einen Überraschungseffekt: Die dominante Rückenansicht ist absolut weiblich modelliert, von der anderen Seite jedoch entdeckt man die männlichen Geschlechtsmerkmale. Das Kunsthistorische

the public paid a great deal of attention, although the matter was treated with surprising discretion. Male tendencies can already be seen in a picture of Jutta, and a kind of transvestism is often the first step towards sexual modification.

The various social problems that arise become apparent only sporadically. One example was when Giovanna Franelli went in for the Italian beauty contests in 1992. It turned out that she was born as Giovanni, had only been a woman for a year, and had thus broken the rules.

The British woman **Caroline Cossey**, who had previously been a man named Charles, was not permitted to marry a man, because her birth certificate was in the original name of Charles.

The life of the American man **Richard Raskind**, a successful New York oculist and tennis champion, met with great public interest. He very much felt that he was a woman, and at night he often used to put on women's clothes and roam the streets. His girl friend nevertheless became pregnant, and Richard Raskind then decided to have a sex change. Now called Renée Raskind, she met a man who encouraged her to play tennis again, but her androgyny became evident during a women's tennis tournament, and she went on to fight for her womanhood. The film called *Second Service*, describing her life, was made in 1986, with Vanessa Redgrave in the main rôle.

Walter Schiffels was born in Saarbrücken in 1944. The book about him is called *Im falschen Körper* (*In the wrong body*). Walter proceeded intelligently and very consistently in working to change himself into Waltraud, and he carried out an open »outing«. In 1988, after several surgical operations, she was allowed the official name Waltraud. (Kamprad, 1991) Waltraud Schiffels (1992) gave her account very openly and in a clear literary style, but it is also evident from it that some traces of the male element remain. Schiffels even describes herself as bisexual and, apart from the permanent girl friend who is her life's partner, men also have an erotic significance where she is concerned, with the result that there is actually a sexual encounter. This personality structure might be said to possess some androgynous aspects, considering that it has repeatedly been made clear that every person has within himself or herself some more or less definite trace elements of the opposite sex.[31]

6. Androgyny in Modern Art

6.1. Pictorial Art: Renaissance, Mannerism, Baroque, Classicism

Werner Hofmann considers (1987) that antithesis as an artistic principle is one of the sources of **Mannerism**, or, to put it better, of Mannerisms. Like the Kali of Hinduism, Medusa, in her ambivalence, becomes a symbol of antithesis. »The child whom Mars and Venus, his loved one, procreate continues this self-contradiction: harmonia est discordia concors. This classical formula is, perfectly logically, also reversed and becomes concordia discors. ... Harmonious discord and discordant harmony are a concept which denotes two things: the first is that every thing contains its opposite within itself, and the second is that artistic creations are assembled from opposites.

In going back to Plutarch and making use of Plato's and Plotin's doctrine of opposites, Pico delle Mirandola defines beauty as an assembled principle which consists of man and woman, Mars and Venus, and is antithetical within itself. The work of artists derives from this a characteristic theme of Mannerism, namely the androgyne.

In the **Renaissance**, the motif of hermaphroditism and androgyny draws mainly on the reserves found in classical mythology and in the writings of Plato. One of the most interesting motifs derives from the myth of Hermaphroditos and Salmacis, referred to above.

The classical tradition of hermaphroditic depictions is continued with considerable accuracy: the upper part of the body is a woman with breasts, represented as having a female physiognomy and a female hairstyle, while the abdomen is usually boyishly narrow, but always has a penis.

The preferred position for a hermaphrodite is recumbent. This guarantees a surprise effect: the dominant rear view is fashioned in an absolutely female way, but the male sexual characteristics can be found by looking from the other side. A depiction of this type, by **Giovanni Francesco Susini** (later than 1639), is preserved in the Museum of Art History in Vienna. The unity, and at the same time the duality, of the bodies is represented on a wedding medallion from the late 17th century. The heads are joined by a lock as in a door, and a child, the product of the union, is seen where the palm leaves cross.

Museum in Wien bewahrt eine solche Darstellung von **Giovanni Francesco Susini** auf (nach 1639). Auf einer Hochzeitsmedaille vom Ende des 17. Jahrhunderts ist die Einheit und gleichzeitig Zweiheit der Körper dargestellt. Ein Schloß verbindet die Köpfe und das Ergebnis der Verschmelzung, ein Kind, zeigt sich an der Kreuzung der Palmenblätter.

Noch eindringlicher ist eine andere Kleindarstellung eines androgynen Wesens: Auf der schon zitierten Medaille des Paduaner Humanisten **Marcantonio Passeri** sind Mann und Frau mit Bauch und Brust aneinandergewachsen, die Köpfe sind zum Rücken gedreht, der Mann trägt den Penis am Gesäß. Zweifellos handelt es sich um eine Interpretation der Platonschen Androgynen. Die Medaille trägt die kaum deutbare Umschrift »Philosophia comite regredimur« – »Mit der Philosophie als Begleiterin kehren wir zurück!«

Die Annäherung an die Androgynie in der Bildnerei der Renaissance erfolgt von beiden Seiten: Weibliches wird männlich interpretiert, und Männliches bekommt weibliche Züge. (Orchard, 1990) Es sind sowohl effeminierte Männer als auch virilisierte Frauen, die die Künstler des Cinquecento bewegen. Inbesondere in den Physiognomien und Körperhaltungen werden die Geschlechter austauschbar.

Im Zusammenhang mit den Darstellungen Christi und der Heiligen (vgl. Kapitel 4.6) wurde bereits auf die ikonographische Austauschbarkeit der Geschlechter hingewiesen.

Das profane »Kultbild« der *Mona Lisa* von **Leonardo da Vinci** (1472–1519) ist mancherlei Deutungen und Manipulationen ausgesetzt. Daß unter den vielen Interpretationen eine androgyne nicht fehlt, überrascht nicht. »... daß sie mit ihrem sprichwörtlichen Lächeln als Androgyne betrachtet und karikiert wurde, ist ein Hinweis auf Leonardos Menschenbild.« (Raehs, 1990)

Der Gedanke, daß es sich bei Leonardos »Gioconda« um einen »weiblich verkleideten Jüngling« (Hocke, 1959) handelt, taucht immer wieder auf. Hocke betont jedoch, »daß für Leonardo kein ›poormonster‹ im Sinne Shakespears dargestellt ist, kein ›seltsames‹ Zwittergebilde für Wunderkabinette, sondern ein kosmisches Symbol: der Zusammenfall des Männlichen und Weiblichen, jeder Polarität in Gott«, womit einmal mehr auch in der Kunst die »coincidentia oppositorum« sichtbar wird.

Die scheinbare Vollkommenheit, die kultisch-ikonische Erhebung zu einem unerreichbaren und unantastbaren Idealbild der abendländischen Kunst hat vor allem die Surrealisten (und später noch die Pop-Künstler) zu einer provokanten Demontage der Ikone gereizt. Die bekannteste Umgestaltung erfolgte 1919 durch **Marcel Duchamp**: Eine Reproduktion wurde mit einem Schnurrbart und einem kleinen Spitzbart versehen. Duchamp selbst kommentierte diesen Vorgang: »Das Seltsame an diesem Schnurr- und Spitzbart ist, daß ... die ›Mona Lisa‹ ein Mann wird. Es ist keine Frau, die als Mann verkleidet ist, es ist ein richtiger Mann.« (Raehs, 1990)

Auch **Salvadore Dalí** (1904–1989) versucht sich surreal-ironisch an der Mona Lisa, und sie bekommt ebenfalls ein Bärtchen verpaßt, es entsteht ein Selbstporträt Dalis.

Durch diese fiktive Geschlechtsumwandlung werden die latenten maskulinen Aspekte sichtbar gemacht, die Geschlechtergegensätze werden, ähnlich wie bei einem Wechselbild, aufgehoben.

Another small depiction of an androgynous being is still more compelling. In the above-mentioned medallion by **Marcantonio Passeri**, a humanist from Padua, a man and a woman are seen joined at belly and breast, their heads are turned towards their backs, and the man's penis is on his posterior. This is undoubtedly an interpretation of the Platonic androgyne. The medallion bears the barely interpretable legend »Philosophia comite regredimur« – »We return with philosophy as our companion«.

Androgyny is approached from both sides in Renaissance sculpture: femininity is interpreted as masculinity, and masculinity is given female traits. (Orchard, 1990) The creativity of the cinquecento artists was aroused both by effeminate women and by virile men. It is particularly in the physiognomies and in the deportment that the sexes became interchangeable.

The iconographical interchangeability of the sexes has already been referred to in connection with the representations of Christ and the Saints (see Chapter 4.6).

The profane cultic image of the »Mona Lisa« by **Leonardo da Vinci** (1472–1519) is the subject of various interpretations and manipulations. It is not surprising that the many interpretations do not fail to include an androgynous one. »... the fact that, what with her proverbial smile, she was regarded as an androgynous being and was caricatured as such is an indication of Leonardo's view of mankind.« (Raehs, 1990)

The idea that Leonardo's »Gioconda« is a »young man disguised as a woman« (Hocke, 1959) occurs repeatedly. But Hocke stresses that, for Leonardo, this depiction was not a »poor monster« in the Shakespearian sense, and was not a »strange« hermaphroditic creation intended for exhibitions of curiosities, but was instead a cosmic symbol: the coincidence, in God, of male and female and of all polarity, and here the »coincidentia oppositorum« once again becomes visible in art.

It was an ostensible perfection, a cultic and iconic elevation of things into an unattainable and untouchable ideal of western art, that aroused the surrealists in particular, and later the pop artists, into provocatively dismantling those icons. The best-known transformation was carried out by **Marcel Duchamp** in 1919: a reproduction was given a moustache and a small goatee beard. Duchamp himself commented as follows on this procedure: »The strange feature of this moustache and goatee is that ... Mona Lisa becomes a man. This is not a woman disguised as a man, but a proper man.« (Raehs, 1990)

Salvador Dalí (1904–1989) also tried a surrealistic, ironic depiction of the Mona Lisa, and she too was given a little beard: a self-portrait of Dali thus came into being.

This fictitious transformation of the sexes makes the latent male aspects visible, and, like in an alternating picture, the contrasts between the sexes are eliminated.

In 1993, Susanne Giroux, a photographic artist from Quebec, propounded a scurrilous theory on the male character of the Mona Lisa: she claimed that, when the mouth is enlarged and the picture is turned through 90°, the rear view of a nude young man can be discerned.

When the classical ideals of beauty were revived in around 1800, the classical depictions were again recalled, and even though explicitly hermaphroditic depictions were rare, the male figures acquired a feminine style which could border on androgyny.

The paintings of **Angelika Kaufmann** (1741–1807) represent »heroes as delicate boys or disguised girls« (Spickernagel, 1985), and A. W. Schlegel expressed the view that the male figures looked as if they »would be only too pleased to have a girl's bosom and, if possible, a girl's hips too«. (Spickernagel, 1985)[32]

6.2. Pictorial Art in the 19th and 20th Centuries

The subject of a two-sexed nature once again became a matter for discussion in the late 19th century, at the »fin de siècle«, when sexuality was increasingly becoming a problem. Symbolism and Art Nouveau provided abundant material for dealing with the »intermediate sexual stages« (Hirschfeld, 1903), and Sigmund Freud's psychoanalysis completely opened up the door to a new view of mankind's sexual structure.

The topic of hermaphroditism is repeatedly encountered in the work of **Aubrey Beardsley**. In 1895, Beardsley drew the title page for the frontispiece of the book of poems called *Love's Mirror*, but the publisher rejected the sheet because he considered the figure depicted to be a hermaphrodite. Gert Mattenklott gave a detailed analysis (1970) of the drawing on the title page, designed by Beardsley, of *Threat and the Path* by Raffalovich. In addition to the evidently hermaphroditic representation of the central figure, Mattenklott also points out that

Eine skurrile These zum maskulinen Charakter der Mona Lisa hat 1993 Susanne Giroux, eine Photokünstlerin aus Quebec, aufgestellt: In einer Vergrößerung des Mundes, und bei einer Drehung um 90° will sie den Rückenakt eines Jünglings erkennen.

Mit der Erneuerung der klassischen Schönheitsideale um 1800 besinnt man sich neuerdings auf die antiken Darstellungen, und wenn auch explizite Hermaphroditendarstellungen selten sind, gewinnen die männlichen Figuren einen femininen Duktus bis an den Rand der Androgynie.

In der Malerei von **Angelica Kaufmann** (1741–1807) werden »Helden wie zarte Knaben oder verkleidete Mädchen« dargestellt und A. W. Schlegel äußert, daß die männlichen Figuren aussähen, als ob sie »gar zu gern einen Mädchenbusen hätten und womöglich auch solche Hüften«. (Spickernagel, 1985) [33]

6.2. Bildende Kunst: 19. und 20. Jahrhundert

Im späten 19. Jahrhundert, im »fin de siècle«, wird mit der zunehmenden Problematisierung der Sexualität, das Thema der Doppelgeschlechtlichkeit erneut zur Diskussion gestellt. Symbolismus und Jugendstil liefern reichhaltiges Material für die Auseinandersetzung mit den »sexuellen Zwischenstufen« (Hirschfeld, 1903), und durch die Psychoanalyse Sigmund Freuds wird das Tor zu einer neuen Sicht der Sexualstruktur des Menschen vollends aufgestoßen.

In der Arbeit von **Aubrey Beardsley** begegnet uns wiederholt das Thema des Hermaphroditischen. Für das Frontispiz des Gedichtbandes *Liebesspiegel* zeichnet Beardsley 1895 das Titelblatt, der Verleger weist das Blatt jedoch zurück, da er in der Figur einen Hermaphroditen erkennt. Gert Mattenklott (1970) widmet der Zeichnung des von Beardsley entworfenen Titelblattes zu *Threat and the Path* von Raffalovich eine ausführliche Analyse. Über die offenkundig hermaphroditische Darstellung der zentralen Figur hinaus verweist Mattenklott auf die phallische Symbolik der Kerzen, auf die Assoziation zum androgynen Dionysos und Priaps durch die Weintrauben, auf die Verwandtschaft zu Amor und zu den Engeln, »... eine Symbiose von Engel und Christus, von Eros und Apoll, von antikem Mythos und christlicher Religion ...«

Völlig eindeutig als Hermaphrodit erkennbar ist die diabolische Gestalt, die Beardsley für das Titelblatt von *Salome* gezeichnet hat. Die Illustration Beardleys zu Malorys *Morte d'Arthur* zeigt einen Hermaphroditen, der, in einem Rosengestrüpp gefangen, gleichwohl die Blüten liebkost.[34]

Aus der Zeit des Jugendstils, aus der Kunst der Wiener Secession, sind uns Darstellungen von Androgynen bekannt, die jedoch nur wenig überzeugen. Differenzierung und Spannung der Geschlechter, das Weib als »femme fatale«, eine neue Artikulation des Weiblichen, waren die eigentlichen künstlerischen Themen, die den Hermaphroditen in den Hintergrund drängten.

Erst im Vorfeld des Surrealismus erwacht neuerlich das Interesse an dem Thema. **Marc Chagall** (1887–1985) widmet 1911/12 ein Bild seinem Freund Guillaume Apollinaire: Es ist ein ähnliches Zwitterwesen dargestellt wie jenes der Alchimisten, doch ist die rechte Seite nun der Frau vorbehalten.

Auch **Niki de Saint Phalle** (geb. 1930) ordnet die rechte Seite der Weiblichkeit zu. *Adam und Eva* nennt sie eine Skulptur, die 1976 entstanden ist, und sie bekräftigt damit die These, wonach der erste Mensch als androgyn gedacht werden kann.

Eine abstruse Komposition, die deutlich die sexuelle Überlappung illustriert, ist die Zeichnung von **Yves Tanguy** (1900–1955), *A ma petite chaussure son Ami Yves Tanguy* aus dem Jahre 1932.[35] »Ein Zwittergeschöpf, das sich in der Art der Cadavre-exquis-Zeichnungen trotz des fließenden Duktus in Schichten von unten nach oben lesen läßt. Ein nach links blickender weiblicher Kopf, aus dessen Haarkrause sich zwei Schamlippen herausschälen. Hutähnlich steht auf dem Kopf eine Figurine, auf deren Nacken ein steifer, spargeldünner Phallus sitzt. Das alles wird von einem mannweiblichen Körper gefaßt, aus dessen Mittelvertikale eine Trennlinie hervorwächst, die sich in einen riesigen Schwanz verfestigt, der zugleich einen weiblichen Körper krönt. Die sorgfältige Linearität kontrastiert mit dunklen, moosigen Flecken, die als erotisierende Körperöffnungen zu lesen sind. Selten wurde der Androgyn-Gedanke so verwirrend komprimiert dargestellt ...« (Hofmann, 1987)

Die merkwürdige »Doppelkodierung« von Penis und Figur ist uns schon aus den archaischen Kulturen bekannt und begegnet uns öfter in der Kunst der Gegenwart. Als *Fillette* bezeichnet die Amerikanerin **Louise Bourgeois** (geb. 1911) eine 60 cm hohe »Figur«, die eindeutig als erigierter Penis zu erkennen ist. Gleichzeitig soll es ein junges Mädchen sein, und wir

82. Aubrey Vincent Beardsley, *Der Liebesspiegel*, 1895.
83. Aubrey Vincent Beardsley, Titelblatt zu *Salome* von Oscar Wilde, 1894. Ausschnitt.
84. Marc Chagall, *Hommage à Guillaume Apollinaire*, 1911.

82. Aubrey Vincent Beardsley, *the Love's Mirror*, 1895.
83. Aubrey Vincent Beardsley, title page of *Salome* by Oscar Wilde, 1894. Detail.
84. Marc Chagall, *Hommage à Guillaume Apollinaire*, 1911.

there is phallic symbolism in the candles, that the grapes provide an association with the androgynous Dionysos and Priapus, and that there is an affinity with Amor and the angels, »... a symbiosis of angel and Christ, of Eros and Apollo, of classical myth and Christian religion ...«

The diabolical figure which Beardsley drew for the title page of »Salome« is very clearly identifiable as a hermaphrodite. Beardsley's illustration for Malory's *Morte d'Arthur* portrays a hermaphrodite who, although caught in a thicket of roses, is nevertheless caressing the blossoms.[33]

Depictions of androgynes, albeit not very convincing, are known from the Art Nouveau period and the art of the Viennese Secession. The real artistic themes, which thrust the hermaphrodite into the background, were: the differentiation and tension between the sexes; woman as »femme fatale«; and a new articulation of femininity.

Interest in this topic only arose again at the stage preceding surrealism. In 1911/12, **Marc Chagall** (1887–1985) dedicated a picture to his friend Guillaume Apollinaire: it depicts a hermaphroditic being similar to that of the alchemists, but the right-hand side is now reserved for the woman.

Niki de Saint Phalle (born 1930) also assigned the right-hand side to femininity. She gave the name of *Adam and Eve* to a sculpture created in 1976, thus corroborating the theory according to which the first human being can be thought of as having been androgynous.

An abstruse composition which clearly illustrates an overlapping of the sexes is the drawing *A ma petite chaussure son Ami Yves Tanguy* (1932) by **Yves Tanguy** (1900–1955).[34] »A hermaphroditic creature which, despite the flowing style, can be read in layers from the bottom upwards, in the manner of the Cadavre exquis drawings. A leftwards-looking female head, out of whose frizzy hair two vulval wings appear. A figurine, in the nape of whose neck there is a stiff phallus as thin as an asparagus, stands on this head like a hat. All this is enclosed by a male-female body from whose central vertical a dividing line grows and solidifies to form an enormous penis which at the same time crowns a female body. Painstaking linearity contrasts with dark mossy patches which are to be interpreted as being sexually stimulating bodily orifices. Rarely has the androgynous idea been depicted in such a confusingly compressed way ...« (Hofmann, 1987)

A strange »double coding« of penis and human figure is known from archaic cultures and is frequently encountered in present-day art. The American woman artist **Louise Bourgeois** (born 1911) gives the name of *Fillette* to a figure, 60 cm high, which is clearly discernible as an erect penis. It is at the same time meant to be a young girl, and we are reminded of the archaic anthrophallic depictions which unite, in one figure, a woman's body and a phallus.

An initial step towards a spatial and structural interpretation, a matter of particular importance in architecture, is to be found in the work of **Hans Bellmer** (1902–1975). Androgyny is a major preoccupation of Bellmer's, as can be plainly seen from his »Puppen« (»Dolls«) and his erotic drawings, and we must agree with Peter Webb, who (1986) says the following about the sculpture called *Maschinengewehr im Zustand der Gnade* (*Machine Gun in a State of Grace*) – 1937, reconstructed in 1961): »This extraordinary creation consists of a small bullet surrounded by rods. The rods are related to various parts of the anatomy, such as: a woman's head which also resembles a vulva; breasts; and a few ambiguous elements which suggest not only parts of the female body but also male testicles. ... The various elements are male and female. ... This androgyne was used to cast doubt upon that pleasant conflict between male and female upon which our culture is based.«

Bellmer's attitude towards double sexuality may be illustrated by an interpretation given by Wieland Schmied (1973): »Bellmer takes the view that only things which exist in a double way exist at all, and that everything that appears can only be one part coming from the other; this is a dualistic view of the world, a view in which everything has its equivalent. Bellmer says: An object which is identical only to itself has no reality.

The axis upon which Bellmer's dualistic principle rests, or around which it moves, is the god of love. It is the desire felt by one form which longs for the presence of the other form, it is the desire which turns virtuality into reality, it is, to put it plainly, the desire which conjures up the male and female sexes simultaneously and makes them coincide in the final fulfilment of dualism.« (Schmied, 1973)

According to Bellmer, »Male and female have become ... interchangeable images; each of them aims at the amalgam of both of them, namely the hermaphrodite«. (Bellmer, Gorsen, 1969)

erinnern uns der archaischen anthrophallischen Darstellungen, die (Frauen)-Körper und Phallus in einer Figur vereinigen.

Einen ersten Schritt zu einer räumlich-strukturellen Interpretation, die für die Architektur besonders wichtig ist, finden wir bei **Hans Bellmer** (1902–1975). Aus seinen »Puppen« und aus den erotischen Zeichnungen ist deutlich abzulesen, daß für Bellmer das Androgyne ein wichtiger Gedankenkomplex ist, und wir müssen Peter Webb (1986) rechtgeben, der über die Skulptur *Maschinengewehr im Zustand der Gnade* (1937, rekonstruiert 1961) sagt: »Diese außergewöhnliche Schöpfung besteht aus einer kleinen, von Stäben umgebenen Kugel. Die Stäbe sind mit verschiedenen anatomischen Teilen verbunden, wie beispielsweise einem Frauenkopf, der auch einer Vulva gleicht, Brüsten und ein paar doppeldeutigen Gliedern, die sowohl weibliche Körperteile als auch männliche Hoden suggerieren ... Die verschiedenen Elemente sind männlich und weiblich ... Dieser Androgyn wurde benutzt, um den angenehmen Zwiespalt zwischen männlich und weiblich, auf der unsere Kultur fußt, in Frage zu stellen.«

Eine Interpretation von Wieland Schmied (1973) mag die Haltung Bellmers zur Doppelgeschlechtlichkeit noch verdeutlichen. »Bellmer meint: Nur was in doppelter Weise existent ist, ist überhaupt existent; alles was erscheint, kann nur eins aus dem anderen dasein – im Sinne eines dualistischen Weltbildes, in dem alles seine Entsprechung hat. Er sagt: Das Objekt, das nur mit sich selbst identisch ist, bleibt ohne Wirklichkeit.«

»Die Achse, auf der das dualistische Prinzip Bellmers ruht – oder um die es sich bewegt – ist der Eros. Es ist die Begierde der einen Form, die die andere herbeisehnt, es ist die Begierde, die das Virtuelle zum Reellen macht, es ist, um ganz deutlich zu sein, die Begierde, die die Gleichzeitigkeit männlichen und weiblichen Geschlechts hervorruft, sie zur Deckung bringt als endliche Erfüllung des Dualismus«. (Schmied, 1973)

Nach Bellmer sind »Das Männliche und das Weibliche ... vertauschbare Bilder geworden; das eine wie das andere zielen zu ihrem Amalgam hin, dem Hermaphroditen«. (Bellmer/Gorsen, 1969)

Ein schönes psychoanalytisches Spektrum erschließt sich in der italienischen »**pittura metafisica**«.

Dem Surrealismus nahestehend ist es eine Malerei, die geprägt ist von einer traumhaft erscheinenden Symbolik. Ihr Hauptvertreter ist **Giorgio de Chirico** (1888–1978). In seinen Bildern ist in Gebäuden, Plätzen, Arkaden, Mauern, Bahnhöfen, Lokomotiven, Uhren, Skulpturen und wenigen menschlichen Figuren ein enigmatisches Vokabular des Geschlechtlichen dargestellt, spannungsreiche Bezugsfelder, die nach einer tiefenpsychologischen Deutung verlangen.

Neben ihm sind die Arbeiten von **Carlo Carrà** (1881–1966) von Interesse. 1927 malt er das Bild *Dopo il tramonto*. Ein phallischer Turm, am Rande des Meeres, ein Boot – Vulva-Symbol – und ein einsamer Platz sind die beziehungsvollen Versatzstücke des Bildes, das eine gleichsam androgyne Landschaft bildet. »L'idolo ermafrodito« von Carlo Carrà ist freilich kein Hermaphrodit, da ihm jedwede Geschlechtsmerkmale fehlen, und er wäre daher als geschlechts-loses Wesen zu bezeichnen, wenn man ihn nicht spontan als männliches Wesen identifiziert.

Pierre Klossowski wird noch als Romanautor zu erwähnen sein. (Vgl. Kap.6.4). Seine Erzählung vom Baphomet hat er selbst illustriert. Im Bild *Le Baphomet offrant ses services au Grand Maître*[36] (1982) ist der Androgyn in einer subtilen Buntstiftzeichnung dargestellt.

Viktor Brauner greift auf uralte Mythen zurück und zeichnet 1961 eine *Selbstbefruchtende Mutterfigur*, die jede sexuelle Deutlichkeit vermissen läßt. Zwar sind Köpfe, Gliedmaßen, Augen, Mund vielleicht auch eine Figur zu erkennen, aber der Akt der Selbstbefruchtung ist in der Tradition der großen Mythologien als das Ideal der Selbstvollkommenheit im transzendenten Sinne anzusehen.

Wolfgang Hutter (geb. 1929) – in der legitimen Nachfolge des Surrealismus – und als einer der Hauptvertreter des »Wiener phantastischen Realismus« anzusehen, findet in seinen Bildern zu einer traumhaften Synthese zwischen zarten, erotischen Frauengestalten und hypertrophen, vegetativen Formationen. Einige Male tauchen in den Blumen- und Blattlandschaften auch Hermaphroditen mit der Fülle des Frauenhaares auf. Ganz im Sinne der Antike dominiert der weibliche Habitus, doch sind sie mit einem erigierten Penis ausgestattet.

Zwei Darstellungen von **Rudolf Hausner** (1914–1995) setzen sich mit dem Thema des Hermaphroditen auseinander: In dem Bild *Forum der einwärts gewendeten Optik* aus dem Jahre 1948 ist der Künstler selbst als Hermaphrodit zu sehen, jedoch reziprok zu den meisten antiken Darstellungen: Der Oberkörper ist männlich, während der Unterleib, durch die breiten Hüften und das Geschlechtsorgan ausgewiesen, weiblich ist. Die rechte Hand balanciert zwei

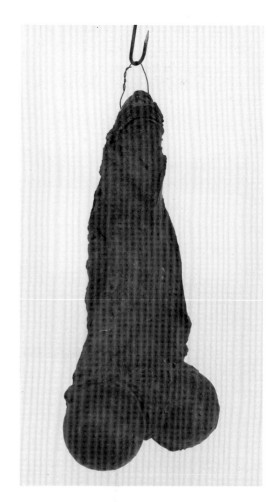

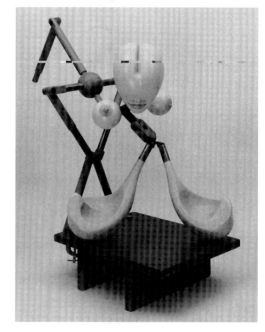

85. Louise Bourgeois, *Fillette*, 1968.
86. Hans Bellmer, *Maschinengewehr im Zustand der Gnade*, 1937, 1961.
87. Yves Tanguy, *A ma petite chaussure*, 1932.
88. Carlo Carrà, *Dopo il tramonto*, 1927.

85. Louise Bourgeois, *Fillette,* 1968.
86. Hans Bellmer, *Machine Gun in the State of Grace*, 1937, 1961.
87. Yves Tanguy, *A ma petite chaussure*, 1932.
88. Carlo Carrà, *Dopo il tramonto*, 1927.

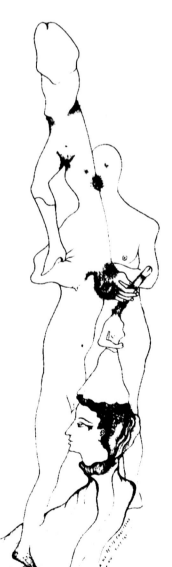

A beautiful psychoanalytical spectrum opens up in the Italian »**pittura metafisica**«. This is a kind of painting which is close to surrealism and is characterized by an apparently dreamlike symbolism. **Giorgio de Chirico** (1888–1978) is its chief exponent. His pictures portray an enigmatic vocabulary of sexuality seen in buildings, squares, arcades, walls, railway stations, locomotives, clocks, sculptures and few human figures. These are tension-ridden fields of reference which require to be interpreted in terms of depth psychology. Apart from Chirico's works, those by **Carlo Carrà** (1881–1966) are also of interest. His painting *Dopo il tramonto* dates from 1927. A phallic tower by the seashore, a boat which is a vulval symbol, and a lonely square, constitute the setting, rich in references, of this picture, in which a kind of androgynous landscape is created. »L'idolo ermafrodito« by Carlo Carrà is admittedly not a hermaphrodite, as he has no sexual characteristics, and if he were not spontaneously identified as a male, he would therefore be called a sexless being.

Pierre Klossowski will be mentioned as a novelist later on (see chapter 6.4) He himself illustrated his story of Baphomet. *Le Baphomet offrant ses services au Grand Maître*[35] (1982) is a subtle drawing in crayons, depicting that androgyn.

In a reversion to ancient myths, **Viktor Brauner** drew a *Selbstbefruchtende Mutterfigur* (*Mother Fertilizing Herself*, 1961), but there is no sexual clarity here. It is true that heads, limbs, eyes, mouth, and perhaps also a human figure, are discernible but, in the tradition of the great mythologies, the act of self-fertilization is here to be regarded in a transcendental sense, as being the ideal of self-perfection.

Wolfgang Hutter (born 1929) is part of the legitimate succession of surrealism and is to be regarded as a leading protagonist of »Viennese fantastic realism«. In his pictures he finds a way of depicting a dreamlike synthesis between delicate, erotic women figures and hypertrophic, vegetative formations. Hermaphrodites with abundant feminine hair sometimes appear here in the landscapes of flowers and leaves. The female body posture dominates, as in classical antiquity, but they have an erect penis.

Two depictions by **Rudolf Hausner** (1914–1995) deal with the topic of the hermaphrodite. In the picture called *Forum der einwärts gewendeten Optik* (*Forum of an inwards-turning Perspective*) dating from 1948, the artist himself is to be seen in the form of a hermaphrodite, but this is the reverse of most of the classical depictions: the upper part of the body is male, while the abdomen, as is shown by the wide hips and the sexual organ, is female. Two eggs are balanced in the right hand. In another picture called *Adam selbst* (*Adam himself*, 1960), the male figure – once again it is the artist himself – is carrying a woman's body within himself, as in a magical pregnancy.

The hermaphrodite depicted by **Francesco Clemente** (born 1952) follows the tradition of Hinduism and the alchemists. The figure is divided vertically, and the right-hand side is re-

Eier. Auf einem anderen Bild *Adam selbst* (1960) trägt die männliche Figur – wieder ist es der Künstler selbst – wie in einer magischen Schwangerschaft einen Frauenkörper in sich.

Francesco Clemente (geb. 1952) schließt mit seinem Hermaphroditen an die Tradition des Hinduismus und der Alchemisten an und teilt die Figur vertikal, die rechte Seite ist der Frau vorbehalten. In wohl ironisierender Weise fügt Clemente in achtteiligen Tableaus das konventionelle Inventar des weiblichen und des männlichen Alltags an.

Auf der »alternativen« Ausstellung zur documenta 9 von 1992 in Kassel hat in Hann. Münden ein chinesischer Künstler, **Liang Sun** eine eigenartige Darstellung präsentiert. Auf dem einen Bild sehen wir ein androgynes Wesen in neuer, von der traditionellen Darstellung abweichenden Form: Das Wesen hat zwei geschlechtslose Köpfe, einander zugewandt, zwei Brüste, voneinander abgewandt, und ein männliches Geschlechtsorgan. Darüber schwebt ein Hermaphrodit in der konventionellen antiken Darstellungsart. Am Rande des Bildes ist ein Androgyn mit einem Phantasie-Tierkopf dargestellt. Tiersymbole und Masken füllen die Bildfläche.

Manfred Scharpf (geb. 1945) gehört zu den wenigen zeitgenössischen Künstlern, die ihr Werk explizit von der Idee des Hermaphroditischen und Androgynen bestimmt sehen. Ein großer, blauer Ring etwa wird von einer Schwertklinge überlagert und gleichzeitig durchstoßen. Vor das goldgerahmte und mit magischen Zeichen versehene Bild stellt Scharpf eine Tonschale mit einem Tonei, eine reziproke Paraphrase des Bildinhaltes. Scharpf sieht sich aber auf den Spuren der Alchimisten, wenn er seine Bilder mit symbolischen Materialien wie etwa Eisen/Kupfer, Silber/Gold, Wismut/Schwefel gestaltet. In den »Materialbildern« versucht er die Synthese aus Geist, Bewußtsein und Material und in dieser Weise das Androgyne in seiner allgemeinen Formulierung zu realisieren. Die Material-Bilder werden mit Objekten arrangiert, so daß nach Scharpf »Heilräume« entstehen.

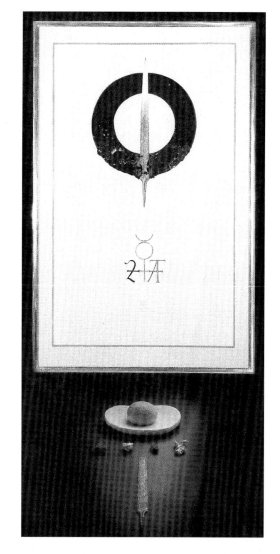

Die skulpturale Tradition der hermaphroditischen Darstellungen der Antike wird in unserem Jahrhundert kaum aufgegriffen, eher schließen die Künstler an die (alchimistischen) Darstellungen des 16. und 17. Jahrhunderts an.

Gleichsam als eine zeitgenössische plastische Ausbildung der alten Androgynvorstellungen kann die Arbeit von **Hans Turba** (geb. 1942) gelten: Ein Torso läßt deutlich erkennen, daß Mann und Frau zu einer Einheit verschmolzen sind.

Die plastische Auseinandersetzung dialektischer Formprinzipien findet auf einer anderen Ebene statt. Auch wenn wir nicht zwingend »Körper« und »konvex« dem Männlichen und »Raum« und »konkav« dem Weiblichen zuordnen können, so sind es doch entscheidende morphologische Kategorien der Dreidimensionalität, die in der Architektur, aber auch in der Plastik abgehandelt werden.

Die späten Skulpturen von **Henry Moore** (1898–1986) kreisen um den Formkomplex konkav-konvex, innen-außen. Doch ist die Synthese dieser Prinzipien in ihrer Bedeutung weit über eine formalistische Übung hinaus zu deuten. Moore gelingt es, die formalen Dichotomien zu einer bruchlosen Einheit zusammenzuführen, so daß tatsächlich eine virtuose »coincidentia« entsteht, bei der die Elemente zwar nicht eliminiert sind, aber im einzelnen nicht mehr abgegrenzt werden können.

Eine andere höchst überraschende coincidentia können wir aus der Skulptur von **Jacques Lipschitz** (1891–1973) herauslesen. *Der Schrei* (1928/29) erlaubt eine doppelte Ausdeutung: Das verschlungene Liebespaar, zu einem Wesen verschmolzen, kann auch als Tier mit offenem Rachen gesehen werden.

Die Unmöglichkeit, ein oder zwei Wesen zu unterscheiden – so sehr sind sie ineinandergeflossen, ohne ihr Wesen aufzugeben – kennzeichnet auch die Arbeit *Der Kuss* von **Max Ernst** (1891–1976) aus dem Jahre 1927. Selbst die Farben, das Blau des Himmels und das Braun der Erde haben teil an der großen Synthese.

Textile Produkte haben nicht nur von jeher eine enge Beziehung zum Kultischen, sondern auch zum Erotischen. In den Arbeiten von **Edda Seidl-Reiter** (geb. 1940), wird dies besonders deutlich, und ihre unschlüssige Benennung von einigen Werken könnte als androgyner Ansatz verstanden werden. Eine Arbeit von 1975 betitelt sie mit *männlich (weiblich?)* und eine andere von 1976 mit *weiblich (männlich?)*. Beide Arbeiten setzen sich mit den Archetypen von Kreis und Quadrat auseinander. In einem quadratischen Stahlrahmen (männlich?) ist einmal ein Kreis eingespannt (weiblich?), ein anderes Mal ein Quadrat. Und in beiden Fällen haben diese Figuren wieder Öffnungen: Einmal quillt eine dicke Schnur heraus (oder hinein?, männlich?), das andere Mal ist es ein harter Metallring (weiblich?). Die Fragezeichen der Bildtitel sind also durchaus berechtigt, denn die metaphorischen Elemente weisen mindestens zwei Deutungsebenen auf und sind schon dadurch androgynen Charakters.

89. Manfred Scharpf, *Hermaphroditisches Bild*,
1990.
90. Francesco Clemente, *Hermaphrodit*, 1985.
91. Rudolf Hausner, *Forum der einwärts gewendeten Optik*, 1948. Ausschnitt.
92. Wolfgang Hutter, *Hermaphrodit mit Zeremo-
nienstab*, 1970. Ausschnitt.

89. Manfred Scharpf, *Hermaphroditic Picture*,
1990.
90. Francesco Clemente, *Hermaphrodite*, 1985.
91. Rudolf Hausner, *Forum of an Inwards-Turning
Perspective*, 1948. Detail.
92. Wolfgang Hutter, *Hermaphrodite with a Cere-
monial Baton*, 1970. Detail.

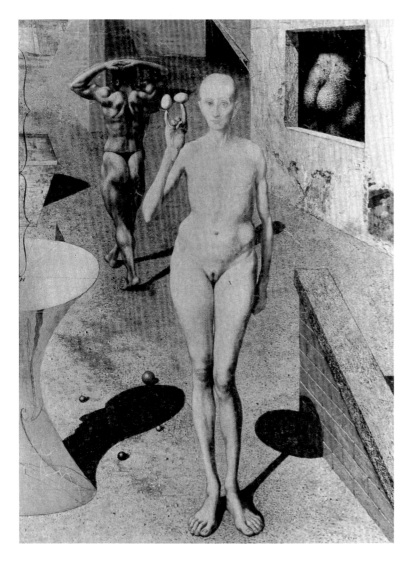

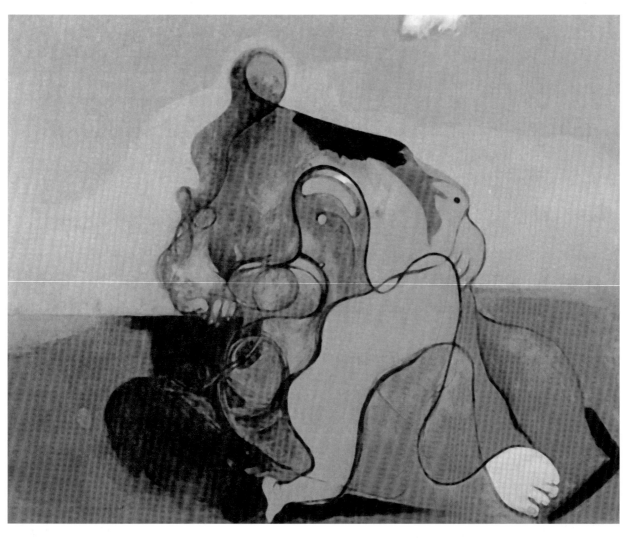

served for the woman only. There are tableaux in eight parts in which Clemente, probably iron- ically, adds the conventional inventory of women's and men's daily lives.

At a location in Hann. Münden, the Chinese artist **Liang Sun** presented a strange creation at the »alternative« exhibition held on the occasion of the »documenta 9« exhibition mounted in Kassel in 1992. In one picture, we see an androgynous being in a new form deviating from the traditional representation: this being has two sexless heads turned towards one another, two breasts turned away from one another, and a male sexual organ. Above this there hovers a hermaphrodite, depicted in the conventional classical way. An androgyn with a fantastic animal's head is seen at the edge of the picture. The surface of the picture is filled with masks and animal symbols.

Manfred Scharpf (born 1945) is one of the few contemporary artists who regard their works as explicitly determined by the idea of hermaphroditism and androgyny. For example, a large blue ring is simultaneously superimposed by a sword blade and pierced by that sword blade. In front of this gold-framed picture with its magic symbols, Scharpf places a clay bowl containing a clay egg, a reciprocal paraphrase of the picture's content. But Scharpf considers that he is on the trail of the alchemists when creating his pictures by the use of such symbolic materials as iron/copper, silver/gold, and bismuth/sulphur. In these »material pictures«, he is trying to achieve a synthesis of spirit, consciousness and material, and in this way to attain a general formulation for androgyny. The material pictures are seen in an arrangement with other objects and, according to Scharpf, »healing rooms« are thereby created.

The sculptural tradition of the hermaphroditic depictions of classical antiquity has scarcely been continued in the 20th century, and instead artists tend to follow up the (alchemic) repre- sentations of the 16th and 17th centuries.

A work by **Hans Turba** (born 1942) can be regarded as a kind of contemporary sculptural development of the old androgynous ideas: a single torso makes it plain that man and woman have become amalgamated into one.

When dialectic principles relating to different shapes are expressed in sculpture, this takes place on another level. Even if we cannot conclusively assign »body« and »convex« to the male element and »space« and »concave« to the female, these are nonetheless essential mor- phological categories under which three-dimensionality is classified, and they are treated of in architecture and also in sculpture.

The later sculptures of **Henry Moore** (1898–1986) rotate around the concave-convex, in- ward-outward complex of shapes. But the synthesis of these principles signifies much more than a mere formalistic exercise. Moore succeeds in combining the formal dichotomies into an uninterrupted whole, so that in fact a masterly »coincidentia« arises whose elements, although not eliminated, can no longer be individually delimited.

Another very surprising »coincidentia« can be read into a sculpture by **Jacques Lipschitz** (1891–1973). *Der Schrei* (*The Shout*) (1928/29) permits a double interpretation: the entwined loving couple, united into a single being, can also be interpreted as an animal with its jaws open.

The impossibility of distinguishing whether there is one being or two, because of the extent to which they have flowed into one another without renouncing their individual beings, is also characteristic of the work by **Max Ernst** (1891–1976) called *Der Kuss* (*The Kiss*, 1927). Even the colours, the blue of the sky and the brown of the earth, take part in the great synthesis.

Textile products and textile art have since time immemorial been closely related not only to ritual but also to eroticism. This becomes especially clear in the works of **Edda Seidl- Reiter** (born 1940), and the inconclusive names she gives to some of her works might be understood as an androgynous tendency. She gives the title of *männlich (weiblich?)* (*male (fe- male?)*) to a work dating from 1975, and that of *weiblich (männlich?)* (*female (male?)*) to one from 1976. Both these works deal with the archetypes of circle and square. On one occasion a circle (female?), and on another occasion a square, is set within a square steel frame (male?). In both cases, these figures have orifices: a thick cord protrudes from an orifice (or passes into it?, male?) in one case, and in the other the orifice is a hard metal ring (female?). Thus the question marks in the pictures' titles are certainly justified, because the metaphorical elements can be interpreted on at least two levels, and are androgynous in character for that reason alone.

There is another motif which found favour with Seidl-Reiter from about 1972 onwards: the pig- tail. This hair sometimes really does end in a small plait, so that a plainly feminine association with luxuriant hair intrudes upon the onlooker's mind, but in general this woman artist regards

Noch ein anderes Motiv ist bei Seidl-Reiter seit etwa 1972 beliebt: der gedrehte Zopf. Manchmal endet er tatsächlich in einem geflochtenen Zöpfchen, so daß sich die – eindeutig weibliche – Assoziation zu üppigem Haar aufdrängt, ganz allgemein gilt aber das Weiche für die Künstlerin als vorwiegend weiblich. Das Frauenhaar gewinnt in der kraftvollen Verdichtung phallischen Charakter, und in Verbindung mit der Öffnung ist eine Penetration dargestellt.

Sehr verschlüsselt ist der Begriff der Androgynie bei **Allessandro Mendini** (geb. 1931). Eine Installation mit dem Titel *Androgyner Raum* von 1981 zeigt ein halbnacktes weibliches Wesen in einem geometrischen Raum. Durch kleine Öffnungen schieben sich Kußmünder, mit Efeu verziert.

Das Werk von **Walter Pichler** (geb. 1936) ist wie kaum ein anderes dazu angetan, die Präsenz des Geschlechtlichen im Übergangsbereich von Architektur zur Skulptur zu demonstrieren.

Die frühen Arbeiten von 1963 setzen sich mit unterirdischen Städten auseinander: Die vollkommene Geborgenheit der mütterlichen Erde wird gesucht, aber einzelne Bauteile ragen über die Erde hinaus und bergen die Behausungen der »Eliten«.

Bei einem anderen unterirdischen Gebäude stellt sich Pichler einen beweglichen Kern vor, und er baut davon ein Modell, eine eindrucksvolle Skulptur aus Beton und Zinn, der Kern kann tatsächlich ausgefahren werden. Es ist das machtvoll-männliche Element, das sich, allmählich erigierend, aus dem mütterlichen Schoß herauslöst, herauswächst, um wieder darin zu versinken.

Es bedarf keiner androgynen Spekulation bei der Deutung einer Zeichnung aus dem Jahre 1972: *Zwei Figuren, nach Angabe von Pierre gezeichnet* sind ineinander verschlungen, tatsächlich zu einer Einheit geworden, lediglich in der Farbzeichnung erkennen wir eindeutig, daß links eine Frau, rechts ein Mann steht, ergänzt durch einen großen Penis. Stäbe und Äste durchbohren und verbinden gleichzeitig die Motive.

Im *Schlafsaal* aus dem Jahre 1968 sind vier Betten aufgestellt, mit weißem Linnen überzogen. Bei einer Liegestatt läßt sich ein »Hosentürl« abknöpfen, und es werden, perfekt und glänzend, zwei Metallstäbe und -kugeln sichtbar: Das Männliche ist eingebettet in jungfräulich weißes Linnen. Auf einem anderen Bett liegt eine *Skulptur im Organza Kleid*, die Interpretationen auf verschiedenen Ebenen provoziert. Zum einen ist es eine weibliche Figur mit gespreizten Beinen und mit reizvoller Unterwäsche ausgestattet, zum anderen erinnert das Objekt an einen Doppel-Penis, einen Godmiché, wie er für verschiedene Sonderformen geschlechtlicher Befriedigung verwendet wird. Ein Vorbild dieser Figuration können wir in den prähistorischen Lochstäben sehen (vgl. Kap. 3.1), wie etwa im Fund aus der Gorge d' Enfer, der eindeutig einen Doppelphallus erkennen läßt. Nicht zuletzt werden wir an jene androgynen Symbole gemahnt, wie sie in der Form eines Y auf hermaphroditischen Darstellungen des 17. Jahrhunderts als Symbol des Einen und des Doppelten erscheinen.

In einer Arbeit aus dem Jahre 1995 – die Zeichnung harrt noch der Umsetzung in die Realität – hat sich Pichler noch mehr von der sexuellen Symbolik entfernt und ist zur Allgemeingültigkeit sich ergänzender Wesenheiten vorgedrungen: In einem Haus steht auf einem Holzblock eine metallische »Schlucht«, davor auf einer Schiene ein »Grat«, der sich auf der Schiene der Schlucht nähert, um schließlich in ihr zu münden, in sie einzugehen, sie auszufüllen: eine vollendete »coincidentia«.

Der Doppelphallus begegnet uns nicht nur bei Walter Pichler. Als *Blumengeschmückter Janus* bezeichnet **Louise Bourgeois** eine Bronzeplastik, die deutlich die Verdoppelung des Penis erkennen läßt.

An der Grenze von Kunst, Provokation und Objektwelt steht eines der *ready made* von **Marcel Duchamp**: Ein Urinoir wird um 90° gekippt, zum Kunstobjekt erklärt und als *Fontaine* bezeichnet. Damit ist im Französischen nicht nur der Springbrunnen gemeint, sondern im Vulgärgebrauch auch der Harnstrahl. So gesehen ist die Fontaine weiblich in der Schale und männlich im Anschlußstück.

6.3. Objektwelt. Design

Die Androgynie in Kunst und Architektur hat ein hohes Maß an Symbolbildung zur Voraussetzung. Die Wahrnehmung und Deutung von Symbolen in der Malerei und Plastik bereitet auch in der Gegenwart keine nennenswerte Schwierigkeit. In der Architektur ist ein wesentlich größerer Symbolverfall zu registrieren, und durch die langen Phasen einer rationalen und funktionalistischen Architektur haben wir das metaphorische Denken verlernt.

97. Edda Seidl-Reiter, *Weiblich – (männlich ?)*, 1976.
98. Edda Seidl-Reiter, *Ende des Knotens im Fenster*, 1977.
99. Walter Pichler, *Unterirdisches Gebäude mit ausfahrbarem Kern*, 1963.
100. Walter Pichler, *Haus für zwei Skulpturen*, 1995. Ausschnitt.
101. Walter Pichler, *Schlafsaal mit vier Betten*, 1968.
102. Walter Pichler, *Zwei Figuren, gezeichnet nach Angaben von Pierre*, 1972.

97. Edda Seidl-Reiter, *Female – (male ?)*, 1976.
98. Edda Seidl-Reiter, *End of the Knot in the Window*, 1977.
99. Walter Pichler, *Underground Building with a Telescopic Nucleus*, 1963.
100. Walter Pichler, *Building for two sculptures* 1995. Detail.
101. Walter Pichler, *Dormitory with four Beds*, 1968.
102. Walter Pichler, *Two Figures drawn to Pierre's Description*, 1972.

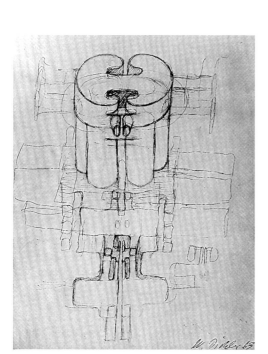

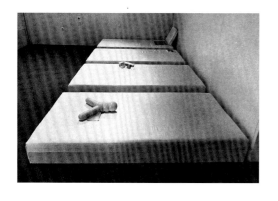

softness as mainly feminine. The vigorous density of women's hair attains a phallic character, and a penetration is depicted in connection with the orifice.

The concept of androgyny appears in a very encoded form in the work of **Allessandro Mendini** (born 1931). An installation called *Androgyner Raum (Androgynous Area)*, which is an installation dating from 1981, displays a semi-nude female being in a geometrical area. Kissing mouths adorned with ivy push their way through little orifices.

The work of **Walter Pichle**r (born 1936) is, more than that of almost any other artist, calculated to demonstrate the presence of sexuality in the transitional area between architecture and sculpture. The early works dating from 1963 deal with the topic of underground towns: the complete security of mother earth is sought for, but individual building components project above the ground and harbour the dwellings of the »élite«.

In another underground building, Pichler imagines a movable core, and he builds a model of it, an impressive sculpture of concrete and tin whose core really can be moved out. This is the powerful male element which, gradually becoming erect, releases itself from the maternal womb and grows out of it, then sinking back inside it.

No androgynous speculation is required to interpret a drawing produced in 1972: *Zwei Figuren, nach Angabe von Pierre gezeichnet (Two figures drawn to Pierre's Description)* are intertwined and have in fact become a single unity, and only the colours of the drawing make it plain that there is a woman standing on the left and a man, supplemented by a large penis, on the right. Rods and tree branches pierce the motifs and at the same time link them.

Four beds covered with linen are seen set up in the work called *Schlafsaal (Dormitory)* from 1968. In one of the beds, a »trouser fly« can be unbuttoned, and two metal rods and spheres, perfect and shining, are then seen: the male element is bedded in linen of a virginal whiteness. A *Skulptur im Organza Kleid (Sculpture in an Organza Dress)* is seen lying on another bed, and it gives rise to various layers of interpretation. On the one hand it is a female figure with spread-out legs and alluring underwear, while on the other this object is reminiscent of a double penis, a godmiché such as is used for various special forms of sexual gratification. A precedent for this figuration is to be seen in the prehistoric holed rods (see Chapter 3.1). An example of it is the object found in the Gorge d'Enfer, a work in which a double phallus is clearly discernible. Not the least significant feature here is that we are reminded of the androgynous symbols which, in 17th-century hermaphroditic depictions, appear in the shape of a Y, as being a symbol of oneness and duality.

In a work dating from 1995 – this drawing is still waiting to become a reality – Pichler has departed still further from sexual symbolism and has advanced to the stage of the universal validity of entities which complement one another: a metal »chasm« stands on a wooden

Vollends Gebrauchsgegenstand, hat sich der Designgegenstand unserer Objektwelt in unserem Jahrhundert nahezu völlig dem geistig interpretierbaren Symbol entzogen. Erst in den beiden letzten Jahrzehnten wird wieder versucht, Design-Objekte auch mit Symbolgehalt, weit über das Pragmatische hinaus, auszustatten. Gleichwohl sind mann/weibliche Metaphern überaus schwer auszumachen, wenn wir nicht neuerdings bei der Psychoanalyse anfragen und von vornherein etwa eine Schale als weiblich, ein Messer als männlich apostrophieren.

Das Gefäß – vor allem Krug und Schale – wird dem Weiblichen zugeordnet. Aus der Unzahl der figurativen **archaischen Gefäßformen** sollen zwei herausgegriffen werden. Ein Fund aus Palästina, etwa aus dem 13. vorchristlichen Jahrhundert, wird als »Gravidenflasche« bezeichnet. Sie hatte vermutlich eine therapeutische Aufgabe während der Schwangerschaft. In einem Figurengefäß aus Troja (um 2000 v. Chr.) erblickt man eine Gefäßgöttin.

Daß Gefäße als Frauen gestaltet werden oder daß die Frau als Gefäß interpretiert wird, ist in unserem Jahrhundert noch aktuell. Die Vasen des Jugendstils haben bisweilen einen deutlich erotisch-femininen Charakter, so die Arbeiten von Tiffany. Eine um 1899 hergestellte Vase aus böhmisch-österreichischer Produktion von Joh. Lötz Witwe (Klostermühle) ist zwar nicht direkt anthropomorph gestaltet, erlaubt aber Assoziationen an die Erotik des weiblichen Körpers.

Edelbert Köb (geb. 1942) gibt einem Gefäß die Form eines liegenden Frauen-Unterleibes, aus der Öffnung scheint eine zähe Flüssigkeit zu rinnen. Eine andere liegende Vase wird als *Amphora* bezeichnet, doch ist unverkennbar, daß sie einer Frauenfigur nachgebildet ist.

Die *weiche Vase* hatte ursprünglich den Arbeitstitel *schwangere Vase*, das »Bauchige« des Gefäßes wird direkt mit einer Frauenfigur assoziiert.

Für **René Magritte** (1889–1967) kann auch die Flasche weiblichen Charakter haben und wird zu einer *Femme Bouteille* (1955).

Krug und Flasche können als androgyne Objekte bezeichnet werden: Sie weisen einen bergenden, bauchigen Behälter auf, dessen Mündung sich jedoch phallisch verengt, um eine lebensspendende Flüssigkeit freizugeben. Flaschen mit manieriert langen Hälsen, evozieren Männliches, während Krüge eher dem Weiblichen zuzuordnen sind. Auf einem chinesischen Tongefäß aus dem 3. Jahrtausend v. Chr. ist eine Figur dargestellt, die als Mann oder Frau, besser wohl als Androgyn gedeutet werden kann.

Nach Devereux (1981) hat die Reziprozität von Vagina und Penis eine Entsprechung in den Kategorien konkav/konvex und, noch konkreter, in der Relation Behälter/Inhalt. Die gefüllte Schale wäre demnach ein androgynes Objekt oder noch deutlicher: Die Obstschale mit der Banane ist eine reale Entsprechung des Linga/Yoni-Symbols.

Hofmann (1974) stellt die gedankliche Verbindung zwischen Frucht und Schale her: »Zwei Lebensvorgänge der feuchten Sphäre sind dem Weiblichen wesensverwandt: das stille Bewahren und das selbsttätige Gebären, das verborgene Ausreifen, und das mühelose Hervorquellen der Frucht. Seit jeher hat die künstlerische Phantasie diesen Doppelaspekt bedacht und der weiblichen Gestalt sowohl Frucht- als auch Gefäßform verliehen. Der Behälter birgt den Inhalt, den er bis zur Reife austrägt. Und diese Leibesfrucht wird von der Vorstellung auf das umhüllende Gefäß projiziert – der bewahrende Körper wird selbst zur Frucht.«

Die Interpretation des Hohlgefäßes als weibliches Element kann selbstverständlich auch bei der halbierten Kugel oder Eiform ansetzen: Es ist die Schale, die Cuppa (=Kuppel), die offene, empfangende, bergende, behütende Form. Die offene Schale hat aber zunächst eine kultische Bedeutung, so etwa beim Gral, den wir in mancherlei Modifikationen in Sagen und Mythen finden. Bei den Kelten gibt es den »Kessel der Fülle« als rituelles Gerät, er wird zum Symbol der Weisheit und der Wiedergeburt und erinnert an den Ur-Kessel, an den Schoß der Muttergöttin. In Spanien finden wir schöne Hochzeitsbecher, die aus Rhinozeroshorn hergestellt und außen reich reliefiert sind. In die Schale selbst legt man einen Bezoar, die Magenausscheidung einer Ziege oder eines Lamas. Beide Elemente haben eine entgiftende Wirkung und sind gleichzeitig auch Symbole für Glück und Reichtum. Die Deutung nach weiblicher Schale und männlicher Kugel und somit nach einer magischen coincidentia scheint durchaus legitim.

Betrachten wir eine noch kleinere Dimension unserer Objektwelt, den **Schmuck**. Die Konfrontation des Körpers mit Objekten hatte von jeher zwei Motivationen: das Kultische und das Erotische. Moderne Schmuckgestalter haben diese Quellen wieder neu erschlossen. **Peter Skubic** (geb. 1935) gestaltet einen Ring, der mit zwei Türmchen ausgestattet ist, der eine trägt eine silberne, der andere eine schwarze »Kuppel«: Stehen das Material, die Oberfläche, die Farbe für das Weibliche und das Männliche wie im Yin/Yang Symbol? Der Zweifel über die erotischen Intentionen bei Peter Skubic wird durch einen anderen Ring zerstreut, bei dem der Charakter der erotischen Penetration nicht zu übersehen ist.

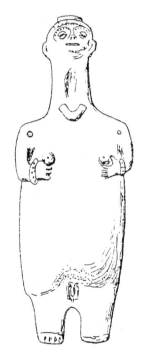

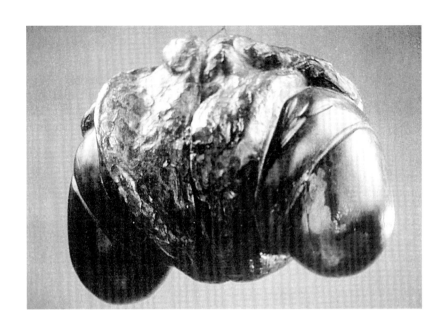

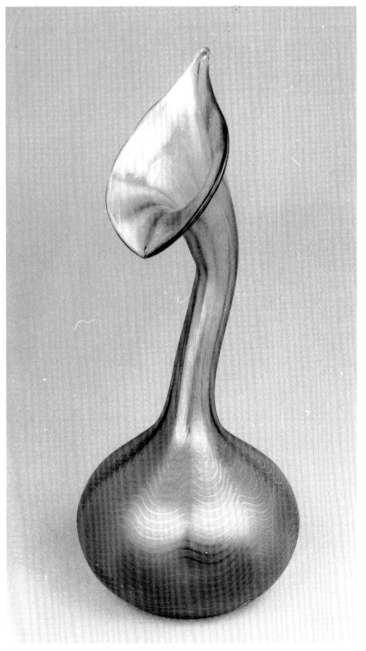

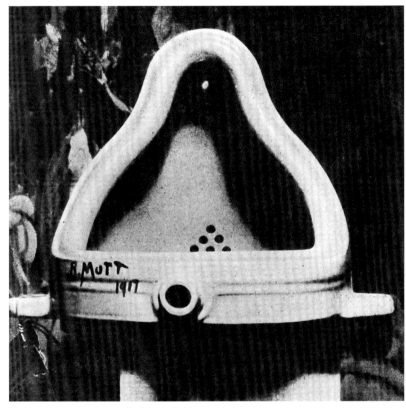

108. Edelbert Köb, *Amphora*, 1990.
109. Schale aus Rhinozeros-Horn mit Bezoarstein aus Spanien, um 1608.
110. René Magritte, *Femme Bouteille*, 1955.

108. Edelbert Köb, *Amphora*, 1990.
109. Bowl made of rhinoceros horn with a bezoar stone from Spain, ca. 1608.
110. René Magritte, *Femme Bouteille*, 1955.

block in a house. In front of the chasm there is a »ridge« on a rail. Moving along the rail, the ridge approaches the chasm and finally leads into it, enters it and fills it up: a completed »coincidentia«.

The double phallus is found not only in the work of Walter Pichler. **Louise Bourgeois** gives the name of *Blumengeschmückter Janus* (*Janus Decorated with Flowers*) to a bronze sculpture in which the doubling of the penis can be clearly discerned.

One of the »ready made« works by **Marcel Duchamp** stands on the borderline between art, provocation and the world of objects: a urinal is turned through 90°, declared to be an art object and given the name *Fontaine*. This French word means not only a fountain but also, in vulgar usage, a stream of urine. But when looked at in this way, the fontaine is feminine in its bowl, and masculine in its connecting piece.

6.3. The World of Objects. Design

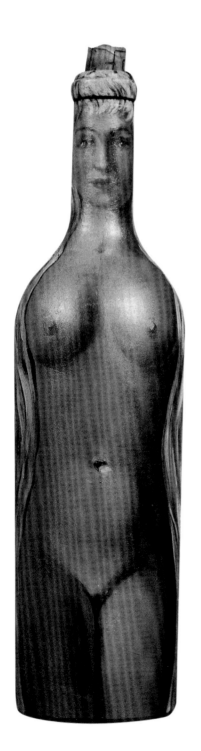

Androgyny in art and architecture presupposes a high degree of symbolism. Even today, no difficulty worth mentioning arises when it comes to perceiving and interpreting symbols in painting and sculpture. A considerably greater decline in symbolism is to be noted in architecture, and the lengthy phases of rational and functionalist architecture have made us forget how to think metaphorically.

In the world of objects, design objects – being entirely utilitarian – have in our century become almost completely removed from any idea of being symbols which can be interpreted spiritually. It is only in the last two decades that the attempt has once again been made to give design objects a symbolic content extending far beyond anything pragmatic. It is nevertheless very difficult to discern any male/female metaphors unless we once again raise the issue of psychoanalysis and start out by, for example, apostrophizing a bowl as female and a knife as male.

Vessels, particularly jugs and bowls, are assigned to the feminine element. Of the vast number of **figurative vessel shapes** from the archaic period, two will be mentioned here. A find from Palestine, dating from about the 13th century BC, is described as a »pregnancy flask«. It probably performed a therapeutic function during pregnancy. A vessel in the form of a goddess is to be seen in a figurative vessel from Troy (ca. 2000 BC)

Vessels designed in the shape of women, or the reverse situation where a woman is interpreted as a vessel, are still a topical notion in the 20th century. Art Nouveau vases, for example the works of Tiffany, sometimes have a plainly erotic feminine character. A vase (ca. 1899) by Joh. Lötz Witwe (Klostermühle), of Bohemian-Austrian production, is not of undoubted anthropomorphic design, but permits associations with the eroticism of the female body.

Edelbert Köb (born 1942) gives a vessel the shape of a recumbent female abdomen, and a viscous liquid seems to be running out of the orifice. Another recumbent vase is described as *Amphora*, but it is unmistakably an imitation of a female figure.

The working title of the *Soft Vase* was originally *Pregnant Vase*, and the »bulginess« of the vessel is directly associated with a female figure.

For **René Magritte** (1889–1967), a bottle too can have a feminine character, and then becomea a *Femme Bouteille* (1955).

Jugs and bottles may be described as androgynous objects: they have a concealing, bulging container, but with an opening that is phallically narrowed so that it can release a life-giving fluid. Bottles with manneristically long necks evoke male ideas, whereas jugs tend instead to have a feminine character. A figure which can be interpreted as either a man or a woman, but probably better as an androgyne, is depicted on a Chinese clay vessel from the 3rd millennium BC This once again relates to the androgynous character of vessels.

According to Devereux (1981), the reciprocity of vagina and penis has an equivalent in the categories of concave and convex and, still more specifically, in the relation of container to contents. This would mean that a filled bowl is an androgynous object or, to put it still more plainly, that a fruit bowl containing a banana is a material equivalent of the linga/yoni symbol.

Hofmann (1974) established a psychological link between fruit and bowl: »Two living processes within this moist sphere are intrinsically related to femininity. The first is quiet retention and the second is the spontaneous giving of birth: there is a concealed ripening on the one hand, and an effortless issuing forth of the fruit on the other. The artistic imagination has at all times taken this double aspect into account and given the female form the shape both of a

6.4. Literatur

Die Darstellung androgyner, hermaphroditischer Aspekte in der Literatur ist außerordentlich umfangreich. Im schriftlichen Medium ist jene Deutlichkeit und Anschaulichkeit, wie sie die visuellen Medien erfordern, nicht notwendig, so daß vielfache Zwischenformen, Andeutungen, Affinitäten möglich sind und die Modelle geschlechtlicher Übergangssituation wesentlich diffiziler dargestellt werden können.

Achim Aurnhammer (1986) stellt die Androgynie ausführlich als ein »Motiv in der europäischen Literatur« dar. Eine Reihe von Zitaten wurde bereits in anderen Zusammenhängen erwähnt, insbesondere auch die literarisch-mythologischen Quellen.

Johann Jakob Christoffel von Grimmelshausen (1622–1676) war die Thematik des Hermaphroditen geläufig. Im 19. Kapitel seines Romans *Der Abenteuerliche Simplicissimus Teutsch*« wird Simplicius von einem Offizier untersucht, dessen Geschlecht nicht eindeutig identifizierbar ist: »Ich wuste nicht/ob er Sie oder Er wäre/dann er trug Haar und Bart auff Frantzösisch/zu beyden Seiten hatte er lange Zöpff herunder hangen ... Nicht weniger setzten mich seine weiten Hosen/seines Geschlechts halber in nicht geringen Zweiffel ...«, so daß Simplicius ihn als »Ach mein lieber Hermaphrodit« anredet.

Eine überraschende Interpretation einer Art früher Androgynie findet sich in dem phantastischem Roman *Eduard und Elisabeth* von **Giacomo Casanova** (1725–1798). Danach findet sich im Inneren des Erdballes eine Art Paradies (wenn auch mit mancherlei Fehlern), das von »Megamikren« bewohnt ist. Und bei ihnen »gibt es nur ein Geschlecht; da sie alle männlich und weiblich zugleich sind, können sie folgerichtig weder Mann noch Frau sein; die Heilige Schrift nennt sie nur ›sie‹, um uns begreiflich zu machen, daß die Fortpflanzung nicht von einem der beiden Partner mehr abhängt als vom anderen ... Hütet Euch, sie Hermaphroditen zu nennen, denn ihr würdet damit nur ungeziemende Vorstellungen verbinden und ihnen Unrecht tun, weil sie es in Wirklichkeit nicht sind.«

Schüchtern und diskret behandelt **Friedrich von Schlegel** in seinem Roman *Lucinde* die Androgynie, löste aber trotzdem mit dem Buch 1799 einen Skandal aus.

Fast naiv wird zunächst das Thema des Rollentausches angeschnitten: »... wenn wir die Rollen vertauschen und mit kindischer Lust wetteifern, wer den anderen täuschender nachäffen kann ... Ich sehe hier eine wunderbare, sinnreiche bedeutende Allegorie auf die Vollendung des Männlichen und Weiblichen zur vollen ganzen Menschheit.«

Die Identität von männlicher und weiblicher Liebe wird als großes Ideal ausgesprochen: »Der dritte und höchste Grad ist das bleibende Gefühl von harmonischer Wärme. Welcher Jüngling das hat, der liebt nicht mehr bloß wie ein Mann, sondern zugleich auch wie ein Weib. In ihm ist die Menschheit vollendet ...«

Und noch einmal wird die idealistische Idee der Einheit angeschnitten: »Wir beide werden noch einst in einem Geiste anschauen, daß wir Blüten einer Pflanze oder Blätter einer Blume sind ...«

Die Unbestimmtheit und Unausgesprochenheit des Geschlechtlichen kann als weiteres verdecktes Symptom einer Androgynie angesehen werden. Das klassische Beispiel dafür mag die Mignon im *Wilhelm Meister* von **Johann Wolfgang von Goethe** (1748–1832) sein. »Besonders fesselt ihn Chlorinde mit ihrem ganzen Tun und Lassen. Die Mannweiblichkeit, die ruhige Fülle ihres Daseins haben mehr Wirkung auf den keimenden Geist der Liebe, der sich im Knaben zu entwickeln anfing, als die gemachten Reize Armindens, ob er gleich ihren Garten nicht verachtete.«

Eine poetische Formulierung für die Idee der Einheit findet **Novalis** (Friedrich Leopold Freiherr von Hardenberg, 1772–1801): »Wer hat des irdischen Leibes / Hohen Sinn erraten? / Daß er das Blut versteht ? / Einst ist alles Leib / EIN LEIB / Im himmlischen Blut / Schwimmt das selige Paar.« Und weiter heißt es: »Der Mann ist gewissermaßen auch Weib, so wie das Weib Mann.« (Novalis, 1980)

Literarisch gut artikuliert ist das Androgyn-Motiv bei **Honoré de Balzac**. In seinem Roman *Seraphita* ist der/die Titelheld/in gleichzeitig Seraphitus, ein engelsgleiches Wesen, das beide Geschlechter in sich vereint. Minna und Wilfried treffen auf dieses Wesen und lieben es, es wird Bruder und Schwester zugleich und schließlich zu einem himmlischen Seraph, aber auch Minna und Wilfried erleben die geistige conjunctio. (Balzac, 1922) Mircea Eliade (1962) weist darauf hin, daß Balzac in seiner *Seraphita* » l'androgyne considère comme l'image exemplaire de l'homme parfait«[37], sie/er besitzt ein »être total«. »Balzacs Androgyn erscheint nur wenig auf der Erde. Sein geistiges Leben ist gänzlich auf den Himmel gerichtet. Seraphitus/Seraphita lebt einzig und allein, um sich zu reinigen und um zu lieben.« (Eliade, 1962)

fruit and of a vessel. The container harbours the contents which it carries until the time of maturity. This fruit of the womb is, in the artist's imagination, projected on to the surrounding vessel: the retaining body itself becomes a fruit.«

An interpretation of the hollow vessel as being a female element can of course also begin with a sphere or an egg-shape that is cut in half: this is a bowl, a cuppa (dome), an open, receiving, sheltering, protective shape. But the initial significance of the **open bowl** is ritualistic, an example being the grail which, in various modifications, is to be found in sagas and myths. The Celts' »kettle of plenitude« was a ritual utensil. It became a symbol of wisdom and rebirth, and is reminiscent of the original hollow, the womb of the maternal goddess. Some beautiful wedding bowls made of rhinoceros horn, with rich reliefs on the outside, are to be found in Spain. A bezoar, a stone voided from the stomach of a goat or a llama, is placed in the bowl. Both elements have a detoxifying effect and are also symbols of happiness and wealth. It seems perfectly legitimate to interpret them as a female bowl and a male sphere, and thus as a magical coincidentia.

Let us look at a still smaller dimension of our world of objects, namely **jewellery**. The placing of objects against the human body has always had two motives: cultic and erotic. Modern jewellery designers have once again opened up these sources. **Peter Skubic** (born 1935) designed a ring which has two turrets, one of them bearing a silver dome and the other a black one. Do the material, the surface, the colour, represent both femininity and masculinity as in the yin/yang symbol? Any doubt about Peter Skubic's erotic intentions is dispersed by another ring in which the character of the erotic penetration is impossible to overlook.

6.4. Literature

There is an extremely abundant literature describing androgyny and hermaphroditism. The clarity and vividness required in the visual media are not necessary in writing, with the result that multifarious intimations, affinities and intermediate forms are possible and the models of a transitional sexual situation can be depicted much more meticulously.

Achim Aurnhammer (1986) gives a detailed description of androgyny as a »motif in European literature«. A number of quotations, particularly the literary and mythological sources, have already been mentioned in other contexts.

Johann Jakob Christoffel von Grimmelshausen (1622–1676) was familiar with the topic of the hermaphrodite. In the 19th chapter of his novel *Der Abenteuerliche Simplicissimus Teutsch* (*The Adventures of Simplicissimus the German*), Simplicius is examined by an officer whose sex is not clearly identifiable: »I did not know whether he was a she or a he, for he wore his hair and beard in the French style. He had long pigtails hanging down on both sides... His wide trousers put me in an equally considerable doubt regarding his sex...«, so that Simplicius addresses him as »O my dear hermaphrodite«.

A surprising interpretation of an early kind of androgyny is to be found in *Edward and Elizabeth*, a fantastical novel by **Giacomo Casanova** (1725–1798). Here, a kind of paradise (although it does have some errors) is to be found inside the Earth, and is inhabited by »megamicros«. These »have only one sex; they are all male and female at the same time, and they consequently can be neither men nor women; Holy Writ refers to them only as ›they‹ in order to make us understand that procreation does not depend more on one of the two partners than on the other ... Beware of calling them hermaphrodites, because you would only associate unseemly ideas with that notion and you would be wronging those beings, because in reality they are not hermaphrodites.«

Friedrich von Schlegel treats of androgyny bashfully and discreetly in his novel *Lucinde*, but nevertheless caused a scandal with this book in 1799.

He initially touches upon the topic of role reversal in an almost naive way: »...when we reverse our roles and, with a childish delight, compete to see which of the two can more misleadingly imitate the other... I can see here a wonderful, meaningful, significant allegory of the consummation of male and female in a full and complete humanity.«

The identity of male and female love is declared to be a great ideal: »The third and highest degree is the continuing feeling of harmonious warmth. Any young man who has it is no longer loving only like a man, but also like a woman. Humanity is consummated in him ...«

The idealistic idea of unity is touched upon once again: »The two of us will, as one spirit, one day see that we are the blossoms of a plant or the leaves of a tree ...«

111. Peter Skubic, Ring aus Weißgold, 1975.

111. Peter Skubic, Ring made of white gold, 1975.

In Balzacs *Sarrasine* verliebt sich der Titelheld, ein Bildhauer, grenzenlos in die schöne Sängerin Zambinella. Als er endlich zum Rendezvous kommt, deutet Zambinella an, daß sie keine Frau sei – für Sarrasine völlig unglaubwürdig: »Nur eine Frau kann einen so runden, vollen Arm, eine so elegante Erscheinung haben.« Aus Verzweiflung will Sarrasine Zambinella töten – wird aber vorher von der Rache eines Kardinals, dem Mäzen Zambinellas, getroffen.

Im Werk von **Joséphin Peladan** (eigentlich Joseph P., 1859–1918) nimmt das Thema der Androgynie eine dominierende Stellung ein. In seinen Romanen – um 1890 entstanden – behandelt er das Problem der geschlechtlichen Transformationen.

Das Thema der Zweigeschlechtlichkeit ist in **Pierre Klossowskis** Roman *Der Baphomet* angesprochen, freilich vielfältig verschlüsselt, in einer verknoteten Handlung, bei der die Zeiten, die Orte, die Personen ständig ihre Realitätsebene wechseln und geistige wie körperhafte Existenzen beliebig springen, so daß die Identität der Personen undurchschaubar wird. Baphomet ist nach der Überlieferung ein »zweigeschlechtliches Idol, das die Templer angebetet haben sollen. Die heilige Therese erkennt mit Schaudern in Roberte, dem weiblichen Dämon ... eine ihrer späten Reinkarnationen, und der Bruder Damiens, der Gast der Templer bei ihrem Erinnerungsmahl, weiß sich eins mit ihrem perversen Gatten, dem Theologen Octave«.

Wie wenig homoerotische Neigungen und androgyne Dispositionen zu trennen sind, wird in *Narziß und Goldmund* von **Hermann Hesse** (1877–1962) deutlich. Narziß ist der über Goldmund Erhabene, der Führende. Er bewundert den »hübschen, hellen, lieben Jungen« und hat den Wunsch, »mit zärtlichen Händen durch sein hellblondes Haar zu streichen«. (Hesse, 1930)

Im *Mann ohne Eigenschaften* von **Robert Musil** (1880–1942) sieht Raehs (1990) in der inzestuösen Beziehung der Geschwister einen direkten Hinweis auf eine Art des Hermaphroditismus: »Dieses Verlangen nach einem Doppelgänger im anderen Geschlecht ist uralt. Es will Liebe eines Wesen, das uns völlig gleichen, aber doch ein anderes als wir sein soll, eine Zaubergestalt, die wir sind, die aber doch eine Zaubergestalt bleibt, und vor allem was wir uns bloß ausdenken, den Atem der Selbständigkeit und Unabhängigkeit voraushat. Unzählige Male ist dieser Traum vom Fluidum der Liebe, das sich, unabhängig von den Beschränkungen der Körperwelt, in zwei gleich-verschiedenen Gestalten begegnet, schon in einsamer Alchemie den Retorten der menschlichen Köpfe entstiegen.«

Beträchtliche Mühe wendet Karl Pufler (1990) auf, um die »Androgynität« im Werk von **Ingeborg Bachmann** (1926–1973) aufzuzeigen. Bachmanns Gedicht *Das Spiel ist aus* vergleicht er mit Musils *Isis und Osiris*. Als Gemeinsamkeit läßt sich die inzestiöse Beziehung Bruder/ Schwester herauslösen, die für Pufler eine ausreichende Argumentation zur Androgynie darstellt: »Das heißt, daß der Inzest die unterdrückte Suche nach dem eigenen Wesen ist. Wenn man berücksichtigt, daß das Selbst eine Ganzheit darstellt, so kann der Inzest als Versuch gewertet werden, Ganzheit zu erlangen. Insoweit hängt dieser mit Androgynie zusammen. Auch in der *Karfunkelfee*, ebenfalls ein Gedicht von Ingeborg Bachmann, sieht Pufler »das androgyne Wesen, das die Einheit des Selbst, nach dem das lyrische Ich strebt, schon in sich vollendet hat«.

Mit diesen wenigen Beispielen ist das Thema der Androgynie in der Literatur des 19. und 20. Jahrhunderts keineswegs erschöpft. Androgyne Themen finden wir bei Franz Kafka, Gustav Meyrink, Stefan George, Hugo von Hofmannsthal, Hermann Broch, Marcel Proust, Rainer Maria Rilke und vielen anderen. Einige weitere bedeutende literarische Zeugnisse im Hinblick auf die Geschlechtsumwandlung wurden im Kapitel 5.7 zitiert.

7. Sexualsymbolik in der Architektur

7.1. »Erotische« Architektur

Wenn wir davon ausgehen, daß Architektur – und dies gilt auch für unser Jahrhundert – mehr ist, als die bloße »utilitas«, die Rationalität und Funktionalität, die Nützlichkeit und Zweckerfüllung, dann kann kein Zweifel darüber bestehen, daß sie eine hohe **Symbolfähigkeit** besitzt, daß sie Metaphern und Gleichnisse bilden kann, daß die ganze Breite und Tiefe menschlicher Existenz und deren Ausdeutung auch in der Architektur – ebenso wie in den anderen Künsten – ihren Platz hat.

Somit muß auch die Architektur ein Bezugsfeld zu den existenziellen Problemen von Liebe, Eros und Sexus aufweisen.

In der Architektur unseres Jahrhunderts – und dies gilt weitgehend auch für das vorangegangene Jahrhundert – wird es nicht leicht fallen, nach einer Epoche der Symbolverluste – die

The idea that sexuality is not determined and remains unspoken can be regarded as a further hidden symptom of androgyny. The classical example of this may be the mignon in *Wilhelm Meister* by **Johann Wolfgang von Goethe** (1748–1832). »Chlorinde particularly captivated him by all that she did and did not do. The male-female element, the quiet profusion of her existence, had more of an effect on that budding spirit of love which began to develop in the boy than did the affected charms of Arminden, although he did not despise her garden.«

Novalis (pen-name of Friedrich Leopold Freiherr von Hardenberg, 1772–1801) found a poetic formulation for the idea of unity: »Who has guessed the Higher Meaning of the terrestrial human body? Does that body understand blood? At one time, everything is a body, ONE BODY, and the blissful couple swims in heavenly blood.« He went on to write: »A man is to a certain extent also a woman, and a woman a man.« (Novalis, 1980)

Honoré de Balzac articulated the androgynous motif in good literary style. In his novel *Seraphita*, the hero/heroine of the title is at the same time Seraphitus, an angelic being who combines both sexes within him/herself. Minna and Wilfried meet this being and love him/her. He/she simultaneously becomes both a brother and a sister, and finally a heavenly seraph, but Minna and Wilfried themselves also experience the spiritual conjunctio. (Balzac, 1922) Mircea Eliade pointed out (1962) that Balzac in his *Seraphita* »considère l'androgyne comme l'image exemplaire de l'homme parfait«[36], and that she/he possesses an »être total«. »Balzac's androgyne does not put in much of an appearance on earth. His/her spiritual life is entirely directed towards heaven. Seraphitus/Seraphita lives for the sole purpose of cleansing himself/herself and of loving.« (Eliade, 1962)

In Balzac's *Sarrasine*, the eponymous hero, a sculptor, falls immeasurably in love with Zambinella, a beautiful songstress. When he finally arrives at the rendezvous, Zambinella intimates that she is not a woman, but to Sarrasine this is entirely unbelievable: »Only a woman can have such a round and full arm and such an elegant appearance.« Sarrasine intends to kill Zambinella out of despair, but is himself first struck down by the revenge of a cardinal who is Zambinella's Maecenas.

The subject of androgyny occupies a dominant position in the work of **Joséphin Peladan** (real name Joseph P., 1859–1918). In his novels, which were written around 1890, he treats of the problem of sexual transformations.

The topic of a two-sexed nature is addressed in the novel *Baphomet* by **Pierre Klossowski**, but in a diversely coded way and in a tangled plot in which the times, locations and characters are constantly moving to another level of reality and spiritual and physical bodies jump around as they please, so that the identity of the characters becomes obscure. According to tradition, Baphomet is a »two-sexed idol said to have been worshipped by the Knights Templar. Saint Theresa is horrified to realize that the female demon Roberte ... is one of the late reincarnations of Theresa herself, and Damien's brother, who is the guest of the Knights Templar at their commemorative banquet, knows that he is one and the same as Theresa's perverted husband, Octave the theologian.«

The difficulty of separating homoerotic tendencies from androgynous dispositions becomes clear in *Narziß und Goldmund* by **Hermann Hesse** (1877–1962). Narziß is more sublime than Goldmund, he is the leader. He admires the »pretty, bright, dear boy« and feels a wish »to stroke, with delicate hands, his light-blond hair«. (Hesse, 1930)

Der Mann ohne Eigenschaften (*The Man Without Qualities*) is a work by **Robert Musil** (1880–1942) regarding which Raehs (1990) considers that the incestuous relationship between the brothers and sisters is a direct reference to a kind of hermaphroditism: »This is the age-old longing for a double of the opposite sex. It is a longing that desires the love of a being which is to be exactly identical to us but at the same time different from us, a magical figure which is us but still remains a magical figure. In particular, this figure has an advantage over the things which we merely think up: that advantage is the breath of autonomy and independence. This is a dream of the aura of love, an aura which, independently of the limitations imposed by the physical world, encounters itself in two figures which are both identical and different. That dream has on innumerable occasions arisen from the retorts of human heads in a kind of lonely alchemy.«

Karl Pufler took considerable trouble (1990) to point out the »androgyny« in the work of **Ingeborg Bachmann** (1926–1973). He compares Bachmann's poem *Das Spiel ist aus* (*The Game Is Over*) with Musil's *Isis und Osiris* (*Isis and Osiris*). The common factor which can be extracted is the incestuous brother-sister relationship which, to Pufler, is a sufficient argument to support the notion of androgyny: »This means that incest is a suppressed search for one's

ersten Anzeichen können wir schon in der Renaissance feststellen – Symbole und Metaphern aufzuzeigen.

Die Kritik am Funktionalismus, die schon in den sechziger Jahren vehement einsetzt, die Zuwendung der Künste zu »privaten Mythologien«, die Entdeckung von »Bedeutung« auf dem Umweg der Semiotik ermutigen uns jedoch dazu, auch in der Architektur des 20. Jahrhunderts den Symbolen nachzuspüren.[38]

Die Beziehung der Künste zum Eros wird heute kaum in Frage gestellt – ausgenommen in der Architektur, die wir nach wie vor zu den Künsten zählen sollten.

Otto Antonia Graf (1990) erinnert uns zu Recht an elementare, heute vergessene Zusammenhänge: »Die Baukunst ist dem erotischen Geschehen am unmittelbarsten und nächsten.« »Die Götter, die Baukunst und der Eros sind die Dreieinigkeit des kulturellen Geschlechtsverkehrs Menschheit.«

Die Macht der Architektur kommt nach Graf »aus der Macht und dem Neumachen des Eros, des Geschlechtswesens und dessen Verkehr mit der gesamten, dem Menschen zugänglichen Welt seiner Tätigkeit«. Architektur ist untrennbar verbunden mit den göttlichen Zeugungsakten, mit dem »hierós gamós«. »Die heilige Hochzeit zwischen Göttern und Menschen, Politik und Eros ist Dasein für den Menschen, das ihm seliges Leben gewähren soll. Der rechte Same Gottes und der Mutterschoß seiner Gemahlin zeugen den Bau ... aus diesem sicheren Wissen der Zeiten folgt die Konstanz gewisser Formen, wie des Schoßes, der eine Kuppel ist, des aufrechten Zeugungsorganes, das Säule oder Turm darstellt ...«

Bei der Erörterung einer **erotischen Architektur** wäre eine terminologische Klärung nützlich. Über die Abgrenzung der vielgebrauchten Begriffe Erotik und Sexualität (die durch weitere, unterschiedlich definierte Begriffe ergänzt werden) konnte jedoch bis heute kein Konsens erzielt werden.

Versuchen wir, in der antiken Mythologie anzufragen. Mit dem Kriegsgott Ares betrügt die schöne Aphrodite ihren Gatten Hephaistos und bringt den Gott **Eros** zur Welt. Er ist ursprünglich als das ordnende Prinzip der Weltentstehung gedacht, als Kind von Kraft und Schönheit.

Nach einer anderen Mythe wird auch Harmonia – die Ordnung – als Kind der Aphrodite und des Ares angesehen – Grund genug also, die Architektur, die »Erzfügung«, mit dem Eros in Zusammenhang zu bringen.

In Platons »Gastmahl« wird Eros zum Sinnbild der reinen Freundschaft und der inspirierenden Liebe zum Wahren, Guten und Schönen. Eros schließt die geschlechtliche Liebe nicht aus, aber reicht über sie hinaus und wird zur höchsten metaphysischen Aufbau- und Einigungskraft im Menschenleben und in der Welt. Die Flügel, mit denen Eros meist dargestellt wird, sind die Flügel des Geistes. Sie sollen zeigen, daß Eros über den Sexus, über die körperliche, ja animalische Geschlechtlichkeit erhaben ist und zur Liebe führt: zu dem großen, geistigen und seelischen Geschehen, in dem Liebe, Eros und Sexus zu einer metaphysischen Einheit unter Patronanz der Götter oder des Gottes werden. Eros ist vor allem die liebevolle Zuwendung, die Hingabe jeglicher Art, wohl auch ohne Geschlechtlichkeit, es ist die Begeisterung und das volle Aufgehen in der Idee.

Auch die Architektur erfordert »Eros« als liebevolle Auseinandersetzung wie mit einem Partner, einem Problem, fordert das tiefe Versenken in eine Aufgabe.

Eros ist aber auch den Sinnen zugewandt: Körperlichkeit und Freude, Spiel und Lust, Illusion und Traum sind seine Domänen. Es sind jene Dimensionen jenseits der Rationalität und Funktionalität, die wir heute in der Architektur weitgehend verloren haben.

»Sinnenhaftigkeit« oder »Sinnlichkeit« hängt nicht immer mit Üppigkeit, mit Hypertrophie, mit Formenschlemmerei, mit Kulinarischem zusammen: Auch die straffe Askese der Form kann uns zu einer tiefen sinnlichen Aufnahme führen. Keine neue Dekorationskunst ist erforderlich, kein Neo-Klassizismus oder Neo-Barock muß uns die neue Sinnenhaftigkeit lehren. Wir verfügen über ein genügend reiches zeitgenössisches Vokabular, um die ganze Breite der Sinnesempfindungen des Menschen anzusprechen.

Sinnenhaftigkeit bedeutet in der Architektur nicht nur den Appell an das Auge, sondern – zumindest im gleichen Maße – auch an den Tastsinn. Architektur ist eine Kunst, die an die Haut geht, eine taktile Kunst wie die Skulptur. Architektur muß begriffen werden, mit den Augen, mit den Händen und mit den Füßen – ja eigentlich mit dem ganzen Körper.

Zu der komplexen sinnenhaften Information des Raumes, der Architektur zählen auch Klang, Geruch und Geschmack. Wie selten kommt es vor, daß diese Informationen bewußt eingesetzt werden. Der Anspruch auf das Gesamtkunstwerk, der noch immer besteht, ist erst dann gerechtfertigt, wenn alle menschlichen Sinne am Architekturerlebnis beteiligt sind.

own being. When it is considered that the human self is an entirety, incest can be judged to be an attempt to attain entirety. Incest is to this extent related to androgyny. In the *Karfunkelfee (Carbuncle Fairy)*, another poem by Ingeborg Bachmann, Pufler once again sees »an androgynous being which has already consummated within itself the oneness of that selfness for which the lyrical ego is striving«.

These few examples by no means exhaust the theme of androgyny in the literature of the 19th and 20th centuries. Androgynous themes are to be found in Franz Kafka, Gustav Meyrink, Stefan George, Hugo von Hofmannsthal, Herman Broch, Marcel Proust, Rainer Maria Rilke and many others. Some further significant literary evidence relating to a change of sex has been referred to in Chapter 5.7.

7. Sexual Symbolism in Architecture

7.1. »Erotic« Architecture

If it is assumed – and this also applies to the 20th century – that architecture is more than mere »utilitas«, more than mere rationality, functionality, usefulness and purpose-fulfilment, then there can be no doubt that it is very capable of generating symbols, that it can create metaphors and allegories, and that the entire breadth and depth of human existence and of its interpretation also have their place in architecture as they do in the other arts.

Thus architecture must also be able to relate to the existential problems of love, Eros and sex.

After an epoch in which symbols were being lost – the first signs of this were to be observed as long ago as the Renaissance –, it will not be easy to point to any symbols or metaphors in the architecture of the 20th century, and the same is also largely true of the 19th century.

However, some factors which encourage us to trace the symbols to be found in 20th-century architecture are: that criticism of functionalism which set in with vehemence in the 1960s; the way in which art addresses itself to private mythologies; and the discovery of meaning by taking a circuitous route through semiotics.[37]

It is scarcely doubted today that there is a relationship between the arts and Eros, except in the case of architecture, which should even now be reckoned among the arts.

Otto Antonia Graf (1990) rightly reminds us of elemental relationships which have been forgotten today: »Architecture has the closest and most immediate relationship with erotic happenings.« »The gods, architecture and Eros are the trinity of the cultural sexual relations which constitute humanity.«

According to Graf, the power of architecture derives »from the power and renewal of Eros, of sexuality, and its relationship with all those of its activities which are accessible to mankind«. Architecture is inseparably linked to the divine acts of procreation, to the »hierós gamós«.»The holy wedding between gods and humans, between politics and Eros, is, to humans, an existence intended to give them a life of bliss. God's rightful seed and his wife's womb generate the structure ... from this secure knowledge of the times, there follows the constancy of certain shapes such as the womb which is a dome, and the erct organ of procreation which is a column or a tower ...«

It is useful to clarify the terminology when discussing **erotic architecture**. An agreement on how to delimit the much-used terms »eroticism« and »sexuality« (which are supplemented by other terms defined in different ways) has though not yet been reached even today.

Let us make an attempt by consulting classical mythology on the subject. The beautiful Aphrodite is unfaithful to her husband Hephaistos, goes with Ares the god of war, and gives birth to the god **Eros**. He is originally thought of as the ordering principle behind the world's creation, as the child produced by strength and beauty.

According to another myth, Harmonia – that is to say orderliness – is regarded as the child of Aphrodite and Ares, and this is sufficient reason to find a connection between architecture – that is to say the notion of a pre-eminent structure – on the one hand, and Eros on the other.

In Plato's »Symposium«, Eros becomes a symbol of pure friendship and of the inspiring love for truth, goodness and beauty. Eros does not exclude sexual love, but goes beyond it and becomes the highest metaphysical structural and unifying power in human life and the world. The wings which Eros is usually depicted as having are the wings of the spirit. They are

Architektur auch zum Hören, zum Riechen, zum Essen und Schmecken könnte unseren Eros zur Architektur neu entfachen. Der sinnenhafte Eros hat einen Vorsprung gegenüber der Architektur: Das erotische Erlebnis umfaßt alle Sinne in einer wunderbaren Ganzheit.

Anatol Ginelli läßt sich fiktiv von einer Frau befragen: »Was und wie baust du denn: wie man eine Frau verführt: kühn und gewagt, überwältigend, heiß von Atemzügen? Du erinnerst dich doch der Bacchantinnen, Faunen, Satyrn und Centauren, des Priapos und Pan und der Leda: du kennst Sapphos lyrisch-verzehrende Glut, Dantes göttliche Liebe zu Beatrice, Petrarcas phantastische Zärtlichkeit zu Laura; da hast du die ganze Zartheit des Minnegesanges und die Abenteuerlichkeit der Renaissance, die Innerlichkeit der Romantik und die Sinnenfreude des Barock verstanden. Du hast die indische, persische, die fernöstliche Liebe, die hellenistische Körperfreude, die etruskisch-römische amor, die germanorum erotica, du hast all' die erotischen Kulturen studiert, aber was fängst du damit an, wo ist deiner Häuser Lust? Und da kommst du mir mit der numerischen Ästhetik, mit der rationalen Architektur und dem absoluten Werk?« (Ginelli, 1986)

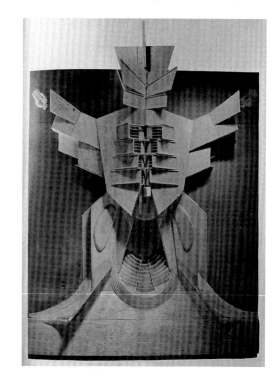

Architektur ist noch mehr als die statische Sinnenfreude: Sie ist eine Kunst des »Perambulatorischen«, des Umwanderns, des Herumgehens, eine Kunst der Erfahrung im Zeitablauf, eine prozessuale Kunst – erst in der Bewegung ist es möglich, die ganze Palette der Erlebnisse auszuschöpfen und mit allen Sinnen Architektur aufzunehmen.

Und nicht zuletzt sollte an einen weiteren Faktor erinnert werden, der aus der Architektur verdrängt wurde, aber in enger Nachbarschaft zur Erotik zu sehen ist: das Spiel. (Huizinga, 1956)

Ein wesentlicher Aspekt einer sinnenhaften Architektur ist die Wiederentdeckung des Körperhaft-Modellierten, des Plastischen und Skulpturalen in der Architektur. Eine Fülle von Beispielen ließe sich dafür anführen, daß die Grenzen zwischen Architektur und Plastik verschwinden. Bisweilen geht die Annäherung so weit, daß wir von einer physiognomischen, von einer **anthropomorphen** und zoomorphen (theriomorphen) Architektur sprechen können. (Feuerstein, 1992)

Für die deutliche Zuordnung von Architektur und menschlichem Körper sollen nur zwei Beispiele aus der jüngeren Zeit angeführt werden – zahlreiche ähnliche könnten wir aus dem historischen Befund zitieren.

Der Architekt selbst, **Ricardo Porro** (geb. 1925) – von dem noch die Rede sein wird – bezeugt, daß das Jugendzentrum in Vaduz, Liechtenstein, (Projekt 1972) eine anthropomorphe Architektur darstellt. Körper und Kopf sowie die Gliedmaßen sind deutlich zu erkennen und zwischen den weit gespreizten Beinen liegen Eingang und Versammlungsraum. Die Brust ist weit geöffnet und läßt das Licht ein, doch bleiben wir im ungewissen, ob es sich um einen männlichen oder weiblichen Körper handelt. Porro jedoch definiert den Bau als einen jungen Mann, dessen Brust zerbirst und dessen Kopf und Hände auffliegen.

In einem anderen Entwurf bedient sich Porro weicher, gerundeter, gekurvter Formen, die eher an den Körper einer Frau denken lassen. Das Feriendorf, 1972 für die Insel Korcula im damaligen Jugoslawien entworfen, wird von Porro als ein Riese interpretiert, der dem Meer entstiegen ist und an die Bilder von Arcimboldo erinnern soll: Die Verwaltung ist der Kopf, das Restaurant der Magen, das Labyrinth die Gedärme, die öffentlichen Räume die Hände und das Amphitheater das Schambein, von dem der Penis ausgeht.

7.2. Carl Gustav Jung und Sigmund Freud

Die Betrachtung der historischen Architektur macht deutlich, daß im Repertoire der Symbolbildung der Architektur der Problemkreis Sexualität und Fruchtbarkeit, insbesondere in den frühen Kulturen eine wichtige Rolle spielt. Die Bildung von »Archetypen« schöpft einen Großteil ihrer metaphorischen Gehalte aus den zwei uralten, elementaren Erlebnissen des Männlichen und Weiblichen. Im kollektiven Unterbewußtsein von **Carl Gustav Jung** (1875–1961) spielen die personalen Archetypen eine wichtige Rolle. Sie sind auch der jeweils ergänzende Teil der menschlichen Psyche: Jung beobachtete, daß alle Menschen ein gegengeschlechtliches Element in der Psyche haben, Männer eine weibliche »Anima« und Frauen einen männlichen »Animus«..

Sigmund Freud (1940) gewinnt aus der Deutung der Träume den unmittelbaren Zusammenhang zwischen Bauwerk und Sexualität: »Die einzige typische, d. h. regelmäßige Darstellung der menschlichen Person als Ganzes ist die als Haus. ... Es kommt im Traume vor, daß man, bald lustvoll, bald ängstlich von Häuserfassaden herabklettert. Die mit ganz glatten

112. Ricardo Porro, Jugendzentrum in Vaduz, Liechtenstein, 1972.
113. Ricardo Porro, Feriendorf in Vela Luca, Korčula, 1972.

112. Ricardo Porro, youth centre in Vaduz, Liechtenstein, 1972.
113. Ricardo Porro, holiday village in Vela Luca, Korčula, 1972.

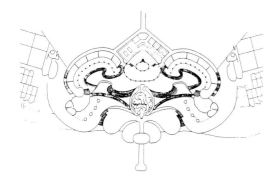

intended to show that Eros is elevated above sex and above physical, and even animal, sexuality, and leads the way to love, to the great psychological and spiritual event in which love, Eros and sex become a metaphysical unity under the patronage of the god or gods. Above all else, Eros is a loving attention, and is dedication of any kind, probably also when there is no sexuality involved: Eros is enthusiasm and complete absorption in an idea.

Architecture also requires »Eros« as a way of dealing with things in a loving way, as with a problem or a sexual partner. It demands profound absorption in a task.

But Eros is also devoted to the senses: physicality, joy, play, desire, illusion and dream are the domains of Eros. These are the dimensions which lie beyond rationality and functionality and which we have largely lost in architecture today.

»Sensuality« is not always related to »voluptuousness«, to hypertrophy, to a gluttony of shapes, or to culinary matters. The austere asceticism of a shape can itself lead us to a deep sensual reception. No new decorative art is required, and the new sensuality does not have to be taught us by any Neo-Classicism or Neo-Baroque. Our contemporary vocabulary is rich enough to address the entire spectrum of human sensual perception.

Sensuality in architecture is an appeal not merely to the eye, but also – and at least to the same extent – to the sense of touch. Architecture is an art which touches the skin. It is a tactile art like sculpture. Architecture must be grasped with the eyes, the hands and the feet – in fact, with the whole body.

The complex range of sensual information provided by space and by architecture also includes sound, smell and taste. How rarely indeed is this information consciously employed. The claim to the entire work of art still exists, but is only justified if all the human senses are taking part in the architectural experience.

An architecture which can be heard, smelt, eaten and tasted might kindle anew our erotic feeling towards architecture. The sensuality of Eros has the advantage over architecture: the erotic experience encompasses all the senses in a wonderful entirety.

Anatol Ginelli produced (1986) a work of fiction in which a woman asks him: »What do you build and how do you build it: do you do it in the same way as one seduces a woman: boldly, daringly, and overwhelmingly, while breathing hotly? You remember the bacchantes, fauns, satyrs and centaurs, Priapos, Pan and Leda; you know of Sappho's lyrical and consuming ardour, Dante's divine love for Beatrice, Petrarch's fantastic tenderness towards Laura; you understood all the tenderness of the minnesang, the adventurousness of the Renaissance, the fervency of romanticism and the sensual enjoyment of the Baroque. You studied Indian, Persian and Far Eastern love, Hellenistic physical joy, the Etruscan-Roman amor, the germanorum erotica, and all the erotic cultures, but what are you going to do with them, where can desire be found in your houses? And then you start telling me about numerical aesthetics, rational architecture and the absolute work?« (Ginelli, 1986)

Architecture is more than a static sensual joy: it is an art of »perambulation«, of wandering about, of going around, it is an art of experiencing the passage of time, an art consisting of a process. Only by movement is it possible to explore the full gamut of experiences and to receive architecture with all the senses.

Another important factor, which has been driven out of the field of architecture but must be seen in close proximity to eroticism, should be remembered. We are here referring to playing. (Huizinga, 1956)

One chief aspect of sensual architecture is the rediscovery of bodily shaping, of the sculptural aspects of architecture. An abundance of examples could be quoted to show the disappearance of the borders between architecture and sculpture. This mutual approximation sometimes even reaches the stage where it is possible to speak of a physiognomical, anthromorphic and zoomorphic (theriomorphic) architecture. (Feuerstein, 1992)

Only two examples from recent times will be quoted here to show how architecture can be clearly allocated to the human body. We might adduce numerous similar examples from history.

Ricardo Porro, (born 1925) who is himself the architect – further reference will be made to him later on –, testifies that the youth centre in Vaduz, Liechtenstein, (a project dating from 1972) is an anthromorphic piece of architecture. The body, head and limbs are clearly discernible, and the entrance and meeting room are between the widely spread legs. The chest is wide open and lets the light in, but we remain uncertain as to whether it is a male or a female body. But Porro defines the structure as a young man whose chest is bursting and whose head and hands are flying upwards.

Mauern sind Männer; die aber mit Vorsprüngen und Balkonen versehen sind, an welchen man sich anhalten kann, das sind Frauen.« Dementsprechend sind die Öffnungen des Gebäudes – Fenster, Türen, Tore – die Analogien zu den menschlichen Körperöffnungen, insbesondere den Geschlechtsteilen.

Gleichsam als eine Illustration zu Sigmund Freud können die Zeichnungen von **Louise Bourgeois** angesehen werden. Die Häuser werden mit der menschlichen Figur identisch, es sind Frauenkörper, die mit einem turmartigen Haus oder einer Tempelfassade verschmelzen.

Die Assoziation zur Körperöffnung drängt sich vor allem dann auf, wenn eine gleichsam »organhafte« Architektur sich von der rationalen Rechtwinkeligkeit distanziert.

Aus der Fülle der Beispiele – einige sind noch in anderen Zusammenhängen zu zitieren – seien nur einige wenige herausgegriffen.

In einer Studie für ein Einfamilienhaus von **André Bloc** (1896–1966) – in einem Modell dargestellt – werden die Gebäudeöffnungen zu anonymen, undifferenzierten Körperöffnungen. Das Gebäude verzichtet auf den Ausdruck des Tektonischen, des Gefügten und Gebauten und weckt die Erinnerung an äußere und innere Organe des Animalischen.

Christian Hunziker (1926–1990) hat seine Beziehung zur Körperhaftigkeit verbal und graphisch wiederholt dokumentiert. Bei einigen seiner Wohnbauten – z. B. bei *Le Stroumpf* in Genf – erinnern die Fenster an Körperöffnungen, insbesondere an die Vulva.

Die Vereinigung der Geschlechter findet in den Träumen nach Freud eine bauliche Symbolik: »Leiter, Stiege, Treppe, respektive das Gehen auf ihnen, sind sichere Symbole des Geschlechtsverkehrs.« (Freud, 1940)

7.3. »Männlich« und »weiblich« in der Architektur

Im Kapitel 2.5. wurde die schwierige Unterscheidung nach »männlich« und »weiblich« oder nach »maskulin« und »feminin« angesprochen. Wenn von männlicher Symbolik, oder allgemein von »männlicher Architektur« die Rede ist, müssen neuerdings die Inhalte des typisch »Männlichen« reflektiert werden.

Auch im Zusammenhang mit der Architektur wird es nicht gelingen, weibliche und männliche Geschlechtsmerkmale ohne Einbeziehung des Biologischen, des Genitalen zu formulieren.

Nochmals bedarf es der Erwähnung, daß die Reduktion von »männlich« und »weiblich« auf den genitalen Bereich problematisch ist und daß damit nicht einmal annähernd die komplexe Existenz menschlicher Wesen charakterisiert werden kann.

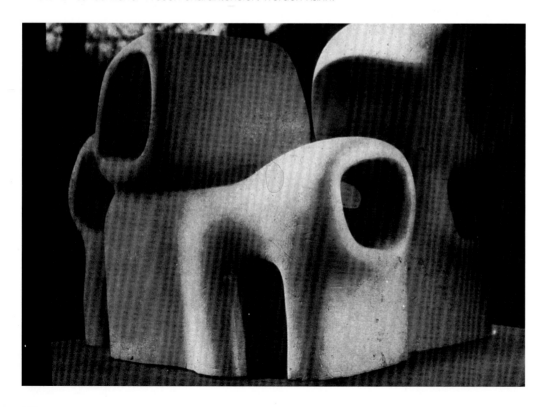

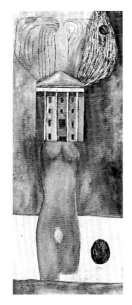

In another design, Porro makes use of soft, rounded, curving shapes which tend rather to make one think of a woman's body. The holiday village designed in 1972 for the island of Korcula in what was then Yugoslavia is interpreted by Porro as a giant who has risen from the sea and is intended to be reminiscent of pictures by Arcimboldo: the office building is the head, the restaurant is the stomach, the labyrinth is the bowels, the public rooms are the hands, and the amphitheatre is the pubis from which the penis emerges.

7.2. Carl Gustav Jung and Sigmund Freud

A consideration of historical architecture makes it clear that the group of problems relating to sexuality and fertility is an important part of the repertoire of symbolism in architecture, particularly in early cultures. When »archetypes« are being created, much of their metaphorical content is taken from the two, age-old elemental experiences: masculinity and femininity. Personal archetypes play an important part in the collective subconscious of **Carl Gustav Jung** (1875 to 1961). Each of them is also a complementary part of the human psyche. Jung observed that all human beings have in their psyche an element of the opposite sex: men have a female »anima« and women a male »animus«.

Sigmund Freud derived (1964), from the interpretation of dreams, a direct link between architectural structure and sexuality: »The one typical – that is regular – representation of the human figure as a whole is a house ... It may happen in a dream that one finds oneself climbing down the façade of a house, enjoying it at one moment, frightened at another. The houses with smooth walls are men, the ones with projections and balconies that one can hold on to are women.« The apertures in the building – windows, doors, gates – are accordingly analogies to the apertures of the human body, and in particular to the genitals.

The drawings by **Louise Bourgeois** may be regarded as a kind of illustration of Sigmund Freud's ideas. The houses become identical to the human figure. They are women's bodies which merge with a tower-like house or with a temple façade.

An association with a bodily orifice most commonly imposes itself upon the onlooker when an »organ-like« kind of architecture is no longer associated with rational rectangularity.

Only a few examples will be selected from the abundance available. Some of them will be mentioned in other connections.

In a study which **André Bloc** (1896–1966) – in the form of a model – produced for a single-family house, the apertures in the buildings become anonymous, undifferentiated body apertures. The building does not trouble to express anything tectonic, structured or built, and arouses memories of external and internal animal organs.

Christian Hunziker (1926–1990) repeatedly documented, in both words and pictures, his relationship with matters of the body. In some of his residential buildings, such as *Le Stroumpf* in Geneva, the windows are reminiscent of body apertures, especially the vulva.

According to Freud, architectural symbols for the unification of the sexes are to be found in dreams. »Ladders, steps and staircases, or, more precisely, walking on them, are clear symbols of sexual intercourse.« (Freud, 1964)

7.3. »Male« and »Female« in Architecture

The difficult distinction between »male« and »female«, or between masculine and feminine, was addressed in Chapter 2.5. When reference is being made to masculine symbolism, or to »masculine architecture« generally, the essence of what is typically »masculine« must be reflected anew.

In connection with architecture, success will not be achieved in formulating female and male sexual characteristics without including biological and genital matters.

It must be repeated that any reduction of »male« and »female« to the genital area alone is problematical, and that the complex existence of human beings cannot even be approximately characterized by such means.

The observation that women and men relate differently to the two elements which are space and body, that is to say to the factors which chiefly constitute architecture, might be the starting point for a sexually specific architecture. Erik H. Erikson used experiments (1970) to provide evidence of the differing behaviour: »Girls emphasize the internal space, boys the

114. André Bloc, Einfamilienhaus, 1965.
115, 116. Louise Bourgeois, *Frau-Haus*, 1945/ 1946.

114. André Bloc, one-family house, 1965.
115, 116. Louise Bourgeois, *Woman House*, 1945/ 1946.

Die Beobachtung, daß Frauen und Männer eine unterschiedliche Beziehung zu den Elementen Raum und Körper aufweisen, also zu jenen Faktoren, die wesentlich Architektur konstituieren, könnte ein Anhaltspunkt zu einer geschlechtsspezifischen Architektur sein. Erik H. Erikson (1970) belegt das unterschiedliche Verhalten durch Experimente: »Die Mädchen betonen den inneren, die Jungen den äußeren Raum.« Diese Differenzierung ist aber letztendlich auch wieder auf biologische Dispositionen zurückzuführen: Für den Knaben ist die Entdeckung des Penis – ähnlich wie es Freud formuliert – ein entscheidendes Erlebnis. Für ihn ist der »äußere Raum« bedeutend und trägt zu seiner Identität bei. Beim Mädchen hingegen ist der »innere Raum« dominierend. Er entsteht durch die Erfahrung einer potentiellen Gebärfähigkeit und bestimmt die weibliche Identität.

Im vollen Bewußtsein dieser Kritik, jedoch ohne tragfähige Alternative, werden daher auch die folgenden Ausführungen, zwar nicht zur Gänze, aber vorwiegend, aus dem Biologischen abzuleiten sein. Eine gewisse Auffächerung mag sich immerhin dadurch ergeben, daß nicht nur die Fortpflanzungsorgane, sondern auch die sekundären und tertiären Geschlechtsmerkmale als Kriterien für Mann und Frau angesehen werden sollen.[39]

117. Christian Hunziker, Wohnhausanlage *Le Stroumpf*, Genf, 1982.

117. Christian Hunziker, residential estate *Le Stroumpf*, Geneva, 1982.

outer.« But this differentiation can ultimately also again be traced back to biological dispositions: to a boy, the discovery of the penis is – somewhat like the way in which Freud puts it –
a decisive experience. To a boy, the external space is important and contributes to his identity.
To a girl, on the other hand, the internal space is dominant. It comes into being by experiencing the potential ability to give birth, and it controls the female identity.

In full awareness of this criticism, but in the absence of a sufficient alternative to it, most
though not all of the following remarks will be derived from biology. The field may nonetheless
be spread somewhat wider in that not only the organs of procreation, but also the secondary
and tertiary sexual characteristics, are to be regarded as criteria for men and women.[38]

7.4. Male Symbolism

7.4.1. Primary Sexual Characteristics. Masts, Poles, Columns, Towers

Using dream symbolism, Freud argues as follows: the male organ »finds symbolic substitutes
in the first instance in things that resemble it in shape – things, accordingly, that are long and
up-standing, such as sticks, umbrellas, posts, trees and so on.« Columns, masts, towers, and
even high-rise buildings, would of course have to be added. However, Freud also states that
pillars and columns are symbols of legs.

The **setting upright** of elements such as stones, branches and trunks, which had previously been lying down, is an analogy to the phallic erection and is probably one of the **original acts** of architecture which are closely related to the archetypes. (Feuerstein, 1966)

The blending or identifying of ritualism with sexuality is a self-evident matter in early and
primitive cultures. »Right into historic times, the phallus and the vulva loom large in village ritual,« wrote Lewis Mumford (1961). »In monumental form they make their way later into the
city, not merely disguised as obelisks, columns, towers, domed enclosures, but in such naked
forms as the huge penis, broken off but erect, still on view at Delos.«

Norberg-Schulz links (1928) stones – which are set up like monuments and are part of the
cult of tombs and ancestors – to **phallic symbolism**: »Although the ancestors' souls do produce an effect, it is not intended that they should drift around too freely. A stone is an appropriate place for them to reside, because its hardness and heaviness express continuance and
deathlessness. Thus a stone becomes a manifestation of the procreative powers of the ancestors, an expression of how the generations continue. Specifically, the erected stone, the
menhir, was understood as being the place where the vital powers resided, as being a representation of the phallus. The erected stone also symbolizes power, as anything erected requires energy.«

It is possible, in the stone columns of China, to discern the »unconscious final stages of
age-old phallic symbolism ... such as is still customary in a diminished form in the Ainos tombs
today.« (Münsterberg, 1990)

Many, perhaps all, of the monumental stones found in numerous early cultures are based
on phallic motifs. According to Gassner (1989), the origin of the cultic buildings reaching hea-
venwards (e. g. minarets, church towers, stupas, etc.) which are met with in various religions
is to be looked for in prehistoric, phallic, monumental stones. »The round towers of England
and Ireland, and also the towers of Christian churches, are the remains of original phallic
monoliths.«

Where the history of Western architecture is concerned, it is rather difficult to interpret **towers** as phallic elements, especially when religious buildings are involved. Concentration on a
religious symbolism, in which sexuality is largely left out of account, means that phallic interpretation belongs to the realm of speculation.

Only by a circuitous route can an approach be made: religion and church are undoubtedly
potential power structures in Western history, and they are certainly male powers, »potencies«, which are striving to express themselves. From this point of view, the phallic association
is perfectly plausible. It is supported by the fact that most church towers do not have a real
function. Their task of serving as bell towers, and sometimes as watchtowers, is only secondary, whereas the symbolic meaning, the marking of the location, and the manifestation of
power, are primary factors.

Some particularly striking examples are the towers which grow directly up from the ground,
such as the Stephansturm in Vienna and the type of the free-standing campanile. Quarrels

7.4. Männliche Symbolik

7.4.1. Primäre Geschlechtsmerkmale. Mast, Pfahl, Säule, Turm

Freud argumentiert anhand der Traumsymbolik: »... das männliche Glied findet symbolischen Ersatz ... durch Dinge, die ihm in der Form ähnlich sind, wie: Stöcke, Schirme, Stangen, Bäume und dergleichen.« Selbstverständlich wären Säulen, Masten, Türme, ja selbst Hochhäuser anzufügen. Pfeiler und Säulen werden bei Freud allerdings auch als Symbol für die Beine genannt.

Die **Aufrichtung**, Aufstellung von zuvor liegenden Elementen wie Steinen, Ästen, Stämmen stellt eine Analogie zur phallischen Erektion dar und gehört wohl zu den **Urakten** der Architektur, die mit den Archetypen in engem Zusammenhang stehen. (Feuerstein, 1966)

In den frühen und primitiven Kulturen ist die Vermengung oder Identät des Kultischen und des Sexuellen eine Selbstverständlichkeit. »Bis in die geschichtliche Zeit hinein spielen Phallus und Vulva im Kultleben des Dorfes eine wichtige Rolle,« schreibt Lewis Mumford (1961). »In monumentaler Gestalt ziehen sie später in die Stadt ein, nicht nur als Obelisken und Säulen, Türme und kuppelgeschmückte Gewölbe, sondern in der unverhüllten Form des abgebrochenen, aber aufrechten Penis, wie er heute noch auf Delos zu sehen ist.«

Norberg-Schulz (1928) bringt die malartig aufgestellten Steine des Grab- und Ahnenkultes mit der **Phallussymbolik** in Zusammenhang: »Die Seelen der Vorfahren wirken zwar, sollen aber nicht frei umhertreiben. Der Stein bietet ihnen eine angemessene Bleibe, weil in seiner Härte und Schwere Dauer und Unvergänglichkeit zum Ausdruck kommen. So wird der Stein eine Manifestation der Zeugungsmächte der Ahnen, ein Ausdruck der Kontinuität der Generationen. Namentlich der aufgerichtete Stein, der Menhir, wurde als Aufenthaltsort der Lebenskräfte, als Repräsentation des Phallus verstanden. Der aufgerichtete Stein symbolisiert zudem Macht, da das Aufgerichtete Energie erfordert.«

In den Steinsäulen Chinas können wir den »unbewußten Ausklang uralter Phallussymbolik ... wie sie auch bei den Ainosgräbern in verkümmerter Gestalt noch heute üblich ist«, erkennen. (Münsterberg, 1990)

Den »Malsteinen« zahlreicher früher Kulturen liegen zum Großteil, vielleicht zur Gänze phallische Motive zugrunde. Nach Gassner (1989) ist der Ursprung himmelstrebender Kultbauten verschiedener Religionen (z. B. Minarette, Kirchtürme, Stupas usw.) in vorgeschichtlichen, phallischen Malsteinen zu suchen. »Es sind die Rundtürme Englands und Irlands ebenso wie die Türme christlicher Kirchen Reste ursprünglicher phallischer Monolithe.«

In der abendländischen Architekturgeschichte stößt die Deutung der **Türme** als phallisches Element auf beträchtliche Schwierigkeiten, insbesondere im Bereich des Sakralbaues. Die Konzentration auf eine religiöse Symbolik, bei der das Sexuelle weitgehend ausgeklammert ist, verweist die phallische Interpretaion in den spekulativen Bereich.

Lediglich über einen Umweg ist eine Annäherung möglich: Religion und Kirche sind zweifellos Machtpotentiale in der abendländischen Geschichte, und es sind sicherlich männliche Mächte, »Potenzen«, die nach Ausdruck streben. So gesehen ist die phallische Assoziation durchaus plausibel. Sie wird dadurch unterstützt, daß die meisten Kirchtürme keine eigentliche »Funktion« haben. Die Aufgabe, als Glockenträger zu dienen, manchmal auch als Wachttürme, ist durchaus sekundär, während die zeichenhafte Bedeutung, die Markierung des Ortes und die Machtmanifestation im Vordergrund stehen.

Als besonders markante Beispiele können jene Türme angesehen werden, die direkt aus dem Boden emporwachsen, wie etwa der Stephansturm in Wien und der Typus des freistehenden Campaniles. Die aus verschiedenen Städten überlieferten Streitigkeiten hinsichtlich der Höhe der Türme (z. B. zwischen Linz und Wien) erinnern in etwa an die absurden Wettstreite um einen längeren Penis.

Die Machtkonkurrenzen des späten Mittelalters kommen auch darin zum Ausdruck, daß, mit zunehmender Bedeutung des Stadtbürgertums, das Turmmotiv der Kirchen von den Rathäusern usurpiert wird, besonders signifikant etwa in den flämisch-belgischen Rathäusern.

Der Turm als weltliches Machtsymbol begegnet uns vor allem in den Geschlechtertürmen der italienischen Städte (Bologna, S. Gimignano u. a.). Auch hier tritt das Phänomen auf, daß durch die Höhe – jenseits jeder Funktion – die Macht dargestellt werden soll. [40]

Aus dem Bereich profaner und weitgehend zweckfreier Türme soll stellvertretend für viele nur ein Beispiel herausgegriffen werden: In Horton (Donset, England), (Mott 1989) steht ein eigenartiger Turm aus Backstein auf einem sechseckigen Grundriß, der 1765 von dem lokalen

(such as one between Linz and Vienna) in various towns regarding the height of the towers have been recorded, and are somewhat reminiscent of absurd competitions for a longer penis.

The power struggles of the late Middle Ages were also expressed in the fact that, as the citizens grew in importance, the tower motif of the churches came to be usurped by the town halls. An especially significant example of this is the Flemish-Belgian town halls.

The tower as a symbol of secular power is mostly encountered in the family towers of Italian towns such as Bologna, S. Gimignano and others. A phenomenon again occurring here is that the height – over and above any function – is intended to represent power.[39]

One example, representative of many others, may be selected from the field of profane and largely purposeless towers:

Baumeister, Humphrey Sturt, errichtet, jedoch Thomas Archer zugeschrieben wurde. Der Turm dient keinem erkennbaren Zweck und war bestenfalls ein Aussichtsturm.

In der Architektur unseres Jahrhunderts spielt das Turmmotiv eine herausragende Rolle, wir finden jedoch kaum direkte Zeugnisse, um es im Sinne phallischer Symbole deuten zu können, und so muß die assoziative Spekulation bemüht werden.

Hervorragende Beispiele zweckfreier, ja nicht einmal besteigbarer Türme sind jene am (urprünglichen) Stadtrand von Mexico-Stadt. **Mathias Goeritz** (1915–1990) hat sie (gemeinsam mit L. Barragán) 1957 erbaut, und sie sollten lediglich Identifikationszeichen, Male, Orientierungspunkte darstellen.

Als Zeugnisse der Macht – und somit als legitime Fortsetzung der historischen Turmbauten – können die Hochhäuser, die Wolkenkratzer angesehen werden. Das Wohnhochhaus stellt eher die Ausnahme dar und liegt auch zunehmend im Kreuzfeuer der Kritik.

Die Mehrzahl der Hochhäuser repräsentiert tatsächlich Macht, wie sie sich in der politischen Verwaltung, in den Konzernen und den großen Unternehmen zeigt. Nur in wenigen Entwürfen und Realisierungen tritt uns das Phallische der aufragenden Architektur unverschlüsselt entgegen.

Hans Hollein (geb. 1934) zeichnet 1958 auf ein bedrucktes Papier eine Skizze für einen Wolkenkratzer. Zweifelsfrei ist dieses »Gebäude« als erigierter Penis zu erkennen.

In einem kleinen Detail entsteht gleichsam ein Doppel-Penis, der aus dem Scrotum herauswächst: Die Lüftungs- und Klimaröhren beim ORF Landesstudio in Graz (1969–1981) von **Gustav Peichl** (geb. 1928) haben unverkennbar einen dynamisch-phallischen Charakter.

Ein Hotelentwurf, das *Dildo Hilton* von **Maria Auböck** (geb. 1951) aus dem Jahre 1974, bekennt sich bewußt zum phallischen Symbol. »Im angelsächsischen Sprachgebrauch ist ein Dildo ein künstliches Geschlechtsorgan. ... Aus der Weite des Stadtparks bricht ein glänzender, stahlumkrusteter, gläserner, unwirklich schimmernder Turm der Lüste, ein neues Wahrzeichen Wiens.« (Auböck, 1974) Der Zimmertrakt weist einen elliptischen Grundriß auf, der auf einen doppelt gekurvten Flachbau aufgesetzt ist, dessen Rundungen als Brüste oder Hoden definiert werden können.

Im Randfeld der Architektur bewegt sich die **Objektkunst**, sie stellt jedoch häufig eine Interpretationshilfe insofern dar, als in provisorischen oder konzeptionellen Bauwerken, von der Funktion abstrahiert, Ideen und Konzepte sinnfälliger zum Ausdruck kommen. Der Turm aus Luft und Plastikfolie, den **Christo** (geb. 1935) bei der Documenta IV in Kassel 1968 errichtet, läßt keinen Zweifel aufkommen, daß es sich um eine gigantische Phallusnachbildung handelt. Die phallische Assoziation wird erleichtert, wenn der Turm nicht in einer Spitze, sondern in einer Rundung endet und somit Ähnlichkeit mit der Glans evoziert, wie dies bei Christos »Turm« aus Luft eindeutig zu sehen war.

Ein anderer pneumatischer Turm war auf der Expo 1970 in Osaka installiert, eine sich nach oben verjüngende schlanke Konstruktion, die Übersetzung eines Obelisken oder Kirchturms in die Technologie der Gegenwart. Das Bemerkenswerte aber war, daß er in rhythmischen Abständen in sich zusammensank und sich dann allmählich wieder aufrichtete: Die Assoziation zur erectio phalli war unvermeidbar und wurde durch die rote Spitze noch unterstützt.

Die **Haus-Rucker-Co** stülpen – allerdings nur im Projekt – über einen kleinen Denkmal-Obelisken in Neuenkirchen, Deutschland, den Obelisken der Place de la Concorde in Paris, eine Nachbildung aus Stahlgitter. Die Bezeichnung *Provisorium der Macht* könnte ebenso »geschwächte Potenz« heißen, denn auch dieses Herrschaftszeichen verliert seine Kraft, die Spitze scheint sich zu neigen wie eine warme Wachskerze.

Männlich-genitale Formen als **Grundrißfigurationen** stellen die Ausnahme dar. Das »klassische« Beispiel des *Oikema*, des Liebestempels von **Claude-Nicolas Ledoux** (1736–1806) wurde zu Beginn des 19. Jahrhunderts aufgezeichnet. Über einen Portikus betritt man das Vestibül, von dem aus die Gesprächszimmer und die Galerien zugänglich sind, deren halbkreisförmiger Grundriß der Rundung der Hoden entspricht. Das Vestibül vermittelt zu einem Flur, von dem aus man die einzelnen Zimmer erreicht. Ein ovaler Salon schließlich ist in der Glans untergebracht. Ledoux versteht sein Oikema keineswegs als gewöhnliches Bordell, sondern ganz im Sinne der aufklärerischen Tendenzen seiner Zeit, als eine Erziehungsanstalt: Der junge Mann soll durch sexuelle Erfahrungen heranreifen, um schließlich für die Ehe fähig zu werden.

Derartig »genitale« Pläne haben nur wenige Nachahmer gefunden. Das Motiv des Phallischen im Grundriß ist in der Realität optisch kaum wahrnehmbar, und so ist es nicht erstaunlich, daß es nur selten auftaucht. **Paul Thiersch** skizziert 1923 für München-Nymphenburg ein

119. Hans Hollein, *Wolkenkratzer*, 1958.
120. Maria Auböck, *Dildo Hilton*, 1974.

119. Hans Hollein, *Skyscraper*, 1958.
120. Maria Auböck, *Dildo Hilton*, 1974.

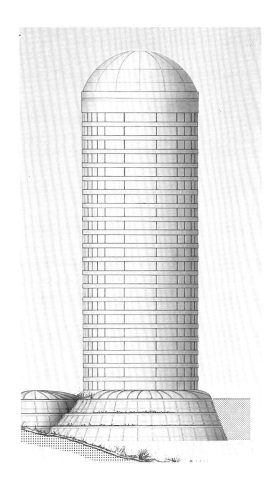

A peculiar brick tower stands on a hexagonal ground plan in Horton (Dorset, England). (Mott, 1989) It was built in 1765 by Humphrey Sturt, the local architect, but attributed to Thomas Archer. The tower serves no discernible purpose and was at best a lookout tower.

The tower motif plays a prominent role in 20th-century architecture, but we can hardly find any direct evidence of its interpretability as a phallic symbol. Associative speculation is therefore required.

Some outstanding examples of purposeless towers, which cannot even be climbed, are those on the original outskirts of Mexico City. **Mathias Goeritz** (1915–1990) built them in 1957 jointly with L. Barragán, and they are only intended to be identifying marks, signs, landmarks.

High-rise buildings, skyscrapers, can be regarded as evidence of power, and thus as a legitimate continuation of historical tower structures. Residential high-rise buildings are more of an exception and are also coming under increasing critical crossfire.

The majority of high-rise buildings really do represent power, such as is seen in political administration, in groups of companies and in large businesses. It is only in a few designs and realizations that the phallic character of the towering architecture is encountered in uncoded form.

Hans Hollein (born 1934) drew, in 1958, a sketch for a skyscraper on a printed sheet of paper. This »building« can undoubtedly be discerned to be an erect penis.

The forming of a kind of double penis growing out of the scrotum can be seen in a small detail, namely the ventilation and air conditioning pipes in the regional studio of the Austrian radio broadcasting company in Graz (1969–1981). The pipes are the work of **Gustav Peichl** (born 1928), and have an unmistakably dynamic-phallic character.

A design for a hotel, the *Dildo Hilton* (1974) by **Maria Auböck** (born 1951) consciously accepts phallic symbolism. »In Anglo-Saxon language usage, a dildo is an artificial sexual organ... A shining tower of delights, made of glass, with a surrounding crust of steel and an unreal shimmer, breaks forth – a new landmark of Vienna – from the expanses of the city park.« (Auböck, 1974) The wing with the hotel rooms in it has an elliptical ground plan placed upon a doubly curving flat structure whose curvatures can be defined as being breasts or testicles.

The **art of objects** is a marginal area of architecture. But it is often an aid to interpretation in that ideas and concepts are more obviously expressed in provisional or conceptual buildings which are abstracted from any specific function. That Tower made of air and plastic sheeting which **Christo** (born 1935) set up in 1968 at the Documenta IV exhibition in Kassel leaves one in no doubt that it is a gigantic imitation of a phallus. The phallic association is made easier if the tower does not end in a peak but in a curvature, thus evoking a similarity with the glans, and this could be clearly seen in Christo's »Tower« made of air.

Another pneumatic tower was installed at Expo 1970 in Osaka, a construction which tapered towards the top and converted an obelisk or church tower into present-day technology. But the notable factor was that it sank down within itself at rhythmical intervals and then gradually raised itself up again. There was an inevitable association with an erectio phalli, confirmed by the red tip.

There is a design in which the **Haus-Rucker-Co** places an imitation, made of steel lattice, of the obelisk in the Place de la Concorde in Paris on top of a small obelisk, which is a monument, in Neuenkirchen, Germany. The name *Provisional Power Structure* which is given to this work might just as well be »Weakened Potency«, because this symbol of domination is also losing its power, and the tip seems to be leaning over like a hot wax candle.

Male genital shapes in **ground-plan figurations** are an exception. The »classical« example, which is *Oikema*, the temple of love by **Claude-Nicolas Ledoux** (1736–1806), was drawn in the early 19th century. From the vestibule, which is entered via a portico, the meeting rooms and the galleries lead off. Their semicircular ground plan corresponds to the curvature of the testicles. The vestibule leads to a corridor from which the individual rooms are gained. Finally, an oval drawing room is housed in the glans. Ledoux does not mean his Oikema to be a common brothel, but understands it as being an educational institution pursuing the tendencies towards enlightenment which were prevalent in his day: the young man is intended to grow up by means of sexual experiences, so that he will finally be capable of marriage.

Such »genital« designs found only a few imitators. The motif of the phallus in the ground plan is scarcely visible in reality, and it is therefore not surprising that it occurs only rarely. **Paul Thiersch** sketched in 1923 a residential house for the Nymphenburg district of Munich. Its rooms are not defined in any detail. Pehnt noted (1973) that, for the architects of this epoch, the designs »secretly become sexual symbols« and that a »building is re-interpreted to form an erotic metaphor«.

121. Gustav Peichl, ORF-Landesstudio Graz, 1969–1981. Detail der Lüftungsanlage.
122. Haus-Rucker-Co, *Provisorium der Macht*, Neuenkirchen, Deutschland, 1976.
123. Pneumatischer Turm auf der Expo '70, Osaka.
124. Claude-Nicolas Ledoux, *Oikema*, 1804.
125. Paul Thiersch, Wohnhaus für München-Nymphenburg, 1923.
126. Christo, *5600 Cubic Meter Package*, 1968.
127. Willi Schelkes, Unterkunftshaus im Hochgebirge, 1931.

121. Gustav Peichl, ORF-Landesstudio Graz, 1969–1981. Detail of the ventilation system.
122. Haus-Rucker-Co, *Provisional Power Structure*, Neuenkirchen, Germany, 1976.
123. Pneumatic tower on Expo '70, Osaka.
124. Claude-Nicolas Ledoux, *Oikema*, 1804.
125. Paul Thiersch, Wohnhaus for Nymphenburg, Munich, 1923.
126. Christo, *5600 Cubic Meter Package*, 1968.
127. Willi Schelkes, accomodation in the high-mountain region, 1931.

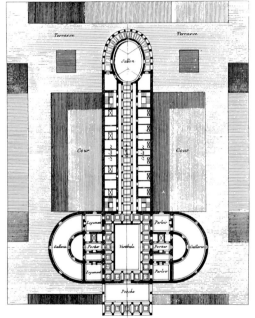

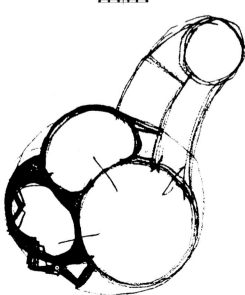

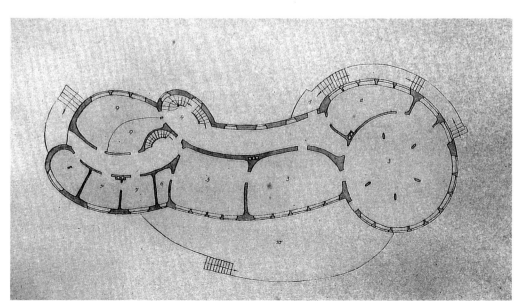

Wohnhaus, dessen Räume nicht näher definiert sind, Pehnt (1973) stellt fest, daß den Architekten dieser Epoche die Entwürfe »unter der Hand zu Geschlechtssymbolen« geraten und das »Bauwerk zu einer erotischen Metapher umgedeutet wird«.

Vielleicht können wir auch den Grundriß des Unterkunftshauses im Hochgebirge (1931) von **Willi Schelkes** mit dem männlichen Genital assoziieren.

Christian W. Thomsen (1991) interpretiert den Grundriß des *Daisy House* (1975–1978) von **Stanley Tigerman** (geb. 1930) als erotisches Symbol: »Dieser Plan weist das Haus insgesamt als männliches Genital aus, wobei sich in den Fenstern des Wohnbereiches männliches und weibliches Prinzip durchdringen. Tigerman, der Panerotiker, läßt ungewöhnlicherweise den Schlitz der Fronttür direkt in die Küche münden, auch dies natürlich eine erotisch-kulinarische Anspielung ...«

7.4.2. Sekundäre Geschlechtsmerkmale

Wie schon in Kap 2.5 dargestellt, fällt die Unterscheidung nach »männlich« und »weiblich« jenseits der genitalen Fakten sehr schwer, und so ist es auch nicht leicht, die sekundären (und eventuell tertiären) Geschlechtsmerkmale allgemeingültig zu definieren. Statistisch ist es zweifellos so, daß der spezifische Körperbau, die Körpergröße, der höhere Muskelanteil, die Atemtätigkeit, Körper- und Barthaar als Charakteristika des Mannes angesprochen werden können. Wenn wir jenseits des Genitalen die Frage nach einer »männlichen« Architektur stellen, könnte bestenfalls das »Kraftvolle«, das Kantige, Spitze, Scharfe, vielleicht auch das Aggressive angeführt werden. So wird etwa die scharfkantige, dunkle Wand, die Kiesler zu seinem Rollendom stellt, als »männlich« interpretiert. Vielleicht kann die Wand, die **Mauer** allgemein als männliches Element angesehen werden, das freilich wieder dem Weiblich-Mütterlichen der Erde entspringt, daraus hervorwächst, darauf aufruht.

Die Mauern gehören in der antiken Mythologie zu den res sanctae, den »göttlichen Dingen«. Die aus den Tiefen emporsteigenden Mauern sind »eine aus dem Mutterleibe hervorgehende Geburt, die in den finsteren Gründen so lange schlief, bis sie die Einwirkung der männlichen Kraft aus dem Schlummer aufweckte und ans Licht hervorzog.« (Bachofen, 1954) »Also sind die Mauern wie die Bäume eine Geburt der Mutter Erde, und durch die Fundamente, wie die Bäume durch die Wurzeln, mit dem Mutterleibe auch nach der Geburt in fortdauernder fester Verbindung.« (Bachofen, 1954)

Die Mauern wurden bei den Römern oft mit dem Bild des Phallus ausgestattet, weil sie ihm die Entstehung verdanken, und weil er das Böse abwehrt.

Freud (1940) findet ein generalisierendes Symbol des Männlichen in der Maschine und meint, daß alle Arten von schwer zu beschreibenden komplizierten Maschinen Symbole desselben (Männlichen) werden. »Eine problematische Geschlechtsfixierung ist daraus wiederum abzuleiten, nämlich insofern, als das Mechanische, Funktionale, Komplizierte, Rationale allein dem Manne zugeordnet wird.«

7.5. Weibliche Symbolik

7.5.1. Primäre äußere Geschlechtsmerkmale. Tor, Tür, Spalte, Wunde

Die notwendige Unterscheidung nach den äußeren und inneren primären Geschlechtsmerkmalen ist in Freuds Traumsymbolik nicht ganz klar artikuliert: »Das weibliche Genitale wird symbolisch dargestellt durch alle jene Objekte, die seine Eigenschaft teilen, einen **Hohlraum** einzuschließen, der etwas in sich aufnehmen kann. Also durch Schächte, Gruben und Höhlen, durch Gefäße und Flaschen, durch Schachteln, Dosen, Koffer, Büchsen, Kisten, Taschen usw. ... aber auch durch Höhlen, Schiffe und alle Arten von Gefäßen.«

»Die komplizierte Topographie der weiblichen Geschlechtsteile macht es begreiflich, daß diese sehr häufig als Landschaft mit Fels, Wald und Wasser dargestellt werden ...« (Freud, 1940). Abgeleitet aus dem Bereich der ethnologischen Forschung ergänzt Winthuis (1928) das Repertoire der weiblichen Symbolik für Vulva und Vagina. Es sind Körperteile wie der Bauch, das Auge, das Ohr, der After, die Nasenlöcher, der Kopf, der Magen, der Mund und verständlicherweise die gespreizten Beine, die stellvertretend für die Sexualorgane stehen. Aus der Naturerfahrung werden überraschenderweise dem Berg (wohl dem Inneren des

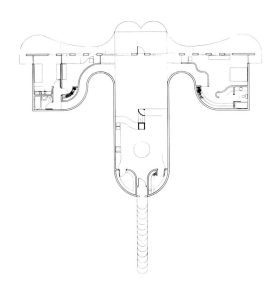

The ground plan of the residential house (1931) in the high mountains, the work of **Willi Schelkes**, can perhaps be associated with the male genitals.

Christian W. Thomsen interpreted (1991) the ground plan of the *Daisy House* (1975-1978) by **Stanley Tigerman** (born 1930) as an erotic symbol: »This plan shows that the house as a whole is the male genitals, with the male and female principles penetrating one another in the windows of the residential section. Tigerman, the pan-erotic, unusually allows the slot of the letter box in the front door to lead directly into the kitchen, and this too is of course an erotic-culinary allusion ...«

7.4.2. Secondary Sexual Characteristics

As already described in Chapter 2.5., it is very difficult to distinguish between »male« and »female« when no genital facts are involved, and it is therefore also not easy to give a generally applicable definition to the secondary, and possibly tertiary, sexual characteristics. It is an undoubted statistical fact that the specific anatomy, the body height, the higher proportion of muscles, the breathing, and the facial and body hair, can be regarded as male characteristics. If, outside the genital field, we ask what a »male« architecture is, the answer given might at best be: a vigorous architecture, an angular, pointed, sharp, and maybe also aggressive architecture. For example, the sharp-edged, dark wall which Kiesler places against his cylinder-type dome is interpreted as »male«. Perhaps a **wall** in general can be regarded as a male element, which does though in turn arise from, grow out of, and rest on, the female motherly earth.

In classical mythology, walls are res sanctae, »divine things«. The walls rising up from the depths are »a birth which rises from the womb and had been sleeping in the sombre depths until the effect of male power roused it from its slumbers and drew it forth to the light.« (Bachofen, 1954) »Thus walls, like trees, are born from mother earth, and even after birth the foundations continue to link them firmly to that womb, just as trees are linked by their roots.« (Bachofen, 1954)

The Romans often equipped walls with an image of a phallus, because they owed their existence to it and because it warded off evil.

Freud considered (1940) that a machine was a generalizing symbol of the male principle, and took the view »that all the types of complicated machines which are hard to describe become symbols of that same male principle.« A problematical sexual fixation can in turn be derived from this to the extent that anything mechanical, functional, complicated, rational is attributed to male humans alone.

7.5. Female Symbolism

7.5.1. Primary External Sexual Characteristics. Gate, Door, Cleft, Wound

The necessary distinction based on the external and internal primary sexual characteristics is not very clearly articulated in Freud's dream symbolism: »The female genitals are symbolically represented by all such objects as share their characteristic of enclosing a **hollow space** which can take something into itself: by pits, cavities and hollows, for instance, by vessels and bottles, by receptacles, boxes, trunks, cases, chests, pockets, and so on. Ships, too, fall into this category.«

»The complicated topography of the female genital parts makes one understand how it is that they are often represented as landscapes, with rocks, woods and water ...« (Freud, 1964) Deriving his ideas from the field of ethnological research, Winthuis added (1928) to the repertoire of the female symbolism which represents the vulva and the vagina. These are such parts of the body as: belly, eye, ear, anus, nostrils, head, stomach, mouth, and, understandably enough, the spread-out legs, which are representative of the sexual organs. When nature is being experienced, vaginal meanings are also, surprisingly, attributed to mountains (probably the inside of mountains), and also to bays of the sea, thickets, rocky ledges, caves, and, of course, the fertile soil.

It has already been mentioned that – in dream symbolism – **gates**, **doors** and **windows** represent bodily orifices, and it is a particular fact that the vulva is not only, in reality, the way

128. Stanley Tigerman, *Daisy House,* Porter, Indiana, 1975–1977.

Berges) vaginale Bedeutungen zugeordnet, ebenso der Meeresbucht, dem Dickicht, der Felsplatte, der Höhle und selbstverständlich dem fruchtbaren Boden.

Daß die **Tore, Türen** und **Fenster** in der Traumsymbolik ganz allgemein Körperöffnungen darstellen, wurde bereits erwähnt, und ganz besonders gilt, daß die Vulva nicht nur realiter Ausgang für jedes neugeborene Leben ist, sondern auch den Eingang, das Tor, die Türe für den von draußen Kommenden symbolisiert. Sie ist auch die empfangende Öffnung, die das Befruchtende aufnimmt, und sie ist der Eingang zum bergenden schützenden Urraum, sie ist gleichsam die Grenze zwischen einer äußeren und einer inneren Welt.

Das weite Deutungsspektrum des Räumlich-Architektonischen als Gleichnis des Biologischen geht weit in die Vorgeschichte zurück.

Die Vulva, die zumeist als Spalte, Tür oder Tor symbolisiert wird, kann sich zum Kreis erweitern. Um den Kreis, den Ring als weibliches Element zu verstehen, helfen uns prähistorische Funde. Ein ringförmiges Frauenidol aus Jasa Tepe, Bulgarien, stammt aus dem Äneolithikum, der Kupfersteinzeit (ca. 2500 v. Chr.). Die Kreisöffnung wird als die geöffnete Vulva bei der Geburt interpretiert, die angedeuteten Brüste und der Kopf weisen die Figur zweifelsohne als weiblich aus. In weitergehenden Abstraktionen bleibt oft nur der Kreisring übrig.

Für den Urmenschen bedeutet die **Höhle** wesentlich mehr als nur physischen Schutz. Sie wird, über das Gleichnishafte hinaus, zu einem realen Uterus. Sonach versinnbildlicht auch der Höhleneingang die Vulva, die Pforte in die Urgeborgenheit. Dieser Gedanke taucht in der Architekturgeschichte, explizit oder latent, immer wieder auf.

Selbst im **Christentum**, das mit der Sexualsymbolik sehr sparsam umgeht, können wir zahlreiche Metaphern aufspüren. Die Kirche ist im theologischen Sinne die Mutter, und sie ist damit auch als weibliches Element zu interpretieren: »... so gibt es auch Deutungen der Kirchentür als Sinnbild der Gnadenmutter und Gottesgebärerin, durch die das Heil in die Welt kam; als die porta clausa oder porta coeli, wiederum in Beziehung zu der Heiligen Jungfrau, weil durch deren Leib die Erlösung geschah.« (Scheltema, 1950)

Vor allem ist es der trichterförmige Eingang, der die psychoanalytische Symbolik zu bestätigen scheint: Das romanische und gotische Portal mit den zahlreichen Abstufungen und dem symbolträchtigen Figurenschmuck sind die Pforten zur großen mütterlichen Geborgenheit der Kirche, sind die Eingänge in den beschützenden, sakralen Bereich als Antizipation des kommenden Paradieses.

Das Tor der Kirche als Symbol für die Vulva finden wir selten explizit artikuliert. Ein Fresko der Kirche in Schwarzrheindorf bei Bonn legitimiert eine entsprechende Interpretation. Christus wird geboren aus Maria der Jungfrau: Diese Darstellung zeigt Christus, wie er eben aus dem Tor einer Kirche (die Jungfrau Maria und gleichzeitig die Mutter Kirche) segnend heraustritt. Die Darstellung ist von zwei Engeln flankiert. Folgen wir einer Assoziationskette, dann ist nicht nur die Kirche, sondern auch die Grotte Sinnbild Mariens und die Öffnung der Grotte ihr Eingang und Ausgang: die Immaculata der Wundererscheinung von Massabielle ereignet sich in einer Grotte, die Lourdesgrotte findet tausendfache Nachahmung in der katholischen Welt. Und noch ein Vergleich mag zulässig sein: Venus wird nicht nur aus dem Schaum geboren, sie entsteigt auch einer Muschel, und in der Darstellung von Odilon Redon wird diese zu Tor und Vulva. (Vgl. Kap. 7.5.2.)

Diese Motive leiten über zu einer anderen im Mittelalter sehr beliebten Figuration, zur **Mandorla.** Christus erscheint in einer mandelförmigen Gloriole, die seine ganze Figur umfaßt. Auch hier finden wir häufig zwei flankierende Engel, und so könnte der Eindruck eines Tores noch verstärkt werden. Bolsena (1980) sieht in der Mandorla grundsätzlich ein Symbol für die Vulva, für das lebens- und heilspendende Element. Maria selbst, etwa in Santa Maria del Fiore in Florenz, bisweilen auch die Darstellung des Gnadenstuhls ist von der Mandorla umgeben.

Eine gewagte Spekulation verbindet einmal mehr Adam mit Christus: Wenn wir nicht der androgynen Interpretation Adams folgen, dann ist Eva aus dem Körper Adams entsprungen: Seine geöffnete Seite war eine Wunde und gleichzeitig ein Geburtsorgan, dem Eva entsteigt.

Auch der »zweite« Adam, Christus, trägt eine Wunde durch den Lanzenstich des Soldaten, und aus dieser Wunde fließen Blut und Wasser, mehr noch: Aus ihr entspringt nun die Ecclesia, die Mutter Kirche, von Christus geboren. (Pfister, 1993)

Für **Graf Ludwig von Zinzendorf** (1700–1760) ist das »Seitenhöhlchen«, die Wunde Christi das weibliche Genitale, und zwar einerseits als Geburtsorgan, andererseits als »Ort der maximalen Befriedigung des mit allen Merkzeichen der primären gleichgeschlechtlichen Sexualbetätigung ausgestatteten religiösen Eros ...« (Pfister, 1925)

129. Trichterportal der Kirche der Zisterzienser-
abtei Lilienfeld, Niederösterreich, um 1250.
130. Maria in der Mandorla im Dom in Florenz,
um 1430.
131. Fresko in der romanischen Kapelle in Schwarz-
Rheindorf bei Bonn, um 1150. Stilisierte Nach-
zeichnung.

129. Funnel-shaped portal of the church of the
Cistercian abbey in Lilienfeld, Lower Austria, ca.
1250.
130. Maria in the mandorla in the Dome in Florence, ca. 1430.
131. Fresco in the Romanic chapel in Schwarz-
Rheindorf near Bonn, ca. 1150. Stylized copy.

out for any new-born life, but is also the way in, the gate, the door for the one coming from outside. It is also the receiving aperture which takes in that which fertilizes, and is the entrance to the sheltering, protective, original space. It is a kind of border between an outer and an inner world.

The wide range of interpretation which is given to space and architecture as biological metaphors goes far back into prehistory.

The vulva, usually symbolized as a cleft, door or gate, can expand into a circle. Prehistoric finds help us to understand a circle, a ring, as being a female element. A ring-shaped female idol from Jasa Tepe, Bulgaria, dates from the Aeneolithic period, the copper age (ca. 2500 BC) The opening of the circle is interpreted as a vulva open during birth, while the lightly outlined breasts and the head undoubtedly identify the figure as female. In abstractions which go further than this, only the ring of the circle remains.

To prehistoric man, a **cave** meant considerably more than mere physical protection. Over and above anything metaphorical, it became a real uterus. Thus the entrance to the cave symbolizes the vulva, the gateway to the original shelter. This idea, either explicitly or latently, recurs repeatedly in the history of architecture.

Numerous metaphors can be detected even in **Christianity**, which is very sparing in its use of sexual symbolism. The church is the mother in the theological sense, and is thus also to be interpreted as a female element: »... thus there are also interpretations of a church door as a symbol of the mother both of grace and of God, the mother by whom salvation came into the world; interpretations as the porta clausa or porta coeli, again related to the Blessed Virgin, because redemption took place through her body.« (Scheltema, 1950)

But it is chiefly the funnel-shaped entrance which seems to confirm the psychoanalytical symbolism: the Romanesque and Gothic portals with their numerous gradations and the heavily symbolic decorative figures are the gateways to the great maternal shelter of the church. They are the entrances to the protecting, sacred region, as being an anticipation of the paradise to come.

A church door is rarely explicitly articulated as a vulval symbol. But a fresco in the church in Schwarzrheindorf near Bonn legitimizes such an interpretation. Christ is seen being born of the Virgin Mary: this depiction shows Christ giving his blessing while stepping out of the door of a church (the Virgin Mary and at the same time the Church as Mother). This depiction is flanked by two angels. If we follow a chain of association, then both the church and the grotto are the symbol of the Virgin Mary, and the entrance to the grotto is her way in and way out: the Immaculata of the Appearance of Miracles in Massabielle takes place in a grotto, and the Lourdes grotto is imitated a thousand times over in the Catholic world. Another comparison may also be permissible: Venus is not only born from foam, but also emerges from a shell which, in a depiction by Odilon Redon, becomes a gate and a vulva. (Cf. chap. 7.5.2.)

These motifs provide the transition to the **mandorla**, another figuration very popular in the Middle Ages. Christ appears in an almond-shaped halo which surrounds his entire figure. Here too, we often find two flanking angels, and this might strengthen the impression given of a gate. Bolsena (1980) regarded the mandorla as being in principle a symbol of a vulva, of the element that gives life and salvation. The Virgin Mary herself, for example in Santa Maria del Fiore in Florence, is surrounded by a mandorla, and so too, sometimes, is the depiction of the throne of grace.

Durch die Gleichsetzung von Wunde und Geburtsorgan erhält Christus einen androgynen Charakter. Es gibt Herz-Jesu-Darstellungen, die überraschend einem Munde ähneln: Einmal mehr interpretieren wir die Freudsche Affinität zwischen Wunde, Vulva und Mund.

In der **zeitgenössischen Kunst und Architektur** fehlt es nicht an sehr direkten Ausformulierungen von Eingängen, die als weibliche Geschlechtsorgane angesehen werden können.

André Masson (1896–1987) versucht das Bild der *Erde* darzustellen. Sie ist ein verwirrendes, komplexes Gebäude, von Spiralnebeln umgeben, aber unschwer erkennen wir eine liegende Frauengestalt mit gespreizten Beinen. Die Vulva in Form einer Raute – ähnlich den graphischen Vulgärdarstellungen und den archaischen Kürzeln – bildet das Tor zum Erdgebäude.

In einer anonymen erotischen Darstellung um 1930 ist eine Frau als Zirkuszelt dargestellt, der Zelteingang ist die Vulva, und die Männer eilen mit erigiertem Penis der Öffnung zu.

Kaum zu leugnen – so verblüffend ist die Ikonizität – ist die Darstellung des weiblichen Geschlechtsteiles bei einer Entwurfszeichnung zum Vondelpark – Theater in Amsterdam, 1919 von **H. TH. Wijdeveld** (1889–1985) zu Papier gebracht: Eine Frau mit weit gespreizten Beinen und aufragendem Bauch scheint sich den auf sie zuströmenden Besuchern darzubieten.

Hans Dieter Schaal (geb. 1943) interpretiert das freudianische Körpergebäude in der Zeichnung einer liegenden Frau mit gespreizten Beinen: Der Geschlechtsteil ist als Pforte ausgebildet. Schaal, der seine Zeichnung als »Tor zum Leben« charakterisiert, knüpft damit an eine Arbeit von **Gustave Courbet** (1819–1877) an: Sein Gemälde *L'origine du monde* von 1866 gewährt einen direkten Einblick in die Vulva, und es ist begreiflich, daß diese Darstellung damals einen Skandal ausgelöst hat. Ganz eindeutig zu verstehen war die große Plastik, die **Niki de Saint Phalle** 1966 mit Jean Tinguely und Per-Olof Ultvedt im Moderna Museet in Stockholm gebaut hat. Eine gigantische, schwangere Frauengestalt spreizt ihre Beine und bietet das »Tor des Lebens« als Eingangstür in ihren Körper an, der eine Reihe von Lustbarkeiten enthält.

Hon – en catedral – Sie – eine Kathedrale war der Name des Exponates. Ulf Linde (hon 1967) erläutert diese scheinbar blasphemische Bezeichnung: »Sie erinnert sowohl an die Hagia Sophia als auch an die Venus von Willendorf; eine aufgespannte Legerin ist sie – gleichzeitig ähnelt sie einem Ei. (Vielleicht weil Niki de Saint Phalle sie angemalt hat, wie Kinder zu Ostern Eier anmalen). Sie verkörpert das Gebären, ist die uralte große Mutter mit weit auseinander gespreizten Knien – ausgedorrter Boden wartet auf Regen und Gewitter, oder Hingegebenheit eines Muttertieres – nicht nur einer Frau. Man kann auch, wenn man so will, sehr deutliche Anspielungen auf den vorchristlichen Fruchtbarkeitskult finden. Der Teich mit Fischen – z. B. gleich nach dem Eintritt in den kolossalen Körper – diesen Teich gab es schon in den Tempelgärten der Göttin Astarte in Babylonien. In einer Brust trägt sie das von Tinguely gebaute Planetarium. Dies erscheint vielleicht begreiflich, wenn man weiß, daß man früher glaubte, Sterne seien Milchtropfen, von sehnsüchtigen Erdenbürgern aus einem göttlichen Rieseneuter gemolken. Der Erotismus, der in diesem Gebäude herrscht, ist mit anderen Worten mythisch und poetisch. Doch ist die Kenntnis der antiken Fruchbarkeitssymbole nicht ausreichend, um sie zu erfassen. Dazu ist die Welt des Jetzt sicher ein besserer Schlüssel.«

Das Thema der begehbaren Frau beschäftigt Niki de Saint Phalle auch in den folgenden Jahren. Nördlich von Rom entsteht der großangelegte Garten mit phantastischen *Tarot*-Figuren. Die »Herrscherin« betritt man durch eine Tür, die knapp unterhalb der mächtigen, bunten Brüste angebracht ist. Für die Künstlerin ist die Riesenfigur eine Muttergöttin, »in deren Innerem sie selbst wieder zur Mutter wurde«. (*art*, 1993/6)

In der Austauschbarkeit der Motive »Öffnung« verweist Freud noch auf andere Analogien. Demnach wird der Mund der Frau zur Vertretung der Genitalöffnung, die **Vagina dentata**, die mit Zähnen ausgestattete Scheide, illustriert die Identität von Mund und Geschlechtsorgan, übrigens ein Motiv, das immer wieder in der Werbung eingesetzt wird.

Aber noch eine andere Identität lehrt uns die Psychoanalyse: Auch die Wunde, die Verletzung kann eine sexuelle Metapher sein.

Der »Neo-Manierismus« in der Architektur der siebziger Jahre hat sich sehr häufig mit dem Thema der »schönen Wunde« beschäftigt, die gleichzeitig Sexualöffnung bedeutet.

Diese Identität wird beim ersten Geschäft Schullin von **Hans Hollein** am Graben in Wien (1972–1974) anschaulich illustriert. In die perfekte marmorspiegelnde Oberfläche schlägt Hollein eine aufgerissene Wunde, die sich bis in die Türöffnung fortsetzt und mit kostbarem Material: Gold (= Messing) ausgelegt ist. Wunde und Vagina, preziös behandelt, sind nicht zu trennen.

Neben diesen gleichsam direkten Aussagen stehen **Spalten, Schlitze, Schluchten**, Engpässe begreiflicherweise als Ersatzmotiv für die Vulva.

132. André Masson, *La terre*, um 1930.
133. H. Th. Wijdeveld, Vondelpark-Theater, Amsterdam, 1919.
134. Le cirque (L'entrée), Paris, um 1930.
135. Hans Dieter Schaal, *Tor zum Leben*, 1978.
136. Niki de Saint Phalle mit Jean Tinguely und Per-Olof Ultvedt, *Hon – en catedral*, Stockholm, 1966.

132. André Masson, *La terre*, ca. 1930.
133. H. Th. Wijdeveld, Vondelpark-Theatre, Amsterdam, 1919.
134. Le cirque (L'entrée), Paris, ca. 1930.
135. Hans Dieter Schaal, *Gateway to Life*, 1978.
136. Niki de Saint Phalle with J. Tinguely and Per-Olof Ultvedt, *Hon – en catedral*, Stockholm, 1966.

132   133
  134 135
  136

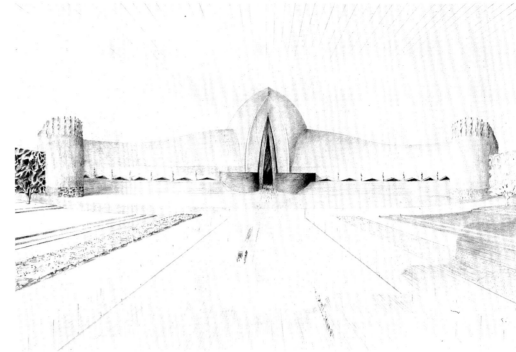

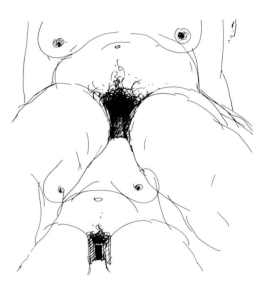

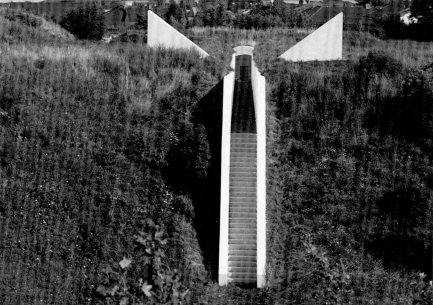

137. Hans Hollein, Juwelierladen Schullin 1, Wien, 1972–1974.
138. Peter Noever, *Die Grube*, Breitenbrunn, Österreich, 1971–1980.

137. Hans Hollein, Schullin jewellery store 1, Vienna, 1972–1974.
138. Peter Noever, *The Pit*, Breitenbrunn, Austria, 1971–1980.

A daring speculation again links Adam to Christ: if we do not follow the androgynous interpretation of Adam, then Eve arose from Adam's body. His open side was a wound and at the same time an organ of birth from which Eve had her origin.

Christ, the »second« Adam, is given a wound by the soldier stabbing him with a spear. Blood and water flow from this wound and, more than that, the ecclesia, the Mother Church, born of Christ, also springs from it. (Pfister, 1993)

To **Count Ludwig von Zinzendorf** (1700–1760), »the hollow in the side, that is to say Christ's wound, is the female genitals, being on the one hand an organ of birth and on the other the place where the religious Eros, bearing all the signs of primary homosexual activity, receives maximum satisfaction ...« (Pfister, 1925)

Christ is given an androgynous character by equating the wound with the sexual organ. There are Sacred Heart depictions which are surprisingly similar to a mouth: we once again interpret this as the Freudian affinity between wound, vulva and mouth.

In contemporary art and architecture, there is no lack of depictions of entrances which, in detailed fashion and very directly, are expressed as being female sexual organs.

André Masson (1896–1987) made an attempt to produce an image of the *Earth*. It is a confusing and complex building surrounded by spiral mists, but we have little difficulty in recognizing a recumbent female shape with her legs spread out. The vulva in the form of a lozenge – similar to vulgar drawn depictions and to archaic abbreviations – is the gate into the building which is the Earth.

In an anonymous erotic depiction from ca. 1930, a woman is represented as a circus tent, the entrance to the tent is the vulva, and men with erect penises are hurrying towards the opening.

So baffling is the iconicity that one can scarcely deny that a female sexual organ is being depicted in a draft drawing of the Vondelpark theatre in Amsterdam, set down on paper by **H. TH. Wijdeveld** (1889–1985) in 1919. A woman with her legs spread wide apart and her belly towering up seems to be presenting herself to the visitors who are thronging towards her.

In a drawing of a recumbent woman with her legs spread out, **Hans Dieter Schaal** (born 1943) interprets the Freudian building which is a body: the sexual organ is in the form of an entrance. Schaal, who characterized his drawing as »Gateway to Life«, is here linking up with a work by **Gustave Courbet** (1819–1877), whose painting *L'origine du Monde* dating from 1866 provides a direct view into the vulva, and it is understandable that this picture caused a scandal at the time. The large sculpture which **Niki de Saint Phalle**, together with Jean Tinguely and Per-Olof Ultvedt, built (1966) in the Moderna Museet in Stockholm could be very clearly understood. A gigantic, pregnant woman figure is spreading her legs and offering the »Gateway to Life«: this is the entrance door into her body, which contains a number of entertainments.

Hon – en catedral (*She – A Cathedral*) – that was the name of the exhibit. Ulf Linde explained (1967) this title, which is on the face of it blasphemous, as follows: »It is reminiscent both of Hagia Sophia and of Venus von Willendorf; she is a stretched-out laying bird, and at the same time she resembles an egg, perhaps because Niki de Saint Phalle painted on her in the way in which children paint on eggs at Easter time. She embodies the giving of birth, and she is the age-old great mother with knees spread wide apart – either these knees are parched earth waiting for rain and thunderstorms, or they are the devotion of a mother animal. These are not only a woman's knees. If one so desires, one can also find some clear allusions to a pre-Christian fertility cult. A pond with fish in it – this can occur just inside the entrance of a colossal body-like building – was encountered in the temple gardens of the goddess Astarte in Babylon. She carries in one of her breasts the planetarium built by Tinguely. This may seem understandable if it is known that it was formerly believed that stars were drops of milk which the yearning denizens of the earth milked from an enormous divine udder. In other words, the eroticism reigning in this building is mythical and poetical. But a knowledge of ancient fertility symbols is not sufficient to comprehend that eroticism. The present-day world is certainly a better key to it.

The topic of a woman who can be entered was to keep Niki de Saint Phalle occupied in the following years too. A large-scale garden with fantastic tarot figures was laid out to the north of Rome. The female ruler is entered through a door located just below the mighty, brightly-coloured breasts. To this woman artist, this giant figure is a mother goddess, inside whom the artist herself again became a mother.« (*art*, 1993/6).

As regards the replaceability of the »orifice« motifs, Freud refers to other analogies, in which the woman's mouth comes to represent the genital orifice, the **vagina dentata**, the toothed

In Malabar in Südindien hat eine Felsspalte die gleiche Bedeutung wie die Yoni: Wird ein Kranker durch diesen Spalt hindurchgezogen, erlebt er seine Wiedergeburt und wird so gesund.

In Cornwall (England) steht aufrecht ein kreisförmiger Stein, der »Menetol«, mit einer Perforation von mehr als einem halben Meter Durchmesser. Er wurde zur Heilung kranker Kinder verwendet, wobei diese durch die Öffnung geschoben wurden. (Giedeon, 1962) Der neben dem Menetol aufgestellte Menhir läßt die Assoziation des männlichen Elementes zu.

Die römischen Imperatoren, die aus den Schlachten zurückkehrten, befreiten sich von ihrer Blutschuld, indem sie durch das Triumphtor hindurchgingen. Damit waren sie entsühnt.

Einen faszinierenden Symbolablauf schafft **Peter Noever** (geb. 1941) bei der *Grube*, einem großen Projekt zwischen Architektur und Land-Art in Breitenbrunn im Burgenland. Von der Straße her betritt man die tonnenförmige Höhle eines Weinkellers, sie mündet auf der anderen Seite in eine große, tiefe, kreisförmige Grube, einen Krater mit nicht ersteigbaren Böschungen. Von dort geht ein schmaler Weg, eine Erdspalte weiter zu zwei Treppenaufgängen, deren »Brüst«ungen wie spitze Brüste aus dem Erdreich ragen. Schließlich endet der Weg in einem Steinbruch. Noever hat hier ein erstaunliches Kompendium menschlicher Geschlechtlichkeit realisiert, wobei das weibliche Element dominiert: Die mütterliche Schlucht ist tief in die Erde eingegraben.

Walter Pichlers *Eingang zu einem unterirdischen Raum* ist ein schmaler Spalt, durch dessen Enge man in die mütterliche Erde hinabsteigen kann. Gleichzeitig aber ist es eine Vulva, die in die Topographie einer Körperlandschaft eingebettet ist.

Die Felsenschlucht ist das zentrale Thema in einem Entwurf von **Christiane Pressel** (geb. 1965) für ein Zentrum für Grenzfragen. Die Felsenspalte wird von einem langgestreckten Baukörper begleitet, eine Brücke vermittelt zu einer zentralen Gruppe teils offener teils höhlenartiger Bauten: eine umfangreiche, freilich unbewußte Ikonographie sexueller Symbole, gleichzeitig aber auch eine Annäherung an androgyne Konzepte insofern, als die männlichen und weiblichen Elemente die Tendenz zum Dialog, zur Synthese erkennen lassen.

Gleichsam den Übergang von der Vulva zum Uterus ist in der Symbolik der **Muschel** zu finden, die beides symbolisieren kann, sie wird zu einer doppelten Metapher: Auf der einen Seite ist sie der umhüllende, schützende Uterus, der in seinem Inneren etwas Kostbares birgt (die Perle, das neue Leben), gleichzeitig aber ist die sich öffnende Spalte auch Ausgang, Öffnung nach außen und somit Pforte des Weiblichen.

Gaston Bachelard (1987) zitiert J. B. Robinet's Vergleiche der Muscheln mit menschlichen Körperteilen: »... es sind Stücke vom Mann, Stücke von der Frau. Robinet gibt eine Beschreibung der Venusmuschel, die die Vulva einer Frau darstellt ... Darstellungen von Phantasmen wie etwa der Vagina mit Zähnen ...«

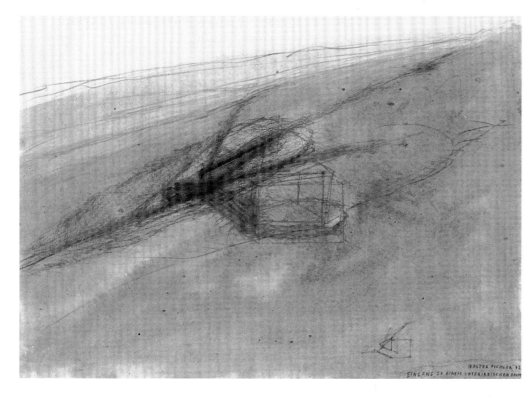

vagina, and also illustrates the identity of mouth and genital organ. Incidentally, this motif is employed again and again in advertising.

But psychoanalysis teaches us yet another identity: a wound, an injury, can also be a sexual metaphor.

»Neo-Mannerism« in the architecture of the 1970s often dealt with the topic of the beautiful wound, which at the same time signifies a genital organ.

This identity is vividly illustrated in the first shop of the Jeweller Schullin in the Graben in Vienna (1972–1974), a work by **Hans Hollein**. Hollein knocks, into the perfect surface of reflective marble, an open wound which continues into the doorway and is tiled with a costly material, namely gold (= brass). Wound and vagina, when treated sumptuously, are inseparable.

Apart from these semi-direct statements, **clefts**, **slits**, **chasms**, bottlenecks are, understandably enough, substitute motifs for the vulva.

A rocky cleft in Malabar in southern India has the same meaning as the yoni: if a sick person is pulled through a rocky cleft, he experiences his rebirth and thus becomes healthy.

A circular stone, the Menetol, with a perforation more than half a metre in diameter, stands upright in Cornwall, England. It was used to cure sick children, who were pushed through the aperture. (Giedeon, 1962) The menhir which is set up next to the Menetol permits an association with a male element.

The Roman imperators returning from their battles liberated themselves from their blood guilt by passing through the triumphal gate. They were thus expiated of guilt.

Peter Noever (born 1941) created a fascinating sequence of symbols in the Grube (Pit), a large project located somewhere between architecture and land art in Breitenbrunn in the Burgenland in Austria. A barrel-shaped cave, a wine cellar, is entered from the street and leads on its other side into a large, deep, circular pit, a crater whose slopes cannot be climbed. From there, a narrow path passes through another crevice to two staircases whose parapets (»Brüstungen«, the German word for parapets, contains a pun on »Brüst(e)«, breasts) project from the ground like pointed breasts. The path finally ends in a quarry. Noever has here brought off an astonishing compendium of human sexuality, with the female element dominant: the maternal chasm is sunk deep into the earth.

The *Entrance to an Underground Room* by **Walter Pichler** is a narrow shaft through whose confined passage one can climb down into Mother Earth. But it is at the same time a vulva bedded into the topography of a landscape of bodies.

A rocky chasm is a central theme of a design by **Christiane Pressel** (born 1965) for a Zentrum für Grenzfragen (Centre for Borderline Questions). The rocky cleft is accompanied by an elongated building, while a bridge leads the way to a central group of partly open and partly cave-like structures: this is an extensive though unconscious iconography of sexual symbols, but at the same time also an approach towards androgynous concepts in that the male and female elements render discernible a tendency towards dialogue and synthesis.

Something like the transition from vulva to uterus is to be found in the symbolism of the **shell**, which can symbolize both of them and becomes a double metaphor: on the one hand the shell is the enveloping, protective uterus which harbours within itself something costly, namely the pearl which is new life, but at the same time the opening cleft is also a way out, an aperture towards the outside, and thus the gateway of femininity.

Gaston Bachelard cites (1987) the way in which J. B. Robinet more than once compares the shells with human body parts: »... they are pieces of a man, pieces of a woman. Robinet describes the Venus shell which depicts a woman's vulva ... depictions of fantastic forms such as a vagina with teeth ...«

Venus or Aphrodite, born from the foam, steps out of a shell. **Sandro Botticelli** (1445 to 1510) gave a good depiction (ca. 1478) of this mythological scene. This is the scallop, in the Greek language a Kteis – and this at the same time means a female womb.

Odilon Redon (1840–1916), in his images of Venus, surrounds the goddess with a large shell shape, somewhat as if she was stepping out of a dark gateway into the world's light, but the shell is at the same time reminiscent of an enormous mouth or the female »gateway«.

Symbols are repeatedly developed directly from iconographical analogies. Eliade gives a detailed treatment of the symbolism of shells, and their iconicity also makes them symbolize the female sexual organ.

Eliade finds (1986) a »similarity between an ark shell and the female genitals...« The gynaecological and embryological symbolism of the pearl which forms in an oyster stands for divine

139. Walter Pichler, *Eingang zu einem unterirdischen Raum*, 1972.
140. Menetol und Menhir in Cornwall, England, um 7000 v. Chr.
141. Christiane Pressel, *Zentrum für Grenzfragen*, 1991.

139. Walter Pichler, *Entrance to an Underground Room*, 1972.
140. Menetol and menhir in Cornwall, England, ca. 7000 BC.
141. Christiane Pressel, *Centre for Borderline Questions*, 1991.

Venus oder Aphrodite, die Schaumgeborene, entsteigt einer Muschel. **Sandro Botticelli** (1445–1510) hat diese mythologische Szene gültig dargestellt (um 1478). Es ist die Kamm-Muschel, im Griechischen Kteis – was gleichzeitig weiblicher Schoß bedeutet.

Odilon Redon (1840–1916) umgibt in seinen Venusbildern die Göttin mit einer großen Mu-schelform, gleichsam als ob sie aus einem dunklen Tor heraustreten würde in das Licht der Welt, aber die Muschel erinnert gleichzeitig an einen riesigen Mund oder an die weibliche »Pforte«.

Immer wieder entwickeln sich Symbole im direkten Wege aus ikonographischen Analogien. Eliade behandelt ausführlich die Symbolik der Muscheln und auch auf Grund ihrer Ikonizität wird sie zum Symbol des weiblichen Geschlechtsorganes.

Eliade (1986) sieht eine »Ähnlichkeit zwischen der Seemuschel und den weiblichen Genita-lien ... Die gynäkologische und embryologische Symbolik der Perle, die sich in der Auster bil-det«, sind Sinnbilder für heilige Kräfte, »von der Prähistorie angefangen bis in die Gegenwart. Besondere Bedeutung hat dabei die Kauri-Muschel, die manchmal als Auge, zumeist aber als Vulva interpretiert wird«.

Bemerkenswert ist, daß auch parthenogene Motive auftauchen, deren Affinität zu andro-gynen Vorstellungen wiederholt aufgezeigt wurde. »Im fünften vorchristlichen Jahrhundert be-merkt Mo-tsi (China) zuerst, die Perlenauster Pang werde geboren ohne Mitwirkung eines männlichen Elementes.« (Eliade, 1986)

Daß Muschel und Perle zwei verschiedene, gleichwohl einander ergänzende Prinzipien darstellen, wird in einem Traktat aus dem 3. Jahrhundert. v. Chr. deutlich: Demnach ist die Muschel das Yang und die in ihr befindliche Perle das Yin. (Vgl. Kap. 9.4.1.)

Die Metapher der klaffenden Muschel für die Vulva und der geschlossenen Muschel mit der Perle für die Gebärmutter mit Leibesfrucht ist bei zahlreichen Völkern auch der Hinter-grund für magische Rituale, die mit der Frau, der Fruchtbarkeit und der Geburt zusammen-hängen.

Die Muschelform als direkt ikonisches architektonisches Motiv ist in der Baukunst selten zu finden. Die Bezeichnung »Konche« (Muschelschale) für meist viertelkugelförmige Raum-teile des frühchristlichen und mittelalterlichen Kirchenbaus gibt aber einen bemerkenswerten sprachlichen Hinweis. Tatsächlich ist die Konche der Ort der Auszeichnung, des Schutzes, des Bergens, in der römischen Basilika der Sitz des Richters, in der frühchristlichen Basilika des Priesters, insbesondere des Bischofs.

Das Thema Muschel hängt unmittelbar mit dem der Grotte zusammen, beide Motive haben eine Affinität zum Wasser. Die (künstliche) Grotte und analoge Raumformen haben vielfältige Ausprägungen in der Architektur erfahren. Sie werden im nächsten Kapitel behandelt.

7.5.2. Primäre innere Geschlechtsmerkmale. Raum, Höhle, Grotte, Kuppel, Schale, Frucht

Freud (1940) leitet ein ergänzendes Objekt- und Architekturvokabular aus den inneren Ge-schlechtsteilen, aus dem **Uterus** ab: »Manche Symbole haben mehr Beziehung auf den Mut-terleib als auf das Genitale des Weibes, so: Schränke, Öfen und vor allem das Zimmer ... Von Tieren sind wenigstens Schnecke und Muschel als unverkennbar weibliche Symbole anzu-führen, von Bauwerken Kirche und Kapelle ... « Und an anderer Stelle: »Das Wohnhaus (ist) ein Ersatz für den Mutterleib, die erste, wahrscheinlich noch immer ersehnte Behausung, in der man sicher war und sich wohl fühlte.« (Freud, 1972)

Neumann (1949) ergänzt, oder besser er korrigiert das Repertoire von Freud, und er sieht im Archetyp des Mütterlichen auch »Tiefe, Abgrund, Tal, Urgrund, aber auch Meer und Meeresgrund, Brunnen, See und Teich ebenso wie Erde, Unterwelt, Höhle, Haus und Stadt«.

Der **Raum**, das Gehäuse, das innere Volumen könnten ganz allgemein mit dem Uterus, dem primären inneren Geschlechtsmerkmal der Frau in Zusammenhang gebracht werden. Das Schützende, Umhüllende und Bewahrende sind die gemeinsamen Merkmale.

Betrachten wir die Lage des Embryos im Mutterleibe, so bietet sich die optimale räumliche Umhüllung dar: Ein eiförmiger Raum mit einer Erweiterung für den Kopf und dem engen »Aus-gang«. Das Urmodell der bergenden Höhlung ist damit vorgeprägt – es wiederholt sich hun-dertfach in jeder **Höhle, Grotte** oder **Kuppel**, im Ei und in der Kugel, in jedem schützenden Raum. Nach Carl Gustav Jung ist »die Höhle der Ort der Wiedergeburt, jener geheime Hohl-

142. Odilon Redon, *Geburt der Venus*, 1910.

142. Odilon Redon, *Birth of Venus*, 1910.

forces »beginning in prehistory and continuing to the present day. The cowrie shell, which is sometimes interpreted as an eye but usually as a vulva, is of particular significance.«

Parthogenetic motifs, whose affinity with androgynous ideas has repeatedly been pointed out, are also met with. »Mo-tsi (China) was the first to note, in the fifth century BC, that the pearl oyster, the Pang, was born without the cooperation of a male element.« (Eliade, 1986)

A treatise from the 3rd century BC makes it plain that a shell and a pearl represent two different principles which nonetheless complement one another. According to this, the shell is the yang and the pearl inside it is the yin. (Cf. chap. 9.4.1.)

The metaphor of a gaping shell which represents a vulva, and of a closed shell which contains a pearl and represents a womb with an embryo in it, is to numerous peoples also the background to magical rituals related to woman, fertility and birth.

A shell shape as a direct, iconic, architectural motif is rarely found in architecture. The term »concha« (scallop shell) for usually quadrant-shaped areas in early Christian and medieval churches is though a notable linguistic indication. A concha is in fact a place of distinction, of protection, of shelter. It is the seat of the judge in Roman basilicas, and in early Christian basilicas it is the seat of the priest, especially the bishop.

The topic of the shell is directly related to that of the grotto. Both motifs have an affinity with water. The artificial grotto, and analogous spatial shapes, have experienced diverse forms in architecture. They will be dealt with in the next chapter.

raum, in den man eingeschlossen wird, um bebrütet und erneuert zu werden ...« Die wärmende, schützende, nahrungsspendende Mutter ist auch der Herd, die schützende Höhle oder Hütte.

Die natürlichen **Höhlen** waren wohl die ersten Zufluchtstätten der Menschen, im Inneren der Berge gelegen und Schutz gewährend. Die Höhlen waren auch die Wohnungen oder die Heiligtümer der großen Erdgöttin, so etwa der Rhea auf Kreta, die identisch ist mit Era, der Erde oder mit ihrer Mutter Gäa, der Mutter Erde.

»Die großen Höhlen galten als Ausgang des Leibinneren der Erde und als Eingang in ihre Unterwelt. Daher gebar sie (Rhea) ihren Sohn und Heros, den kretischen Zeus, jedes Jahr in einem Strom von Blut und blitzendem Feuer aus dieser Höhle wieder.« (Göttner-Abendroth, 1980)

Mircea Eliade (1959) interpretiert die Höhle als eine »mystische Rückkehr zur ›Mutter‹ ... Diese archaischen Anschauungen haben ein langes Leben. Die Bezeichnung ›delph‹ (Uterus) blieb noch im Namen eines der höchsten Heiligtümer des Hellenentums, Delphi, erhalten.

Pausanias spricht von einem Ort Argos, der sich Delta nannte und als Heiligtum der Demeter galt ... Man weiß, daß bei den Griechen das Wort Delta die Frau symbolisiert«.

Das Thema der Höhle könnten wir überall dort aufspüren, wo der Charakter des Schutzes, des Bergens, häufig verbunden mit einer chthonischen Dunkelheit, auftritt. Sigfried Giedion (1969) meint, das Dunkel sei »mit der Erdmutter, mit der Gebärerin des Lebens verbunden«.

Zahlreich sind die durchaus glaubwürdigen Thesen, wonach in den frühen und primitiven Kulturen die Höhlen nicht nur Symbole der weiblichen Leibeshöhle, sondern auch realiter mit deren Eigenschaften ausgestattet waren. Magische Zeichen von Vulva, Klitoris und Phallus auf den Höhlenwänden sollten nicht nur die Fruchtbarkeit des Menschen, sondern auch die der Tiere beschwören. Hans Peter Duerr (1985) zitiert einen australischen Volksstamm, für den die Höhle mit dem Vorgang der Geburt verbunden ist. Heute noch wird dieser Felsenuterus durch die Felsenvulva von schwangeren Frauen betreten, die hierherkommen, um zu gebären.

Zu den ältesten, gleichsam architektonisch nachgebauten Frauengestalten zählen die »organischen« Bauten des matriarchalischen Malta, höhlenartige, annähernd elliptische Räume, die aneinandergereiht werden. Die **maltesischen Höhlen** können als direkte Abbilder der großen Muttergöttinnen gesehen werden, wobei »vor allem der Bauch und die Brüste durch die Architektur dargestellt wurden« (Duerr, 1985). Der Vergleich mit weiblichen Figuren aus der gleichen Kultur läßt diese These plausibel erscheinen. Das Hineintreten in die Höhle kann – durchaus im psychoanalytischen Sinne – verschieden gedeutet werden. Es ist eine Rückkehr in den uterinen Schutzbereich, vielleicht um im Schoß zu »sterben und wiedergeboren zu werden« (Duerr, 1985), ein Thema, das wir, in Verbindung mit dem Wasser, im frühchristlichen Taufritus explizit ausgedrückt finden. Das Eintreten durch die »Vulva« in die Höhle kann aber auch den Koitus mit der großen Göttin repräsentiert haben.

»Daß der regressum ad uterum bisweilen als Geschlechtsakt gesehen wurde, mag zunächst mit der schlichten Tatsache zusammenhängen, daß es eine ›umgekehrte Geburt‹ realiter nicht gibt und daß das einzige Beispiel dafür, daß in gewissem Sinne ein Mensch in einen anderen ›eingeht‹ eben der Beischlaf ist.« (Duerr, 1985)

Abt Suger und Durandus bezeichnen die Kirchengebäude als »die eigentliche Braut Jesu Christi«, gleichzeitig aber auch als »Leib der Heiligen Jungfrau«. Dieser Gedanke ist auch im Kirchenbau unseres Jahrhunderts noch tragfähig. **Otto Mauer** (1907–1973) liefert eine schöne Interpretation der Marien-Wallfahrtskirche Ronchamp (1954) von Le Corbusier: »... Alles ist Innenraum der Geborgenheit, nur durch Luken bricht das Licht, durch tiefe Schächte. Aber im Innern ist Wärme, Innigkeit, Geborgensein. Wie im Mutterleib der katholischen Kirche, wie im Schoß Marias das Kind in Gotteshut ... Die Arche ist gestrandet, und Gottes Haus hat sich bei uns niedergelassen, die Jungfrau, die Mutter, die Kirche.« (Mauer, 1993)

Der großartige Torso von **Paolo Soleri** (geb. 1919), das *Arcosanti*, steht in der Wüste von Arizona. Soleri, Schüler und Mitarbeiter von F. L. Wright, hat schon vor Jahrzehnten begonnen, seine Idee einer ganz neuen Idealstadt zu konzipieren, ein gewaltiges Gebilde mit Hunderttausenden von Einwohnern. Nur weniges, gleichwohl Exemplarisches konnte davon realisiert werden: Es sind segmentförmige Tonnen bzw. Kuppeln, und obwohl sie sich an einer Seite der Landschaft Arizonas öffnen, haben sie doch einen höhlenartigen Charakter.

Armancio Guedes (geb. 1925) entwirft ein Hotel, das gleichsam aus organhaften Nischen, aus bergenden Höhlen zusammengesetzt ist. Die feminine Interpretation wird bestätigt durch

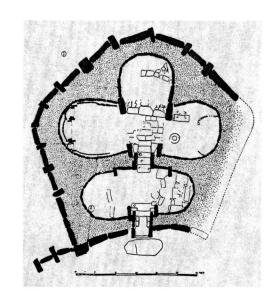

7.5.2. Primary Internal Sexual Characteristics. Space, Cave, Grotto, Dome, Bowl, Fruit

Freud (1964) derives a complementary vocabulary of architecture and objects from the internal sexual organs, from the **uterus**. »Some symbols have more connection with the uterus than with the female genitals: thus, cupboards, stoves and, more especially, rooms. ... Among animals, snails and mussels at least are undeniably female symbols; ... among buildings churches and chapels.« And elsewhere: »The home is a substitute for the mother's body, the first accommodation in which we were secure and felt well, which we probably still long for.« (Freud, 1964)

Neumann (1949) adds to, or rather corrects, Freud's repertoire and also places »depths, abysses, valleys, sources, but also the sea and the sea-bed, lakes and pools and also earth, underworld, cave, house and city« within the maternal archetype.

The **room**, the casing, the inner volume can all be quite generally linked with the uterus, the woman's primary internal sexual characteristic. Things that protect, enclose and preserve are the common characteristics.

If we consider the position of the embryo in the mother's womb, we find the best possible spatial enclosure: an ovoid space, broadening for the head and the narrow »exit«. This predetermines the primordial model of the protecting hollow – and it is repeated a hundred times over in every **cave**, **grotto** or **dome**, in eggs and spheres, in every protective space. According to Carl Gustav Jung the »cave is the place of rebirth, that common hollow space in which one is enclosed to be incubated and renewed ...« The warming, protecting, warmth-providing mother is also the hearth, the protecting hollow or hut.

Natural **caves** were probably man's first places of refuge, inside mountains and offering protection. Caves were also the homes or shrines of the great earth-goddesses like for example the Rhea on Crete, which is identical with Era, the earth, or her mother Gaia, the earth mother.

»The great caves were thought to be the exits form the inside of the earths body and an entrance to her underworld. For this reason she (Rhea) bore her son and Heros, the Cretan Zeus, again each year in a stream of blood and flashing fire from this cave.« (Göttner-Abendroth, 1980)

Mircea Eliade (1959) interprets the cave as a »mystical return to the ›mother‹ ... These archaic views are long-lived. The term ›delph‹ (uterus) survived in the name of one of the loftiest Hellenic shrines, Delphi.

Pausanias speaks of a place Argos that called itself Delta and was thought to be a shrine of Demeter. ...We know that for the Greeks the word delta symbolizes woman«.

The cave theme could be traced in all places where the character of protecting and rescuing occurs, frequently combined with a chthonic darkness. Sigfried Giedion (1969) thinks that darkness is »linked with the earth mother, with the bearer of life«.

There are numerous entirely credible theories according to which caves in early and primitive cultures were not just symbols of parts of the female body, but were actually furnished with its characteristics. Magic signs of vulva, clitoris and phallus on cave wall were intended to conjure up the fertility of animals as well as that of human beings. Hans Peter Duerr (1985) cites an Australian tribe for which caves are linked with the birth process. Even today this rock uterus is entered through the rock vulva by pregnant women who come here to give birth.

The »organic« buildings of matriarchal Malta, series of cave-like, approximately elliptical rooms, are among the oldest female shapes to be copied in architecture, as it were. The **Maltese caves** can be seen as direct copies of the great mother-gods, with »the belly and the breasts in particular represented by architecture«. (Duerr, 1985) Comparison with female figures from the same culture makes this thesis plausible. Entering the cave can be interpreted in various ways – entirely in the psychoanalytical sense. It is a return to the protected area of the womb, perhaps to »die and be born again« there. (Duerr, 1985), a theme that we find expressed explicitly, linked with water, in the early Christian ritual of baptism. But entering the cave through the »vulva« can also have represented coitus with the great goddess.

»The fact that the regressum ad uterum was sometimes seen as a sexual act may be linked first of all with the simple fact that in reality there is no such thing as a ›reversed birth‹ and that the only example of one person ›going into‹ another in some way is in fact intercourse.« (Duerr, 1985)

Abbot Suger and Durandus call church buildings »the actual bride of Jesus Christ«, but at the same time the body of the Blessed Virgin. This idea is still valid in church building in our

ein Einfamilienhaus mit ähnlicher Formensprache: Guedes nennt es *Habitable women*, die bewohnbare Frau. Der Grundriß erinnert tatsächlich verblüffend an »organische« Formen in unserem Körper, aber die Konchen und Nischen sind auch Rückzugsbereiche in eine schützende Grotte.

Eine sehr ähnliche Formensprache weist ein Hausentwurf aus dem Jahre 1970 des Malers **Jean Dubuffet** (geb. 1901) auf. Sowohl die Höhle und die Grotte als auch das Innere einer organischen Existenz können als Inspirationsquellen angesprochen werden. Mit der Höhle verwandt ist die **Grotte**. »Natürliche« Grotten sind Höhlen, die dank ihrer phantastischen geologischen Formation eine Fülle von Assoziationen zulassen und mit magisch-mythischen Ideen verbunden sind.

Damit wird der Berg, der a priori männlichen Charakter hat, gleichsam uterin ausgehöhlt und gewinnt androgyne Merkmale. Die scheinbar »gewachsenen« üppigen Mineral-Figurationen erinnern an organische, biologische Formen und verstärken so den uterinen Charakter. Die oft turmartig aufragenden, mächtigen Stalagmiten wecken phallische Vergleiche, und das Gesamtsystem hat androgynen Charakter.

Die natürliche Grotte, etwa die gigantische Anlage von Postojna (Adelsberg), ermöglicht auch das tiefe Eindringen in den Berg, den Felsen, also in zumeist männliche Kategorien.

Die künstliche Grotte ist ein beliebtes Thema in der Renaissance, im Manierismus und im Barock und evoziert ebenfalls das Gefühl, in einem Berg und in einem Wesen zu sein.[41]

Die Makrowelt der Grotte scheint sich in einer mineralischen Mikrowelt zu wiederholen. In einer Bergkristall-Druse können wir die weibliche Form erkennen, aber sie ist mit zahlreichen phallischen Elementen bestückt. Diese Assoziation ist offenkundig schon in der Zeit der Art Nouveau in Frankreich aufgetaucht, denn die silberne Fassung des Minerals zeigt eine nackte Frauenfigur, die von einem bärtigen Männerkopf betrachtet wird.

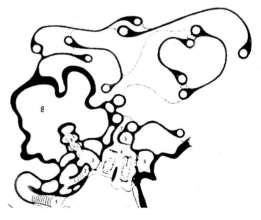

Die künstlichen Grotten sind mit zahlreichen mythologischen Versatzstücken ausgestattet, aber der elementare magische Bezug ist verlorengegangen. So stellen etwa die künstlichen Grotten des 17. und 18. Jahrhunderts mit ihren amüsanten Wasserspielen nur mehr Lustbarkeiten für die höfische Gesellschaft dar.

In mancherlei Formen lebt die Idee der Grotte auch im 19. Jahrhunderts weiter. Zunächst ist sie ein beliebtes Versatzstück der Romantik und begegnet uns häufig in Verein mit künstlichen Ruinen.

Auf eine seltsame Ausprägung der Grotte nach der Mitte des 19. Jahrhunderts wurde schon im Kap. 7.5.1 hingewiesen: Es ist die **Lourdesgrotte** mit der Immakulata. Die schützende Muttergottes selbst erscheint hier in einer gleichsam nach außen projizierten Muschelgrotte, die noch einmal das Helfend-Mütterliche unterstreicht.

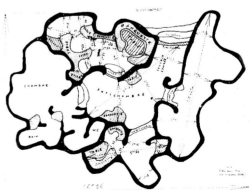

Der Grotten- und Höhlencharakter ist oft genug auch in der Architektur unseres Jahrhunderts ausgeprägt. Manche Innenräume des **Goetheanums** in Dornach (1924–1928) von

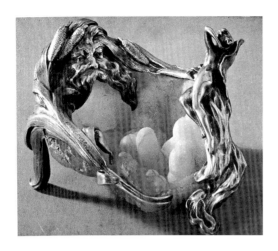

century. Otto Mauer (1907–1973) provides a beautiful interpretation of Le Corbusier's pilgrimage chapel Ronchamp (1954): »... Everything is the internal space of seclusion, light is admitted only through small openings, through deep shafts. But inside is warmth, intimacy, safety. As in the womb of the Catholic Church, as the child in the womb of Mary, in the keeping of God ... The ark is on dry land, and God's house has set itself down with us, the Virgin, the Mother, the Church.« (Mauer, 1993)

Paolo Soleri's magnificent torso (born 1919), the *Arcosanti*, stands in the Arizona desert. Soleri, a pupil and colleague of Frank Lloyd Wright, started to conceive his idea of an entirely new ideal city decades ago, a massive structure with hundreds of thousands of inhabitants. Only a little material, standing for the project as a whole, has been realized: segmental barrels or domes that have a cave-like character even though they open on to the landscape of Arizona on one side.

Armancio Guedes (born 1925) is designing a hotel that is made up of organ-like niches, of protecting caves. This feminine interpretation is confirmed by a detached house with a similar formal language: Guedes calls it Habitable woman, and the ground plan is indeed strikingly similar to »organic« forms in our body, but the conches and niches are also areas for retreat into a protecting grotto.

A house designed by the painter **Jean Dubuffet** (born 1901) uses a very similar formal language. Both the cave and the grotto and also the interior of an organic existence can be addressed as sources of inspiration. Related to the cave is the **grotto**. Natural ›grottoes‹ are caves which, thanks to their fantastic geological formation admit an abundance of associations and are linked with magical and mythical ideas.

In this way mountains, which are essentially masculine in character, are hollowed out like wombs, so to speak, and acquire androgynous characteristics. The abundant mineral formations that have apparently »grown« are reminiscent of organic, biological forms and thus reinforce the womb-like character. The massive stalagmites, which often soar up like towers, stimulate phallic associations, and the system as a whole is androgynous in character.

The natural grotto, like the gigantic Postojna (Adelsberg) complex, for example, also make it possible to penetrate deeply into the mountain, the rock, in other words into mainly masculine categories.[40]

Artificial grottoes are a popular theme in the Renaissance, in Mannerism and the Baroque, and also evoke the feeling of being inside a mountain and a being.

The macro-world of the grotto seems to repeat itself in a mineral micro-world. We can recognize the female form in a drusy cavity of rock crystal, but it is equipped with numerous phallic elements. This association obviously cropped up in the Art Nouveau period in France, as the silver setting of the mineral shows a naked female figure being observed by a bearded man's head.

Artificial grottoes are equipped with numerous mythological set-pieces, but the elemental magic link is lost. Thus the artificial grottoes of the 17th and 18th centuries with their amusing water-games are just pieces of fun for court society.

The idea of the grotto also survives in many forms in the 19th century. First it is a popular property in Romanticism, frequently manifested in association with artificial ruins.

A strange form of the grotto after the mid 19th century is mentioned in chapter 7.5.1 the **Lourdes Grotto** with the Immaculata. The protecting Mother of God herself appears here in a shell grotto that is projected outwards, as it were, which once more underlines the quality of the helping mother.

Grotto and cave character appears often enough in the architecture of our century as well. Many interiors in **Rudolf Steiner's** Goetheanum in Dornach (1924–1928) are cave-like in character as a result of the »organic« formal language, in the vestibule, for example and the stairwell. The concrete that Steiner used for the second Goetheanum (instead of wood for the first) is the material that is perceived to be closest to stone and rock.

The *Merzbau* (1920–1936) by Kurt Schwitters (1887–1948) is subtitled «Cathedral of erotic misery«, and its bewildering spatial quality is reminiscent of grottoes. Schwitters abandons all structural »logic«, and the building looked as though it has grown by chance. But ultimately grottoes are chance phenomena for our eyes only, in reality they follow physical and geological laws that we are hardly likely to be able to formulate.

The meditation grotto drawn by **Frederick Kiesler** for New Harmony in Indiana in 1963 leaves no doubt that it was inspired by organ-like, biological structure: it was a fish motif that gave a morphological stimulus. As well as this, comparison with the anatomical cut through

Rudolf Steiner haben Höhlencharakter. Er wird durch die gleichsam »organische« Formensprache hervorgerufen, etwa bei der Vorhalle und beim Stiegenhaus. Der Beton, den Rudolf Steiner beim zweiten Goetheanum verwendet (anstatt des Holzes beim ersten) ist jenes Material, das in der Rezeption ganz nahe an Stein und Fels herankommt.

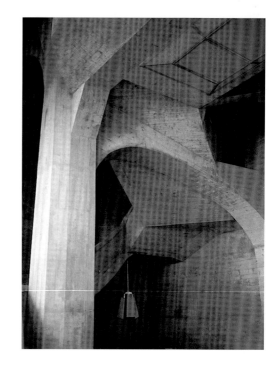

Der *Merzbau* (1920–36) von **Kurt Schwitters** (1887–1948) trägt den Untertitel »Kathedrale des erotischen Elends«, und seine verwirrende Räumlichkeit läßt an Grotten denken. Schwitters verzichtet auf jede strukturelle »Logik«, der Bau scheint zufällig so gewachsen zu sein. Doch letzten Endes sind auch Grotten nur für unser Auge Zufallsergebnisse, in Wahrheit sind es physikalisch-geologische Gesetzmäßigkeiten, deren Formulierung uns freilich kaum gelingen wird.

Die Meditationsgrotte, die **Frederick Kiesler** 1963 für New Harmony in Indiana gezeichnet hat, läßt keinen Zweifel darüber aufkommen, daß er von einem organhaften, biologischen Gebilde inspiriert wurde: Es ist zunächst das Motiv eines Fisches, der eine morphologische Anregung gegeben hat. Darüber hinaus drängt sich der Vergleich mit dem anatomischen Schnitt durch das Becken einer Frau auf. Weich gekurvte Formen und die gleichsam fraulichen Kuppelräume lassen an eine feminine Architektur denken, die geistige Versenkung gleicht einer Rückkehr in den mütterlichen Leib.

Auch andere Entwürfe wie etwa der für das *Endless House* (1958) sind »offene Grotten«, leiten aber bereits zum Thema der androgynen Architektur über.

Die Wohnbauten von **Christian Hunziker** (teilweise mit Frei, Berthood), die 1976–1983 in Genf entstanden sind, nennt der Architekt *Les Grottes*, und zumindest die Vorhallen können Erinnerungen an die Grottenromantik erwecken. Der Übergang vom Außenraum erfolgt gleichsam über eine »Schwelle«, in der wir einiges von der Rationalität der Welt abstreifen können, bevor wir unseren eigentlichen Lebensbereich, die Wohnung, betreten.

Engelbert Kremser (geb. 1938) baut in Deutschland Spielhäuser, Spielhöhlen für Kinder, die im Inneren einen deutlich grottenartigen Charakter haben und im Äußeren eine skulpturale Architektur bilden. Das Zurückziehen in eine Höhle, die Distanzierung von einer rational-funktionalistischen Architektur ist ganz besonders für Kinder ein wichtiges psychisches Bedürfnis. Zur Bundesgartenschau 1985 baut Kremser ein Ensemble aus Seebühne, Café und einem Arkadengang (1977–1985), den er selbst als Grotte bezeichnet. Die Anklänge an Gaudí sind nicht zu übersehen.

Die Vielzweckhalle (1974–1977) von **Günther Domenig** (geb. 1934) in Graz gibt uns das Gefühl einer offenen Geborgenheit in einem organischen Gebilde, das die Erinnerung an Höhlen und Grotten provoziert. Auch der phantastische Raum des Sparkassengebäudes von Domenig in Wien-Favoriten (1975–1979) läßt bei aller Transparenz den Höhlengedanken zu.

Selbst der sehr kühle Raum des Kerzengeschäftes Retti (1964/65) von **Hans Hollein** erfährt durch Thomsen (1991) eine sexual-symbolische Deutung: »Das Betreten des Geschäftes ist vergleichbar dem gewaltlosen Eindringen in einen uterischen Raum, der sich nach einer engen Eingangspassage weitet und seinerseits wieder nach dem Prinzip pulsierender Expansion und Kontraktion gestaltet ist.«

Eine völlig neue Interpretation erfährt der kleine, bergende Raum durch die pneumatischen Gebilde der 60er Jahre. Die **Haus-Rucker-Co** basteln 1968 das *Gelbe Herz*: Durch eine enge Pforte kriecht man in einen uterinen, aber weitgehend transparenten Raum.

Über die Motive der Höhle und Grotte weit hinausgehend kann jeder bergende, schützende, organische Raum als weiblich angesehen werden, in erster Linie selbstverständlich die **Kuppel**. Als Symbol des Himmels ist sie aber häufig auch männlicher Natur.

Die Dimension ist nicht entscheidend: Die kleinen Kragkuppelräume der süditalienischen Trulli bergen eine Familie, der gigantische Kenotaph der Revolutionsarchitektur von E. L. Boullée war als Huldigung für Newton als kosmische Analogie gedacht. Dazwischen liegt das umfangreiche Vokabular der Kuppelbauten der gesamten Baugeschichte.

Die Kuppel kann primär als das Weibliche, Mütterliche, Bergende charakterisiert werden. Betrachten wir die Außenerscheinung der Hagia Sophia, so läßt die sanfte Kuppelrundung die Assoziation zur Frau ohne weiteres zu. Verfolgen wir die Entwicklung der Kuppel in der Renaissance, dann registrieren wir eine zunehmende Streckung des Kuppelmotivs: Der Tambour wird eingeschoben, die äußere und die innere Kuppelschale divergieren mehr und mehr. Tatsächlich erhält das Äußere der Kuppel eine zusätzliche Aufgabe: Auf weite Sicht hat sie sich zu behaupten, muß repräsentieren, wird auch zum Machtsymbol. Dieser erste, noch kaum registrierbare Schritt zu einer Androgynisierung wird in den folgenden Kapiteln noch weiter zu verfolgen sein. Die Kuppel erhält aber nun ein deutliches Herrschaftszeichen: die Laterne. Viel-

149. Rudolf Steiner, zweites Goetheanum, Dornach, Schweiz, 1924–1928.
150. Kurt Schwitters, *Merzbau – Kathedrale des erotischen Elends*, 1920–1936.
151. Schnitt durch ein weibliches Becken.
152. Frederick Kiesler, Meditationsgrotte für New Harmony, Indiana, 1963.

149. Rudolf Steiner, second Goetheanum, Dornach, Switzerland, 1924–1928.
150. Kurt Schwitters, *Merzbau – Cathedral of Erotic Misery*, 1920–1936.
151. Section through the pelvis of a woman.
152. Frederick Kiesler, meditation grotto for New Harmony, Indiana, 1963.

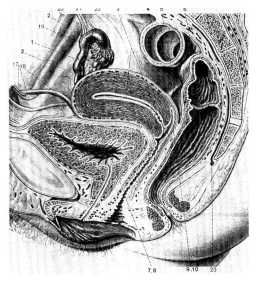

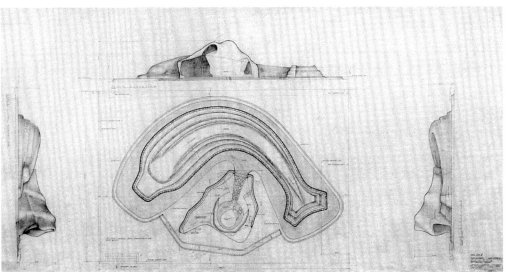

the pelvis of a woman suggests itself. softly curving forms and the essentially female domed spaces suggest female architecture, and spiritual absorption is like a return to the mother's body.

Other designs, like the one for the *Endless House* (1958) are »open grottoes« as well, but form a link with the theme of androgynous architecture.

Christian Hunziker's residential buildings (some with Frei, Berthood) in Geneva, 1976 to 1983, are called *Les Grottes* by the architect, and the entrance halls at least can be reminiscent of grotto romanticism. Transition from the outside world takes place via a »threshold« in which we can shake off some of the rationality of the world, before we enter our actual life-sphere, the dwelling.

Engelbert Kremser (born 1938) builds play-houses and play-caves for children, and their interiors have a grotto-like quality, with sculptural exteriors. Withdrawing into a cave, distancing from rationalist-functionalist architecture is an important psychological requirement for children in particular. Kremser built an ensemble of lake stage, café and an arcade (1977–1985) for the 1985 Bundesgartenschau, and he called this a grotto himself. Hints of Gaudí cannot be overlooked.

The multi-purpose hall in Graz (1974–1977) by **Günther Domenig** (born 1934) gives us a feeling of open seclusion inside an organic structure reminiscent of caves and grottoes. The fantastic space of Domenig's bank building in the Favoriten district of Vienna (1975–1979) admits the notion of a cave despite all its transparency.

Even the very cool space of **Hans Hollein's** Retti candle shop (1964/65) is interpreted as a sexual symbol by Thomsen (1991): »Entering the shop is comparable with penetrating a uterine space by force; it widens after a narrow entrance passage and is again designed on the principle of pulsing expansion and contraction.«

The small, protective space is completed re-interpreted by the pneumatic structures of the 60s. The **Haus-Rucker-Co** put the *Yellow Heart* together in 1968: you crawl through a narrow gateway into a uterine but largely transparent space.

Beyond the motif of cave and grotto any concealing, protecting, organic space can be seen as female, with the **dome** at the top of the list. But as a symbol of the sky it is frequently male by nature as well.

The scale is not crucial: the small corbel-domed rooms in Trulli in southern Italy accommodate a family, the gigantic cenotaph of Boullée's Revolutionary Architecture was intended as a cosmic analogy in homage to Newton. In between the two is the copious vocabulary of all the domes in architectural history.

153. Günther Domenig, Mehrzweckhalle in Graz-Eggenberg, 1974–1977.
154. Günther Domenig, Filiale der Zentralsparkasse der Stadt Wien in Wien-Favoriten, 1975 bis 1979.
155. Haus-Rucker-Co, *Gelbes Herz*, 1968.
156. Engelbert Kremser, Café am See, Berlin-Neukölln, 1977–1985.

153. Günther Domenig, Multi-purpose hall in Eggenberg, Graz, 1974–1977.
154. Günther Domenig, branch of Zentralsparkasse der Stadt Wien in Favoriten, Vienna, 1975 to 1979.
155. Haus-Rucker-Co, *Yellow Heart*, 1968.
156. Engelbert Kremser, Café am See, Neukölln, Berlin, 1977–1985.

leicht ist es zu spekulativ, diesem Motiv bereits phallischen Charakter zuzusprechen, einige weitere Entwicklungen dürften diese Interpretation jedoch rechtfertigen.

Die Muschel und die Höhle sind gleichsam naturgeformte Schalen, organische oder geologische Behälter. Aber auch der von Menschen geformte Behälter wird zum Gleichnis des Weiblichen. Der Gedanke, den Gefäßen, insbesondere den keramischen, die Gestalt eines Menschen zu geben, tritt vor allem in den frühen Kulturen auf. Nach dem bisher Gesagten ist es begreiflich, daß der weibliche Körper bevorzugt wird, und häufig finden wir auch die Andeutung einer weiblichen Brust. »Wenn wir die Körper-Welt-Gleichung des Frühmenschen in ihrer ersten und unspezifischen Form mit der symbolischen Grundgleichung des Weiblichen, Weib = Körper = Gefäß verbinden, dann kommen wir zu einer, symbolischen Universalformel der menschlichen Frühzeit die lautet: Weib = Körper = Gefäß = Welt.« (Neumann, 1956)

Der Mikro-Ausbildung des weiblichen Schutzraumes können wir im Gefäß, in der Schale wie im Krug begegnen. (Vgl. Kap. 6.3.)

7.5.3. Sekundäre Geschlechtsmerkmale. Außenkuppel, Halbkugel, Rundung

Von den sekundären Geschlechtsmerkmalen sind es die weibliche **Brust**, das Gesäß, die Hüfte, das Becken und im weitestem Sinne das spezifische Unterhautfettgewebe, der Knochenbau und die Körpergröße, die Inhalt abbildhafter oder sinnbildhafter Darstellungen sein können. Und wieder kann die Freudsche Traumsymbolik zitiert werden: »Zu den Genitalien müssen die Brüste gerechnet werden, die wie die größeren Hemisphären des weiblichen Körpers ihre Darstellung finden in Äpfeln, Pfirsischen, Früchten überhaupt.« (Freud, 1940)

Wir haben es also auch hier mit »Mehrfachcodierungen«, mit unterschiedlichen Deutungen der gleichen morphologischen Elemente zu tun. Im vorhergehenden Kapitel wurde ausgeführt, daß manche Früchte sowohl als Vulva oder Vagina als auch als Uterus interpretiert werden können. Nun kommt laut Freud eine dritte Deutungsebene hinzu, die der weiblichen Brust.

Ergänzend zu den Zitaten Freuds kann angenommen werden, daß auch das Äußere von Kuppeln und Halbkugeln, von Rundungen ganz allgemein in die Symbolik einbezogen werden kann.

Neumann (1956) spricht generell vom »großen Runden«, das immer dem Weiblichen zuzuordnen wäre. Dennoch ist es kritikwürdig in allem Weichen, Gekurvten, Gerundeten, Anschmiegsamen das Weibliche schlechthin zu erblicken. Ebensowenig geht es an, generell eine liebliche, gemütvolle, friedliche, kleinteilige, gar »humane« Architektur als spezifisch fraulich zu apostrophieren.

An einigen wenigen authentischen Aussagen zur Architektur unseres Jahrhunderts (wobei Architektur wieder im weitesten Sinne zu verstehen ist) können wir die Analogie gebauter Formen zu weiblichen Formen exemplifizieren.

Einen in seiner Direktheit trivialen Entwurf finden wir bei einem französischen Architekten: **Nicolas Schöffer** (geb. 1912) (Studio Yves Hervochon) zeichnete – im Zuge der utopischen Projekte der 60er Jahre – ein *Zentrum für sexuelle Freizeit*. Ähnlich wie Ledoux meint er: » ... sie werden richtige Liebestempel sein, wo es keinerlei Tendenz zur Pornographie gibt, sondern alles dazu beiträgt, die Paare auf die sexuelle Liebe vorzubereiten, die dann endlich entmystifiziert, für alle erreichbar, ungekünstelt und nicht mehr erniedrigt sein wird.

Die wandernden Zuschauer bewegen sich in einer Atmosphäre, die die sexuellen Funktionen stimuliert. Am Ende des abwärts führenden Weges befindet sich ein Tanzsaal und ein Hotel-Restaurant, um die Paare zu empfangen. Diese Zentren werden eine ungeheuer wichtige soziale Aufgabe erfüllen. Ist das sexuelle Tabu erst einmal entmystifiziert, dann wird sich der von jedem falschen Zwang befreite Mensch endlich entfalten und Zugang zu einem normalen Sexualleben und auch zur Liebe finden können«, soweit Nicolas Schöffer (1970). Die Frage nach den gesellschaftlichen, ethischen und psychologischen Problemen läßt der Künstler freilich offen – falls es sich nicht einfach um ein Bordell handeln sollte.[42]

Auch bei einem Projekt der **Haus-Rucker-Co** können wir auf die interpretative Spekulation verzichten und uns direkt auf die Aussagen der Gestalter stützen: »Im selben Jahr (1968) aber kam es zu einer Zusammenarbeit an einem Projekt für die 1970 geplante Weltausstellung in Osaka. *Max Bra*, die Architektur einer überdimensionalen, weiblichen Brust, gefüllt mit audiovisuellen und haptischen Sensationen ...« (Haus-Rucker-Co, 1984)

Bernhard Strecker (geb. 1940) baut für Oldenburg eine »frauliche« Brücke, und sie heißt »Amalie«. Darüber hinaus »sind nicht nur die runden Formen der Frau, der Busen, der Hintern,

157. Nicolas Schöffer, *Centre des Loisirs Sexuels,* 1968.

The dome can be seen primarily as female, maternal and sheltering. If we consider the external appearance of Hagia Sophia then the soft curve of the dome undoubtedly admits the association with a woman. If we pursue the development of the dome in the Renaissance then we register an increasing extension of the dome motif: the drum is inserted and the inner and outer shells of the dome diverge more and more. In fact the outside of the dome is given an additional task: it has to assert itself over a distance, exude prestige and be a symbol of power. The first, as yet barely perceptible, step towards androgyny will be further pursued in subsequent chapters. But the dome now acquires a clear sign of dominance: the lantern. Perhaps it is too speculative to suggest that this motif is already phallic in character, but some further development must justify this interpretation, however.

The shell and the cave are like naturally formed shells, organic or geological containers. But man-made containers are also an allegory of the female. The idea of making vessels, especially ceramic ones, in human shape appears above all in early cultures. In the light of the above it is understandable that the female body is preferred, and frequently we also find a hint of a female breast. »If we combine this body-world equation of early man in its first unspecific form with the fundamental symbolic equation of the feminine, woman = body = vessel, we arrive at a universal symbolic formula for the early period of mankind: woman = body = vessel = world.« (Neumann, 1955)

We come across the micro-form of the female protecting space in the vessel, the dish and the jug. (Cf. chap. 6.3.)

7.5.3. Secondary Sexual Characteristics. Outer Dome, Half-dome, Curve

Of the secondary sexual characteristics it is the female **breast**, the buttocks, the hip, the pelvis and in the broadest sense the specific sub-cutaneous fatty tissue, the bone structure and the body size that can be the content of copied or symbolic representations. And once more Freud's dream symbolism can be cited: »The breast have to be counted as genitals; they like the great hemispheres of the female body are represented in apples, pears, peaches and all kind of fruit.« (Freud, 1964)

So here we are dealing with »multiple coding«, with different interpretations of the same morphological elements. In the previous chapter it was pointed out that many fruits can be interpreted both as vulva or vagina or as uterus. Now according to Freud a third level of interpretation comes along, the female breast.

In addition to Freud's quotations it can be accepted that the exterior of domes and half-domes, of curves can be included in the symbolism in a quite general way.

Neumann (1955) speaks generally of the »great curve« that should always be classified as female. Despite this is not acceptable to see everything soft, curved, rounded or clinging as the epitome of the female. And it is equally unacceptable to describe any pleasing, warm-hearted, peaceful, intricate or even »humane« architecture as specifically female.

We can give examples of the analogy of built forms to female forms in a few authentic statements about the architecture of our century (once more meaning architecture in the broadest possible sense).

We find a design that is trivial in its directness in the work of a French architect: **Nicholas Schöffer** (born 1912) (Studio Yves Hervochon) designed – as one of the Utopian projects of the 60s – a Zentrum für sexuelle Freiheit (*Sexual Freedom Centre*). Similarly to Ledoux, he thought: »... they will be real temples of love, where there is no tendency to pornography, but everything contributes to preparing the couples for sexual love, which will then at last be demystified, available to all, not artificial and no longer debased.

The wandering spectators move in an atmosphere that stimulates the sexual functions. At the end of the way leading down is a dance hall and a hotel-restaurant to receive the couple. These centres will fulfil and enormously important social task. Once the sexual taboo has been demystified the people, liberated from all false compulsions, will finally develop and have access to normal sexual life and also to love.« Thus Nicholas Schöffer (1970). Of course the artist leaves open the question of social, ethical and psychological problems – if it is not simply to be a brothel.[41]

There is also a **Haus-Rucker-Co** project where we can go without any interpretative speculation and rely directly on the designers' statement: »But in the same year (1968) we came to co-operate on a project for the World Fair planned for Osaka in 1970. ›Max Bra‹, the architec-

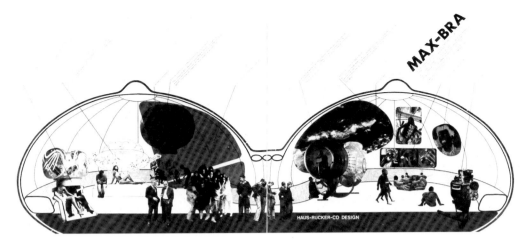

die schön gewölbte Augenbraue usw. in die Brücke eingegangen, sondern das Wichtigste der Frau ist auch direkt mit dem Bauwerk verwirklicht worden: die Fruchtbarkeit der Frau. Auf der Brücke wachsen Bäume! Die Brücke ist nicht nur fraulich, sie ist auch eine Mutter, sie bringt etwas hervor«. (Strecker, 1984)

Diese etwas naive Schilderung fordert zweifellos Kritik heraus, ist aber als explizite Aussage des Gestalters von Interesse. Wenn also das »Runde« und »Gekurvte« für die physische Erscheinungsform des Weiblichen reklamiert werden darf, dann wecken zweifellos die »pneumatischen« Konstruktionen Assoziationen zum weiblichen Körper. Eine Arbeit von **Carlfried Mutschler** (geb. 1926) und **Frei Otto** (geb. 1925) kann dies illustrieren. Die Multihalle von Mannheim, 1973–1975 für die Bundesgartenausstellung errichtet, erweckt den Eindruck einer riesigen liegenden Figur, eines weiblichen Körpers, und die Eingänge legen freudianische Interpretationen nahe.

Daß die **Phänomenologie des Runden** mit dem Frauenkörper in Verbindung gebracht werden kann, wird von einer Frau selbst bestätigt: **Anne Rossberg** (geb. 1963) definiert in ihrer Dissertation *Das Damenzimmer als Abbild von Frauenbild und -körper*. (Rossberg, 1996)

Der Innenraum der Kuppel wurde im Kapitel 7.5.2 dem Weiblich–Uterinen zugeordnet. Kann die Außenerscheinung mit der weiblichen Brust in einen Zusammenhang gebracht werden? Die geodätischen Kuppeln von **Richard Buckminster Fuller** (1895–1983), z. B. jene für die Union Tank Company in Baton Rouge, Louisiana (1958/59), könnten zu dieser Spekulation anstiften. Im Zenit der Kuppel befindet sich ein laternenartiger Aufsatz, der als weibliche Brustknospe gelesen werden könnte und die Assoziation verstärkt.

Der Entwurf für ein *Intimate Theatre* von **Norman Bel Geddes** (1893–1958) weist einen kreisförmigen Grundriß für eine totale Raumbühne auf. Die in einer Spitze endende Kuppel ist nicht allein durch die Statik bestimmt, sondern verstärkt die Assoziation zu weiblichen Formen.

Theoretisch läßt sich wohl unterscheiden – und dies gilt für die gesamte architektonische Sprache – ob eine Form semantisch intendiert ist, oder ob sie lediglich unsere Assoziationen herausfordert, möglicherweise auch unbeabsichtigt. Neben diesen wenigen authentischen Aussagen scheint es aber neuerdings zulässig, der Assoziation einen gewissen Stellenwert zu geben. Die projektiven Metaphern sind zwar nur bedingt durch das Unbewußte und Unterbewußte abgedeckt, scheinen aber trotzdem eine legitime Interpretationsmethode darzustellen.

Auch in Bezug auf die Frau sollen die tertiären Geschlechtsmerkmale, etwa jene, die im Bereich des Psychischen, des Sozialen, der Verhaltensweisen, speziell des Rollenverhaltens liegen, ausgeklammert werden.

7.6. Doppelkodierung, Mehrfachkodierung

Die morphologischen Zuordnungen von Bauformen zum »Männlichen« oder »Weiblichen« ist keineswegs immer eindeutig. Schon im prähistorischen Formenvokabular sind wechselseitige Interpretationen möglich, vielleicht vergleichbar mit dem wahrnehmungspsychologischen Phänomen der »Wechselbilder«, bei denen die Deutungen ohne Veränderung der Bildgestalt »umspringen« können.

Die Mehrfachdeutungen könnten im Sinne der neueren Informationsästhetik als eine Art von **Doppelkodierung** bezeichnet werden, und sie könnten auch ein Indikator für die Rever-

ture of an outsize female breast, filled with audio-visual and tactile sensations ...« (Haus-Rucker-Co, 1984)

Bernhard Strecker (born 1940) built a »womanly« bridge for Oldenburg, and it is called »Amalie«. As well as this, »not only the rounded female forms, the bosom, the behind, the beautifully curved eyebrow etc. have gone into the bridge, but woman's most important quality has been realized with the bridge: her fertility. There are trees growing on the bridge! The bridge is not only womanly, it is also a mother, it produces something«. (Strecker, 1984)

This somewhat naïve description indubitably invites criticism, but it is of interest as an explicit statement by the designer. So if the »rounded« and the »curved« can be claimed as the physical manifestation of the female, then there is no doubt that »pneumatic« constructions produce associations with the female body. A work by **Carlfried Mutschler** (born 1926) and **Frei Otto** (born 1925) will serve to illustrate this. The Multihalle von Mannheim, built 1973 to 1975 for the Bundesgartenschau, gives the impression of a gigantic recumbent figure, of a female body, and the entrances suggest Freudian interpretations.

The fact the **phenomenology of curves** can be associated with the female body is actually confirmed by a woman: Ann Rossberg (born 1953) defines *Das Damenzimmer als Abbild von Frauenbild und -körper* (*The Lady's Room as a Copy of the Woman's Image and Body*) in her dissertation. (Rossberg, 1996)

The interior of the dome was classified as female and uterine in chapter 7.5.2. Can the outward appearance be linked with the female breast? The geodesic domes, e. g. the one built for the Union Tank Company in Baton Rouge, Louisiana (1958/59), by **Richard Buckminster Fuller** (1895–1983)could give rise to this speculation. The zenith of the dome is topped by a lantern-like structure that could be read as a female nipple, thus strengthening the association.

The design for an *Intimate Theatre* by **Norman Bel Geddes** (1893–1958) has a circular ground plan for a total stage-space. The dome ends in a point and is not determined by statics alone, but reinforces the association with female forms.

Theoretically it is possible to distinguish – and this is true of all architectural language – whether a form is intended semantically or whether it merely challenges our associations, possibly unintentionally, as well. But alongside these less authentic statements it has recently seemed admissible to give a certain place value to the association. The projective metaphors are covered by the unconscious and the subconscious only to a limited extent, but nevertheless seem to represent a legitimate interpretative method.

In terms of women as well tertiary sexual characteristics, for instance those that are in the realms of the psychological, the social and of modes of behaviour , especially role behaviour, should be bracketed out.

7.6. Double Coding, Multiple Coding

Morphological classification of building forms as »male« or »female« is by no means always unambiguous. Even in prehistoric formal vocabulary contradictory interpretations are possible, perhaps comparable with the perceptual-psychological phenomenon of »alternate images«, in which interpretations can »twist round« without any change to the pictorial image.

Multiple interpretations can be seen as a kind of »double coding« in the terms of the new information aesthetic, and they could also be an indicator of the reversibility and reciprocity of

sibilität und Reziprozität von männlich und weiblich sein. Dies wäre jedoch keineswegs eine Abschwächung, sondern vielmehr eine Bestätigung für die These von einer androgynen Architektur.

Die Idee einer *Kirche für alle Religionen*, wie sie **Niki de Saint Phalle** hatte, gewinnt in einem bunten Modell Gestalt. Es kann als Kopf gedeutet werden – dann ist der Eingang der Mund, oder als Körper – dann ist die einladende Pforte die Vulva.

Interessanter als die weiblich-weibliche ist die weiblich-männliche Doppelkodierung, bei der vor allem Hoden und Brüste gleichgesetzt werden. Über die Doppelkodierung hinaus könnten wir auch von Mehrfachkodierungen sprechen. Wir begegnen ihnen bereits bei prähistorischen Idolen. Schwellende, gerundete Formen können als Frauenfiguren (Gesäß), als Frauenbrüste oder als Hoden interpretiert werden.

Überraschenderweise können wir solche Phänomene – bei einiger interpretatorischen Freiheit – auch in unserem Jahrhundert beobachten.

Die Doppeldeutigkeit der Kuppel wurde schon erwähnt: Sie ist der mütterlich bergende Raum, in der Außenerscheinung erinnert vor allem die Doppelkuppel an weibliche Brüste. Als Beispiel könnten wir das erste Goetheanum **Rudolf Steiners** erwähnen, ein Holzbau aus dem Jahre 1913, der 1922 abgebrannt ist. Die Kuppeln stehen für die geistige Gemeinschaft, den spirituellen Schutz, sie evozieren aber auch den Charakter des Üppig-Fruchtbaren. Ein Nebengebäude, ein Rest vom ersten Goetheanum in Dornach, zeigt im Mittelteil eine physiognomische Gestaltung, die beiden seitlichen Kuppeln, können dank ihrer paarweisen Anordnung als weibliche Brüste interpretiert werden. Ähnliches gilt auch für das Heizhaus beim **zweiten Goetheanum** (1924–1928). Der steil aufragende Schornstein in Form einer Pflanze verleitet aber zu einer zweiten Bedeutungsebene. Das Bauwerk kann phallisch, mit Hoden ausgestattet, gesehen werden.

Beim Palast von **Sintra** (14. Jahrhundert) in Portugal finden wir seltsame bauliche Gebilde, die ihre Gestalt zweifellos aus sehr einfachen funktionalen Bedingungen ableiten: Es sind hochaufragende, spitz zulaufende und leicht bombierte Türme. Sie enthalten die Klosterküchen, die sich unmittelbar in den Schornsteinen fortsetzen. Die androgyne Deutung ist auch hier wieder rein projektiver und spekulativer Art, die Symbolisierung entsteht lediglich auf Grund der Interpretationsfähigkeit des Menschen: Der runde Küchenraum mit der Assoziation zu Feuer, Nahrung, Fruchtbarkeit ist zweifellos weiblicher Natur, der Schornstein, der den Rauch ausstößt, turmartig und dominant ausgebildet, läßt maskuline Assoziationen zu. Eine weitere Deutungsebene bietet sich an: Die Türme stehen paarweise nebeneinander und legen so den Vergleich mit den phallischen Brüsten nigerianischer Holzskulpturen nahe.

Der im Kapitel 7.4.1 phallisch gedeutete Grundriß des *Daisy House* in Indiana (1977) von **Stanley Tigerman** könnte dank der gerundeten Form auch mit dem Weiblichen in Verbindung gebracht werden. Ähnliches gilt vom Gebäude der Anti-Cruelty-Society in Chicago (1983) von Tigerman.

Die Annäherungen in den Skulpturen von **Heinz Tesar** – er nennt die Gebilde »Homotypen« – evozieren zweifellos Erotisches, ohne daß uns eine eindeutige biologische Zuordnung gelingt: Gleich den Wechselbildern können wir weibliche Brüste oder Phallisches identifizieren, um 90° gedreht würden wir eine androgyne Architektur erkennen, bei der aus der weiblichen Bergkuppel-Rundung das Männliche herauszuwachsen scheint.

male and female. This would not weaken the androgynous architecture thesis, however. On the contrary, it would confirm it.

Niki de Saint Phalle's idea of a *Church for all Religions* takes shape in a colourful model. It can be interpreted as a head, in which case the entrance is the mouth, or as a body, in which case the inviting portal is the vulva.

More interesting than female-female double coding is the female-male version, in which testicles and breasts are the main things to be equated. We could go further than double coding and talk about multiple coding. We come across this as early as prehistoric idols. Swelling, rounded forms can be interpreted as female figures (buttocks), as breasts or as testicles.

Surprisingly we can observe phenomena of this kind – if some interpretative freedom is permitted – in our century as well.

The ambiguity of the dome has already been mentioned: it is a maternal, protecting space, and the outward appearance of the double dome in particular is reminiscent of women's breasts. We can take **Rudolf Steiner's** first Goetheanum as an example, a wooden building dating from 1913 that burned down in 1922. The domes stand for the spiritual community, spiritual protection, but they also evoke the element of luxurious fertility. A surviving side building from the first Goetheanum in Dornach has a face-like design in its central section, and the two side domes are arranged as a pair, which means that they can be interpreted as breasts. The same is true of the boiler-house in the second Goetheanum (1924–1928). But the steeply thrusting chimney in the form of a plant suggests a second plane of interpretation. The building can be seen as phallic, with testicles.

In the palace of **Sintra** (14th century) in Portugal we find strange building structures that undoubtedly derive their shape from very simple functional conditions: they are slightly dished towers, towering up high and tapering to a point. They contain the monastery kitchens, which continue directly into the chimneys. Here too the androgynous interpretation is purely projected and speculative, and the symbolism derives merely from man's ability to interpret: the round kitchen space associated with fire, food and fertility is undoubtedly female in nature, and the chimney, which emits the smoke, is tower-like and dominantly shaped, admitting masculine associations. Another associative plane is possible: the towers are placed in pairs, thus suggesting the phallic breasts of Nigerian wooden sculptures.

The phallically interpreted ground plan of the *Daisy House* in Indiana (1977) by Stanley Tigerman, mentioned in chapter 8.5.1, could also have female associations because of its rounded form. Tigerman's Anti-Cruelty-Society building in Chicago (1983) could be similarly interpreted.

The approaches made in **Heinz Tesar's** sculptures – he calls the structure »Homotypen« – undoubtedly evoke something erotic, without the possibility of unambiguous biological classification: as with the changing images we can identify breast or something phallic, turned through 90° we would see androgynous architecture, in which the female mountain-dome curve seems to grow out of the male areas.

Several interpretations suggest themselves in the case of **Ricardo Porro's** fine art school in Havana, Cuba. The artist himself legitimizes some interpretations when he says that the »image of Eros« should be seen a key to the design. Unlike Frederick Kiesler he by no means denies that the domes with their glazed tips are reminiscent of a woman's breasts. »The whole city became a copy of a woman's breast because there are so many domes that look like breasts, it became an image of Eros.« But that is not all: the central square is dominated by a fountain inspired by the exotic fruit of the papaya, and this is a metaphor, or more than that, a copy of the female sexual organs, iconic and yet metaphysical. In this way Porro has also succeeded in creating a link with magic and the myth of the black population. In the school garden there are some very slender plants with long leaves that Porro feels are reminiscent of pubic hair. The architect chooses an ellipse for the individual studios, and this, translated into three-dimensional terms, always stands for the egg, »the quintessential symbol of emerging life.« (Porro, 1994)

Let us try to spin these metaphors out further: the building complex, the »city«, can be interpreted as a single (female) organism protecting numerous eggs. Then the organically narrowing entrance is undoubtedly the vagina and the square the uterus. The domes themselves can then be seen as double-coded in a way that we have come across before: they are not just breasts, but also the concealing and protecting uterine female space. If I move on to another coding level, then the ground plan can also be interpreted as two »organs«, as bodies, as beings that have moved very close to each other, admittedly without it being possible to

Mehrere Interpretationen bieten sich bei **Ricardo Porros** Schule für bildende Kunst in Havanna, Kuba, an. Für einige Deutungen gibt uns der Architekt selbst die Legitimation, wenn er
davon spricht, daß das »Bild des Eros« als wesentliche Entwurfsidee anzusehen sei. Im Gegensatz zu Frederick Kiesler leugnet er keineswegs, daß die Kuppeln mit ihren verglasten Spitzen an die Brust einer Frau erinnern. »Die ganze Stadt wurde zum Abbild einer Frauenbrust,
aufgrund der Vielzahl der Kuppeln, die wie Frauenbrüste aussehen, zum Abbild des Eros.«
Damit nicht genug: Den zentralen Platz beherrscht ein Brunnen, der von der exotischen Frucht
der Papaya inspiriert ist, und diese ist eine Metapher, ja mehr, ein, wenngleich ikonisches,
dennoch metaphysisches Abbild des weiblichen Geschlechtsteiles. Damit ist es Porro auch
gelungen, die Verbindung zur Magie und zum Mythos der schwarzen Bevölkerung herzustellen. Im Garten der Schule stehen sehr dünne Pflanzen mit langen Blättern, die nach Meinung
Porros an Schamhaare erinnern. Für die einzelnen Ateliers wählt der Architekt die Ellipse, und
diese, ins Dreidimensionale übersetzt, steht immer auch für das Ei »das Symbol schlechthin
für entstehendes Leben«. (Porro, 1994)

Versuchen wir die Metaphern weiterzuspinnen: Man kann den Gebäudekomplex, die
»Stadt«, als einen einzigen (weiblichen) Organismus interpretieren, der in seinem Schutz
zahlreiche Eier birgt. Dann ist zweifellos der organisch sich verengende Eingang die Vagina
und der Platz der Uterus. Die Kuppeln selbst wiederum kann man in einer Doppelkodierung
verstehen, die uns schon einige Male begegnet ist: Sie sind eben nicht nur die weiblichen
Brüste, sondern auch der schützende und bergende uterine weibliche Raum. Beschreite ich
noch eine Ebene der Codierung, dann kann man den Grundriß auch als zwei »Organe« interpretieren, als Körper, als Wesen, die sich einander ganz stark angenähert haben, ohne daß
ich freilich zwischen einem männlichen oder weiblichen Wesen unterscheiden könnte, die als
männlich deutbaren Elemente sind aber eher bescheiden.[43]

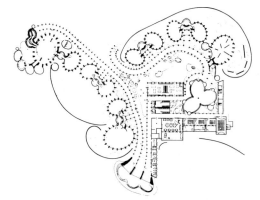

Die amerikanische Gruppe **Ant-Farm** baut 1973 in Texas das skurrile *House of Century*:
Ein verlockendes Interpretationsfeld mit einer spekulativen Mehrfachcodierung bietet sich dar.
Die kuppelförmigen, gerundeten Bauteile können als Brüste, Hoden oder Gesäßbacken gedeutet werden, während Eingang und Turmelement, die nebeneinander liegen, jene Doppelgeschlechtlichkeit signalisieren, die wir etwa in den alchimistischen Androgyn-Darstellungen
finden.

Ein umfangreiches Repertoire an Metaphern beschert uns auch **Frederick Kieslers** Shrine
of the Book in Jerusalem (1959–1965).[44] Kiesler umgibt die heiligen Schriftrollen mit einer Ab-
folge von Schutzschichten, auch wenn diese nur symbolischer Natur sind, um die Kostbarkeit
des Gutes zu unterstreichen. »Der Hauptraum bewahrt den vorgeburtlichen, dem Mutterleib
ähnlichen Charakter des Endlosen.«

Die kosmischen Relationen von Kreis und Quadrat, die uns in zahlreichen kosmogonischen
Architekturen und Symbolen begegnen, werden dialektisch ausgespielt. Das große Welt-Qua-
drat ist aufgefüllt mit Wasser – ähnlich wie der Indische Berg Meru von Flüssen umgeben ist.
Die riesige Zwiebel des Schreins ist abgesenkt in das Wasser, in ihm gleichsam schwimmend.
Im Inneren ermöglicht ein Umgang das ehrfurchtsvolle Umschreiten und das weitere Hinabsteigen zwischen einem Schutzwall, um sogleich wieder aufzusteigen auf die Plattform mit
dem zentralen Sanktuarium. Und hier endlich, in der Innersten »Pyxis«, liegen die wichtigsten
heiligen Schriften, zur Ehrfurcht, fast zur Anbetung präsentiert: die letzten Wesenheiten in den
schützenden Hüllen.

Die Trommel mit den heiligen Schriften wird durch ein merkwürdiges Element überhöht: Ein
Kolben oder riesiger Handgriff ragt in die Höhe, der Lichtöffnung entgegen. Tatsächlich sind
mehrere Deutungen möglich: Zunächst ist es das »Wesen im Wesen«, ähnlich dem indischen
Linga in der Garbhagriha. Die Lingas werden bei der »Puja« mit Wasser begossen, das über
Shivas Pfahl hinabfließt in die Yoni Schale und über schmale Kanäle ins Freie rinnt. Bei dem
Kolben im Dome hingegen war ursprünglich daran gedacht, daß aus seiner Spitze eine Fon-
täne hochstrahlt, durch die Deckenöffnung spritzt, außen über die Keramikplatten der Kuppel
rieselt und schließlich in das Wasserbecken rinnt.

Im Sinne einer Mehrfachkodierung können wir diesem Konzept noch weitere Metaphern
unterlegen: Die gleichsam organhafte Ausstülpung des Doms erhält die Bedeutung einer le-
bensspendenden Brust, aus der die Flüssigkeit quillt, ähnlich den Renaissancebrunnen mit
den üppigen Göttinnen. In einer Zeichnung ist diese Idee angedeutet. Eine deutlichere Darstellung des Fruchtbarkeitsaktes ist wohl kaum denkbar. Indes wurde dieses Konzept nicht realisiert, sondern das Wasser spritzt nun – sofern es nicht abgestellt ist – aus vielen kleinen
Düsen von außen auf die Kuppel. Der Kolben im Zentrum hat jedoch jenseits psychoanalyti-

distinguish between a male and a female being, though the elements that can be interpreted as male are very modest. [42]

The American group **Ant Farm** built the droll *House of Century* in Texas in 1973. It presents an enticing field for interpretation with speculative multiple coding. The dome-shaped, rounded parts of the building can be interpreted as breasts or testicles or buttock cheeks, while the entrance and the tower elements, which are juxtaposed, signal the kind of dual sexuality that we find in the androgynous presentations of alchemy, for instance.

Frederick Kiesler's Shrine of the Book in Jerusalem (1959–1965)[43] presents us with a copious range of metaphors. Kiesler surrounds the sacred scrolls of scripture with a sequence of protective layers, even when these are only symbolic by nature, in order to underline the precious quality of the scrolls. »The main room preserves the character of the infinite, before birth and similar to the mother's womb.«

The cosmic relations of circle and square, which we encounter in numerous cosmogonic architectures and symbols are developed out dialectically. The great world-square is filled with water – similarly to the way in which the Indian Mount Meru is surrounded by the rivers. The giant onion of the shrine is sunk into the water, effectively floating in it. Inside a gallery makes it possible to walk round reverently and climb further down inside a protective wall, then immediately climbing up again to the platform with the central sanctuary. And here at last, in the innermost »Pyxis« are the most important of the sacred writings, presented for reverence, almost for worship: the last essentials within the protective covers.

The dome containing the sacred scriptures has a remarkable element placed above it: a cylinder or gigantic handle towers up, thrusting towards the lighting aperture. In fact several interpretations are possible: first it is the »being in a being«, similar to the Indian linga in the Garbhagriha. The lingas have water poured over them during the »Puja«, flowing over Shiva's stave into the yoni bowl and running into the open air in narrow channels. The original intention for the cylinder in the dome was that a fountain should shoot out of its tip through the opening in the ceiling, trickle down over the ceramic tiles of the dome and finally run into the pool of water.

We can establish further metaphors for this concept in the sense of multiple coding: the effectively organ-like outward thrust of the dome acquires the meaning of a life-giving breast from which the liquid pours, similar to a Renaissance fountain with its voluptuous goddesses. This idea is indicated in a drawing. A clearer representation of the act of fertility can scarcely be conceived. However, this concept was not realized, but the water now spurts – so long as it has not been turned off – down on to the dome from a number of small jets. But the cylinder in the centre has been interpreted in an entirely superficial and plausible way beyond psychoanalytical interpretation: it is simply the handle on the thora scroll.

The »being in the being« (cf. chap. 9.3.1.) was probably also the basic idea behind one of Kiesler's early designs, in which the dome was simply to be placed inside a library chamber. It would then be in a protected zone, waiting for birth, for rebirth.

166, 167. Ricardo Porro, Kunstschule in Havanna, 1963.
168, 169. Frederick Kiesler mit Armand Bartos, Shrine of the Book, Jerusalem, 1959–1965.
170. Ant Farm, *House of the Century*, Texas, 1972.

166, 167. Ricardo Porro, art school in Havanna, 1963.
168, 169. Frederick Kiesler with Armand Bartos, Shrine of the Book, Jerusalem, 1959–1965.
170. Ant Farm, *House of the Century*, Texas, 1972.

166 168 169
167 170

scher Deutungen auch eine durchaus vordergründige und plausible Interpretation erfahren: Er ist einfach der Griff der Thorarolle.

Das »Wesen im Wesen« (vgl. Kap. 9.3.1) war wohl auch der Grundgedanke eines ersten Entwurfes Kieslers, bei dem die Kuppel einfach in einen Bibliotheksraum hineingestellt werden sollte, sie befindet sich dann in einer Schutzzone und harrt der Geburt, der Wiedergeburt.

Kiesler hat diesen Gedanken sehr deutlich dem Rollendom zugeordnet: »Der Schrein ist dem Konzept der Wiedergeburt gewidmet, ist ihr plastischer Ausdruck. Aber es ist nicht allein die Wiedergeburt Israels. Es ist auch unsere eigene Wiedergeburt. Das wichtigste Ereignis in unserem Leben ist, uns selbst zu gebären. Nicht auf die natürliche Geburt zu vertrauen, sondern uns selbst zu zeugen, solange wir noch auf der Erde sind.«

»Sich selbst gebären – nicht mit der Geburt durch eine Mutter zufrieden sein, sondern im Bilde der eigenen Lebenserfahrung sein eigenes Wesen wiedererschaffen. Das ist natürlich nicht die Wiedergeburt nach dem Tod, sondern die Wiedergeburt während unserer allereigensten Lebenszeit.«

Kiesler rekapituliert eine Vorstellung, die wir in vielen Religionen finden: die der menschlichen Wiedergeburt. Ist es im Hinduismus eine schwer zu unterbrechende Kette der ständigen Wiedergeburt, so ist es im Christentum eine Wiedergeburt durch die Taufe Christi. Es genügt aber nicht, einmal geboren zu werden. Wir haben eine große Sehnsucht nach einer geläuterten, neuen Existenz.

Das Motiv des Wassers wird von Kiesler mit dem der Wiedergeburt in Zusammenhang gebracht – genau der Gedanke, der das christliche Taufritual bestimmt. »...Vielleicht würde ein Heiligtum der Stille – das fließende und wiederkehrende Wasser – jedermann das zweite Kommen seiner selbst einflößen ...« Kiesler dementiert heftig, daß der Dom einer Frauenbrust nachgebildet ist, aber eben dieses Dementi kann die Assoziation nur bestärken: »... Diese Kuppel ist aber weder einer Zwiebel noch einer Frauenbrust oder einer Pagode nachgebildet, sondern hat die Form eines alten Gefäßes für Wein mit einem breit ausladenden Bauch und einem offenen Hals.« Kieslers Dementi geht sogleich in anthropomorphe Metaphern über.

In einer weiteren Ebene archetypischer Dispostionen wird dem weiblichen Element der Kuppel das männliche phallische nicht nur implantiert, sondern dialektisch gegenübergestellt. Dieses Motiv ist freilich aus dem Spannungsfeld der schwarzen Basaltscheibe zur Kuppel kaum abzuleiten. Zwei Zeichnungen Kieslers geben aber Aufschluß über den originären Gedanken: In einer Schnittzeichnung sehen wir im Schutze der umgebenden Mauern tatsächlich ein hoch aufgerichtetes, malartiges Zeichen, dessen Deutung als phallisches Element wohl zulässig ist. Eine ähnliche Disposition zeigt eine Skizze aus dem Jahre 1959.

Damit ist ein sehr häufiges Architekturmotiv zitiert: Die dialektische Gegenüberstellung von Kuppel und Turm ist die Metapher für den Dialog unterschiedlicher Wesenheiten wie etwa Mann und Frau. (Vgl. Kap. 8.2) Kiesler spricht zwar nicht vom phallischen Symbol, aber von einer »hartkantigen männlichen Architektur«, so daß eine Deutung der scharfkonturierten Basaltplatte als die eines maskulinen Elements zulässig erscheint.

Die Dialektik wird auch aus der Farbe offenkundig: Die Kuppel erstrahlt in glänzendem Weiß, die Mauer hingegen ist in einem satten Schwarz gehalten.

So finden wir in Kieslers Anlage des Rollendoms ein weites, nicht nur doppelt, sondern mehrfach kodiertes Spektrum an Bedeutungen, das in seiner Gesamtheit jedenfalls als eine androgyne Architektur bezeichnet werden kann.

Über das permanente Streben Kieslers nach einem grenzenlosen, »endlosen« Gesamtkunstwerk hinaus werden noch wesenhaftere existenzielle Probleme angesprochen: die uralte Sehnsucht nach der Einheit von Theos, Eros und Thanatos.

8. Zueinander

8.1. Partner

Ein gestaltpsychologisches Phänomen der menschlichen Wahrnehmung zwingt uns dazu, als menschliche Wesen solche Erscheinungen zu interpretieren, die in etwa der menschlichen Proportion entsprechen und die Andeutung eines Kopfes oder einer Physiognomie, zumindest aber ein »Vorn« und ein »Hinten« aufweisen. So können Turmelemente unter gewissen Voraussetzungen als anthropomorph gedeutet werden.

Kiesler applied this concept to the dome of the scrolls very clearly: »The shrine is dedicated to the concept of rebirth, and expresses it sculpturally. But it is not just the rebirth of Israel. It is also our rebirth. The most important event in our life is that of bearing ourselves. Not trusting in natural birth, but reproducing ourselves for as long as we are on earth.«

»Bearing oneself – not being content with being born to a mother, but recreating one's own being in the image of one's own experience of life. This is of course not rebirth after death, but rebirth during our very own lifetime.«

Kiesler is recapitulating a notion that we find in many religions: that of human rebirth. In Hinduism it is a chain of constant rebirth that it is difficult to interrupt, while in Christianity it is rebirth through the baptism of Christ. But it is not enough to be born once. We express a great longing for a purified, new existence.

The motif of water is linked with rebirth by Kiesler – precisely the thought defined by the Christian ritual of baptism. »... Perhaps a shrine of silence – water flowing and returning – could make someone's own second flow into them...« Kiesler denies vehemently that the dome is modelled on a woman's breast, but this very denial can only strengthen the association: »But this dome is not modelled on an onion or a woman's breast or a pagoda; it is in the shape of an old wine vessel with a broad, swelling belly and an open neck.« Kiesler's denial has immediate recourse to anthropomorphic metaphors.

On another level of archetypal dispositions the male phallic element is not just implanted into the female element of the dome, but dialectically juxtaposed. Admittedly this motif can scarcely be derived from the field of tension between the black basalt slab and the dome. But two drawings by Kiesler cast light on the original thought: in a cross-section drawing we do in fact see a vertical, monument-like sign under the protection of the surrounding walls, and it is probably admissible to interpret this as a phallic element. A sketch dated 1959 shows a similar disposition.

Thus a very frequent architectural metaphor is quoted: the dialectical juxtaposiiton of dome and tower is a metaphor for dialogue between different beings like man and woman, for example. (Cf. chap. 8.2.) Kiesler does not actually speak of a phallic symbol, but talks about »hard-edged, masculine architecture«, so that it seems admissible to interpret the sharp outlines of the basalt slab as a masculine element.

The dialectic is also made obvious by the colouring: the dome shines out in gleaming white, but the wall remains deepest black.

Thus in Kiesler's Shrine of the Book we find a broad spectrum of meaning, coded not just doubly but multiply, and which can certain be called androgynous architecture overall.

Beyond Kiesler's permanent striving for a boundless, »infinite« universal art work, even more fundamental existential problems are addressed: our ancient longing for the unity of theos, eros and thanatos.

8. Together

8.1. Partners

A »gestalt«-psychological phenomenon of human perception forces us to interpret as human beings phenomena that approximate to human proportions and at least hint at a head or a face, but at least have a »front« and a »back«. Thus in certain conditions tower elements can be interpreted anthropomorphically.

They are wayside shrines (Lower Austria, France) that are in shape of slender **conch columns**: they »stand« at the roadside and turn their »face« forwards. Perhaps **Le Corbusier** (1887–1965) took up this motif and used it in the pilgrimage church at Ronchamp (1950–1954). If we interpret the towers as (asexual) beings they are obviously turning their back on each other, as we are inclined to interpret the opening as a face and the curve as a back.

Seen in this way, the sections of the *Grünes Haus (Green House)* (1978/79), connected by a hall, by **Michael Szyskowitz** (born 1944) and **Karla Kowalski** (born 1941) have their »backs« to each other.

In contrast with »turned away« we feel the opposite when to sections of a building seem to »look« at each other and are also connected to each other. **Peter Cook** (born 1936) and **Christine Hawley** (born 1949) designed something that is almost a reversal of the Corbusier towers in 1978/79. We are given the impression that the *Trickling Towers* by are about to copulate.

Es gibt Wegkapellen (Niederösterreich, Frankreich), die in der Art von schlanken **Konchen-säulen** gebildet sind: Sie »stehen« am Straßenrand und wenden das »Gesicht« nach vorn. Vielleicht hat **Le Corbusier** (1887–1965) dieses Motiv aufgegriffen und bei der Wallfahrtskirche von Ronchamp (1950–1954) verwendet. Wenn wir die Türme als (geschlechtslose) »Wesen« interpretieren, dann wenden sie freilich einander den Rücken zu, da wir geneigt sind, die Öffnung als Gesicht und die Krümmung als Rücken zu interpretieren.

So gesehen stehen auch die durch eine Halle verbundenen Bauteile des *Grünen Hauses* (1978/79) in Graz von **Michael Szyszkowitz** (geb. 1944) und **Karla Kowalski** (geb. 1941) mit dem »Rücken« zueinander.

Im Gegensatz zum »Abgewendet« haben wir die umgekehrte Empfindung, wenn zwei Bauteile gleichsam zueinander »schauen« und zusätzlich noch miteinander verbunden sind. Gleichsam die Umkehrung der Corbusier-Türme haben **Peter Cook** (geb. 1936) und **Christine Hawley** (geb. 1949) 1978/79 gezeichnet. Man hat den Eindruck als ständen die *Trickling Towers* knapp vor einer Kopulation.

Die beiden Teile eines Häuserblockes (1920–1924) in Amsterdam von **H. Th. Wijdeveld** scheinen sich, bis auf eine knappe Distanz, einander genähert zu haben; sie bilden sozusagen ein »Paar«. Auch die Türme in einer Autofabrik in Toluka in Mexiko (1963/64) von **Mathias Goeritz** stehen »paarweise«, wenngleich in einer gewissen Distanz. Die Kegelstümpfe sind ungleich hoch und breit. Damit ist noch keine Geschlechtsspezifikation ausgedrückt, doch wenn wir eine Zuordnung versuchen sollten, müßten wir den größeren Turm als den männlichen interpretieren. Allmählich kommen wir dazu, den »Paaren« geschlechtsspezifische Charakteristika zuzuweisen.

Eine unübertroffen schöne Darstellung des partnerschaftlichen Zueinanders gelingt **Walter Pichler** in seiner Arbeit *Zwei Tiegel mit Zuflüssen* (1971). Pichler vermerkt auf der Entwurfs-skizze: »Ich möchte eine gute Beziehung zwischen einer Frau und einem Mann darstellen.« Die zwei Tiegel sind in einem sie beide vereinigenden Sandhügel eingesetzt (in der Zeichnung noch auf Böcken aufgestellt). Sie setzen sich in große Messinglappen mit Rinnen fort. »Man muß das Modell im Regen aufstellen« so der Künstler, dann sammelt sich in den Rinnen das Wasser und fließt in die Röhren. Ab einer gewissen Höhe gibt es ein Überfließen bei verschieden hohem Wasserstand: die Gefäße »kommunizieren« – eine berührende Metapher zum Thema einer beginnenden Vereinigung.

Die Annäherung der Körper, nun in der horizontalen Lage, ist in einem Projekt von **Heinz Tesar** sinnfällig dargestellt. Der Entwurf für das Naturmuseum in Berlin (1988, 1992) sieht zwei langgestreckte Baukörper vor, zwischen denen sich zwar eine schmale Schlucht einschiebt, die aber zweifellos eine Annäherung, ja Synthese anstreben: Die »Köpfe« neigen sich zuein-ander, der eine Kopf umklammert ein Ei (das Haus enthält ein Embryomuseum) und scheint es dem anderen anzubieten. Eine Skizze von Tesar mag diese Interpretation unterstreichen: »Künstliche Frau, Raumzerriß Ohnmacht Knicklos« lautet der verschlüsselte Titel. Ähnlich wie beim Museumsentwurf entziffern wir ein geteiltes- oder ein doppeltes Wesen, das gleichwohl zu einer neuen Einheit generiert. Das Thema des »Zueinander« wird von **Stanley Tigerman** in origineller Weise in die Architektur umgesetzt: Das *Zipp House* wird von Tigerman sehr ein-deutig beschrieben: »Continuing in the mildly scatological vein of the Daisy House, the site plan is organized about and around the shape of a zipper with the genitals as entry stairs (landscaping having obvious pubescent overtones). Thus the project has an anthropomorphic (symmetrical) sense.«[45]

Die Dualität, die Wiederholung und Spiegelung stellt ein wichtiges Detail in den Arbeiten **Hans Holleins** dar. Die Entstehung einer neuen Ganzheit aus der Zweiheit kann durchaus auch als erotischer Akt gesehen werden. Die zur Einheit verschmolzene Doppelsäule in der Feigen-Galerie in New York hat ihr Vorbild an der Westfassade von St. Stephan. Die Spiege-lung im Retti-Laden in Wien führt in die Dualität eines realen-irrealen Raums.

8.2. Nebeneinander

Im vorherigen Kapitel waren die »Wesen«, die anthropomorphen Architekturelemente, gleich-sam in einer Geschlechtslosigkeit einander zugeordnet. Das menschliche Interpretationsbe-dürfnis scheint jedoch so geartet zu sein, daß **Paare** auch dort mit geschlechtsspezifischen Eigenschaften ausgestattet werden, wo es dafür nur wenige konkrete Hinweise gibt.

Eine erste Annäherung an eine androgyne Architektur könnte man dann sehen, wenn die Grundprinzipien artikuliert weiblich/männlich dialektisch einander gegenübergestellt werden.

171. Le Corbusier, Wallfahrtskirche Notre-Dame-du-Haut, Ronchamp, Frankreich, 1950–1954.
172. Peter Cook und Christine Hawley, *Trickling Towers*, 1978.
173. Michael Szyszkowitz und Karla Kowalski, *Grünes Haus*, Graz, 1978/1979.
174. H. Th. Wijdeveld, Wohnkomplex in Amsterdam, 1920–1924.
175. Mathias Goeritz, Automex-Türme, Toluca, Mexiko, 1963/1964.

171. Le Corbusier, pilgrimage church of Notre-Dame-du-Haut, Ronchamp, France, 1950–1954.
172. Peter Cook, Christine Hawley, *Trickling Towers*, 1978.
173. Michael Szyszkowitz, Karla Kowalski, *Green House*, Graz, 1978/1979.
174. H. Th. Wijdeveld, residential complex, Amsterdam, 1920–1924.
175. Mathias Goeritz, Automex towers, Toluca, Mexico, 1963/1964.

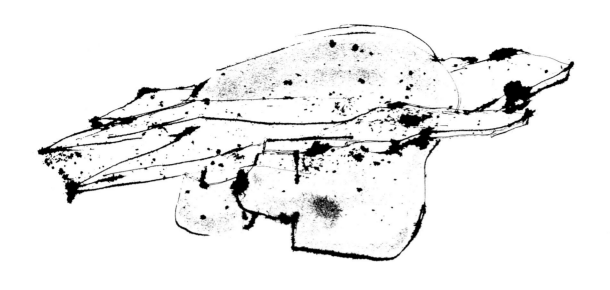

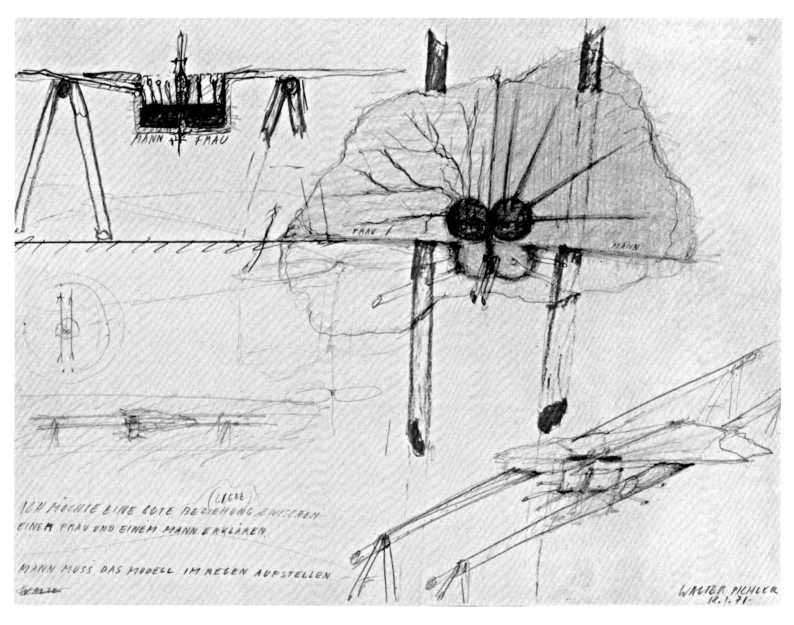

ICH MÖCHTE EINE GUTE BEZIEHUNG ZWISCHEN
EINEM FRAU UND EINEM MANN ERKLÄREN.

MANN MUSS DAS MODELL IM REGEN AUFSTELLEN

WALTER PICHLER
18.1.71.

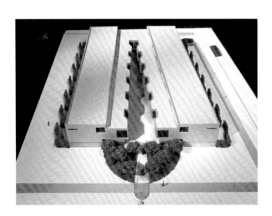

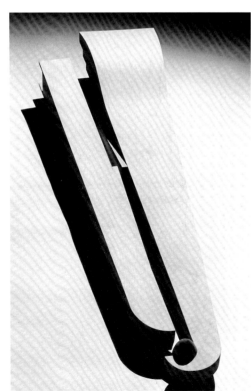

The two parts of a block of houses (1920–1924) in Amsterdam by **H. Th. Wijdeveld** seem to have come up close to each other, while keeping a certain distance; they make a »couple«, as it were. The towers in a car factory in Toluka in Mexico (1963/64) by **Mathias Goeritz** also stand »in pairs«, although keeping their distance. The conical stumps are different in height and breadth. This does not express specific sexuality, but if we were to attempt a classification we would have to interpret the larger tower as the male one. We gradually find ourselves endowing the »couples« with sexually specific characteristics.

Walter Pichler achieves an unsurpassedly beautiful representation of partners together in his work *Zwei Tiegel mit Zuflüssen* (*Two Pans with Inflows*, 1971). Pichler notes in the design sketch: »I wanted to show a good relationship between a woman and a man.« The two pans are set in a mound of sand that unites them (still set on trestles in the sketch). They continue into large brass leaves with channels. »The model is to be set up in the rain« said the artist, so that the water collects in the channels and flows into the tubes. From a certain height there is overflowing at a certain water level: the vessels are »communicating« – a touching metaphor on the subject of unification that is beginning.

Bodies coming closer, now in a horizontal position, is strikingly demonstrated in a project by **Heinz Tesar**. The design for the Naturmuseum in Berlin (1988, 1992) anticipates two long buildings between which there is indeed a small gap, but they are nevertheless trying to get closer to each other. The »heads« bow towards each other, with one head holding an egg (the building contains an embryo museum), which it seems to be offering to the other one. A sketch by Tesar may confirm this interpretation: »Artificial woman, space-rip powerlessness uncreased« runs the cryptic title. As with a museum design we decipher a divided or a double being, which nevertheless generates into a new unity. **Stanley Tigerman** translates the »together« theme into architecture in an original way: the *Zipp House* is described very unambiguously by Tigerman himself: »Continuing in the mildly scatological vein of the Daisy House, the site plan is organized about and around the shape of a zipper with the genitals as entry stairs (landscaping having obvious pubescent overtones). Thus the project has an anthropomorphic (symmetrical) sense.«

Duality, repetition and reflection are represented by an important detail in the work of **Hans Hollein**. The emergence of a new totality from duality can be seen as an erotic act through and through. The double column on the Feigen Gallery in New York, fused into unity, has its model in the west façade of St. Stephan. The reflection in the Retti shop in Vienna leads into the duality of a real-unreal space.

8.2. Juxtaposed

In the previous chapter the »being«, the anthropomorphic architectural elements, are arranged together in an essentially asexual fashion. But the human need for interpretation seems to be such that **couples** are provided with sexually specific qualities even when there is very little concrete indication of this.

A first approach to an androgynous architecture could be seen at the point where the basic female/male principles are set against each other dialectically. For it is not only balanced harmony in the spirit of the Renaissance that has its place in architecture, but also living dialogue, as has already been shown. In many buildings or groups of buildings we find the male and the female principle represented in juxtaposition to an equal extent, without a complete synthesis emerging.

If we look at the west façade of **St. Stephan in Vienna** then no female or male symbols can be made out at first glance. But Bolsena (1980) does discover metaphors: »The image of a most lavish symbolism and the most complete sense of the Gothic hermaphrodite can still be admired in St. Stephan in Vienna ... the male part that symbolizes Eros is paired with a clock, with time renewing itself, while the belly of Venus, the female part, can be recognized in the signs of the zodiac, which stands for the universal.

The two apertures for the clock and the signs of the zodiac form the tip of two long slender columns, similar to candelabra, from which light is emitted. The columns, applied to the wall like relief, have the cross-section of a Y, the Greek Eros. The left-hand column, which ends in the clock, is concluded by a mushroom in the shape of a glans penis, and the other, which ends in the signs of the zodiac, has a kind of mons veneris with a book and two twigs running together downwards on top of it; they are in the shape of a mandorla. In the upper point they

Denn nicht allein die ausgeglichene Harmonie im Sinne der Antike oder der Renaissance hat ihren Platz in der Architektur, sondern auch, wie schon dargestellt, der lebendige Dialog. Wir finden bei vielen Bauwerken oder Bauwerkgruppen gleicherweise das männliche und das weibliche Prinzip nebeneinander vertreten, ohne daß sich eine vollkommene Synthese abzeichnet.

Betrachten wir die Westfassade von **St. Stephan in Wien**, so können wir auf den ersten Blick keinerlei weibliche oder männliche Symbole erkennen. Bolsena (1980) jedoch entdeckt Metaphern: »Das Abbild der reichsten Symbolik und das vollständigste des gotischen Hermaphroditen kann man noch an St. Stephan in Wien bewundern ... der männliche Teil der den Eros symbolisiert ist gepaart mit einer Uhr, der sich erneuernden Zeit, während der Bauch der Venus, der weibliche Teil, am Tierkreis, soviel wie das Universum, erkennbar ist. Die zwei Öffnungen für die Uhr und den Tierkreis bilden die Spitze von zwei langen, schlanken Säulen, ähnlich Kerzenleuchtern, aus denen das Licht entspringt. Die Säulen, reliefartig an der Wand appliziert, haben den Querschnitt des Y, des griechischen Eros. Die linke Säule, die als Uhr endet, ist von einem Pilz in der Form der männlichen Glans abgeschlossen, die andere, die im Tierkreis endet, mit einer Art Venushügel, auf dem ein Buch und zwei nach unten zusammenlaufende Zweige liegen, die die Form einer Mandorla haben. Im oberen Teil sind sie durch Blätter vereint, was jedoch von unten schlecht zu erkennen ist. Es ist evident, daß es sich um das weibliche Geschlechtsorgan handelt. In der Mitte des Tierkreisbandes mit den 12 Konstellationen, die mit den 12 Stunden der gegenüberliegenden Uhr korrespondieren, sieht man die Sonne mit dem Mondviertel, das wahrsagerische H, der universelle Hermaphrodit. Derartige Symbole mußten auch an den Bändern zwischen den Säulen des Hauptportales gewesen sein, aber sie wurden auf Verlangen der Jesuiten von Maria Theresia entfernt.« (Bolsena, 1980)

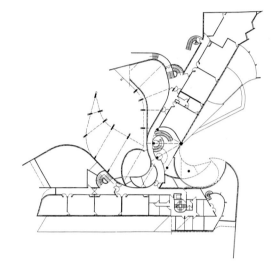

In eindrucksvoller Weise läßt sich das Prinzip der Annäherung an ein androgynes Prinzip an einem Bauwerk **Ricardo Porros** darstellen. Es ist das Collège Fabien in Montreuil, Frankreich. Allerdings müssen wir den Grundriß des Gebäudes heranziehen, um die – wie bei Porro so häufige – Anthropomorphie eines Gebäudes entschlüsseln zu können. Wir sind jedoch nicht auf Spekulationen angewiesen, sondern können uns auf die authentische Interpretation des Architekten berufen. Das Gebäude besteht aus zwei Flügeln, die sich in einem Gelenk, der Eingangshalle treffen. »Die beiden Flügel sind in zwei seltsame Tiere gewandelt, ein männliches und ein weibliches. Das männliche Tier scheint das weibliche beschützen zu wollen. Beide Körper schwingen in einer großen kreisförmigen horizontalen Bewegung und bilden auf diese Weise das Yin/Yang-Symbol, das Symbol des Gleichgewichts zwischen einem Gegensatzpaar.« (Porro, 1994)

Der Gedanke der »coincidentia oppositorum« liegt also hier ganz nahe, wenngleich wir es mit einer gleichsam animalischen Androgynie zu tun haben.

Toshio Nakamura (1994) beschreibt Porros Werk als »androgynous« und charakterisiert damit gleichzeitig das System von Gegensatzpaaren: »... it well be turned out by a close examination that his planning consists of juxtaposition of two different elements like linear and curvilinear, free curve and rectangular, axial and non axial, and baroque and classic. These are not in relation of counterpoint but of conglutination. They do not form a layering of meanings nor ambiguity. But they violent bring about contamination of meanings or hybridization. As a result, the occurred a combination of two opposites for example concave and convex, cryptogam and phanerogam, and male and female, androgynous.« [46]

Wenn in den vorhergehenden Kapiteln, vereinfachend, dem Männlichen das Turmmotiv, dem Weiblichen die Kuppel zugeordnet wurde, dann scheint es gerechtfertigt, im Nebeneinander dieser Bauformen ein Vorstadium zur Androgynie zu sehen. Für das **Nebeneinander von Turm und Kuppel** lassen sich zahlreiche Beispiele in der gesamten Baugeschichte bis in unsere Gegenwart hinein finden, einige wenige sollen zitiert werden.

Wenn wir den Typus Kuppel auf Hohlraum, Innenraum allgemein erweitern, dann kann jeder Kirchenbau mit einem Campanile oder mit einem abgelöst artikulierten Turm als ein solch dialektisches Nebeneinander der Prinzipien gesehen werden.

Die Karlskirche in Wien (1716–1739) von **Johann Bernhard** (1656–1723) und **Joseph Emanuel Fischer v. Erlach** (1693–1742), die großartige Umsetzung der Habsburger Macht in ein Bauwerk, orientiert sich an römischen Vorbildern und stellt Kuppel und Säule einander gegenüber.

Hans Sedlmayr (1956) gelingt der überzeugende Nachweis des umfangreichen Symbolgehaltes. Über das Sinnbildhafte hinausgehend spricht Sedlmayr von einer »abbildenden« Archi-

are joined by leaves, but it is difficult to see this from below. It is evident that this represents a female sexual organ. In the middle of the signs of the zodiac with the 12 constellations cor-responding with the 12 hours on the clock opposite can be seen the sun with the crescent moon, the prophetic H, the universal hermaphrodite. There must have been symbols of this kind on the bands between the columns of the main portal as well, but these were removed at the request of Maria Theresa's Jesuits.« (Bolsena, 1980)

The principle of approaching an androgynous principle can be shown impressively in a building by **Ricardo Porro**. It is the Collège Fabien in Montreuil, France. However, we have to look at the ground plan of the building if – as is so often the case with Porro – we are going to be able to decode the anthropomorphy of a building. But we do have to rely on speculation, but can cite the architect's authentic interpretation. The building consists of two wings, which meet at a joint, the entrance hall. »The two wings are transformed into two strange animals, one male, one female. The male animal seems to want to protect the female one. Both bodies curve in a great circular horizontal movement, thus forming the yin/yang symbol, the symbol of balance within a contrasting pair.« (Porro, 1994)

The notion of the »coincidentia oppositorum« is thus clearly suggested here, although we are dealing with an androgyny that is essentially animal.

Toshio Nakamura (1994) describes Porro's work as »androgynous«, and thus at the same time established the character of the system of opposing pairs: »It will be turned out by a close examination that his planning consists of juxtaposition of two different elements like lin-ear and curvilinear, free curve and rectangular, axial and non-axial, and baroque and classic. These are not in relation of counterpoint but of conglutination. They do not form a layering of meanings nor ambiguity. But they violent bring about contamination of meanings or hybridiza-tion. As a result there occurred a combination of two opposites for example concave and con-vex, cryptogram and phanerogam, and male and female, androgynous.«

If in the preceding chapters, for the sake of simplicity, the male was allotted the tower mo-tif and the female the dome, then it seems justifiable to see androgyny in the juxtaposition of these building forms. They are numerous examples throughout architectural history of **tower and dome together**, right down to the present, and a few of them should be quoted.

If we broaden the dome over hollow, internal space type generally, then every church build-ing with a campanile or a separately articulated tower can be seen as this kind of dialectical juxtaposition of the principles.

The Karlskirche in Vienna (1716–1739) by **Johann Bernhard** (1656–1723) and **Joseph Ema-nuel Fischer von Erlach** (1693–1742), a magnificent translation of Habsburg power into a building, follows Roman models and sets dome and column against each other.

Hans Sedlmayr (1956) successfully establishes the high level of symbolic content. Going beyond this, he talks about an »copying« architecture. Although the two colossal columns nar-rate the life of St. Charles Borromeo, they are, almost as a copy of Trajan's Column in Rome, therefore masculine power symbols and can be compared with the Pillars of Hercules, which marked the limits of the earth. The oval dome on the other hand is a quotation of Hagia So-phia, the temple of wisdom, according to Sedlmayr, and thus of a female being. Thus the in-terpretation of a male-female field of tension seems justified.

The Catholic church of St. Michael in Frankfurt (1953–1961) by **Rudolf Schwarz** (1897–1961) and **Karl Wimmenauer** (b. 1914) takes up the notion of the campanile: an austerely cylindrical tower enters into a beautiful dialogue with the body of the church, which is a slender ellipse.

Remarkable examples from **Iran** can be cited. Usually the mosques have only one minaret, and then the character of dialogue interplay between tower and housing becomes particularly clear. In Mashad the gate makes the tower and the dome into an architectural trinity.

In our century, in the German Expressionist period, we find some very significant examples of contrasting forms being juxtaposed in dialogue. **Bruno Taut's** (1880–1938) fantastic drawing *Die große Blume* (*The big flower*) was created in the idealistic days of the »Gläserne Kette«, 1920. A giant lotus flower symbolizes the female principle, and next to it, tall and straight, is a tower-like structure. The interpretation in this case is by no means speculative, as Bruno Taut accompanied the drawing with revealing textual material, including this statement: »Ancient wis-dom is alive again. Complete lack of concealment in sexual matters – overcoming instincts by oneself – phallus and rosette a sacred symbol again, the dirty joke impossible ...«

The large flow is divided up into individual zones: an outer, widely spreading one, a second, supported on arches, on which the tower is leaning and flanked by four turrets and a third zone of blossom with a crater-like aperture.

tektur. Obgleich die beiden Kolossalsäulen vom Leben des Heiligen Karl Borromäus erzählen, sind sie, fast als Kopien der römischen Trajansäule, kaiserliche, also männliche Machtsymbole und können mit den erdbegrenzenden Säulen des Herkules in Verbindung gebracht werden. Die ovale Kuppel hingegen ist nach Sedlmayr ein Zitat der Hagia Sophia, des Tempels der Weisheit, also eines weiblichen Wesens. Somit scheint die Interpretation eines männlich-weiblichen Spannungsfeldes durchaus gerechtfertigt.

Die katholische Kirche St. Michael in Frankfurt (1953–1991) von **Rudolf Schwarz** (1897 bis 1961) und **Karl Wimmenauer** (geb. 1914) greift den Gedanken der Campanile auf: Ein streng zylindrisch geformter Turm steht in einem schönem Dialog zum Kirchenbau in Gestalt einer schlanken Ellipse.

Aus dem **Iran** können bemerkenswerte Beispiele zitiert werden. Die Moscheen sind zumeist nur mit einem Minarett ausgestattet, der Charakter der dialogischen Wechselwirkung von Turm und Gehäuse wird dann besonders sinnfällig. In Mashad ergänzt das Tor den Turm und die Kuppel zu einer architektonischen Trinität.

In unserem Jahrhundert finden wir zur Zeit des Expressionismus in Deutschland einige sehr signifikante Beispiele für das dialogische Nebeneinander kontrastierender Formen. Die phantastische Zeichnung *Die große Blume* hat **Bruno Taut** (1880–1938) in der idealistischen Zeit der »Gläsernen Kette«, 1920, angefertigt. Eine riesige Lotosblume symbolisiert das weibliche Prinzip, daneben befindet sich, hoch aufgerichtet, ein turmartiges Gebilde. Die Deutung ist in diesem Fall keineswegs spekulativ, denn Bruno Taut begleitet die Zeichnung mit aufschlußreichen Texten. So heißt es unter anderem: »Uralte Weisheit ist wieder lebendig. Völlige Unverhülltheit in Geschlechtsdingen – Überwindung der Triebe durch sich selbst – Phallus und Rosette wieder heiliges Symbol, die Zote unmöglich ...«

Die große Blume ist in einzelne Zonen aufgeteilt: eine äußere, breit ausladende, eine zweite, arkadengestützte, an die sich der Turm anlehnt und die von vier Türmchen flankiert wird und eine dritte Blütenzone, die eine kraterartige Öffnung aufweist.

In einem Modell, das einem großen Knochen nachgebildet ist, wird bei **Hermann Finsterlin** (1887–1973) die bipolare Dialektik deutlich ausgedrückt: Der *Entwurf für eine Kathedrale auf dem VIII. Hügel Roms* (1920–1924) ist ein »organisches« Gebilde, bei dem Kuppel und Turm, obgleich noch nebeneinanderstehend, durch die topographische Basis miteinander verbunden sind. Finsterlin fordert den anthropomorphen Innenraum und formuliert: »Architektur ist die Kunst der Raumcurve. Nichts kommt gleich den Curven der organischen Höhlen ... Nur wenn wir den Raum vor uns als Organismus empfinden wollen, können wir optimale Architektur schaffen.« (1988)

In ganz ähnlicher Weise wie bei Finsterlin tritt in einer Zeichnung von **Hans Luckhardt** (1890–1954) die Spannung eines aufragend turmartigen Elementes – entfernt an eine gotische Kathedrale erinnernd – zu einer gewaltigen, spiralförmigen Höhlung auf. Wie ein Wasserwirbel scheint das Gebäude in eine geheimnisvolle Tiefe zu führen, in einer dynamischen Rotationsbewegung, die im Begriff ist, die statische Ruhe des Turms zu erfassen. Über die Begriffe »männlich« und »weiblich« hinaus können wir das Bedeutungsvokabular beliebig erweitern: da ist auch »hoch« und »tief«, »Ruhe« und »Bewegung«, »linear« und »zyklisch«.

Die hohe Bedeutung, die nach der russischen Revolution dem Buche zukommt, wird in den Entwürfen für die Lenin-Bibliothek in Moskau deutlich.

Die bedeutendste Arbeit liefert **Iwan Iljitsch Leonidow** (1902–1959). Das Auditorium hat die konsequente Form einer Kugel, die sich vom Boden abhebt und von Stahltrossen stabilisiert wird. Daneben steht der gewaltige Bücherturm: das Zeichen der Macht des Wortes gegenüber der bergenden Hülle für die Gemeinschaft.

Die Dialektik der elementaren Formen taucht in einem Bild von **Hugh Ferriss** (1889–1962) auf, dem phantastischen Realisten und Visionär der New Yorker Wolkenkratzer in den zwanziger und dreißiger Jahren. Im Vordergrund steht machtvoll aufgerichtet ein gewaltiger, phallischer Wolkenkratzer, weit zurückgedrängt ein monumentaler Kuppelbau mit Satelliten, alles in ein feierliches Licht eingetaucht.

Für die New Yorker Weltausstellung baut 1939 **Wallace K. Harrison** (geb. 1932) zwei charakteristische Symbole: den *Trylon*, eine schlanke Turmnadel, die an F. L. Wrights *High mile tower* von 1956 erinnert und die *Perisphere*, ein Kugelbau als Vorwegnahme von Fullers Kuppel bei der Expo 1970 in Montreal. In einer klaren und spannungsreichen Weise sind hier zwei elementare Grundprinzipien, wie immer man sie benennen mag, einander gegenübergestellt.

Eine großartige Kombination der Archetypen können wir in den Bauten für Braslia von **Oscar Niemeyer** (geb. 1907) entdecken. Von den Bauten des Wettbewerbs von 1956 wurden

183. Iwan Iljitsch Leonidow, Lenin-Bibliothek, Moskau, 1927.
184. Moschee mit Minarett in Mashad, Iran, 16. Jh.
185. Aldo Rossi, Deutsches Historisches Museum in Berlin, 1986.
186. Hans Luckhardt, Architekturphantasie, 1921.
187. Hermann Finsterlin, Entwurf für eine Kathedrale auf dem VIII. Hügel Roms, 1920.

183. Ivan Ilich Leonidov, Lenin Library, Moscow, 1927.
184. Mosque with minaret in Mashad, Iran, 16th cent.
185. Aldo Rossi, Deutsches Historisches Museum, Berlin, 1986.
186. Hans Luckhardt, architectural fantasy, 1921.
187. Hermann Finsterlin, cathedral on the VIIIth Hill of Rome, 1920.

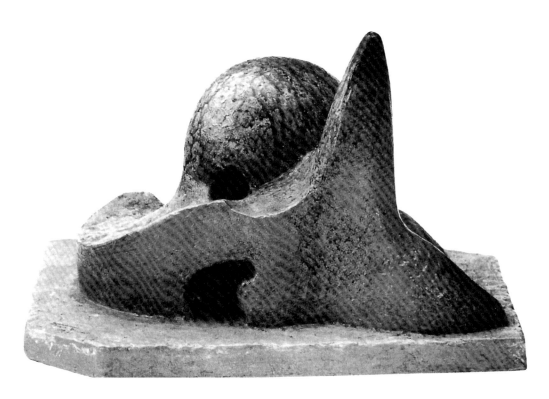

DIE GROSSE BLUME

Heiligtum zur Aufsaugung der Sonnenenergie mit Glasplatten und Brennlinsen und spiegeln. Anstauung in Lichttürmen — Flugwegweiser

Technik ist jetzt etwas ganz anderes als in der Fabrikschorn-Steinzeit

Der Mensch ist so umgebildet, dass er keine Arbeit tun kann, die nicht Freude ist. Es geht an auch nicht bei Zwang. Die Hundegesellschaft hat der Mensch verloren

Uralte Weisheit ist wieder lebendig: Völlige Unverhülltheit in Geschlechtsdingen — Überwindung der Triebe durch sich selbst — Phallus und Rosette — wieder heiliges Symbol, die Zote unmöglich ohne Verstecken und Verschweigen . . .

Der Begriff des Besitzes ist verschwunden — also auch die Ehe. Alles ist geliehenes Pfund — Lust ist nur Freude

188. Bruno Taut, *Die große Blume*, 1920.
189. Clemens Holzmeister, Kathedrale für Rio de Janeiro, 1956.
190. Hugh Ferriss, Center of Philosophy, New York, 1929.
191. Wallace K. Harrison, Trylon and Perisphere, Weltaustellung New York, 1939.
192. Rudolf Schwarz mit Karl Wimmenauer, St. Michael, Frankfurt am Main, 1953–1961.
193. Karl Schwanzer, BMW-Hauptverwaltung, München, 1970–1972.

188. Bruno Taut, *The Big Flower*, 1920.
189. Clemens Holzmeister, cathedral for Rio de Janeiro, 1956.
190. Hugh Ferriss, Center of Philosophy, New York, 1929.
191. Wallace K. Harrison, Trylon and Perisphere, World Exposition New York, 1939.
192. Rudolf Schwarz with Karl Wimmenauer, St. Michael, Frankfurt am Main, 1953–1961.
193. Karl Schwanzer, BMW headquarters, Munich, 1970–1972.

Hermann Finsterlin (1887–1973) clearly expresses the bipolar dialectic in a model based on a large bone. His *Entwurf für eine Kathedrale auf dem VIII. Hügel Roms* (*Design for a Cathedral on the VIIIth Hill of Rome,* 1920–1924) is an »organic« structure in which dome and tower, although still placed next to each other, are linked by the topographical basis. Finsterlin challenges the anthropomorphic interior and formulates: »Architecture is the art of the spatial curve. Nothing can equal the curves of organic caves. ... Only when we intend to perceive the space in front of us as an organism can we create optimal architecture.« (1988)

In a similar way to Finsterlin a drawing by **Hans Luckhardt** (1890–1954) confronts the tension of a soaring tower-like element – distantly reminiscent of a Gothic cathedral – with a powerful, spiral hollow. The building seems to lead into mysterious depths like a whirlpool, in a dynamic rotating movement which is in the act of seizing the static calm of the tower. We can expand the vocabulary of meaning beyond the concepts »male« and »female« as much as we wish: there is also »high« and »deep«, »peace« and »movement«, »linear« and »cyclical«.

The great significance attributed to books after the Russian Revolution is clear from the designs for the Lenin Library in Moscow.

The most important work is submitted by **Ivan Illich Leonidov** (1902–1959). The auditorium has the consistent shape of a sphere rising from the floor and stabilized by steel cables. Next to this is the massive book tower: a sign of the power of the word set against the protective covering for the community.

The dialectic of elemental forms appears in a picture by **Hugh Ferriss** (1889–1962), the fantastic realist and visionary of the New York skyscrapers in the twenties and thirties. In the foreground is the tall and powerful shape of a massive phallic skyscraper, and thrust far to the back a monumental domed building with satellites, all bathed in a solemn light.

Wallace K. Harrison (born 1932) built two characteristic symbols for the New York World Fair in 1939: the *Trylon* a slender needle tower, reminiscent of Frank Lloyd Wright's *High mile tower* of 1956 and the *Perisphere*, a spherical structure anticipating Fuller's dome for the Expo Montreal in 1970. Two elemental basic principles, whatever one might wish to call them, are juxtaposed here in a very lucid and exciting way.

We find a magnificent combination of archetypes in the buildings for Brasilia by **Oscar Niemeyer** (born 1907). Of the buildings produced for the 1956 competition, the first to be built were the congress building (1958–1970) and the government building (1958–1960). The former takes the shape of a dish that apparently open towards the top, and the latter is in the form of a dome. The massive double towers of the Supreme Court buildings date from 1966 to 1972. This staked out the dimensions for a fundamental formal language: the soaring towers are juxtaposed with the large-scale covering, even though this is not entirely open to spatial experience.

The large dish of the museum, apparently open towards the top is placed in front of the two massive tower cylinders in the BMW building in Munich by **Karl Schwanzer** (1918–1975). In fact the tower, which is additionally distinguished by the archetypal ground plan of the four circles, is the seat of the administration, the organization, the direction, in others words of power over a technical empire. The dish on the other hand conceals, protects, preserves: the museum as a place of protection uses the female-maternal primordial from. The phallic element moves a step closer to the protecting one in the design for a cathedral in Rio (1956) by **Clemens Holzmeister** (1886–1983). The pointed cone of the tower has come so close to the powerful embrace of the cathedral's arms that they have fused together in the lower sections.

Not only dome and dish, but also circle and annulus stand for the female-protective element. Seen in this way we can also see an image of partnership in **Aldo Rossi**'s (born 1931) design for the Historical Museum in Berlin: a large circular centrally planned building is joined by a tower that tapers towards the top.[44]

A group of residential buildings by **Hans Scharoun** (1893–1972) in Stuttgart was given the name *Romeo and Juliet*, and now their is no doubt at all about the attribution.

The lower building – Julia – forms a invitingly open courtyard, and the tower-like one – Romeo – is placed contrapuntally in the first design; it seems to intend to penetrate the protective space of the courtyard, and one could imagine that an androgynous unit will then be produced.[45]

If we risk moving to the boundaries of interpretational tolerance, then the Traisenpavillons in St. Pölten, Lower Austria (1988), by **Adolf Krischanitz** (born 1946), could also be interpreted in a spirit of dialectical partnership: the great cylinder of the hall is accompanied by a long narthex, a recumbent tower motif, as it were.

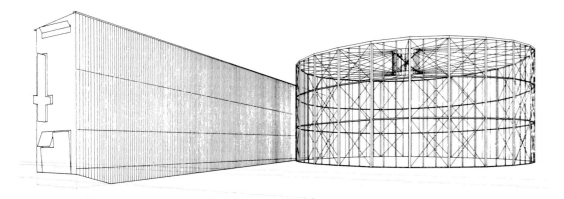

zunächst das Kongreßgebäude (1958–1970) und das Regierungsgebäude (1958–1960) errichtet, ersteres in Form einer scheinbar nach oben sich öffnenden Schale, letzteres in Form einer Kuppel. 1966 bis 1972 entstanden die Bauten für den Obersten Gerichtshof als machtvolle Doppeltürme. Damit war die Dimension einer elementaren Formensprache abgesteckt: Die aufragenden Türme werden der großformatigen, wenngleich räumlich nur bedingt erlebbaren bergenden Hülle zugesellt.

Den vier mächtigen Turmzylindern des BMW–Gebäudes in München von **Karl Schwanzer** (1918–1975) ist die große nach oben offen wirkende Schale des Museumsbaus vorgelagert. Tatsächlich ist der Turm, der zusätzlich durch den archetypischen Grundriß der vier Kreise ausgezeichnet ist, der Sitz der Verwaltung, der Organisation, der Direktion, also der Macht über ein technisches Imperium. Die Schale hingegen birgt, bewahrt, konserviert: Das Museum als Ort des Schutzes bedient sich der weiblich-mütterlichen Urform. Einen Schritt weiter bewegt sich das phallische Element auf das schützende hin im Entwurf für eine Kathedrale in Rio (1956) von **Clemens Holzmeister** (1886–1983). Der spitze Konus des Turmes hat sich den machtvoll umfangenden Armen der Kathedrale so weit genähert, daß in den unteren Bereichen eine Verschmelzung stattgefunden hat.

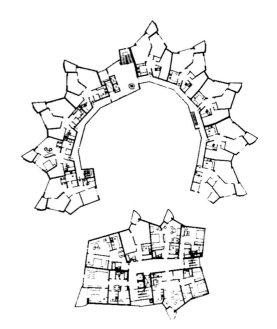

Nicht nur Kuppel und Schale, sondern auch Kreis und Kreisring stehen für das Weiblich-Schützende. So gesehen können wir auch im Wettbewerbsentwurf von **Aldo Rossi** (geb. 1931) für das Projekt des Deutschen Historischen Museums in Berlin ein partnerschaftliches Bild sehen: Ein großer kreisrunder Zentralbau wird von einem nach oben sich verjüngenden Turm assistiert.[47]

Eine Wohnhausgruppe von **Hans Scharoun** (1893–1972) in Stuttgart erhält die Bezeichnung *Romeo und Julia*, und nun besteht kein Zweifel mehr über die Zuschreibung.

Der niedere Baukörper – Julia – bildet einen aufnehmend-offenen Hof, der turmartige – Romeo – ist im ersten Entwurf kontrapunktisch gegenübergestellt, er scheint die Absicht zu haben, in den schützenden Hofraum einzudringen, und man könnte sich vorstellen, daß dann eine androgyne Einheit entstehen wird.[48]

Wenn wir uns an die Grenze der Interpretationstoleranz wagen, dann könnten auch die Traisenpavillons in St. Pölten, Niederösterreich (1988), von **Adolf Krischanitz** (geb. 1946) im Sinne der dialektischen Partnerschaft gedeutet werden: Dem großen Zylinder der Halle ist ein langgestreckter Narthex beigesellt, gleichsam ein umgelegtes Turmmotiv.

In der Kirche Santa Croce in Parma hat **Aurelio Cortesi** (geb. 1931) im Zuge der liturgischen Reformen einen Altar und einen Ambo geschaffen. In breit ausladender, konkaver Geste der eine, als zylindrischer Pfahl der andere. Stefano Malvenuti (1991) interpretiert die beiden Elemente als weiblich und männlich, als »symbolische Repräsentation der menschlichen Natur«. Einmal mehr hat sich eine sexuelle Metapher in den weitgehend tabuisierten Raum der christlichen Kirche eingeschlichen.

Eine andere Art der Annäherung unterschiedlicher »Temperamente« stellt **Walter Michael Pühringer** (geb. 1945) in seinen Arbeiten für Heuberger in Thalgau, Salzburg, dar. In der *Power connection* ist die conjunctio schon ziemlich weit fortgeschritten: der sperrig-kantige Teil hat schon kräftig nach dem rundem Gehäuse gegriffen, der Umhüllung einer alten Maschine, eine neue Einheit bahnt sich an.

194. Adolf Krischanitz, Traisenpavillon, St. Pölten, Niederösterreich, 1988.
195. Hans Scharoun, Wohnhauskomplex Romeo und Julia, Stuttgart, 1954–1959.
196. Aurelio Cortesi, Altar und Ambo in der Chiesa di S. Croce, Parma, Italien, 1990.
197. Walter Michael Pühringer, Power Connection für Heuberger, Thalgau, Oberösterreich, 1996.

194. Adolf Krischanitz, Traisenpavillon, St. Pölten, Lower Austria, 1988.
195. Hans Scharoun, residential complex Romeo and Julia, Stuttgart, 1954–1959.
196. Aurelio Cortesi, altar and ambo in the Chiesa di S. Croce, Parma, Italy, 1990.
197. Walter Michael Pühringer, Power Connection for Heuberger, Thalgau, Upper Austria, 1996.

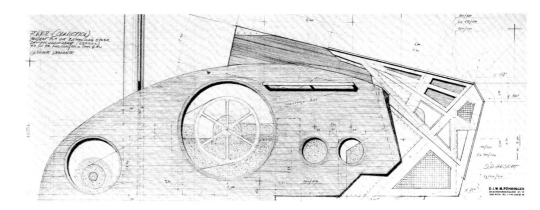

In the church of Santa Croce in Parma, **Aurelio Cortesi** (born 1931) has created an altar and an ambo which is a part of the liturgical reforms. The altar is a broad, sweeping concave gesture, and the ambo is a cylindrical post. Stefano Malvenuti (1991) has interpreted the two elements as female and male, as a »symbolic representation of human nature«. Once again a metaphor of sexuality has crept in amongst the extensive taboos of the Christian church.

Walter Michael Pühringer (born 1945) represents another kind of approach by different »temperaments« in his works for Heuberger in Thalgau, Salzburg. The conjunctio has already made considerable progress in the *Power connection*: the bulky and angular section has already reached out powerfully towards the round casing, the cover for an old machine: a new unity is in the offing.

9. Androgynous Architecture

9.1. First Synthesis: One on Top of the Other

9.1.1. Space/Body and Column/Tower

If we continue to work on the simplifying hypothesis that column- and tower-like elements represent the male principle and elements like a casing or housing the female, then the first additional approach that we could anticipate would be when the column or the tower is placed on the housing, on top of a dome, for example.

Now if we stay with the anthropomorphic metaphor there is no doubt that we could interpret this position as the female being dominated, indeed controlled by the male, or draw conclusions from the predominantly coital positions. This has to be set against the fact that the opposite position could scarcely be realized structurally. But an arrangement in which the male is surrounded, covered, protected, captured by the female is perfect possible structurally, and the subject »being in being« will be dealt with in chapter 9.3.1. A **superimposed column** cannot be detected from inside, and its outward appearance is often inorganic, like a collage. When the tower space is not visible from the inside, then this is only the first stage towards synthesis of the dialectical elements, as the spatial and the corporeal have not yet been transformed into a superordinated structure.

But very often we find an aperture in the lower spatial element (usually a dome) which at least gives an inkling of the presence of the tower above it. If this aperture broadens, then the elements can fuse together. Finally if the tower, which is frequently in the shape of a cone, becomes wider at the base, and lower, it becomes a shallow cone, or a cropped cone, a shallow conical stump. (Cf. chap. 9.1.3.)

The essentially male archetype of the »tower« has moved closer towards the bisexual form of the »hill«, and a start has been made towards the female archetype of the »hall« or »dome«.

The **ridge turret**, which is at first very modest, above the crossing of churches, can be seen as an historical example of placing a tower above a hall in occidental architecture. **Crossing towers**, often massive, which develop in northern France in particular, are rather more convincing. One of the most beautiful examples is St. Sernin in Toulouse (1095–1180), where the crossing tower is the dominant architectural motif. This overcomes the original an-

9. Androgyne Architektur

9. 1. Erste Synthese: Das Aufeinander

9.1.1. Raum/Körper und Säule/Turm

Gehen wir weiterhin von der vereinfachenden Hypothese aus, daß säulen- und turmartige Elemente das männliche Prinzip und gehäuseartige Elemente das weibliche Prinzip repräsentieren, so wäre eine weitere Annäherung zunächst dann festzustellen, wenn die Säule oder der Turm auf das Gehäuse, auf ein Kuppelelement beispielsweise, aufgesetzt wird.

Nun könnten wir zweifellos, bei der anthropomorphen Metapher verharrend, aus dieser Position auch eine Dominanz, ja Beherrschung des Weiblichen durch das Männliche ablesen oder Rückschlüsse auf die vorherrschenden coitalen Positionen ziehen. Dem ist entgegenzuhalten, daß eine umgekehrte Position im Baulichen wohl kaum realisierbar erscheint. Hingegen ist die Disposition, daß das Maskuline vom Femininen umgeben, umhüllt, beschützt, gefangen ist, durchaus baulich realisierbar und das Thema »Wesen im Wesen« wird im Kap. 9.3.1 noch zu behandeln sein.

Die **aufgesetzte Säule** ist von innen nicht wahrnehmbar, und sie wirkt in der Außenerscheinung oft unorganisch, collageartig. Wenn der Turmraum von innen nicht sichtbar ist, können wir nur von der ersten Stufe einer Synthese der dialektischen Elemente sprechen, da das Räumliche und das Körperhafte sich noch nicht zu einem übergeordneten Gebilde verwandelt haben.

Sehr häufig finden wir jedoch im unteren Raumelement (zumeist eine Kuppel) eine Öffnung, die zunächst den darüber befindlichen Turmraum erahnen läßt. Erweitert sich diese Öffnung, kann es zu einer Verschmelzung der Elemente kommen. Wenn schließlich der Turm, der häufig als Kegel ausgebildet ist, an Basisbreite gewinnt und an Höhe verliert, wird er zum flachen Konus oder zu einem gekappten Konus, einem flachen Kegelstumpf. (Vgl. Kap. 9.1.3.)

Der gleichsam männliche Archetypus »Turm« hat sich an den neutralen oder beidgeschlechtlichen des »Berges« angenähert, und eine Verschmelzung mit dem weiblichen Archetypus »Raum« oder »Kuppel« hat sich angebahnt.

Als historisches Beispiel für das Aufsitzen des Turmes auf dem Raum in der abendländischen Baukunst kann der zunächst sehr bescheidene **Dachreiter** über der Vierung von Kirchen angesehen werden. Überzeugender sind die oft gewaltigen **Vierungstürme**, die sich speziell in Nordfrankreich entwickeln. Als eines der schönsten Beispiele kann St. Sernin in Toulouse (1095–1180) genannt werden, wobei der Vierungsturm zum dominierenden baulichen Motiv wird. Damit gelingt eine großartige Überwindung der ursprünglichen Antagonismen von Turm und Gehäuse, die oft beziehungslos nebeneinanderstehen oder am Gebäude appliziert erscheinen.

Der dominante Turm über der Vierung ist auch ein beliebtes Motiv im orthodoxen Kirchenbau des Ostens. Ein signifikantes Beispiel dafür ist die Klosterkirche von Dealù in Rumänien (1499).

In Georgien finden wir in der Himmelsfahrtskirche von Kolomenskoje (1532) eine überzeugende Lösung für den Übergang vom Körper zum Turm. Schuppenartige Motive vermitteln zwischen den beiden Elementen und stellen die Einheit her – eine weitere Annäherung an die androgyne Architektur.

In den Zeichnungen der Revolutionsarchitekten wird die Kombination heterogener Elemente zu einem Gestaltungsprinzip.

Ein beliebtes Motiv ist eine meist stark verkürzte oder turmartige Säule, die auf einen Unterbau aufgesetzt wird. Bei **Jean-Jacques Lequeu** (1757–1825) erreicht die Stilklitterung skurrile Formen. Bei der *Indischen Pagode* werden Reiseberichte aus der Türkei, aus Persien und Indien verarbeitet, die an die damals beliebte »indian gothic« erinnern.

Ein stark verkürztes Turmelement wird auf ein dreifach abgestuftes Gebäude aufgesetzt. Grundriß und Widmung sind nicht näher bekannt, doch kann angenommen werden, daß es bergende Innenräume sind, die von einem phallischen Element gekrönt werden. Auch bei **Claude-Nicolas Ledoux**, einem Zeitgenossen Lequeus, stoßen wir auf ähnliche Motive. In einem der nicht ausgeführten Entwürfe für die *Pariser Barrierès*, die Zollschranken, stellt Ledoux die typische römische Triumphsäule, die den Barocksäulen vor der Wiener Karlskirche gleicht, auf ein quadratisches Haus, das festungsartig von einer Mauer mit Türmchen umschlossen ist.

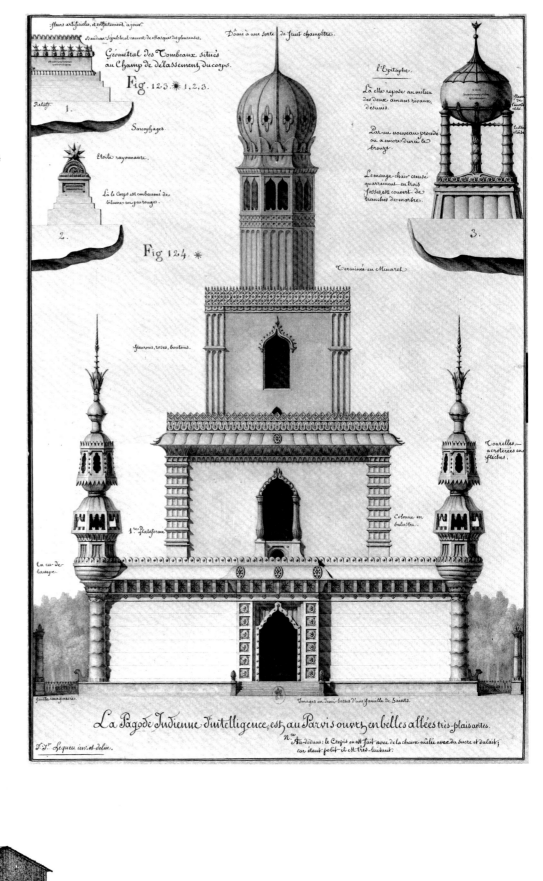

202. Giacomo Trombara, Leuchttum, um 1800.
203. Herkules, Kassel-Wilhelmshöhe, 1713–1718.
204. Giorgio de Chirico, *La Nostalgia dell'Infinito*, 1916.

202. Giacomo Trombara, lighthouse, ca. 1800.
203. Herkules, Wilhelmshöhe, Kassel, 1713–1718.
204. Giorgio de Chirico, *La Nostalgia dell'Infinito*, 1916.

tagonism of tower and housing magnificently. Often they stand next to each other without any real relationship, or seem to be merely applied to the building.

The dominant tower over the crossing is also a popular motif in the orthodox church architecture of the East. A significant example of this is the monastery church of Dealù in Romania (1499).

We find a convincing solution of the transition from body to tower in the Kolomenskoje Resurrection Church (1532) in Georgia. Shed-like motifs link the two elements and produce unity – another step closer to androgynous architecture.

Combining heterogeneous elements becomes a design principle in drawings by the Revolutionary architects.

A popular motif is a column, usually highly foreshortened or tower-like, which is placed on a substructure. The stylistic hotch-potch reaches the bounds of the absurd in the work of **Jean-Jacques Lequeu** (1757–1825). An *Indian Pagoda* incorporates travellers' tales from Turkey, Persia and India, reminiscent of the »Indian Gothic« that was popular at the time.

A highly abbreviated tower element is placed on top of a building that moves back in three steps. Nothing more is known about ground plan and use, but it can be assumed that these are protective inner chambers, which are crowned by a phallic element. We come across similar motifs in the work of **Claude-Nicolas Ledoux**, a contemporary of Lequeu. In one of the unbuilt *Pariser Barrières (Designs for the Barrières)*, the Paris customs barriers, Ledoux places a typical Roman triumphal column, like the Baroque columns of the Karlskirche in Vienna, on top of a square building, which is enclosed by a wall with turrets, like a fortress.

The theme of an essentially phallic-male culmination for a building is clearly articulated in the so-called Hercules in Kassel. This extensive building was built in at the top of a hill on the edge of the city by **Giovanni Francesco Guerniero** (1665–1745) in 1701–1717. The substructure is a 60 m high octagon with round-arched apertures, a gigantic palace whose feminine interpretation is supported by the presence of grottoes (cf. chapter 7.5.2). The crowning stone pyramid's proportions are such that first of all it is not possible to make an unambiguous »tower« or »mountain« attribution. But it is topped by the monumental 8 metre high figure of Hercules, and this seems to make the masculine character – in the powerful form of Hercules, whose masculinity is firmly underlined by his club – unambiguously recognizable.

Giacomo Trombara (1742–1808) drew a lighthouse in about 1800. This is an interesting collage of structural elements that are close to Classicism but used in such a contradictory way that they suggest free handling of formal elements that has been clearly present from the early 19th century to the present day. The building rises from a broadly based substructure with open staircases, firmly placed on the ground; it tapers gradually, and is topped by a delicate tempietto.

Giorgio de Chirico tackles a quite different theme, though substantially reduced in formal terms, in his picture *La Nostalgia dell'Infinito*. The tower rises, narrowing at three points, from a broad substructure, surrounded by columns; it is topped by a tempietto with four pennants fluttering from it.

The design for a monument to Frederick the Great (1794) by **Friedrich Weinbrenner** (1766–1826) is characterized by a highly abbreviated, Trajan's column, effectively sunk in the ground. The massive, closed cube represents the earth's maternal protection in the grave as a kind of cenotaph, and the upright column stands for the king's ruling power, and masculine power is further illustrated by four flanking figures of Hercules. The monument stands in a courtyard, forming a surrounding protecting area.

At almost the same time (1797) **Friedrich Gilly** (1772–1800) designed the Königshütte, showing clear parallels with Ledoux's cannon foundry. The chimneys are – as was common practice in the 19th century – in the form of columns, or better, column stumps – and thus once more negate the classical laws of proportion. But around the turn of the century a new power factor had long since been established: industry. It is therefore not surprising that it should use traditional symbols of power like the column, and comparison with Frederick the Great's column is hard to resist. Two other planes of interpretation suggest themselves: if we compare Gilly's design with Ledoux's cannon foundry, then the fire and smoke columns positively »shoot« out of the tubes. But cannons – as instruments of conflict and power – are also phallic elements. The bursts of fire from the cannon-like chimneys can be read as a copious, yet aggressive ejaculation.

In another design Gilly remembers the spiral reliefs on Roman and Baroque triumphal columns. His drawing of a lighthouse shows androgynous tendencies: provision stores (fertility) or

Das Thema einer gleichsam phallisch-männlichen Krönung eines Bauwerkes ist beim sogenannten *Herkules* in Kassel deutlich artikuliert. Auf der Spitze eines Hügels am Rande der
Stadt wurde das weitläufige Bauwerk 1701–1717 von **Giovanni Francesco Guerniero** (1665
bis 1745) errichtet. Den Unterbau bildet ein 60 m hohes, sich in Rundbogen öffnendes Okto-
gon als ein riesiges Schloß, dessen feminine Deutung durch Grotten (vgl. Kap. 7.5.2) unterstützt wird. Die krönende Steinpyramide weist jene Proportionen auf, die zunächst eine eindeutige Zuweisung zu »Turm« oder »Berg« unmöglich macht. Sie wird jedoch von der monumentalen 8 m hohen Figur des Herkules gekrönt, und damit scheint der maskuline Charakter
in der Kraftgestalt des Herkules, dessen Männlichkeit durch die Keule wirksam unterstrichen
wird, eindeutig erkennbar.

Giacomo Trombara (1742–1808) zeichnet um 1800 einen Leuchtturm, eine interessante
Collage aus Bauelementen, die zwar dem Klassizismus nahestehen, aber in der Art ihrer
widersprüchlichen Verwendung einen freien Umgang mit Formelementen ankündigen, den wir,
im 19. Jahrhundert beginnend, bis in unsere Gegenwart feststellen können. Aus einem breit
gelagerten, der Erde verbundenen Unterbau mit feierlichen Freitreppen wächst das Bauwerk
empor, allmählich sich verjüngend, und endet an der Spitze mit einem zarten Tempietto.

Ein gänzlich ähnliches Thema, wenn auch formal wesentlich reduziert, behandelt **Giorgio
de Chirico** in seinem Bild *La Nostalgia dell'Infinito* (*Heimweh des Unendlichen*). Von einem
breiten Unterbau, der von einer Säulenstellung umgeben ist, steigt nach dreifacher Verjüngung
der Turm auf, gekrönt durch ein Tempietto, auf dem vier Wimpel wehen.

Die stark verkürzte, gleichsam in den Boden abgesunkene Trajanssäule charakterisiert den
Entwurf für ein Denkmal Friedrichs des Großen (1794) von **Friedrich Weinbrenner** (1766 bis
1826). Der mächtige, geschlossene Kubus repräsentiert als eine Art Kenotaph den mütterlichen Grabesschutz der Erde, die aufgestellte Säule steht für die herrschaftliche Macht des
Königs, vier flankierende Herkulesfiguren illustrieren zusätzlich die männliche Kraft. Das Denkmal steht in einem Hof, einem schützenden Bereich, der es umgibt.

Fast zur gleichen Zeit (1797) zeichnet **Friedrich Gilly** (1772–1800) die Königshütte mit deutlichen Parallelen zur Kanonengießerei von Ledoux. Die Schornsteine sind, wie es im 19. Jahrhundert oft genug praktiziert wurde, als Säulen ausgebildet, besser noch als Säulenstümpfe,
und damit einmal mehr die klassischen Proportionsgesetze negierend. Um die Jahrhundertwende hat sich aber längst ein neuer Machtfaktor etabliert: die Industrie. Es ist daher nicht
verwunderlich, wenn sie sich der traditionellen Machtsymbole wie der Säule bedient, und der
Vergleich mit dem Denkmal Friedrichs des Großen drängt sich auf. Zwei weitere Deutungsebenen liegen nahe: Vergleichen wir Gillys Entwurf mit Ledouxs Kanonengießerei, dann »schie-
ßen« die Feuer- und Rauchsäulen gleichsam aus den Rohren hervor. Kanonen sind aber – als
Mittel des Kampfes und der Macht – auch phallische Elemente. Die Feuergarben aus den ka-

pilots' rooms (protection) were to be accommodated on the second floor in the base. A spiral staircase with tower leads to the keeper's accommodation, to the signalling light.

The reverence for the ancient formal vocabulary by **Adolf Loos** (1870–1933) is expressed in a design that for a long time was considered an absurd extravagance: Loos sent a drawing of a massive Doric column set on a cubic substructure to the Chicago Tribune competition (1922). Here again a non-bearing column, here enlarged to gigantic proportions, with a possible office inside, becomes a symbol of potency: it is one of the new powers of our century, the medium of the press. When we remind ourselves of the fact that Classicism was a significant source of inspiration for Adolf Loos, then comparison with the cited works by Ledoux, Weinbrenner and Gilly seems justified.

Loos was perfectly aware that his column would not be built at the time, but his self-confidence or expedient optimism seem to have convinced him that it would be realized at a later date when the writes: »This column will be built, if not now, then at a later date, and if not in Chicago, then in another city.« In fact history seems to prove Loos right: habitable »columns« were built, and built in Chicago, not far from the competition area, and not as offices, but as residential buildings: the Marina City by **Bertrand Goldberg** (born 1913) with its »fluting« is surprisingly reminiscent of Loos's Doric column, in its proportions as well.[46]

Two projects in the Gothic style continue the idea of St. Sernin in Toulouse – a tower over a housing – and they are placed at the point where the sacred meets the profane.

James Wyatt captured a magnificent example of combining tower and palace in a watercolour: this is the so-called *Fonthill Abbey* in Wiltshire by the poet **William Beckford** (1760 to 1844). (Beckford, 1964) It seems reasonable to speculate about androgynous architecture because the mother-son problem was of fundamental importance to Beckford. In his novel *Vathek*, subtitled an »Arabian tale«, he deals with the fantastic life of a caliph who is introduced as Harun-al-Raschid's grandson. Karathis, Vatheks's mother, plays an important role – partly as a magnificent protectress, partly as a cruel avenger – and reminds us of the many faces of the Indian goddess Kali. It is also the mother who hurries on to the scene »to test her power over the spirit of her son«. (Beckford, 1964) Beckford's own mother played a central role in his life as well: detaching the son from the great protecting mother became a fundamental problem for the eccentric poet. Dominance of the male by the female can scarcely be represented in architecture. But the triumph of the tower over the hall below it can be seen as Beckford's desire ultimately to dominate the female, or in an androgynous interpretation the self-confident tower and the hall beneath it can represent a synthesis of male and female. The fantastic palace building in the English »Gothic revival« style, in ruins today, seems like an ecclesiastical building, but was simply the wealthy writer's country seat, perhaps a suggestion of Vathek's magnificent palace, whose five massive wings had lavish names with a poetic ring to them.

nonenartigen Schornsteinen können als ein üppiges, gleichwohl aggressives Ejakulat gelesen werden.

Bei einem anderen Entwurf erinnert sich Gilly an die Spiralreliefs römischer und barocker Triumphsäulen. Die Zeichnung für einen Leuchtturm läßt androgyne Annäherungen erkennen: Im 2. Sockelgeschoß sollten Vorratskammern (Fruchtbarkeit!) oder Räume für Lotsen (Schutz) untergebracht werden. Eine gewendelte Treppe mit Turm führt zur Wohnung des Wächters, zum Signallicht.

Die Verehrung von **Adolf Loos** (1870–1933) für das antike Formenvokabular kommt in einem Entwurf zum Ausdruck, der lange Zeit als skurrile Extravaganz eingestuft wurde: Zum Wettbewerb für die Chicago Tribune (1922) schickt Loos die Zeichnung für eine mächtige dorische Säule, die auf einem kubischen Unterbau aufsitzt. Einmal mehr wird die nichttragende Säule, hier ins Gigantische vergrößert und im Inneren als Büro nutzbar, zum Zeichen der Potenz: Es ist eine der neuen großen Mächte unseres Jahrhunderts, das Medium Presse. Wenn wir uns die Tatsache vergegenwärtigen, daß für Adolf Loos der Klassizismus eine bedeutende Inspirationsquelle war, dann scheint auch der Vergleich mit den zitierten Arbeiten von Ledoux, Weinbrenner und Gilly gerechtfertigt.

Loos war sich darüber im klaren, daß seine Säule nicht gebaut wird, aber in seinem Selbstbewußtsein oder Zweckoptimismus scheint er von der späteren Realisierung überzeugt zu sein, wenn er schreibt: »Diese Säule wird gebaut werden, wenn nicht jetzt, dann in späteren Zeiten, wenn nicht in Chicago, dann in einer anderen Stadt.« Tatsächlich scheint die Geschichte Loos rechtzugeben: Es wurden bewohnbare »Säulen« gebaut, sogar in Chicago, unweit des Wettbewerbsgebietes, zwar nicht als Büro, sondern als Wohnbauten: die Marina City von **Bertrand Goldberg** (geb. 1913) mit ihren »Kanneluren« erinnert auch in den Proportionen verblüffend an Loos' dorische Säule.[49]

Zwei gotisierende Projekte führen den Gedanken von St. Sernin in Toulouse – der Turm auf dem Gehäuse – weiter, sie sind im Schnittpunkt des Profanen und Sakralen angesiedelt.

Ein großartiges Beispiel der Verbindung von Turm und Schloß hat James Wyatt in einem Aquarell festgehalten: Es ist die sogenannte *Fonthill Abbey* des Dichters **William Beckford** (1760–1844) in Wiltshire. (Beckford, 1964) Die Spekulation zu einer androgynen Architektur findet insofern eine Basis, als das Mutter-Sohn-Problem für Beckford eine elementare Bedeutung hatte. In seinem Roman *Vathek*, der im Untertitel als eine »arabische Erzählung« bezeichnet wird, geht es um das phantastische Leben eines Kalifen, der als Harun-al-Raschids Enkel vorgestellt wird. Karathis, die Mutter Vatheks, spielt eine wichtige Rolle – teils als großartige Beschützerin, teils als grausame Rächerin – und erinnert an die Vielgesichtigkeit der indischen Göttin Kali. Die Mutter ist es auch, die herbeieilt, »um ihre Macht über den Geist des Sohnes zu versuchen«. (Beckford, 1964) Auch in Beckfords Leben spielt seine Mutter eine zentrale Rolle: Die Loslösung des Sohnes von der großen schützenden Mutter wird zu einem elementaren Problem für den exzentrischen Dichter. Die Dominanz des Weiblichen über das Männliche ist in der Architektur kaum darzustellen. Der Triumph des Turms über die darunter liegende Halle kann aber als der Wunsch Beckfords angesehen werden, endlich über das Weibliche zu herrschen, oder es können in einer androgynen Deutung der selbstbewußte Turm und die darunter liegende Halle eine Synthese des Männlichen und Weiblichen repräsentieren. Der phantastische Schloßbau im Stile des englischen »Gothic revival«, der heute eine Ruine ist, erweckt den Anschein eines Kultbaues, war aber lediglich der Landsitz des reichen Schriftstellers, vielleicht eine Ahnung vom prächtigen Palast Vatheks, dessen fünf mächtige Flügel mit üppig klingenden, poetischen Namen ausgestattet waren. Als Beckford 1822 Fonthill verkaufen muß, zieht er nach Bath – und setzt dem Haus, das er erwirbt, sogleich wieder einen machtvollen Turm auf.

Fast hundert Jahre später zeichnet **Hans Makart** (1840–1884) eine *Grabkapelle*, die englische Gotik mündet in die Neo-Gotik des Historismus und ist noch üppiger mit Detailformen ausgestattet. In einer durchaus kontinuierlichen Formation – der Stephansturm in Wien ist sicher Pate gestanden – steigt das Bauwerk von der Basis bis zu einem schlanken Turm empor. Bringen wir den funeraren Charakter mit der Erde und dem Mutterschoß in Verbindung und interpretieren wir wieder den Turm als Machtemblem des Männlichen, dann scheint die Zuweisung zu einer androgynen Architektur gerechtfertigt.

Eine für ihre Zeit geniale technische Leistung ist die Kuppel von San Gaudenzio in Novara, 1858–1864 von **Alessandro Antonelli** (1798–1888) erbaut, eine interessante Kombination frühhistoristischer Bauformen mit den Errungenschaften des Eisenbaues. Der Kuppelraum über der Vierung weist eine beträchtliche Höhenentwicklung auf, die Kuppel öffnet sich breit in ei-

208. Hans Makart, gotische Grabkirche, 1883.
209. William Beckford, *Fonthill Abbey*, 1798.
210. Adolf Loos, Chicago Tribune Tower, 1922.

208. Hans Makart, Gothic mortuary church, 1883.
209. William Beckford, *Fonthill Abbey*, 1798.
210. Adolf Loos, Chicago Tribune Tower, 1922.

When Beckford had to sell Fonthill in 1822 he moved to Bath – and immediately topped the house he bought there with a massive tower.

Almost a hundred years later **Hans Makart** (1840–1884) drew a tomb chapel; here English Gothic merged with the neo-Gothic of historicism, and is even more lavishly decorated with detailed shapes. The building rises with complete continuity – certainly modelled on the Stephansdom in Vienna – from its base to a slender tower. If we link its funerary character with the earth and the mother's womb and again interpret the tower as an emblem of male power, then it seems justifiable to count this as androgynous architecture.

A technical achievement that is an act of genius for its time is the dome of San Gaudenzio in Novara, 1858–1864, by **Alessandro Antonelli** (1798–1888). This is an interesting combination of early historical building forms with the achievements of iron construction. The some above the crossing rises to a considerable height, and the dome broadens further into another ovoid space, and this again shifts into a conical spatial structure that penetrates another semi-ellipsoid space (a steel structure). And that is not all: yet another turret is set on top of the cone, and this penetrates the apex of the ovoid space. We can find a remarkable accumulation of metaphors in the structure, which is undoubtedly absurd to an extent: the dome and the dual ovoid shapes can stand for the female principle, the cone can be interpreted as a »building within a building«, and the thrusting tower can be interpreted as a phallic element. But we can also detect another motif (and this will be discussed later) in the many closures, thrusts and intersections, that of penetration.

A few years later (1893–1890) Antonelli tried his hand at iron structure again. He built a kind of dome in Turin that was originally intended to house a synagogue. The silhouette of this *Mole Antonelliana* is particularly interesting: the »dome« theme is taken over into the »tower« theme with astonishing continuity, and thus the building could be addressed as androgynous architecture.

Placing a phallic element on a massive cubic substructure with a semicircular apse surging out of it identifies a monumental building in a small German town as androgynous. It was designed by **Otto Kohtz** (1880–1956) in 1909. He calmly places the building among the Romantic roofs of the little town, which is not identified any further. In contrast with the buildings and designs mentioned so far, Kohtz abandons harmonious and continuous transition between the individual sections of the building. The tower sits on the building as abruptly as Weinbrenner placed his column on Frederick the Great's cenotaph.

Josef Hoffmann (1870–1956) designed a temporary imperial pavilion for the jubilee parade at almost the same time as Otto Kohtz. A tower is placed on an attractively articulated structure, not quite as abruptly as in Kohtz's »monumental building«, but with very similar proportions and topped by the symbol of power, the stylized imperial crown. The phallic character of hat, crown and tiara has already been indicated, and it is remarkable that the second, the Habsburg imperial crown, seems to confirm this theme in Hoffmann's design.

Wassili Luckhardt (1889–1972) imagines his *Denkmal der Arbeit* (*Labour monument*, 1919) in massive dimensions. Very optimistically, he calls it »An die Freude« (»Ode to Joy«), probably a borrowing from Schiller's or Beethoven's jubilant cry, and absolutely in the spirit of the optimistic drama of fantastic Expressionism in Germany after the First World War, which he found above all in the »Gläserne Kette« association in his home town. A gigantic rotunda is given monumental quality by a powerful tower, which is however structured as it rises. Expressive metaphors are found for protection and community on the one hand, power and signal on the other.

This indicates the transfer of monumental building from the ecclesiastical and feudal area into a new social field. Admittedly the dream of new democratic community buildings was not fulfilled; at best the monumentalization of domestic building in the inter-war period successfully usurped important historical forms.[47]

The *Architekturidee* (1918) by **Johannes Molzahn** (1892–1965) can be seen as a convincing approximation to androgynous architecture, even though the expressive character of the drawing does not admit any clear three-dimensional interpretation. The biological gesture made by the substructure with its »erotic« entrance and light radiating from a sun-like gloriole could have feminine associations, and the tower on top, linked together by numerous facets, stands for the masculine principle.

Given generous interpretation, we could also find the theme of »room and tower« in the »Einstein Tower« (1917–1921) by **Erich Mendelsohn** (1887–1953).

The building opens its flanks wide and invites us to pass through a gate. The actual research room is in the basement, in the earth, so to speak. The three-dimensionally developed

nen weiteren eiförmigen Raum, und dieser wiederum geht über in ein konisches Raumgebilde, das einen weiteren halbellipsoiden Raum (eine Stahlkonstruktion) penetriert. Damit nicht genug: Auf den Konus ist noch ein Türmchen aufgesetzt, das den Scheitel des Eiraums durchstößt. Wir finden eine merkwürdige Anhäufung von Metaphern in dem zweifellos skurrilen Gebilde: Die Kuppel und die zweifachen Eiformen können für das weibliche Prinzip stehen, der Konus kann als ein »Haus im Haus« interpretiert werden, und der durchstoßende Turm ist als phallisches Element zu deuten. In den vielfältigen Verklammerungen, Durchdringungen, Verschneidungen können wir aber auch noch ein anderes Motiv erkennen (das noch abzuhandeln sein wird), das der Penetration.

Wenige Jahre später (1893–1890) setzt sich Antonelli noch einmal mit der Eisenkonstruktion auseinander und baut in Turin eine Art Kuppel, die ursprünglich den Raum einer Synagoge bilden sollte. Bei der *Mole Antonelliana* ist besonders die Silhouette interessant: Das Thema »Kuppel« wird mit einer erstaunlichen Kontinuität in das Thema »Turm« überführt, und sonach könnte der Bau als androgyne Architektur angesprochen werden.

Das Aufsetzen eines phallischen Elementes auf einen mächtigen kubischen Unterbau mit halbkreisförmig hervorquellender Apsis weist einen Monumentalbau in einer deutschen Kleinstadt als androgynes Bauwerk aus. **Otto Kohtz** (1880–1956) hat 1909 den Entwurf gezeichnet, und er setzt den Bau unbekümmert zwischen die romantischen Dächer des Städtchens, das nicht näher definiert ist. Zum Unterschied von vorher zitierten Bauten und Entwürfen verzichtet Kohtz auf den harmonischen und kontinuierlichen Übergang zwischen den einzelnen Baukörpern, der Turm sitzt so unvermittelt auf dem Gebäude, wie Weinbrenner seine Säule auf den Kenotaph Friedrichs des Großen aufstellt.

Fast gleichzeitig mit Otto Kohtz entwirft **Josef Hoffmann** (1870–1956) einen provisorischen Kaiserpavillon für die Jubiläumsparade. Auf einen schön gegliederten Bau wird ein Turm aufgesetzt, nicht ganz so unvermittelt wie bei dem »Monumentalbau« von Kohtz, aber in einer sehr ähnlichen Proportion und gekrönt vom Zeichen der Macht, der stilisierten Kaiserkrone. Auf den phallischen Charakter von Hut, Krone und Tiara wurde bereits hingewiesen, und es ist bemerkenswert, daß die zweite, die habsburgische Kaiserkrone, diese These in Hoffmanns Entwurf zu bestätigen scheint.

In gewaltigen Dimensionen stellt sich **Wassili Luckhardt** (1889–1972) sein *Denkmal der Arbeit* (1919) vor, dem er, sehr optimistisch, den Titel »An die Freude« verleiht, wohl in Anlehnung an den Jubelgesang Schillers bzw. Beethovens und ganz im Sinne des optimistischen Pathos des phantastischen Expressionismus in Deutschland nach dem Ersten Weltkrieg, der vor allem in der Vereinigung der »Gläsernen Kette« seine Heimstatt gefunden hat. Ein riesiger Rundbau wird durch einen mächtigen, doch gegliedert aufstrebenden Turm monumentalisiert. Schutz und Gemeinschaft einerseits, Macht und Signal andererseits finden ihre expressiven Metaphern.

Der Transfer des Monumentalbaus aus dem sakralen und feudalen Bereich in ein neues, soziales Feld ist damit angedeutet, freilich hat sich der Traum von den neuen demokratischen Gemeinschaftsbauten nicht erfüllt, sondern bestenfalls in der Monumentalisierung des Wohnbaues der Zwischenkriegszeit gelingt die usurpatorische Aneignung bedeutsamer historischer Formen.[50]

Die *Architekturidee* (1918) von **Johannes Molzahn** (1892–1965) kann als überzeugende Annäherung an eine androgyne Architektur angesehen werden, wenngleich der expressive Charakter der Zeichnung keine klaren räumlichen Identifikationen zuläßt. Der biologische Gestus des Unterbaus mit dem »erotischen« Eingangstor, das Überstrahlen durch eine sonnenartige Gloriole lassen Weibliches assoziieren, der aufsitzende und mit vielen Facetten sich verbindende Turm steht für das Männliche.

Das Thema »Raum und Turm« könnten wir, bei großzügiger Interpretation, auch aus dem »Einsteinturm« (1917–1921) von **Erich Mendelsohn** (1887–1953) herauslesen.

Das Gebäude öffnet weit die Flanken und läßt uns in ein Tor eintreten. Im Tiefgeschoß, gleichsam in der Erde, befindet sich der eigentliche Forschungsraum. Der plastisch durchgebildete Turm mit dem halbkugelförmigen Abschluß ist als phallisches Element auf den Basisbau aufgesetzt. Turm und Basisgeschoß bilden eine harmonische Einheit, die durch die konsequente expressive Formensprache (aus Ziegel, nicht aus Beton gebildet) noch unterstützt wird.

Einen Turm auf ein Gebäude, einen Kuppelraum aufzusetzen, war schon immer ein technologisch schwieriges Problem, so daß es nicht verwunderlich ist, wenn wir im historischen Fundus mehr Projekte als Realisierungen vorfinden. Trotz der technologischen Fortschritte ist das

tower with its hemispherical conclusion is set on the base as a phallic element. Tower and base floor form a harmonious unit that is further supported by the consistent and expressive formal language (using bricks, not concrete).

Placing a tower on top of a building, a domed area, has always been a difficult technical problem, and so it is not surprising to find more projects than actual building in the historical stock. Despite technological progress the structural problems remain, and so we can adduce only a few examples from the more recent architectural scene. Just a single work will represent them.

The design for the television tower in Barcelona (1988) by **Santiago Calatrava** (born 1951) is an elegant, pointed, aggressive needle, a spindle placed over a shallow dome.

9.1.2. Mountain and Column/Tower

The ambivalent interpretation of the hill as male or female will be dealt with further in chapter 9.4.2. The artificial hill or mountain is one of the oldest archetypal forms.

Two fundamental starting points motivate the principle of serial **accumulation**: firstly the grave mound, which develops to the tumulus, the monumental mound of the dead, the mausoleum. The grave mound is an emanation, a protrusion of that maternal earth that takes in the dead man, and allows him to return to primordial security. The other interpretation is that of the divine hill on which are placed the thrones of the gods, the gods themselves. If we work on the first interpretation, then the monumental tomb hill can be seen as a female-maternal element. Now from time to time we find a phallic element on the hills, pyramids and mountains: obelisks, steles, towers, outlook posts top the mound, fuse with it and thus approach androgynous unity. The Indian or Nepalese **stupa** is a mound and within it, installed like a phallus, as it were, the world column is to be found.

The legend of building the stupa of Svayambhunath (Wiesner, 1976) includes the actual manufacturing process of the Nepalese stupa. First a hole is dug, and the sacred flame is placed inside this. A tree-trunk, notionally the same height as the sacred Mount Meru, is placed on the stone and brick- and clay-built stupa is piled up around this mast, with no hollow space inside it, therefore. The five Buddhas are placed on the outside, thus significantly disturbing the archetypal order of the figure four, following the four points of the compass, as the fifth image in the centre of the stupa cannot be accommodated visibly and thus stands somewhat to the side of the eastern image. The stupa, as a protecting element and the place in which the Buddha is concealed can be associated with the female. Set on top of the stupa, crowning it like a tower, is a cube with pairs of eyes and forehead marks: it is Buddha, looking to the four points of the compass. On top of the cube are thirteen discs or square slabs laid one on top of the other: they symbolize heaven, and are supported by the central mast, thus underlining its phallic character. An umbrella-like top concludes the structure.

Buildings in Burma show remarkable modifications to Indian temple construction. The 12th century Sabaññu temple in Pagan demonstrates three basic architectural elements: the square temple hall (with a smaller square building added on), a stepped roof, a rudiment of

bautechnische Problem geblieben, und so können wir aus der neueren Architekturszene nur wenige Beispiele dieses Typus anführen. Stellvertretend soll nur eine Arbeit genannt werden:

Der Entwurf des Fernsehturms in Barcelona (1988) von **Santiago Calatrava** (geb. 1951) zeigt eine elegante, spitze, aggressive Nadel, eine Spindel, die ihren Platz über einer flachen Kuppel findet.

9.1.2. Berg und Säule/Turm

Die ambivalente Deutung des Berges als männlich oder weiblich wird in Kap. 9.4.2 noch ausführlich zu erörtern sein. Der künstliche Hügel, der artifizielle Berg gehört zum uralten Bestand archetypischer Formen.

Zwei grundsätzliche Ausgangspunkte motivieren das Prinzip der **Aufhäufung:** zum einen der Grabhügel, der sich zum Tumulus, zum monumentalen Totenberg, zum Mausoleum entwickelt. Der Grabhügel ist eine Emanation, eine Ausstülpung jener mütterlichen Erde, die den Toten aufnimmt, ihn zurückkehren läßt in die Ur-Geborgenheit. Die andere Deutung ist die des Götterberges: Auf ihm thronen die göttlichen Tempel, die Götter selbst. Gehen wir von der ersten Deutung aus, dann könnte der monumentale Grabhügel als weiblich-mütterliches Element interpretiert werden. Nun finden wir bisweilen auf den Hügeln, Pyramiden, Bergen ein phallisches Element vor: Obelisken, Stelen, Türme, Aussichtwarten krönen die Berghügel, verschmelzen mit ihnen und nähern sich damit einer androgynen Einheit. Der **Stupa** Indiens oder Nepals ist ein Berg, in seinem Inneren befindet sich, gleichsam phallisch eingebaut, die Weltensäule.

In der Legende über die Errichtung des Stupa von Svayambhunath (Wiesner, 1976) ist der tatsächliche Herstellungsprozeß der nepalesischen Stupas inkludiert. Zunächst gräbt man ein Loch, in das die heilige Flamme eingesetzt wird. Diese wird mit einem Stein bedeckt, der in der Mitte durchbohrt worden ist. Ein Baumstamm, der »gedanklich« die Höhe des heiligen Berges Meru hat, wird auf den Stein aufgesetzt, und um diesen Mast herum wird der Stupa aus Ziegeln und Lehm aufgeschichtet, er birgt also keinerlei Innenraum. An den Außenseiten werden die fünf Buddhas aufgestellt, wobei die archetypische Ordnung der Vierzahl nach den vier Himmelsrichtungen eine bedeutende Störung erfährt, da das fünfte Bild im Zentrum des Stupa nicht sichtbar untergebracht werden kann und daher etwas seitlich des Ost-Bildes steht. Der Stupa, als schützendes Element und als bergender Ort der Buddhas, kann mit dem Weiblichen assoziiert werden. Auf dem Stupa aufsitzend, ihn turmartig bekrönend, befindet sich ein Kubus mit Augenpaaren und Stirnzeichen: Es ist Buddha, der in die vier Himmelsrichtungen blickt. Auf dem Kubus liegen dreizehn aufeinandergeschichtete Scheiben oder Quadratplatten: Sie symbolisieren den Himmel und werden vom zentralen Mast gehalten, womit der phallische Charakter unterstrichen wird. Ein schirmartiger Aufsatz bildet den Abschluß.

Die Bauten von **Burma** zeigen bemerkenswerte Modifikationen der indischen Tempelbauten. Der Sabaññu-Tempel in Pagan aus dem 12. Jahrhundert weist drei archetypische Grundelemente auf: die quadratische Tempelhalle (mit einem kleineren quadratischen Zubau), darauf aufgesetzt das abgestufte Dach, ein Rudiment des heiligen Berges Meru, und darauf wieder ein Stupa in der typischen, bombierten Silhouette, aber mit einem Türmchen gekrönt.

Das Motiv des heiligen Berges ist beim Ananda-Tempel noch viel eindeutiger ausgesprochen: Die siebenfache Abstufung führt zum bekrönenden Stupa.

Sind bei diesem Tempel die Grundelemente Berg und Turm noch deutlich unterschieden, so verschmelzen sie zu einer gewaltigen Synthese beim **Wat-Arum** in Bangkok. Die drei architektonischen Zonen sind nur durch kleine Absätze getrennt, die aber in keiner Weise die großartige Einheitlichkeit des Baues beeinträchtigen. Bemerkenswert ist vor allem, daß der bekrönende Stupa nun zu einem deutlich phallischen Ausklang umgewandelt ist.

In der *Hypnerotomachia Poliphilii* des **Francesco Colonna** (1434–1527) finden wir eine interessante Zeichnung: Auf eine steile Pyramide mit begehbarem Unterbau ist ein Obelisk aufgesetzt, und dieser trägt eine drehbare Statue. Der Vergleich mit den vorhin zitierten Bauten Asiens liegt nahe: Kein Zweifel, daß die Pyramide als Berg interpretiert werden kann und der Obelisk die männlich sakrale Überhöhung darstellt.

Wir können einen Sprung von dreihundert Jahren machen und entdecken ein ganz ähnliches Motiv, offenkundig aber mit einer massiven Pyramide ohne Innenraum. In einem Entwurf von **C. Ries** aus dem Jahr 1805 wird die Pyramide von einem Obelisken gekrönt, gleichsam die Aufrichtung eines Steines.

Meru, the sacred mountain, and on top of that again a **stupa** with its typical dished silhouette, but topped with a turret.

The sacred mountain motif is expressed much less ambiguously in the Ananda Temple: the seven-fold terrace leads to the crowning stupa.

The basic elements of mound and tower are still quite distinct in this temple, but in the **Wat-Arum** in Bangkok they fuse into a powerful synthesis. The three architectural zones are separated only by small ledges, but these in no way spoil the building's magnificent unity. It is remarkable above all that the crowning stupa is now transformed into a clearly phallic final note.

We find an interesting drawing in the *Hypnerotomachia Poliphilii* by **Francesco Colonna** (1434–1527): an obelisk is placed on a steep pyramid with a substructure on which it is possible to walk, and the obelisk supports a revolving statue. Comparison with the above-mentioned Asian buildings suggests itself: there is no doubt that the pyramid can be interpreted as a mound and the obelisk represents the sacred male raised element.

We can now make a leap of three hundred years and discover a very similar motif, but apparently one with a massive pyramid without an interior space. In a design by **C. Ries** dating from 1895 the pyramid is topped with an obelisk, like a stone.

9.1.3. Dome and Cone

In the mosque of Ibn Tûlûn in Cairo a terraced body mediates between the dome and the square substructure, and further development of this form can be addressed as androgynous architecture. The external outline of the dome in the examples quoted forms a kind of pointed arch, thus coming closer to the **cone**.

When establishing terminology for the upper conclusion of buildings it is not possible to say with certainty when a »tower roof« becomes a »centralized« roof. This is particularly true of truncated conical roofs (cone roofs). In the same way sexual metaphor produces a gradual transition from »male« to »female«.

A shape like ill. 220 a should undoubtedly be addressed as a tower roof – and perhaps like ill. 220 b as well – and could be classified as male. The outline of ill. 220 c corresponds approximately to medieval charnel houses and can already be called a centralized roof, or more particularly a conical spire. The shape shown in ill. 220 d appears in numerous examples of conical roofs of centralized buildings or those with crossing towers. We frequently find this shape in orthodox churches, especially in Georgia, Armenia and Russia.

Classifications as »towering« on the one hand and »protecting« (behütend in German; this word contains the notion of the Hut = hat) on the other are scarcely possible any longer. If the silhouette becomes even more shallow, like ill. 220 e and f, for example, the tower character is lost completely.

9.1.3. Kuppel und Konus

Bei der Moschee Ibn Tûlûn in Kairo vermittelt ein abgetreppter Körper zwischen Kuppel und quadratischem Unterbau. Die Weiterentwicklung dieser Form kann als androgyne Architektur angesprochen werden. Die äußere Kuppelkontur bildet bei den zitierten Beispielen eine Art Spitzbogen und nähert sich damit dem **Konus**.

In der terminologischen Festlegung von oberen Gebäudeabschlüssen kann nicht mit Bestimmtheit gesagt werden, wann ein »Turmdach« in ein »Zentralbaudach« übergeht. Dies gilt insbesondere für Kegelstumpfdächer (Konusdächer). So ergibt sich auch aus der Sexualmetaphorik ein allmählicher Übergang des »Männlichen« in das »Weibliche«.

Eine Formation gemäß Abb. 220 a wird zweifellos als Turmdach anzusprechen sein – vielleicht auch noch jene gemäß Abb. 220 b – und könnte dem Männlichen zugeordnet werden. Die Kontur der Abb. 220 c entspricht in etwa den Karnern des Mittelalters und kann schon als Zentralbaudach, speziell als Kegeldach bezeichnet werden. Die Gestalt gemäß 220 d tritt bei zahlreichen kegelförmigen Dächern von Zentralbauten oder von Vierungstürmen auf. Wir finden diese Form häufig bei orthodoxen Kirchen, insbesondere in Georgien, in Armenien und Rußland.

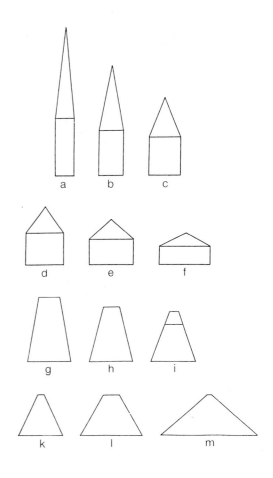

Die Zuordnungen zum »Aufragenden« einerseits und zum »Behütenden« andererseits (der Begriff Hut ist enthalten) sind kaum mehr möglich. Wird die Silhouette noch flacher, etwa nach 220 e und f, verliert sie vollends den Charakter eines Turmes.

Ist die Spitze gekappt, so handelt es sich um Kegelstumpfdächer (220 g–l), wobei diese Formen häufig auch ohne Unterbau vorkommen und dann zum Tumulus überleiten, zum künstlichen Hügel, zum Berg (216 m), der wieder vorwiegend männlich, jedoch sekundär auch als weiblich zu interpretieren ist. Das in der Zeichnung schematisch skizzierte morphologische Thema wird im folgenden noch öfter anzuschneiden sein, insbesondere wenn auf die erstaunliche Präferenz des monumentalen Konus im 19. und 20. Jahrhundert eingegangen wird.

Aus der Baugeschichte können wir einige konkrete Beispiele zu diesen morphologischen Phänomenen zitieren. Zunächst ist der **Kegel auf Kubus oder auf Zylinder** zu nennen.

Die Pagode Bai-Te (1279) in Peking, ein Werk der lamaistischen Kunst, weist zusätzlich zu dem kegelförmigen Aufsatz auf einem leicht nach unten sich verjüngenden Zylinder den typischen schirmartigen Abschluß auf, der ergänzend zum Himmel vermittelt.

Die äußerst einfache geometrische Kombination von Zylinder und Konus bildet die Grundform bei mittelalterlichen Rundbauten, etwa bei den Karnern. Als Beispiel soll der Karner von Burg Schlainitz, Niederösterreich, zitiert werden. In einer geometrisch sehr klaren Form sitzt der Konus, etwas zurückspringend, auf dem zylindrischen Unterbau auf, der durch einfache Wandsäulen gegliedert ist. Wie so häufig findet auch hier die Spitze durch eine Art Knauf ihre Akzentuierung.

Die Rundkirche von Petronell, Niederösterreich, zeigt, vom Konus abweichend, ein geschweiftes Dach, vielleicht eine Reminiszenz an Rundzelte. Der bergende Rundraum vertritt als Grabstätte das Erdhaft-Mütterliche, das Trichterportal als Zugang zu dunklen, fensterarmen Räumen hat vaginalen Charakter. Die konusartigen Dächer als phallische Erinnerung, aber auch als steiler Berg oder Fels, können dem Männlichen zugeordnet werden. Die baulich überzeugende Einheit verweist auf eine androgyne Architektur.

Der Typus »Kegel auf Zylinder« weist sich dadurch als Archetypus aus, daß sein Vorkommen ohne kulturhistorische Beeinflussung in entfernten geographischen Bereichen zu verzeichnen ist.

So ist etwa die **Türbe** ein Grabbau, der im islamischem Bereich verbreitet ist. Als Beispiel soll die Türbe des Emirs Hassan bei Ahlal am Vansee in Ostanatolien (1275) genannt werden.

Unter den nicht ausgeführten Entwürfen von **Friedrich von Schmidt** (1825–1891) finden wir auch eine Gruftkapelle (1880). Die Anlehnung – thematisch durchaus motiviert – an die mittelalterlichen Karner ist nicht zu übersehen. Auf einem mächtigen Sockel, über eine monumentale Stiege mit Portikus erreichbar, sitzt der zylindrische Unterbau. Der aufgesetzte Konus hat genau die Proportion des Karners von Burg Schlainitz.

Der Konus, aufsitzend auf einem Zylinder, ist auch der anonymen volkstümlichen Architektur nicht fremd. Die **Trulli** Süditaliens, insbesondere in Alberobello, dürfen nicht nur als profane Ergebnisse der »falschen Wölbung« verstanden werden, in den frühen Kulturen hat auch das Wohnhaus gleichsam sakralen Charakter. Der weiblich-bergende Raum erscheint phallisch überhöht, was durch das zapfenartige Element an der Spitze noch unterstrichen wird.

Für Klassizismus und Revolutionsarchitektur um 1800 war der Konus als elementare geometrische Form ein beliebtes Motiv, vor allem in den zahlreichen Entwurfszeichnungen.

If the tip is cut off, then we are dealing with truncated conical roofs (ill. 220 g-l). These forms often occur without substructure and then move lead on to the tumulus, to the artificial mound, the hill (260 m), again to be interpreted as predominantly male, but secondarily as female. The theme that is sketched morphologically in the drawing will often be addressed below, especially when dealing with the astonishing preference for the monumental cone in the 19th and 20th centuries.

Building history provides us with some concrete examples of this morphological phenomenon. The first to be dealt with is the **cone on cube or on cylinder**.

The *Bai-Te Pagoda (*1279) in Peking, a work of lama art, has the typical umbrella-like conclusion, additionally mediating with heaven, as well as the conical top on a cylinder tapering slightly towards the bottom.

The extremely simple geometrical combination of cylinder and cone is the basic form for medieval centralized buildings, the charnel houses, for example. Let us take the charnel house at Burg Schlainitz, Lower Austria, as an example. The cone, set slightly back, geometrically very clear in form, sits on the cylindrical substructure, which is articulated by simple engaged columns. As so often happens, the tip here is also accentuated by a kind of pommel.

The round church in Petronell, Lower Austria, deviates from the cone and has a curved roof, perhaps a reminiscence of round tents. The protective round room represents the earthly and maternal as a place of burial, and the squinch portal as access to dark spaces with very few windows is vaginal in character. The cone-like roofs are a phallic reminiscence, but can also be seen as a steep mound or rock, and can be classified as male. The architecturally convincing unity indicates androgynous architecture.

The »cone on cylinder« type thus shows that is an archetype by the fact that it occurs without culture-historical influence in distant geographical areas.

The same is true of the **türbe**, a tomb structure common in the Islamic world. An example is the türbe of Emir Hassan at Ahlal on Lake Van in east Anatolia (1275).

We also find a crypt chapel (1880) among the unbuilt designs of **Friedrich von Schmidt** (1825–1891). It is impossible to miss his – thematically entirely justified – borrowing from the medieval charnel house. The cylindrical substructure is set on a massive base reached by a monumental flight of steps with portico. The cone on top has exactly the same proportions as the charnel house at Burg Schlainitz.

The cone, set on a cylinder, is also not alien to anonymous folk architecture. The **trulli** of southern Italy, especially in Alberobello, should not be understood simply as secular results of »false vaulting«, as even the dwelling house was effectively sacred in character in early cultures. The female-protecting room seems to be raised in a phallic manner, which is further underlined by the pine-cone-like element on the tip.

The cone as a fundamental form was a popular motif for classical and Revolutionary Architecture, especially in the numerous design drawings.

James Paine II (1745–1829) designed a national monument for the Earl of Chatham ca. 1781. The closed cone is placed on a square substructure, with strange torsos from Doric temple façades in front of it.

There is an interesting cross-section of **Giannantonio Selva's** (1751–1819) planned memorial for Napoleon on Monte Cenisio (1813). It shows that the coffered dome and the pointed once on top of it are not linked spatially in any way and form a unit only in outward appearance. Nevertheless this is s typical example of androgynous architecture: the concrete element, the »female« cavity of the dome, which has light funnels at the sides, has a compact, conical and tower-like element on top of it, but outside the two parts fuse into a unit. This theme has remained just as interesting in our century.

The side chapel of the church in Neu-Ulm (1926) by **Dominikus Böhm** (1880–1955) is an expressively faceted, small centralized space, which runs into a pointed turret that can be made out inside as well. This transition is achieved by means of a shallow conical stump, which takes up the stelliform points of the circular space at the base. The tower itself is a cone, but considerably steeper than those found on Romanesque charnel houses or of the gigantic cones drawn in designs around 1800. Thus it is more tower-like in character, but the mediating shallow cone means that it can form an organic unit with the round space.

Böhm himself, in 1926, speaks of a »light turbine«, a term that the ground plan makes particularly comprehensible. Thus the idea of movement as a fundamental human process and the idea of rotation as an element that is equally cosmic and mechanical is introduced into architecture.

James Paine II (1745–1829) entwirft um 1781 ein Nationalmonument für den Earl of Chatham. Der geschlossene Konus sitzt auf einem quadratischen Unterbau, dem seltsame Torsi von dorischen Tempelfassaden vorgestellt sind.

Für das für Napoleon auf dem Monte Cenisio (1813) von **Giannantonio Selva** (1751–1819) geplante Denkmal gibt es einen informativen Querschnitt. Ihm ist zu entnehmen, daß der kassettierte Kuppelraum und der darauf sitzende spitze Kegel keinerlei räumliche Verbindung aufweisen und nur in der äußeren Erscheinung eine Einheit bilden. Trotzdem handelt es sich hier um ein charakteristisches Beispiel einer androgynen Architektur, da dem konkreten Element, dem »weiblichen« Hohlraum der mit seitlichen Lichttrichtern versehenen Kuppel ein kompaktes, kegelförmig-turmartiges Element aufgesetzt ist, wobei aber die beiden Teile außen zu einer architektonischen Einheit verschmolzen sind. In unserem Jahrhundert hat das Thema keineswegs an Interesse verloren.

Die Seitenkapelle der Kirche in Neu-Ulm (1926) von **Dominikus Böhm** (1880–1955) ist ein expressiv facettierter, kleiner Zentralraum, der in ein auch innen räumlich wahrnehmbares, spitz zulaufendes Türmchen übergeht. Dieser Übergang wird durch einen flachen Kegelstumpf bewerkstelligt, der an der Basis die sternförmigen Zacken des Rundraumes aufnimmt. Der Turm selbst ist ein Kegel, jedoch wesentlich steiler als etwa jene von romanischen Karnern oder die in den Entwürfen um 1800 gezeichneten riesigen Koni. Somit trägt er stärker den Turm-Charakter, der vermittelnde Flachkegel läßt ihn jedoch mit dem Rundraum zu einer organischen Einheit werden.

Böhm selbst spricht 1926 von einer »Lichtturbine«, eine Bezeichnung, die vor allem aus dem Grundriß verständlich wird. Damit ist auch die Idee der Bewegung als eines elementaren menschlichen Prozesses und die Idee der Rotation als gleicherweise kosmisches wie mechanisches Element in die Architektur eingebracht.

Josef Plečnik (1872–1957) zeichnet 1947 einen Entwurf für ein slowenisches Parlament in Ljubljana. Das monumentale Kerngebäude steht, etwas exzentrisch, in einem annähernd quadratischen, niederen Gebäudeblock. Der große Zentralraum wird durch schräggestellte Säulen, die an Gaudí erinnern, und eine flache Segmentkuppel gebildet. Dieser aufgesetzt ist ein streng geometrischer Kegel als turmartige Überhöhung, die aber im Innern nicht wahrnehmbar, räumlich nicht wirksam gewesen wäre. (Hofmann, 1987) Vielmehr war vorgesehen, die Turmspitze über eine große Rampenanlage erreichbar zu machen. Die Steilheit des Kegels ist wieder derart, daß die Bezeichnung »Turm« gerechtfertigt erscheint. In der Kombination mit dem zentralen Kuppelraum scheint die männliche und weibliche Symbolik zu einer Einheit verschmolzen zu sein.

Eine morphologische Sonderentwicklung, die uns in den beiden letzten Jahrhunderten überraschend häufig begegnet, ist der **Kegelstumpf**, also ein Konus mit gekappter Spitze. Für die symbolische Deutung gibt es nur wenige Aussagen, die oberste, kreisrunde Schnittfläche wird jedoch häufig zur Raumbelichtung herangezogen. Wie schon an Abb. 220 dargelegt, hängt die metaphorische Zuordnung weitgehend vom Neigungswinkel ab. Die flachere Neigung werden wir eher dem »Berg« zuordnen, den steileren Neigungswinkel eher dem »Phallus«, der jedoch dann seiner aggressiven Spitze beraubt ist. In den Arbeiten der Revolutionsarchitekten um 1800 taucht wiederholt das Motiv des gekappten Konus auf.

Das um diese Zeit beliebte Thema des Leuchtturmes, metaphorisch weit über die Funktion hinausgehend, greift **Étienne-Louis Boullée** (1728–1799) auf, und er verleiht dem Gebäude in einer Zeichnung die Form eines breiten Konus, aufgestellt auf einen mächtigen Unterbau, der von einem Säulenumgang gekrönt ist. Eine ganz ähnliche Form schlägt Boullée für einen Kenotaph vor, der Basiskranz ist mit Bäumen bepflanzt. Es kann angenommen werden, daß das Innere des Leergrabes ähnlich konzipiert war, wie jenes in Form einer gekappten Pyramide.

Guido Fiorini (1891–1965), ein Bologneser Architekt, ist nach seiner barocken und »Modernismo« Phase von den französischen Revolutionsarchitekten beeinflußt. Weiterverarbeitet ergeben diese Impulse eine pathetisch-monumentale Architektur. Die Zeichnung zum *Santuario* entsteht 1928/29 und erlaubt Assoziationen zu weiblichen und männlichen Geschlechtssymbolen. Der vulvaartige Eingang führt zu einem androgynen Bauwerk, das sowohl als bergend – schützend als auch als machtvoll-phallisch angesprochen werden kann. (Pepponi, 1991) Es ist wieder ein Kegel bzw. ein Kegelstumpf von einer derartigen Steilheit, daß man das Gebilde sowohl dem Typus »Turm« als auch dem Typus »Berg« zuordnen kann. Da sich innen offenkundig ein erdhaft-schützender Raum befinden sollte, scheint die androgyne Zuordnung naheliegend.

Die megalomane Formensprache der französischen Revolutionsarchitektur um 1800 ist wohl nicht ohne Einfluß auf die totalitäre Architektur des Faschismus geblieben.

224, 225. Josef Plečnik, Parlamentsgebäude in Ljubljana, 1947.
226. Giannantonio Selva, Denkmal für Napoleon auf dem Monte Cenisio, 1813.
227. James Paine II, Denkmal für den Earl of Chatham, 1781.
228. Étienne-Louis Boullée, Kenotaph, um 1800.
229. Étienne Louis Boullée, Leuchtturm, um 1800.
230. Wilhelm Kreis, Totenmal am Dnjepr, 1942.
231. Clemens Holzmeister, Mausoleum für Kemal Atatürk, 1951.

224, 225. Josef Plečnik, Parliament building in Ljubljana, 1947.
226. Giannantonio Selva, monument to Napoleon on the Monte Cenisio, 1813.
227. James Paine II, Monument to the Earl of Chatham, 1781.
228. Étienne-Louis Boullée, cenotaph, ca. 1800.
229. Étienne-Louis Boullée, lighthouse, ca. 1800.
230. Wilhelm Kreis, mortuary monument on the Dnjepr, 1942.
231. Clemens Holzmeister, mausoleum for Kemal Atatürk, 1951.

```
      226  227
224   228  229
225   230  231
```

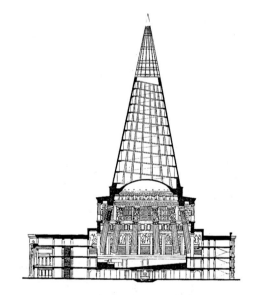

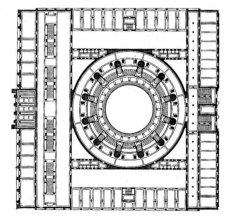

Das Totenmal am Dnjepr, ein Entwurf von **Wilhelm Kreis** (1873–1955) aus dem Jahr 1942, kann die direkte Verwandtschaft mit Boullée nicht verleugnen.

Der Kegel ist an der Spitze nur wenig abgeflacht und mit einem kleinen Rundbau abgeschlossen, der von einer Skulptur gekrönt wird. Der Neigungswinkel ist nun derart flach, daß das Bauwerk als architektonische Monumentalisierung eines Tumulus angesehen werden kann. Die Transfiguration des erdhaften Grabhügels zu einem monumentalem Machtzeichen rückt den Entwurf in die Nähe eines androgynen Bauwerks.

Lange vor den memorialen Machtzeugnissen des Faschismus beschäftigt sich der schwedische Architekt **Sigurd Lewerentz** (1885–1975) mit dem Thema des Todes. Der Entwurf eines Krematoriums für Malmö, ein Wettbewerb aus dem Jahre 1926, schlägt drei Kegelstümpfe auf einem quadratischen Unterbau vor. Portikus und Obelisken unterstreichen den feierlichen Ernst. Trotz der verschiedenen Funktionen der Koni wird die Assoziation zum Tumulus-Hügel und zur schützenden Hülle gleicherweise geweckt. **Clemens Holzmeister** (1886–1983) knüpft an den archaischen Gedanken des Mausoleums auch formal an: Der Entwurf für das Grabmal Kemal Atatürks in Ankara aus dem Jahre 1951 ist eine erstaunliche Synthese des Weiblichen und des Männlichen: Dieses manifestiert sich in dem nur wenig gekappten, steil aufsteigenden Konus, jenes im großen Rund des Kuppelraumes. Einmal mehr gelingt es, das Machtvoll-Männliche und das Schützend-Weibliche in einer »coincidentia« zu überlagern.

Das Motiv des Konus, des Kegelstumpfes, erfreut sich in einigen Architekturrichtungen der siebziger und achtziger Jahre im Umfeld der sogenannten Postmoderne überraschender Beliebtheit.

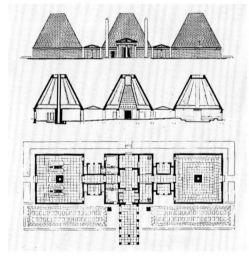

Offenkundig sind es neoklassizistische Tendenzen und die erneute Besinnung auf die französische Revolutionsarchitektur, die dieses einfache geometrische Motiv begünstigen. Diese Form bildet in etlichen Entwürfen von **Aldo Rossi** einen Orientierungs- und Kristallisationspunkt. Im Wettbewerb für das Rathaus in Muggio von 1972 ist der Konus von einfachen Blockbauten eingeklammert, beim Friedhof für Modena (1971–1978) ist der Turm aufgeschnitten. Trotz der vielfältigen Wandlungen im Werke Rossis scheint er einem Topos treu geblieben zu sein: Auch bei einer seiner letzten Arbeiten aus dem Jahre 1995 hat das Thema des Konus eine dominante Position. Für Barialto, einer Neustadt bei Bari, baut Aldo Rossi gleichsam ein neues Stadttor in Form eines Kegelstumpfes, eingebaut in die Rudimente einer neuen Stadtmauer. Der Konus ist oben offen, und im Zentrum steht ein Olivenbaum, das Symbol der Region. Damit ist noch ein anderes Thema angeschnitten: das Wesen im Raum, das biologisch-wachsende Element in der schützenden Umhüllung. (Vgl. Kap. 9.3.2.)

In einem Entwurf von **Hans Hollein** gewinnt der Konus ein beachtliches Interpretationsspektrum. Der für die Ausführung bestimmte Wettbewerbsentwurf von 1995 für ein Vulkanmuseum in der Auvergne, zeigt als dominierendes Element einen großen Konus, der zunächst für den Archetypus »Berg« steht. Der Konus ist aufgeschlitzt, und die erotische Spalte bietet Einblick und Eintritt in das Innere: Wir befinden uns nicht nur im Berginneren, sondern gleichzeitig auch unter der Erde: Das uns umgebende Gold ist das Feuer der Tiefe, und Hollein konfrontiert seine Arbeit mit den Illustrationen Gustave Dorés zu Dantes »Inferno«. Gleichzeitig haben wir mit Jules Verne die *Reise nach dem Mittelpunkt der Erde* vollzogen und sind tief in deren mütterlichen Leib eingedrungen: Die Entstehung der Welt aus dem Feuer, und die Entstehung

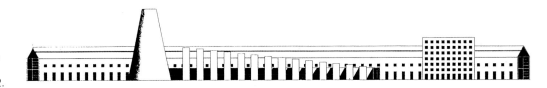

	232	238
	233	236
234	235	237

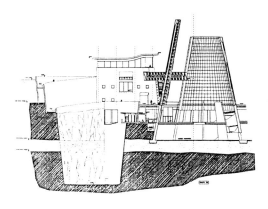

Josef Plečnik (1872–1957) produced a design for a Slovenian parliament in Ljubljana in 1947. The monumental core building stands, somewhat eccentrically, in an approximately square, low block of buildings. The large centralized space is formed by sloping columns reminiscent of Gaudí and a shallow segmental dome. This is topped by a strictly geometrical cone as a tower-like raised feature, but this would not have been perceptible inside, would have had no three-dimensional effect. (Hofmann, 1987) On the contrary, the intention was to provide access to the tip of the tower from a large system of ramps. The steepness of the cone is again such that the word »tower« seems justified. In combination with the central domed space the male and female symbolism seems to have fused into a unit.

A special morphological development, which we come across surprisingly frequently in the last two centuries, is the **truncated cone**, in other words a cone with its top cut off. Little has been said about its symbolic significance, but the uppermost, circular surface is often used for lighting purposes. As ill. 250 has already shown, metaphorical classification often depends on the angle of inclination. The shallower angle is more likely to be classified as a »mound«, and a steeper angle as a »phallus«, even though it is then robbed of its aggressive tip. The truncated cone occurs repeatedly in the work of the Revolutionary Architects around 1800.

The lighthouse theme was popular at this time, going well beyond its function in metaphorical terms. It was taken up by **Étienne-Louis Boullée** (1728–1799). In one drawing he gives the building the shape of a broad cone, set upright on a massive substructure topped by a columned gallery. Boullée suggests a very similar form for a cenotaph, with its circular base planted with trees. It can be assumed that the interior of the empty tomb was conceived similarly, like the former in the shape of a truncated pyramid.

Guido Fiorini (1891–1965), a Bolognese architect, was influenced by French Revolutionary architecture after his Baroque and »Modernismo« phase. Taken further, these impulses produce dramatic and monumental architecture. The drawing for the *Santuario* was produced in 1928/29 and permits associations with female and male sexual symbols. The vulva-like entrance leads to an androgynous structure that can be seen both as concealing and protecting and also powerful and phallic. (Pepponi, 1991) It is again a cone or a truncated cone that is so steep that it can be classified both as a »mound« and a »tower«. Obviously the interior is intended to be an earth-like, protecting space, and so classification as androgynous suggests itself.

The megalomaniac formal language of French Revolutionary Architecture around 1800 probably influenced the totalitarian architecture of Fascism.

The memorial to the dead on the Dnjepr, a design by **Wilhelm Kreis** (1873–1955) dating from 1942, cannot deny its direct relationship with Boullée.

The cone is only slightly flattened at the tip and concludes with a small circular structure with a sculpture on top of it. The angle of inclination is now so shallow that the building can be seen as an architectural monumentalization of a tumulus. The transfiguration of the earth-like tomb mound into a monumental power symbol brings the design close to an androgynous structure.

Sigurd Lewerentz (1885–1975) addressed the subject of death long before the memorial manifestations of Fascist power. His design for a crematorium for Malmö, a competition dating from 1926, proposes three truncated cones on a square substructure. Portico and obelisks underline the solemnity of the building. Despite the various functions of the cones, it suggests associations with the tumulus mound and the protective covering to an equal extent. **Clemens Holzmeister** (1886–1983) also makes a formal link with the idea of the mausoleum: his design for the tomb of Kemal Atatürk in Ankara, dating from 1951, is an astonishing synthesis of the male and the female: the former shows in the steeply rising cone, which is only slightly truncated, and the latter in the great round, domed space. Once more the concepts of powerful and male and female and protecting overlap successfully in a »coincidentia«.

The motif of the cone, the truncated cone, enjoyed surprising popularity in some architectural approaches in the seventies and eighties in the context of so-called Post-Modernism.

Obviously this simple geometrical motif is favoured by neo-classical tendencies and renewed consideration of French Revolutionary Architecture. This form is an orientation and crystallization point in numerous designs by **Aldo Rossi**. In the 1972 competition for the town

des Lebens aus dem Frauenleib überlagern sich in den chtonischen Tiefen der Erde, fruchtbar und tödlich zugleich.

Das Motiv des spitzen Kegels, das **Gustav Peichl** bei der Bundeskunsthalle in Bonn (1994) als weitere Bereicherung der Dachlandschaft verwendet, erfährt eine Modifikation beim Projekt für den Palazzo Tergesteo in Triest (1996) gemeinsam mit Franco Fonatti geplant. Der Kegelstumpf endet nicht mit der oberen Schnittfläche, vielmehr ist noch ein Zylinder aufgesetzt, der das Motiv des »faro«, des Leuchtturmes assoziiert und auch als Verweis auf Boullées konischen Leuchtturm gelesen werden kann.

Die traumhaften Architekturbilder von **Massimo Scolari** (geb. 1943) zeigen den konischen Turm-Berg in der Art eines neuen babylonischen Turmes und versetzen ihn in eine mythologische Umgebung. Im Bild *Di la del cielo* (1982) erscheint der Konus in einer ähnlichen Proportion wie bei Boullée.

Die Verdoppelung des Kegelstumpfes, gleichsam ein »Paar« bildend, wurde bereits erwähnt: Mathias Goeritz akzentuiert damit die Autofabrik in Toluca, Mexico (vgl. Kap. 8.1)

9.1.4. Kuppel und Pyramide

Eine der zahlreichen Deutungen der ägyptischen Pyramide besagt, daß sie einen künstlichen Berg in der endlosen Weite der Wüste bildet. Sie hat damit eine Ähnlichkeit zum Tumulus, dem künstlichen Grabhügel und ist, wie dieser, den Toten gewidmet, ohne jedoch einen nennenswerten Innenraum zu bilden.

Im Klassizismus und in der Revolutionsarchitektur erfreut sich die Pyramide einer besonderen Beliebtheit, doch wird sie jetzt architektonisch dadurch völlig neu interpretiert, daß sie auch mit einem Innenraum ausgestattet ist – freilich vorwiegend in zahllosen Zeichnungen.

Das Leergrab von **Étienne-Louis Boullée** in Gestalt einer gekappten Pyramide birgt im Innern einen mächtigen halbkreisförmigen Kuppelbau mit einer zentralen Öffnung ähnlich der des Pantheons, durch die man in den Hohlraum der Pyramide blicken kann. Dieser ist, aus der Schnittzeichnung zu schließen, offenbar kegelförmig im Gegensatz zur Außenpyramide.

Sehen wir die Pyramide als Berg eher männlich an, und interpretieren wir den Kuppelraum mit seiner Öffnung zum männlichen Raumkonus als weiblich, so könnte dieser Entwurf als ein weiterer Schritt zu einer androgynen Architektur verstanden werden.

Dieses Thema nimmt **Franz Engel** (1776–1827) im Entwurf für ein Mausoleum in Keszthely (1820) auf, und wieder ist es ein Grab- und Memorialbau, bei dem eine steile »männliche« und machtvolle Pyramide mit dem »weiblichen« bergenden Kuppelraum verknüpft wird. Durch eine große Öffnung in der Kuppel ist ein Überfließen der beiden Räume gewährleistet. Der oberste Teil der Pyramide dient als Glockenträger und ist mit ziemlich kleinen Schallöffnungen ausgestattet. Die Basis der Turmpyramide weist eine dorisierende Architektur ganz im Sinne des Klassizismus auf.

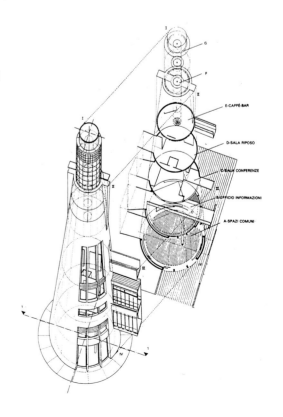

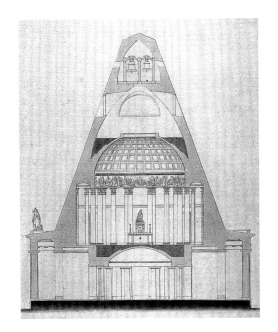

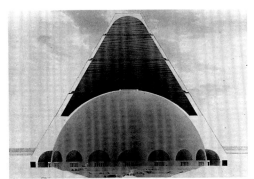

hall in Muggio the cone is set within simple block structures, and in the Modena cemetery (1971–1978) the tower is cut open. Despite many changes in Rossi's work he seems to have remained faithful to one topos: even in his latest work in 1995 the cone theme is dominant. For Barialto, a new town near Bari, Aldo Rossi builds what is effectively a new town gate in the form of a truncated cone, built into the rudiments of a new town wall. The cone is open at the top and at the centre is an olive tree, the symbol of the region. This also brings in a new theme: the being in space, the biological and growing element in the protective covering.

The cone acquires a broad spectrum of interpretation in a design by **Hans Hollein**. The 1995 design, which is to be built, for a volcano museum in the Auvergne has a large cone as its dominant element, standing first of all for the »mountain« archetype. The cone is slit open, and this erotic slit offers a view of and access to the interior: we are not only inside the mound, but at the same time inside the underground as well: the gold surrounding us is the fire of the depths, and Hollein confronts his work with Gustave Doré's illustrations for Dante's »Inferno«. At the same time we have competed a *Journey to the Centre of the Earth* with Jules Verne, and have penetrated deeply into its maternal body: the world emerging from fire and life emerging in the mother's womb overlap in the chthonic depths of the earth, fertile and deadly at the same time.

The motif of the pointed cube, used by **Gustav Peichl** for the Bundeskunsthalle in Bonn as further enrichment for the roofscape, is modified in the project for the Palazzo Tergesteo in Trieste, planned jointly with Franco Fonatti. The truncated cone no longer ends with the upper cut surface; in fact a cylinder is placed on top, suggesting the motif of the »faro«, the lighthouse. It can also be seen as a reference to Boullée's conical lighthouse.

The dreamlike architectural images **Massimo Scolari** (born 1943) show the conical tower-mound as a new Tower of Babel and place it in mythological surroundings. In the picture *Di la del cielo* (1982) the cone appears in proportions similar to Boullée's.

Doubling the truncated cone, effectively forming a »couple«, has already been mentioned: Mathias Goeritz uses it to accentuate the car factory in Toluca, Mexico (cf. chapter 8.1).

9.1.4. Dome and Pyramid

One of the many interpretations of the Egyptian pyramid states that it forms an artificial mound in the infinite breadth of the desert. Thus it is similar to the tumulus, the artificial grave mound, and like this it is dedicated to the dead, but without providing a significant interior.

The pyramid enjoyed particular popularity in Classicism and Revolutionary Architecture, but it is completely reinterpreted architecturally in that it is also provided with an interior – admittedly predominantly in countless drawings.

Étienne-Louis Boullée's cenotaph in the shape of a truncated pyramid has a massive semi-circular domed structure inside with a central opening similar to the one in the Pantheon, through which one can look into the cavity of the pyramid. The cross-section suggests that this is cuboid, in contrast with the outer pyramid.

If we seen the pyramid as an essentially male mound and interpret the domed space with its opening to the male cone space as female then this design could be seen as a further step towards androgynous architecture.

Franz Engel (1776–1827) takes up this theme in his design for a mausoleum in Keszthely (1820), and again it is a tomb and memorial building in which a steep »male« and powerful pyramid is connected with the »female« protecting domed space. The two spaces are allowed to overflow through a large opening in the dome. The uppermost part of the pyramid serves as a belfry with fairly small sound apertures. The base of the tower pyramid is Doric-style architecture entirely in the spirit of Classicism.

9.2. Second Synthesis: Penetration

9.2.1. Cupid and Angel

If we ask about the next step in the synthesis of polar forms, a closing up, then the process of thrusting in, breaking through, drilling through, should be mentioned a process that we can observe in architecture – although rarely – as in human beings.

9.2. Zweite Synthese: Die Penetration

9.2.1. Amor und Engel

243. Gian Lorenzo Bernini, *Verzückung der heiligen Theresia*, Rom, 1646.
244. Tempel in Südindien, 18. Jh.
245. Claude-Nicolas Ledoux, *Oikema*, um 1800.

243. Gian Lorenzo Bernini, *The Ecstasy of St. Teresa*, Rome, 1646.
244. Temple in South India, 18th cent.
245. Claude-Nicolas Ledoux, *Oikema*, ca. 1800.

Fragen wir nach dem nächsten Schritt einer Synthese polarer Formen, einer Verklammerung, dann ist der Vorgang des Eindringens, des Durchstoßens, des Durchbohrens, zu nennen, ein Prozeß, den wir gleicherweise beim Menschen wie – wenn auch sehr selten – in der Architektur beobachten können.

Die **Penetration** tritt uns in zwei typischen Erscheinungsformen entgegen, die scheinbar völlig gegensätzlicher Natur sind: in der Sexualität und im Kampf. Die Verbindung, ja Identität dieser beiden elementaren menschlichen Kategorien wurde immer wieder aufzuzeigen versucht, am deutlichsten wohl von Sigmund Freud. Demnach hat der Geschlechtsakt durchaus aggressiven Charakter, und in der Traumsymbolik stehen u. a. auch die Waffen stellvertretend für den Penis.

Die Penetration im geschlechtlichen Akt kann der Ausgangspunkt für neues Leben sein, die Penetration durch die Waffe kann den Tod bedeuten. Das oft gewaltsame Eindringen des Mannes in die Frau kann ein kämpferischer Akt sein, das Eindringen der Waffe in den menschlichen Körper kann Substanzen des Eros auslösen. Einmal mehr liegen Eros und Thanatos ganz nahe beisammen.

Es ist nicht von ungefähr, daß in der antiken Mythologie Amor oder Eros mit einer Waffe ausgestattet ist, daß die von der Liebe Getroffenen von einem Pfeil durchbohrt werden: das signifikanteste Beispiel einer schmerzhaften Penetration, die gleichzeitig die Liebe auslöst.

In den zahllosen Darstellungen der antiken Mythologie ist Eros ein junges Wesen, ein Knabe mit sehr mädchenhaften Zügen, haufig geflügelt.

Eine Neuinterpretation Amors begegnet uns in jenem Engel, der mit seinem Pfeil die Verzückung der heiligen Theresia auslöst. Vor allem **Gian Lorenzo Bernini** (1598–1680) hat in seiner berühmten Skulptur in Rom die durchaus erotische Bereitschaft in Erwartung einer lustvollen Verletzung und die völlige Hingabe in den göttlichen Anruf gleicherweise dargestellt. Im Altarbild der Karmeliterkirche in Vicenza von **Sebastiano Ricci** (1659–1734) wird die Heilige von Engeln emporgetragen, der Pfeil des Amor-Engels endet in einer rotflammenden Spitze.[51]

9.2.2. Historische Architektur

Die Penetration ist ein sehr seltenes Motiv in der historischen Architektur. In der Baukunst Südindiens finden wir in zahlreichen Tempeln hoch aufragende, schlanke Säulen, manchmal kanneliert, die das Dach des Tempels so durchstoßen, daß noch ein Stück des Himmels sichtbar bleibt. Die Säule wächst gleichsam in den Kosmos hinaus.

Für den *Oikema*, den Liebenstempel, hat **Claude-Nicolas Ledoux** noch eine erweiterte Variante gezeichnet: Der penisartige Grundriß ist in den mütterlich-fraulichen Kreis der Gesamtanlage eingedrungen.

In der erotischen Aufladung der Kunst um 1900 wird neuerlich die Tür, **das Tor**, zum Eingang in einen Körper. Wolfgang Pehnt (1973) formuliert es so: »In die verschatteten Portale, manchmal parabelförmig, manchmal wie ein Omega-Bogen ausgebildet, von Ornamentgewächsen halb zugewuchert oder von Gorgonenhäuptern bewacht, dringt man nicht ohne Schaudern ein, wie in ein verbotenes, erogenes Geheimnis. So haben Joseph Maria Olbrich oder Fedor Schechtel, Pierre Roche, Raimondo d'Aronco oder Giuseppe Sommaruga den Eintritt in ihre Häuser inszeniert. ... Wo die Art-Nouveau-Künstler ihrer Phantasie die Zügel ließen, wurde das Betreten des Hauses zu einem Vorgang, der sexuelle Penetration ebenso wie einen umgekehrten Geburtsvorgang assoziieren konnte. Der ausgesetzte und vereinsamte Mensch kehrt zurück in den Schoß der großen Hetäre oder der großen Mutter, in Carl Gustav Jungs ›schützende Höhle‹«.

9.2.3. Architektur des 20. Jahrhunderts

Das Thema der Penetration in der Architektur des 20. Jahrhunderts gewinnt an Bedeutung in der Szene der siebziger und achtziger Jahre im Zusammenhang mit dem Neo-Manierismus, der als eine Architektur der Verletzung und Verwundung charakterisiert werden kann.

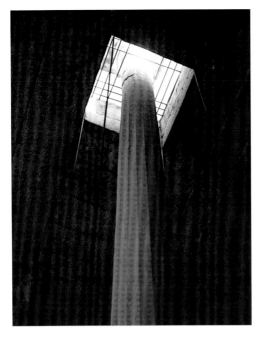

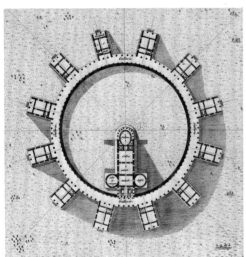

We come across **penetration** in two typical manifestations, apparently of quite opposite natures: in sexuality and in battle. Attempts have repeatedly been made to show the link between, indeed the identity of these two fundamental human categories, probably most clearly by Sigmund Freud. According to him the sexual act is entirely aggressive in character and in dream symbolism weapons among other things stand for the penis.

Penetration in the sexual act can be the starting-point for new life, and penetration by a weapon can mean death. A man's often violent penetration of a woman can be a combative act, and penetration of the human body by a weapon can release erotic substances. Once more Eros and Thanatos are very close together.

It is no coincidence that Cupid or Eros carries a weapon in ancient mythology, and that people who fall in love are penetrated by an arrow: this is the most significant example of painful penetration that also triggers love.

In the countless depictions of ancient mythology Eros is a young creature, a boy with very girlish features, and frequently winged.

We find a new interpretation of Cupid in the angel who sends St. Theresa into ecstasy with an arrow. **Gian Lorenzo Bernini** (1598–1680) in particular, in his famous sculpture in Rome, showed entirely erotic readiness in expectation of a joyous wound and compete acquiescence with the divine call to an equal extent. In **Sebastiano Ricci's** (1659–1734) altarpiece for the Carmelite church in Vicenza the saint is borne aloft by angels and the arrow of the Cupid-angel ends in a flaming red point.[48]

9.2.2. Historical Architecture

Penetration is a very rare motif in historical architecture. In the architecture of southern India we find numerous temples with soaring, slender columns, sometimes fluted, which thrust through the temple roof in such a way that a piece of the sky can still be seen. The column grows out into the cosmos, as it were.

For the *Oikema*, the temple of love, **Claude-Nicolas Ledoux** produced an extended variant: the penis-like ground plan has penetrated the maternal-feminine circle of the complex as a whole.

When art acquired an erotic charge around 1900 the door, the **gateway** became an entrance into a body. Wolfgang Pehnt (1973) formulates it like this: »It is not without a shudder that one penetrates the shaded portals, sometime in the shape of a parabola, sometimes like an omega-bow, half overgrown with ornamental plants or guarded by Gorgon's heads, as if into a forbidden, erogenous secret. This is how Joseph Maria Olbrich or Fedor Schechtel, Pierre Roche, Raimondo d'Aronco or Giuseppe Sommaruga staged the entrances to their buildings. ... When the Art Nouveau artists gave their imagination the reins, entering the building became a process that could be associated with sexual penetration as much as a reversed birth process. The rejected, lonely human being return to the womb of the great hetaera or the great mother, into Carl Gustav Jung's ›protecting cave‹.«

9.2.3. 20th-Century Architecture

In 20th-century architecture the theme of penetration becomes more important in the seventies and eighties in the context of Neo-Mannerism, which can be characterized as an architecture of injury and wounding.

The subsequent »Deconstructivist«[49] movement takes up some motifs of Neo-Mannerism, especially criticism of harmonizing and perfectionist architecture. The theme of injury is modified particularly as a complex penetration process.

The **Coop Himmelblau**[50] experimental group (founded 1968) embraces dynamic architecture in its verbal statements as well, and is no stranger to the theme of aggression and here above all penetration. »If there is a poetry of desolation, then it is the aesthetic of the architecture of death in white cloth. Of death in tiled hospital rooms. The architecture of sudden death on concrete. The architecture of the steering column smashing through the thorax, the shot canal of the dealer on 42nd Street.« (Feuerstein, 1988) Interpenetration of heterogeneous elements in dynamic aggression is one of the basic design motifs in the designs and realizations. The theme of the arrow that injures and inflames acquires a new level of interpretation.

Die darauffolgende Richtung des »Dekonstruktivismus«[52] greift einige Motive des Neo-Manierismus auf, vor allem die Kritik an einer harmonisierenden und perfektionistischen Architektur. Das Thema der Verletzung wird vor allem als vielschichtiger Vorgang zur Penetration modifiziert.

Die Experimentalgruppe der **Coop Himmelblau**[53] (gegr. 1968) bekennt sich auch in ihren verbalen Äußerungen zu einer dynamischen Architektur, der das Thema der Aggression und hier vor allem der Penetration nicht fremd ist. »Wenn es eine Poesie der Trostlosigkeit gibt, so ist es die Ästhetik der Architektur des Todes in weißen Tüchern. Des Todes in verfliesten Spitalszimmern. Die Architektur des plötzlichen Sterbens auf Beton. Die Architektur des von der Lenksäule durchbrochenen Brustkorbes, der Schußkanal des Dealers in der 42. Straße.« (Feuerstein, 1988) In den Entwürfen und Realisierungen ist die Durchdringung heterogener Elemente in einer dynamischen Aggression eines der gestalterischen Grundmotive. Das Thema des Pfeils, der verletzt und entzündet, erfährt eine neue Deutungsebene.

Ein Projekt für die Wiener Secession, in Zeichnung und Modell präsentiert, zeigt einen schlanken, spitzen Pfahl, der blitzartig schräg durch den Bau von Joseph Maria Olbrich hindurchschießt. In einem kleinen Maßstab wird diese Idee realisiert: Bei der Reissbar in Wien durchsticht ein transluzider Stab eine Mauer und kommt in einem Nebenraum wieder zum Vorschein.

Gestänge, Platten und Glaswände durchbohren, durchdringen die Mauern der Liederbar Roter Engel in Wien. (1981)

Beim Projekt *Hot flat* für den Neuen Markt in Wien (1978) ist ein riesiger Pfahl durch das Gebäude gesteckt, an dessen Ende eine Flamme züngelt.

Thomson (1991) interpretiert dieses Projekt sehr eindeutig in einem sexuellen Sinn: »In gewalttätiger Deflorations- und Penetrationssymbolik durchbohrt in der Höhe des goldenen Schnittes ein alternativ als Stahl- oder Glasträger ausgebildetes Element von doppelter Geschoßhöhe schräg das Haus, an einem Ende ein gläserner Flammenflügel, der seinerseits die Wohnungen der obersten Geschosse durchschneidet.«

Die Gruppe **Haus-Rucker-Co**[54] (gegr. 1967) errichtet auf der Wiener Messe von 1980 ein Werbezeichen für die Idee des Industrial Design. Das phallische Zentralelement der pneumatischen Konstruktion durchstößt einen Ring und dieser selbst ist durch zwei Ringe durchgezogen, gleichsam eine Mehrfachpenetration, in der Verknüpfung der Elmente aber gleichzeitig ein androgynes Denkmal.

Das Thema der Penetration wird verdeutlicht an einem Entwurf von **Günther Feuerstein** (geb. 1925) für die Erweiterung des Technischen Museums in Wien. Die Zubauten, großräumige Hallen in Quadrat- und Rautenform, haben eine weibliche Charakteristik, sie werden, ebenso wie der Altbau, überlagert und durchbohrt von begehbaren Gitterträgern, die ein Durchwandern der Räume ermöglichen .

Die Kunsthalle am Karlsplatz Wien wurde 1992 als Provisorium eröffnet. **Adolf Krischanitz** hat eine einfache Stahlkonstruktion in der Art eines Containers aufgestellt. Eine reizvolle Spannung erhält das schlichte Gebilde durch die kraftvolle Penetration eines riesigen hochliegenden Rohrs, das die Besucher über eine Stiege erreichen und so durch die Halle hindurchspazieren können.

Das Thema der »Penetration« ist für **Walter Michael Pühringer** ein zentrales Problem der Dialektik von Bauwerk und Skulptur. Dem üblichen beziehungslosen Nebeneinander von Architektur und Plastik antwortet Pühringer mit der größtmöglichen Verknüpfung: der Durchdringung, dem Durchbohren, Durchstoßen, Einschießen der Skulpturteile in den Bau, wobei sich die merkwürdige Ambivalenz jeder Penetration offenbart, die ebenso ein aggressives Durchstoßen wie eine liebevolle Vereinigung sein kann. In einer Hauptschule in Wien-Ottakring läßt Pühringer seinen *Grenzflieger* (1995) abstürzen, er landet in der Halle, aber die Hälfte ragt zeichenhaft in den Platzraum.

Als eine gleichsam beginnende Penetration können drei weitere zeitgenössische Beispiele angesehen werden: **Rob Krier** (geb. 1938) macht die Eingangsspalte bei einem Wohnhaus aufnahmebereit für ein säulenartiges Bau-»Glied«.

Bei einer Sparkasse in Wien-Josefstadt zitiert **Boris Podrecca** (geb. 1940) in einem Motiv zwei androgyne Gedanken. Die aufstrebende Doppelsäule erinnert an jene von St. Stephan und von Hans Hollein in der Feigen-Galerie, doch haben Podreccas Säulen noch Distanz bewahrt. Der eigentlich erotisch-androgyne Prozeß besteht darin, daß die Säulen die Raumdecke durch eine kreisrunde Öffnung souverän durchstoßen. Die Assoziation zu den erwähnten indischen Tempelsäulen liegt nahe.

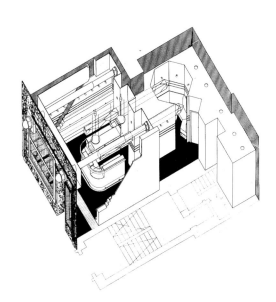

A project for the Vienna Secession, presented as drawing and model, shows a slender, pointed staff shooting straight through the building by Joseph Maria Olbrich like lightning. This idea is realized on a small scale: in the Reissbar in Vienna a translucent staff pierces a wall and reappears in a side room.

Struts, slabs and glass walls bore drill through and penetrate the walls of the Roter Engel lieder bar in Vienna.

In the *Hot flat* project for the Neuer Markt in Vienna a gigantic pole is thrust through the building, with a flame flickering at the end of it.

Thomson (1991) interprets this project as unambiguously sexual: »An element, a glass or steel bearer, twice the height of a storey, thrusts through the building diagonally at the level of the golden section in violent symbolism of defloration and penetration. At one end is a glass wing of flame, which for its part cuts through the flats in the upper storeys.«

The **Haus-Rucker-Co** group[54] (founded 1967) built an advertising sign for the idea of Industrial Design at the 1980 Vienna Trade Fair. The phallic central element of the pneumatic structure thrusts through a ring and this is itself drawn through two rings, a multiple penetration, as it were, but at the same time an androgynous monument in the linking of the elements.

The theme of penetration is illustrated in a design by **Günther Feuerstein** (born 1925) for the extension to the Technical Museum in Vienna. The additional buildings, spacious halls in the shape of squares and lozenges, are feminine in character, and like the old building they are overlapped and penetrated by promenade braced girders upon which it is possible to move through the rooms.

191

Eine gewaltige Durchdringung baut **Oswald Mathias Ungers** (geb. 1926). Der monumentale Torbau im Frankfurter Messegelände (1983/1984) findet den oberen Abschluß in einer tiefen Schlucht. Doch von oben schiebt sich ein dunkler Pfahl in den Spalt und scheint den Körper zu durchstoßen.

Identität und gleichzeitige Divergenz des Außen und Innen lassen den Entwurf **Heinz Tesars** für das Prähistorische Museum in München (1990) zu einer androgynen Architektur werden. Bemerkenswert daran ist, daß nicht, wie in den bisher gezeigten Beispielen, das Weibliche ein Männliches einschließt, sondern umgekehrt. Deuten wir den scharfkantigen Würfel des Außenkörpers als rational männliches Element, dann ist der sich einbohrende vaginale Schacht, durch eine sanft geschwungene Spiraltreppe charakterisiert, als ein reziprok penetrierendes weibliches Element zu interpretieren.

9.3. Dritte Synthese: Das Ineinander

9.3.1. Wesen im Wesen

Wenn die im vorhergehenden Kapitel geschilderte Penetration vollzogen ist, befindet sich ein Element in einem anderen: Der Pfeil sitzt im Herzen des in Liebe Entbrannten – oder im Herzen des Feindes, die indische Säule steht im Himmel, die Pfähle der Coop Himmelblau stecken im Raum, im Gebäude.

Die biologische Analogie ist einleuchtend: Der Penis hat das Hymen durchstoßen, ist in die Vagina eingedrungen, wird von einem »Raum« umschlossen, ja noch mehr: Sandor Ferenczi (1924) geht sogar von der Hypothese aus, der Koitus stelle den Versuch des Mannes dar, in den Uterus zurückzukehren.

Wenn wir uns die Freudsche These vor Augen halten, wonach in der Traumsymbolik die menschliche Figur als Sexualsymbol generell, insbesondere als männliches zu sehen ist, und wenn der Eintritt durch ein Tor in ein Gebäude, gleichsam als Doppelkodierung, den Geschlechtsakt ebenso wie die Rückkehr in den Uterus bedeutet, dann scheint die entsprechende Analogie zur Architektur durchaus plausibel.

Das elementare Schutzbedürfnis des Menschen manifestiert sich in mannigfaltigen Phänomenen, nicht zuletzt in der Architektur. Das »Drinnensein« in einem Gebäude, einem Raum, einer Höhlung, einem Körper bedeutet offenbar jene Geborgenheit, die wir in unserer pränatalen Existenz »erlebt« haben.

Das (lebende) Wesen in einem lebenden Wesen hat demnach ein Urmodell, dem unsere unentwegte Sehnsucht gilt: das **Embryo im Mutterleib**. Alle folgenden Darstellungen dieses Kapitels können unter diesem Gesichtspunkt interpretiert werden.

Im mythologischen Bereich finden wir nicht selten die Auffassung, daß Menschen Tiere gebären und umgekehrt, daß Tiere Menschen zur Welt bringen. Die Vorstellung, daß der Mensch sich in einem Tier aufhält, gehört zum Fundus der Mythen, Sagen und Märchen.

Das Thema des menschlichen Wesens in einem tierischen Wesen findet in der biblischen Erzählung von Jonas, der drei Tage im Bauch des Walfisches verbrachte und somit in Analogie zum Tode Christi tritt eine bekannte Formulierung.

Ähnliches erlebt Münchhausen mit seinem Schiff, das von einem Seeungeheuer verschlungen wird, und erst nach trickreichen Erfindungen gelingt die Befreiung.

In dem Märchen vom Rotkäppchen hält sich die Großmutter im Bauch des bösen Wolfes auf, bevor sie durch den Jäger befreit wird.

Ein riesiger, wohl toter Fisch scheint in der *Versuchung des Heiligen Antonius* (1556) von **Pieter Bruegel d. Ä.** (1530–1569) eine Behausung abzugeben.

Die Verdammten werden in spätmittelalterlichen Darstellungen im Rachen eines riesigen Ungeheuers dargestellt, bisweilen ist es auch die Vorhölle, aus der sie von Christus befreit werden.

Das Verschlucken und Ausspeien nach einer angemessenen Aufenthaltsdauer kann, neben der Bedeutung von Tod und Auferstehung, auch als Metapher für die Befruchtung und die Geburt angesehen werden.

Die Analogie zwischen einer schwangeren Frau und einer Stadtstruktur taucht im indischen Kulturkreis einige Male auf. Häufig sind die Figuren Muttergottheiten, so etwa jene für die Stadt **Suchindram** in Südindien: »Die weibliche Stadtgottheit, repräsentiert durch vier Tempel in den Himmelsrichtungen, geht mit dem männlichen Shiva-Tempel im Zentrum schwanger.« (Pieper, 1987)

251. Adolf Krischanitz, Kunsthalle am Karlsplatz, Wien, 1992.
252. Walter Michael Pühringer, *Grenzflieger*, Schule Koppstraße, Wien, 1995.
253. Rob Krier, Wohnhaus bei Stuttgart, 1968–1973.
254. Oswald Mathias Ungers, Messetor, Frankfurt am Main, 1983/1984.
255. Boris Podrecca, Bankfiliale in Wien-Josefstadt, 1991–1993.
256. Heinz Tesar, Prähistorisches Museum, München, 1990.

251. Adolf Krischanitz, Kunsthalle am Karlsplatz, Vienna, 1992.
252. Walter Michael Pühringer, *Border Pilot*, Schule Koppstraße, Vienna, 1995.
253. Rob Krier, residential building near Stuttgart, 1968–1973.
254. Oswald Mathias Ungers, Messetor, Frankfurt am Main, 1983/194.
255. Boris Podrecca, bank branch in Josefstadt, Vienna, 1991–1993.
256. Heinz Tesar, Prähistorisches Museum, Munich, 1990.

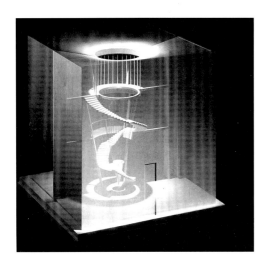

The Kunsthalle am Karlsplatz in Vienna was opened as a temporary building in 1992. **Adolf Krischanitz** put up a simple steel structure like a container. The plain structure gains attractive tension from powerful penetration by a huge, high-set tube that visitors reach via a flight of steps, and thus can walk through the hall.

For **Walter Michael Pühringer** the theme of penetration is central problem in the dialectic of building and sculpture. Pühringer responds to the usual unrelated juxtaposition of architecture and sculpture with the greatest possible degree of linkage: penetration, drilling through, breaking through, including sculptural sections in the building. This reveal the remarkable ambivalence of every penetration, which can be just as much an aggressive breaking through as a loving union. Pühringer has his *Grenzflieger* (*Border pilot*) crash in a secondary school in Ottakring, a suburb of Vienna. He lands in the hall, but half the work juts symbolically into the square.

Two other contemporary examples can be seen as something that is in fact the start of a penetration: **Rob Krier** (born 1938) makes the entrance slit of a residential building in ready to take a column-like building »element«. **Boris Podrecca** (born 1940) quotes two androgynous thoughts in a motif in a bank in the Vienna suburb of Josefstadt. The upward-thrusting double column is reminiscent of the one in St. Stephan and the one by Hans Hollein in the Feigen Gallery, but Podrecca's columns have kept their distance. The actual erotic-androgynous process lies in the fact that the columns thrust through the ceiling in a sovereign fashion through a circular opening. This suggests an association with the Indian temple columns that have been mentioned.

Oswald Mathias Ungers (born 1926) is building a massive penetration. The monumental gateway on the Frankfurt Trade Fair site (1983/1984) is concluded at the top in a deep gorge. But from above a dark pole thrusts into the gap and seems to penetrate the body.

Identity and simultaneous divergence of inside and outside make **Heinz Tesar's** design for the prehistoric museum in Munich (1990) into androgynous architecture. The remarkable feature of this is that it is not a female feature including a male one, as in previous examples, but vice versa. If we interpret the sharp-edged cube of the outer body as a rationally male element, then the vaginal shaft, characterized by a gently curving spiral staircase, that thrusts its way in is to be interpreted as a reciprocally penetrating female element.

9.3. Third Synthesis: One Inside the Other

9.3.1. Being in a Being

When the penetration described in the previous chapter has taken place, then one element is inside the other: the arrow sits in the heart of the person inflamed with love – or in the heart of the enemy, the Indian column is in heaven, Coop Himmelblau's poles are in the space, in the building.

The biological analogy is plausible: the penis has broken through the hymen, has penetrated the vagina, is surrounded by a »space«, indeed more: Sandor Ferenczi (1924) even works on the hypothesis that coitus is the man's attempt to return to the womb.

If we keep an eye on the Freudian thesis that suggests that in dream symbolism the human figure is to be seen as a sexual symbol in general, and particularly as a masculine one, and if going through a door into a building, as double coding, as it were, means the sexual act as well as return to the womb, then the corresponding analogy with architecture seems entirely plausible.

Man's fundamental need for protection manifests itself in a number of phenomena, not least in architecture. »Being inside« a building, a room, a hollow, a body obviously stands for the kind of security that we have »experienced« in our prenatal existence.

According to this the (living) being in a living being has a primordial model for which we persistently long: the **embryo in the mother's womb**. All the rest of the illustrations in this chapter can be interpreted according to this point of view.

In the mythological sphere it is not unusual to come across the image of human beings giving birth to animals and animals bringing human beings into the world. The idea of man existing in an animal is part of the stock of myth, legend and fairy-tale.

The theme of a human being within an animal is famously formulated in the Biblical tale of Jonah, who spent three days in the belly of a whale, in analogy with the death of Christ.

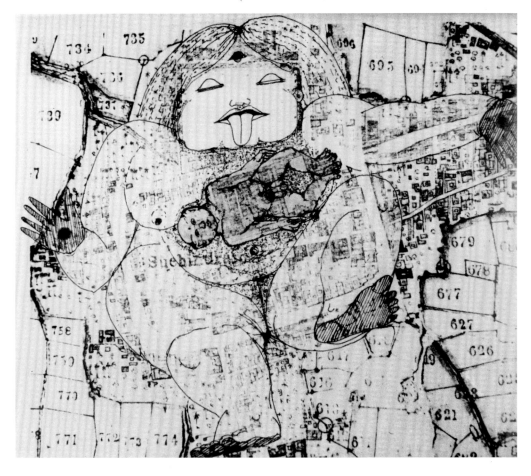

Über die Städte hinaus wird die ganze Welt, ja der gesamte Kosmos als menschliche Figur gedeutet, die Kosmogonien beschreiben die Entstehung der Welt als anthropomorphe Prozesse, oft mit ungewöhnlichen sexuellen Vorgängen.

Das Thema »Wesen im Wesen« begegnet uns in der christlichen Ikonographie in einer seltenen Interpretation der Schutzmantelmadonna.

Eine Holzfigur, die Darstellung der Heiligen Maria läßt sich wie ein Schrein öffnen, und wir sehen, geborgen unter dem Schutzmantel, aber eigentlich schon im Leibe der Jungfrau, die Schutzbefohlenen, manchmal sogar die Darstellung eines Gnadenstuhles mit Gott Vater und dem Gekreuzigten. Die **Vièrge ouvrante**, die öffenbare Jungfrau, ist also mehr als die mit dem Mantel beschützende: Die Schutzbefohlenen, selbst Gott Vater und Christus, sind in ihren Leib eingezogen.

Im christlichen Bereich bedarf es bisweilen spekulativer Deutungen, um das Thema »Wesen im Wesen« aufzuzeigen. Pieper (1987) deutet mit Recht die Wallfahrtskirche von Notre Dame de Puy in Frankreich als anthropomorphe Architektur, wobei nicht zu übersehen ist, daß die Muttergottes die archaischen Muttergottheiten zu ersetzen hatte, ihre jungfräuliche Empfängnis ist ein uralter mythischer Topos. Bedingt durch die Hanglage und die Kirchenerweiterung folgt der Pilger einem überraschenden Weg: »Man betritt unsere liebe Frau von Puy durch den Bauch-Nabel und man verläßt sie durch die Ohren«, wie es im Kirchenführer – und bei den Jakobspilgern – heißt. Das ist sicherlich eine Abschwächung gegenüber dem freudianischen Eintreten in die Architektur durch die Vulva, trotzdem ist die »Interpretation des Kirchenbaues als Leib und Schoß der Muttergottes« gerechtfertigt. (Pieper, 1987)

Die im Kapitel 7.5 zitierten **begehbaren Frauen** von den Mutterhöhlen Maltas bis zu Niki de Saint Phalles »Hon« erfahren ihren Sinn erst durch das Betreten, und wir selbst werden tatsächlich zu den »Wesen im Wesen«, wenn wir in den gebauten Körper eintreten.[55]

Nicht nur der ganze Körper, sondern auch der Kopf des Menschen ist bevölkert, bewohnt. In der *Versuchung des Heiligen Antonius* (1556) von **Pieter Bruegel d. Ä.** ist ein schrecklicher Kopf, groß wie ein Haus, im Wasser liegend, von allerlei Menschen okkupiert, die ihr wildes Unwesen treiben und scheinbar vergebens Schutz und Geborgenheit erwarten.

In einer Zeichnung für einen *Liebesgarten* von **Johann Wilhelm Baur** (1607–1642) von 1630 wird ein Kopf mit Hut zu einem riesigen Rundbau, von allerlei munterem Volk umgeben.

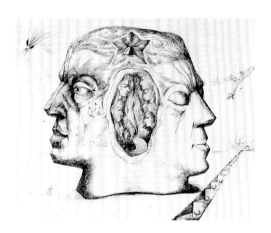

Münchhausen experiences something similar when his ship is swallowed by a sea monster and liberated only by a series of inventive tricks.

In the fairy-tale of Little Red Riding Hood the grandmother spends time in the belly of the wolf before she is freed by the huntsman.

A gigantic fish, probably dead, appears to be offering accommodation in the *Temptation of St. Anthony* (1556) by **Pieter Bruegel the Elder** (1530–1569).

In late-medieval depictions the damned are shown in the maw of a gigantic monster; sometimes this is also Purgatory, from which they are freed by Christ.

Being swallowed and then spat out again after an appropriate period can also be seen as a metaphor for death and resurrection, and also as a metaphor of fertilization and birth.

The analogy between a pregnant woman and the structure of a town occurs several times in Indian culture. Frequently the figures are mother-goddesses, like for example the one for the city of **Suchindram** in Southern India: »The female goddess of the city, represented by four temples on the points of the compass, is pregnant with the male Shiva temple in the centre.« (Pieper, 1987)

Beyond the cities the entire world, indeed the whole cosmos is interpreted as a human figure, and the cosmogonies describe the emergence of the world as an anthropomorphic process, often with unusual sexual occurrences.

We find the »being in a being« theme in Christian iconography in a rare interpretation of the Madonna of the Misericordia.

A wooden figure, representing the Virgin Mary, can be opened like a shrine and we see, hidden under a protective mantle, but actually already within the body of the Virgin, her charges, sometimes even a depiction of a throne of grace with God the Father and Christ Crucified. The **Vièrge ouvrante**, the opening Virgin, is thus more than the Virgin protecting with a mantle: the charges, even God the Father and Christ, are drawn into her body.

In the Christian world it is occasionally necessary to use speculative interpretations to establish the »being in a being« theme. Pieper (1987) rightly sees the Notre Dame de Puy pilgrimage church in France as anthropomorphic architecture, but we must not overlook the fact that the Mother of God had to replace the archaic mother goddesses; her virgin conception is an ancient mythical topos. Pilgrims are constrained by the sloping site and the church extension to follow a surprising path: »One enters Our Lady of Puy through the navel and leaves her through the ears«, as it is put in the guide to the church – and by the Santiago pilgrims. This is certainly weaker than the Freudian architectural notion of entering by the vulva, but nevertheless the »interpretation of the church building as the body and womb of the Mother of God« is justified. (Pieper, 1987)

The **women who can be entered** mentioned in chapter 7.5, from the maternal caves of Malta to Niki de Saint Phalle's »Hon« become meaningful only when they are walked on, and we ourselves actually become »beings in a being« when we enter the built body.[52]

Not just the whole body, but the head of the human being as well is populated, lived in. In **Pieter Bruegel the Elder's** *Temptation of St. Anthony* (1556) a terrible head, as large as a house, lying in the water, is occupied by all sorts of people behaving in a wild fashion and apparently waiting in vain for protection and seclusion.

In a drawing for a garden of love by **Johann Wilhelm Baur** (1607–1642) dating from 1630 a head with a hat becomes a gigantic rotunda, surrounded by all sorts of happy people.

André Masson, moved by the events of the war, drew a portrait of André Breton as a Janus head in 1941. »With open and closed eyes, Breton perceives war and peace as an ambivalent conflict between death and Eros. This possible allusion by Masson to the contemporary situation leads to a double function for the seeing person, who successfully achieves a coincidentia oppositorum. Inside his head, which opens up like a gigantic auricle, the conscious male side meets the unconscious female one. Both are divided by a ›vulva-shaped flame‹ ...« (Lachnitz, 1987)

Promenade heads were in fact realized very impressively in the fantastic garden, Bomarzo's Sacro Bosco. The grotesque stone garden pavilion (1551), inside which one can sit around a stone table, is attributed to **Pirro Ligorio** (1510–1583). When the candles are lit for the evening banquet, then the open maw and the eyes glow in the eerie light.

Arnaldo Pomodoro (b. 1926) bursts open the most perfect shape, the sphere, torn apart by an inner explosion or by a second sphere, also broken open. The sculpture stands in the pine courtyard of the Vatican, conveying perfection and vulnerability, security and breaking apart simultaneously: the »being in the being« theme is made abstract and idealized.

André **Masson** zeichnet 1941, beeindruckt vom Kriegsgeschehen, ein Porträt André Bretons als Januskopf. »Offenen und geschlossenen Auges nimmt Breton Krieg und Frieden als Ambivalenzkonflikt von Tod und Eros wahr. Diese mögliche Anspielung Massons auf die Zeitsituation mündet in die Doppelfunktion des Sehers, dem die coincidentia oppositorum gelingt. Im Innern seines Kopfes, der sich gleich einer riesigen Ohrmuschel öffnet, trifft die bewußte männliche auf die unbewußte weibliche Seite. Beide trennt ›a vulva-shaped flame‹ ...« (Lachnitz, 1987)

Begehbare Köpfe wurden tatsächlich realisiert, sehr eindrucksvoll im phantastischen Garten, im Sacro Bosco von Bomarzo. Dem **Pirro Ligorio** (1510–83) wird der fratzenhafte, steinerne Gartenpavillon (1551) zugeschrieben, in dessen Innerem man sich um einen Steintisch setzen kann. Werden die Kerzen zum abendlichen Gelage entzündet, dann glühen der offene Rachen und die Augen in unheimlichem Lichte.

Arnaldo Pomodoro (geb. 1926) sprengt die vollkommenste Form, die Kugel, auf, gleichsam zerrissen von einer inneren Explosion oder von einer zweiten, ihrerseits wieder aufgebrochenen Kugel. Im Pinienhof des Vatikans steht die Skulptur, die Vollkommenheit und Verletzbarkeit, Geborgenheit und Aufbrechen gleichzeitig mitteilt: Das Thema »Wesen im Wesen« ist abstrahiert und idealisiert.

9.3.2. Wesen im Haus

Im vorigen Kapitel wurde schon deutlich, daß das »Seiende«, das »Wesen« uns auch in der Metapher des Gebäudes, des Hauses entgegentritt, daß die menschliche Figur und das Bauwerk in ihrer Symbolträchtigkeit austauschbar sind.

»Alles Umfassende, Große, das ein Kleines enthält, umgibt, birgt, schützt, erhält und nährt gehört zum mütterlichen Bezirk« (Neumann, 1949).

Im sakralen und kultischen Bereich wird das »Wesen« von bedeutender, verehrungswürdiger, heiliger Art sein, eine Kostbarkeit, die für das Göttliche oder Heilige steht, oder das Göttliche selbst oder dessen Rudimente werden im Haus aufbewahrt.

Die Cella, der **Schrein**, das Sanktuarium gehören zu den architektonischen Typen, die für die Aufnahme bedeutsamer Wesenheiten geeignet erscheinen. Als bevorzugte Figur im schützenden Gehäuse treffen wir immer wieder die Standbilder von Göttern oder vergöttlichten Wesen oder stellvertretend Teile oder Repräsentanten des Göttlichen an.

Von besonderem Interesse sind dominante, raumbeherrschende, oft raumfüllende (Kolossal-)Figuren. Die kleine Zella des griechischen Tempels wird, weit über die optimale Rezeptionsmöglichkeit hinaus, von einem mächtigen Götterbild beherrscht.

260. Pieter Bruegel d. Ä., *Die Versuchung des heiligen Antonius*, 1556.
261. Arnaldo Pomodoro, *Kugel in der Kugel*, Vatikan, Rom, 1986.
262. Papanatha-Tempel mit Gharbagriha, Pattadakal, Südindien, um 750.
263. Nandi in einem Tempel in Khajuraho, Indien, 11. Jh.

260. Pieter Bruegel d. Ä., *The Temptation of St. Anthony*, 1556.
261. Arnaldo Pomodoro, *Sphere in the Sphere*, Vatican, Rome, 1986.
262. Temple of Papanatha with gharbagriha, Pattadakal, South India, ca. 750.
263. Nandi in a templel in Khajuraho, India, 11th cent.

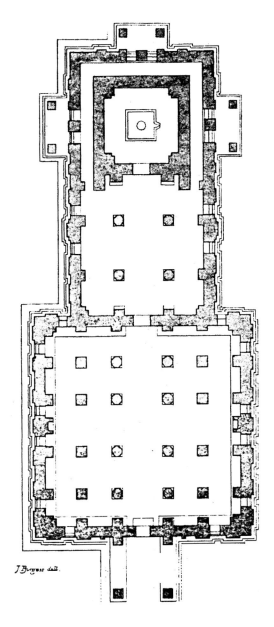

J. Burgess del.

9.3.2. Being in a House, or Building

In the previous chapter it became clear that we also come across the »being« in the metaphor of the building, the house, and that the human figure and the building are interchangeable in their symbolic quality.

»Everything that embraces and is large, and that contains, surrounds, conceals, protects, sustains and feeds something small is part of the maternal sphere.« (Neumann, 1949)

In the ecclesiastical and cultic sphere the »being«, will be of a significant, venerable, sacred nature, a precious object that stands for the divine or sacred, or the divine object itself or its rudiments are kept in the building.

The cella, the **shrine**, the sanctuary are among the architectural types that seem appropriate to accommodate significant beings. We constantly find statues of gods or deified beings, or representative parts or beings standing in for the divine presence as preferred figures in the sacred building.

Dominant figures, controlling or often filling the space (colossal figures) are particularly interesting. The small cella in the Greek temple is dominated by a powerful image of the god, well beyond the possibility for reaction.

Quantitative increases in Buddha statues are of central significance throughout the cultural sphere of **Buddhism**. They are either accumulations of Buddhas (or Bodhisattwas), representations of the »thousand Buddhas« or gigantic increases in scale. Recumbent, seated or standing Buddhas then fill the entire temple or shrine, one is intended to be overwhelmed by the size, and there is no optical distance from which one can take in the figure as a whole. Colossal figures of this kind are found in southern India, Japan, Burma and other countries. (Pieper, 1987)

The **Hindu religion** has developed very attractive shrine types. In southern India, the bull Nandi, representing the power of Shiva, is usually found filling most of a temple section. Juxtaposed with this in the Indian religion, representing the essential being, the divine, Shiva and his powers of reproduction, is the linga, the phallic pole. In southern India it is enclosed, wrapped up, protected in a cell that is often surprisingly small, the gharbagriha. This small room in fact signifies the original cell, the womb, the uterus. Accordingly it is a geometrical abstraction of the principle of being in the being, or of being in the house, in an enclosure, a shrine.

Indian travelling altars are furnished with an interesting system of little doors, featuring a huge number of painted religious scenes. After opening the last door the actual image of the god is reached.

This idea of the shrine, accommodating the sacred being himself or his representative, is a fixed component of cultic practice in numerous regions. The idea of keeping something precious, shutting away and protecting, mysterious concealment are the basic motifs.

In the Christian and particularly the Catholic sphere the **tabernacle** is a fixed component of every church. The host, the small piece of white bread that is identical with the body of Christ and needs protection, represents the divine being, but really and not symbolically. The medieval house of the sacrament is in fact a lavish architecture derived from the art of the cathedral, and it guards the host, separately from the altar. In later development the tabernacle moves on to the altar table or is placed above it, but it retains the character of a little house and has a small closed door. Christ »lives« in this shrine.

Walter Pichler's work illustrates the topicality of the »shrine« in the present day. In 1976 he made a case for a crucifix wrapped in bandages. This is directly linked with the idea of the Christian tabernacle, but there is also an unmistakable analogy with Indian travelling altars. The shrine can be completely opened up and then forms a *Großes Kreuz (Large Cross)*. Pichler builds cases for his figures, in other words for beings that represent man. The *Mobile Figure* (1981) has found its place in the attic of the glass house.[53]

These examples are intended to show that the thing housed and the housing become an indivisible unit, similar to the woman and the embryo.

Are we allowed to speak of androgynous unity, when the embryo can also be male by nature?

We should point out once more that expanded androgyny points beyond the sexual and represents the fundamental synthesis of opposites, however they manifest themselves.

Thus the unity of protector and protected can represent a further aspect of protector and protected.

Im gesamten Kulturbereich des **Buddhismus** haben die quantitativen Steigerungen der Buddhastatuen zentrale Bedeutung. Es sind entweder Additionen von Buddhas (oder Bodhisattwas), die Darstellungen der »tausend Buddhas«, oder gigantische Maßstabsvergrößerungen. Liegende, sitzende oder stehende Buddhas füllen dann den gesamten Tempel oder Schrein aus, man soll überwältigt sein von der Größe, und es gibt keine Augdistanz, von der aus man die gesamte Gestalt erfassen kann. In Südindien, Japan, Burma und anderen Ländern finden wir derartige Kollossalfiguren. (Pieper, 1987)

Die **hinduistische Religion** hat sehr schöne Schreintypen ausgebildet. Der Stier Nandi, die Kraft Shivas repräsentierend, liegt in Südindien meist raumfüllend in einem Tempelteil. Ihm gegenübergestellt, stellvertretend für das wesenhaft Seiende, für das Göttliche, für Shiva und dessen Zeugungskraft steht in der indischen Religion der Linga, der phallische Pfahl. Er ist umschlossen, eingehüllt, behütet in einer im südindischen Bereich oft überraschend kleinen Zelle, in der Gharbagriha. Dieser kleine Raum hat tatsächlich die Bedeutung der Ursprungszelle, des Mutterschoßes, des Uterus. Sonach handelt es sich gleichsam um eine geometrische Abstraktion des Prinzipes Seiendes im Seienden, bzw. Seiendes im Haus, im Gehäuse, im Schrein.

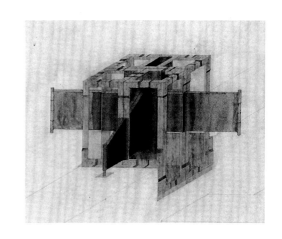

Die indischen Reisealtäre sind mit einem interessanten System von Türchen ausgestattet, die eine Unzahl von gemalten religiösen Szenen aufnehmen. Nach dem Öffnen des letzten Türchens gelangt man zum eigentlichen Götterbild.

Diese Idee des Schreins, der das Heilige selbst oder dessen Darstellung aufnimmt, gehört in zahlreichen Religionen zum fixen Bestandteil des kultischen Gebrauches. Die Idee des Aufbewahrens einer Kostbarkeit, das bergende Verschließen, das geheimnisvolle Verstecken sind die Grundmotive.

Im christlichen und insbesonders im katholischen Bereich zählt der **Tabernakel** zum fixen Bestandteil jeder Kirche. Stellvertretend für das göttliche Wesen, aber dieses realiter und nicht nur symbolisch repräsentierend, steht die Hostie, das kleine Weißbrot, das mit dem Corpus Christi identisch ist und des Schutzes bedarf. Das mittelalterliche Sakramentshaus ist tatsächlich eine reiche Architektur, aus der Kunst der Kathedrale abgeleitet, und es behütet, vom Altar getrennt, die Hostie. In der späteren Entwicklung rückt der Tabernakel auf die Mensa des Altares oder wird darüber angeordnet, behält aber den Charakter des Häuschens und ist mit einem verschlossenen Türchen ausgestattet. Christus »wohnt« in diesem Schrein.

Die Aktualität der Idee eines »Schreins« in unserer Gegenwart kann am Werke **Walter Pichlers** verdeutlicht werden. In unmittelbarem Anschluß an die Idee des christlichen Tabernakels, aber auch in nicht zu übersehender Analogie zu den indischen Reisealtärchen, entsteht 1976 ein Gehäuse für ein Kruzifix, das mit Binden umwickelt ist. Der Schrein kann weit geöffnet werden und bildet dann ein *Großes Kreuz*. Pichler baut Gehäuse für seine Figuren, für We-

264. Walter Pichler, *Bewegliche Figur*, 1981.
265. Walter Pichler, *Großes Kreuz*, 1976.
266. Stupa in einem Tempel in Karli, Indien.
267. Gian Lorenzo Bernini, Baldacchino, St. Peter, Rom, 1623–1633.

264. Walter Pichler, *Mobile Figure*, 1981
265. Walter Pichler, *Large Cross*, 1976.
266. Stupa in a temple in Karli, India.
267. Gian Lorenzo Bernini, Baldacchino, St. Peter, Rome, 1623–1633.

9.3.3. Object in a Building, Building in a Building, Building in a Courtyard

Phallic representation of Shiva in the linga becomes an object in its abstraction and can be interpreted architecturally as a column or truncated column. We come across a series of other objects in architecture, objects that effectively need to be wrapped and protected, that are buildings in a larger space. Columns or piers, steles, tombstones, altars and shrines look for protection inside a building. They are always objects that are particularly precious, dignified or sacred.

The housings usually also accommodate one or more adoring persons.

A clear link between the principle of »object in a building« and »building in a building« are India's **Buddhist cave temples**. A nave-like space, reminiscent of occidental types, almost of cathedrals, is hewn subtractively out of the rock. But despite the structural »imitation« of piers and ribs the space remains a cave in the rocks, and the massive quality of the mountain massif is present.

The maternal cave accommodates the free-standing stupa, a modification of the sacred mountain. The stupa is often furnished with Buddha figures, in other words with male accents, so that the religious classification becomes even clearer. If we think of the massive dimensions of the open-air stupa, they are probably also to be addressed as buildings.

In the case of pagodas in **Chinese cave temples**, which are also monolithic, the transition to architecture, and thus to the »building in a building« becomes even clearer. The cave temple of Yün-Kang, Shensi has a massive column in the centre that simultaneously represents a building in its five-fold terracing. The surfaces are lavishly decorated with Buddha reliefs.

In the Christian church the concept of the tabernacle, as presented in the previous chapter, is extended in scale, so that architecture actually is produced. The baldacchino-like **ciborium** is found even in the early Christian basilica, and it undoubtedly represents an analogy with Roman and Byzantine representative signs, similar to conches. In further development ciboria become monumental architectural structures.

Gian Lorenzo Bernini's tabernacle in St. Peter's in Rome is one of the most outstanding examples. It is more a baldacchino than a building, and undeniably draws on textile art.

There are may reasons for »building in a building« architecture, often memorial in character, and often identifying a significant place, which is furnished with a monument, usually a small building or chapel, and then built around subsequently. Where it was not possible to create a building in this way, the chapels and small buildings carry a memory of the original chapels into the new monumental building.

The most significant example of a »building in a building« is the **Porziuncola chapel** in the church of Santa Maria degli Angeli near Assisi. This tiny chapel was built by St. Francis as the centre of his first small religious community. It is a simple unit room built of undressed stone with a saddleback roof, a round-arched gate and a ridge turret, a plain and touching space in the spirit of the saint. But the chapel soon became too small for the crowds of pilgrims. In the Baroque period a massive, dramatic church was built over it, with a magnificent façade and dominant dome to proclaim extroversion from then on.

The magnificent centralized building of **Santa Maria della Consolazione** in Todi, probably wrongly attributed to Bramante, originally housed an utterly austere chapel of grace, probably very similar in character to the Porziuncola in Assisi. (Pieper, 1989)

We find a great deal of material for the building in a building in Baroque architecture, where the ciborium acquires a shrine-like closed quality. The increase in pilgrimages to places of grace, which were originally marked only by a chapel, encouraged the magnificent decoration of the **primordial chapels**, which then has lavish basilicas built over them.

The character of a protecting building emerges clearly in the lavishly decorated chapel in the **basilica of Mariazell** in the Steiermark. A magnificent edifice, lavishly decorated with gold and silver emblems, stands in the centre of the church, with space around it on all sides, as processions require. It has all the architectural characteristics of a building and goes well beyond the baldacchino type.

This procedure of subsequently **building over** an important topos goes back to ancient times and is found repeatedly in Christendom. The **tomb of Christ** in Jerusalem, originally free-standing, first had a small chapel built over it, standing in an arcaded courtyard. The imposing Church of the Holy Sepulchre was then built over it. Numerous sepulchre churches and chapels in the West have been furnished with a copy of the Church of the Holy Sepulchre from the outset.

sen also, die den Menschen repräsentieren. Ein Torso sitzt hieratisch in einem hellen, weißen Raum. Die *Bewegliche Figur* von 1981 hat ihren Platz im Dachboden des Glashauses gefunden.[56]

Die Beispiele sollten zeigen, daß das Behauste und das Gehäuse zu einer untrennbaren Einheit werden, ähnlich wie die Frau und das Embryo.

Können wir von androgyner Einheit sprechen, wo das Embryo doch auch männlicher Natur sein kann?

Einmal mehr soll darauf verwiesen werden, daß eine gleichsam expandierte Androgynie über das Geschlechtliche weit hinaus weist und die grundsätzliche Synthese der Oppositorien darstellt, wie auch immer sie sich manifestieren.

So kann die Einheit des Schützenden und Beschützten einen weiteren Aspekt einer coincidentia darstellen.

9.3.3. Objekt im Haus, Haus im Haus, Haus im Hof

Die phallische Repräsentation Shivas im Linga gerät in ihrer Abstraktion zu einem Objekt und kann architektonisch als Säule oder Säulenstumpf interpretiert werden. Eine Reihe von anderen Objekten begegnet uns in der Architektur, Objekte, die gleichsam der Umhüllung, des Schutzes bedürfen, die behaust sind in einem größeren Raum. Säulen oder Pfeiler, Stelen, Grabmäler, Altäre, Heiligtümer suchen Schutz in einem Gebäude. Immer sind es Objekte von besonderer Kostbarkeit, Würde oder Heiligkeit.

Die umhüllenden Gehäuse nehmen zumeist auch eine oder mehrere adorierende Personen auf.

Ein deutliches Bindeglied zwischen dem Prinzip »Objekt im Haus« und »Haus im Haus« stellen die **buddhistischen Höhlentempel** Indiens dar. Ein Langhausraum, der an abendländische Typen, fast an Kathedralen erinnert, ist substraktiv aus dem Felsgestein herausgehauen. Trotz der strukturellen »Imitationen« von Pfeilern und Rippen bleibt der Raum jedoch Felsenhöhle, und die Mächtigkeit des Bergmassives ist präsent.

Die mütterliche Höhle nimmt den freistehenden Stupa auf, eine Modifikation des heiligen Berges. Der Stupa wird häufig mit Buddha-Figuren, also mit männlichen Akzentuierungen, ausgestattet, so daß die quasi sakrale Zuordnung noch deutlicher wird. Bedenken wir die mächtigen Dimensionen des Stupas im Freien, so sind sie wohl auch als Bauwerke anzusprechen.

Bei den ebenfalls monolithischen Pagoden in den **chinesischen Höhlentempeln** wird der Übergang zur Architektur und damit zum »Haus im Haus« noch deutlicher. Der Höhlentempel von Yün-Kang, Shensi, weist im Zentrum eine mächtige Säule auf, die in ihrer fünffachen Abstufung gleichzeitig ein Bauwerk repräsentiert. Die Flächen sind reichlich mit Buddha-Reliefs ausgestattet.

In der christlichen Kirche wird der Begriff des Tabernakels, wie er im vorstehenden Kapitel dargestellt wurde, in der Dimension erweitert, so daß tatsächlich eine Architektur entsteht. Das baldachinartige **Ziborium** finden wir bereits in der frühchristlichen Basilika, und es stellt zweifellos eine Analogie zu den römischen und byzantinischen Repräsentationszeichen dar, ähnlich den Konchen. In der weiteren Entwicklung werden die Ziborien zu monumentalen, architektonischen Gebilden gestaltet.

Gian Lorenzo Berninis Tabernakel im Dom zu St. Peter in Rom zählt zu den prominentesten Beispielen. Mehr Baldachin als Haus, kann es die vielfältigen Anregungen aus der textilen Kunst nicht verleugnen.

Die Anlässe zu einer »Haus im Haus«-Architektur sind mannigfaltig, meist haben sie memorialen Charakter, oft sind sie Auszeichnung eines bedeutsamen Ortes, der mit einem Mal, meist mit einem Häuschen oder mit einer Kapelle ausgestattet ist, und dann sekundär umbaut wurde. Sofern ein solches **Einhausen** nicht möglich war, tragen die Kapellen und Häuschen die Erinnerung an die Ursprungskapellen in den neuen Monumentalbau hinein.

Das bedeutendste Beispiel für ein »Haus im Haus« ist die **Porztiuncola-Kapelle** in der Kirche Santa Maria degli Angeli bei Assisi. Die winzige Kapelle wurde vom heiligen Franziskus als Zentrum seiner ersten kleinen Glaubensgemeinschaft erbaut, ein einfacher Einheitsraum aus Bruchsteinen mit einem Satteldach, einem Rundbogentor und einem Dachreiter, ein schlichter berührender Raum im Geiste des Heiligen. Aber für die Heerscharen an Pilgern war die Kapelle bald zu klein geworden. Sie wurde in der Barockzeit von einer gewaltigen, pathetischen

The notion of the sepulchre or Jerusalem church has also been realized in many different ways in Europe: the Holy Sepulchre was assimilated into the traditional church structure. Probably the most important »copy« of the Holy Sepulchre is in the Capella Rucellai near San Pancrazio in Florence. It was designed by **Leon Battista Alberti** (1404–1472).

Pieper (1987) records that this is not precisely imitative architecture, although Alberti knew exactly what the sepulchre chapel looked like. It is probably enough to take over just some characteristics of the model to guarantee iconic quality.

We find over a hundred sepulchre churches of this kind in Europe. They show a remarkable breadth of formal interpretation and make the point that precise copying is by no means a condition for worship.

The **Mauritiusrotunde** of the Liebfrauenmünster in Konstanz is a significant example of the »building in a building«. A dodecagonal Gothic pavilion with clear oriental reminiscences was built in a rib-vaulted rotunda by the Minster between 1250 and 1300. A »copy« of the Holy Sepulchre (no longer there today) was installed in this pavilion, probably filigree, open-work sarcophagus architecture. (Pieper, 1987)

Strongly reduced elements of the Holy Sepulchre are also found in almost every Catholic church at Easter. They also acquire liturgical significance in the »entombment« on Good Friday.

Pieper (1987) describes this »building in a building« principle in his study of the churches of Jerusalem, but extends the comparison to other buildings, suggesting: »The **rotunda**, pregnant with the aedicule, corresponds with one of the most fundamental gestures in the natural world, where it occurs in many hundreds of variants, from the pearl in the oyster to the vein of ore in the bedrock.«

Pieper uses a number of examples to demonstrate this »pregnant« architecture. For example, on the **Sacro Monte** in Varallo an octagonal pavilion with a pyramid roof is placed inside a small domed space, and in another building on the Sacro Monte there is an Ascension Chapel in the rotunda whose obelisk soars into the lantern of the rotunda, another example of »penetration« as described in chapter 9.2. These two buildings are particularly interesting because the inserted pavilions take up a great deal of space, and thus underline the unity of the exterior and interior of the building. There is room to walk round the pavilion, but in a sense one is walking between two shells of an identical structure, which makes the definition of a »pregnant« building understandable.

An interesting occasion for the »building in a building« in the Christian sphere is the **Loreto motif**. The **Casa santa** is to be found in this Italian town, the sacred house in Nazareth in which the Holy Family lived. According to legend it was borne by angels to Loreto in Italy on 7 September 1295 and since then (demonstrably since the 15th century) it has been a goal for numerous Virgin pilgrimages down to the present day. A basilica was built over the Casa santa from 1468, the significance of the place increased rapidly and Loreto was made a bishopric under Pope Sixtus V in 1584.

The Casa santa was much imitated, particularly in the Baroque period, in Hergiswald in Switzerland, for example, or in Loretto in Burgenland.

The **sarcophagus**, man's last »house«, as it were, is also a secondary space, surrounded by the primary space of the church, the crypt, the mausoleum.

A sarcophagus is not enough for the solemn **funerals** of prominent personalities. In the same way that the tabernacle is completed and elevated in the ciborium, architecture, usually temporary, is set up for the funeral ceremony, especially in the pageantry-loving Baroque period.

For example, the prestigious structure set up for King John I. in about 1731 in the Church of St. Anthony in Portugal was in the form of a ciborium altar. The wooden architecture was furnished with festive fabric decorations, and the funeral structure was completed with figurative and decorative adornments. The *catafalque* set up for Carlo Barberini in a church in Ferrara was not quite so splendid, but much more compact and reminiscent of a chapel. Comparison with stupas in Indian cave complexes suggests itself.

The »building in a building« theme develops remarkably in the formal language of **Revolutionary Architecture**, and Classicism, which is close to it. **Étienne-Louis Boullée** designed a gigantic, pyramid-shaped tomb monument with a truncated top in the style of his megalomaniac designs. The monumental semicircular entrance arch accommodates a Doric temple with twelve columns.

The spectrum of architectural and spiritual interest is clearly expressed. The Greek temple has lost significance. It is completely subordinated to the mighty pyramid, which was far more suitable for Boullée's gigantic ideas. The temple is guarded and protected, assimilated.

Kirche überbaut, eine prunkvolle Fassade und dominante Kuppel künden von der nunmehrigen Extrovertiertheit.

Der großartige Zentralbau von **Santa Maria della Consolazione** in Todi, wohl fälschlich dem Bramante zugeschrieben, beherbergte ursprünglich eine überaus schlichte Gnadenkapelle, im Charakter wohl sehr ähnlich der Porziuncola von Assisi. (Pieper, 1989)

In der Barockarchitektur finden wir reichliches Material für das Haus im Haus, das Ziborium gewinnt eine schreinartige Geschlossenheit. Die Zunahme an Wallfahrten zu den Gnadenorten, die anfangs nur durch eine Kapelle markiert waren, fördert die prunkvollen Ausstattungen der **Ursprungskapellen** und deren Überbau durch großzügige Basiliken.

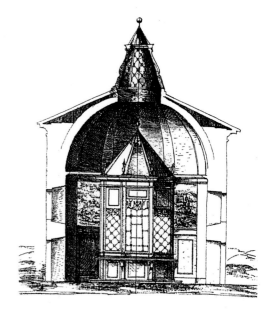

Der schützende Hauscharakter tritt deutlich hervor bei der reich ausgestatteten Kapelle in der **Basilika in Mariazell** in der Steiermark. Ein prunkvoller, mit Gold- und Silberemblemen reich ausgestatteter »Korpus« steht, allseitig umschreitbar, wie es die Prozessionen verlangen, im Zentrum der Kirche. Er trägt alle architektonischen Kennzeichen eines Gebäudes und geht weit über den Typus des Baldachins hinaus.

Dieser Vorgang des nachträglichen **Überbauens** eines bedeutsamen Topos geht schon auf die Antike zurück und findet sich wiederholt im Christentum. Das zunächst freistehende **Grab Christi** in Jerusalem wird zuerst mit einer kleinen Kapelle überbaut, die in einem Arkadenhof steht. Später wird der imposante Bau der Grabeskirche darübergestülpt. Die zahlreichen Grabeskirchen und -kapellen im Okzident stattet man gleich von Anfang an mit einer Nachbildung des Heiligen Grabes aus.

Die Idee der Grabeskirche, der Jerusalemkirche, hat auch in Europa zahlreiche Realisierungen erfahren: Das Heilige Grab in Jerusalem wurde dem traditionellen Kirchenbau einverleibt. Die wohl bedeutendste »Nachbildung« des Heiligen Grabes steht in der Capella Rucellai bei San Pancrazio in Florenz und wurde von **Leon Battista Alberti** (1404–1472) entworfen.

Pieper (1987) zeigt auf, daß es sich um keine präzise imitative Architektur handelt, obwohl das genaue Aussehen der Grabkapelle bekannt war. Es genügt wohl, nur einige Merkmale vom Vorbild zu übernehmen, um die Ikonizität zu gewährleisten.

Mehr als hundert solcher Grabeskirchen finden wir in Europa. Sie zeigen eine bemerkenswerte formale Interpretationsbreite und bekunden, daß eine naturgetreue Nachbildung keineswegs Bedingung für die Verehrung war.

Ein signifikantes Beispiel für das »Haus im Haus« stellt die **Mauritiusrotunde** des Liebfrauenmünsters in Konstanz dar. In einer kreuzrippengewölbten Rotunde wurde neben dem Münster zwischen 1250 und 1300 ein zwölfeckiger, gotischer Pavillon eingebaut, der deutlich orientalische Reminiszenzen aufweist. In diesen Pavillon wurde eine »Kopie« des Heiligen Grabes eingestellt (heute nicht mehr vorhanden), wohl eine filigrane, durchbrochene Sarkophagarchitektur. (Pieper, 1987)

Die stark reduzierten Elemente des Heiligen Grabes finden wir um die Osterzeit in fast jeder katholischen Kirche. Bei der »Grablegung« am Karfreitag erhalten sie auch liturgische Bedeutung.

Pieper (1987) beschreibt in seiner Studie über die Jerusalem-Kirchen dieses »Haus im Haus«-Prinzip, aber er dehnt den Vergleich auf andere Bauwerke aus und meint: »Die **Rotunde**, die mit der Ädikula schwanger geht, entspricht einer der elementarsten Gesten der natürlichen Welt, die dort in viel hundertfacher Abwandlung immer wieder begegnet, von der Perle in der Muschel bis zum Erzgang im Muttergestein.«

An einer Reihe von Beispielen demonstriert Pieper die gleichsam »schwangere« Architektur. Am **Sacro Monte** in Varallo etwa ist ein achteckiger Pavillon mit Zeltdach in einen kleinen Kuppelraum eingestellt, bei einem anderen Bau des Sacro Monte steht in der Rotunde eine Himmelfahrtskapelle, deren Obelisk in die Laterne der Rotunde hineinragt, ein weiteres Beispiel einer »Penetration«, wie sie im Kap. 9.2 dargestellt wurde. Die beiden Bauten sind deswegen von besonderen Interesse, weil die eingestellten Pavillons ziemlich raumfüllend sind und dadurch die Einheit von äußerem und innerem Haus unterstrichen wird. Es bleibt der Platz zum Umschreiten des Pavillons, aber man bewegt sich gleichsam zwischen zwei Schalen eines identischen Gebildes, so daß die Bezeichnung eines »schwangeren« Gebäudes verständlich ist.

Ein interessanter Anlaß für die »Haus im Haus«-Darstellung im christlichen Bereich ist das **Loreto-Motiv**. In dieser italienischen Stadt befindet sich die **Casa santa**, das heilige Haus von Nazareth, in dem die Heilige Familie gelebt hat. Der Legende nach wurde es am 7. September 1295 von Engeln nach Loreto in Italien getragen und bildet seither (nachweislich seit dem 15. Jahrhundert) das Ziel zahlreicher Marienwallfahrten bis in unsere Zeit. Die Casa Santa wurde

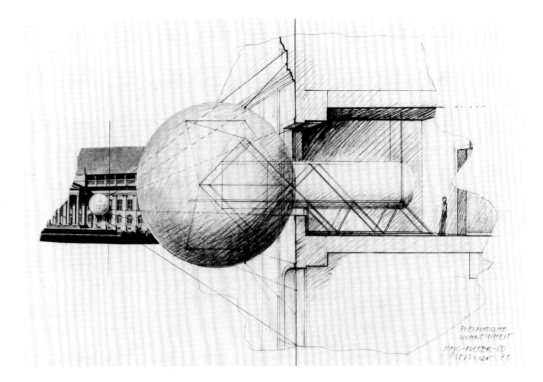

Peter Speeth (1772–1831) uses a similar motif much more modestly: the Doric temple accepts the protection of a simple pyramid (1810) or a semicircular arch (1807), which represents the façade of the building. Both buildings are intended as memorials to the dead.

If we see death as a return to prenatal existence, then it is possible to justify an intellectual connection with »gravid« architecture.

The protecting element can itself be a little house that now itself accommodates a shrine, a reliquary, a container. Here we are approaching the »Russian doll« principle, in which one body is inside yet another body, then another, and another.

The »building in a building« idea could expand according to the various dimensions, and we would have a hierarchical system of the various protective zones: the town protects the building and this again protects the dwelling, in the dwelling we find the room and in this the cupboard, the chest. They contain the casket, and in that is the box that finally hold the jewel.

The »building in a building« theme has acquired a new topicality in recent architectural development through the work of **Oswald Mathias Ungers** in particular. Ungers presented the theme very consistently in the Deutsches Architekturmuseum in Frankfurt (1979–1984). The inside of an old patrician house was removed and a new, very tightly articulated »house« placed inside it; it can be recognized by its steep gable roof, on the top floor, under the glass skylight.

The first prize for the competition for the President's Office in Berlin in 1994 was awarded to **Helmut Kleine-Kraneburg** (born 1961) and **Martin Gruber** (born 1963) *(Bauwelt*, 1994). The large courtyard of the elliptical building is by no means an airy open space, but a kind of »narthex«, a bar is placed in the courtyard. This leads to a second plane of interpretation: if we interpret the egg as a wrapping, protecting, perhaps uterine structure, then the phallic bar has penetrated as a »building in a building« and is at the same time an embryonic being with a protective covering. Comparison with Ledoux's *Oikema* suggests itself.

We could see a modification of the »building in a building« principle in the rare »building out of a building« that should be cited here, because effectively it represents a »birth process«. This interesting aspect is not found only in drawings by the **Haus-Rucker-Co**, but also presented in reality: a building »emanating« from another building. The first simple realization was the *Balloon for two* in Vienna, 1967.

A set of rods is run out of the window of a block of rented flats in a reciprocal penetration. They support a pneumatic structure that is gradually blown up, the birth of an architectural volume. The same motif, although more mature technically, crops up at documenta 5, 1972, in Kassel: *Oasis no. 7* effectively penetrates a window, an expansion of the volume, of the building in the form of a transparent sphere dominates the square. The possibility of an isolated and protected container as a new sphere of life is put up for discussion by the installation of a palm oasis.

ab 1468 mit einer Basilika überbaut, die Bedeutung des Ortes wuchs rasch und 1584 wurde unter Papst Sixtus V. zum Bischofssitz ernannt.

Die Casa Santa fand, vor allem in der Barockzeit, zahlreiche Nachahmungen, so etwa in Hergiswald in der Schweiz oder in Loretto im Burgenland.

Auch der **Sarkophag**, als gleichsam letzte »Behausung« des Menschen, ist ein Sekundärraum, der vom Primärraum der Kirche, der Krypta, des Mausoleums umschlossen wird.

Zu den festlichen **Funerarien** prominenter Persönlichkeiten begnügt man sich nicht mit dem Sarkophag allein. Ähnlich wie der Tabernakel eine Ergänzung und Überhöhung im Ziborium erfährt, wird, insbesondere in der Barockzeit mit ihrem Prunkbedürfnis, eine meist provisorische Architektur für die Totenfeier aufgestellt.

Der repräsentative Aufbau etwa, der für König Johann I. um 1731 in der St. Antoniuskirche in Portugal aufgestellt wurde, hat die Gestalt der Ziborienaltäre. Die hölzerne Architektur wird mit festlichen textilen Dekorationen ausgestattet, figurativer und dekorativer Schmuck ergänzen den Funeralbau. Nicht ganz so prunkvoll, dafür wesentlich kompakter und an eine Kapelle erinnernd, ist der *Katafalk* ausgebildet, der für Carlo Barberini 1630 in einer Kirche in Ferrara aufgestellt wurde. Der Vergleich mit den Stupas in den indischen Höhlenanlagen drängt sich auf.

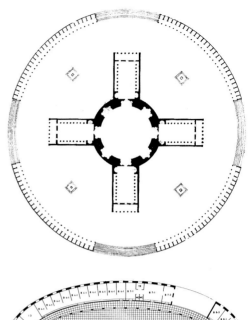

Eine überaus merkwürdige Ausformung erfährt das Thema »Gebäude im Gebäude« in der Formensprache der **Revolutionsarchitektur** und dem ihr nahestehenden **Klassizismus**. **Étienne-Louis Boullée** zeichnet in der Art seiner megalomanen Entwürfe ein riesiges, pyramidenförmiges Grabmonument mit gekappter Spitze. Der monumentale, halbrunde Eingangsbogen nimmt einen zwölfsäuligen dorischen Tempel auf.

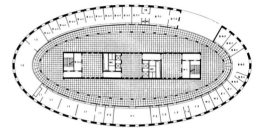

Das architektonische und geistige Interessenspektrum kommt deutlich zum Ausdruck. Der griechische Tempel hat an Bedeutung verloren, er ist völlig der mächtigen Pyramide untergeordnet, die den gigantischen Vorstellungen Boullées wesentlich adäquater war. Der Tempel wird gleichsam behütet, beschützt, einverleibt im direkten Wortsinne.

Wesentlich bescheidener gibt sich **Peter Speeth** (1772–1831) mit einem sehr ähnlichen Motiv: Der dorische Tempel begibt sich in den Schutz einer einfachen Pyramide (1810) oder eines halbkreisförmigen Bogens (1807), der die Front eines Gebäudes darstellt. Bei beiden Zeichnungen handelt es sich ebenfalls um die Darstellung von Totendenkmälern.

Wenn wir den Tod als eine Rückkehr in die prenatale Existenz ansehen, dann kann die gedankliche Verbindung zu einer gleichsam »graviden« Architektur ihre Berechtigung haben.

Das beschützende Element kann selbst wieder ein Häuschen sein, das nun seinerseits einen Schrein, ein Reliquiar, einen Behälter aufnimmt. Wir kommen gleichsam zum Prinzip der »russischen Puppe«, bei der im Körper noch ein Körper steckt, noch einer und noch einer.

Die Idee »Haus im Haus« könnte nach den verschiedenen Dimensionen expandieren, und wir bekämen gleichsam ein hierarchisches System der einzelnen Schutzzonen: Die Stadt schützt das Haus und dieses wieder die Wohnung, in der Wohnung finden wir das Zimmer und darin den Schrank, die Truhe. Sie bewahren die Schatulle auf, und darin liegt die Dose, die schließlich das Kleinod aufnimmt.

In der jüngsten Architekturentwicklung hat das Thema »Haus im Haus« vor allem durch **Oswald Mathias Ungers** eine ganz neue Aktualität erhalten. Sehr konsequent hat Ungers das Thema beim Deutschen Architekturmuseum in Frankfurt (1979–1984) vorgetragen. Ein altes Patrizierhaus wurde entkernt und ein neues, sehr straff artikuliertes »Haus« hineingestellt, das im obersten Geschoß, unter dem Glasoberlicht, sich mit seinem steilen Giebeldach zu erkennen gibt.

Der 1. Preis beim Wettbewerb für das Bundespräsidialamt in Berlin im Jahr 1994 fiel an **Helmut Kleine-Kraneburg** (geb. 1961) und **Martin Gruber** (geb. 1963) (*Bauwelt*, 1994). Der große Hof des elliptischen Gebäudes ist keineswegs ein luftiger Freibereich, vielmehr ist eine Art »Narthex«, ein Stab in den Hof eingelegt. Das verleitet zu einer zweiten Interpretationsebene: Deuten wir das Ei als umhüllendes, bergendes, vielleicht uterines Gebilde, dann ist der phallische Stab als »Haus im Haus« eingedrungen und ist gleichzeitig ein embryonales Wesen, das schützend umhüllt wird. Der Vergleich mit dem *Oikema* von Ledoux liegt nahe.

Eine Modifikation des Prinzips »Haus im Haus« könnten wir in dem seltenen Vorgang »Haus aus dem Haus« sehen, der hier zitiert werden soll, weil er gleichsam einen »Geburtsvorgang« darstellt. Dieser interessante Aspekt wird von den **Haus-Rucker-Co** nicht nur in Zeichnungen, sondern auch real vorgetragen: die »Emanation« des Hauses aus dem Haus heraus. Eine erste einfache Realisierung war der *Ballon für Zwei* in Wien, 1967.

In einer reziproken Penetration wird aus dem Fenster eines Mietshauses ein Gestänge ausgefahren, das einer pneumatischen Konstruktion, die allmählich aufgeblasen wird, als Träger

Prima Claffe Primo Premio Giorgio Duran Spagnuolo 1795.

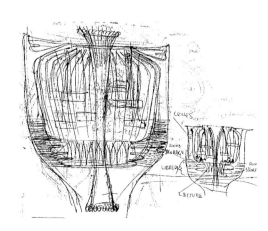

The building or object does not always have to be in a closed space for the protective, wrapping role to be expressed. We move from the »building in a building« to the **building in a courtyard**. Basically every walled area, every courtyard, every square of buildings is an enclosed area at the centre of which buildings rise, seeking protection but phallically dominant, effectively trusting in maternal protection.

The Utopian novel *Christianopolis* by **Johann Valentin Andreae** shows an ideal town plan in one of the few illustrations: the square town structure with its right-angled alleyways leaves a square free in the centre. It is accentuated by a tower-like church that makes an entirely phallic impression.

The period around 1800 provides us with ideal designs that represent the enclosure of buildings very convincingly. **Giorgio Duran** drew his project for a tomb chapel in 1795. A circular temple stands in the middle of a generous courtyard formed by a gigantic circle of arches.

Leo von Klenze's (1784–1864) ideal design is related to this plan: again it is a gigantic round courtyard, accommodating a centralized building with four long wings.

The forecourts of early Christian basilicas usually feature a cantharus, a fountain which was used for ritual cleansing in the oriental style. Protecting one of the most precious commodities, water, by a courtyard, an enclosure or a wall, which we come across particularly in hot countries that are short of water is also a theme of contemporary architecture.

The **Kaaba** in Mecca, Saudi Arabia, a kind of »textile« building in a gigantic courtyard that accommodates the crowds of pilgrims, has been much imitated in stone. for example there is a very fine pavilion of this kind in the courtyard of the Friday Mosque in Isfahan, Iran.

We can cite only a few examples of the building (or phallus) in a courtyard from our own century.

In **Paolo Soleri's** design for a philosophical centre (1960–1970) the »paternal« tower stands in the middle of the large »maternal« building crater, like a gigantic demonstration of the linga/yoni principle.

The concept of the post in a ring is convincingly demonstrated in a temporary building. **Adolf Krischanitz** built the Austria Pavilion for the Frankfurt Book Fair in 1995. Regardless of the polygonal realization it is in fact a large ring with an inner courtyard featuring an obelisk: the male element that protects the great harmony.

Massimo Scolari's *Turris Babel* stands isolated in a desert landscape, and far behind it is a slender version of Boullée's massive lighthouse, with mythological figures in front of it. But the tower is not a mound, but hollowed out, torn open, articulated into two storeys, each accommodating and protecting a post: tower and sphere-crowned obelisk conjure up not just history, but also magical and artistic associations.

It may be that in the case of the »building in a building« theme the sexual dichotomy cannot be made out quite accurately. Even if the great covering, the area under the dome, for instance, is seen as maternal and the inserted element as male, then chapel, ciborium or shrine become entirely female in character as well, and once more we are faced with »double coding«.

dient, die Geburt eines architektonischen Volumens. Das gleiche Motiv, technisch nur ausgereifter, treffen wir bei der documenta 5, 1972, in Kassel an: Die *Oase Nr. 7* penetriert gleichsam ein Fenster, eine Expansion des Volumens, des Hauses in Gestalt einer transparenten Kugel beherrscht den Platzraum. Die Möglichkeit eines isolierten und geschützen Containers als neuer Lebensbereich wird durch die Installation einer Palmen-Oase zur Diskussion gestellt.

Das Haus oder Objekt muß nicht immer in einem geschlossenen Raum stehen, wenn die schützende, umhüllende Aufgabe zum Ausdruck kommen soll. Vom »Haus im Haus« kommen wir zum **Haus im Hof.** Im Grunde genommen ist jede Ummauerung, ist jeder Hofraum, jedes Gebäudegeviert ein umfriedeter Bereich, in dessen Zentrum sich Bauten schutzsuchend, gleichwohl aber phallisch – dominant erheben, gleichsam auf den mütterlichen Schutz vertrauend.

Der utopische Roman *Christianopolis* von **Johann Valentin Andreae** zeigt in einer der wenigen Illustrationen den idealen Stadtplan: Das quadratische Stadtgebilde mit seinen rechtwinkeligen Gassen läßt in der Mitte einen Platz frei. Er ist akzentuiert durch eine durchaus phallisch wirkende, turmartige Kirche.

Die Zeit um 1800 liefert uns einige Idealentwürfe, die sehr überzeugend die Umfriedung von Bauwerken darstellen. **Giorgio Duran** zeichnet 1795 das Projekt für eine Grabkapelle. Ein Rundtempel steht inmitten eines großzügigen Hofes, der durch einen riesigen Arkadenkreis gebildet wird.

Der Idealentwurf von **Leo von Klenze** (1784–1864) ist diesem Plan verwandt: Wieder ist es ein gewaltiger Rundhof, er nimmt einen Zentralbau mit vier ausgreifenden Flügeln auf.

Die Vorhöfe frühchristlicher Basiliken nahmen zumeist einen Cantharus, einen Brunnen auf, der nach orientalischem Muster der rituellen Reinigung diente. Der Schutz eines der kostbarsten Güter, des Wassers, durch einen Hof, eine Umfriedung oder eine Mauer, den wir vor allem in heißen und wasserarmen Gegenden antreffen, ist auch heute ein Thema der Architektur.

Die **Kaaba** in Mekka, Saudi-Arabien, ein gleichsam »textiles« Gebäude in einem riesigen Hof, der die Pilgerscharen aufnimmt, hat zahlreiche Nachbildungen in Stein gefunden. So steht beispielsweise ein schöner Pavillon im Hofe der Freitags–Moschee in Isfahan, Iran.

Nur wenige Beispiele für das Prinzip Haus (oder Phallus) im Hof können wir aus der Architektur unseres Jahrhunderts zitieren.

Beim Entwurf zu einem philosophischen Zentrum (1960–1970) von **Paolo Soleri** steht der »väterliche« Turm inmitten des großen »mütterlichen« Gebäudekraters, gleichsam eine riesige Darstellung des Linga/Yoni-Prinzips.

Das Konzept des Pfahls im Ring wird bei einem temporären Bau überzeugend dargestellt. **Adolf Krischanitz** baut 1995 den Österreich-Pavillon für die Frankfurter Buchmesse. Unbeschadet der polygonalen Realisierung ist es doch ein großer Ring mit einem Innenhof, der einen Obelisken aufnimmt: das männliche Element, dem die große Harmonie Schutz bietet.

Massimo Scolaris *Turris Babel* steht einsam in einer Wüstenlandschaft, weit hinter ihm eine schlanke Version von Boullées gewaltigem Leuchtturm, vor ihm mythologische Gestalten. Der Turm aber ist kein Berg, sondern ausgehöhlt, aufgerissen, in zwei Etagen gegliedert, und jede von ihnen nimmt schützend einen Pfahl auf: Turm und kugelgekrönter Obelisk beschwören nicht nur die Historie, sondern auch magisch-künstlerische Assoziationen.

Es mag sein, daß beim Thema »Haus im Haus« die Geschlechter-Dichothomie nicht mehr ganz genau auszumachen ist. Wenn auch die große Hülle, etwa der Kuppelraum, als das Mütterliche und das eingestellte Element als das Männliche angesprochen wurde, gewinnen Kapelle, Ziborium oder Schrein durchaus auch weiblichen Charakter, wir sehen uns neuerlich einer »Doppelcodierung« gegenüber.

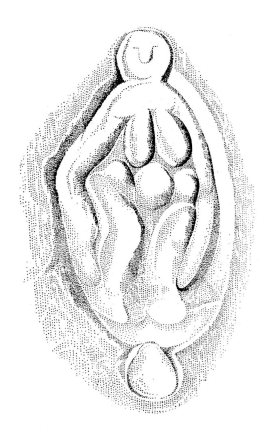

9.4. Fourth Synthesis: The Coincidentia

9.4.1. Surface Connection

Before we move on to architecture we must discuss a very important phenomenon in the two-dimensional field: surface connection, generally a semantic coincidence.

The essence of surface connection is that two (or more) forms that are autonomous as such complement each other so completely that a new and more significant form is produced that is more than just a sum of the individual forms.

We know of some interesting prehistoric depictions that do admit several interpretations, but that can be adduced as an argument for **androgynous surface connection**.[54]

»In the fertility shrine in Laussel, France ... a strange relief with two figures was discovered, of which one is clearly female, while the other is puzzling because it has been partly destroyed by weathering. Both figures are enclosed in a deeply incised, joint outline. This is an approximately egg-shaped oval. Only the circle of the heads protrudes outside this at opposite ends.« (Giedion, 1964)

Interpretations of this image vary between birth and coitus, which is more probable, but »the remarkable enclosure of the two bodies can just as well be interpreted as an androgynous being.« (Giedion, 1964)

If we compare these archaic figurative images with magical symbols, with the further symbolism of the ovoid form, with the countless representations and ideas of unity in duality, then we can probably postulate a very early symbol of a coincidentia of two beings into one, though rare in prehistoric times.

The theme of uniting beings into one compact form can also be studied in an early Neolithic stone relief from Catal Hüyük. Four people are represented, on the left a man and woman, perhaps in the hierós gamós, the sacred wedding, and on the right a woman with a small figure, certainly to be interpreted as mother and child. (Biedermann, 1987)

A leap through the millennia, to contemporary art, brings us to a very similar structure: **Helmut Lander's** *Couple* can be put together in such a way that it produces a compact, harmonious overall form.

The abstract idea of unification has produced numerous symbols that usually produce surface connection.

We are most familiar with the example of the **yin/yang** principle. Yin has stood for the female, the soft and passive and yang for the male, hard and active in Chinese philosophy of nature since 400 BC. But the principles are not separate, but have their origins in an absolute. According to Thiele (1986) both signs have an element in common, the sign for four – hill. But in the first character it is the »shady« hill, and thus becomes secret, mysterious, cold – and the female principle, and in the second character it is the sunlit hill, and this means radiant, shining, bright, sunny – and male principle.

This dualism is expressed visually in the yin/yang sign, two bladder-like figures that complement each other to form unity, completeness, perfection. And the two small circles in the bladders indicate that something of the other is included in each principle. This sign simultaneously represents the cosmic balance between east and west, north and south, heaven and earth, sun and moon: once again we come across the great contrasting pairs of humanity and attempts at synthesis.

The graphic model of yin and yang is complemented by number magic. Here the odd numbers correspond to yang, the male, and the even numbers to yin, the female. We also find this classification in other cultures, in the Aegean area, for example. The figure two in particular is seen as female, and the three, generally the odd number, as male. But among the Bambars of West Sudan the female sex is associated with the number four, and the perfect human being – the androgyne – is accordingly represented by the figure seven, the sum of three and four.

The **bladder motif**, similar to yin/yang, is also found in Gothic tracery, alongside other surface connection systems.

A small work by **Frederick Kiesler** should confirm the topicality of androgynous surface connection in our century. A »female« kidney-shaped table and a »male« pine cone-shaped table can be pushed together in such a way that they form a circle. This is a crucial idea in visual form: two entirely disparate elements are synthesized to make something that is more than the sum, a new quality: that of (formal) perfection.

9. 4. Vierte Synthese: Die Coincidentia

9.4.1. Flächenschluß

Bevor auf die Architektur eingegangen wird, ist noch ein überaus wichtiges Phänomen im zweidimensionalen Gestaltbereich zu erörtern: der Flächenschluß, allgemein eine semantische coincidentia.

Das Wesen des Flächenschlusses besteht darin, daß zwei (oder mehr) an sich autonome Formen einander so völlig ergänzen, daß eine neue, bedeutsamere Form entsteht, die mehr ist, als die bloße Summierung der Einzelformen.

Aus der Vorgeschichte sind uns einige interessante Darstellungen bekannt, die zwar mehrere Deutungen zulassen, aber zur Argumentation eines gleichsam **androgynen Flächenschlusses** herangezogen werden können.[57]

»In dem Fruchtbarkeitsheiligtum von Laussel, Frankreich, wurde ... ein seltsames Relief mit zwei Figuren entdeckt, von denen die eine deutlich weiblich ist, während die andere durch teilweise Verwitterung Rätsel aufgibt. Ein tiefeingegrabener, gemeinsamer Umriß umspannt beide Gestalten. Er ist von annähernd eiförmig ovaler Gestalt. Nur das Kreisrund der Köpfe ragt an entgegengesetzen Enden darüber hinaus«. (Giedion, 1964)

Die Interpretationsbreite dieser Darstellung schwankt zwischen Geburtsakt und, was wahrscheinlicher ist, Koitus, aber »die merkwürdige Umschließung der beiden Körper kann ebensogut als ein androgynes Wesen aufgefaßt werden.« (Giedion, 1964)

Vergleichen wir diese archaischen figurativen Darstellungen mit magischen Symbolen, mit der weiten Symbolik der Eiformen, mit den zahllosen Darstellungen und Ideen der Einheit in der Zweiheit, so können wir wohl auch ein sehr frühes, wenngleich für die Prähistorie seltenes Symbol einer coincidentia von zwei Wesen zu einem einzigen postulieren.

Das Thema der Vereinigung von Wesen in einer kompakten Form können wir auch bei einem Steinrelief des Frühneolithikums aus Catal Hüyük studieren. Es sind vier Menschen dargestellt, links Mann und Frau, vielleicht in der hierós gamós, der heiligen Hochzeit, rechts eine Frau mit einer kleinen Figur, sicherlich als Mutter und Kind zu deuten. (Biedermann, 1987)

Ein Sprung über die Jahrtausende, in die Kunst der Gegenwart, führt uns zu einem sehr ähnlichen Gebilde: Das *Paar* von **Helmut Lander** kann man in der Weise zusammenstecken, daß eine kompakte, harmonische Gesamtform entsteht.

Die Idee der Vereinigung hat in ihrer Abstraktion zahlreiche Symbole hervorgebracht, die zumeist einen Flächenschluß bilden .

Am geläufigsten ist uns das Beispiel des **Yin/Yang**-Prinzips. In der chinesischen Naturphilosophie seit 400 v. Chr. steht Yin für das Weibliche, das Weiche und Passive, Yang hingegen für das Männliche, Harte, Aktive. Trotzdem sind die Prinzipien nicht getrennt, sondern haben ihren Ursprung in einem Absoluten. Nach Thiele (1986) haben beide Zeichen ein gemeinsames Element, das Zeichen für Fou = Hügel. Im ersten Schriftzeichen ist es jedoch der »schattige« Hügel, also wird damit geheim, dunkel, mysteriös, kalt – aber auch das weibliche Prinzip ausgesagt, im zweiten Schriftzeichen ist es der sonnige Hügel, der strahlend, glänzend, hell, sonnig bedeutet und das männliche Prinzip repräsentiert.

Die visuelle Ausprägung dieses Dualismus ist das Yin/Yang-Zeichen, die zwei fischblasenartigen Figuren, die einander zum Kreis, also zur Einheit, Ganzheit, Vollkommenheit ergänzen. Und die beiden kleinen Kreise in den Fischblasen deuten an, daß in jedem Prinzip auch etwas vom anderen enthalten ist. Dieses Zeichen repräsentiert gleichzeitig das kosmologische Gleichgewicht zwischen Ost und West, Nord und Süd, Himmel und Erde, Sonne und Mond: Wieder treten uns die großen Gegensatzpaare der Menschheit und die Versuche nach Synthesen entgegen.

Das graphische Modell des Yin/Yang wird durch die Zahlenmagie ergänzt. Die ungeraden Zahlen entsprechen demnach dem Yang, dem Männlichen, die geraden Zahlen dem Yin, dem Weiblichen. Diese Zuordnung finden wir auch in anderen Kulturen, etwa im ägäischen Raum. Insbesondere der Zweier entspricht dem Weiblichen, der Dreier, allgemein die ungerade Zahl, dem Männlichen. Bei den Bambar im Westsudan ist das weibliche Geschlecht jedoch mit vier charakterisiert, der vollkommene Mensch – der Androgyn – ist demnach in der Zahl sieben, der Summe aus drei und vier repräsentiert.

Das **Fischblasenmotiv**, dem Yin/Yang ganz ähnlich, finden wir, neben anderen Flächenschlußsystemen, auch im Maßwerk der Gotik.

Die Aktualität des androgynen Flächenschlusses in unserem Jahrhundert soll ein kleiner Entwurf von **Frederick Kiesler** bestätigen: Ein »weibliches« Nierentischchen und ein »männ-

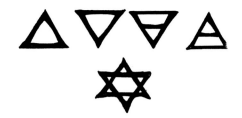

Edelbert Köb's work lies on the border between object world and sculpture. His three-dimensional »figures«, abstract, often vase-like structures, tackle the theme of formal reciprocity. A single, highly precise contact line produces a perfect formal connection from the complementary quality of concave and convex form, where the individual parts themselves have concave and convex elements. Köb models forms that can be entirely classified as female and male (the bowl female, the piston male), and the perfect formal completion is reminiscent of the yin/yang symbol and the surface connection theme.

We could once again draw abstract conclusions from the sexual specification of forms and simply talk about basic forms. Two vase-like elements, juxtaposed in formal connection, actually show no specific sexual qualities. But anthropomorphic associations cause us to interpret one form as broad-shouldered and the other as broad-hipped, which is the first step towards male-female classification. An additional feature is the contrasting blue and yellow of the two bodies. The female/male classification may be all the clearer for an object consisting of a gently curving dish with a club-like element in it, nestling snugly up to the dish. (*The Birth of Venus,* 1992) If we look at the two elements in their absolute and indivisible relationship to each other, then an aspect of the androgynous can probably be accepted. »Just as Botticelli's Venus is a symbol of flawless beauty and perfection, for Köb the vessel is a female principle and expresses the eternal search for perfection.« (Köb, 1992)

In **alchemy** the elements fire, water, earth and air are presented by **triangular figures**. When the overlap they represent the great symbiosis and form a hexagram, a figure that is in fact identical with the Star of David, but is by no means unique to Jewish culture. The sigillum Salomonis shows a linking of the triangles, we find a depiction in a mosaic in the church of S. Maria Anagni in Frosinone.

In **Indian symbolism** the downward-pointing triangle is the vulva, and the upward-pointing version the phallus. When they overlap they produce a star (in the same way as the Star of David), or complicated figurations that are nevertheless woven into a unit. O. A. Graf shows the persisting presence of the vulva triangle in his history of forms.

The **linga/yoni** principle is presented exhaustively in chapter 3.5. We are also given another wonderful overall show by the **mandalas** of the Far East. They do not in fact achieve surface connection, but in dualistic elements they produce complex complete systems representing a superordinated cosmic unity. Numerous types in various religious and philosophical forms, especially in Tantrism, articulate the possible connection between mind and matter, gods and world, heaven and earth.

Archetypal mandalas concerned with the relation of circle, square and the number four are especially interesting for architecture. The circle is usually reserved for the divine, the perfect, the cosmic, while the square corresponds to man, reason, the earthly. (Feuerstein, 1966)

Fertility and sexuality were crucial factors in early man's existence. If a **conjunctio** is represented, then, at a high level of abstraction, those sexual symbols are adequate that are strikingly symbolized as terse signs and are always generated to form a »super-sign«.

The door-leaf of a prehistoric tomb in the necropolis of Casteluccio in Sicily (ca. 1800 BC) has a depiction of the union of male and female elements: the phallus seems to be penetrating a slit from below.

An scratched drawing from Notgasse am Stoderzinken near Gröbming (Steiermark) shows a convincing shorthand sign of the unification of male and female: the vulva sign is penetrated by the phallus in such a way that the tip of the penis also forms the cleft of the vulva. This depiction – and countless other prehistoric scratchings – is also interesting because it moves away from the frequent triangular representations and represents the vulva in the form of a lozenge. Thus this shorthand sign comes close to the trivial and vulgar drawings, mainly infantile, that are still found today on the walls of buildings and in toilets.

The oldest signs of the fusion of male and female come from the Palaeolithic period. According to Graf the »juxtaposition of the male and female organs« produces »a curve that is used later under the name ›spiral‹ and ›running dog‹. One side of the penis forms the side of the female form.«

A major field for interpretation is to be found in the numerous **labyrinth depictions**.

Cohabitation is certainly plausible among the many interpretations, but it appears in such an abstract form that »male« and »female« run into each other seamlessly, making it possible to speak of an androgynous symbol.

The so-called vulva image from the Stone Age was found in Luzzanas in Sicily. The lines form an organic, open, essentially uterine dish; a line has worked its way in, penetrated,

286. Yin/Yang Prinzip mit den acht Trigrammen.
287. Gotisches Fischblasenmaßwerk.
288. Frederick Kiesler, Aluminiumtische, 1938.
289. Zeichen der Alchemie: Feuer, Wasser, Luft, Erde (in Indien: männlich und weiblich, vereinigt in Sternfigur).
290. Yantra aus neun Dreiecken, 1938.

286. Yin/yang principle with the eight trigrams.
287. Gothic vesica piscis tracery.
288. Frederick Kiesler, aluminium tables, 1938.
289. Signs of alchemy: fire, water, air, earth (in India: male and female, united in the star figure).
290. Yantra combined of nine triangles, 1938.

liches« Zapfentischchen können so ineinander geschoben werden, daß sie in etwa einen Kreis bilden. Es ist ein essentieller Gedanke, der hier visualisiert wird: Aus den zwei durchaus verschiedenen Elementen entsteht durch die Synthese etwas, das mehr ist als die Summe, eine neue Qualität: die der (formalen) Vollkommenheit.

Im Grenzbereich von Objektwelt und Skulptur liegen die Arbeiten **Edelbert Köbs.** Seine plastischen »Figuren«, abstrakte, oft vasenartige Gebilde, behandeln das Thema der formalen Reziprozität. Jeweils nur in einer einzigen Berührungslinie von großer Präzision ergibt sich ein vollkommener Formenschluß aus der Komplementarität von Konkav- und Konvexform, wobei die einzelnen Teile selbst Konkav- und Konvexelemente aufweisen. Köb modelliert Formen, die durchaus dem Weiblichen und dem Männlichen zugeordnet werden können (die Schale weiblich, der Kolben männlich), die perfekte formale Ergänzung erinnert an das Ying/Yang-Symbol, an das Thema des Flächenschlusses.

Einmal mehr könnten wir von der geschlechtlichen Spezifikation der Formen abstrahieren und einfach von Grundformen sprechen. Zwei vasenartige Elemente, die formschlüssig nebeneinanderstehen, weisen tatsächlich keine Geschlechtsspezifika auf. Anthropomorphe Assoziationen veranlassen uns jedoch dazu, die eine Form als breitschultrig, die andere als breithüftig zu interpretieren, womit bereits eine männlich-weibliche Zuordnung angebahnt ist. Hinzu kommt das kontrastierende Blau und Gelb der beiden Körper. Noch deutlicher mag die Zuweisung weiblich/männlich bei einem Objekt sein, bei dem in einer großen, sanft geschwungenen Schale ein keulenartiges Element liegt, das sich vollkommen an die Schale anschmiegt (*Die Geburt der Venus,* 1992). Sehen wir die beiden Elemente in ihrer absoluten untrennbaren Bezogenheit zueinander, so kann wohl ein Aspekt des Androgynen angenommen werden. »So wie Botticellis Venus Sinnbild für makellose Schönheit und Vollkommenheit ist, ist für Köb das Gefäß ein weibliches Prinzip und Ausdruck der ewigen Suche nach Vollkommenheit.« (Köb, 1992)

In der **Alchimie** werden die Elemente Feuer, Wasser, Erde, Luft durch **Dreiecksfiguren** dargestellt. In der Überlagerung stehen sie für die große Symbiose und bilden das Hexagramm, eine Figur, die mit dem Davidstern zwar identisch, aber keineswegs nur dem jüdischen Kulturkreis eigen ist. Das Sigillum Salomonis zeigt eine Verknüpfung der Dreiecke, eine Darstellung finden wir in einem Mosaik der Kirche S. Maria Anagni in Frosinone.

In der **indischen Symbolik** ist das nach unten zeigende Dreieck die Vulva, das nach oben zeigende der Phallus. Überlagert ergeben sie einen Stern (analog dem Davidstern) oder komplizierte Figurationen, die gleichwohl zu einer Einheit verflochten sind. Die unentwegte Präsenz des Vulvadreiecks zeigt O. A. Graf in seiner Formengeschichte auf.

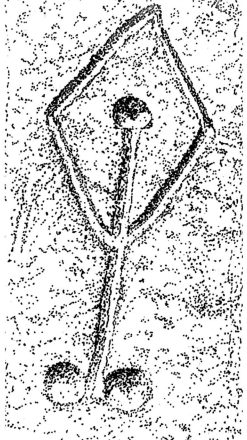

Das Prinzip **Linga/Yoni** wurde in Kap. 3.5 ausführlich dargestellt.

Eine weitere großartige Gesamtschau liefern uns die fernöstlichen **Mandalas.** Sie bilden zwar keinen Flächenschluß, ergeben aber in dualistischen Elementen komplexe Gesamtsysteme, die eine übergeordnete kosmische Einheit repräsentieren. Zahlreiche Typen in den unterschiedlichen religiösen und philosophischen Ausprägungen, insbesondere im Tantrismus, artikulieren die mögliche Verbindung zwischen Geist und Materie, Götter und Welt, Himmel und Erde.

Für die Architektur sind jene archetypischen Mandalas besonders interessant, die sich mit der Relation von Kreis, Quadrat und Vierzahl beschäftigen, wobei der Kreis zumeist dem Göttlichen, Vollkommenen, Kosmischen vorbehalten ist, während das Quadrat dem Menschen, der Ratio, dem Irdischen entspricht. (Feuerstein, 1966)

Für die Menschen der Frühzeit sind Fruchtbarkeit und Sexualität die wesentlichen Faktoren ihrer Existenz. Wenn eine **conjunctio** dargestellt wird, dann genügen in einem sehr hohen Abstraktionsgrad die Sexualsymbole, die als knappe Kürzel überaus eindringlich symbolisiert und jeweils zu einem »Superzeichen« generiert werden.

Die Türplatte eines prähistorischen Grabes der Nekropole von Casteluccio in Sizilien (um 1800 v. Chr.) zeigt die Darstellung der Vereinigung von weiblichen und männlichen Elementen: Der Phallus scheint von unten in eine Spalte einzudringen.

Eine Ritzzeichnung aus Notgasse am Stoderzinken bei Gröbming (Steiermark) zeigt ein überzeugendes Kürzel der Vereinigung des Weiblichen mit dem Männlichem: Das Vulvazeichen wird vom Phallus in der Weise durchstoßen, daß die Penisspitze gleichzeitig die Vulvaspalte bildet. Diese Darstellung – und zahlreiche andere prähistorische Ritzungen – sind auch deswegen interessant, weil sie von den häufigen Dreiecksdarstellungen abweichen und die Vulva in Form einer Raute darstellen. Damit nähert sich dieses Kürzel den bis heute gebräuchlichen meist infantilen Trivial- und Vulgärdarstellungen an Hauswänden und in Toiletten.

through this opening. It is recognizably a phallus, but completely fused with the surrounding lines. Doubts can be raised about the interpretation of the vulva image. But then there is still a lavish stock of prehistoric depictions which undoubtedly represent the union of male and female signs. In a Bronze Age rock scratching (ca. 900–500 BC) from Laxe de Rotea de Mendo in Spain we can make out a labyrinthine figure being penetrated by a phallic anthropomorphic figure. (Kern, 1982)

The *Tragliatella*, a representation on an Etruscan vase from ca. 620 BC is similar. The copulating couples admit no doubts about how the labyrinthine depiction should be interpreted.

Labyrinths are called »entrails« in a Babylonian depiction, which is understandable given the intertwining and convolution of the intestinal tract. A »palace of the entrails« is mentioned, and the »palace portal«, it counted as vulva and vagina, and the convolutions of the labyrinth figure as the unfathomable quality of the womb, and descent into the labyrinth is an erotic symbol of sexual union. (Kerenyi, 1951)

9.4.2. Mountains and Caves

»In the history of evolution, the **sheltering cave**, as being part of a **mountain**, is the natural form of those cultural symbols which – whether they are temples, temenoses, huts, houses, villages, towns, lattices, fences, or walls – all signify something which both protects and completes.« (Giedion, 1964)

The first connecting links with androgynous architecture might again lie in the natural field, in geological topography.

The chain of association with a high mountain is, at the outset, undoubtedly male in nature: mountains are »mighty«, »tremendous«, »unconquerable« and the like. A steeply rising mountain becomes a horn, that is to say a male element: the Matterhorn, the Zwölferhorn, etc. In Mfact, a steep mountain also becomes a phallic symbol.

But mountains also have another noteworthy property: they harbour caves, caverns, grottoes, that is to say those spatial areas which have since time immemorial provided protection for humans, even before the latter built any dwellings.

Mountains and caves are directly related in mythical thinking. Caves as we imagine them are always located in mountains (although this is not necessarily always geologically correct), and mountains are full of caves. Thus it is that mountains and rocks, which are described in masculine terms (Berg and Fels, the German words for mountain and rock, are both masculine in gender in German), turn into a synthesis with caves and grottoes, which are given a feminine designation (Höhle and Grotte, cave and grotto, are feminine in German).

The history of architecture does not give us any very comprehensive material, because the climbable mountains of the gods, the ziggurats, the pre-Colombian step-shaped mountains, the pyramids – that is to say the age-old mountain symbols – do not possess an interior worth mentioning, and thus tend rather to represent masculinity, but by no means androgyny.

But instructive depictions are again found in the occult doctrines of the 16th century, especially in the »Alchemy« of 1654. *Alchimia* (1654) by **Stephan Michelspacher** depicts the *Mountain of the Adepts* – that is to say the initiates or the elect. The four elements and the zodiac surround a mountain which consists of four stages and at the same time forms not only a large cave or an enormous gate, but also part of a strange building, the temple of the wise. By traversing seven steps which are given the names of alchemic processes, one enters the magic pavilion of knowledge or inauguration. (Jung, 1984) In this depiction we once again en-

Die ältesten Zeichen der Verschmelzung des Männlichen und Weiblichen stammen aus dem Paläolithikum. Nach Graf entsteht aus dem »Nebeneinander des weiblichen und männlichen Organs eine Kurve, die später unter dem Namen ›Spirale‹ und ›laufender Hund‹ geführt wird. Die eine Seite des Gliedes bildet die Seite der weiblichen Form«.

Ein großer Interpretationsbereich besteht bei den zahlreichen **Labyrinthdarstellungen**.

Unter den vielen Deutungen ist die der Kohabitation sicher plausibel, sie erscheint aber derart abstrahiert, daß »männlich« und »weiblich« ineinander bruchlos übergehen, so daß wir von einem androgynen Symbol sprechen können.

Das sogenannte Vulvenbild aus der Steinzeit wurde in Luzzanas in Sizilien gefunden. Die Lineaturen bilden eine organische, geöffnete, gleichsam uterine Schale; durch diese Öffnung hat sich eine Linie eingefädelt, ist eingedrungen und als Phallus erkennbar, aber völlig verschmolzen mit den umhüllenden Linien. An der Deutung des Vulvenbildes können Zweifel gehegt werden. Dann bleibt aber noch immer ein reichlicher Bestand an prähistorischen Darstellungen, die zweifelsfrei eine Vereinigung männlicher und weiblicher Kürzel darstellen. In einer bronzezeitlichen Felsritzung (ca. 900–500 v. Chr.) aus Laxe de Rotea de Mendo in Spanien, erkennen wir eine labyrinthoide Figur, in die eine phallische anthropomorphe Figur eindringt. (Kern, 1982)

Ähnlich ist die *Tragliatella*, eine Darstellung auf einer etruskischen Vase um 620 v. Chr. Die beigesellten kopulierenden Paare lassen keinen Zweifel über die Deutung der labyrinthischen Darstellung aufkommen.

In einer babylonischen Darstellung werden Labyrinthe als »Eingeweide« bezeichnet, was verständlich ist, angesichts der Verschlingungen und Windungen des Darmtraktes. Es ist von einem »Palast der Eingeweide« die Rede und von der »Palastpforte«, sie galt als Vulva und Vagina, und die Windungen der Labyrinthfigur als Unergründlichkeit des Mutterschoßes, der Abstieg ins Labyrinth als erotisches Symbol für die sexuelle Vereinigung. (Kerenyi, 1951)

9.4.2. Berg und Höhle

»Die **bergende Höhle** als Teil des **Berges** stellt entwicklungsgeschichtlich die Naturform der Kultursymbole dar, die als Tempel und Temenos, als Hütte und Haus, als Dorf und Stadt ebenso wie Gatter, Zaun und Mauer Schützendes und Abschließendes bedeuten.« (Giedion, 1964)

Die ersten Anknüpfungspunkte zu einer androgynen Architektur könnten wieder im Naturbereich, in der geologischen Topographie liegen.

Die Assoziationskette mit dem (hohen) Berg ist zunächst zweifellos männlicher Natur: Berge sind »mächtig«, »gewaltig«, »unbezwingbar« und dergleichen. Der steilaufragende Berg wird zum »Horn«, also zu einem männlichen Element: das Matterhorn, das Zwölferhorn usw. Tatsächlich wird der steile Berg auch zu einem Phallussymbol.

Der Berg hat aber auch noch eine andere merkwürdige Eigenschaft: Er »birgt« die Höhlen, die Kavernen, die Grotten, also jene Raumbereiche, die seit urdenklichen Zeiten den Menschen Schutz geboten haben, noch bevor sie sich Behausungen errichteten.

Berg und Höhle stehen im mythischen Bewußtsein in einem unmittelbaren Zusammenhang. Höhlen befinden sich in unserer Vorstellung (nicht immer unbedingt geologisch richtig) in Bergen, und die Berge sind von Höhlen durchzogen. So wird das gleichsam Männliche (**der** Berg, **der** Fels) zu einer Synthese mit dem Weiblichen (**die** Höhle, **die** Grotte).

Die Architekturgeschichte liefert uns kein allzu umfassendes Material, denn die besteigbaren Götterberge, die Zikkurats, die präkolumbianischen Stufenberge, die Pyramiden, also die uralten Bergsymbole weisen keinen nennenswerten Innenraum auf und stehen daher eher für das Männliche, keineswegs aber für das Androgyne.

Hingegen finden wir einmal mehr in den Geheimlehren des 16. Jahrhunderts aufschlußreiche Darstellungen. In **Stephan Michelspachers** *Alchimia* von 1654 ist der »Berg der Adepten«, der Eingeweihten oder Auserwählten dargestellt. Die vier Elemente und der Tierkreis umgeben einen vierstufigen Berg, der gleichzeitig eine große Höhle oder ein riesiges Tor bildet und teilweise ein seltsames Bauwerk, den Tempel der Weisen, birgt. Über sieben Stufen, die mit alchimistischen Prozessen bezeichnet sind, gelangt man in den magischen Pavillon der Erkenntnis oder Weihe. (Jung, 1984) In dieser Darstellung begegnen wir wieder dem »Haus im Haus«-Thema, aber der über geistige Stufen erreichbare Pavillon scheint sich dem schützenden Bereich der Berg-Höhle anzuvertrauen.

296. Stephan Michelspacher, *Der Berg der Adepten*, 1654.
297. Schule von Lucas von Valckenborgh, *Der Turm von Babel*, 1587.

296. Stephan Michelspacher, *The Mountain of the Adepts*, 1654.
297. School of Lucas von Valckenborgh, *The Tower of Babel*, 1587.

counter the theme of the »house within a house«, but the pavilion which can be reached by spiritual stages seems to be entrusting itself to the protective area of the mountain cave.

The numerous depictions of **Babylonian towers** are also instructive. In a painting from the school of **Lucas van Valckenborgh** (1530–1597), the building really does pass from the motif of a gradated mountain into that of a tower shape.

If we regard the lower part as a step-shaped mountain, and the upper part as a tower, then there are two male symbols flowing into one another. But if we are justified in assuming that the building also has some female, protective rooms in its interior – and the dark openings of the arcade do permit such a conclusion –, then it is allowable to interpret it as a piece of androgynous architecture.

Some significant examples, which were actually put into effect, are to be found in the **mountain churches** of the Baroque period: a Mount Calvary, which can be climbed, harbours a church or chapel in its interior.

The Kalvarienberg (Mount Calvary) was built in Maria Lanzendorf in Lower Austria in 1699. It is an extensive rocky structure with chapels and grottoes, completed by the Crucifixion scene at its summit. The mountain can be climbed by a series of curving staircases, and inside it there is a chapel. An imitation of the Scala Santa is to be found in the rock.

The Mount Calvary with the Chapel of Grace was, on the instructions of **Prince Paul Esterházy** (1635–1713), built as mountain church in Eisenstadt, probably on the model of Maria Lanzendorf. The various surrounding clamped-on structures, both outside and inside, are a magnificent spatial achievement. This building was completed in 1705.

A Mount Calvary of very similar design, but on a considerably more modest scale, was constructed in the Viennese suburb of Hernals a few years later.

Apart from these witnesses to Baroque piety against an archaic background, there are only a few examples of buildings in whose interior it is possible to walk about, but whose exterior can also be climbed.

We can give from the more recent past some examples for which at least the designs exist. **Richard Teschner** (1879–1948) painted a scurrilous picture of the *Berg der deutschen Arbeit (Mountain of German Work*, 1915). In the interior, people are working assiduously in cave-like but brightly lit workshops. The outside of the terraced mountain can be climbed by flights of stairs, and on the summit there is a festival ground crowned by a phallic pavilion.

The step-shaped mountain with its mysterious orifices may become an ominous monster whose nose has turned into a phallus. In the fantastic drawings by **Lebbeus Woods** (born 1940) for a private architectural cosmos, we may discover diverse erotic symbols, and some

Aufschlußreich sind auch die zahlreichen Darstellungen des **babylonischen Turmes**. Aus der Schule von **Lucas van Valckenborgh** (1530–97) stammt ein Gemälde, bei dem das Gebäude tatsächlich aus dem abgestuften Bergmotiv in eine Turmform übergeht.

Wenn wir den unteren Teil als Stufenberg ansehen, den oberen jedoch als Turm, dann wären es zwei männliche Symbole, die ineinanderfließen. Ist die Annahme gerechtfertigt und die dunklen Arkadenöffnungen lassen darauf schließen –, daß das Gebäude in seinem Inneren auch weiblich-schützende Räume aufweist, dann ist die Interpretation als androgyne Architektur zulässig.

Signifikante realisierte Beispiele finden wir in den **Bergkirchen** der Barockzeit: Der besteigbare Kalvarienberg birgt in seinem Inneren eine Kirche oder Kapelle.

In Maria Lanzendorf in Niederösterreich wurde 1699 der Kalvarienberg errichtet, eine weitläufige Felsenanlage mit Kapellen und Grotten, am Gipfel abgeschlossen durch die Kreuzigungsszene. Über geschwungene Treppenanlagen ist der Berg besteigbar, in seinem Inneren liegt eine Kapelle. Im Felsen finden wir auch eine Nachbildung der Scala Santa.

Im Auftrag des **Fürsten Paul Esterházy** (1635–1713) wurde der Kalvarienberg mit der Gnadenkapelle, die Bergkirche in Eisenstadt gebaut, wohl nach dem Vorbild von Maria Lanzendorf. Die vielfache Verklammerung von außen und innen stellt eine großartige räumliche Leistung dar. Das Bauwerk wurde 1705 fertiggestellt.

Wenige Jahre später wurde auch in Wien-Hernals ein Kalvarienberg mit einer sehr ähnlichen Konzeption, wenn auch wesentlich bescheidener errichtet.

Über diese Zeugnisse einer barocken Frömmigkeit mit archaischem Hintergrund hinaus gibt es nur wenige Beispiele von Bauwerken, die innen begehbar und außen besteigbar sind.

Aus jüngster Zeit können wir einige, zumindest projektierte Beispiele nennen. **Richard Teschner** (1879–1948) zeichnet ein skurriles Bild vom *Berg der deutschen Arbeit* (1915). Im Inneren arbeiten die fleißigen Menschen in höhlenartigen, gleichwohl hellen Werkstätten. Der terrassierte Berg ist außen über Stiegen besteigbar, auf seinem Gipfel liegt eine Festwiese, die durch einen phallischen Pavillon gekrönt wird.

Der Stufenberg mit seinen geheimnisvollen Öffnungen wird zu einem unheildrohenden Monster, dessen Nase sich in einen Phallus verwandelt hat. In den phantastischen Zeichnungen zu einem privaten architektonischem Kosmos von **Lebbeus Woods** (geb. 1940) entdecken wir mancherlei erotische Symbole, und in den vielfältigen Verflechtungen und Verklammerungen gerät auch einiges zu androgynen Dispositionen.

Das Völkerschlachtdenkmal in Leipzig (1898–1913) von **Bruno Schmitz** (1858–1916), findet tatsächlich eine androgyne Interpretation. Der riesige Innenraum, höhlenartig gebildet, in den man eintritt, in dem man hinaufsteigt, wäre das weibliche Prinzip, der machtvolle Außenbau, Berg und Turm gleichzeitig, stellt das männliche Prinzip dar. Der mächtige Steinhaufen, durch die martialischen Kriegerfiguren noch akzentuiert, wird nicht von außen erklettert, sondern man steigt im Inneren empor.

Beim nicht minder pathetischen Kyffhäuser-Denkmal, ebenfalls von Bruno Schmitz, mögen wir ähnliche Motive entdecken. Über einen Felsenhof betreten wir eine Kuppelhalle, die im Turmkörper liegt. Sie hat zwei Seitenkammern, die allerlei patriotische Reliquien aufnehmen.

Die Idee, durch einen Berg hindurchzuklettern, um an den Gipfel zu gelangen, ist ein kultisch-archaisches Motiv. In Triruchirapalli in Südindien führen 437 Stufen im Inneren des Berges zu einem Tempel an der Spitze.

Die Idee eines innen und außen begehbaren Bauwerkes, hat überraschenderweise in jüngster Zeit in einigen Projekten Niederschlag gefunden.

Giovanni Michelucci (1891–1990) hat seine Autobahnkirche an der Strada del Sol in der Nähe von Florenz (1960–1963) als begehbares Bauwerk konzipiert; leider wurde die Idee so nicht realisiert. Im expressiv höhlenartigen Innenraum gibt es Treppen zu einem oberen Niveau, von dort aus führt (im Konzept) eine Tür ins Freie, man befindet sich nun auf dem Bauwerk wie auf einem Felsen. Über Galerien und Treppen wäre ein weiteres Erklimmen des künstlichen Berges möglich gewesen. Michelucci hat die Idee der Kalvarienbergkirchen in die Formensprache der Gegenwart übersetzt. Eine der Handzeichnungen von Michelucci macht jedoch deutlich, daß der bergende Raum eine wesentliche Bedeutungserweiterung erfährt: Die Höhle steigt empor zu einem Gebilde, das Berg und Turm zugleich ist und im Inneren von einem »Baum« getragen wird, der sich anschickt, durch den Gipfel des Turmberges hindurchzuwachsen. Der Vergleich mit einer Zeichnung von Frederick Kiesler drängt sich auf: Der *Architekturentwurf* von 1947 läßt keine funktionalen Zuordnungen zu, doch scheinen die von der Schale ausgehenden Ausstülpungen für Emanationen, welcher Art auch immer, gedacht zu sein.

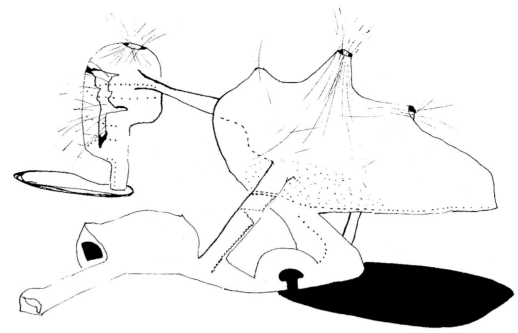

of the various intertwinements and clamped-on structures take on an androgynous arrangement.

The Völkerschlachtdenkmal in Leipzig (Battle of the Nations Monument in Leipzig, 1898 to 1913), the work of **Bruno Schmitz** (1858–1916), can in fact be interpreted androgynously. The female principle is the enormous interior – formed in the manner of a cave – which the visitor enters and then climbs up, and the male principle is the mighty exterior structure, both mountain and tower at the same time. The powerful heap of stones, accentuated by the martial warrior figures, is not climbed from the outside. Instead the visitor goes up on the inside.

Similar motifs may be discovered in the Kyffhäuser monument, another work by Bruno Schmitz which is no less emotive. We cross a rocky courtyard and enter a domed hall inside the body of the tower. At the sides of the hall are two chambers containing all kinds of patriotic relics.

The idea of climbing through a mountain to reach the summit is an archaic cultic motif. In Triruchirapalli in southern India, 437 steps inside the mountain lead to a temple at its peak.

The idea of an edifice in which it is possible to walk about not only in the interior but also on the exterior has, surprisingly enough, found expression in some recent designs.

Giovanni Michelucci (1891–1990) designed his motorway church (1960–1963), which is located near Florence on the Strada del Sol, as an edifice which could be walked on both on the inside and on the outside. The idea was unfortunately not put into effect in this way. Flights of stairs in the expressively cave-like interior lead up to a higher level, from which (in the design) a door leads into the open air and the visitor is now standing on the edifice as on a rock. Galleries and flights of stairs would have made it possible to climb further up this artificial mountain. The idea of the Mount Calvary churches was transformed by Michelucci into today's language of shapes. But one of Michelucci's freehand drawings makes it plain that the sheltering room undergoes a considerable expansion in meaning: the cave ascends into a structure which is at once both a mountain and a tower and whose interior is supported by a »tree« which is preparing to grow through the peak of the tower/mountain. A comparison with a drawing by Fredrick obtrudes here: no function can be assigned to the *Architekturentwurf* (*Architectural Design*) of 1947, but the bulges which proceed from the bowl seem intended to represent emanations of one kind or another.

Hans Hollein repeatedly treated the theme of the climbable edifice. A drawing for a theatre in St. Louis, USA, was produced in 1963 and is thus one of his early works. This edifice grows, so to speak, out of the slanting slopes of the topography, and the closed cubes evoke geological associations. The idea of three-dimensional structures whose exterior can be walked on takes on a specific shape in the design which was produced for the Zentralsparkasse (Central Savings Bank) in Floridsdorf, in Vienna, but was unfortunately not put into effect. Hollein designed a roof landscape, which could be walked on, climbed and planted with vegetation, but was linked to the interior by large glass apertures.

The inspiration for the buildings which can be walked on both on the outside and on the inside undoubtedly came from the American pueblos, whose roof landscapes, similarly to the houses in Jaipur, India, provide a second usable level.

Hans Hollein hat wiederholt das Thema des besteigbaren Bauwerkes behandelt. Eine Zeichnung für ein Theater in St. Louis, USA, entstand schon 1963 und zählt somit zu seinen frühen Arbeiten. Das Bauwerk wächst gleichsam aus den schrägen Böschungen der Topographie heraus, die geschlossenen Kuben geben geologische Assoziationen. Die Idee außen begehbarer Volumen nimmt konkrete Gestalt an beim Entwurf für die Zentralsparkasse in Wien-Floridsdorf, der leider nicht ausgeführt wurde. Hollein baut eine Dachlandschaft, begehbar, ersteigbar und bepflanzt, die aber durch große Glasöffnungen mit dem Innenraum in Verbindung steht.

Zweifellos kam die Inspiration zu den begehbaren Bauwerken von den amerikanischen Pueblos, deren Dachlandschaften, ähnlich wie die Häuser in Jaipur, Indien, eine zweite Nutzungsebene bilden.

Eine meisterhafte Auseinandersetzung mit dem Thema Berg und Höhle ist das von Hans Hollein geplante Museum im Salzburger Mönchsberg, das einen Teil der Guggenheim-Sammlung aufnehmen sollte. Man steigt in der untersten Ebene gleichsam in den Berg hinein, zahlreiche dunkle, grottenartige Räume gruppieren sich um den Mittelbereich, in dem der Felsen besonders stark spürbar wäre. Die Halle ist mit einem großen Oberlicht ausgestattet, gleichsam eine immaterielle Penetration des Berges. Die Treppen an den Felswänden ermöglichen das innere »Erklettern« der Berg-Höhle.

Nicht immer ist der »Berg« tatsächlich besteigbar, wir begnügen uns mit der Metapher. So hat etwa **Frank Lloyd Wright** (1867–1959) in seiner Beth Sholom Synagoge (1958/59) in der Nähe von Chicago in Zusammenarbeit mit dem Oberrabbiner tatsächlich ein Sinnbild des heiligen Berges Sinai gebaut, der aber, unbeschadet seiner wunderbaren Transparenz, mit dem bergenden und schützenden Raum für die gläubige Gemeinde identisch ist. Die Synthese des behütenden, uterinen, mütterlichen Raumes mit der Idee des männlichen, machtvollen, phallischen Berges oder Felsens kann als vollendete Metapher für die Androgynie angesehen werden.

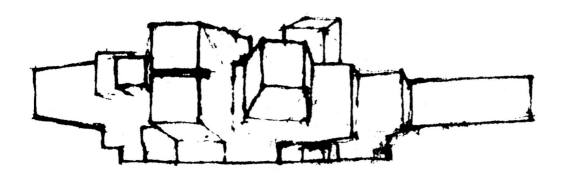

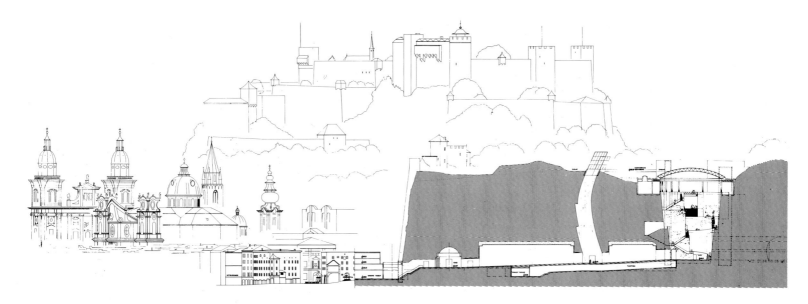

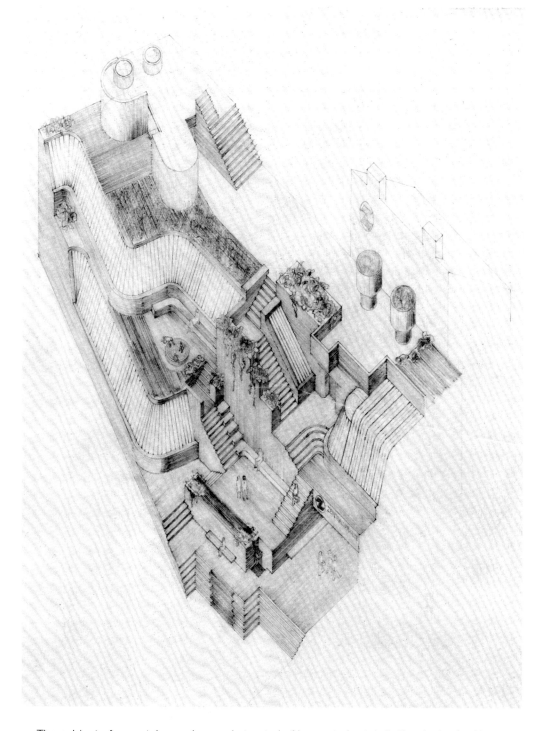

304. Frank Lloyd Wright, Beth Sholom Synagogue, Elkins Park, Pennsylvania, 1958/1959.
305. Hans Hollein, Theater, 1963.
306. Hans Hollein, Mönchsberg- (Guggenheim-) Museum, Salzburg, 1989.
307. Hans Hollein, Zweigstelle der Zentralsparkasse der Stadt Wien in Wien-Floridsdorf, 1966.

304. Frank Lloyd Wright, Beth Sholom Synagogue, Elkins Park, Pennsylvania, 1958/1959.
305. Hans Hollein, theatre, 1963.
306. Hans Hollein, Mönchsberg- (Guggenheim-) Museum, Salzburg, 1989.
307. Hans Hollein, branch of the Zentralsparkasse der Stadt Wien, Floridsdorf, Vienna, 1966.

The subject of mountains and caves is treated of in masterly style in the design by Hans Hollein for the Museum im Salzburger Mönchsberg. The museum was intended to house part of the Guggenheim collection. The visitor on the lowest level enters the mountain, as it were, and there are numerous dark, grotto-like rooms grouped around the central area in which the presence of the rock would be particularly noticeable. The hall has a large skylight, which is a kind of insubstantial penetration of the mountain. The flights of stairs on the rocky walls enable the visitor to climb up the inside of the mountain cave.

The »mountain« cannot really always be climbed, and we have to content ourselves with a metaphorical notion. For example, **Frank Lloyd Wright** (1867–1959), in his Beth Sholom Synagogue *(1958/59)* near Chicago, collaborated with the Chief Rabbi to build a symbol of the holy Mount Sinai. The latter, in spite of its wondrous transparency, is identical to the room which shelters and protects the community of the faithful. The synthesis of the guarding, uterine, motherly room on the one hand, and the idea of the powerful male phallic mountain or rock on the other, may be regarded as a consummated metaphor of androgyny.

9.4.3. Turmkuppeln/Kuppeltürme

Im Verlauf der historischen Entwicklung können wir zumeist die dominierenden Elemente der Baugestalt eindeutig bezeichnen. Wir haben kaum Schwierigkeiten, etwa die Kuppel und den Turm nach klaren Kriterien zu unterscheiden. Im Kapitel 9.1.3 wurde jedoch an Hand von Skizzen erläutert, daß sich einige morphologische Spektren einschieben, deren Elemente wir nicht präzise benennen können.

Typologisch könnten wir noch eine andere Gebäudeform analysieren, die wir sprachlich weder als Kuppel noch als Turm bezeichnen wollen. Diese terminologische Schwierigkeit ist mit ein Indiz dafür, daß es sich eben um eine weitere coincidentia handelt, um eine androgyne Architektur.

Verwenden wir den Begriff **Turmkuppel**- oder auch **Kuppelturm**, um diese Bauform zu benennen, wobei darunter keineswegs der Turm **auf** einer Kuppel zu verstehen ist. Es handelt sich vielmehr um ein Gebilde, das nach außen hin hoch und steil aufragt und einen zumeist abgerundeten Abschluß aufweist, so daß sich die Assoziation zu einem, wenngleich sehr voluminösen Phallus einstellen kann.

Eine weitere Bedingung besteht darin, daß das Bauwerk bergende, schützende, vielleicht höhlenartige Räume oder Kuppelräume enthält, im Idealfall einen einzigen Kuppelraum. Damit sind beide Charakteristika, die des Männlichen und Weiblichen präsent, jedoch in einer vollständigen Synthese und keineswegs zur Unkenntlichkeit reduziert.

In der **orientalischen Architektur** finden wir zahlreiche signifikante Beispiele, die diesen Bautyp repräsentieren. Eine Medrese in Damaskus zeigt einen gleichsam schützenden Unterbau, der in einzelnen Abstufungen in ein turmartiges Element organisch und bruchlos übergeht. Der obere Abschluß läßt eine Kuppel assoziieren, kann aber auch als Glans gedeutet werden.

Der Typus der nordindischen Tempelbauten der Provinz Orissa ist durch die in etwa parabelförmige Kontur charakterisiert. Aus der sehr klar artikulierten phallischen Ikonographie der indischen Kunst und im Hinblick auf den bergenden Charakter ist eine androgyne Architektur von großer Ausdruckskraft entstanden.

Zur Illustration der Turmkuppel im Bereich der westlichen Hochkultur stehen uns in erster Linie Entwürfe zur Verfügung. Eine Zeichnung von **Antonio Sant'Elia** (1888–1916), die zwischen 1909 und 1910 entstand, somit noch vor der Formulierung des Futurismus, zeigt eine monumentale Kombination von machtvollem Turm mit abschließender Kuppel, von vier Halbkuppeln begleitet. Durch den stark gestreckten Tambour, der unmittelbar in die Kuppel übergeht, entsteht der phallische Charakter. Mit Sicherheit kann angenommen werden, daß im Inneren eine riesige Kuppel geplant war.

Vielleicht hat diese Zeichnung ihr Vorbild in einer Arbeit des Wagner-Schülers **Otto Schönthal** (1878–1961), einem Entwurf für eine Friedhofskirche. In der Skizze sind dem Kuppelbau zwei flankierende Säulen, ähnlich wie bei der Karlskirche, zugeordnet. Die detaillierte Farbzeichnung läßt einen physiognomischen Eingang erkennen, die Kuppel zeigt eigenartige Schwellungen, eine Art Entasis.

Diese »Schwellkuppel« ist keineswegs neu: So wurde sie beispielsweise um 1400 beim Mausoleum des Timur in Samarkand angewendet, ein Bau, der ebenfalls als Turmkuppel angesprochen werden kann.

Ein ganz ähnliches Erscheinungsbild wie das Mausoleum in Samarkand bietet ein Hotel in Japan, freilich mit völlig anderen funktionellen und technologischen Voraussetzungen. Die Fuller-Kuppel am Hoteldach überdeckt die Terrasse und das Restaurant, aber Volker Fischer sieht die »schwellende Form des Gebäudekopfes wie auch die Gesamtanlage des Gebäudes ... bis hinunter zu Ausstattungsdetails ... als symbolische, phallische Anspielungen«. (Klotz, 1986) Sehen wir jedoch die bergende, transparente Kuppel als weibliches Element, dann käme dem Bau auch eine androgyne Deutung zu.

Hans Scharoun bringt seinen Volkshausgedanken in einer expressiven Farbskizze zu Papier. Die Turmkuppel wird als ein tranzsluzider, ausstrahlender Berg interpretiert, ganz im Sinne der Glashauseuphorie der Gruppe um die »Gläserne Kette«. Zu der androgynen Interpretation kommt noch die Assoziation zur Frucht und zur Blume, also zu durchaus weiblichen Metaphern, die das männliche Symbol überlagern.

In der Architekturszene nach dem Zweiten Weltkrieg gibt es einige wenige Beispiele von Turmkuppeln, die weitgehend aus den statischen Konzepten der Parabelkonstruktionen in Stahlbeton abzuleiten sind. Als ein Kompendium verschiedener historischer Formen bei gleich-

308. Medrese Al Nuriya, Al Kubra, Damaskus,
Syrien, 1172.
309. Stupa in Bhubanesvar, Orissa, Indien.
310. Antonia Sant'Elia, Monumentalbau, 1909
311. Hans Scharoun, *Volkshausgedanke*, 1919.
312, 313. Otto Schönthal, Friedhofskirche, 1901.

308. Medrese Al Nuriya, Al Kubra, Damaskus,
Syria, 1172.
309. Stupa in Bhubanesvar, Orissa, India.
310. Antonia Sant'Elia, monumental building, 1909.
311. Hans Scharoun, *Volkshausgedanke*, 1919.
312, 313. Otto Schönthal, cemetery church, 1901.

308 310 311
309 312 313

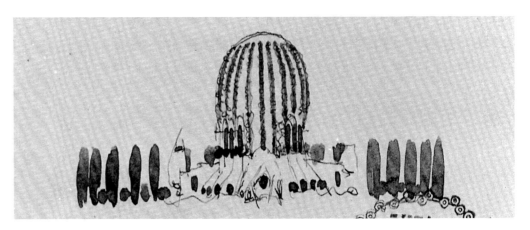

314. Mausoleum des Timur, Samarkand, Usbeki-
stan, um 1400.
315. Minoru Takeyama, Hotel Beverly Tom, Toma-
komai, Hokkaido, 1972.
316. Marabu in Marokko, 19. Jh.
317. Weingärtner-Unterstand in Flonheim, Deutschland, 20. Jh.
318. Paul Schneider-Esleben, St. Rochus, Düsseldorf, 1950–1955.

314. Mausoleum of Timur, Samarkand, Uzbekistan,
um 1400.
315. Minoru Takeyama, Hotel Beverly Tom, Toma-
komai, Hokkaido, 1972.
316. Marabu in Morocco, 19. cent.
317. Winer grower's shelter in Flonheim, Deutschland, 20th cent.
318. Paul Schneider-Esleben, St. Rochus, Düsseldorf, 1950–1955.

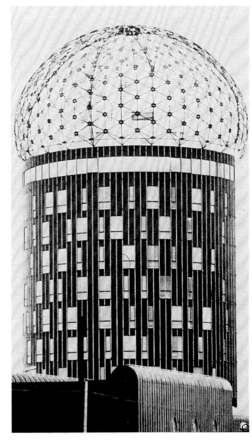

9.4.3. Tower-type Domes / Domed Towers

The dominant elements of the shape of a building as they evolved throughout history can usually be clearly defined. For example, hardly any difficulties arise in finding clear criteria by which to distinguish between domes and towers. However, in Chapter 9.1.3, sketches were used to explain that certain ranges of shapes also become involved to whose elements no precise names can be given.

We might analyse the typology of another building shape and, where the language to be employed to describe it is concerned, we wish to refer to it neither as a dome nor as a tower. This terminological difficulty is one indication that it is another coincidentia, an androgynous type of architecture.

Let us use the term **tower-type dome** or **domed tower** to designate this particular structural shape, although this term certainly does not mean a tower **above** a dome. Rather, it is a structure which, on the outside, rises up steeply and high and has a usually rounded-off conclusion, so that an association with a phallus, albeit a very voluminous one, may be formed. Another requirement is that this building has to contain some sheltering, protective, possibly cave-like or domed rooms – ideally, a single domed room. This means that both the male and the female characteristic are present, but they are in a complete synthesis and are by no means reduced to unrecognizableness.

Numerous significant examples of this type of structure are to be found in **Oriental architecture**. There is a medrese in Damascus with a kind of protective substructure which, in individual gradations, passes organically and uninterruptedly into a tower-like element. The upper conclusion permits an association with a dome, but can also be interpreted as a glans.

The type of northern Indian temple buildings found in Orissa province is characterized by its approximately parabolic contour. A very expressive androgynous architecture has been created: firstly there is the very clearly articulated phallic iconography of Indian art, and secondly the structure has a sheltering character.

The chief examples of tower-type domes in very advanced Western civilizations consist of drafts. A drawing by **Antonio Sant'Elia** (1888–1916), produced between 1909 and 1910, before futurism had been formulated, displays a monumental combination consisting of a mighty tower and a concluding dome, accompanied by four semidomes. The phallic character is created by the greatly extended tambour which passes directly into the dome. It can be safely assumed that an enormous dome was planned for the interior.

The model for this drawing is perhaps to be found in a work by Wagner's pupil **Otto Schönthal** (1878–1961). This is a design for a church with a graveyard. In the sketch, the dome structure is provided with two flanking columns, similar to those in the Karlskirche. This detailed coloured drawing allows a physiognomical entrance to be discerned, while the dome displays some peculiar swellings, a kind of entasis.

This »Swelling dome« is by no means new. It was for example used in ca. 1400 in the Mausoleum of Timur in Samarkand. That building may itself be regarded as a tower-type dome.

There is a hotel in Japan whose outer appearance is very similar to that of the mausoleum in Samarkand, although its functional and technological aspects are entirely different. The Fuller dome on the hotel roof stands above the terrace and the restaurant, but Volker Fischer considers that »not only the swelling shape of the head of the building, but also the general plan of the edifice ... right down to the details of the appointments ... are symbolic, phallic allusions«. (Klotz, 1986) But if we regard the sheltering, transparent dome as a female element, this building can also be interpreted in an androgynous sense.

Hans Scharoun set his Idea of a House for the People down on paper in an expressive coloured sketch. The tower-type dome is interpreted as a translucent, radiating mountain, very much in the sense of the glasshouse euphoria of the group surrounding the »Gläserne Kette«. Apart from the androgynous interpretation, there is also an association with fruits and flowers, that is to say with definitely female metaphors which overlie the male symbol.

The architectural scene after World War 2 contains a few examples of tower-type domes which can largely be derived from static plans for parabolic designs in reinforced concrete. The Rochus church in Düsseldorf (1950–1955) by **Paul Schneider-Esleben** (born 1915) might be regarded as a compendium of various historical forms, though at the same time it is radically abstract. This brings us back to the thesis from which we began: although structural motives predominate, the great idea of perfection in the shape of an egg seems also to have been made comprehensible for modern times.

zeitiger radikaler Abstraktion könnte die Rochuskirche in Düsseldorf (1950–1955) von **Paul Schneider-Esleben** (geb. 1915) angesehen werden. Damit kehren wir zurück zur Ausgangsthese: Obgleich die konstruktiven Motivationen überwiegen mögen, scheint doch auch der große Gedanke der Vollkommenheit in der Eiform für unsere Gegenwart verständlich gemacht.

Im Bereich der anonymen, naiven Architektur begegnet uns eine Reihe von Turmkuppeln in oft sehr bescheidener Ausprägung. In einem Weingarten bei Flonheim im Rheinland finden wir einen Unterstand für den Weingärtner und meinen, uns auf einer Mittelmeerinsel zu befinden: Ein Rundbau mit der typischen Spitzei-Kontur, weiß getüncht, ist ein ferner Verwandter mediterraner Zentralbauten.

Über die Kontinente hinweg finden wir ganz ähnliche morphologische Phänomene in Marokko. Die *Marabus* sind Grab- und Gedächtnisstätten für heilige Männer des Islam. Sie bergen einen relativ kleinen Innenraum, der häufig mit bescheidenen Opfergaben wie beispielsweise Pflanzen, Blumen und Steinen ausgestattet ist. Wieder einmal ist der bergend-mütterliche Raum des Todes mit einem aufragenden, im oberen Teil annähernd kegelförmigen Element verbunden, das die typische Übergangsform vom Berg zum Turm aufweist und als eindeutig männlich interpretiert werden kann; der Gesamtbau ist als androgyne Architektur zu erkennen.

Mit diesen Darstellungen ist keineswegs ein androgynes Idealmodell beschrieben worden, und sicherlich bilden sie auch keinen Abschluß in den Reflexionen über mann-weibliche Architektur. Ebenso wie es den idealen androgynen Menschen nicht geben kann – unbeschadet der zahlreichen kulturhistorischen Darstellungen – sondern nur Annäherungen an ein Lebensprinzip, kann es auch in der Architektur nur möglich sein, Grundlinien von Denkprozessen aufzuzeigen.

10. Abschluß

Androgyne Architektur kann nicht erfunden, nicht konstruiert werden. Sie ist kein Stil und keine Tendenz, sondern eine latente Wirklichkeit in der gebauten Umwelt. »Ambisexualität und Androgynie sind sichtbare Zeichen einer neuen Epoche, eines Zeitalters, in dem die Relevanz intensiver zwischenmenschlicher Beziehungen zunehmend erkannt wird. Ambisexuelle Daseinsweisen können Ausdruck einer Persönlichkeit sein, die in ihrem Fühlen, Denken und Handeln eine Synthese willkürlich hergestellter Gegensätze anstrebt und die in einer androgynen Lebensform ihre Ablehnung tradierter Rollenkonzepte kundtut.[58]

Wir müssen ... den Mut haben, ideologischen Ballast abzuwerfen und in ein Gebiet vorzustoßen ... dessen intensive Erforschung vorangetrieben wird durch die Sehnsucht des Menschen, das Innerste seines Wesens zu ergründen. Ambisexualität und Androgynie sind elementare Bestandteile dieses Wesens ... dessen mannigfaltige Erscheinung eine Herausforderung des Geistes darstellen.«

Androgynie ist »der bewußt stilisierte Versuch, die Trennung zwischen Objektivem und Subjektivem, zwischen dem Individuum und der Gesellschaft, ja zwischen Menschsein und Göttlichkeit zu überwinden.« (Tegetmeier, 1986)

Die Überzeugung, daß auch heute, wie zu allen Zeiten, die Baukunst die Fähigkeit besitzt, in Symbolen, Metaphern und Gleichnissen Aussagen über die Existenz des Menschen zu machen, sollte uns dazu ermutigen, den Begriff der Androgynie auch auf die Architektur auszudehnen.

A number of tower-type domes, often in a very modest form of expression, are to be found in the field of anonymous, naive architecture. In a vineyard near Flonheim in the Rhineland, there is a shelter for the vintner which makes us imagine that we are on an island in the Mediterranean: a whitewashed rotunda having the typical contour of a pointed egg is a distant relative of centrally planned Mediterranean buildings.

Passing beyond the European continent, we can find some very similar morphological phenomena in Morocco. The marabouts are tombs and memorial sites for holy men of Islam. They harbour within themselves a relatively small inner room, often decked out with modest sacrificial offerings such as plants, flowers and stones. Once again, the sheltering, motherly room of death is linked to a rising element whose upper section is approximately conical in shape. This element has a typical shape passing from a mountain into a tower, and can be interpreted as clearly masculine. The overall structure is a discernibly androgynous piece of architecture.

These descriptions have by no means provided an ideal model of androgyny, and they certainly do not constitute the last word in any reflections on male-female architecture. In spite of the numerous depictions to be found in the history of civilization, there cannot be an ideal androgynous person. Instead, there can only be approximations towards a living principle. In the same way, only the main features of thought processes can be indicated in architecture.

10. Conclusion

Androgynous architecture cannot be invented or fabricated. It is not a style or a tendency, but a latent reality in the world of buildings surrounding us. »Ambisexuality and androgyny are visible signs of a new epoch, of an era in which the relevance of intensive interpersonal relationships is increasingly becoming recognized. Ambisexual modes of existence can be the expression of a personality which, in its feelings, thoughts and actions, aims to achieve a synthesis of arbitrarily generated contrasts and which, in an androgynous life pattern, announces that it rejects traditional role concepts.[55]

»We must ... have the courage to jettison any ideological ballast and to advance into an area ... whose intensive investigation is being stimulated because humans long to fathom the innermost parts of their being. Ambisexuality and androgyny are elemental components of that same being ... whose manifold manifestations are a challenge to the human spirit.«

Androgyny is »a deliberately stylized attempt to overcome the division between objectivity and subjectivity, between the individual and society, indeed, between being a human and being divine.« (Tegetmeier, 1986)

The conviction that architecture today, as at all times, has the ability to employ symbols, metaphors and allegories in order to make statements about human existence should encourage us to extend the concept of androgyny to architecture too.

Anmerkungen

[1] 1882 unternahm E. Du Bois-Reymond den Versuch, »Die sieben Welträtsel« zu postulieren und kam zu dem Schluß: »ignoramus et ignorabimus« (Wir wissen es nicht und werden es nie wissen). 1892 veröffentlichte Ernst Haeckel *Die Welträtsel* als »Gemeinverständliche Studie über monistische Philosophie«.

[2] Neben dem »ethischen Dualismus« (gut – böse) und dem »anthropologischen Dualismus« (Seele – Leib) verzeichnet die Ideengeschichte noch eine Reihe weiterer Dualismen: »Naturphilosophischer Dualismus« (Geist – Materie), »erkenntnistheoretischer Dualismus« (Sinnlichkeit – Verstand), »metaphysischer Dualismus« (vergängliche Erscheinungswelt – ewige Ideenwelt), »methodischer Dualismus« (Geisteswissenschaft – Naturwissenschaft). René Descartes (1596–1650) unterscheidet die denkende Substanz der Seele (res cogitans) von der ausgedehnten Substanz der Materie (res extensa).

[3] Bisweilen wird auch der Terminus »Androgynität« verwendet.

[4] »Wer von der Androgynie spricht, berührt mit einer doppelten Antenne die Tiefen seines eigenen Unbewußten.«

[5] »Ein bevorzugtes Beispiel aus der reinen Mythe.«

[6] Geläufig ist auch der Terminus »Transvestitismus«.

[7] Die Begriffe werden in der Literatur sehr unterschiedlich verwendet. Dies ist auch daraus verständlich, daß die Phänomene nicht klar abgegrenzt werden können; Übergänge und Verklammerungen sind möglich, insbesondere bei den Begriffen Transsexualismus (Transsexualität), Transvestismus und Intersexualität. Das Begriffsfeld wird noch ergänzt durch einige Affinitäten zur Homosexualität. Der medizinische und psychologische Teil muß im Zusammenhang mit dieser Arbeit weitgehend ausgeklammert werde. Von Interesse sind die frühen (19. Jahrhundert) Auseinandersetzungen mit dem Thema. Dazu nur einige Stichworte: Hermaphroditus verus, Zwitter, »Erreur de sexe«, Urning, Geschlechtsdrüsen – Keimdrüsen, Chromosomen X, Y, Chromosomenanomalien, Eierstock- und Hodengewebe, Hormonstaus, chromosomales und gondales Geschlecht, sexuelle Zwischenstufen.

Aus der Literatur des 19. Jahrhunderts sollen einige Namen genannt werden: Wilhelm Fließ (1858–1928), Sigmund Freud (1856–1939), Alfred Adler (1870–1937), Carl Gustav Jung (1875–1961), Otto Weininger (1880–1903), Magnus Hirschfeld (1868–1935).

[8] Diesen Mythos finden wir bei den Phöniziern, den Indern, in China, in Japan, in Peru, bei den Polynesiern, Finnen und Slawen, vor allem aber in der griechischen Mythologie.

[9] Architekturwettbewerbe und Projekte sind eine reiche Quelle für morphologische Tendenzen der Gegenwartsarchitektur, und die Ellipse taucht immer häufiger auf. Bei einem Wettbewerb für das Technologiezentrum in Hagen schlagen die Gewinner des 2. Preises, A. Janssen und R. Beckerwahl, drei dominate Baukörper in Ellipsenform vor (1991). Auf den Wettbewerb von Kleine-Kraneburg und Gruber für das Bundespräsidialamt in Berlin wird im Kap. 9.3.3 hingewiesen.

Der nicht ausgeführte preisgekrönte Entwurf von Wilhelm Holzbauer für das Regierungsviertel in St. Pölten (1990) versucht, die einzelnen Baukörper in eine eiförmige Megaform zusammenzufassen, wobei Holzbauer bei diesem Wettbewerb nicht der einzige war, der mit der Ellipse operierte.

[10] Die Aktualität dieser Idee wird in der Kunst deutlich. Constantin Brancusi etwa formte 1924 aus Marmor ein Ei. Er gab der Arbeit den Titel *Weltenanfang*.

[11] Die Zugehörigkeit der biologischen und psychologischen Phänomene zu sekundären und tertiären Geschlechtsmerkmalen ist keineswegs eindeutig geklärt, das Existieren tertiärer Geschlechtsmerkmale wird vielfach geleugnet.

[12] Diese Werte weisen eine beträchtliche ethnologische Streuung auf und sind außerdem stark altersabhängig.

[13] Der Begriff »Gender« ist mit »Geschlecht« nicht identisch. »Lenses of Gender«: die Sichtweisen, Linsen, der Focus des Genus.

[14] »Polarisierung des Genus, Mannzentrierung, biologische Wesenheit.« »Diese drei Sichtweisen des Genus gewährleisten die Begründung für eine Theorie, wie Biologie, Kultur und die individuelle Psyche im historischen Zusammenhang zusammenwirken, um die Männerdominanz zu reproduzieren.«

[15] Das Henkelkreuz gehört in erster Linie der ägyptischen Symbolwelt an und hat verschiedene Deutungen erfahren, vor allem als Lebenssymbol, als eine Figur mit ausgebreiteten Armen. Eine andere Interpretation, die ebenfalls mit dem Leben zusammenhängt, sieht darin das Gerät zum Abnabeln der Neugeborenen.

[16] Beschneidungen als rituelle Operationen im Zusammenhang mit Initiationsriten. Subinzision: Aufschneiden des Penis oder der Harnröhre, Zirkumzision: Auf- und Wegschneiden der Vorhaut (Judentum). Bisweilen bei Mädchen: Entfernen der Klitoris oder der kleinen Schamlippen.

[17] Die »Knabenliebe« entfaltete sich zwischen erwachsenen reiferen Männern und Knaben im Entwicklungsstadium der Pubertät. Sie umfaßte erotisch bis genital-sexuelle Beziehungen. Durch den femininen Habitus der Knaben ergibt sich ein Randphänomen der Androgynie.

[18] Lekythos: Henkelkrug mit schmalem Hals, figurativ geschmückt.

[19] Auch Lingam/Yoni.

[20] Weiterhin finden wir unter den Urgottheiten der Mexikaner, der Inkas, der Babylonier, der Sumerer u. a. zweigeschlechtliche, göttliche Wesen.

[21] Trinitätsvorstellungen sind keineswegs auf das Christentum beschränkt, sondern stellen gleichsam einen Archetypus dar. Besonders deutlich ist er im Hinduismus ausgeprägt.

[22] Im jüdischen Talmud wird die Zuordnung von Mann und Frau sehr radikal formuliert: »Wer ohne Frau lebt, ist kein Mensch, denn es heißt, als Mann und Frau erschuf er sie ... und nannte ihren Namen Mensch.«

[23] Die Vorstellung einer tatsächlichen androgynen »Ehe« ist sehr aufschlußreich auf einer Hochzeitsmedaille aus dem Italien des 17. Jh. dargestellt: Das Ehepaar ist zu einem einzigen Körper verschmolzen, aber die Gesichter sind einander zugewandt. (Vgl. Kap. 6.1.)

[24] Es darf nicht übersehen werden, daß im Christentum auch die Jungfräulichkeit, die Ehelosigkeit um Gottes Willen einen hohen Stellenwert inne hat.

Georg Koepgen (1939) sieht allerdings auch im Zölibat durchaus androgyne Ansätze: »... der jungfräuliche Priester ... vollzieht in seiner Seele die androgyne Einheit des Männlichen und Weiblichen.«

[25] Außer von Franz von Baader wurden die Gedanken noch von Jakob Böhme weitergetragen und modifiziert von Johann Georg Gichtel (1638 bis 1710), Gottfried Arnold (1666–1714), Friedrich Christoph Oetinger (1702–1782) und Michael Hahn (1758–1819).

[26] Die historische, theologische und ikonographische Abgrenzung zwischen Johannes dem Täufer und Johannes dem Evangelisten (und Apostel) kann nicht eindeutig vollzogen werden.

Der Apostel Johannes (der »Liebling« des Herrn) wird ebenfalls bartlos und feminin dargestellt, häufig in erotischer Position zu Christus.

[27] In den Tänzen vieler Völker wird der Transvestismus praktiziert. So etwa in Rajasthan, wobei die magisch-kultischen Bezüge entscheidend sind.

[28] Im westlichen Kulturkreis gehören neben den Schotten auch die katholischen Priester zu den männlichen Rockträgern. Im asiatischen Bereich hat sich diese Thematik nicht polarisiert.

[29] Zu den beliebtesten Hosenrollen im Film zählt die Gestalt des Peter Pan: Der fröhliche, dynamische, junge und flotte Knabe findet in der weiblichen Darstellung eine adäquate Interpretation.

Von den ernsten Themen, denen sich der Film gewidmet hat, kann noch *Das Bildnis des Dorian Gray* genannt werden: 1983/84 spielte Veruschka von Lehndorff die Titelrolle.

[30] »Unverwirklichbare Realisation der Vereinigung von Tadzio und Aschenbach.«

[31] Der Travestie im Kino widmet Kaltenecker (1993) eine ausführliche Analyse. Das Crossdressing-Phänomen wird vor allem anhand des Films *Tootsie* analytisch-spekulativ erörtert.

Weitere Filme werden zur Reflexion des Phänomens herangezogen: *Aus eines Mannes Mädchenzeit* (Deutschland 1912), *The perfect Lady* (USA 1915, Charlie Chaplin), *The Playhouse* (USA 1921, mit Buster Keaton), *Our Hospitality* (USA 1923, mit Buster Keaton), *Viktor und Viktoria* (Deutschland, 1933), *Crimson Pirat* (USA 1953, Richard Siodmak, mit Burt Lancaster), *The Magic Christian* (USA 1969, Joseph Mc Grath, mit Yul Brynner), *They Got me Covered* (USA 1964), *Das süße Leben des Graf Bobby* (Deutschland 1963, mit Peter Alexander), *I was a Male War Bride* (USA 1949, mit Cary Grant), *What Did You Do In The War, Daddy?* (USA 1966, Blake Edwar, mit Dick Shawn), *Babes On Broadway* (USA 1941, Buybs Bekeley, mit Mickey Rooney), *Some Like it Hot* (USA 1959, Billy Wilder, mit Jack Lemmon, Tony Curtis, Marilyn Monroe), *Thunderbold and Lightfood* (USA 1973, Michael Ciminos, mit Jeff Bridges), *Der Fürst von Pappenheim* (Deutschland 1927), *Charleys Tante* (Deutschland 1955/Österreich 1963, mit Heinz Rühmann, und Geza von

Cziffra), *That's My Wife* (USA 1932, mit Stan Laurel), *Paradise ist not for Sale* (Dänemark 1984, Teit Ritzan, Christine Jorgensen, Han-ne Rasmussen, Thomas Holck).

Androgyne Ansätze lassen sich bei einiger Interpretationstoleranz auch in folgenden Filmen aufspüren: *Fahrenheit 451* (England 1966, François Truffaut), *Modesty Blaise* (England, 1965, Josef Losey), *Barbarella* (Italien/Frankreich 1967, Roger Vadim), *Alphaville* (Frankreich/Italien 1965, Jean-Luc Godard), *Unheimliche Begegnung der dritten Art*, (USA 1977, Steven Spielberg).

Die Aktualität des Themas zeigt sich auch daran, daß man ihm umfassende Würdigung in festivalartigen Veranstaltungen zuteil werden läßt.

[32] Einige der Grenzfälle zur Androgynie wurden schon erwähnt: die Homosexualität und der Transsexualismus. Weitere Randprobleme können nur zitiert werden: die Geschlechtslosigkeit (ikonographisch etwa bei den Engeln), der Narzißmus (Selbstverliebtheit mit Verzicht auf das andere Geschlecht), das Zölibat (Ehelosigkeit aus ideellen Motiven), die Endogamie (Partner aus engerer sozialer Gruppe), der Inzest (Goethe: Lilien sind Gatte und Gattin auf einem Stengel), die Mensch-Tier-Coincidentia (mythische Wesen), die Mensch-Pflanze-Coincidentia u. a. m.

[33] Auch In der Kunst der Nazarener ab 1810 und der Malerei der Präraffeliten ab 1848 treten häufig deutliche androgyne Züge auf.

[34] Im Werk des belgischen Symbolisten Fernand Khnopff finden sich offenkundig weitere androgyne Motive.

[35] »An meinen kleinen Schuh sein Freund Yves Tanguy«.

[36] »Der Baphomet bietet dem großen Meister seine Dienste an.«

[37] »... betrachtet den Androgyn wie das exemplarische Bild des perfekten Menschen ... totales Sein«.

[38] Der Symbolbegriff wäre wesentlich zu erweitern: Die Termini einer manifesten, latenten, projektiven und interpretativen Symbolsprache wurden an anderer Stelle erörtert. (Feuerstein 1985)

[39] Der Antike ist das Problem »männlich«/»weiblich« in der Architektur durchaus geläufig: Die Tempel, die Säulenordnungen werden als männlich, weiblich oder jungfräulich bezeichnet. Und noch Humboldt spricht von »männlicher und weiblicher Form« in der Architektur.

[40] Die schiefen Türme infolge mangelhaften Baugrundes wurden als Attraktion bisweilen absichtlich gebaut. Hans Hollein konzipiert 1995 in Wien einen »schiefen Turm« für eine Versicherungsgesellschaft.

[41] Die künstlichen Grotten in den Boboli-Gärten in Florenz, im Garten der Villa d'Este in Tivoli, in Hellbrunn bei Salzburg und später noch in der Romantik sollen zitiert werden.

[42] Durch die Begehbarkeit der Brust wird sie gleichzeitig zur Kuppel, zur Höhle. Vgl. Kap. 7.6. über Doppelkodierung.

[43] Die »Revolutionsarchitektur« Porros im Auftrag Fidel Castros fiel bald in Ungnade und verfällt heute zusehends.

[44] Gebaut gemeinsam mit Armand Bartos.

[45] »In Fortsetzung der sanften pornographischen Neigung des Daisy House ist der Lageplan in Gestalt eines Zippverschlusses organisiert. Die Genitalien sind Eingangsstiegen, die Grünanlage zeigt unverkennbar die Zeichen der Mannbarkeit.«

[46] »Eine sorgfältige Prüfung wird aufzeigen, daß seine Planungen auf dem Nebeneinander von zwei unterschiedlichen Elementen beruhen wie linear und geradkurvig, freikurvig und rechtwinklig, axial und nicht-axial, barock und klassisch. Diese Elemente stehen nicht im Kontrapunkt zueinander, sondern in einer Vereinigung. Sie formen keine Schichten von Bedeutungen oder Zwitter. Im Endergebnis bilden sie eine Kombination von zwei Gegensätzen: konkav und konvex, Sporenpflanzen und Samenpflanzen, männlich und weiblich, androgyn.«

[47] Der Turm nimmt bewußt oder unbewußt die Proportionen von St. Stephan in Wien auf.

[48] Im realisierten Bau ist diese Dialektik nicht mehr so deutlich spürbar wie im ersten Entwurf.

[49] Das Thema der bewohnbaren Säule war schon um 1800 bekannt. Barbier beispielsweise baute für den Park in Marly eine bewohnbare, scheinbar abgebrochene Säule.

[50] Die signifikanten Beispiele baute das »Rote Wien« in den pathetischen Großformen der Gemeindebauten. Auch in Berlin und Amsterdam hat die große Gestik des Wohnbaues Anklang gefunden.

[51] Nochmals sei der heilige Sebastian erwähnt: Trotz der Durchbohrung mit den Pfeilen weisen die Sebastian-Darstellungen ein verzücktes, erotisches Antlitz auf.

[52] Erstmals in Szene gesetzt durch Philip Johnsons Ausstellung *Deconstructivist Architecture*, New York 1987.

[53] Wolf-Dieter Prix (geb. 1942) und Helmut Swiczinsky (geb. 1944).

[54] Laurids Ortner (geb. 1941), Günter Zamp-Kelp (geb. 1941), Klaus Pinter (geb. 1940), später Manfred Ortner (geb. 1943).

[55] Nicht ganz so deutlich ist der erotische Eintritt bei den kolossalen Frauenfiguren wie etwa der Freiheitsstatue in New York oder der Bavaria in München.

[56] Der Schrein des Buches von Frederick Kiesler wurde in Kap. 7.6 behandelt.

[57] Eine Vorstufe zur Vereinigung, eine Art Flächenschluß, sind die gegenseitig übergeschlagenen Beine der Liebenden in der Ikonographie. Nach Orchard (1992) ist es eine Metapher für die Kopulation.

[58] Der Autor arbeitet an dem Thema weiter in einem umfangreichen Forschungsprojekt mit dem Titel »Androgynie – coincidentia oppositorum«.

Literatur

Amrain, Susanne, »Der Androgyn. Das poetische Geschlecht und sein Aktus«, in: *Frauen, Weiblichkeit, Schrift*, Tagungsschrift, Bielefeld 1984, Berlin 1985.

»Tadao Ando«, *El Croquis* (Madrid), 58, XII, 1993.

Andreae, Johann Valentin, *Christianopolis*, Stuttgart 1972.

Androgyn. Sehnsucht nach Vollkommenheit, Ausstellungskatalog, Berlin 1986.

Der Architekt (Stuttgart), Heft 6, 1977.

Arnold, Christina, »Die Rezeption der feministischen Theologie«, in: *Religionspädagogische Schriften*, o. O. 1990.

Louise Bourgeois, *art* (Hamburg), Heft 6, 1993.

Assunto, Rosario, *Die Theorie des Schönen im Mittelalter*, Köln 1963.

Auböck, Maria, »Das Vienna Eros Hilton«, *Architektur aktuell* (Wien), Heft 41, 1974.

Aurnhammer, Achim, »Zum Hermaphroditen in der Sinnbildkunst der Alchemisten«. in: C. Meinel (Hrsg.), *Die Alchemie in der europäischen Kultur- und Wissenschaftsgeschichte*, Wiesbaden 1986.

Aurnhammer, Achim, *Androgynie*, Köln und Wien 1986.

Baader, Franz von, *Sätze aus der erotischen Philosophie und anderen Schriften*, hrsg. v. G. K. Kaltenbrunner, Frankfurt 1966.

Baader, Franz von, *Ausgewählte Schriften zum androgynen Menschenbild*, Bensheim 1991.

Bachelard, Gaston, *Poetik des Raumes*, Frankfurt am Main 1987.

Bachelard, Gaston, *Die Bildung des wissenschaftlichen Geistes. Beitrag zu einer Psychoanalyse der objektiven Erkenntnis*, Frankfurt am Main 1978.

Bachofen, Johann Jakob, *Eine Auswahl*, hrsg. von Rudolf Marx,Stuttgart 1941.

Bachofen, Johann Jakob, *Mutterrecht und Urreligion*, Stuttgart 1954.

Badinter, Elisabeth, *Ich bin Du, Die neue Beziehung zwischen Mann und Frau oder Die androgyne Revolution*, München und Zürich 1991.

Balzac, Honoré de, *Seraphita*, Wien 1922.

Balzac, Honoré de, *Gesammelte Werke. Sarrasine* (u. a. Novellen), Berlin o. J.

Barbier, Patrick, *Farinelli – Der Kastrat der Könige*, Düsseldorf 1995.

Bastin, Georges, *Wörterbuch der Sexualpsychologie*, Freiburg-Basel, Wien 1972.

Bataille, Georges, *Der heilige Eros*, Neuwied 1963.

Baumann, Hermann, *Schöpfung und Urzeit des Menschen im Mythos der afrikanischen Völker*, Berlin 1936.

Baumann, Hermann, *Das doppelte Geschlecht – Ethnologische Studie zur Bisexualität in Ritus und Mythos*, Berlin 1955, 1986.

Beardsley, Aubrey; *The Collected Drawing of Aubrey Beardsley*, New York 1967.

Beauvoir, Simone de, *Das andere Geschlecht, Sitte und Sexus der Frau*, Berlin und Darmstadt 1981.

Becker, Gerhold, *Die Ursymbole in den Religionen*, Graz und Wien 1988.

Becker-Schmidt, Regina, *Geschlechtertrennung, Geschlechterdifferenz*, Bonn-Bad-Godesberg 1989.

Beckford, William, *Vathek – Eine arabische Erzählung*, München 1964.

Begegnung mit den anderen, Ausstellungskatalog (»Gegen-documenta«), Hann. Münden 1992.

Bell-Metereau, Rebecca, *Hollywood Androgyny*, New York 1985.

Beltz, Walter, *Die Mythen der Ägypter*, Düsseldorf 1982.

Bem, Sandra L., »Die Harten und die Zarten«, *Psychologie heute,* (Weinheim und Basel) Heft 2, 1976.

Bem, Sandra L., *Sex Role Adaptility*, New Haven (Conn.) 1975.

Bem, Sandra L., *The Measurement of Psychological Androgyny*, New Haven (Conn.) 1974.

Benz, Ernst, *Der vollkommene Mensch nach Jacob Boehme*, Stuttgart 1937.

Benz, Ernst, Adam, *Der Mythos vom Urmenschen*, München 1955.

Berdjajew, Nikolaj, *Die Bestimmung des Menschen*, Bern und Leipzig 1935.

Berne, Eric, *Spiele der Erwachsenen*, Hamburg 1967.

Berner, Ole, *Hermaphroditismus und sexuelle Umstimmung*, Leipzig 1938.

Bernsdorff, Madeleine, und Stefanie Hetze, *Frauen in Hosen*, München 1989.

Bertholet, Alfred, *Das Geschlecht der Gottheit*, Tübingen 1934.

Bieber, M., *The Sculpture of the Hellenistic Age*, New York 1955.

Biedermann, Hans, »Das Androgyn-Symbol in der Alchemie«, in: *Androgyn. Sehnsucht nach Vollkommenheit*, Berlin 1986.

Biedermann, Hans, *Die großen Mütter. Die schöpferische Rolle der Frau in der Menschheitsgeschichte*, Graz und Wien 1987.

Bierhoff-Alfermann, Dorothee, *Psychologie der Geschlechtsunterschiede*, Köln 1977.

Bierhoff-Alfermann, Dorothee, *Androgynie – Möglichkeiten und Grenzen der Geschlechterrollen*, Opladen 1989.

Bischof, Norbert und Holger Preuschoft (Hrsg.); *Geschlechtsunterschiede. Entstehung und Entwicklung, Mann und Frau in biologischer Sicht*, München 1980.

Blavatsky, H. P., *Die Geheimlehre. Die Vereinigung von Wissenschaft, Religion und Philosophie*, 4 Bde. (*Kosmogenesis, Anthropogenesis, Esoterik, Index*), Wien 1899, Ulm 1958.

Bleibtreu-Ehrenberg, Gisela Ingeborg, *Sexuelle Abartigkeit im Urteil der abendländischen Religions-, Geistes- und Rechtsgeschichte im Zusammenhang mit der Gesellschaftsentwicklung*, Diss., Bonn 1970.

Bleibtreu-Ehrenberg, Gisela Ingeborg, *Der Weibmann, Kultischer Geschlechtswechsel im Schamanismus*, Frankfurt am Main 1989.

Bloc, André, *De la Sculpture à l'architecture*, Boulogne 1964.

Bloch, Ernst, *Geist der Utopie*, Frankfurt am Main 1964.

Bock, Ulla, *Androgynie und Feminismus. Frauenbewegung zwischen Institution und Utopie,* Ber-

lin und Basel 1988 (*Ergebnisse der Frauenforschung*, Bd. 16).

Bock, Ulla, »Androgynie. Ein Modell für ein verändertes Verhältnis von Frau und Mann?«, 5. Würzburger Symposion, Februar 1991: *Mann und Frau – Frau und Mann*, Würzburg 1991.

Böckelman, F., »Zur Auflösung der Geschlechtsrollen«, in: H. Kentler (Hrsg.), *Texte zur Sozio-Sexualität*, Opladen 1973.

Böhme, Jakob, *Sämtliche Schriften*, Stuttgart 1958.

Böhme, Jakob, *Mysterium Magnum oder Erklärung über Das Erste Buch Mosis* (1623), Stuttgart 1958.

Boff, Leonardo, *Das mütterliche Antlitz Gottes*, Düsseldorf 1985.

Bogner, Dieter (Hrsg.), *Friedrich Kiesler 1890 bis 1965*, Ausstellungskatalog, Wien 1988.

Bolsena, Pietro, *La iconologia bisessuale, segreto di Raffaelo*, Wien 1980.

Bornemann, Ernest, *Das Patriarchat. Ursprung und Zukunft unseres Gesellschaftssystems*, Frankfurt am Main 1975.

Bornemann, Ernest, *Der Mythos vom Doppelten Geschlecht*, München 1981

Boullée, Étienne-Louis, *Architektur. Abhandlung über die Kunst,* mit einer Einführung und einem Kommentar von Adolf Max Vogt, Zürich und München 1987.

Braun, Christiane von, »Männliche Hysterie – weibliche Askese«, in: Karin Rick (Hrsg.), *Das Sexuelle, die Frauen und die Kunst*, Tübingen 1987.

Braunschweig, Rosa v., »Felicita von Vestvali«, in: Magnus Hirschfeld (Hrsg.), *Jahrbuch für sexuelle Zwischenstufen*, Leipzig 1903.

Breitner, Burghard, *Das Problem der Bisexualität*, Wien 1951.

Brückner, Margit, »Die Sehnsucht nach dem Kugelmenschen oder vom Wunsch nach Aufhebung der Geschlechtertrennung«, in: C. Hagemann-White und Maria S. Rerrich (Hrsg.), *Frauen, Männer, Bilder*, Bielefeld 1988.

Burchard, Johann M., *Struktur und Soziologie des Transvestitismus und Transsexualismus*, Stuttgart 1961.

Burri, Josef, *Als Mann und Frau schuf er sie*, Zürich, Einsiedeln und Köln 1977.

Busst, A. J. L., »The Image of the Androgyne in the 19th Century«, in: Jan Fletcher (Hrsg.), *Romantic Mythologies*, New York 1967.

Bynum, Caroline Walker, *Jesus as mother*, Berkeley (Calif.) 1982.

Carrà, Carlo, *L'opera completa di Carrà dal futurismo alla metafisica e al realismo mitico 1910–1930*, Mailand 1970.

Casanova, Giacomo, *Eduard und Elisabeth oder die Reise in das Innere unseres Erdballs*, Frankfurt am Main und Berlin 1968.

Christ, Felix, *Jesus Sophia*, Zürich 1970.

Clemen, Carl, *Die Religionen der Erde. Ihr Wesen und Ihre Geschichte*, München 1966.

Colegrave, Sukie, *The Spirit of the Valley. Androgyn and Chinese Thought*, London 1979.

Colonna, Francesco (Francesco Giorgio Martin), *Hypnerotomachia poliphilii*, Padua 1499.

Comenius, Johann Amos, *Vorspiele – Prodromus Pansophiae, Vorläufer der Pansophie*, Düsseldorf 1963.

Conrads, Ulrich, und Hans G. Sperlich, *Phantastische Architektur*, Stuttgart 1960.

Cranston, Jones, *Architecture Today and Tomorrow*, New York 1961.

Daidalos (Berlin), Heft 45, 1992.

Daniels, Dieter, *Duchamp und die anderen. Der Modellfall einer künstlerischen Wirkungsgeschichte in der Moderne*, Köln 1992.

Degenhart, Annette, und Hans Martin Trautner (Hrsg.), *Mann und Frau in psychologischer Sicht*, München 1979.

Dekker, Rudolf und Lotte van de Pol, *Frauen in Männerkleidern. Weibliche Transvestiten und ihre Geschichte*, Berlin 1989/90.

Delcourt, Marie, *Hermaphrodite. Mythes et rites de la bisexualité dans l'antique classique*, Paris 1958.

Delcourt, Marie, *Hermaphroditea. Recherches sur l'être double, promoteur de la fertilité dans la monde classique*, Brüssel 1960.

Devereux, Georges, *Baubo. Die mythische Vulva*, Frankfurt am Main 1981.

Dieterich, Albrecht, *Mutter Erde. Ein Versuch über Volksreligion*, Leipzig 1905 (1913, 1925).

Döhl, Reinhard, *Hermann Finsterlin. Eine Annäherung*, Stuttgart 1988.

Douglas, Mary, *Ritual, Tabu und Körpersymbolik. Sozialanthropologische Studien in Industriegesellschaft und Stammeskultur*, Frankfurt am Main 1974.

Jean Dubuffet, Ausstellungskatalog, Kunsthaus Wien, Wien 1995.

Duerr, Hans Peter (Hrsg.), *Sehnsucht nach dem Ursprung. Zu Mircea Eliade*, Frankfurt am Main 1983.

Duerr, Hans Peter (Hrsg.), *Die Mitte der Welt. Aufsätze zu Mircea Eliade*, Frankfurt am Main 1984.

Duerr, Hans Peter, *Sedna oder Die Liebe zum Leben*, Frankfurt am Main 1985.

Duerr, Hans Peter, *Der Mythos vom Zivilisationsprozeß*, Bd. 1: *Nacktheit und Scham.* Frankfurt am Main 1988.

Duerr, Hans Peter, *Der Mythos vom Zivilisationsprozeß*, Bd. 2: *Intimität.*, Frankfurt am Main 1990.

Ehmann, Peter, *Zur Ätiologie und Phänomenologie ambisexueller und androgyner Daseinsweisen. Versuch einer Überwindung des Bisexualitäts-Konzepts*, Diss., Bonn 1976.

Eibl-Eibesfeldt, Irenäus, *Die Biologie des menschlichen Verhaltens. Grundriß der Humanethologie*, München und Zürich 1984.

Eliade, Mircea, *Ewige Bilder und Sinnbilder. Vom unvergänglichen menschlichen Seelenraum*, Freiburg im Breisgau 1952 und Frankfurt am Main 1986.

Eliade, Mircea, *Der Mythos der ewigen Wiederkehr*, Düsseldorf 1953.

Eliade, Mircea, *Schmiede und Alchemisten*, Stuttgart 1956.

Eliade, Mircea, *Das Heilige und das Profane. Vom Wesen des Religiösen*, Hamburg 1957.

Eliade, Mircea, *Mephistophélès et l'Androgyne*, Paris 1962.

Eliade, Mircea, *Archaic techniques of ecstasy*, London 1970.

Eliade, Mircea, *Die Religionen und das Heilige*, Darmstadt 1976.

Eliade, Mircea, *Mythos und Wirklichkeit*, Frankfurt am Main 1988.

Ellis, Havelock, und J. A. Symonds, *Das konträre Geschlechtsgefühl*, Leipzig 1896.

Ellis, Havelock *Studies in the Psychology of Sex*, vol. 7: *Eonism and Other Supplementary Studies*, Philadelphia 1928.

Erikson, Erik Homburger, *Jugend und Krise. Die Psychodynamik im sozialen Wandel*, Stuttgart 1970.

Erikson, Erik Homburger, »Genitale Modi und räumliche Modalitäten«, *Bauwelt* (Berlin), Heft 31/32, 1979.

Erler, Gisela Anna, *Frauenzimmer. Für eine Politik des Unterschiedes*, Berlin 1985.

»Erotik und Architektur – gibt es eine Beziehung?«, *Der Architekt* (Stuttgart), Heft 6, 1977, mit Beiträgen von I. Bielicki, O. Jacobsen, G. Feuerstein, W. Pehnt, A. Ginelli, V. Marg, R. Gieselmann, H. Hollein, H. J. Guckel, W. Bunsmann, R. Häuser, G. Gruner und P. Vehling.

Femininmasculin, Le sexe de l'art, Ausstellungskatalog, Centre Pompidou, Paris 1995.

Ferenczi, Sándor, *Versuch einer Genitaltheorie*, Leipzig und Wien 1924.

Fergusson, James, *A History of Indian and Eastern Architecture*, London und New York 1899.

Feuerstein, Günther, *Archetypen des Bauens*, Diss., Wien 1966.

Feuerstein, Günther, *Visionäre Architektur: Wien 1958/1988*, Berlin 1988.

Feuerstein, Günther, »Eros – Architektur – Sexualität«, *Transparent* (Wien), Heft 1/2, 1988.

Feuerstein, Günther, »Architektur als ›sprechende Person‹«, *Daidalos* (Berlin), Heft 45, 1992.

Field Belenky, M., u. a., *Das andere Denken. Persönlichkeit, Moral und Intellekt der Frau*, Frankfurt am Main 1989.

Film-Kurier (Wien), Heft 318, 1983.

Fink, Gerhard, *Who's who in der antiken Mythologie*, München 1993.

Fleischer, Robert, *Die römischen Bronzen aus Österreich*, Mainz 1967.

Fletcher, Ian (Hrsg.), *Romantic Mythologies*, New York 1967.

Fliess, Wilhelm, *Der Ablauf des Lebens. Grundlegung zur exakten Biologie*, Leipzig und Wien 1923.

Forcher, Eberhard, »Who's bad? Mythos Jackson«, *Wiener* (Wien), Heft 97, 1988.

Frauen, Weiblichkeit, Schrift, Tagungsschrift, Bielefeld 1984 und Berlin 1985.

Freud, Sigmund, *Totem und Tabu*, London 1940.

Freud, Sigmund, *Über Psychoanalyse*, Wien 1947.

Freud, Sigmund, *Abriß der Psychoanalyse. Das Unbehagen in der Kultur,* mit einer Rede von Thomas Mann, Frankfurt am Main 1972.

Freud, Sigmund, *Werkausgabe in 2 Bänden*, hrsg. von Anna Freud und Ilse Grubrich-Simitis, Frankfurt am Main 1978.

Frobenius, Leo, *Die Weltanschauung der Naturvölker*, Weimar 1898.

Gail, A., »Die zweigeschlechtliche Gottheit in Indien«, in: *Jahrbuch für Kunstgeschichte*, Bd. 17, Graz 1981.

Galahad, Sir, *Mütter und Amazonen. Ein Umriß weiblicher Reiche*, München 1932.

Gallas, Klaus, *Iran, Kulturstätten Persiens. Zwischen Wüsten, Steppen und Bergen*, Köln 1976.

Garber, Marjorie, *Verhüllte Interessen. Transvestismus und kulturelle Angst*, Frankfurt am Main 1993.

Gassner, Jutta, *Phallische und ithyphallische Darstellungen und Kulte*, 3 Bde., Wien 1989.

Gassner, Jutta, *Phallos – Fruchtbarkeitssymbol oder Abwehrzauber?*, Wien 1993.

Gauster, Hannelore, »Zu Hermaphroditen-Darstellungen in der Antike«, in: *Frauen, Weiblichkeit, Schrift*, Tagungsschrift, Bielefeld 1984 und Berlin 1985.

Gautier, Theophile, *Mademoiselle de Maupin*, Hellerau 1926.

Geisler, Eduard, *Psychologie für Architekten. Eine Einführung in dle Architekturpsychologische Denk-Arbeitsweise*, Stuttgart 1978.

Giedion, Sigfried, *Ewige Gegenwart. Die Entstehung der Kunst. Ein Beitrag zu Konstanz und Wechsel*, Köln 1964.

Giedion, Sigfried, *Architektur und das Phänomen des Wandels. Die drei Raumkonzeptionen in der Architektur,* Tübingen 1969.

Giese, Fritz, *Der romantische Charakter,* Bd. I: *Die Entwicklung des androgynen Problems in der Frühromantik*, Langensalza 1919.

Giese, Hans, und E. V. Gebsattel (Hrsg.), *Psychopathologie der Sexualität*, Stuttgart 1962.

Gildemeister, Regine, »Weibliches Denken – Männliches Denken. Oder: Sind zwei Geschlechter genug?«, *Wissenschaft ist Frauensache* (Kassel), Heft 6.

Ginelli, Anatol, »Bauten und Entwürfe«, *Bauwelt* (Berlin), Heft 21, 1986.

Glas und Keramik des Jugendstils in Österreich. Aus den Sammlungen des österreichischen Museums für angewandte Kunst in Wien, Ausstellungskatalog, Wien 1989.

Glück, H., und E. Diez, *Die Kunst des Islams*, Berlin 1925.

Goebel, Gerhard, »Locus Amoenus oder die Architektur der Lust«, in: *Kunstforum international* (Köln)*,* Nr. 69, 1984.

Gomperz, Th. (Hrsg.), *Auswahl herkulanischer kleiner Schriften*, o. O. 1993.

Görlich, Walter, *Der Hermaphrodit von Virunum*, Wien 1941.

Gorsen, Peter, *Das Bild Pygmalions*, Reinbek bei Hamburg 1969.

Gorsen, Peter: *Das Prinzip Obszön. Kunst, Pornographie und Gesellschaft*, Reinbek bei Hamburg 1969.

Gorsen, Peter, *Sexualästhetik. Zur bürgerlichen Rezeption von Obszönitat und Pornographie*, Hamburg 1972.

Gorsen, Peter; »Intersexualismus und Subkultur« in: A. Matthes (Hrsg.), *Maskulin-Feminin*, München 1975.

Gotlieb, Howard, *William Beckford of Fonthill. Writer, Traveller, Collector, Caliph 1760–1844*, New Haven (Conn.) 1960.

Göttner-Abendroth, Heide, *Die Göttin und ihr Heros. Die matriarchalen Religionen in Mythos, Märchen und Dichtung*, München 1980.

Göttner-Abendroth, Heide, »Matriachale Mythologie«, in: B. Wartmann (Hrsg.), *Weiblich–Männlich*, Berlin 1980.

Grabovsky, Norbert, *Die mannweibliche Natur des Menschen. Mit Berücksichtigung des psychosexuellen Hermaphroditismus*, Leipzig 1896.

Graf, Otto Antonia, *Otto Wagner*, Bd. 3: *Die Einheit der Kunst. Weltgeschichte der Grundformen*, Wien und Köln 1990.

Green, Richard, »Die Suche nach der Geschlechtsrolle«, *Psychologie heute* (Weinheim und Basel), Mai 1976.

Grimm, Jacob, *Über den Liebesgott*, Berlin 1851.

Gusenberg, Richard M., und Dietmar Meyer, *Die dreißiger Jahre*, Berlin, Darmstadt und Wien 1970.

Gutschow, Niels, *Stadtraum und Ritual der newarischen Städte im Kathmandu-Tal*, Berlin, Köln und Mainz 1982.

Gutschow, Niels, und Jan Pieper, *Indien – Bauformen und Stadtgestalt einer beständigen Tradition*, Köln 1978.

Gutschow, Niels, und Jan Pieper, *Indien – Von den Klöstern im Himalaya zu den Tempelstädten Süd-Indiens,* Köln 1981.

Hacker, Friedrich, *Aggression. Die Brutalisierung der modernen Welt*, Wien, München und Zürich 1971.

Hacker, Friedrich, *Materialien zum Thema Aggression*, Wien 1972.

Hacker, Friedrich, *Terror. Mythos – Realität – Analyse*, Wien, München und Zürich 1973.

Haeckel, Ernst, *Monismus als Band von Religion und Wissenschaft*, o. O. 1892.

Haeckel, Ernst: *Die Welträtsel. Gemeinverständliche Studien über Monistische Philosophie*, Bonn 1902.

Haerle, Gerhard, *Männerweiblichkeit.· Zur Homosexualität bei Klaus und Thomas Mann*, Frankfurt am Main 1988.

Hagemann-White, C., und Maria S. Rerrich (Hrsg.): *Frauen Männer Bilder. Männer und Männlichkeit in der feministischen Diskuission*, Bielefeld 1988.

Halley des Fontaines, Jean, *La notion d'androgynie dans quelques mythes et quelques rites*, Paris 1938.

Hassauer, Friederike, *Félicien Rops*, Zürich 1984.

d'Harnoncourt, Anne, und Kynaston Mc Shine (Hrsg.), *Marcel Duchamp*, New York 1973, 1989.

Hauser, Arnold, *Der Ursprung der modernen Kunst und Literatur. Die Entwicklung des Manierismus seit der Krise der Renaissance*, München 1973.

Haus-Rucker-Co. 1967–1983, Braunschweig 1984.

Heberer, G. (Hrsg.), *Die Evolution der Organismen*, Stuttgart 1943, 1959

Herdick, Reinhard, »Kosmisch, sozial, leiblich. Gestalt – Ordnungen in Nepal und Marokko«, *Daidalos* (Berlin), 45, 1992.

Hesse, Hermann, *Narziss und Goldmund*, Berlin 1930.

Hesse, Hermann, *Piktors Verwandlungen*, Frankfurt am Main 1954.

Highwater, Jamake, *Sexualität und Mythos*, Freiburg im Breisgau 1992.

Hirschfeld, Magnus (Hrsg.), *Jahrbuch für sexuelle Zwischenstufen*, I.–V. Jg., Leipzig 1900 bis 1903.

Hirschfeld, Magnus, *Die Transvestiten: Eine Untersuchung über den erotischen Verkleidungstrieb*, Berlin 1910.

Hirschfeld, Magnus, *Sexualpathologie*, Bd. 1: *Geschlechtliche Entwicklungsstörungen*, Bonn 1917 (1922), Bd. 2: *Sexuelle Zwischenstufen.– Das männliche Weib und der weibliche Mann*, Bonn 1918.

Hirschfeld, Magnus, *Geschlechtskunde*, Bd. 1: *Die körperseelischen Grundlagen*, Stuttgart 1926 (1928).

Hocke, Gustav René, *Die Welt als Labyrinth. Manier und Manie in der europäischen Kunst*, München 1957.

Hofmann, Werner, *Das irdische Paradies. Motive und Ideen des 19. Jahrhunderts*, München 1960.

Hofmann, Werner, *Zauber der Medusa – Europäische Manierismen*, Wien 1987.

Hollein, Hans, »Zukunft der Architektur«, *Bau* (Wien), 1, 1965.

Hans Hollein, Ausstellungskatalog, Historisches Museum der Stadt Wien, Wien 1995.

Holtmont, Alfred, *Die Hosenrolle. Variationen über das Thema: Das Weib als Mann*, München 1925.

Hon, hon-en katedral/historia, Ausstellungskatalog, Moderna Museet Stockholm, Stockholm 1967.

Huizinga, Johan, *Homo Ludens. Vom Ursprung der Kultur im Spiel*, Hamburg 1956.

Hulten, Pontus, *Niki de Saint Phalle*, Ausstellungskatalog, Bundeskunsthalle, Bonn 1992.

Humboldt, Wilhelm von, »Über den Geschlechtsunterschied. Über die männliche und weibliche Form«, in: *Werke*, Band 1, Stuttgart 1841, Berlin 1917, Darmstadt 1960, 1981.

Hummel, Siegbert, *Die lamaistische Kunst*, Leipzig 1955.

Huysmans, J. K., *Felicien Rops – L'Œuvre graphique complète*, Paris 1977.

James, E. O., *Prehistoric Religions*, London 1957.

Jaspers, Karl, *Nikolaus Cusanus*, München 1987.

Jensen, A. E., *Mythos und Kult bei Naturvölkern. Religionswissenschaftliche Betrachtungen*, Wiesbaden 1951.

Jung, Carl Gustav, *Symbolik des Geistes. Studien über psychische Phänomenologie*, Zürich 1948.

Jung, Carl Gustav, *Der Mensch und seine Symbole*, Olten 1968.

Jung, Carl Gustav, *Psychologie und Alchemie*, Olten und Freiburg im Breisgau 1972, 1984, 1985.

Kähler, Gert, »Das Ei und ich oder: Warum ausgerechnet Hagen?«, *Baumeister* (München), Heft 2, 1992.

Kamprad, Barbara, und Waltraud Schiffels, *Im falschen Körper*, Hamburg 1991.

Kaufmann, Emil, *Architecture in the Age of Reason. Baroque and Post-Baroque in England, Italy and France*, New York 1955.

Keel, Othmar (Hrsg.), *Göttinnen, Götter und Gottessymbole*, Freiburg, Basel und Wien 1992.

Kiesler, Frederick, *Transparent* (Wien), Heft 3/4, 1984.

Kiesler, Frederick, *The Book of the Shrine*, Graz 1992.

Kirsch, Sarah, Irmtraud Morgner und Christa Wolf, *Geschlechtertausch. Drei Geschichten über die Umwandlung der Verhältnisse*, Frankfurt am Main 1980.

Klausmann, Ulrike, und Marion Meinzerin, *Piratinnen*, München 1992.

Klein, W., *Vom antiken Rokoko*, Wien 1921.

Kleinspehn, Thomas, *Der flüchtige Blick. Sehen und Identität in der Kultur der Neuzeit*, Hamburg 1989.

Klimowsky, Ernst W., *Das mann-weibliche Leitbild in der Antike*, München 1972.

Klimowsky, Ernst W., *Geschlecht und Geschichte. Sexualität im Wandel von Kultur und Kunst*, Wien 1956, München 1972.

Klossowski, Pierre, *Der Baphomet*, Hamburg 1968.

Klossowsky, Pierre, *Anima*, Ausstellungskatalog, Wiener Secession, Wien 1995.

Klotz, Heinrich (Hrsg.), *Vision der Moderne. Das Prinzip Konstruktion*, Ausstellungskatalog, München 1986.

Köb, Edelbert, *Ambivalenz*, Ausstellungskatalog, Wien 1990.

Köb, Edelbert, *Ausstellungsfolder*, Wien 1992.

Koenig, Otto, *Urmotiv Auge. Neuentdeckte Grundzüge menschlichen Verhaltens*, München 1975.

Koepgen, Georg, *Die Gnosis des Christentums*, Salzburg 1939.

Köhler, Wolfgang, *Die Aufgabe der Gestaltpsychologie*, Berlin 1971.

König, Oliver, *Nacktheit – Soziale Normierung und Moral*, Opladen 1990.

Kohtz, Otto, *Gedanken über Architektur*, Berlin 1909.

Jeff Koons, Ausstellungskatalog, Museum of Modern Art, San Francisco 1992.

Kraemer, Hans, *Das XIX. Jahrhundert in Wort und Bild*. Bd. 3: *1871-1899*, Berlin, Leipzig, Stuttgart und Wien o. J.

Kraft-Ebing, Richard v., *Psychopathia Sexualis*, München 1984.

Krätschmer, Renate und Jörg Schwarzenberger, *Über das männliche und weibliche Prinzip. Eine Ausstellung von Kusch*, Wiener Secession, Wien 1980.

Engelbert Kremser. Baukunst 1967–1987, Berlin 1986

Kšica, Miroslav und Eva und Olga Kšicová, *Frauenidole der Eiszeit und Nacheiszeit. Realität und Abstraktion von Muttergottheiten aus 30 Jahrtausenden*, Ausstellungskatalog, Linz, Brünn und Düsseldorf 1989.

Lachnit, Edwin, »Zur Geschichtlichkeit des Manierismusbegriffs«, in: Werner Hofmann (Hrsg.), *Zauber der Medusa*, Wien 1987.

Claude-Nicolas Ledoux. Architecte du Roi. Projets et Divagations, étude d' Yvan Christ, Paris 1961.

Leeuw, Gerardus v. d., *Der Mensch und die Religion. Anthropologischer Versuch*, Basel 1941 (*Philosophia Universalis*, Bd. 2).

Lempicka, Tamara, *Passion by Design*, Oxford 1987.

Leroi-Gourhan, André, *Prähistorische Kunst. Die Ursprünge der Kunst in Europa*, Freiburg, Basel und Wien 1971.

Lersch, Philipp, *Vom Wesen der Geschlechter*, München 1947.

Leupold-Löwenthal, *Handbuch der Psychoanalyse*, Wien 1986.

Lexicon Iconographicum Mythologiae Classicae (LIMC), Bd. V/I: *Herakles – Keuchrias*, Zürich und München 1981.

Lindemann, Gesa, *Das paradoxe Geschlecht. Transsexualität im Spannungsfeld von Körper, Leib und Gefühl*, Frankfurt am Main 1993.

Loidolt, Herbert, »Kontrastierende und konforme Entwurfslösungen«, *Transparent* (Wien), Heft 8, 1975.

Lommel, Hans, »Die iranische Religion«, in: *Die Religionen der Erde, ihr Wesen und ihre Geschichte*, München 1966.

Lüthi, Kurt, *Gottes neue Eva. Wandlungen des Weiblichen*, Stuttgart 1978.

Lurker, Manfred, *Symbol, Mythos und Legende in der Kunst. Die symbolische Aussage in Malerei, Plastik und Architektur*, Baden-Baden und Straßburg 1958.

Magnago Lampugnani, Vittorio (Hrsg.), *Hatje-Lexikon der Architektur des 20. Jahrrhunderts*, Stuttgart 1983.

Mahlsdorf, Charlotte v., *Ich bin meine eigene Frau. Ein Leben*, hrsg. von Peter Süß mit einem Photoessay von Burkhard Peter, St.Gallen, Berlin und Sao Paulo 1992.

Malke, Lutz S., »Weibmann und Mannweib in der Kunst der Renaissance«, in: *Androgyn*, Ausstellungskatalog, Berlin l986.

Malvenuti, Stefano, »Aurelio Cortesi – Maschile – Femminile«, in: *Materia, Rivista d'Architettura*, Viano 1991.

Manfredini, Alberto, »Considerazioni su Ideologia e Prassi nella Progettazione architettonica«, *Parametro* (Emilia Romana), Heft 185, 1991.

Marcuse, Herbert. *Eros und Kultur. Ein philosophischer Beitrag zu Sigmund Freud*, Stuttgart 1957.

Marcuse, Max., *Handwörterbuch der Sexualwissenschaft*, Bonn 1923, Bern 1926.

Maria Lanzendorf, Führer zur Kirche, Maria Lanzendorf 1964.

Marsh, H. W. und M. Myers , »Maskulinity, femininity and androgyn: A methodological and theoretical critique«, in: *Sex Roles*, 1986.

Mattenklott, Gert, *Der übersinnliche Leib. Beitrag zur Metaphysik des Körpers*, Hamburg 1982.

Mattenklott, Gert, *Bilderdienst. Ästhetische Opposition bei Beardsley und George*, Frankfurt am Main 1985, München 1970.

Mauer, Otto, *Über Kunst und Künstler*, Salzburg 1993.

Mead, Margret, *Male and female*, Hardmondsworth 1975.

Meesmann, Hartmut, und Bernhard Sill (Hrsg.), *Androgyn*, Weinheim 1994.

Meinel C. (Hrsg.), *Die Alchemie in der europäischen Kultur und Wissenschaftsgeschichte*. (Beitrag Aurnhammer), Wiesbaden 1986.

Meyer-Thoss, Christiane, *Louise Bourgeois*, Zürich 1992.

Meyers Neues Lexikon, 8 Bde., Mannheim, Wien und Zürich 1978.

Minckwitz, Johannes, *Illustriertes Taschenwörterbuch der Mythologie aller Völker*, Leipzig 1878.

Molinier, Pierre, *Le Chaman et ses Créatures*, Perigueux 1995.

Mollenkott, U. R., *Gott eine Frau?*, München 1985.

Mona Lisa im 20. Jahrhundert., Ausstellungskatalog, Wilhelm-Lehmbruck-Museum, Duisburg 1978.

Money, John, und Anke Erhardt, *Männlich-Weiblich. Die Entstehung der Geschlechtsunterschiede*, Reinbek bei Hamburg 1975.

Moore, Henry, *Hauptthemen. Monographien zur Kunstgeschichte*, hrsg. von Heinz Spielmann, Hamburg 1976.

Morris, Jan (früher James), *Conundrum: An Extraordinary Narrative of Transsexualism*, New York 1974, 1986.

Mott, Georg, *Follies and pleasure Pavilions, England, Ireland, Scotland, Wales*, New York 1989.

Müller, Ernst (Hrsg.), *Der Sohar, das heilige Buch der Kabbala, nach dem Urtext herausgegeben*, Wien 1932.

Mulack, Christa, *Maria. Die geheime Göttin im Christentum*, Stuttgart 1985.

Mulack, Christa, Die Weiblichkeit Gottes, Stuttgart 1983, Berlin 1991.

Münsterberg, Hugo, *Frühe Schriften zur Soziologie*, Berlin 1990.

Mumford, Lewis, *Die Stadt. Geschichte und Ausblick*, Teufen 1961.

Mythen der Welt, mit Beiträgen von A. Eliot, M. Eliade, J. Campell, D. Lauf und E. Bührer, Luzern und Frankfurt am Main 1976.

Nerdinger, Winfried, Klaus Jan Philipp und Hans Peter Schwarz (Hrsg.), *Revolutionsarchitektur. Ein Aspekt der europäischen Architektur um 1800*, Ausstellungskatalog, München 1990.

Neugebauer, Franz Ludwig von, »17 Fälle von Koincidenz von Geistesanomalien mit Pseudohermaphroditismus« in: Magnus Hirschfeld (Hrsg.), *Jahrbuch für sexuelle Zwischenstufen*, Leipzig 1900.

Neugebauer, Franz Ludwig von, »Chirurgische Überraschungen auf dem Gebiete des Scheinzwittertums«, in: Magnus Hirschfeld (Hrsg.), *Jahrbuch für sexuelle Zwischenstufen*, Leipzig 1903.

Neugebauer, Franz Ludwig von, *Hermaphroditismus beim Menschen*, Leipzig 1908.

Neumann, Erich, *Ursprungsgeschichte des Bewußtseins*, mit einem Vorwort von Carl Gustav Jung, Zürich 1949.

Neumann, Erich, *Die große Mutter. Der Archetyp des großen Weiblichen*, Zürich 1956.

Niki de Saint Phalle, »Ein magischer Garten der Mutter-Göttin«, *art* (Hamburg), Heft. 6, 1993.

Nikolaus von Kues, *Aller Dinge Einheit ist Gott*, Zürich, Einsiedeln und Köln 1984.

Norberg-Schulz, Christian, *Genius Loci. Landschaft-Lebensraum-Baukunst*, Stuttgart 1982.

Nornengast, Urda, *Der androgyne Mensch*, Bellnhausen über Gladenbach 1970.

Oberösterreichische Nachrichten (Linz), 28. 9. 1990 und 18. 3. 1992.

Oerter, Rolf, *Moderne Entwicklungspsychologie*, Donauwörth 1970.

Ohlbaum, Isolde, *Denn alle Lust will Ewigkeit. Erotische Skulpturen auf europäischen Friedhöfen in 77 Lichtbildern*, Nördlingen 1986.

Orchard, Karin, *Annäherung der Geschlechter. Androgynie in der Kunst des Cinquecento*, Münster und Hamburg 1992.

Orlan, Pierre Mac und Joris-Karl Huysmans, *L'Œuvre gravé de Felicien Rops*, Paris 1975.

Ortkemper, Hubert, *Engel wider Willen – Die Welt der Kastraten*, Berlin 1993.

Overzier, Claus (Hrsg.), *Die Intersexualität*, Stuttgart 1961.

Ovid, *Metamorphosen (Verwandlungen)*, Zürich 1958, Zürich und München 1989.

Papus, *Die Kabbala*, autorisierte Übersetzung, Ulm 1962.

Parametro (Faenza), Nov./Dez. 1991.

Paulsen, Wolfgang (Hrsg.), *Die Frau als Heldin und Autorin*, Berlin und München 1979.

Pehnt, Wolfgang, *Die Architektur des Expressionismus*, Stuttgart 1973.

Peladan, *Weibliche Neugier*, München 1923.

Peladan, *Das höchste Laster*, München 1923.

Peladan, *Einweihung des Weibes*, München 1923.

Peladan, *Das allmächtige Gold*, München 1923.

Peladan, *Der Androgyn*, München 1924.

Peladan, *Gynandria*, München 1925.

Pepponi, Maria Cecilia, »Guido Fiorini Architetto 1891–1965«, *Parametro*, (Faenza), Heft 187, 1991.

Pevsner, Nikolaus, John Fleming und Hugh Honour, *Lexikon der Weltarchitektur*, München 1966.

Piaget, Jean, *Nachahmung, Spiel und Traum*, Stuttgart 1969.

Walter Pichler, Katalog der Galerie Schapira & Beck, Wien 1976.

Walter Pichler. Bilder, Salzburg und Wien 1986.

Walter Pichler. Skulptur, Ausstellungskatalog, Salzburg und Wien 1990.

Walter Pichler. Skulpturen, Gebäude, Projekte, Salzburg und Wien 1983.

Walter Pichler. 111 Zeichnungen, mit einem Essay von Max Peintner und einem Prosatext von Thomas Bernhard, Salzburg 1973.

Walter Pichler. Skulpturen, Zeichnungen, Modelle, Salzburg und Wien 1987.

Pieper, Jan, *Das Labyrinthische. Über die Idee des Verborgenen, Rätselhaften, Schwierigen in der Geschichte der Architektur*, Braunschweig und Wiesbaden 1987.

Pieper, Jan, »Jerusalemkirchen«, *Bauwelt* (Berlin), Heft 3, 1989.

Pieper, Jan: »Architektonische Toposforschung«, *Bauwelt* (Berlin), Heft 3, 1989.

Pieper, Jan, »Häuser des Narziß. Architektur nach des Menschen Bild und Gleichnis«, *Daidalos* (Berlin) Heft 45, 1992.

Pirchan, Emil, *Therese Krones. Die Theaterkönigin Altwiens*, Wien und Leipzig 1942.

Platon, *Über die Freundschaft, die Liebe und das Schöne*, München und Zürich 1960.

Pleck, Joseph H., *The Myth of Masculinity*, Cambridge (Mass.) 1981.

Plečnik, Josef. *Wiener Arbeiten von 1896 bis 1914*, hrsg. von D. Prelovšek, Wien 1979.

Ricardo Porro. Architekt, Klagenfurt 1994.

Die Portugiesen in Indien. Die Eroberungen Dom João des Castros auf Tapisserien 1538 bis 1548, Ausstellungskatalog, Wien 1992.

Prinz, U., » Androgyn – Sehnsucht nach Vollkommenheit«, in: Katalog der gleichnamigen Ausstellung, Berlin 1986.

Pufler, Karl, *Androgynität im Werk Ingeborg Bachmanns*, Diss., Wien 1990.

Putscher, Marielene, »Das ›Buch der Heiligen Dreifaltigkeit‹ und seine Bilder in Handschriften des 15. Jahrhunderts.« in: C. Meinel (Hrsg.), *Die Alchemie in der europäischen Kultur- und Wissenschaftsgeschichte*, Wiesbaden 1986.

Raehs, Andrea, *Zur Ikonographie des Hermaphroditen. Begriff und Problem von Hermaphroditismus und Androgynie in der Kunst*, Frankfurt am Main 1990.

Ranke-Graves, Robert von, *The White Goddes*, New York 1958.

Ranke-Graves, Robert von, *Griechische Mythologie, Quellen und Deutung*, 2 Bde., Reinbek bei Hamburg 1960.

Remmler, Helmut, *Das Geheimnis der Sphinx, Archetyp für Mann und Frau*, Olten/Freiburg im Breisgau 1988.

Rentmeister, Cillie, »Die Quadratur des Kreises, Die Machtergreifung der Männer über die Bauformen«, *Bauwelt* (Berlin), Heft, 31/32, 1979.

Revolutionsarchitektur. Boullée, Ledoux, Lequeu, Ausstellungskatalog, Baden–Baden 1970.

Rick, Karin (Hrsg.), *Das Sexuelle, die Frauen und die Kunst*, Tübingen 1987.

Ringel, Erwin, *Die österreichische Seele*, Graz und Wien 1984.

Roheim, Geza, *Heros, phalliques et symbols maternels dans la mythologie australienne*, o. O. 1970.

Römer, L. S. und A. M. v. Amsterdam, »Über die androgynische Idee des Lebens«, in: Magnus Hirschfeld (Hrsg.), *Jahrbuch für sexuelle Zwischenstufen*, Leipzig, 1903.

Aldo Rossi. Bauten und Projekte 1981–1991, Zürich und München 1991.

Ruhbach, Gerhard und Josef Sudbrack (Hrsg.), *Große Mystiker. Leben und Wirken*, München 1984.

Sartre, Jean Paul, *Baudelaire*, London 1949, Hamburg 1953.

Schaal, Hans Dieter, *Denkgebäude*, Braunschweig und Wiesbaden 1984.

Schaden-Tholen, Sigrid, Monika Wagner und Sigrid Weigel (Hrsg.), *Allegorie und Geschlechterdifferenz*, Wien 1994.

Scharpf, Manfred, *Heilräume, Splendor Artis*, Broschüre mit Beilagen, o. O., o. J.

Schaup, Susanne, *Sophia, das Weibliche in Gott*, München 1994.

Schelsky, Helmut, *Soziologie der Sexualität, Über die Beziehung zwischen Geschlecht, Moral und Gesellschaft*, Hamburg 1955.

Scheltema, F. Adama van, *Die geistige Mitte. Umrisse einer abendländischen Kulturmorphologie*, München 1950.

Schiffels, Waltraud, *Frau werden: Von Walter zu Waltraud. Authentischer Bericht einer Transsexuellen*, Zürich 1992.

Schleberger, Eckhard, *Die indische Götterwelt. Gestalt, Ausdruck und Sinnbild*, Köln 1986.

Schlegel, Friedrich, *Lucinde*, Berlin 1985.

Schlesier, Karl H., »Anmerkungen über Tsistsistas (Cheyenne), Hehmaneh und Hohnuhka oder die Coincidentia oppositorum«, in: H. P. Duerr (Hrsg.), *Sehnsucht nach dem Ursprung. Zu Mircea Eliade*, Frankfurt/M. 1983.

Schmied, Wieland, *Zweihundert Jahre phantastische Malerei*, Berlin 1973.

Schmutzler, Robert, *Art Nouveau – Jugendstil*, Stuttgart 1962.

Schöffer, Nicolas, *Die kybernetische Stadt*, München 1970.

Scholze, Herta, *Geschlechtswechsel im österreichischen Brauchtum*, Wien 1948.

Schwarzrheindorf 1832 –1982. Katholischer Gottesdienst in Schwarzrheindorf. Schwarzrheindorf 1982

Schwarz–Winklhofer und H. Biedermann, *Das Buch der Zeichen und Symbole*, Graz 1972.

Schrödter, Willy, *Geschichte und Lehren der Rosenkreuzer*, Villach 1956.

Schutting, Jutta, *Liebesroman*, Salzburg 1985.

Sedlmayr, Hans, *Johann Bernhard Fischer von Erlach*, Wien und München 1956.

Sedlmayr, Hans, *Epochen und Werke*, Wien 1976.

Seeßlen, »Die Frau in Blau. Zum Film *Blue Steel* von Kathryn Bigelow«, *Die Zeit* (Hamburg) 19, 1990.

Seidl-Reiter, Edda. Alles ist weben. Tapisserien, Ildeen, Objekte. Projekte 1957–1987, Wien, Köln und Graz 1988.

Seifert, Edith, »Einheit – Zweiheit – Ganzheit«, in: B. Wartmann (Hrsg.), *Weiblich-Männlich*, Berlin 1980.

Sekler, Eduard F., *Josef Hoffmann. Das architektonische Werk*, Salzburg und Wien 1982.

Serres, Michel, *Der Hermaphrodit*, Frankfurt am Main 1989.

Sgan Cohen, Michael, »Zur Ikonographie des Endless House«, in: D. Bogner (Hrsg.), *Friedrich Kiesler 1890–1965*, Wien 1988.

Sichtermann, Barbara, *Glaubt mir kein Wort* (über Marlene Dietrich), *Standard*, (Wien) 6. 12. 1991.

Sichtermann, Barbara, *Weiblichkeit. Zur Politik des Privaten*, Berlin 1983.

Sigusch, Volkmar, und Gunter Schmidt, *Zur Frage des Vorurteils gegenüber sexuell devianten Gruppen*, Stuttgart 1967.

Silbermayr, Ernst, *Untersuchungen über den Zusammenhang von Geschlechtsidentität und psychischer Stabilität bei erwachsenen Männern. Ein Beitrag zur Androgynitätsforschung,* Wien 1988.

Sill, Bernhard, *Androgynie und Geschlechtsdifferenz nach Franz von Baader*, Regensburg 1980.

Sill, Bernhard, *Die Kunst der Geschlechterliebe*, Mainz 1989.

Singer, June, *Boundaries of the Soul. The practice of Jung's psychology*, London 1973.

Singer, June, *Nur Frau – nur Mann? Wir sind auf beides angelegt*, München 1981.

Singer, June, *Androgyny*, London 1977.

Skip Kinomagazin, Interview mit Charlotte von Mahlsdorf (»Immer als Frau gefühlt«), Dez./Januar 1992/93.

Slama, Beatrice, *Anna, Anne und die anderen,* in: K. Rick (Hrsg.), *Das Sexuelle, die Frauen und die Kunst*, Tübingen 1987.

Smith, B.,*The Dome*, Princeton, New Jersey, 1950.

Spickernagel, Ellen, »›Helden wie zarte Knaben oder verkleidete Mädchen‹. Zum Begriff der Androgynität bei J. J. Winckelmann und A. Kauffmann«, in: *Frauen, Weiblichkeit, Schrift* (Tagungsschrift), Bielefeld 1984, Berlin 1985.

Steiner, Rudolf, *Der Baugedanke des Goetheanums*, Dornach 1932, Stuttgart 1958.

Strecker, Bernhard, »Ego und Genius Loci, Amalie – Eine Stadtbrücke«, *Kunstforum international*, (Köln), Heft 69, 1984.

Sulzer, J. J., *Allgemeine Theorie der Schönen Künste*, 4. Teil, Leipzig 1794.

Staudacher, Willibald, *Die Trennung von Himmel und Erde. Ein vorgriechischer Schöpfungsmythus bei Hesiod und den Orphikern*, Tübingen 1942.

Swoboda, Erich, *Carnuntum*, Graz und Köln 1964.

Szeemann, Harald (Hrsg.), *Junggesellenmaschinen. Der Hang zum Gesamtkunstwerk*, Ausstellungskatalog, Aarau 1983.

Tenschert, Roland, *Mozart. Ein Leben für die Oper*, Wien 1944/45.

Theweleit, Klaus, *Männerphantasien*, 2 Bde., Hamburg 1977.

Thiel, Josef Franz, »Androgynie in Afrika«, in: *Androgyn*, Ausstellungskatalog, Berlin 1986.

Thiele, Peter, »Yin und Yang«, in: *Androgyn*, Ausstellungskatalog, Berlin 1986.

Thomsen, Christian W., »Architektur und Erotik«, in: *Architektur für die Sinne*, Düsseldorf 1992.

Thomsen, Christian W., *Liter-Architektur. Wechselwirkungen zwischen Architektur, Literatur und Kunst im 20. Jahrhundert,* Köln 1989.

Thomsen, Christian W., *Bauen für die Sinne. Gefühl, Erotik un d Sexualität in der Architektur*, München 1996.

Der Traum vom Raum. Gemalte Architektur aus 7 Jahrhunderten, Eine Ausstellung der Albrecht-Dürer-Gesellschaft, Nürnberg und Marburg 1986.

Venturi, Adolfo, *Leonardo da Vinci und seine Schule*, Wien 1941.

Vernon, M. D., *The Psychology of Perception*, Hartmondsworth 1962.

Vidler, Anthony, *Claude Nicolas Ledoux*, Basel, Boston und Berlin 1988.

Vogt, Adolf Max, *Russische und französische Revolutionsarchitektur, 1917, 1789*, Köln 1947.

Vogt, Adolf Max, *Boullées Newton Denkmal. Sakralbau und Kugelidee*, Basel 1969.

Wagner, Susanne, »Selbstverliebter Knabe als Märtyrerin getarnt«, *art* (Hamburg), Heft 6, 1992.

Wartmann, Brigitte (Hrsg); *Weiblich-Männlich. Kulturgeschichtliche Spuren einer verdrängten Weiblichkeit*, Berlin 1980.

Webb, Peter, »Hans Bellmer«, in: *Androgyn*, Ausstellungskatalog, Berlin 1986.

Wedekind-Schwertner B., *Daß ich eins und doppelt bin. Studien zur Idee der Androgynie unter besonderer Berücksichtigung Thomas Manns*, Münster 1984.

Wehr, Gerhard, *Der Urmensch und der Mensch der Zukunft. Das Androgyn Problem im Lichte der Forschungsergebnisse Rudolf Steiners*, Freiburg im Breisgau 1964.

Wehr, Gerhard, *C. G. Jung und Rudolf Steiner*, Stuttgart 1972.

Wehr, Gerhard, *Alle Weisheit ist von Gott. Gestalten und Wirkungen christlicher Theosophie: Weigel, Böhme, Andreae u. a.*, Gütersloh 1980.

Wehr, Gerhard, *Die deutsche Mystik. Mystische Erfahrungen und theosophische Weltsicht – Eine Einführung in Leben und Werk der großen deutschen Sucher nach Gott*, Bern, München und Wien 1988.

Weininger, Otto, *Geschlecht und Charakter*, Wien und Leipzig 1917.

Weinreb, Friedrich, *Zahl, Zeichen, Wort. Das symbolische Universum der Bibelsprache*, o. O. 1948.

Weinreich, Otto, *Menekrates. Zeus und Salmoneus*, Stuttgart 1933.

Werlhof, Claudia von, *Männliche Natur und künstliches Geschlecht. Aufsätze zu feministischer Wissenschaftskritik*, Wien 1985.

Werlhof, Claudia von, Maria Mies und Veronika Bennholdt-Thomsen*, Frauen – die letzte Kolonie? Zur Hausfrauisierung der Arbeit*, Reinbek bei Hamburg 1983, Wien 1988.

Westendorf, Wolfhart, »Mann-weibliche Konzeption im Alten Ägypten«, in: *Androgyn*, Ausstellungskatalog, Berlin 1986.

Wex, Marianne, »Weibliche« und »Männliche« Körpersprache als Folge patriachalischer Machtverhältnisse, Frankfurt 1980.

Wiener (Wien) Heft 97, 1988.

Winckelmann, J. J., *Sämtliche Werke*, Bd. VIII: *1825 bis 1829,* Osnabrück 1965.

Winckelmann, J. J., *Vorläufige Abhandlungen zu den Denkmalen der Kunst des Altertums*, Donaueschingen o. J.

Winthuis, Josef, *Das Zweigeschlechterwesen bei den Zentralaustraliern und anderen Völkern. Lösungsversuch der ethnologischen Hauptprobleme auf Grund des primitiven Denkens*, Leipzig 1928.

Winthuis, Josef, *Einführung in die Vorstellungswelt primitiver Völker*, Leipzig 1931.

Wolf, Christa, *Bisexualität*, Frankfurt 1981.

Wolter, Gundula, *Hosen-weiblich. Kulturgeschichte der Frauenhosen*, Marburg 1994.

Woolf, Virginia, *Orlando. Eine Biographie, Victoria Sackville-West gewidmet*, Frankfurt am Main 1989.

Wundt, Wilhelm, *Völkerpsychologie*, Bd. I: *Die Sprache*, Bd. II: *Mythus und Religion,* Bd. III: *Die Kunst,* Bd. IV, V: *Mythus und Religion,* Leipzig 1908.

Züger, Armin, *Männerbilder – Frauenbilder. Androgyne Utopie in der deutschen Literatur zwischen 1970 und 1980*, Bern und Frankfurt am Main, 1992.

Notes

[1] In 1882 E. Du Bois-Reymond tried to postulate »The Seven Riddles of the World« and came to the conclusion »ignoramus et ignorabimus« – we do not know, and we never will. In 1892 Ernst Haeckel published his book *Die Welträtsel als allgemeinverständliche Studie über monistische Philosophie.*

[2] As well as »ethical dualism« (good-evil) and »anthropological dualism« the history of ideas lists a series of other dualisms: »natural-philosophical dualism« (mind – matter). »epistemological dualism« (sensuality – reason), »metaphysical dualism« (transient world of appearance – eternal world of ideas), »methodological dualism« (arts– science). René Descartes (1596–1650) distinguishes between the thinking substance of the soul (res cogitans) and the extended substance of material (res estensa).

[3] The term »Androgynität« (androgynity) is sometimes used as well.

[4] »Anyone who speaks of androgyny touches the depths of his own consciousness with double antenna.«

[5] »A preferred example from pure myth.«

[6] The term »Tranvestitismus« (transvetitism) is also current.

[7] These concepts are used in very different ways in literature. This is because the phenomena cannot be clearly demarcated, it is possible for them to overlap and to be blocked off, especially in the case of transsexualism, transvestism and intersexuality.

The conceptual field also includes some affinities with homosexuality.

The medical and psychological element has to be largely omitted in the context of this work. Early (19th century) analyses of the subject are interesting. Just a few headings on the subject:

Hermaphroditismus verus, hermaphrodites, »Erreure de sexe«, urning, sexual glands – germ glands, chromosomes X, Y, chromosome anomalies, ovarian and testicular tissue, hormone blocks, chromosomal and gonadal sex, intermediate sexual stages.

Some names from 19th-century literature should be mentioned:

Wilhelm Fließ (1858–1928), Sigmund Freud (1856–1939), Alfred Adler (1870–1937), Carl Gustav Jung (1875–1961), Otto Weininger (1880–1903), Magnus Hirschfeld (1868–1935).

[8] We find this myth among the Phoenicians, the Indians, in China, Japan, Peru, among the Polynesians, Finns and Slavs, but above all in Greek mythology.

[9] Architectural competitions and projects are a rich source in terms of morphological trends in contemporary architecture, and the ellipse appears increasingly frequently. In the competition for the technology centre in Hagen the winners of the second prize, A. Janssen and R. Beckerwahl, propose three dominant building sections in elliptical shape (1991). Kleine-Kraneburg and Gruber's competition entry for the Präsidialamt (President's Office) in Berlin is mentioned in chapter 9.3.3.

Wilhelm Holzbauer's prize-winning entry, which was not built, for the St. Pölten government quarter in Lower Austria, attempts to draw the individual buildings together as an egg-shaped megaform (1990); Holzbauer was not the only entrant to this competition who worked with ellipses.

[10] The topicality of this idea is clear in art. For example, Constantin Brancusi made a marble egg in 1924 and called the work »Weltenanfang« (»World beginnings«).

[11] Ascription of biological and psychological phenomena to secondary and tertiary sexual characteristics has certainly not been resolved unambiguously, and the existence of tertiary sexual characteristics is often denied.

[12] These values show considerable ethnological scatter and are also strongly dependent on age.

[13] The concept of »gender« is not identical with the German word »Geschlecht« (sex). »Lenses of Gender«: ways of looking, lenses, the focus of the genus.

[14] The ansate cross belongs mainly to the world of Egyptian symbolism and has been interpreted in various ways, above all as a life symbol, as a figure with extended arms. Another interpretation – which is also associated with life – sees it as a device for cutting the new-born child's umbilical cord.

[15] Circumcision as a ritual operation as part of initiation rites. Subincision: cutting open the penis or the urethra; circumcision: cutting the foreskin open or off (Judaism). Sometimes in the case of girls: removal of the clitoris or the labia minora.

[16] »Boy-love« occurs between adult men and pubescent boys. It included erotic to genital-sexual relations. The boys' feminine aura produces a peripheral form of androgyny.

[17] Lekythos: narrow-necked Greek pitcher with handle and figurative decoration.

[18] Also lingam/yoni.

[19] We also find bisexual deities among the primeval gods of the Mexicans, Incas, Babylonians, Sumerians etc.

[20] Notions of trinity are by no means limited to Christianity, but are in many ways an archetype. It is particularly marked in Hinduism.

[21] In the Jewish Talmud the designation of man and woman is formulated particularly radically: »Anyone who lives without a woman is not a man, for its is written that he created them as man and woman ... and called their name man.«

[22] The idea of an actual androgynous »marriage« is shown very revealingly on a 17th-century Italian wedding medallion: the couple is fused into a single body, but their faces are turned to each other. (Cf. chapter 6.1.)

[23] It should not be overlooked that in Christianity chastity, lack of marriage for the sake of God, is rated very highly.

But Georg Koepgen (1939) sees considerable androgynous potential in celibacy: »... the virgin priest ... achieves the androgynous unity of male and female in his soul.«

[24] As well as Franz von Baader, Jakob Böhme's ideas are pursued further and modified by Johann Georg Gichtel (1638–1710), Gottfried Arnold (1666 to 1714), Friedrich Christoph Oetinger (1702–1782) and Michael Hahn (1758–1819).

[25] The historical, theological and iconographic distinction between John the Baptist and John the Evangelist (and Apostle) cannot be resolved unambiguously. The Apostle John (the Lord's »Beloved«) is also shown as beardless and feminine, often relating erotically to Christ.

[26] Transvestism is practised in the dances of many peoples. In Rajasthan, India, for example, where the magical and cultic links are crucial.

[27] In Western cultural circles Catholic priests as well as Scots are skirt-wearers. This idea has not become polarized in Asia.

[28] Peter Pan is one of the most popular breeches roles in film: the cheerful, dynamic, young and attractive boy is well suited to female presentation.

The Picture of Dorian Gray can also be mentioned as one of the serious themes that film has addressed: Veruschka von Lehndorff played the title role in 1983/84.

[29] »Unattainable realization of the union of Tadzio and Aschenbach.«

[30] Kaltenecker (1993) provides a thorough analysis of travesty in the cinema. The »cross-dressing« phenomenon is addressed and analysed speculatively above all in terms of the film »Tootsie«.

Other films also reflect the phenomenon: *Aus eines Mannes Mädchenzeit,* (Germany 1912), *The Perfect Lady,* (USA 1915, Charlie Chaplin), *The Playhouse,* (USA 1921, with Buster Keaton), *Our Hospitality,* (USA 1923, with Buster Keaton), *Viktor und Viktoria,* (Germany 1933), *Crimson Pirate,* (USA 1953, Richard Siodmak, with Burt Lancaster), *The Magic Christian,* (USA 1969, Joseph Mc Grath, with Yul Brynner), *They Got me Covered,* (USA 1964), *Das süße Leben des Graf Bobby,* (Germany 1963, with Peter Alexander), *I Was a Male War Bride,* (USA 1949, with Cary Grant), *What Did You Do in the War, Daddy?,* (USA 1966, Blake Edward, with Dick Shawn), *Babes on Broadway,* (USA 1941, Busby Berkeley, with Mickey Rooney), *Some Like It Hot,* (USA 1959, Billy Wilder, with Jack Lemmon, Tony Curtis, Marilyn Monroe) *Thunderbold and Lightfood,* (USA 1973, Michael Cimino, with Jeff Bridges), *Der Fürst von Pappenheim,* (Germany 1927), *Charleys Tante,* Germany 1955 with Heinz Rühmann and Austria 1963 with Geza von Cziffra), *That's My Wife,* (USA 1932, with Stan Laurel), *Paradise is not for Sale,* (Denmark 1984, Teit Ritzan, Christine Jorgensen, Hanne Rasmussen, Thomas Holck)

Androgynous elements can also be detected in the following films, given a little interpretative leeway: *Fahrenheit 451*, (England 1966, François Truffaut), *Modesty Blaise,* (England 1965, Joseph Losey), *Barbarella,* (Italy/France 1967, Roger Vadim), *Alphaville,* (France/Italy 1965, Jean-Luc Godard), *Close Encounters of the Third Kind*, USA 1977, Steven Spielberg).

The currency of the theme can also be seen in the fact that it is thoroughly appreciated at festival-like event.

[31] Some borderline cases of androgyny have already been mentioned: homosexuality and transsexualism. Other peripheral problems can only be quoted in passing: asexuality (iconographically in the case of angels, for example), narcissism (self-love eschewing the opposite sex), celibacy (re-

maining unmarried for idealistic reasons), endogamy (partners from a close social group), incest (Goethe: lilies are husband and wife on one stem), man-animal unions (mythical beings), man-plant unions etc.

[32] Clear androgynous traits occur frequently in Nazarenes art from 1810 and pre-Raphaelite painting from 1848.

[33] Further androgynous motifs can be seen clearly in the work of the Belgian Symbolist Fernand Khnopff.

[34] »To my little shoe his friend Yves Tanguy.«

[35] The Baphomet offers his services to the great master.

[36] »... considers the androgyne to be the exemplary image of the perfect human being ... total being.«

[37] The symbol concept could be broadened considerably: the terms of a manifest, latent, projective and interpretative symbolic language have been discussed elsewhere (Feuerstein 1985).

[38] Antiquity was completely familiar with the problem of »male/female« in architecture: the temples and column orders are defined as male, female or virginal. And even Humboldt referred to »male and female form« in architecture.

[39] Leaning towers caused by defects in the subsoil were sometimes built deliberately as an attraction. Hans Hollein conceived a »leaning tower« for an insurance company in Vienna in 1995.

[40] The artificial grottoes in the Boboli Gardens in Florence, in the gardens of the Villa d'Este in Tivoli, in Hellbrunn near Salzburg and later still in the Romantic period should be mentioned.

[41] The fact that it is possible to walk on the breast simultaneously makes it a dome, a cave. Cf. chapter 7.6. on double coding.

[42] Porro's »revolutionary architecture« for Fidel Castro soon fell out of favour and is increasingly falling into disrepair.

[43] Built with Armand Bartos.

[44] Consciously or unconsciously the tower adopts the proportions of St. Stephan in Vienna.

[45] This dialectic is not as clear in the realization of the building as in the first design.

[46] The idea of the habitable pillar was known as early as 1800. For example, Barbier built a habitable, apparently broken pillar for the park in Marly.

[47] »Red Vienna« built the most significant examples in the dramatic large-scale forms of the community buildings. The grand gesture in residential building met with approval in Berlin and Amsterdam as well.

[48] St. Sebastian should be mentioned again: although his body is pierced with arrows, images of St. Sebastian always have an ecstatic, erotic face.

[49] Presented for the first time by Philip Johnson's *Deconstructivist Architecture*, New York 1987.

[50] Wolf-Dieter Prix (b. 1942) and Helmut Swiczinsky (b. 1944).

[51] Laurids Ortner (b. 1941), Günter Zamp-Kelp (b. 1941), Klaus Pinter (b. 1940), later Manfred Ortner (b. 1943).

[52] The erotic presence of colossal standing female figures like the Statue of Liberty in New York or Bavaria in Munich is not quite so clear.

[53] Frederick Kiesler's »Shrine of the Book« or »Scroll Cathedral« was dealt with in chapter 7.6.

[54] Mutually intertwined lovers' legs in iconography are a preliminary stage to union, a kind of surface merger. According to Orchard (1992) it is a metaphor for copulation.

[55] The author continues to work on this subject in an extensive research project with the title »Androgynie – coincidentia oppositorum«.

Bibliography

Amrain, Susanne, »Der Androgyn. Das poetische Geschlecht und sein Aktus«, in: *Frauen, Weiblichkeit, Schrift*, conference proceedings, Bielefeld 1984, Berlin 1985.

»Tadao Ando«, *El Croquis* (Madrid), 58, XII, 1993.

Andreae, Johann Valentin, *Christianopolis*, Stuttgart 1972.

Androgyn. Sehnsucht nach Vollkommenheit, exhibition catalogue, Berlin 1986.

Der Architekt (Stuttgart), no. 6, 1977.

Arnold, Christina, »Die Rezeption der feministischen Theologie«, in: *Religionspädagogische Schriften*, n. p. 1990.

Louise Bourgeois, *art* (Hamburg), no. 6, 1993.

Assunto, Rosario, *Die Theorie des Schönen im Mittelalter*, Cologne 1963.

Auböck, Maria, »Das Vienna Eros Hilton«, *Architektur aktuell* (Vienna), no. 41, 1974.

Aurnhammer, Achim, »Zum Hermaphroditen in der Sinnbildkunst der Alchemisten«. in: C. Meinel (ed.), *Die Alchemie in der europäischen Kultur- und Wissenschaftsgeschichte*, Wiesbaden 1986.

Aurnhammer, Achim, *Androgynie*, Cologne and Vienna 1986.

Baader, Franz von, *Sätze aus der erotischen Philosophie und anderen Schriften*, ed. by G. K. Kaltenbrunner, Frankfurt am Main 1966.

Baader, Franz von, *Ausgewählte Schriften zum androgynen Menschenbild*, Bensheim 1991.

Bachelard, Gaston, *La Poètique de la rêverie*, Paris 1960.

Bachelard, Gaston, *Die Bildung des wissenschaftlichen Geistes. Beitrag zu einer Psychoanalyse der objektiven Erkenntnis*, Frankfurt am Main 1978.

Bachofen, Johann Jakob, *Eine Auswahl*, ed. by Rudolf Marx, Stuttgart 1941.

Bachofen, Johann Jakob, *Myth, Religion and Mother Right*, New York and Princeton 1967.

Badinter, Elisabeth, *Ich bin Du, Die neue Beziehung zwischen Mann und Frau oder Die androgyne Revolution*, Munich and Zurich 1991.

Balzac, Honoré de, *Œuvres complètes*, Paris 1935.

Barbier, Patrick, *Farinelli – Der Kastrat der Könige*, Düsseldorf 1995.

Bastin, Georges, *Wörterbuch der Sexualpsychologie*, Freiburg, Basle and Vienna 1972.

Bataille, Georges, *L'Érotisme,* Paris 1957.

Baumann, Hermann, *Schöpfung und Urzeit des Menschen im Mythos der afrikanischen Völker*, Berlin 1936.

Baumann, Hermann, *Das doppelte Geschlecht – Ethnologische Studie zur Bisexualität in Ritus und Mythos*, Berlin 1955, 1986.

Beardsley, Aubrey; *The Collected Drawings of Aubrey Beardsley*, New York 1967.

Beauvoir, Simone de, *Le deuxième sexe,* Paris 1962.

Becker, Gerhold, *Die Ursymbole in den Religionen*, Graz and Vienna 1988.

Becker-Schmidt, Regina, *Geschlechtertrennung, Geschlechterdifferenz*, Bonn-Bad-Godesberg 1989.

Beckford, William, *History of the Calif Vathek*, London 1964.

Begegnung mit den anderen, exhibition catalogue (*Gegen-Documenta*), Hann. Münden 1992.

Bell-Metereau, Rebecca, *Hollywood Androgyny*, New York 1985.

Beltz, Walter, *Die Mythen der Ägypter*, Düsseldorf 1982.

Bem, Sandra L., *The Measurement of Psychological Androgyny*, New Haven (Conn.) 1974.

Bem, Sandra L., »Die Harten und die Zarten«, *Psychologie heute,* (Weinheim and Basle), no. 2, 1976.

Bem, Sandra L., *Sex Role Adaptibility*, New Haven (Conn.) 1975.

Benz, Ernst, Adam, *Der Mythos vom Urmenschen*, Munich 1955.

Benz, Ernst, *Der vollkommene Mensch nach Jacob Boehme*, Stuttgart 1973.

Berdyayev, Nikolay, *Die Bestimmung des Menschen*, Berne and Leipzig 1935.

Berne, Eric, *Spiele der Erwachsenen*, Hamburg 1967.

Berner, Ole, *Hermaphroditismus und sexuelle Umstimmung*, Leipzig 1938.

Bernsdorff, Madeleine, and Stefanie Hetze, *Frauen in Hosen*, Munich 1989.

Bertholet, Alfred, *Das Geschlecht der Gottheit*, Tübingen 1934.

Bieber, M., *The Sculpture of the Hellenistic Age*, New York 1955.

Biedermann, Hans, »Das Androgyn-Symbol in der Alchemie«, in: *Androgyn. Sehnsucht nach Vollkommenheit*, Berlin 1986.

Biedermann, Hans, *Die großen Mütter. Die schöpferische Rolle der Frau in der Menschheitsgeschichte*, Graz and Vienna 1987.

Bierhoff-Alfermann, Dorothee, *Psychologie der Geschlechtsunterschiede*, Cologne 1977.

Bierhoff-Alfermann, Dorothee, *Androgynie – Mögichkeiten und Grenzen der Geschlechterrollen*, Opladen 1989.

Bischof, Norbert, and Holger Preuschoft (ed.); *Geschlechtsunterschiede. Entstehung und Entwicklung, Mann und Frau in biologischer Sicht*, Munich 1980.

Blavatsky, H. P., *Die Geheimlehre. Die Vereinigung von Wissenschaft, Religion und Philosophie*, 4 vols. (*Kosmogenesis, Anthropogenesis, Esoterik, Index*) London 1888, Vienna 1899, Ulm 1958.

Bleibtreu-Ehrenberg, Gisela Ingeborg, *Sexuelle Abartigkeit im Urteil der abendländischen Religions-, Geistes- und Rechtsgeschichte im Zusammenhang mit der Gesellschaftsentwicklung*, diss., Bonn 1970.

Bleibtreu-Ehrenberg, Gisela Ingeborg, *Der Weibtmann, Kultischer Geschlechtswechsel im Schamanismus*, Frankfurt am Main 1989.

Bloc, André, *De la Sculpture à l'architecture*, Boulogne 1964.

Bloch, Ernst, *Geist der Utopie*, Frankfurt am Main 1964.

Bock, Ulla, *Androgynie und Feminismus. Frauenbewegung zwischen Institution und Utopie,* Berlin and Basle 1988 (*Ergebnisse der Frauenforschung*, vol. 16).

Bock, Ulla, »Androgynie. Ein Modell für ein verändertes Verhältnis von Frau und Mann?«, 5. Würzburger Symposion, February, 1991: *Mann und Frau – Frau und Mann*, Würzburg 1991.

Böckelman, F., »Zur Auflösung der Geschlechtsrollen«, in: H. Kentler (ed.), *Texte zur Sozio-Sexualität*, Opladen 1973.

Böhme, Jakob, *Sämtliche Schriften*, Stuttgart 1958.

Böhme, Jakob, *Mysterium Magnum oder Erklärung über Das Erste Buch Mosis* (1623), Stuttgart 1958.

Boff, Leonardo, *Das mütterliche Antlitz Gottes*, Düsseldorf 1985.

Bogner, Dieter (ed.), *Friedrich Kiesler 1890 bis 1965*, exhibition catalogue, Vienna 1988.

Bolsena, Pietro, *La iconologia bisessuale, segreto di Raffaelo*, Vienna 1980.

Bornemann, Ernest, *Das Patriarchat. Ursprung und Zukunft unseres Gesellschaftssystems*, Frankfurt am Main 1975.

Bornemann, Ernest, *Der Mythos vom Doppelten Geschlecht*, Munich 1981

Boullée, Étienne-Louis, *Architektur. Abhandlung über die Kunst,* with an introduction and a commentary by Adolf Max Vogt, Zurich and Munich 1987.

Braun, Christiane von, »Männliche Hysterie – weibliche Askese«, in: Karin Rick (ed.), *Das Sexuelle, die Frauen und die Kunst*, Tübingen 1987.

Braunschweig, Rosa v., »Felicita von Vestvali«, in: Magnus Hirschfeld (ed.), *Jahrbuch für sexuelle Zwischenstufen*, Leipzig 1903.

Breitner, Burghard, *Das Problem der Bisexualität*, Vienna 1951.

Brückner, Margit, »Die Sehnsucht nach dem Kugelmenschen oder vom Wunsch nach Aufhebung der Geschlechtertrennung«, in: C. Hagemann-White and Maria S. Rerrich (ed.), *Frauen, Männer, Bilder*, Bielefeld, 1988.

Burchard, Johann M., *Struktur und Soziologie des Transvestitismus und Transsexualismus*, Stuttgart 1961.

Burri, Josef, *Als Mann und Frau schuf er sie*, Zurich, Einsiedeln and Cologne 1977.

Busst, A. J. L., »The Image of the Androgyne in the 19th Century«, in: Jan Fletscher (ed.) *Romantic Mythologies*, New York 1967.

Bynum, Caroline Walker, *Jesus as mother*, Berkeley (Calif.) 1982.

Carrà, Carlo, *L'opera completa di Carrà dal futurismo alla metafisica e al realismo mitico 1910 al 1930*, Milano 1970.

Casanova, Giacomo, *Eduard und Elisabeth oder die Reise in das Innere unseres Erdballs*, Frankfurt am Main and Berlin 1968.

Christ, Felix, *Jesus Sophia*, Zurich 1970.

Clemen, Carl, *Die Religionen der Erde. Ihr Wesen und Ihre Geschichte*, Munich 1966.

Colegrave, Sukie, *The Spirit of the Valley. Androgyn and Chinese Thought*, London 1979.

Colonna, Francesco (Francesco Giorgio Martin), *Hypnerotomachia poliphilii*, Padua 1499.

Comenius, Johann Amos, *Vorspiele – Prodromus Pansophiae, Vorläufer der Pansophie*, Düsseldorf 1963.

Conrads, Ulrich, and Hans G. Sperlich, *Phantastische Architektur*, Stuttgart 1960.

Cranston, Jones, *Architecture Today and Tomorrow*, New York 1961.

Daidalos (Berlin), no. 45, 1992.

Daniels, Dieter, *Duchamp und die anderen. Der Modellfall einer künstlerischen Wirkungsgeschichte in der Moderne*, Cologne 1992.

Degenhart, Annette, and Hans Martin Trautner (ed.), *Mann und Frau in psychologischer Sicht*, Munich 1979.

Dekker, Rudolf, and Lotte van de Pol, *Frauen in Männerkleidern. Weibliche Transvestiten und ihre Geschichte*, Berlin 1989/90.

Delcourt, Marie, *Hermaphrodite. Mythes et rites de la bisexualité dans l'antique classique*, Paris 1958.

Delcourt, Marie, *Hermaphroditea. Recherches sur l'être double, promoteur de la fertilité dans la monde classique*, Brussels 1960.

Devereux, Georges, *Baubo. Die mythische Vulva*, Frankfurt am Main 1981.

Dieterich, Albrecht, *Mutter Erde. Ein Versuch über Volksreligion*, Leipzig 1905 (1913, 1925).

Döhl, Reinhard, *Hermann Finsterlin. Eine Annäherung*, Stuttgart 1988.

Douglas, Mary, *Ritual, Tabu und Körpersymbolik. Sozialanthropologische Studien in Industriegesellschaft und Stammeskultur*, Frankfurt am Main 1974.

Jean Dubuffet, exhibition catalogue, Kunsthaus Wien, Vienna 1995.

Duerr, Hans Peter (ed.), *Sehnsucht nach dem Ursprung. Zu Mircea Eliade*, Frankfurt am Main 1983.

Duerr, Hans Peter (ed.), *Die Mitte der Welt. Aufsätze zu Mircea Eliade*, Frankfurt am Main 1984.

Duerr, Hans Peter, *Sedna oder Die Liebe zum Leben*, Frankfurt am Main 1985.

Duerr, Hans Peter, *Der Mythos vom Zivilisationsprozeß*, vol. 1: *Nacktheit und Scham.* Frankfurt am Main 1988.

Duerr, Hans Peter, *Der Mythos vom Zivilisationsprozeß*, vol. 2: *Intimität.*, Frankfurt am Main 1990.

Ehmann, Peter, *Zur Ätiologie und Phänomenologie ambisexueller und androgyner Daseinsweisen. Versuch einer Überwindung des Bisexualitäts-Konzepts*, diss., Bonn 1976.

Eibl-Eibesfeldt, Irenäus, *Die Biologie des menschlichen Verhaltens. Grundriß der Humanethologie*, Munich and Zurich 1984. English edition: *The Biology of Behaviour*, New York 1970.

Eliade, Mircea, *Schmiede und Alchemisten*, Stuttgart, 1956.

Eliade, Mircea, *Das Heilige und das Profane. Vom Wesen des Religiösen*, Hamburg 1957.

Eliade, Mircea, *Cosmos and History*, New York 1559.

Eliade, Mircea, *Mephistophélès et l'Androgyne*, Paris 1962.

Eliade, Mircea, *The myth of the eternal return*, Princeton 1971.

Eliade, Mircea, *Die Religionen und das Heilige*, Darmstadt 1976.

Eliade, Mircea, *Ewige Bilder und Sinnbilder. Vom unvergänglichen menschlichen Seelenraum*, Freiburg im Breisgau 1952 and Frankfurt am Main 1986.

Eliade, Mircea, *Mythos und Wirklichkeit*, Frankfurt am Main 1988.

Ellis, Havelock, and J. A. Symonds, *Das konträre Geschlechtsgefühl*, Leipzig 1896.

Ellis, Havelock, *Studies in the Psychology of Sex*, vol. 7: *Eonism and Other Supplementary Studies*, Philadelphia 1928.

Ellis, Havelock, *Psychology of Sex*, London 1941.

Erikson, Erik Homburger, *Identity – Youth and Crisis*, New York 1968. Quotations from the German edition (*Jugend und Krise. Die Psychodynamik im sozialen Wandel*, Stuttgart 1970).

Erikson, Erik Homburger, »Genitale Modi und räumliche Modalitäten«, *Bauwelt* (Berlin), no. 31/32, 1979.

Erler, Gisela Anna, *Frauenzimmer. Für eine Politik des Unterschiedes*, Berlin 1985.

»Erotik und Architektur – gibt es eine Beziehung?«, *Der Architekt* (Stuttgart), no. 6, 1977, with contributions by I. Bielicki, O. Jacobsen, G. Feuerstein, W. Pehnt, A. Ginelli, V. Marg, R. Gieselmann, H. Hollein, H. J. Guckel, W. Bunsmann, R. Häuser, G. Gruner and P. Vehling.

Femininmasculin, Le sexe de l'art, exhibition catalogue, Centre Pompidou, Paris 1995.

Ferenczi, Sándor, *Versuch einer Genitaltheorie*, Leipzig and Vienna 1924.

Fergusson, James, *A History of Indian and Eastern Architecture*, London and New York 1899.

Feuerstein, Günther, *Archetypen des Bauens*, diss., Vienna 1966.

Feuerstein, Günther, *Visionäre Architektur: Wien 1958/1988*, Berlin 1988.

Feuerstein, Günther, »Eros – Architektur – Sexualität«, *Transparent* (Vienna), no. 1/2, 1988.

Feuerstein, Günther, »Architektur als ›sprechende Person‹«, *Daidalos* (Berlin), no. 45, 1992.

Field Belenky, M., and others, *Das andere Denken. Persönlichkeit, Moral und Intellekt der Frau*, Frankfurt am Main 1989.

Film-Kurier (Vienna), no. 318, 1983.

Fink, Gerhard, *Who's who in der antiken Mythologie*, Munich 1993.

Fleischer, Robert, *Die römischen Bronzen aus Österreich*, Mainz 1967.

Fletcher, Ian (ed.), *Romantic Mythologies*, New York 1967.

Fliess, Wilhelm, *Der Ablauf des Lebens. Grundlegung zur exakten Biologie*, Leipzig and Vienna 1923.

Forcher, Eberhard, »Who's bad? Mythos Jackson«, *Wiener* (Vienna), no. 97, 1988.

Frauen, Weiblichkeit, Schrift, conference proceedings, Bielefeld 1984 and Berlin 1985.

Freud, Sigmund, *Totem und Tabu*, Frankfurt am Main 1940.

Freud, Sigmund, *Über Psychoanalyse*, Wien 1947.

Freud, Sigmund, *The Standard Edition of the Complete Psychological Work of Sigmund Freud*, London 1964.

Freud, Sigmund, *Abriß der Psychoanalyse. Das Unbehagen in der Kultur,* mit einer Rede von Thomas Mann, Frankfurt am Main 1972.

Freud, Sigmund, *Werkausgabe in 2 Bänden*, hrsg. von Anna Freud und Ilse Grubrich-Simitis, Frankfurt am Main 1978.

Frobenius, Leo, *Die Weltanschauung der Naturvölker*, Weimar 1898.

Gail, A., »Die zweigeschlechtliche Gottheit in Indien«, in: *Jahrbuch für Kunstgeschichte*, vol. 17, Graz 1981.

Galahad, Sir, *Mütter und Amazonen. Ein Umriß weiblicher Reiche*, Munich 1932.

Gallas, Klaus, *Iran, Kulturstätten Persiens. Zwischen Wüsten, Steppen und Bergen*, Cologne 1976.

Garber, Marjorie, *Verhüllte Interessen. Transvestismus und kulturelle Angst*, Frankfurt am Main 1993.

Gassner, Jutta, *Phallische und ithyphallische Darstellungen und Kulte*, 3 vols., Vienna 1989.

Gassner, Jutta, *Phallos – Fruchtbarkeitssymbol oder Abwehrzauber?*, Vienna 1993.

Gauster, Hannelore, »Zu Hermaphroditen-Darstellungen in der Antike«, in: *Frauen, Weiblichkeit, Schrift*, Tagungschrift, Bielefeld 1984 and Berlin 1985.

Gautier, Theophile, *Mademoiselle de Maupin*, Hellerau 1926.

Geisler, Eduard, *Psychologie für Architekten. Eine Einführung in dle Architekturpsychologische Denk-Arbeitsweise*, Stuttgart 1978.

Giedion, Sigfried, *The Eternal Present – A Contribution on Constancy and Change. The Beginning of Architecture,* Washington, D. C. 1964.

Giedion, Sigfried, *Architektur und das Phänomen des Wandels. Die drei Raumkonzeptionen in der Architektur,* Tübingen 1969).

Giese, Fritz, *Der romantische Charakter,* Band I: *Die Entwicklung des androgynen Problems in der Frühromantik*, Langensalza 1919.

Giese, Hans, and E. V. Gebsattel (ed.), *Psychopathologie der Sexualität*, Stuttgart 1962.

Gildemeister, Regine, »Weibliches Denken – Männliches Denken. Oder: Sind zwei Geschlechter genug?«, *Wissenschaft ist Frauensache* (Kassel), no. 6.

Ginelli, Anatol, »Bauten und Entwürfe«, *Bauwelt* (Berlin), no. 21, 1986.

Glas und Keramik des Jugendstils in Österreich. Aus den Sammlungen des österreichischen Museums für angewandte Kunst in Wien, exhibition catalogue, Vienna 1989.

Glück, H., and E. Diez, *Die Kunst des Islams*, Berlin 1925.

Goebel, Gerhard, »Locus Amoenus oder die Architektur der Lust«, *Kunstforum international* (Cologne)*, Nr. 69, 1984.

Gomperz, Th. (ed.), *Auswahl herkulanischer kleiner Schriften*, n. p. 1993.

Görlich, Walter, *Der Hermaphrodit von Virunum*, Vienna 1941.

Gorsen, Peter, *Das Bild Pygmalions*, Reinbek near Hamburg 1969.

Gorsen, Peter: *Das Prinzip Obszön. Kunst, Pornographie und Gesellschaft*, Reinbek near Hamburg 1969.

Gorsen, Peter, *Sexualästhetik. Zur bürgerlichen Rezeption von Obszönitat und Pornographie*, Hamburg 1972.

Gorsen, Peter; »Intersexualismus und Subkultur« in: A. Matthes (ed.), *Maskulin-Feminin*, München 1975.

Gotlieb, Howard, *William Beckford of Fonthill. Writer, Traveller, Collector, Caliph 1760–1844*, New Haven (Conn.) 1960.

Göttner-Abendroth, Heide, *Die Göttin und ihr Heros. Die matriarchalen Religionen in Mythos, Märchen und Dichtung*, Munich 1980.

Göttner-Abendroth, Heide, »Matriachale Mythologie«, in: B. Wartmann (ed.), *Weiblich-Männlich*, Berlin 1980.

Grabovsky, Norbert, *Die mannweibliche Natur des Menschen. Mit Berücksichtigung des psychosexuellen Hermaphroditismus*, Leipzig 1896.

Graf, Otto Antonia, *Otto Wagner*, vol. 3: *Die Einheit der Kunst. Weltgeschichte der Grundformen*, Vienna and Cologne 1990.

Green, Richard, »Die Suche nach der Geschlechtsrolle«, *Psychologie heute* (Weinheim and Basle), May 1976.

Grimm, Jacob, *Über den Liebesgott*, Berlin 1851.

Gusenberg, Richard M., and Dietmar Meyer, *Die dreißiger Jahre*, Berlin, Darmstadt and Vienna 1970.

Gutschow, Niels, *Stadtraum und Ritual der newarischen Städte im Kathmandu-Tal*, Berlin, Cologne and Mainz 1982.

Gutschow, Niels, and Jan Pieper, *Indien – Bauformen und Stadtgestalt einer beständigen Tradition*, Cologne 1978.

Gutschow, Niels, and Jan Pieper, *Indien – Von den Klöstern im Himalaya zu den Tempelstädten Süd-Indiens,* Cologne 1981.

Hacker, Friedrich, *Aggression. Die Brutalisierung der modernen Welt*, Vienna, Munich and Zurich 1971.

Hacker, Friedrich, *Materialien zum Thema Aggression*, Vienna 1972.

Hacker, Friedrich, *Terror. Mythos – Realität – Analyse*, Vienna, Munich and Zurich 1973.

Haeckel, Ernst, *Monismus als Band von Religion und Wissenschaft*, n. p. 1892.

Haeckel, Ernst: *Die Welträtsel. Gemeinverständliche Studien über Monistische Philosophie*, Bonn 1902.

Haerle, Gerhard, *Männerweiblichkeit. Zur Homosexualität bei Klaus und Thomas Mann*, Frankfurt am Main 1988.

Hagemann-White, C., and Maria S. Rerrich (ed.), *Frauen Männer Bilder. Männer und Männlichkeit in der feministischen Diskussion*, Bielefeld 1988.

Halley des Fontaines, Jean, *La notion d'androgynie dans quelques mythes et quelques rites*, Paris 1938.

Hassauer, Friedericke, *Félicien Rops*, Zurich 1984.

d'Harnoncourt, Anne, and Kynaston Mc Shine (ed.), *Marcel Duchamp*, New York 1973, 1989.

Hauser, Arnold, *Der Ursprung der modernen Kunst und Literatur. Die Entwicklung des Manierismus seit der Krise der Renaissance*, Munich 1973.

Haus-Rucker-Co. 1967–1983, Braunschweig 1984.

Heberer, G. (ed.), *Die Evolution der Organismen*, Stuttgart 1943, 1959

Herdick, Reinhard, »Kosmisch, sozial, leiblich. Gestalt – Ordnungen in Nepal und Marokko«, *Daidalos* (Berlin), 45, 1992.

Hesse, Hermann, *Narziss und Goldmund*, Berlin 1930.

Hesse, Hermann, *Piktors Verwandlungen*, Frankfurt am Main 1954.

Highwater, Jamake, *Sexualität und Mythos*, Freiburg im Breisgau 1992.

Hirschfeld, Magnus (ed.), *Jahrbuch für sexuelle Zwischenstufen*, vols. I–V, Leipzig 1900–1903.

Hirschfeld, Magnus, *Die Transvestiten: Eine Untersuchung über den erotischen Verkleidungstrieb*, Berlin 1910.

Hirschfeld, Magnus, *Sexualpathologie*, vol. 1: *Geschlechtliche Entwicklungsstörungen*, Bonn 1917 (1922), vol. 2: *Sexuelle Zwischenstufen.– Das männliche Weib und der weibliche Mann*, Bonn 1918.

Hirschfeld, Magnus, *Geschlechtskunde*, vol. 1: *Die körperseelischen Grundlagen*, Stuttgart 1926 (1928).

Hocke, Gustav René, *Die Welt als Labyrinth. Manier und Manie in der europäischen Kunst*, Munich 1957.

Hofmann, Werner, *Das irdische Paradies. Motive und Ideen des 19. Jahrhunderts*, Munich 1960.

Hofmann, Werner, *Zauber der Medusa – Europäische Manierismen*, Vienna 1987.

Hollein, Hans, »Zukunft der Architektur«, *Bau* (Vienna), 1, 1965.

Hans Hollein, exhibition catalogue, Historisches Museum der Stadt Wien, Vienna 1995.

Holtmont, Alfred, *Die Hosenrolle. Variationen über das Thema: Das Weib als Mann*, Munich 1925.

Hon, hon-en katedral/historia, exhibition catalogue, Moderna Museet Stockholm, Stockholm 1967.

Huizinga, Johan, *Homo Ludens. Vom Ursprung der Kultur im Spiel*, Hamburg 1956.

Hulten, Pontus, *Niki de Saint Phalle*, exhibition catalogue, Bundeskunsthalle, Bonn 1992.

Humboldt, Wilhelm von, »Über den Geschlechtsunterschied. Über die männliche und weibliche Form«, in: *Werke*, vol. 1, Stuttgart 1841, Berlin 1917, Darmstadt 1960, 1981.

Hummel, Siegbert, *Die lamaistische Kunst*, Leipzig 1955.

Huysmans, J. K., *Felicien Rops – L'Œuvre graphique complète*, Paris 1977.

James, E. O., *Prehistoric Religions*, London 1957.

Jaspers, Karl, *Nikolaus Cusanus*, Munich 1987.

Jensen, A. E., *Mythos und Kult bei Naturvölkern. Religionswissenschaftliche Betrachtungen*, Wiesbaden 1951.

Jung, Carl Gustav, *Symbolik des Geistes. Studien über psychische Phänomenologie*, Zurich 1948.

Jung, Carl Gustav, *Man and his Symbols*, London 1964. Quotations cited from the German edition (*Der Mensch und seine Symbole*, Olten 1968).

Jung, Carl Gustav, *Psychologie und Alchemie*, Olten and Freiburg im Breisgau 1972, 1984, 1985.

Kähler, Gert, »Das Ei und ich oder: Warum ausgerechnet Hagen?«, *Baumeister* (Munich), no. 2, 1992.

Kamprad, Barbara, and Waltraud Schiffels, *Im falschen Körper*, Hamburg 1991.

Kaufmann, Emil, *Architecture in the Age of Reason. Baroque and Post-Baroque in England, Italy and France*, New York 1955.

Keel, Othmar (ed.), Göttinnen, Götter und Gottessymbole, Freiburg, Basle and Vienna 1992.

Kiesler, Frederick, *Transparent* (Vienna), no. 3/4, 1984.

Kiesler, Frederick, *The Book of the Shrine*, Graz 1992.

Kirsch, Sarah, Irmtraud Morgner and Christa Wolf, *Geschlechtertausch. Drei Geschichten über die Umwandlung der Verhältnisse*, Frankfurt am Main 1980.

Klausmann, Ulrike, and Marion Meinzerin, *Piratinnen*, Munich 1992.

Klein, W., *Vom antiken Rokoko*, Vienna 1921.

Kleinspehn, Thomas, *Der flüchtige Blick. Sehen und Identität in der Kultur der Neuzeit*, Hamburg 1989.

Klimowsky, Ernst W., *Das mann-weibliche Leitbild in der Antike*, Munich 1972.

Klimowsky, Ernst W., *Geschlecht und Geschichte. Sexualität im Wandel von Kultur und Kunst*, Vienna 1956, Munich 1972.

Klossowski, Pierre, *Der Baphomet*, Hamburg 1968.

Klossowsky, Pierre, *Anima*, exhibition catalogue, Wiener Secession, Vienna 1995.

Klotz, Heinrich (ed.), *Vision der Moderne. Das Prinzip Konstruktion*, exhibition catalogue, Munich 1986.

Köb, Edelbert, *Ausstellungsfolder*, Vienna 1992.

Köb, Edelbert, *Ambivalenz*, exhibition catalogue, Vienna 1990.

Koenig, Otto, *Urmotiv Auge. Neuentdeckte Grundzüge menschlichen Verhaltens*, Munich 1975.

Koepgen, Georg, *Die Gnosis des Christentums*, Salzburg 1939.

Köhler, Wolfgang, *DIe Aufgabe der Gestaltpsychologie*, Berlin 1971.

König, Oliver, *Nacktheit – Soziale Normierung und Moral*, Opladen 1990.

Kohtz, Otto, *Gedanken über Architektur*, Berlin 1909.

Jeff Koons, exhibition catalogue, Museum of Modern Art, San Francisco 1992.

Kraemer, Hans, *Das XIX. Jahrhundert in Wort und Bild*. vol. 3: *1871–1899*, Berlin, Leipzig, Stuttgart and Vienna, n. y.

Kraft-Ebing, Richard v., *Psychopathia Sexualis*, Munich 1984.

Krätschmer, Renate and Jörg Schwarzenberger, *Über das männliche und weibliche Prinzip*, exhibition catalogue, Wiener Secession, Vienna 1980.

Engelbert Kremser. Baukunst 1967–1987, Berlin 1986

Kšica, Miroslav, and Eva and Olga Kšicová, *Frauenidole der Eiszeit und Nacheiszeit. Realität und Abstraktion von Muttergottheiten aus 30 Jahrtausenden*, exhibition catalogue, Linz, Brno, Paris, Düsseldorf 1989.

Lachnit, Edwin, »Zur Geschichtlichkeit des Manierismusbegriffs«, in: Werner Hofmann (ed.), *Zauber der Medusa*, Vienna 1987.

Claude-Nicolas Ledoux. Architecte du Roi. Projets et Divagations, étude d' Yvan Christ, Paris 1961.

Leeuw, Gerardus v. d., *Der Mensch und die Religion. Anthropologischer Versuch*, Basle 1941 (*Philosophia Universalis*, vol. 2).

Lempicka, Tamara, *Passion by Design*, Oxford 1987.

Leroi-Gourhan, André, *Prähistorische Kunst. Die Ursprünge der Kunst in Europa*, Freiburg, Basle and Vienna 1971.

Lersch, Philipp, *Vom Wesen der Geschlechter*, Munich 1947.

Leupold-Löwenthal, *Handbuch der Psychoanalyse*, Vienna 1986.

Lexicon Iconographicum Mythologiae Classicae (LIMC), vol. V/I: *Herakles – Keuchrias*, Zurich and Munich 1981.

Lindemann, Gesa, *Das paradoxe Geschlecht. Transsexualität im Spannungsfeld von Körper, Leib und Gefühl*, Frankfurt am Main 1993.

Loidolt, Herbert, »Kontrastierende und konforme Entwurfslösungen«, *Transparent* (Vienna), no. 8, 1975.

Lommel, Hans, »Die iranische Religion«, in: *Die Religionen der Erde, ihr Wesen und ihre Geschichte*, Munich 1966.

Lüthi, Kurt, *Gottes neue Eva. Wandlungen des Weiblichen*, Stuttgart 1978.

Lurker, Manfred, *Symbol, Mythos und Legende in der Kunst. Die symbolische Aussage in Malerei, Plastik und Architektur*, Baden-Baden and Straßburg 1958.

Magnago Lampugnani, Vittorio (ed.), *Encyclopedia of 20th-Century Architecture*, London and New York 1986.

Mahlsdorf, Charlotte v., *Ich bin meine eigene Frau. Ein Leben*, ed. by Peter Süß with a photographic essay by Burkhard Peter, St.Gallen and Berlin 1992.

Malke, Lutz S., »Weibmann und Mannweib in der Kunst der Renaissance«, in: *Androgyn*, exhibition catalogue, Berlin 1986.

Malvenuti, Stefano, »Aurelio Cortesi – Maschile – Femminile«, in: *Materia, Rivista d'Architettura*, Viano 1991.

Manfredini, Alberto, »Considerazioni su Ideologia e Prassi nella Progettazione architettonica«, *Parametro* (Emilia Romana), no. 185, 1991.

Marcuse, Herbert, *Eros und Kultur. Ein philosophischer Beitrag zu Sigmund Freud*, Stuttgart 1957.

Marcuse, Max, *Handwörterbuch der Sexualwissenschaft*, Bonn 1923, Berne 1926.

Maria Lanzendorf, Führer zur Kirche, Maria Lanzendorf 1964.

Marsh, H. W., and M. Myers , »Maskulinity, femininity and androgyn: A methodological and theoretical critique«, in: *Sex Roles*, 1986.

Mattenklott, Gert, *Der übersinnliche Leib. Beitrag zur Metaphysik des Körpers*, Hamburg, 1982.

Mattenklott, Gert, *Bilderdienst. Ästhetische Opposition bei Beardsley und George*, Munich 1970, Frankfurt am Main 1985.

Mauer, Otto, *Über Kunst und Künstler*, Salzburg 1993.

Mead, Margret, *Male and female*, Hardmondsworth 1975.

Meesmann, Hartmut, and Bernhard Sill (ed.), *Androgyn*, Weinheim 1994.

Meinel C. (ed.), *Die Alchemie in der europäischen Kultur und Wissenschaftsgeschichte*. (Beitrag Aurnhammer), Wiesbaden 1986.

Meyer-Thoss, Christiane, *Louise Bourgeois*, Zurich 1992.

Meyers Neues Lexikon, 8 vóls., Mannheim, Vienna and Zurich 1978.

Minckwitz, Johannes, *Illustriertes Taschenwörterbuch der Mythologie aller Völker*, Leipzig 1878.

Molinier, Pierre, *Le Chaman et ses Créatures*, Perigueux 1995.

Mollenkott, U. R., *Gott eine Frau?*, Munich 1985.

Mona Lisa im 20. Jahrhundert, exhibition catalogue, Wilhelm-Lehmbruck-Museum, Duisburg 1978.

Money, John, and Anke Erhardt, *Männlich-Weiblich. Die Entstehung der Geschlechtsunterschiede*, Reinbek near Hamburg 1975.

Moore, Henry, *Hauptthemen. Monographien zur Kunstgeschichte,* ed. by Heinz Spielmann, Hamburg 1976.

Morris, Jan (formerly James), *Conundrum: An Extraordinary Narrative of Transsexualism*, New York 1974, 1986.

Mott, Georg, *Follies and pleasure Pavilions, England, Ireland, Scotland, Wales*, New York 1989.

Müller, Ernst (ed.), *Der Sohar, das heilige Buch der Kabbala, nach dem Urtext herausgegeben*, Vienna 1932.

Mulack, Christa, *Maria. Die geheime Göttin im Christentum*, Stuttgart 1985.

Mulack, Christa, Die Weiblichkeit Gottes, Stuttgart 1983, Berlin 1991.

Mumford, Lewis, *The City in History*, London 1961.

Münsterberg, Hugo, *Frühe Schriften zur Soziologie*, Berlin 1990.

Mythen der Welt, with contributions by A. Eliot, M. Eliade, J. Campell, D. Lauf and E. Bührer, Lucerne and Frankfurt am Main 1976.

Nerdinger, Winfried, Klaus Jan Philipp and Hans Peter Schwarz (ed.), *Revolutionsarchitektur. Ein Aspekt der europäischen Architektur um 1800*, exhibition catalogue, Munich 1990.

Neugebauer, Franz Ludwig von, »17 Fälle von Koincidenz von Geistesanomalien mit Pseudohermaphroditismus« in: Magnus Hirschfeld (ed.), *Jahrbuch für sexuelle Zwischenstufen*, Leipzig 1900.

Neugebauer, Franz Ludwig von, »Chirurgische Überraschungen auf dem Gebiete des Scheinzwittertums«, in: Magnus Hirschfeld (ed.), *Jahrbuch für sexuelle Zwischenstufen,* Leipzig 1903.

Neugebauer, Franz Ludwig von, *Hermaphroditismus beim Menschen*, Leipzig 1908.

Neumann, Erich, *The Origins and History of Consciousness*, New York and London 1954. Quotations from the German edition (*Ursprungsgeschichte des Bewußtseins*, Zurich 1949).

Neumann, Erich, *The Great Mother – An Analysis of the Archetype*, New York 1955.

Niki de Saint Phalle, »Ein magischer Garten der Mutter-Göttin«, *art* (Hamburg), no., 6, 1993.

Nikolaus von Kues, *Aller Dinge Einheit ist Gott*, Zurich, Einsiedeln and Cologne 1984.

Norberg-Schulz, Christian, *Genius loci – paesaggio, ambiente, architettura. Towards a phenomenology of architecture,* London 1980. Quotations from the German edition (*Genius loci. Landschaft, Lebensraum, Baukunst*, Stuttgart 1982).

Nornengast, Urda, *Der androgyne Mensch*, Bellnhausen über Gladenbach 1970.

Oberösterreichische Nachrichten (Linz), 28 Sept. 1990 and 18 March 1992.

Oerter, Rolf, *Moderne Entwicklungspsychologie*, Donauwörth 1970.

Ohlbaum, Isolde, *Denn alle Lust will Ewigkeit. Erotische Skulpturen auf europäischen Friedhöfen in 77 Lichtbildern*, Nördlingen 1986.

Orchard, Karin, *Annäherung der Geschlechter. Androgynie in der Kunst des Cinquecento*, Münster and Hamburg 1992.

Orlan, Pierre Mac, and Joris-Karl Huysmans, *L'Œuvre gravé de Felicien Rops*, Paris 1975.

Ortkemper, Hubert, *Engel wider Willen – Die Welt der Kastraten*, Berlin 1993.

Overzier, Claus (ed.), *Die Intersexualität*, Stuttgart 1961.

Ovid, *Metamorphoses*, Warminster 1992.

Papus, *Die Kabbala*, Ulm 1962.

Parametro (Faenza), Nov./Dec. 1991.

Paulsen, Wolfgang (ed.), *Die Frau als Heldin und Autorin*, Berlin and Munich 1979.

Pehnt, Wolfgang, *Expressionist Architecture*, London and New York 1973.

Peladan, *Weibliche Neugier*, Munich 1923.
Peladan, *Das höchste Laster*, Munich 1923.
Peladan, *Einweihung des Weibes*, Munich 1923.
Peladan, *Das allmächtige Gold*, Munich 1923.
Peladan, *Der Androgyn*, Munich 1924.
Peladan, *Gynandria*, Munich 1925.

Pepponi, Maria Cecilia, »Guido Fiorini Architetto 1891–1965«, *Parametro*, (Faenza), no. 187, 1991.

Pevsner, Nikolaus, John Fleming and Hugh Honour, *Lexikon der Weltarchitektur*, Munich 1966.

Piaget, Jean, *Nachahmung, Spiel und Traum*, Stuttgart 1969.

Walter Pichler, catalogue of Galerie Schapira & Beck, Vienna 1976.

Walter Pichler. Bilder, Salzburg and Vienna 1986.

Walter Pichler. Skulptur, exhibition catalogue, Salzburg and Vienna 1990.

Walter Pichler. Skulpturen, Gebäude, Projekte, Salzburg and Vienna 1983.

Walter Pichler. 111 Zeichnungen, with an essay by Max Peintner and a text by Thomas Bernhard, Salzburg 1973.

Walter Pichler. Skulpturen, Zeichnungen, Modelle, Salzburg and Vienna 1987.

Pieper, Jan, *Das Labyrinthische. Über die Idee des Verborgenen, Rätselhaften, Schwierigen in der Geschichte der Architektur,* Braunschweig and Wiesbaden 1987.

Pieper, Jan, »Jerusalemkirchen«, *Bauwelt* (Berlin), no. 3, 1989.

Pieper, Jan: »Architektonische Toposforschung«, *Bauwelt* (Berlin), no. 3, 1989.

Pieper, Jan, »Häuser des Narziß. Architektur nach des Menschen Bild und Gleichnis«, *Daidalos* (Berlin) no. 45, 1992.

Pirchan, Emil, *Therese Krones. Die Theaterkönigin Altwiens*, Vienna and Leipzig 1942.

Plato, *Symposium*, translated by Tom Griffith, Berkeley (Calif.) and Los Angeles 1989.

Pleck, Joseph H., *The Myth of Masculinity*, Cambridge (Mass.) 1981.

Plečnik, Josef. Wiener Arbeiten von 1896 bis 1914, ed. by D. Prelovšek, Vienna 1979.

Ricardo Porro. Architekt, Klagenfurt 1994.

Die Portugiesen in Indien. Die Eroberungen Dom João des Castros auf Tapisserien 1538 bis 1548, exhibition catalogue, Vienna 1992.

Prinz, U., »Androgyn – Sehnsucht nach Vollkommenheit«, exhibition catalogue, Berlin 1986.

Pufler, Karl, *Androgynität im Werk Ingeborg Bachmanns*, diss., Vienna 1990.

Putscher, Marielene, »Das ›Buch der Heiligen Dreifaltigkeit‹ und seine Bilder in Handschriften des 15. Jahrhunderts.« in: C. Meinel (ed.), *Die Alchemie in der europäischen Kultur- und Wissenschaftsgeschichte*, Wiesbaden 1986.

Raehs, Andrea, *Zur Ikonographie des Hermaphroditen. Begriff und Problem von Hermaphroditismus und Androgynie in der Kunst*, Frankfurt am Main 1990.

Ranke-Graves, Robert von, *The White Goddess*, New York 1958.

Ranke-Graves, Robert von, *Griechische Mythologie, Quellen und Deutung*, 2 vols., Reinbek near Hamburg 1960.

Remmler, Helmut, *Das Geheimnis der Sphinx, Archetyp für Mann und Frau*, Olten and Freiburg im Breisgau 1988.

Rentmeister, Cillie, »Die Quadratur des Kreises, Die Machtergreifung der Männer über die Bauformen«, *Bauwelt* (Berlin), no., 31/32, 1979.

Revolutionsarchitektur. Boullée, Ledoux, Lequeu, exhibition catalogue, Baden–Baden 1970.

Rick, Karin (ed.), *Das Sexuelle, die Frauen und die Kunst*, Tübingen 1987.

Ringel, Erwin, *Die österreichische Seele*, Graz and Vienna 1984.

Roheim, Geza, *Heros, phalliques et symbols maternels dans la mythologie australienne*, n. p. 1970.

Römer, L. S., and A. M. v. Amsterdam, »Über die androgynische Idee des Lebens«, in: Magnus Hirschfeld (ed.), *Jahrbuch für sexuelle Zwischenstufen*, Leipzig 1903.

Aldo Rossi. Bauten und Projekte 1981–1991, Zürich and Munich 1991.

Ruhbach, Gerhard, and Josef Sudbrack (ed.), *Große Mystiker. Leben und Wirken*, Munich 1984.

Sartre, Jean Paul, *Baudelaire*, London 1949.

Schaal, Hans Dieter, *Denkgebäude*, Braunschweig and Wiesbaden 1984.

Schaden-Tholen, Sigrid, Monika Wagner and Sigrid Weigel (ed.), *Allegorie und Geschlechterdifferenz*, Vienna 1994.

Scharpf, Manfred, *Heilräume, Splendor Artis*, Broschüre mit Beilagen, n. p., n. y.

Schaup, Susanne, *Sophia, das Weibliche in Gott*, Munich 1994.

Schelsky, Helmut, *Soziologie der Sexualität, Über die Beziehung zwischen Geschlecht, Moral und Gesellschaft*, Hamburg 1955.

Scheltema, F. Adama van, *Die geistige Mitte. Umrisse einer abendländischen Kulturmorphologie*, Munich 1950.

Schiffels, Waltraud, *Frau werden: Von Walter zu Waltraud. Authentischer Bericht einer Transsexuellen*, Zurich 1992.

Schleberger, Eckhard, *Die indische Götterwelt. Gestalt, Ausdruck und Sinnbild*, Cologne 1986.

Schlegel, Friedrich, *Lucinde*, Berlin 1985.

Schlesier, Karl H., »Anmerkungen über Tsistsistas (Cheyenne), Hehmaneh und Hohnuhka oder die Coincidentia oppositorum«, in: H. P. Duerr (ed.), *Sehnsucht nach dem Ursprung. Zu Mircea Eliade*, Frankfurt am Main 1983.

Schmied, Wieland, *Zweihundert Jahre phantastische Malerei*, Berlin 1973.

Schmutzler, Robert, *Art Nouveau – Jugendstil*, Stuttgart 1962.

Schöffer, Nicolas, *Die kybernetische Stadt*, Munich 1970.

Scholze, Herta, *Geschlechtswechsel im österreichischen Brauchtum*, Vienna 1948.

Schwarzrheindorf 1832 –1982. Katholischer Gottesdienst in Schwarzrheindorf. Schwarzrheindorf 1982

Schwarz–Winklhofer and H. Biedermann, *Das Buch der Zeichen und Symbole*, Graz 1972.

Schrödter, Willy, *Geschichte und Lehren der Rosenkreuzer*, Villach 1956.

Schutting, Jutta, *Liebesroman*, Salzburg 1985.

Sedlmayr, Hans, *Johann Bernhard Fischer von Erlach*, Vienna and Munich 1956.

Sedlmayr, Hans, *Epochen und Werke*, Vienna 1976.

Seeßlen, »Die Frau in Blau. Zum Film *Blue Steel* von Kathryn Bigelow«, *Die Zeit* (Hamburg) 19, 1990.

Seidl-Reiter, Edda. Alles ist weben, Tapisserien, Ideen, Objekte. Projekte 1957–1987, Vienna, Cologne and Graz 1988.

Seifert, Edith, »Einheit – Zweiheit – Ganzheit«, in: B. Wartmann (ed.), *Weiblich-Männlich*, Berlin 1980.

Sekler, Eduard F., *Josef Hoffmann. Das architektonische Werk*, Salzburg and Vienna 1982.

Serres, Michel, *L'Hermaphrodite. Sarrasine sculpteur*, Paris 1987.

Sgan Cohen, Michael, »Zur Ikonographie des Endless House«, in: D. Bogner (ed.), *Friedrich Kiesler 1890–1965*, Vienna 1988.

Sichtermann, Barbara, *Glaubt mir kein Wort* (über Marlene Dietrich), *Standard*, (Vienna) 6. 12. 1991.

Sichtermann, Barbara, *Weiblichkeit. Zur Politik des Privaten*, Berlin 1983.

Sigusch, Volkmar, and Gunter Schmidt, *Zur Frage des Vorurteils gegenüber sexuell devianten Gruppen*, Stuttgart 1967.

Silbermayr, Ernst, *Untersuchungen über den Zusammenhang von Geschlechtsidentität und psychischer Stabilität bei erwachsenen Männern. Ein Beitrag zur Androgynitätsforschung,* Vienna 1988.

Sill, Bernhard, *Die Kunst der Geschlechterliebe*, Mainz 1989.

Sill, Bernhard, *Androgynie und Geschlechtsdifferenz nach Franz von Baader*, Regensburg 1980.

Singer, June, *Boundaries of the Soul. The practice of Jung's psychology*, London 1973.

Singer, June, *Androgyny*, London 1977.

Skip Kinomagazin, Interview with Charlotte von Mahlsdorf (»Immer als Frau gefühlt«), Dec. 1992, January 1993.

Slama, Beatrice, *Anna, Anne und die anderen*, in: K. Rick (ed.), *Das Sexuelle, die Frauen und die Kunst*, Tübingen 1987.

Smith, B.,*The Dome*, Princeton (New Jersey) 1950.

Spickernagel, Ellen, »›Helden wie zarte Knaben oder verkleidete Mädchen‹. Zum Begriff der Androgynität bei J. J. Winckelmann und A. Kauffmann«, in: *Frauen, Weiblichkeit, Schrift* (Tagungsschrift), Bielefeld 1984, Berlin 1985.

Steiner, Rudolf, *Der Baugedanke des Goetheanums*, Dornach 1932, Stuttgart 1958.

Strecker, Bernhard, »Ego und Genius Loci, Amalie – Eine Stadtbrücke«, *Kunstforum international*, (Cologne), no. 69, 1984.

Sulzer, J. J., *Allgemeine Theorie der Schönen Künste*, 4th part, Leipzig 1794.

Staudacher, Willibald, *Die Trennung von Himmel und Erde. Ein vorgriechischer Schöpfungsmythus bei Hesiod und den Orphikern*, Tübingen 1942.

Swoboda, Erich, *Carnuntum*, Graz and Cologne 1964.

Szeemann, Harald (ed.), *Junggesellenmaschinen. Der Hang zum Gesamtkunstwerk*, exhibition catalogue, Aarau 1983.

Tenschert, Roland, *Mozart. Ein Leben für die Oper*, Vienna 1944/45.

Theweleit, Klaus, *Männerphantasien*, 2 vols., Hamburg 1977.

Thiel, Josef Franz, »Androgynie in Afrika«, in: *Androgyn*, exhibition catalogue, Berlin 1986.

Thiele, Peter, »Yin und Yang«, in: *Androgyn*, exhibition catalogue, Berlin 1986.

Thomsen, Christian W., »Architektur und Erotik«, in: *Architektur für die Sinne*, Düsseldorf 1992.

Thomsen, Christian W., *Liter-Architektur. Wechselwirkungen zwischen Architektur, Literatur und Kunst im 20. Jahrhundert,* Cologne 1989.

Thomsen, Christian W., *Bauen für die Sinne. Gefühl, Erotik und Sexualität in der Architektur*, Munich 1996.

Der Traum vom Raum. Gemalte Architektur aus 7 Jahrhunderten, Eine Ausstellung der Albrecht-Dürer-Gesellschaft, Nürnberg and Marburg 1986.

Venturi, Adolfo, *Leonardo da Vinci und seine Schule*, Vienna 1941.

Vernon, M. D., *The Psychology of Perception*, Hartmondsworth 1962.

Vidler, Anthony, *Claude Nicolas Ledoux*, Basle, Boston and Berlin 1988.

Vogt, Adolf Max, *Russische und französische Revolutionsarchitektur, 1917, 1789*, Cologne 1947.

Vogt, Adolf Max, *Boullées Newton Denkmal. Sakralbau und Kugelidee*, Basle 1969.

Wagner, Susanne, »Selbstverliebter Knabe als Märtyrerin getarnt«, *art* (Hamburg), no. 6, 1992.

Wartmann, Brigitte (Hrsg), *Weiblich-Männlich. Kulturgeschichtliche Spuren einer verdrängten Weiblichkeit*, Berlin 1980.

Webb, Peter, »Hans Bellmer«, in: *Androgyn*, exhibition catalogue, Berlin 1986.

Wedekind-Schwertner B., *Daß ich eins und doppelt bin. Studien zur Idee der Androgynie unter besonderer Berücksichtigung Thomas Manns*, Münster 1984.

Wehr, Gerhard, *Der Urmensch und der Mensch der Zukunft. Das Androgyn Problem im Lichte der Forschungsergebnisse Rudolf Steiners*, Freiburg im Breisgau 1964.

Wehr, Gerhard, *C. G. Jung und Rudolf Steiner*, Stuttgart 1972.

Wehr, Gerhard, *Alle Weisheit ist von Gott. Gestalten und Wirkungen christlicher Theosophie: Weigel, Böhme, Andreae u. a.,* Gütersloh 1980.

Wehr, Gerhard, *Die deutsche Mystik. Mystische Erfahrungen und theosophische Weltsicht – Eine Einführung in Leben und Werk der großen deutschen Sucher nach Gott*, Berne, Munich and Vienna 1988.

Weininger, Otto, *Geschlecht und Charakter*, Vienna and Leipzig 1917.

Weinreb, Friedrich, *Zahl, Zeichen, Wort. Das symbolische Universum der Bibelsprache*, n. p. 1948.

Weinreich, Otto, *Menekrates. Zeus und Salmoneus*, Stuttgart 1933.

Werlhof, Claudia von, *Männliche Natur und künstliches Geschlecht. Aufsätze zu feministischer Wissenschaftskritik*, Vienna 1985.

Werlhof, Claudia von, Maria Mies and Veronika Bennholdt-Thomsen*, Frauen – die letzte Kolonie? Zur Hausfrauisierung der Arbeit*, Reinbek near Hamburg 1983, Vienna 1988.

Westendorf, Wolfhart, »Mann-weibliche Konzeption im Alten Ägypten«, in: *Androgyn*, exhibition catalogue, Berlin 1986.

Wex, Marianne, »Weibliche« und »Männliche« Körpersprache als Folge patriachalischer Machtverhältnisse, Frankfurt am Main 1980.

Wiener (Vienna) no. 97, 1988.

Winckelmann, J. J., *Sämtliche Werke,* vol. VIII: *1825 bis 1829,* Osnabrück 1965.

Winckelmann, J. J., *Vorläufige Abhandlungen zu den Denkmalen der Kunst des Altertums*, Donaueschingen, n. y.

Winthuis, Josef, *Einführung in die Vorstellungswelt primitiver Völker*, Leipzig 1931.

Winthuis, Josef, *Das Zweigeschlechterwesen bei den Zentralaustraliern und anderen Völkern. Lösungsversuch der ethnologischen Hauptprobleme auf Grund des primitiven Denkens*, Leipzig 1928.

Wolf, Christa, *Bisexualität*, Frankfurt 1981.

Wolter, Gundula, *Hosen-weiblich. Kulturgeschichte der Frauenhosen*, Marburg 1994.

Woolf, Virginia, *Orlando. A Biography*, London 1958.

Wundt, Wilhelm, *Völkerpsychologie*, vol. I: *Die Sprache,* vol. II: *Mythus und Religion,* vol. III: *Die Kunst,* vols. IV and V: *Mythus und Religion,* Leipzig 1908.

Züger, Armin, *Männerbilder – Frauenbilder. Androgyne Utopie in der deutschen Literatur zwischen 1970 und 1980*, Berne and Frankfurt am Main 1992.

Photonachweise/Photo Credits

Accademia Nazionale di San Lucca, Roma 279
Akademie der Künste, Berlin 186, 187, 188, 206, 213, 215, 311
Albertina, Wien 210
Andreae 1972 281
Androgyn, 1986 30
Archäologischer Park Carnuntum 29
Architekturmuseum der TU München 273
Arkitektur Museet Stockholm 233
art, 6, 1993 106, 115, 116
Archiv Tadao Ando 5, 6, 7
Archiv Maria Auböck 120
Archiv Dieter Bogner 1, 170, 288
Archiv Peter Cook 172
Archiv Coop Himmelblau 246, 248, 250
Archiv Günther Domenig 153, 154
Archiv Günther Feuerstein 8, 9, 10, 11, 12, 13, 14, 15, 17, 19, 20, 22, 33, 46, 50, 58, 76, 80, 81, 86, 87, 88, 94, 107, 114, 117, 118, 131, 140, 143, 145, 148, 159, 160, 167, 168, 175, 181, 183, 185, 189, 195, 199, 204, 209, 214, 218, 231, 232, 239, 243, 253, 258, 262, 266, 282, 286, 287, 289, 290, 292, 293, 296, 298, 300, 302, 308
Archiv Haus-Rucker-Co 122, 155, 158, 249, 275
Archiv Hans Hollein 119, 137, 236, 237, 305, 306, 307
Archiv Wolfgang Hutter 92
Archiv Helmut Kleine-Kraneburg 277
Archiv Edelbert Köb 108
Archiv Engelbert Kremser 156
Archiv Adolf Krischanitz 194, 280
Archiv Helmut Lander 285
Archiv Peter Noever 138
Archiv Wolfgang Pehnt 211
Archiv Gustav Peichl 4, 240
Archiv Walter Pichler 99, 100, 101, 102, 139, 177, 264, 265
Archiv Jan Pieper 257, 270, 271, 272, 294, 295
Archiv Christiane Pressel 141
Archiv Walter Michael Pühringer 197, 252
Archiv Hans Dieter Schaal 135
Archiv Manfred Scharpf 89
Archiv Karl Schwanzer 193
Archiv Edda Seidl-Reiter 97, 98
Archiv Peter Skubic 111
Archiv Paolo Soleri 144, 278
Archiv Heinz Tesar 3, 165, 176, 179
Archiv Stanley Tigerman 128, 178
Archiv Hans Turba 96
Ashmolean Museum of Art and Archeology, Oxford 260
Atalanta fugiens, 1618 34
Augustinermuseum Rattenberg, Tirol 43
Aurnhammer 1986 23, 39
Avery Architectural and Fine Art Library, Columbia University, New York 190, 191
Banca Popolare di Lecco, Como 310
Baumann 1986 18, 21
Bauwelt, 5, 1996 234
Aubrey Beardsley, 1967 82, 83
Bibliothèque Nationale, Paris 55, 79, 200, 201, 228, 242, 245
Biedermann 1987 284, 291
Bildarchiv der Österr. Nationalbibliothek, Wien 24, 51, 61, 62, 267, 269

Bildarchiv Foto Marburg 219
Dieter Bogner 1988 2, 303
Cooper-Hewitt Museum, New York 41
Dekker, Pol 1990 54
Deutsche Kinemathek, Berlin 66, 68
Jean Dubuffet, 1995 146
André Emmerich Gallery, New York 152
Feminimasculin, 1995 90
Günther Feuerstein 32, 45, 95, 121, 123, 126, 129, 130, 134, 149, 164, 166, 171, 173, 180, 184, 198, 216, 220, 221, 223, 244, 247, 251, 254, 261, 263, 274, 299, 301, 304, 309, 316, 317
Film-Kurier, 318, 1983 69
Filmladen, 245, 1995 60
Galleria degli Uffizi, Firenze 229
Garber 1992 56, 57
Germanisches Nationalmuseum, Nürnberg 78
Giedion 1964 283
Gusenberg 1970 65
Glück 1925 314
Solomon R. Guggenheim Foundation 93
Harvard Theatre Collection, Cambridge 63, 64
Herzog August Bibliothek, Wolfenbüttel 38
Jung 1985 35
Keel 1992 103
Klossowsky 1995 70
Klotz 1986 315
Kövesdi Presseagentur Wien 74, 75
Kungl. Akademien för de Fria Konsterna, Stockholm 202
Kunsthistorisches Museum, Wien 26, 28, 42, 49, 52, 77, 109
Kurpfälzisches Museum, Heidelberg 297
Lempicka 1987 72
Herbert Lippert, *Anatomie*, 1989 151
Réunion des Musées Nationaux, Paris 47, 48
Magyar Országos Leveltar, Budapest 241
Materia, 1991 196
Moderna Museet Stockholm 136
Molinier 1995 59
Musée des Thermes et de l'Hôtel de Cluny, Paris 259
Musées de la Ville de Paris 142
Museen der Stadt Wien 91, 222
Musei Civici Veneziani 226
Museum der Stadt Wien 91
Museum of Fine Arts, Boston 25, 27
Museum of Modern Art, New York 85
Nederlands Architectuurinstituut, Rotterdam 133, 174
Nerdinger 1990 124, 230
Nevidal 169
Oberösterreichisches Landesmuseum, Linz 71
Österreichische Galerie, Wien 208
Österr. Museum für angewandte Kunst, Wien 105
Orlan 1975 44
Frei Otto 161
Palast der Götter, 1991 31
Pehnt 1973 125, 127
Artur Pfau 192
Plurigraf 268
Ricardo Porro, 1994 112, 113
Aldo Rossi, 1991 235, 238
San Francisco Museum of Modern Art 67
Paul Schneider-Esleben, 1987 318
Schöffer 1970 157

Johannes Schultz-Tesmar, Roman Soumar, *Thailand*, 1990 217
Schutting 1985 73
Schwingenschlögl 179, 256
Sekler 1982 212
Slovenska Akademija, Ljubljana 224, 225
Sprengel-Museum, Hannover 53, 150
Staatens Konstmuseer, Stockholm 132
Staatliche Graphische Sammlung, München 276
Staatliche Kunsthalle Karlsruhe 205
Staatliche Schlösser und Gärten Kassel-Wilhelmshöhe 203
Stedelijk Van Abbe Museum, Eindhoven 84
Rudolf Steiner. Eine Erinnerung an die Rudolf-Steiner-Ausstellung des Jahres 1961, 1961 162, 163
Staatliche Museen Preußischer Kulturbesitz, Berlin 207
Eckart von Sydow, *Afrikanische Plastik*, 1945 16
David Sylvester, *Magritte*, 1992 110
Szeemann 1985 40
Vadiana, St.Gallen 37
Victoria and Albert Museum, London 227
Weiler 1991 104
Iain Boyd Whyte, *Emil Hoppe, Marcel Kammerer, Otto Schönthal*, 1989 312, 313
Siegfried Wichmann, *Jugendstil – Art Nouveau*, 1977 147
Zentralbibliothek Zürich 36
Gerald Zugman 255